The Overland Journey
from Utah to California

The Overland Journey from Utah to California

Wagon Travel from the City of Saints to the City of Angels

EDWARD LEO LYMAN

UNIVERSITY OF NEVADA PRESS

Reno & Las Vegas

University of Nevada Press, Reno, Nevada 89557 USA
Copyright © 2004 by the University of Nevada Press

Manufactured in USA
Book design by Kaelin Chappell

Library of Congress Cataloging-in-Publication Data
Lyman, Edward Leo, 1942–
The overland journey from Utah to California:
wagon travel from the City of Saints to the City of Angels /
Edward Leo Lyman.
    p.   cm.
Includes bibliographical references (p.) and index.
ISBN 0-87417-501-1 (alk. paper)
1. Overland journeys to the Pacific. 2. Trails—West (U.S.)—
History—19th century. 3. Frontier and pioneer life—West
(U.S.) 4. Wagon trains—West (U.S.)—History—19th century.
5. Pioneers—West (U.S.)—History—19th century.
6. Morman pioneers—West (U.S.)—History—19th century.
7. West (U.S.)—description and travel.
8. West (U.S.)—History, Local. I. Title.
F593 .L955 2004
978'.02—dc22
2003019691

The paper used in this book meets the requirements of
American National Standard for Information Sciences—
Permanence of Paper for Printed Library Materials,
ANSI Z39.48-1984. Binding materials were selected for strength
and durability.

First Printing
13 12 11 10 09 08 07 06 05 04
5 4 3 2 1

For Clifford J. Walker,
a longtime teacher and advocate
of the desert and its trails

Contents

Illustrations

Preface

A prominent Mormon leader, Anthony W. Ivins, who had lived near the Utah-to-southern California road a generation after its heyday, wrote in 1923, "one of the most interesting and in its time most important of the old trails, now obliterated, and well nigh forgotten was the Southern Route which connected the Pacific Coast with the Missouri River." He lamented that "the tragedy and romance of the old trail will never be told, nor written; it cannot be because the men who made unrecorded history along its route have long since gone to travel the unknown paths of another world, leaving no written records behind them."[1] A young married couple who had grown to maturity in the same Utah's Dixie, LeRoy R. Hafen and Ann Woodbury Hafen would soon embark on a quest that proved President Ivins wrong by gathering and publishing many documentary accounts of travel over the route, at least during the Hispanic period and the first year of Anglo-American wagon travel. By the present time a rather large body of such materials has emerged, so that the admittedly little-known history of this important roadway may now be properly presented, although Ivins was not entirely wrong about innumerable stories that have been lost. I am proud to have studied with Professor Hafen during the latter portion of his academic career and to be engaged in furthering the work he started.

Along with the Hafens, another nationally prominent historian, Dale Lowell Morgan, biographer of Jede-

diah S. Smith, also devoted much time to studying the route. Working with Eleanor Towles Harris, a coauthor with him on several overland trails projects, Morgan carefully edited the original Vincent A. Hoover diary used herein. This was apparently with full intent to publish, probably under the auspices of the California Historical Society. The date of the typescript in the Morgan papers at the Bancroft Library at Berkeley, California, is 1971, which is the year the great historian was diagnosed with cancer and subsequently died. There is a similar Morgan-edited copy of the William Lorton diary over the same route in 1849, along with a considerable array of associated notes useful in this study and undoubtedly gathered for some larger purpose.

The currently active professional historians Dr. Ronald W. Walker of Brigham Young University and Will Bagley, associated with the Arthur H. Clark Company, publisher of many of the Hafens' books, both read the early draft of this book, and both offered most perceptive and useful criticisms and comments. Both insisted I needed to treat the Mountain Meadows Massacre more fully than I originally intended. Interestingly, both readers became deeply immersed in that subject while themselves preparing their own careful histories of that tragedy. Bagley's book has already been published in three printings. Mormon scholars have alleged that Bagley used too many questionable sources. Yet his general view of the circumstances surrounding that horrible mass murder, and the implication of the highest Mormon leaders therein, does not appreciably differ from my own treatments of those subjects. On the other hand, Ronald Walker, one of the historians I most respect in the entire profession, is currently engaged with two project partners, Richard E. Turley Jr. and Glen M. Leonard, each a loyal Latter-day Saint historian, in writing their own account of the massacre and surrounding events, drawing on church sources never before available. There is certainly room for all three accounts, as interest in resolving this important subject remains at a high pitch.

Similarly, people with more local reputations but direct knowledge of the desert trails have been of immeasurable assistance. The late Arda Haenzel, of Redlands, California, devoted years to the study of the Nevada and California segments of the route and had an invaluable personal library of related materials, always generously shared. Dennis G. Casebier, the preeminent historian of the East Mojave Desert, whose fine Mojave Desert Archives at Goffs, California, now houses much of the Haenzel collection and so much more, was equally helpful. LaVoid Leavitt of St. George, Utah, has a similarly lengthy span of interest and experience with the Utah-Nevada portions of the trail, which he has enthusiastically offered to me on several occasions. Early 1990s conversations with C. Gregory Crampton, another former professor of the author and longtime student of the Old Spanish Trail, were helpful.

Harold A. Steiner, of Las Vegas, another author who has published a history and guidebook of the trail, has been equally impressive in his willingness to help better understand certain aspects of the route. Over a decade ago, high school teacher and trails scholar Todd I. Berens and his students scoured some portions of the desert, locating segments of trail heretofore ignored and neglected. He too has assisted this project in important ways. Larry L. Reese, photographer and coauthor of *The Arduous Road*, an important supplement to this book as a guidebook of the Southern Route, was also an important rediscoverer, with me, of several important forgotten segments of the old road. And Dr. Norman Meek of California State University, San Bernardino, offered invaluable service, providing maps of the entire road. Clifford L. Walker, of Barstow, California, an associate

and friend for more than twenty-five years, has been of such great assistance in helping not only me but also several generations of others to know and understand the desert and its trails that this book is dedicated to him.

When overland routes to the Pacific Coast are discussed in the historical literature, or mapped in the textbooks, there is seldom, if ever, mention of the one that avoided the winter snows blocking routes farther north and that was quite heavily used during the period from the California Gold Rush through completion of the transcontinental railroad. This study, among other things, aims to get the route included with the others when historians discuss emigration and transportation in the Far West. The so-called Southern Route from Utah to southern California was well used precisely because it was an all-season route, although it could be particularly formidable in the summer season. The term *Southern Route*, although widely used and correct, is somewhat confusing, because routes across Texas, New Mexico, and Arizona to California have also been known by that designation.[2] Still, that is the primary name by which the subject of this study has always been known.[3]

Despite the relatively heavy use, it can be cogently argued that this was the most difficult road American pioneers traveled with any consistency in the entire history of the United States. Whereas almost all other emigrant routes followed rivers most of their distance, this road led from desert watering place to sometimes-distant water hole for up to four hundred miles. And except for a two-year span in the mid-1850s when the Las Vegas mission was functioning, there was no haven for the sick, hungry, or otherwise unfortunate such as those served by Fort Laramie, Salt Lake City, and other popular stopping places along the more famous trails. Yet with the exception of the infamous Mountain Meadows Massacre, loss of human life was extremely rare on the route, with virtually none of the deaths to disease so prevalent along many river roadways. And despite the almost total disruption of Native American life along the road and consistent stealing and begging by people who believed tribute was owed by the emigrants for passage through their lands, only a few deaths on either side are attributed to conflicts initiated by Indians.

The overland journey west was the most memorable

common experience in the lives of an entire generation of pioneers. The more historically minded of these recorded their collective experience, including that on the difficult trail to southern California. As with most other aspects of the history of that region, similar chronicling of like events in other areas had been treated long before that of southern California. Similarly, Mormon history of the trek from the Midwest to Utah is as familiar to most citizens there as experiences of their own lives. But the same people know virtually nothing about another important road connecting Mormondom with the outside world, the Southern Route to California. This book seeks to remedy these situations. Despite the movie and television emphasis on the spectacular aspects of the westward migration, the quiet coping with the rigors of the desert environment actually de-monstrates a significance—even heroism—that calls for equal recognition and understanding. The impact of emigrant incursions into Native American domain along the route has also long deserved discussion.

Some will find the recounting of the somewhat repetitive details of many company journeys less desirable than a synthesis of those experiences treated in some more topical format. My purpose in staying with a mainly chronological approach and adding important items of information from each company about which accounts could be located is that subtle variations over time altered the experience of the arduous desert crossing. I hope that gathering so much of this experience will allow interested readers to make their own syntheses of an important aspect of the nation's history. I have been greatly influenced by a paper entitled "The Significance and Value of the Overland Journal," which Dale Lowell Morgan presented at a 1961 conference. He concluded, "[E]ach overland journal is a reflection of a folk experience and a time spirit. In their journals westering Americans set down a collective self-portrait, a mosaic in words. The mosaic can never be altogether filled in, never a final creation. Each journal that is found alters some detail, and gives fresh play to our imagination as well as our understanding."[4]

One student of the wagon road stated, "[I]t is a remarkable thing that the first wagons to traverse the road varied so little from the actual hard-surface highways where cars and trucks speed over these desert areas to-day. Only two alterations have been made in the original trail and in the case of one of these a modern highway exists along the road followed by the creaky wagons."[5] Actually, both places where the pioneer trail varies from the modern highway have automobile roads nearby, but the U.S. Highway 91–Interstate 15 route is a considerable distance (and a mountain range) away from the old road in much of both segments. The routes are entirely separate for a full third of the distance, from Enoch, Utah, to Beaver Dam, Arizona, and from Las Vegas, Nevada, to Yermo, California.[6] I am a veteran of some 270 automobile trips over this road, including innumerable side trips to rediscovered historic spots. In recent years it has been exciting to piece together the sections of the old road, including locating actual wagon ruts and other "artifacts in place" long since forgotten by all but a very few.

Although many assume the Old Spanish Trail—western half—and what is often called the Mormon wagon route are virtually the same road, in fact there are a considerable number of places where the pack mule trail was impracticable for wheeled vehicles.[7] I and other associates, particularly Clifford J. Walker and Larry Reese, have tried to relocate still-visible two track wagon ruts in numerous segments of the route, including efforts made in three actual field classes sponsored through California State University Desert Studies Center headquartered at Zzyzx, California. Each class included road-locating trips to various Nevada and Utah locations as well as California. One of our contributions has been to show with reasonable certainty half a dozen places where the wagon road varied from the mule train trail, including on Utah Hill between the Santa Clara River and Beaver Dam Wash, Arizona, and on the Virgin River, where the packer trail followed the river considerably farther than the wagon road of the teamsters, who pulled away from the river some six miles downstream from Bunkerville, Nevada, then struggled up the Virgin Hill directly north of where Interstate 15 commences its grade up the Mormon Mesa between Mesquite and Glendale, Nevada. In the area of Cottonwood Springs-Blue Diamond, Nevada, mule caravans left the spring directly south heading for Mountain Springs, whereas wagon groups had to circle around the intervening hills before climbing up the mountain grade. Emigrant Pass, just within California, is perhaps the clearest instance of separate roads approaching the summit, and Cajon Pass includes similar distinct variations.[8]

Some portions of the earlier pack train route and the wagon road still need to be located. In an era when many pioneer trails have attracted dedicated advocate organizations that sponsor careful mapping and marking endeavors, the Southern Route from Salt Lake City to Los Angeles awaits adoption by such enthusiasts. Perhaps the increasingly active Old Spanish Trail Association can broaden its interest to more fully include the wagon road and western trail segments, with some appropriate combination name for the route. The automobile highways that later followed the same general route also need to be more fully adopted by promotion enthusiasts. It is doubtful if any American road has anything near the public consciousness or partly media-made mystique of Route 66, but the histories of the at least equally important Arrowhead Trails Highway, U.S. Highway 91, and Interstate 15 have yet received virtually no such attention. These voids will soon be filled. When the parallel natural gas pipelines, railroad, electric power transmission lines, air traffic routes, and the interstate highway are considered together, this historic route is presently one of the most important transportation corridors in the United States.[9]

It can be argued that mapping and publicizing old historic trails invites obliteration by people who would then ride all-terrain vehicles over them, but tradeoffs must be anticipated. There is no way to expect that all the existing road remnants will remain intact, partly because of normal highway construction needs and the

phenomenal growth of Washington County in Utah and the Las Vegas and Mesquite, Nevada, areas, among other factors. But again, organized groups could do much to assist in preserving and policing the trail. The efforts of such interested people virtually saved the historic Amargosa Canyon from semidestruction by ATV (all-terrain vehicle) enthusiasts, by persuading the U.S. Bureau of Land Management to limit such activity to the nearby (and perfectly suited for such use) Dumont Dunes recreational area. There is presently an excellent hiking trail through the canyon. Not far away on any given day one can watch (from the semipublic power line roads) the important military training maneuvers and operations conducted on another significant, but virtually obliterated, portion of the pioneer road between Red Pass and Bitter Springs within the present Fort Irwin army training base. This reservation is presently being expanded even farther northward, endangering another segment of the old road.

Special appreciation is due to Clifford J. Walker for exercising the editorial skills he honed through a career as an English teacher. The editorial staff of the University of Nevada Press have also improved the quality of this work. Las Vegas–based former acquisitions editor Trudy McMurrin and her editorial assistant, Monica Miceli, have been a pleasure to work with. I am particularly appreciative of Joanne O'Hare, editor in chief, for her persistence and patience at an early juncture of the project. Sarah Nestor, a final reader of the manuscript, was a pleasure to work with, as was Sara Vélez Mallea, managing editor. The errors of omission and commission remain, of course, my own.

The Overland Journey
from Utah to California

Chapter One

Contemporary Impressions Along the Southern Route

Because the wagon highway considered herein has never been much discussed, we must first describe the physical features of the route.[1] Perhaps this can best be accomplished by drawing on the descriptions and comments of travelers who experienced it firsthand and recorded their views. Although virtually all who journeyed over the route profoundly respected its challenges, few asserted they were surmounting the most challenging long roadway in the history of U.S. pioneering. But that is exactly what the Southern Route was, and those travelers were battling the nation's most difficult wagon road. Other roads may have had equally formidable mountain grades and certainly more rivers to cross, but none could even approach the difficulties presented by the insufficient livestock feed and water. And yet, although many draft animals succumbed to the harsh desert, no emigrants or freighters who followed the main road are known to have been lost directly to such causes of death. This says much about the serious-

ness and competence with which these heroic pioneers of the Southern Route approached their daunting journeys.

THROUGH THE UTAH SETTLEMENTS

The initial leg of the southern road to California was relatively easy, closely following the later overland automobile routes called at times Arrowhead Trails Highway, Highway 91, and Interstate 15. No settlements lay south of Provo in 1849, but that situation changed rapidly. As Lt. Sylvester Mowry stated in his 1855 report to his superiors, "[T]he march for two hundred and seventy miles [from Utah County] was through a well settled country, the road being dotted every few miles with small towns, their population varying from three or four hundred to as many thousands. The road is an admirable

Longest segment of the Southern Route, through present-day Utah. This is the closest to a north–south direction on the road. See inset at upper left for indication of how the directions of this and the ensuing two maps are oriented.

MAP COURTESY DR. NORMAN MEEK, CALIFORNIA STATE UNIVERSITY, SAN BERNARDINO

one to travel."[2] In the mid-1850s, many Mormon towns were changing their original names, which had been based on physical features, to those they have today. Willow Creek, at the southern edge of Salt Lake Valley, would thereafter be known as Draper. The hill between there and the adjacent Utah Valley was first called Corner of the Mountain but has been known ever since as Point of the Mountain. First in the sequence of towns in the northernmost portion of Utah Valley was Dry Creek, later called Lehi. Lake City later became known as

American Fork, and Battle Creek has been Pleasant Grove since those earliest days. Provost, named for an early mountain man and shortened simply to Provo, has always been the largest town in the valley.

Many of the pioneers over the Southern Route in 1849 gathered for their journey at Hobble Creek, later called Springville. Diarist William Birdsall Lorton described it as "a fine stream six yards wide running westerly from the Timpan-oza [Timpanogos] Mountains into the Utah Lake," a large freshwater lake emptying into the Great Salt Lake. He reported the water pure and cold and the stream banks "covered with a fringe of bushes and cottonwood trees." Pioneers camped there because in every direction the excellent soil lay "covered with a luxuriant growth of grass which affords abundant feed for cattle." The same diarist noted that the neighboring Spanish Fork River might be slightly larger, with similar grass, more interspersed with sagebrush, and banks covered with willows. Eight miles farther south what was called at the time Election Creek or Peteetneet, later Payson, served as the actual point of embarkation for several of the largest pioneer companies over the Southern Route. Lorton described the area as similar to the neighboring ones just passed, although the principal trees there were box elder with a few cottonwoods.

Lorton's traveling companion, Adonijah S. Welch, described what was usually called Salt Creek at future Nephi, some thirty-five miles south of Payson, saying it too was similar to those farther north. This characteristic description included a growth of willows along the banks and grasslands interspersed with cottonwood trees for at least a mile back from the foot of the mountains. Some ten miles farther down the trail, near what was later called the Levan ridge, was a formation some called Cistern Springs. Lorton described these as "a number of large excavations in the earth filled with water which from their singular resemblance to a cistern" received that name. Welch clarified these to be a series of springs about two miles in length and a half mile wide scattered with "excavations" generally eight feet in diameter and twenty feet deep. They were filled with pure, clear water, with bottoms covered with white lime and the nearby ground also white with an encrusted carbonate, with grass well interspersed between them (see note 2). Those afore-mentioned, and smaller streams coursing from the Wasatch Mountains running parallel to the trail

during the first fifty miles, became less frequent farther south. The vegetation also became more sparse, although 1849 diarist Vincent Hoover may have been a little extreme when he stated that the farther they journeyed in that direction, the more the country neared "the aspect of desolation." Hoover traveled the area just prior to the time when the first settlements in southern Utah were planted. Later observers included comments on the human elements of that area as well. Although the grass feed and water for the animals proved sufficiently plentiful for about three hundred miles, the equally essential firewood remained generally scarce near the road. Yet travelers from Lieutenant Mowry in 1855 to photographer William H. Jackson in 1867 noted that wood could be bought "at small cost" at each settlement along the route.

After climbing the hill dividing Utah Valley from adjacent Juab Valley, the emigrant road skirted the foot of Mount Nebo, leading to the Salt Creek–Nephi area. Characteristic of many Mormon settlements in the southern region, clusters of houses there were "well walled in and strong wooden gates fixed." In 1855, when British traveler William Chandless arrived there near midnight his guide, mail carrier David Savage, felt compelled to climb over the barricade, falling into a snowdrift in the ditch on the inside. Although Indians had reportedly burned the "good house for travelers" and it was not soon replaced, passing emigrants could usually obtain a meal, if not lodging, at one of the Nephi homes. Beyond Nephi the road stretched for some fifty miles without passing through a settlement (until Graball-Scipio was established in the 1860s).

Midway from Salt Creek to Cedar Springs, the road crossed the Sevier River, the largest stream encountered on the remainder of the route, some fifty feet across and four feet deep, in many places with even deeper mud. In 1849, before the innumerable passing wagon trains wore down the banks naturally, William Lorton described the banks as "eighteen feet perpendicular." His traveling companion Adonijah Welch noted a "stream fringed with willows and furnishing at intervals a bottom consisting of several acres of fine grass."[3] Mormon work crews erected a good bridge there in 1853, but it was destroyed within a year either by flood or by fire that Native Americans started. Solomon Nunes Carvalho, traveling with a large group of Mormon dignitaries, including Brigham Young, availed himself of a raft associ-ates fashioned from bridge timbers, crossing the river with reasonable ease. Soon after, Europeans Jules Remy and Julius Brenchley experienced considerably more difficulty persuading mules to pull their wagon up the steep south bank after crossing the stream. Another Eu-ropean traveler, William Chandless, passing that obsta-cle nearly a year later, noted that the greatest difficulty was watering the draft animals through a hole chopped in the ice.[4]

Crossing through Round Valley, several diarists com-mented on the agricultural potential and on the abun-dance of jackrabbits. After the valley, the road followed one that Franciscan explorers Sylvestre de Escalante and Atanasio Dominguez used in 1776 as they climbed through Scipio Pass and descended to Cedar Springs (temporarily known as Buttermilk Fort for the standard refreshment offered there). The small community would soon be renamed Holden after a Mormon Battalion vet-eran who died of exposure in the nearby pass. This set-tlement consisted of several houses enclosed by an adobe wall fifty feet square. Ten miles farther south the road brought travelers to Fillmore, for a short time the capital of Utah Territory. Enclosed within a "palisade," presumably tree trunks and cedar posts, this town fea-tured two inns and a "tavern." These facilities were es-tablished to serve the legislators and other government officials who met there on several occasions; they later voted to hold their governing sessions in Salt Lake City. Before the town was abandoned as the center of govern-ment, citizens erected a wing of a "statehouse" just be-yond the enclosure wall. The reddish stone building, which Jules Remy described as being 61 feet by 41 feet, seemed remarkable in that country at the time, if not in the outside world.[5] Meadow Creek was just a few miles farther south, after which Chief Kanosh's main Pahvant Indian village became visible off to the left. Some wag-oners experienced difficulty with the hills adjacent to the present Dog Valley between Kanosh and Cove Fort, then called Prairie Dog Valley. On down the roadway at Cove Creek, Willden's Stockade was to be enlarged and renamed as Cove Fort at the end of the overland emi-grant-freighting era, so late in the period that neither en-closure played any significant role in Southern Route travel. Not far from there a natural juniper tree "bow-ery" called by David Savage "the tavern" had at one time lent much-needed shade to travelers passing that way.

Solomon Carvalho carefully investigated a natural hydrothermal formation, just east of the road some five miles south of Cove Creek, long thereafter known as Sul-phurdale. This world traveler was correct in surmising that the visible mineral deposits had been formed by the action of sulfuric acid on feldspar rock. Farther down the trail another natural grade led travelers into Beaver Val-ley, featuring particularly rugged mountains on the east, as well as well-watered meadowlands, making it Vincent Hoover's favorite campground along the trail. More than a few emigrants attempted to catch fish in the Beaver River, with varying results. Leaving the valley to the south, difficult rocky stretches of road lay in the low pass near Black Mountain, replaced by an alternative route east of that mountain and improved through grading accomplished with congressional funds in 1855. The ad-jacent Parowan Valley featured the longest dry stretch on that portion of the trail, which headed southward toward Paragonah and Parowan and which loomed as a crucial test of the patience and organizational makeup of several emigrant companies early in the annals of the wagon trail's use. For many travelers, the valley north of Parowan proved longer than it first appeared. Government sur-veyor Mark S. Severance, with Lt. George Wheeler's 1872 expedition, lamented that his party was "unable to make Paragonah which seemed to recede as we neared it." This compelled his group and others coming before to camp at Buckhorn Springs, described by Severance as "a poor pool of water in the middle of the barren valley." By the 1870s, a Mormon family was operating a ranch where the surveyors obtained milk for their evening and morning meals.[6]

Solomon Carvalho had known and appreciated the area since his recent winter ordeal in connection with an ill-fated John C. Frémont expedition through the moun-tains just east of Paragonah in 1853–54. He offered a good description of the sheer-sided canyon walls, char-acteristically composed of red rock and soil. Gwin H. Heap, who with Edward Fitzgerald Beale's party inter-sected the main Southern Route trail there in 1853, was particularly impressed with the "excellent wagon road, made and kept in repair and bridged in many places by the Mormons." He also noted finger signposts at all crossroad intersections, along with milestones indicating the distances to various destinations. The expedition chronicler described the typically large lots behind each dwelling at Parowan, the Iron County seat, which enabled the planting of large vegetable gardens and fruit orchards while still allowing sufficient storage space for produce from the outlying farms.[7]

A few miles past Parowan the road climbed out of the valley, with a village naturally called Summit Creek situated near the top of the hill. At this location the Mormons held a major conference of the Church of Jesus Christ of Latter-day Saints: The 1851 colonists heading for southern California met with local church members gathered for the unusual occasion—outside of the center of Zion—of being addressed by four of the Quorum of Twelve Apostles. Just beyond the summit, the Old Spanish Trail branched west, whereas the road kept to the south toward Cedar City, the Iron Mission works, and the Leach Cutoff, built in 1855. During the first half-dozen years of wagon use over the Southern Route, all traffic followed the Old Spanish Trail. This crossed through the valley where Enoch would later be situated and up the western side toward Iron Springs, where many emigrants camped overnight. After passing a few more miles through the hills and continuing west, the trail came to Antelope Springs, a convenient interval for watering livestock near the edge of the Escalante Valley. From these springs, a good road turned southward and intersected a stretch of brushy desert as the road commenced the rather easy climb to the much-appreciated Mountain Meadows.

MOUNTAIN MEADOWS TO THE MUDDY RIVER

The other branch of the road passed through Cedar City, and after construction of the Leach Cutoff it headed southwest, cutting some fifteen miles off the old road distance. In 1855, Iron County Mormons complained that a substantial portion of the funds allocated by Congress for a military and mail road through the area appeared to have been funneled into the pockets of favorite "spoilsmen."[8] They may well have been referring to the supposed cutoff, which people not using the road considered unnecessary. Nevertheless, the contractor substantially improved the road.

Near the southwestern end of that cutoff, beyond the new village of Pinto, lay Mountain Meadows, situated in a valley some ten miles long and a mile wide, rich in nourishing bunchgrass feed, which was then watered by springs. These meadows partially comprise the origins of Magotsu Creek, a tributary of the Santa Clara River, the first stream encountered on the Southern Route that would eventually drain from the Colorado River into the Pacific Ocean instead of into the salton sinks of the Great Basin. Earlier, in the 1840s, John C. Frémont had recognized this distinguishing characteristic of the region and noted a point near the meadows to be the rim of the Great Basin. Virtually all emigrants appreciated the convenience of the meadows as a place for livestock to recuperate before heading into the demanding river bottoms and deserts of the ensuing segments of the route. Solomon Carvalho wrote with characteristically lavish praise of the meadows, saying, "[W]e camped on the banks of a beautiful stream, the Santa Clara, on the margins of which I observed the rose-tree, in full bearing, also cottonwood, ash, besides shrubs of different kinds, all in bloom. The air was filled with fragrance, and the scene presented a harmonious and refreshing landscape." He lamented, "This paradise is without a solitary living human inhabitant. These plants and flowers are literally wasting their sweetness on the desert air." Others with less literary facility demonstrated equal appreciation for the varied beauties and utility of the place, later the scene of the horrible Mountain Meadows Massacre (discussed fully in chapter 6).[9]

Beyond Mountain Meadows the trail headed south, descending the plateaus and mountains well over a thousand feet in a distance of thirty miles. This became regarded as the first difficult segment of roadway most pioneers encountered, being alternately rocky and sandy, with up to a dozen steep-banked crossings demanded, first of Magotsu Creek, then of the Santa Clara River. Vincent Hoover complained that his first large group with wagons in 1849 encountered an undergrowth of trees and shrubs "so thick [they had] to cut the road," slowing progress considerably. The same diarist documented another drawback: lack of nourishing grass available in the canyon bottoms, compelling cattle to "browse on the leaves of the trees." Later companies, often assisted by the numerous Native Americans in the vicinity, drove their livestock up to four miles into side canyons or onto the top of the plateau to graze better grasslands there. Sometimes this grass lay in close proximity to volcanic craters, lava flows, and cinder cones of great interest to some passing travelers, as were the Indian dwellings and fields interspersed throughout the area. Fortunately most wagoners forded the Santa Clara during seasons of low water, but Carvalho encountered the stream when it was "much swollen" and thus "got a wetting as the price of [his] ferriage." He described accomplishing the crossings by attaching each wagon to all the horses with long ropes and pulling over quickly, with the current "so strong as nearly to overturn them." Despite the difficulty, this journey chronicler described the "abrupt rocks" as picturesque, comparing the canyon formations to some he had recently observed in Colorado.

After enjoying a good campsite where the valley of the Santa Clara widened as it curved eastward toward the site of the later Mormon town of that same name, within the present Shivwits Indian reservation, the road left the stream and commenced a difficult climb up what was for a time known as Conger Hill, after the mail carrier Leonard Conger, who frequently used it. Officially called the Beaver Dam Mountains, this range is more commonly known as Utah Hill. Traveling in 1850, Washington Peck reported the trail was up a dry creek bed in a canyon, featuring "loose sand and gravel very heavy on the teams, a steep hill most of the way up. Very deep sand. About 200 feet from the top was an elevation of about 45 degrees."[10] Although some experienced travelers later used Camp Springs—near the higher summit some four miles off the trail—most made this climb one of their first "dry camps," with the livestock forced to pull all day without having water during the night, finally reaching some at Beaver Dam Wash late the next morning. Although the twenty-mile climb and descent proved reasonably manageable, near the apex of the mountain roadway travelers encountered in Hoover's words "a very rocky canyon, dangerous to wagons."

The earlier pack-mule trains could negotiate the lower stream beds, but sometimes teamsters felt compelled to take their wagons up steep grades strewn with loose rocks and along mountain roads not always sufficiently level to keep the vehicles from tipping. Some wagon drivers apparently chose to travel up the stream bed rather than pull over the ridges. After the travelers had surmounted these obstacles, the gradual descent

was easy, although the draft animals could be difficult to hold back as they smelled the water at the foot of the long grade. Near the end of the overland wagon era, a long discussed cutoff road, the Miller cutoff, was eventually constructed from Castle Cliff midway down from the summit due west toward the upper Beaver Dam Wash and toward the foot of Mormon Mountain beyond. But this was primarily for later freighters. Emigrant trains were still compelled to face the rigors presented by Indians, the Virgin River, Virgin Hill, and other similar challenges on down the old trail.

As the road approached the Virgin River, which had just emerged from a rocky gorge several miles to the east, emigrants could see the lower Beaver Dam Wash—often dry—to their right, running approximately parallel to their course of travel. Descending into the wash approximately a half mile before it converged with the Virgin, pioneers found a large grove of cottonwood and willow trees fed by several springs. In 1849, Jefferson Hunt showed Addison Pratt where the namesake beaver dam had spanned the small creek; the dam had been destroyed by the previous season's flood runoff. Pratt also noticed numerous stumps of smaller trees that had been cut by the animals. This was a distinct zone of change insofar as plants and animals as well as climate were concerned—from mountain to desert. Thomas Morris, traveling through the area in 1849, noted the remarkable "transition from winter to summer."[11]

Described by Pratt as ten rods wide, the Virgin River wound along a sandy bottom covered with salt grass on either side, with sometimes perpendicular banks looming on the outer edge of the bottoms, occasionally rising to a height of one hundred feet. Vincent Hoover, who traveled the area at almost the same time, described the water as reddish in color and "brackish owing to many salt springs which flow[ed] into it." The latter diarist described the primary shrub as red locust, but he undoubtedly meant mesquite, which grows profusely along the stream. The numerous river crossings, most of which featured sand, mud, and quicksand footings for the animals and wagons, proved treacherous at best, and the notably sandy road in between ensured hard pulling for the draft livestock. The Hoover-Derr-Gruwell party of 1849 was probably typical of most future travelers who became particularly discouraged and "tired of the trip" after struggling along this portion of the road. Hoover

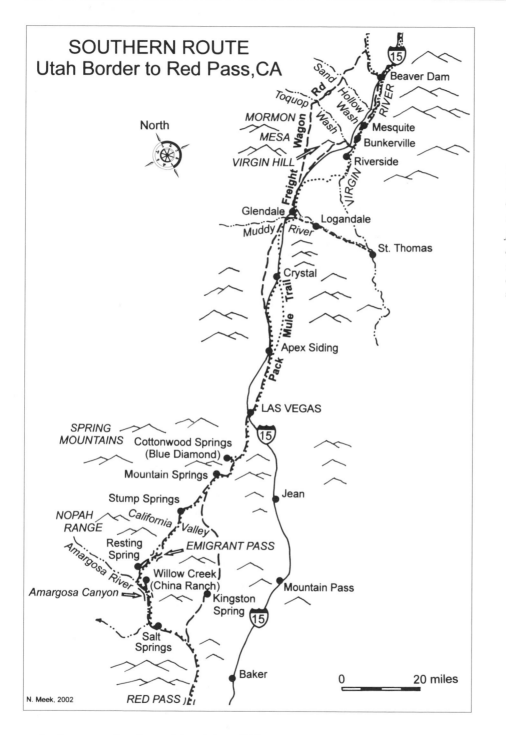

SOUTHERN ROUTE
Utah Border to Red Pass, CA

North

MORMON
MESA

VIRGIN HILL

Toquop Wash

Sand Hollow Wash

Wagon Rd

VIRGIN RIVER

Beaver Dam

Mesquite

Bunkerville

Riverside

Freight

Glendale

Muddy River

Logandale

St. Thomas

Crystal

Pack Mule Trail

Apex Siding

LAS VEGAS

SPRING
MOUNTAINS

Cottonwood Springs
(Blue Diamond)

Mountain Springs

Stump Springs

Jean

NOPAH
RANGE

California Valley

Resting
Spring

EMIGRANT PASS

Amargosa River

Willow Creek
(China Ranch)

Amargosa Canyon

Kingston
Spring

Mountain Pass

Salt
Springs

Baker

0   20 miles

N. Meek, 2002

RED PASS

This section of the Southern Route was doubtless the most difficult stretch of wagon road used regularly by pioneers or freighters anywhere in the continental United States.

MAP COURTESY DR. NORMAN MEEK, CALIFORNIA STATE UNIVERSITY, SAN BERNARDINO

spoke for many when he exclaimed that all his companions appeared elated to be leaving the river, which they did at a point some six miles downstream from present Bunkerville, Nevada, locally called Huntsman's hill. The pack-mule trail continued down the river for some distance before climbing onto what would after the 1870s be called Mormon Mesa.

By unanimous consensus from all who left accounts of travel over the Southern Route, the next obstacle, the Virgin Hill, proved the most difficult on the entire wagon road. After fording the river the last time, the travelers headed north and west with some two miles of heavy pulling up the sandy slope to the foot of the mesa. Addison Pratt described the steep hill as "about two hundred yards long and ris[ing] with a circular sweep," until near the top there loomed a ledge the diarist described as "rocky and nearly perpendicular." Vincent Hoover's company, the first wagon train over the route, had to spend several hours breaking rock to chisel a passageway to the mesa top. This road improvement, still visible, was much appreciated by subsequent groups. These groups pooled their draft animals, usually attached to a long rope or joined chains. This arrangement allowed the long pull while still affording the better traction possible on the top of the mesa than could ever be attained on the steep slope. Pratt had described this slope as "so steep near the top that an ox can barely stand without pulling at all." In fact, some exhausted animals also had to be assisted to the top by the ropes. Many emigrant companies labored through the night getting all their wagons up, which resulted in camps with no water and almost no fuel for cooking fires.[12]

The fourteen-mile road across the mesa served well for wagons but often proved tough on the unshod hooves of the livestock. Peck called it "the hardest roads on teams, for a dry one, I've ever seen." Thomas Flint, whose party was driving a herd of sheep there in 1853, described it as "a rough sharp gravelly trail" with "pebbles like rasps" on the tender feet of his animals, many of which had to be abandoned on the way. The main roadway approximately intersecting the center of the plateau was characterized by several huge chasms cutting the southern half and barring travel across that segment. The latter freight road essentially followed the foothills on the northern edge of the flatlands. At the western rim of the mesa, the brush and willows of the Muddy River were clearly visible in the valley more than a mile distant, below, which could be reached by a rather easy descending road.

Flint asserted the stream to be "rightly named," with the water "generally four feet deep and the mud deeper." He complained the riverbanks were so steep they had to search for a place where his sheep could get down to the water. Some of the accompanying cattle jumped off the high banks, and men had to drive them in the river, with

considerable difficulty, to where they could climb out. Virtually all pioneer companies camped at the Muddy River crossing for several days to let their livestock recuperate before embarking on what Spaniard muleteers had earlier termed the "*jornada del muerto*," the journey of death (also called by some Anglo emigrants the "fifty-mile desert"). On leaving the California Crossing of the Muddy, the road passed up the similarly named California Wash, described by Gwin Heap in 1853 as "six miles up a broad and sandy ravine, issuing from which [they] entered upon an extensive and undulating plain whose sandy and stony soil produced no vegetation except artemisia." Almost all travelers elected to commence this journey at night, primarily for the benefit of the draft animals, who would generally have to pull some thirty-six hours without water to get across. Although no human deaths were recorded during the era of Anglo-American use, this stretch remained an always dreaded fifty-mile ordeal.[13]

LAS VEGAS TO RESTING SPRINGS

Undoubtedly the desert approaches to Las Vegas Springs from either direction made it the most appreciated stopping place on the entire route. Heap lauded it: "[T]his oasis deserves the name of the 'diamond of the desert' so beautiful and bright it appears in the center of the dreary waste that surrounds it." The main artesian area actually had a series of three springs, the largest forming a pool over forty feet in diameter, which watered the *vegas* (meadowlands), the Spanish name from which the place-name was derived. The small stream, with several other springs feeding it en route, ran eastward some two and a half miles to the brow of the plateau, where the Mormons built their fort-outpost in 1855, watering grasslands stretching back from the creek about a quarter mile on each side. Several travelers noted the buoyancy of bathers held up by the upward currents in the main spring and the universally unsuccessful attempts to establish the depth of the water there.

Predictably, Carvalho penned the most vivid contemporary description of the area. He reported his group "camped on a narrow stream of deliciously cool water, which distributes itself about half a mile further down, in a verdant meadow bottom, covered with good grass. . . . We followed up this delicious stream for about three miles." Upon locating the source he reported, "[T]he water bubbled up as if gas were escaping, acacias in full bloom, almost entirely surrounded it—it was forty-five feet in diameter; we approached through an opening, and found it to contain the clearest and purest water I ever tasted; the bottom which consisted of white sand, did not seem to be more than two feet from the surface." He continued that on entering the water to swim, "[W]hat were my delight and astonishment to find all my efforts to sink were futile. I raised my body out of the water, and suddenly lowered myself, but I bounced upwards as if I had struck a springing-board. I walked about in the water up to my arm-pits, just the same as if I had been walking on dry land," propelled upward by the springs current. Investigating, Carvalho discovered that "the water, instead of being two feet deep, was over fifteen, the depth of the longest tent pole we had with us."[14]

After the required rest, each wagon train passed down the trail southwest, climbing gradually through low limestone hills. Addison Pratt described "the ground covered with stones from the size of gravel to that of a man's head [which] was covered with sharp points and corners. . . . This [was] the worst day's travel [they had experienced so far as their] cattle's feet" were concerned. For that reason, some of the best-prepared companies stopped in the area to shoe more of their animals. Toward the end of an eighteen-mile trek from the last campsites, the road headed westward up a dry creek bed with scattered cottonwood trees, eventually arriving at Cottonwood Springs, site of the present town of Blue Diamond, Nevada. This too would have served as a good resting place—if the preceding companies had not depleted the limited grass supply. Jules Remy described the locality as "a spot surrounded by hills, on a small piece of ground covered with verdure, in the midst of which were to be seen willows, cactus, figworts, some poor and lank helianthus, some tall crucifers, a large rumex, all of them completely withered, but still recognizable. Before us," he continued, "on the other side of the hills, rose a peaked rocky, jagged mountain, to which our eyes were attracted by some reddish tints of different shades." This

doubtless described a view of what would later be a portion of Red Rock Canyon State Park visible in the distance.[15] Many other travelers also commented on the appealing scene.

Examination of the still-extant trail near the springs indicates that wagons did not pass through the gap to the main trail, as pack mules undoubtedly did, but were compelled to double back around the hills to intersect with that road. Thereafter the route continued southwest, then climbed rather abruptly through a mountain canyon later called Potosi Pass to Mountain Springs at an elevation of about 5,300 feet above sea level. William Chandless described the summit area as "a pretty spot, among pine and cedar-wood, and high mountain tops; and though a regular camping place on the route, yet with an air of solitude very impressive." He also noted of the weather that "though at a considerable elevation, we found no snow here, nor even saw it on the peaks very much above us."[16] Others would encounter snow there, though no one enjoyed it.

The descent into what was later named Pahrump Valley featured a gradually inclined, good road still heading southwest. Peck observed concerning the vast expanses, "It appears the goddess of desolation and barrenness has erected her throne and reigns without a rival." The valley floor included considerable sandy stretches on the fifteen miles of road heading toward Stump Springs, described by Charles Colson Rich as "a spring under a willow tree." Peck and some others inaccurately called Stump Springs, Willow Springs. Some mentioned several such trees along the bottom of the desert wash. At best the water supply there was sparse. If, as did Amasa Mason Lyman, my great-great-grandfather, in 1851, travelers "managed" the precious commodity properly by digging a storage reservoir to fill through the night, they could adequately water the livestock at that stopping place. Still, the animals would always have to be driven some distance from the spring to find sufficient grass.[17]

The trail thereafter passed into California and over a steep divide seldom mentioned in the available diaries. William Farrar, a young English Mormon convert heading for the gold fields to mine on shares with his grubstake supplier, an older Latter-day Saint from Salt Lake City, noted having "crossed a ridge rather bad descending. Traveled the Valley about 12 miles & turned to the right." At that point, having crossed what was later called the California Valley, the trail came to one of the most difficult climbs of the route, up Emigrant Pass, after which the road reached Resting Springs some thirty miles from the last watering place.[18]

An impressive desert oasis ranked only behind those of Las Vegas and Mountain Meadows, Resting Springs served as an important stopping place for travelers. However, abundant alkali impregnation of the surrounding soil ensured that the only grass available would be salt grass, which many livestock handlers soon concluded to be poor feed, and thus most stopped but a short time at the springs. Rich mentioned an "orchard" there, which must have been simply a reference to a grove of shade trees rather than fruit-bearing ones, or else other travelers would have mentioned that fact. Caroline Barnes Crosby noted that Indians camped near the springs were growing considerable vegetables there in 1858.[19]

AMARGOSA RIVER
TO THE MOJAVE RIVER

A few miles south of Resting Springs, near future Tecopa, California, the trail came to the Amargosa River, known to many pioneers as Salaratus Creek because of the heavy alkali content of the water. Addison Pratt described the entrance to the nearby river canyon as a "short crooked ridge" that divided two dry washes or riverbeds. The lower end of this incline was "steep and descended with much difficulty." Lt. Sylvester Mowry called the Amargosa "a small putrid stream running through a deep narrow canyon the descent into which [was] exceedingly dangerous for wagons." Other companies could attest to the veracity of his statement that "more breakage occurred here than along the whole of the previous march."[20]

William Lorton described Amargosa Canyon in some detail in 1849. After mentioning some cascades on the creek, he observed the "high, erect sand bluffs on each side, and a good spring, though warm." During some seasons numerous small springs run along a fault line along the east wall of the canyon. In mentioning sand, Lorton probably meant sandstone, ancient lake sediment, and conglomerate rock "here piled up perpendi-

cular in shapes, cones and in shapes of columns, domes and perspective edifices with turrets, cupolas, and fantastic shapes." Two of the most descriptive women diarists of the route also commented on this feature as they traveled through Amargosa Canyon. Sarah Pratt in 1852 noted "beautiful scenery, as well as heavy sand." Caroline Crosby, traveling back the other way northeastward toward Salt Lake City in 1858, reported, "[W]e have a very romantic scenery around us. The rocks on all sides of us rise almost perpendicular above our heads, and present a grand and majestic appearance." Vincent Hoover was also much impressed by the landscape in this vicinity.

One of the least-known resources of the entire region skirting Death Valley was Willow Creek, rising in what later became China Ranch just a mile from its confluence with the Amargosa. This freshwater tributary was probably what Mowry in 1855 called "the pure water springs on the Amigosia [sic]." A few other emigrants, such as Amasa Lyman also in 1855, enjoyed this spring water that flowed so close to the unpalatable waters of the Amargosa. But most others, for whatever reasons, did not avail themselves of this opportunity.[21]

After the main trail emerged from the canyon, it ran through perhaps the deepest sand on the entire route, in the vicinity of the later famous off-road-vehicle recreation area, Dumont Dunes, toward Amargosa Springs in the Salt Springs Hills some fourteen miles from the Willow Creek confluence with the Amargosa River. David Cheesman's 1850 report of the area was probably the more typical, stating, "[H]ere we found some of the heaviest roads we had yet pulled through. The sand was so loose and deep it seemed almost impossible to move the wagons through it, the cattle were so weak." The brackish Amargosa Springs lay in a short, narrow canyon adjacent to the mine of the same name discovered by Addison Pratt and his travel companions in 1849. The pack-mule trail cut through this passageway, but wagon trains were compelled to skirt a little farther south and then east, past nearby Salt Springs and the wash of the same name passing around the nearby hills. Joseph Caine, author of the "Mormon Waybill," cautioned pioneers that Salt Spring had "no fresh water" and but "poor feed." However, several companies, including Addison Pratt's, found puddles of standing water since a recent rain, which served the livestock well. Several groups also fed the livestock the reeds they found growing along the usually wet Salt Creek Wash. Similarly, more than a few travelers found "muddy water standing in holes" on the hardpans on or near Silurian (dry) Lake to the south and east. Cheesman's comments on the Salt Springs and creek were less favorable: "[T]he water here [was] so alkaline that the stock would not drink it. They would make the effort and then give up."[22]

In the Silurian (dry) Lake area southeastward a few miles beyond Salt Springs Wash, the main trail intersected the Kingston Springs cutoff, the often-used alternative route that branched off the main road after the descent from Mountain Springs, Nevada. This route bypassed Stump Springs, Emigrant Pass, Resting Springs, the Amargosa River, and Salt Springs, using only Kingston Springs and the nearby Coyote Holes water sources midway on that trail. The most experienced travelers of the Southern Route, the mail carriers, considered the cutoff substantially shorter in distance and time. They were undoubtedly correct about the latter, but modern topographic maps indicate little savings in actual distance, although the only acceptable map of that time seemed to indicate a good shortening in distance as well.[23] William Chandless described the "wide plains of dreary cactus" of the northernmost portion of Pahrump Valley as the trail bypassed Stump Springs and traversed a wide, dry lake bed. He noted that the approach to Kingston Springs also followed a "dry watercourse." Another international traveler, Jules Remy, described the main spring as "scanty," with water "jetting up from a culminating point." He noticed birds playing and bathing "in the rill that flowed from the spring" and away into the saline soil. Chandless reported that the spring "rose out of a small hillock of rotten black earth, covered on the surface with a white crust; the effect of the alkali with which the water is very strongly impregnated and made unpleasant to drink."

Solomon Carvalho met the John and Enoch Reese freight wagon train at Kingston Springs on their return journey toward Utah in early 1854. Because Carvalho's report gave the first published mention of Kingston Springs, the Reeses have sometimes been credited with originating the cutoff. However, it is doubtful that anyone as mistake prone as members of that expedition had

been could have conceived of such an innovation. It is far more likely they followed the advice of some fellow Mormon mail carrier who had probably already traveled that way. Trail veteran William Clark asserted that a longtime California acquaintance, former mail carrier C. L. Kingston, who helped one of the Pomeroy brothers retrieve money hidden during an earlier crisis along the route in 1849, had it named after himself. In the absence of alternatives, this claim should be accepted.[24] As one of the springs in the area, probably the one now named Coyote Holes, was then called Savage Springs, it is entirely likely that mail carrier David Savage should be credited with establishing regular use of the cutoff. This was probably a better route for pack mules and perhaps even mules pulling wagons, but the longer dry stretches on both sides of the main springs doubtless caused mail carrier Jim Williams to advise Lt. Sylvester Mowry to take his horse-mounted army regiment by the old road in 1855.

Caroline Crosby described Silurian (dry) Lake, where the two trails rejoined, as a "great curiosity. It was much larger than [she] had anticipated. The surface was as level as a floor and composed of light colored clay." In fact, she added, "the white clay seem[ed] to affect [their] eyes." Lieutenant Mowry, who had led his extremely thirsty soldiers across the most forbidding stretch of the entire Southern Route, mainly along washes from the dry lake to Red Pass on 2 June 1855, reported that "the severity of this march across the desert can scarcely be imagined. The road for more than half the distance is ascending and heavy with sand. No vegetation exists." He concluded by stating that the desolation of the area strongly reminded him of the biblical curse "[F]rom generation to generation it shall lie waste, none shall pass through it for ever and ever" (Isaiah 34:10). In fact, of the numerous travelers who struggled past that way none are known to have perished there, although literally thousands of draft animals left their bones along that road.

Just two days prior to Mowry, Charles C. Rich had led a small Mormon party that same way. He recorded in his journal that as they approached the Red Pass section, "[W]e came to the point of a mountain jutting out towards the road, said to be about eighteen miles from the Bitter Springs where we stopped and rested about an hour without unharnessing. When we stopped here we were about give out, both men and animals." The temperature posed the most serious threat; the church leader recorded that "the heat has been so intense that all had suffered in consequence, the very air seemed almost suffocating. The rocks of the surrounding mountains and the sand reflected the heat with such intensity that if the air had been blown from heated ovens it seemed as if it could not have been more oppressive." It took the group the rest of a painful day to reach Bitter Springs.[25]

Rich's fellow Mormon, apostle Parley Parker Pratt, accompanying the California colonization company of 1851, also gave a poignant account of this leg of the journey. His group of ten wagons was about fourteen miles from the springs, with some of their oxen having just given out and thus removed from their yokes. Yet, he recorded, "we still rolled slowly, resting every few minutes. We soon found the different portions [of the party of ten wagons that should have been an hour ahead] halted, and lost in slumber—every man and beast, by common consent, sunk in profound slumber, and probably dreaming of water and feed ahead." Most of Pratt's own group "slipped quietly past them and resting often and a few minutes at a time continued to roll."[26]

Solomon Carvalho, probably the best describer of the entire Southern Route, wrote thus of the same area: "[T]his is a howling, barren wilderness; not a single tree or shrub for the last fifty miles, nor is there one in sight now. [He] did not observe during the last day's travel, a lizard or any sign of animal or insect life. There was plenty of food for wolves," because of the numerous dead draft animals, but those scavengers, meaning coyotes, did not dare venture that far from water. The traveler-artist observed of what was always known as Bitter Springs, "[T]hese springs are not bitter, but possess a brackish taste. These are small springs in different places; the largest admitted one horse at a time to drink, the rest would have to wait until the water was replenished from the earth." Then, commenting on available livestock feed, he asserted that "along the whole road there is not a blade of grass for a distance of fifty miles; but in the immediate vicinity of this spring there are hundreds of acres of the best quality of bunch grass." The Jewish Portuguese observer conceded reasonably, "[W]ithout the watchful care of Divine Providence, man

would be unable successfully to traverse these deserts," referring to the strategically placed, if meager, supplies of feed and water.

The numerous messages left pinned to the thorny mesquite bushes for others coming behind became an interesting feature of Bitter Springs. Lorton called it "a regular post office without any master." Much of the information related to the formidable obstacle of a long, dry mountain climb just ahead. Later, a new road cut off to the south from Bitter Springs, undoubtedly blazed in 1860 to connect the military outpost established there with the larger army garrison then maintained at Camp Cady on the Mojave River. At least a few later emigrant groups, such as the Rousseau party of 1864, would go that way.[27]

IMPASSABLE PASS
TO THE MOJAVE RIVER

Just beyond Bitter Springs looms a large rock formation long known as "the whale," around which the main road circled to the west. As Vincent Hoover noted, "[Y]ou then turn to the left and begin to ascend a long and tedious mountain" that was fifteen miles to the top. Most continued up the grade to the southwest, long afterward known as Impassable Pass, many leaving exhausted animals en route. "Wash" Peck vividly described the climb thus: "Our rise was at least 150 feet per mile and much of the way the wheels sinking 1/2 the depth of the fellow [sic; a felloe is the circular segment of the wheel between the rim and the spokes] in sand or gravel. It was hot [in mid-December] so had to rest the animals often." Vincent Hoover's 1849 group made a dry camp not far from the summit, and after supper he set out alone in the dark in a futile attempt to locate grass and water. After about an hour facing a severe windstorm, he reached the top just as the moon came up. For some of this distance the high wind compelled him to crawl on his hands and knees.[28]

A group of Mormon missionaries traveling just days behind Hoover found the climb even worse because of an intervening snowstorm. James S. Brown described their gloomy situation amid mud and snow, with darkness setting in and every rod of the road appearing more steep and difficult. The two-mile climb to the summit, he observed, could only be accomplished in small, exhausting spurts. Some travelers broke a trail through the snow ahead of the team and wagon, whereas others pushed from behind. This effort aimed as much to break a trail for the weaker associates coming behind as to get through themselves. Finally, Brown recalled, "[W]ith a shout of triumph, we reached the summit in two feet of snow, at eleven o'clock at night." Although all in the group would have agreed the pass was properly named, the remaining men got through the next day.[29]

The ensuing leg of the roadway, down Spanish Canyon and on across a moderate desert stretch to the Mojave River, would not have been formidable except for the exhaustion of people and animals. In fact, almost no diarists seemed prone to record anything about this final struggle to get to better feed and water. Peck remarked, "[T]he road to the [Mojave] river is descending all the way and good except a little too much sand in places." However, once there many lavished praise on an area others would later consider a rather drab desert river bottom. James Brown's account commented, "[W]e moved to the Mojave River. When we reached that stream, I presume that we felt as pleased as a man liberated from a life sentence in a dungeon, for we had reason to feel assured that we would succeed in our journey, as we had only one more hard scramble of thirty miles and had pleasant weather and plenty of feed and water for [their] stock, with time to rest in." It probably mattered little that the actual distance was still three times that estimate, as he noted some companions shouting, "[D]aylight once more; thank God for our deliverance!" Having reached that same general vicinity, Parley Pratt was similarly elated and thankful. After confessing the journey "was certainly the hardest time [he] ever saw," he claimed God had heard the prayers of the travelers in his group "to strengthen [them] and [their] teams and He did so in a miraculous manner, and [they] were saved from the horrors of the desert." Peck confessed relief on arrival at the Mojave because his fellow travelers now considered themselves through the desert. He compared the recent ordeal to a difficult ocean voyage, saying they "felt like the dangerous and almost unknown seas when we arrive in a port." He also boasted they had "crossed a desert of 260 miles with only 10 watering

places intervening and part of the water salt, bitter or impregnated with alkali. The grass mostly of inferior quality and scarce."[30]

UP THE MOJAVE RIVER

At the first contact with the Mojave River, usually at a place long known as Forks of the Road (the other fork heading eastward into Arizona), the water seldom ran on the surface of the river bottom. Gwin Heap expressed the common understanding of all travelers that although "the sandy soil through which the Mohaveh [Mojave] flows absorbs nearly all its water, and where we struck it was no longer a running stream." Nevertheless, earlier travelers had dug sufficient shallow wells that the best water since leaving Las Vegas was always available there. Heap observed appreciatively that good grass feed "was everywhere abundant, together with a thick growth of willows, reeds, and mesquite bushes, interlaced with grape-vines; and in some places there were beautiful groves of cottonwoods." But he was probably confessing a disappointment shared by his traveling companion, Edward F. Beale, who had hoped to locate an Indian reservation in the vicinity, when he stated, erroneously, that "except on the edge of the river, however, the land was barren and unproductive, offering no point fit for settlement."[31]

Addison Pratt was more complimentary about the area, describing the bottoms as "a mile or two wide here and it intermixed with willows and grass until it affords some of the finest range I ever saw." He pursued a favorite avocation of deer hunting without any success—his Mormon brethren a day or two ahead had already killed five and had presumably frightened all others away, at least temporarily.[32] And again, Solomon Carvalho continued lauding most appreciatively the river upstream near the last crossing between present Helendale and Oro Grande. After also noting the good livestock feed, he described as his party "rode through a beautiful grove of cottonwood, with willow undergrowth. Rose trees in full bloom, with hundreds of other beautiful flowers. This is a fairy land, indeed. What a contrast to the desert of a few hours ago! Grape vines hang gracefully from the branches of lofty trees, while the air resounds with the songs of birds." He also noticed the abundant California quail, ducks, and herons.[33]

When Gwin Heap and his company passed that same area in 1853, they observed antelope on the river meadows, along with numerous rabbits. He described the river at that point as "a rapid stream, twenty-five yards in breadth and one foot in depth, but its water was too warm to be drinkable." After enjoying the expected rest at the Mojave, the Beale-Heap party took "the road leading up to an extensive plain, thickly covered with cedars and pines, intermingled with palmyra cactus [Joshuas] and aloes." The chronicler noted that about ten miles from the river, in the area of later southwest Victorville, the trails again divided. He continued, "[T]he left-hand fork, which [his group chose] follow[ed] the Old Spanish Trail, whilst the other, which had been recently opened by the Mormons, makes a bend to avoid a rough portion of country. They both join again in the Cajon Pass."[34]

DOWN CAJON PASS

After a usually dry camp in the vicinity of present southwestern Hesperia and Oak Hills, virtually all emigrant parties of 1849 negotiated what some compared to the previous worst ordeal of the journey at Virgin Hill. Vincent Hoover boasted his party "accomplished this day what never has been performed in the annals of wagon era. [They had] descended the back bone of Sierra Nevada [sic; San Bernardino–San Gabriel Mountains]. Persons who have not wagoned much would have thought impossible for us to have got a wagon down it. No person but a determined, resolute set would have ever got down it." He later explained that most had rough-locked [tied or chained to prevent turning] the rear wheels of their wagon to slow the descent, but he had elected to leave his wheels free and had driven "down [the grade] with fear and trembling." Descending the canyon to the area later intersected by California Highway 138, each party camped near the first water encountered in the Coyote–Crowder Creek branch of Cajon Creek.

For Hoover's trailblazing party, the second day proved even more challenging. He reported, "[W]e have been all day fixing the canyon. It is very rocky. You cannot imagine what a place it is. Nothing but rocks upon rock.

The like has never been performed before or since. The distance is one half mile. It took two hours to go it," presumably with teams and wagons. He continued: "[T]he stones are large and in many places small precipices to fill in which we had to do with stones. We completed the road at about three in the evening." The diarist also reported that "in many places we were compelled to let the wagon boxes down and over the rocks." After all this labor, a storm of unusual intensity for the Cajon Pass raised the water level of the creek so high as to compel several emigrant companies to camp in close-packed proximity rather than pull back up the grade.[35]

Addison Pratt, in the same area at that time, described the terrain: "[T]his stream has cut its way though mountains until the perpendicular banks in some places are near a hundred feet high." In that spot, although there was hardly sufficient livestock feed or camping room, "the water rose so high in the creek that [they] were obliged to stay there two days . . . all jammed together in the narrow pass," during which the energetic Mormons explored the surrounding mountains. When it was finally possible to proceed, Pratt boasted that "all [others] had to be helped but our own wagon, it helped itself up and down the rocks but the rest had to be lifted and pried to get them up and down." He must have meant that the men attached to his wagon were able to lift it over the rock obstacles without other assistance. Hoover had to wade down the cold creek, presumably to steady wagons, some of which did capsize.[36]

After that first year of wagon use on the Southern Route, virtually all wagons descended roads constructed in the west Cajon Pass instead of the nearly impossible trail of the forty-niners through Coyote–Crowder Creek Canyon. From the dividing point ten miles from the Mojave, as diarist Sarah Pratt recorded, this way to the summit struck "off to the right." She stated it was a "good road but a little ascending most of the way," along which they encountered "beautiful specimens" of various plants, including huge Joshua trees in what was later the Baldy Mesa–Phelan area.[37]

David Cheesman, traveling to southern California, in 1850 led the first wagon train to attempt the roadway down the west Cajon that William T. B. Sanford had just informed him about and presumably improved. His company approached the summit in mid-afternoon. There they encountered the sandy fifteen-foot "hogback" bank

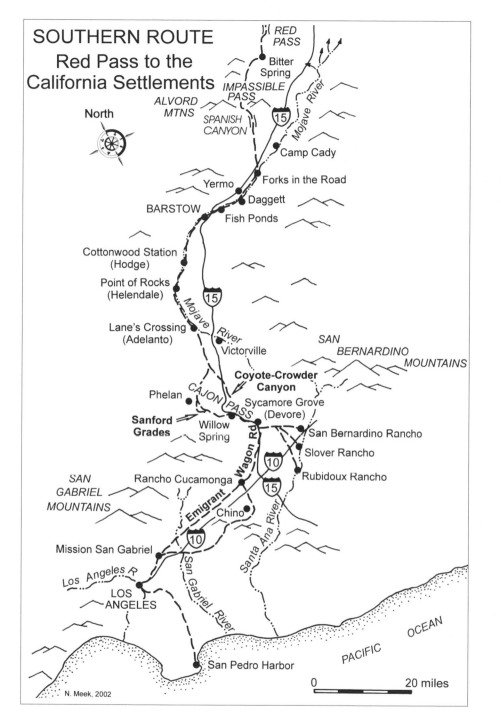

SOUTHERN ROUTE
Red Pass to the California Settlements

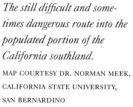

The still difficult and some-times dangerous route into the populated portion of the California southland.

MAP COURTESY DR. NORMAN MEEK,
CALIFORNIA STATE UNIVERSITY,
SAN BERNARDINO

they had to climb before starting the descent. He recorded that "all hands, women and all, pushed, so we reached the long desired summit. Once on the summit, the [intersecting] ridge was so narrow that the fore and hind wheels were on either side." Like most teamsters negotiating this challenging incline, Cheesman locked both hind wheels of his wagon and unhitched all but the wheel oxen and started down. He recalled, "[F]or a distance of fifty or sixty feet it was so steep that the cattle and all slid down. After that the descent was gradual."[38]

Carvalho three years later noted a slightly different method, saying, "[T]he descent of our wagons occupied considerable time; the team was in front, but the whole force of men were attached to long ropes at the end of the wagon, to prevent its too rapid descent; the surface of this saddle [gap in ridge] is perfectly smooth."[39]

The lower Cajon Pass roadway could be traversed with relative ease, with most emigrants stopping to rest at Willow Grove, where the two branches of the trail again joined. The water of the Cajon Creek flows consistently at that spot, and because most draft teams had not enjoyed sufficient water for more than a full day, it remained a much appreciated stopping place. The mouth of the canyon pass featured an even more lauded camping ground, called by contemporaries Sycamore Grove and, more recently, Glen Helen Regional Park at Devore, California. Cheesman was among the considerable number who wrote enthusiastically of this spot so near their immediate destination. He exclaimed, "[W]e arrived at Sycamore Grove in the afternoon and camped. This was a most beautiful spot; a small valley dotted with large sycamores and clover nearly waist high. The only drawback was a strong wind which set in toward the canyon." Such winds are now known as the Santa Ana winds, still a common phenomenon of that area during at least half the year.

As many other companies did later, Cheesman's party remained at Sycamore Grove three days. He then noted leaving "this paradise of a camping spot reluctantly for Cucumonga Ranch [Cucamonga Rancho]," also an almost universal temporary destination for travelers. At that juncture at the end of 1850, Cheesman confessed, "it is impossible to describe our feelings. We had now arrived in the valley of California. The mountains, dreary wastes and deserts were behind us. Here opened up the most lovely country we had ever beheld. The grass was up and seemingly all over the valley, some four inches in height, the climate soft and exhilarating."[40] The diarist spoke for literally all emigrants who had survived this most formidable of ordeals in American pioneering and who now anticipated a new life in California or at least the discovery of sufficient riches to make that life easier elsewhere. Some, like Vincent Hoover and A. S. Welch, lamented ever choosing the Southern Route and forcefully advised others against following it. But for most, difficult as it was, it more than served their purposes.

The Cucamonga rancho became a favorite spot for almost all incoming emigrants, primarily because it included what may have been the first nonmission winery in California. Good Mexican food was also available there at a fair price, even though some considered the premises dirty. Other travelers chose to go straight ahead to the Lugos' rancho at San Bernardino or to the ranchos of former mountain men Isaac Slover or Louis Rubidoux, all of which hosted weary veterans of the desert crossing. Isaac Williams's Rancho del Chino, an impressive complex of buildings (located at the present site of the Heman C. Stark boys' reformatory), earned a deserved reputation as the premier long-term recovery station for weary travelers. Besides the huge and well-stocked cattle range, this ranch included cultivated fields (primarily wheat), a grist mill, and some facilities for room and board. Lorton noted that the John Rowland ranch was "a fine, large ranch fifteen miles [west] from Williams'." It too dispensed some welcome hospitality to exhausted emigrants.[41]

The Hoover party was particularly fascinated by the remnants of the Mission San Gabriel, encountered a day or so after Rowland's ranch. They noted the extensive orchards, including some bearing orange and olive trees "going to decay." The extensive vineyards were equally neglected. The church, still in use, included much-admired murals on the side walls. The family camped near the mission for almost two weeks. Lorton provided comprehensive descriptions, mentioning the mission garden fenced with a "live fence" of "cacti or prickly pears and trees," partly broken down. He observed, "[T]he church is a long, white building, plaster over bricks, eight pilasters on the side, 100 feet long, and a vestry in which hang the chimes. The interior looks like a prison, with the exception of the west end, which is decorated off in the usual Catholic styles, and two effigy figures on each side." He described a "massive 'doby' [adobe] corral formed by a large row of rooms and columns of brick in the front and rear. He lamented that the emigrants had taken possession of most of these rooms and built fires indiscriminately, even though the local alcalde (Spanish for mayor) and the priest resided on the premises.

Moving thereafter to Los Angeles, Hoover was less impressed with the abundance of gamblers and saloons in that town. And when he heard a sermon there on Sunday, he assumed it might have been the first Protestant service ever in the city.[42] Most emigrants quickly learned that the existing road to the northern California gold fields was difficult, and they opted for passage on the coastal steamships making semiregular stops at San Diego and San Pedro harbors before steaming up to San Francisco Bay. In a sense the Southern Route saved some from the harshness of the winter rainy season in the gold fields, yet still allowed the would-be miners to get there in time for the spring and summer season of good placer mining that followed.

This trail extended just over eight hundred fifty miles, more than half of which traversed some of the most forbidding desert terrain ever encountered by American pioneer companies. The comments of those camped at Utah Lake before the first groups embarked over the route fully demonstrate that all understood the severity of the undertaking in following the desert road. Yet this road proved preferable, after August of any given year, to risking the fate of the Donner party in the snows of the Sierra Nevada. And the loss of life along this alternative route remained amazingly small compared to that experienced on any of the other transcontinental roads of the era. The success experienced negotiating the Southern Route is a great testament to the preparedness, as well as resolve, of the people who traveled this most formidable pioneer trail in the annals of the West.

Chapter Two

The Old Spanish Trail— Highway of Diversity

The Old Spanish Trail has sometimes been underrated as an important transportation link between southern California and New Mexico and by extension over the Santa Fe Trail to the United States. A considerable array of differing peoples used the route for a wide range of equally divergent purposes. The trail has received only intermittent scholarly attention. Some have asserted it was misnamed on several counts. David J. Weber is correct that no Spaniards during the time their country ruled the region ever traveled over the entire route. It was only used as a trade route for two decades during Mexican rule prior to acquisition by the United States. Yet the name is not altogether inappropriate, because individual Spaniards did explore major portions of the pack mule trail, which did link two important terminal towns founded by the Spaniards, Santa Fe and Los Angeles. Besides, Anglo-Americans who traveled over parts of the route referred to it as the Spanish Trail from the first year they used it. During the period of greatest use,

an unfortunate heritage of conflict with neighboring Native Americans developed that also carried over into the later era.

Weber was certainly correct in his reminder that Spaniards blazing the various portions for use by European-Americans were "guided almost invariably by Indians." His statement was part of his new introduction to LeRoy and Ann Hafen's classic study of the Old Spanish Trail. There too the authors conceded, "[I]n justice to the Indians, however, one must admit that they had pioneered the trail long before and had made it a regular route of primitive barter prior to the white man's entry."[1] Clifford J. Walker, in his *Back Door to California*, asserted that at least the southwestern portion of the later Old Spanish Trail had "been used by Native Americans for trading and migration in each direction for at least four thousand years."[2] The Mohave Indian residents along the Colorado River were great traders, particularly with the Chumash peoples of the Santa Barbara

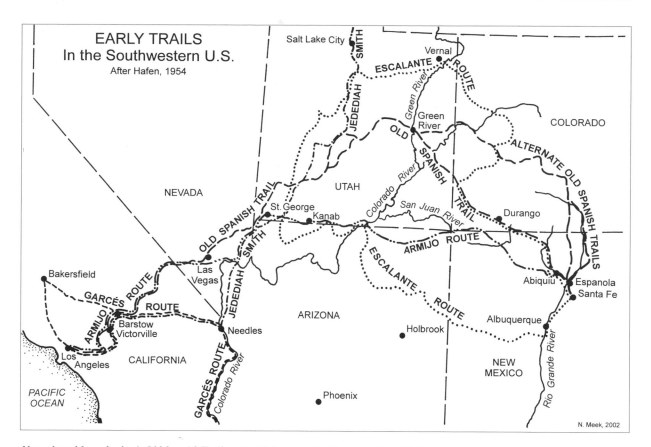

Map adapted from the classic Old Spanish Trail map published in LeRoy Hafen's and Ann W. Hafen's
Old Spanish Trail. Note eastern branches converging on present Utah then essentially following early
route by way of Colorado River and preferred route through Las Vegas, Nevada, area.

MAP ADAPTATION COURTESY ARTHUR E. CLARK COMPANY, DR. NORMAN MEEK, CARTOGRAPHER

channel area, from whom they acquired numerous shell beads. Those beads Padre Francisco Garcés observed in the possession of Serrano chieftains along the Mojave River probably came from the Chumash. Even more extensive trade existed on the eastern portion of the trail, which, except for the through trade with peoples of present California, Utah, and Nevada, is beyond the scope of this study.

GARCÉS'S EXPLORATIONS

The first of the great European explorers of a major portion of the trail was Francisco Hermenegildo Garcés, born in Aragon, Spain, in 1738. Entering the Franciscan missionary order at age fifteen, he came to the northern

Mexican frontier to help replace the Jesuits expelled in the 1760s. He was eventually assigned to the northernmost mission, San Xavier del Bac, near present Tucson, founded by another great explorer, Jesuit Eusebio Kino. Along with his regular duties, for which associate padres swore he was perfectly suited in temperament and interest, Garcés did extensive exploring throughout what was later to become Arizona. When Juan Bautista de Anza, a frontier fighter against the Indians, received assignment to establish an overland route from Tubac, in later southern Arizona, to California, he requisitioned Garcés as one of two priests to accompany the expedition, which commenced in 1773.[3]

On successfully reaching Mission San Gabriel, Garcés went with Junipero Serra, a former acquaintance and head of the Upper California missions, to Mission San

Diego, so Garcés missed the chance to accompany de Anza northward to Monterey, the Spanish capital of Alta California (Upper California, as opposed to Baja, or Lower, California). Nevertheless, these journeys stimulated Garcés's interest in helping locate a more northerly route from Mexico and New Mexico to Monterey. In 1775 he received a copy of a letter written by a fellow Franciscan of similar interests, Fray Silvestre Vélez de Escalante, describing his exploration of a route from New Mexico to the Hopi Indian villages of Arizona. Within the next year both were conceiving of and proposing roadways from Santa Fe to Monterey.

When de Anza subsequently led a company of 240 pioneers over the same route, aiming to settle San Francisco in 1776, Garcés went with them for the first portion of the trip. He left the larger group at Yuma on the Colorado River. Thence, with the guidance of Sebastian Taraval, a former runaway California Indian, perhaps from Mission San Diego, along with a Mohave who, certainly, knew the best way to travel up the great river, the missionary sought the latter's home villages near present Needles, California. Greatly impressed with the receptivity of the Mohave to his message of religion, Garcés not only baptized some but also performed a marriage ceremony for the head chief.[4]

When Garcés expressed desire to visit "the padres that were living near the sea," some of his Mohave hosts not only affirmed they "knew the way" but offered to accompany him on the proposed journey. Less than a week after arriving at the Needles villages, he started for the seacoast with Taraval and three Mohaves. They traveled by way of Piute Springs, Rock Springs, and Cedar Springs, clearly an ancient Indian trail, which became a variant portion of the Old Spanish Trail and later served as the main mail route from southern California to Arizona during parts of the 1860s and 1870s. On reaching the sink of the Mojave River at Soda Lake, the group followed the river upstream through later Afton Canyon. Here the missionary encountered his first Serrano Indians, called Beneme or Vanyume by his guides. These Indians, too, appeared interested in the padre's fervent message.

After one of his guides deserted, Garcés enticed the others to remain by offering each a blanket and shirt and

killing a horse for food. Farther up the Mojave River the party encountered other Serranos, including a head chief who presented a string of white seashell beads. At another village still some forty miles from the closest oak trees, another kika-chief's wife sprinkled the priest with acorns, an essential part of even these desert Native Americans' diet. The first European to cross what became known as the Mojave Desert, the missionary then passed over the San Bernardino Mountains adjacent to Cajon Pass and moved on to Mission San Gabriel, where he arrived three weeks after leaving the Colorado River. Garcés thereby opened—or made known to non-Indians—the western third of what would be the Old Spanish Trail. Historian Joseph P. Sanchez asserts that within a short time thereafter the missionary probably realized he had accomplished that feat.[5]

Commandante Fernando Rivera, with whom Garcés would die at the Yuma massacre (well known in California history) just five years hence, refused to support Garcés's further explorations with either military escort or rations. Nevertheless, Garcés traveled through what was later named the San Fernando Valley into the southern San Joaquin Valley, before crossing Tehachapi Pass back into the Mojave Desert. On reaching the Mojave River, the ardent adventurer essentially retraced his steps, although he visited several Chemehuevi rancherias not on the inbound trail.

Before returning to his mission at San Xavier del Bac, Garcés sought to explore a route to New Mexico by heading east from the Mohave villages. The first Indians he met, the Yavapai, welcomed him and provided guides for the next leg of his trip. But the Hopi, not then friendly to Spaniard missionaries, refused his gifts and essentially blocked his passage through their domain. A friendly Zuni Indian added more information to the great explorer's knowledge about Escalante's visit to the area from the opposite direction the previous year. He thus understood that between the two Franciscans they had already pioneered a direct route later followed quite closely by the Atcheson, Topeka, and Santa Fe Railroad and the famous Route 66-Highway 40.[6]

Garcés promoted excellent relations with all Native Americans he met in California partly, as he stated in his diary, "in order that the foundation of missions may be facilitated," as well as that a travel route could be developed between California and New Mexico. When Garcés returned home, he immediately sent a report of his explorations to Escalante. But as the dispatch was not actually forwarded until 6 July 1776 and the recipient's expedition started before the end of that same month, he probably did not receive it prior to his return later in the year. Yet each explorer already had some idea of the other's similar accomplishments and intentions.[7]

THE DOMINGUEZ-ESCALANTE EXPEDITION

Escalante, eleven years younger than Garcés, who was then thirty-eight years old, enlisted the interest of his church superior, Padre Atanasio Dominguez, about Garcés's age, in his plans for a mission of exploration. Historian Joseph Sanchez suggested they may have proposed the Northern Route through Yuta lands in anticipation of a better chance to get their proposal approved, because the route avoided both the Hopi and Apache, known to be hostile. The expedition drew on the considerable earlier exploration by New Mexico traders among the Yutas, or Utes, particularly a government-sanctioned journey in 1765 led by Juan Maria Antonio Rivera, guided by Ute Indians. The Domingues-Escalante Expedition of 1776 included Andres Muniz, who had been with Rivera. At the San Miguel River in what was later Colorado, the party met a Ute who agreed to guide them farther in exchange for knives and beads. At the Colorado River another Ute agreed for similar pay to lead them on to Utah Lake.

When they arrived there in late September, besides ascertaining the possibilities for establishing a mission the explorers unsuccessfully sought another guide who could take them farther west toward the Pacific Coast. As their secondary goal, the Domingues-Escalante expedition sought to at least get close enough to their destination to "learn about the other padre," by whom they doubtless meant Garcés. They obtained no such assistance. Thereafter venturing farther south, party members became discouraged with the snow in the mountains to the west, depleted provisions, and the knowledge

Padres Dominguez and Escalante and party entering the Utah Valley in 1776, as portrayed by Paul Salisbury.

they were still a long way from the Pacific Coast. The padres finally decided to return to their home base by a shorter route and thereby increase the possibility of more frequent contact with the Timpanogos Utes and perhaps a mission at Utah Lake. Disappointing as the expedition proved to the promoters, it blazed two variations of the eastern third of the Old Spanish Trail.[8] A great deal of travel, trade, and raiding ensued on that segment during the following half century. Unfortunately, the shortsightedness of government officials in New Spain, as well as their inability to maintain good relationships with many of the Native Americans involved in the region, prevented both goals from being accomplished either from New Mexico or California.[9]

THE ANGLO-AMERICAN MOUNTAIN MEN

Equally important as trade with New Mexico in finally opening the western end of the Old Spanish Trail was the increasing Anglo-American involvement in the Rocky Mountain fur trade in the 1820s. As this "restless breed of men" scoured the Intermountain West in search of

*Painting of Jedediah Smith
and his men crossing the
Mojave Desert in 1826.*
COURTESY NEW YORK PUBLIC
LIBRARY

beaver pelts, they also explored its geographic features more thoroughly than anyone else would for many years to come. Foremost of these was Jedediah Strong Smith, born in New York in 1799, who became arguably the greatest pathfinder in American history. A Bible-reading man, he did not smoke, drink, or cohabit with Indian women (contrasting with most mountain men, whose behavior appalled most people of their day) as almost all his peers in the fur trade did. His list of discoveries, including opening new roadways across the continent, through the Rockies and from California to Oregon and first crossing the Sierra Nevada, is well recounted elsewhere.[10] As an owner, with William L. Sublette and David E. Jackson of the Rocky Mountain Fur Company, Smith felt constrained to search for new beaver-trapping areas for his mountain men. At Utah Lake he discovered that local Native Americans could offer no information about the lands to the south and west. Admittedly afflicted with wanderlust anyway, he thus resolved in the late summer of 1826 to take a party of fifteen men, equipped with traps and trading goods, on one of his most significant discovery journeys.

From the eastern shore of Utah Lake, the group followed the Dominguez-Escalante route southward to the Sevier River, then up that stream to Clear Creek, where they crossed into the present Cove Fort area of central Utah. Then, after passing through the Beaver River vicinity and on to Little Salt Lake, Smith remained on Escalante's trail, continuing south approximately on the route of the later main automobile highways into the St. George area, rather than veering west before what later became Cedar City, as the main pack mule trail later did. The party encountered Paiute Indians engaged in agriculture along the Santa Clara River, then followed that stream to its confluence with the Virgin River. There they made the difficult passage through the narrows, which were later extensively blasted and excavated for the present Interstate 15 highway. After probably trapping briefly on the Beaver Dam Wash tributary of the Virgin, the party traveled down the main stream. At a Paiute village the brigade leader met some visiting trader Indians, whom Smith journal editor George R. Brooks correctly identified as Mohave. Smith promptly engaged them as guides.

Although he probably had not intended to go all the way to California, when the Indians told him about abundant beaver near their home villages Smith decided to investigate. He believed that in the moderate climate his men could trap all winter and he could also procure much-needed horses. The company followed the Virgin to its junction with the Colorado River. From there Smith and the guides led the men through terrain he termed "remarkably barren, rocky and mountainous," more than once forcing the party to leave the river for some distance. On one occasion he noted his trappers and their pack animals "clambering and winding among the rocks." Smith's experience shows why not many other groups would follow this variant of the route. After the Indian guides abandoned them, the trappers followed their tracks to where the riverbanks became more timbered and fertile and where the Mohaves and doubtless some Chemehuevi-Paiutes cultivated extensive crops on a forty-mile stretch along the river.[11]

At this point Jedediah Smith had reached the portion of the Old Spanish Trail previously blazed by Padre Garcés and in so doing he linked that portion with what the Domiguez-Escalante expedition pioneered exactly a half century earlier. This was also the first recorded overland journey from the United States at the Missouri River to California and opened a new "central route to the Pacific."[12]

Disappointed in not finding many beaver, the expedition only stayed long enough to trade for a few horses and a good quantity of food. Not all was cordial during the visit: One horse was killed and eaten by Mohaves and another stolen, although later recovered. With difficulty Smith finally procured two Indians, who had lived at the Spaniard settlements, to lead them toward the Pacific Coast. They essentially followed the Garcés route, actually a well-traveled Mohave trail all the way to Mission San Gabriel. Although the priests treated the Americans well, Mexican officials remained suspicious and it proved difficult for Smith to extricate his party from the area. Finally, promising to leave the entire province, they were allowed to depart. Obtaining a good supply of food at the San Bernardino rancho branch of the Mission San Gabriel, they then essentially broke their promise by doubling back into the San Joaquin Valley, where Smith left most of his men trapping beaver on the streams coursing from the western slopes of the Sierra Nevada. Then with two men, Silas Goble and Robert Evans, Smith became the first European known to cross those mountains and the equally formidable deserts to the east, finally returning to the fur trade rendezvous in early July of 1827.[13]

Six months after Jedediah Smith's visit with the Colorado River Indians, Ewing Young and other Taos-based

trappers, including James Ohio Pattie, approached the Mohave villages from the south. But this time the Native Americans appeared hostile and some, afraid. Pattie biographer Richard Batson has suggested that Mexican officials disturbed by Smith's arrival in California by the Colorado River route had encouraged and possibly engaged the Mohaves to discourage other trappers from entering the province from that direction. Jedediah Smith later expressed similar suspicions. For whatever reasons, the Mohaves were far less friendly than previously. Although the Mohaves were still willing to trade vegetables for strips of red cloth, the whites suspected the Native Americans of attempting to lure individual trappers away from the main body where they could be easily attacked.[14]

It is equally likely that the central cause of the new animosity stemmed from the Young-Pattie group exploiting resources the Mohaves believed belonged exclusively to them. Soon after Ewing Young's fur brigade arrived, a "dark and sulky" Indian whom Pattie assumed to be a chief came into their camp, backed by a large number of other Indians. By sign language he demanded a horse, and when the Anglo-Americans refused he indicated through gestures, pointing at the Colorado River and then at the packs on the horses and mules, that because the beaver pelts had been trapped in the Indians' domain, the horse was assumed to be legitimate payment. The Anglos again refused this proposal, which might have been considered fair between whites. The chief turned and according to some reports thrust his spear clear through one of the horses, whereupon the fur trappers shot him. Knowing that this killing invited further retaliation, the trappers constructed a breastwork, and a day later the Mohaves charged, releasing a flurry of arrows. The trappers returned fire with their rifles and then counterattacked, shooting a second volley. Pattie reported sixteen Indians dead. This quelled the attack, and the Native Americans retreated while the perceived trespassers made their escape.[15]

This episode is significant in establishing the pattern of hostility prevailing in the region between Native Americans and the predominantly Anglo-American fur trappers, including some who later led government explorers, soldiers, surveyors, and emigrants. Although a measure of distrust doubtless existed previously, the stubborn refusal of Ewing Young's fur trappers to re-spectfully consider the request for reimbursement for resources taken—beaver plews (pelts)—established the precedent for subsequent practices and conflict. There is little question that Native Americans understood the general principle of business conduct among whites, in-cluding payment for use privileges and goods received. Because the outsiders who so frequently crossed Indian lands, using their trails, livestock feed, water, as well as scarce game, refused to pay willingly, the Native Ameri-cans naturally adopted methods of exacting payment by stealing and wounding passing livestock so that the whites would leave it behind for their use.

Extant sources make clear that Mohave Indians were in frequent contact with their Southern Paiute neighbors at Las Vegas and beyond. Word of the initial dispute and discussions of how to deal with future incursions by out-siders were doubtless extensive. On several instances in subsequent years, recounted in this study, Southern Paiutes made similar requests for payment, occasionally assented to but usually ignored. Many non-Indians who followed the mountain men into the Old Spanish Trail province were more inclined to shoot at Indians who pre-sumed to collect the toll fees they believed were due them. Thus developed an unfortunate climate of hostil-ity and conflict.

The first victims of the altered Mohave policy toward Anglo travelers were members of Jedediah Smith's sec-ond expedition through the region the year after his first journey. Following almost the same route from Utah Lake, his new brigade of trappers frightened the Mo-haves at their first approach. But when the trappers found opportunity to show friendship and conversa-tion through Smith's former guide-interpreter, Francisco, security seemed assured on both sides. Smith learned that a party of Spaniards and Anglo-Americans from the Mexican province of Sonora, which included Arizona, had recently come into their Mohave domain, quarreled among themselves, and split into two separate groups.[16]

After resting briefly among the Native Americans, Smith's party crossed the Colorado, with their horses swimming and some of the trappers pushing much of their outfit on a raft. At that juncture, the Mohaves at-tacked those still on the riverbank, killing ten and taking prisoner two Indian women who had been accompany-ing the trappers. Nine other trappers either fought their way free or were already safely in the river and able to es-cape the onslaught. Thomas Virgin sustained injury from a war club, for which these particular Indians were justly feared. Smith and his companions threw away most of their equipment but left some on a sandbar, hoping the loot might temporarily distract some attackers. With but five pounds of dried meat and five rifles, they prepared for the anticipated final fatal charge. When a few Native Americans appeared in the distance, well-aimed shots felled two and caused the others to retreat. Smith con-cluded that the men remaining with him "were released from the apprehension of immediate death." Because the Mohaves did not press again, the trappers made their escape just before dark and, traveling all night, arrived at a spring next morning, probably Piute Springs beyond what has since been known as Jedediah Smith Butte.[17]

After a difficult crossing of the Mohave trail, the party succeeded in trading for more food among Indians along the Mojave River whom Smith probably mistakenly as-sumed to be Paiutes. This time the great pathfinder traveled down Cajon Pass, instead of following the main Indian-Garcés road over the adjacent mountains. He left the wounded Thomas Virgin at the San Bernardino *asistencia-rancho* and moved on to Mission San Gabriel. Smith reported that the padres "appeared somewhat confused" at his reappearance, doubtless because he had not been officially welcomed previously and had promised to leave the province permanently. Thus the trappers again had considerable difficulty freeing them-selves from the situation, but finally did, before reunit-ing with the men Smith had left trapping in the great Central Valley. Tragically, when the combined group subsequently entered Oregon, Umpqua Indians massa-cred all but Smith and three others. Soon thereafter, Jedediah Smith retired from the fur trade, but he was ul-timately lured back into service leading a train over the Santa Fe Trail and Comanches killed him while he was out scouting alone.[18]

Another Euro-American trapping party reached Cali-fornia across Arizona from New Mexico in 1827. Richard Campbell led a company of thirty-five by way of the Zuni pueblos and the Gila River, crossing the Colorado at

Yuma. But most Euro-American travelers thereafter recognized that the conflicts with Apache, Maricopa, and Mohave were sufficiently bitter that they avoided attempting to traverse those Indian lands. Thus considerably more interest developed in the new routes north of the Grand Canyon.

In 1829 several other trapping expeditions followed portions of the Old Spanish Trail into California. Peter Skene Ogden of the British Hudson's Bay Company, centered in Oregon, was apparently assigned to investigate trapping conditions in regions in which Jedediah Smith had recently demonstrated interest. In fact, one survivor of the Oregon massacre, John Turner, led the rival fur brigade down the Virgin River into the Colorado River area. The cautious Ogden allowed only a few Mohave into his camp at one time, and when they wounded a guard and attempted to steal some horses, he ordered his well-armed men to shoot, massacring twenty-six Indians. The Hudson's Bay Company men did not enter the Los Angeles basin but trapped for the season in the San Joaquin Valley, in association with rival American trappers. The British were probably unimpressed with the area's fur-producing potential, because no evidence shows any company men ever again trapping in southern or central California.[19]

That same year, Ewing Young, accompanied by forty men, including young Kit Carson, trapped across Arizona from Taos. Sending half the men back laden with beaver pelts, Young and the others made their way across difficult deserts to the Colorado River north of the Mohave villages. Although some Mohave doubtless recognized Young as their earlier antagonist, no notable conflicts arose with these often-punished Native Americans. The trapper group then followed the Garcés-Smith route into the San Gabriel area. After a brief stay there, clearly not condoned by Mexican officials, they hurried back to trap on the lower Colorado, then up the Gila River and back to New Mexico.

Still another poorly documented expedition of 1829 involved the legendary Thomas "Pegleg" Smith. His later recollections state he was part of a company trapping on the Santa Clara and Virgin Rivers and that they enjoyed such success that he was dispatched to sell the pelts at Los Angeles. However, his account offers no information on the route followed. The company certainly trapped along a portion of the Old Spanish Trail on the Utah and Nevada rivers, and Pegleg and his two companions probably followed the trail recently blazed by Jedediah Smith into the California southland.[20]

THE PACK MULE TRADE

More important than the fur hunters using portions of the newly broken roadway were the New Mexican traders, with their pack mule trains, who traveled the entire road annually for at least the next two decades. Antonio Armijo remains foremost of these, partly because he improved the route and partly because his group first used a variation of the trail mainly for trade purposes. Sanctioned by New Mexico governor José Antonio Chavez, who was just then obtaining permission from Mexico for trade over the route, Armijo's expedition carried blankets and other goods to trade for mules in California. It was already known that the larger California mules pur78chased for ten dollars could easily bring fifty dollars along the Santa Fe Trail. Starting 6 November 1829, they traveled through what surveyors later established as the Four Corners area, where New Mexico, Colorado, Utah, and Arizona meet. Then, crossing the Colorado River above the Grand Canyon at a place now inundated by manmade Lake Powell, they found inscriptions on the rocks, carved by Dominguez and Escalante. The group essentially followed the later Arizona-Utah border until they reached the Virgin River near later St. George. This was hardly new territory to some of these New Mexicans, who had traded extensively in the region since the time of the Franciscan explorations by Escalante and others. In fact, one of the men with Armijo, Rafael Rivera, had previously been as far as present Hoover Dam.[21]

From the Virgin River vicinity of what later became Mesquite, Nevada, Armijo adopted a "leapfrog" technique of sending out scouts, sometimes days ahead, seeking to locate water in the forbidding desert region. On one of these Rivera absented himself a full week and on returning claimed to have visited both Paiute and Mohave Indian villages. The record offers insufficient detail to determine which villages he encountered. The ones on the Virgin and the Muddy rivers would not have been significant. But if he successfully crossed the desert to the Southern Paiute villages near Las Vegas, the feat would have been of considerable importance. Circumstantial evidence that he did so is that Armijo chose to leave the Colorado River at Las Vegas Wash, thereby avoiding Jedediah Smith's difficult route downstream as well as the Mohaves. Southeast of Las Vegas Springs, the expedition apparently left the wash and followed Duck Creek. Armijo's journal account does not mention the later famous springs. Armijo scholar Elizabeth Warren and recent historian Joseph Sanchez agree the party passed no closer than eight miles to Las Vegas Springs, although they disagree about the route thereafter.[22] The Hafens, Sanchez, and others interpret Armijo as heading for Spring Mountain and Cottonwood Springs at present Blue Diamond. The expedition leader probably bypassed Mountain Springs but used Stump Springs just before his men left present-day Nevada. Their technique of locating and jumping from water hole to water hole may well have discovered Resting Springs so far as Euro-American use is concerned. They were also likely the first non-Indians to use the Amargosa River, Salt Springs, and Bitter Springs before finally reaching the Mojave River. The trip took fifty-six days with no loss of human life. The profits from the mules taken back over the trail ensured other expeditions would follow.[23] And from then on most travelers would take routes through the Las Vegas area rather than farther down the Colorado River.

In 1828, New Mexico resident Ewing Young formed a partnership with an old Missouri friend, William Wolfskill, to conduct business, mainly in liquor at Taos. One of their employees was Kit Carson, who accompanied Young over the Old Spanish Trail the following year. In 1830, Wolfskill made plans for his own expedition to the Pacific Coast. First securing Mexican citizenship, he received a trading license from Gov. Manuel Armijo, which later proved useful in California as well. George Yount, another former Missouri associate, who shared the leadership of the company of twenty-nine trappers, according to Wolfskill biographer Iris Wilson, had previously been with Jedediah Smith among the Mohaves in 1826. She also listed Old Bill Williams and Pegleg Smith among the members of the 1830 expedition.[24]

Significantly, while en route to California the leaders of the party secured permission from Ute Indians to travel and trap on the Sevier River in later central Utah. They secured these rights by making gifts of knives, tobacco, beads, awls, and vermilion. While trapping, the group became almost immobilized in deep snow in the Panguitch, Utah, area and were fortunate to make their way across the intervening mountain range to the west, to the Little Salt Lake area on the main trail to California. The journey down the Santa Clara and Virgin rivers proved less difficult, after which they went on to the Mohave villages. They stayed there but two days, trading red cloth, knives, and trinkets for beans and dried pumpkin. Although apprehensive about possible Indian attack, they departed for the Mojave River in safety. The group arrived at the San Bernardino rancho branch of the Mission San Gabriel in early February 1831.

Although Wolfskill did not prosper sufficiently to pay the debts he left in New Mexico, some of his men made good profits selling their store of woolen blankets called *serapes* and *fresadas* in exchange for mules. When the animals were ultimately sold at the other end of the trail, the participants were well pleased with their success, and trade over the Old Spanish Trail thus became even more firmly established. Concerning the bargains made by Wolfskill's men, observer and future trail veteran J. J. Warner noted, "[T]here sprang up a trade, carried on by means of caravans or pack animals between the sections of the country, which flourished" for some twenty years. Probably most subsequent traders penetrated farther north into Utah, as did the Yount-Wolfskill party, rather than traveling by the more southerly Armijo route. Another group of New Mexican "merchants in wool" followed the former roadway two months later. Because these were not also engaged in fur trapping, some historians consider them the first real traders, but the earlier groups carrying some trade goods and taking mules back over the trail certainly paved the way for subsequent commerce.[25]

The mainstay of this transportation network, both as carriers and the chief return merchandise, was the mule, which for Latino and Anglo-Americans alike would prove better suited than horses or oxen for the formidable desert roadway. The animals were more able to subsist on the inconsistent and sometimes alkaline water

Sketch of portion of a pack mule train such as would have been typical on the Old Spanish Trail during its heyday.

and equally scarce grass feed. For packing the equipment and cargo, an *aparejo*, a square pad of stuffed leather, was placed over a *jerga*, or saddle cloth, with a *salea* or raw, hand-softened sheepskin under it. These were secured by a broad band cinched very tightly around the mule's middle, as was the pack saddle. The more firmly this equipment could be secured, the more comfortably the mule traveled. The *carga*, or burden, might either be placed on top if a single pack, or half on each side, if two packs. The usual load weighed from two to four hundred pounds. Again all was drawn tightly as possible under the animal's belly. A square piece of matting, a *petate*, placed over the load protected it from weather.

Usually, according to Anglo-American contemporary observer George F. Ruxton, the eight or ten muleteers assigned to an *atajo* or caravan of often a hundred pack mules could pack each blindfolded animal in about three minutes and get the entire train under way in an amazingly short time. He also asserted muleteering to be "the natural occupation of the Mexican," with many of them aspiring to attain the rank of mayordomo or captain of a mule train.[26] Although it is known that pack trains traversed the Old Spanish Trail nearly every year until the American acquisition of the region in 1848 and even occasionally after that, LeRoy Hafen and his successor historians have been unable to find a single diary

of any caravan member traveling the road between 1831 and 1848. What is known has thus been pieced together from more fragmentary sources.

HORSE AND MULE THIEVES

It soon became apparent to many, mainly from New Mexico, that they could more easily obtain mules and horses by stealing than by legitimate purchase. This practice became so extensive that in 1832 the Los Angeles *ayuntamiento* or city council felt constrained to pass measures to control the situation. The council designated assembly points where all livestock to be driven over the trail would be inspected. Although not all complied, one of the first incoming caravans inspected by the new regulators enumerated in its cargo "1645 *serapes*, 341 *fresadas*, 171 *colchos* and four *tirutas*."[27]

One of the new rules decreed that purchases would only be deemed legitimate when the alcalde (mayor) of a town or the judge of the plains in a particular rural jurisdiction had been notified. When José Antonio Carrillo, an alcalde from either the Los Angeles or Santa Barbara area, noticed some New Mexicans on the road with a large band of uninspected animals, he dispatched a posse of five men to apprehend them. Catching them at the Mojave River, posse leader Antonio Ignacio Avila took the head rustler, Juan Jesús Villapando, to jail. From jail, however, he soon escaped and presumably rejoined his men as they fled with most of the livestock. Avila subsequently apprehended other thieves farther out on the trail near the Amargosa River, who were attempting to get away with animals stolen from as far away as San Luis Obispo and Tulare.[28]

Jacob Leese, later a prominent Anglo-American California pioneer and merchant, appeared to be one of the most venturesome early livestock traders. In the fall of 1833, he purchased up to four hundred and fifty mules from several California missions at $14 a head and left Los Angeles with nine wranglers to join other herds and drovers on the Mojave River. When he arrived he discovered the others had departed over the trail without him, so he decided to make the journey with just his own group. After pushing the animals hard, trying to catch the parties ahead of them, at what seems from Leese's account to have been Resting Springs, they all camped exhausted, without posting guards. Early in the morning the proprietor-leader noticed fresh tracks from Indian footgear and gave an alarm. Most of his animals had been stolen, but with an easily followed trail the Leese drovers prepared to give chase. Just then one of his men returned from the nearby camp of the New Mexican traders who had been traveling ahead of them and informed Leese they had been attacked by Native Americans and five of their number killed. It became clear that in an extended battle against up to three hundred Indians, the nineteen remaining traders had been fortunate to survive. Leese prudently concluded to return home thankful to escape with his life. He never again ventured into the livestock trade over the Old Spanish Trail.[29]

By the 1840s, other horse thieves proved even more formidable and successful. Among these were many mountain men, whose former fur-trapping enterprises were becoming increasingly unprofitable because of shortages in beaver and changing styles in men's hats. But probably the greatest of all horse thieves in the history of the West was Wakara, a Ute Indian chief from central Utah. When Wakara and his tribesmen joined forces with Old Bill Williams, Pegleg Smith, and other mountaineer associates, the result was probably the most extensive horse-stealing escapade ever documented. In mid-May 1840, Mission San Gabriel officials reported to the Los Angeles alcalde that *changuanosos*—thieves of various nationalities—were raiding ranches from their own area to their branch mission at San Bernardino and on to the sister mission at San Juan Capistrano, with some 1,500 horses being lost. Similar simultaneous actions in the San Luis Obispo area garnered an equal number of horses.

The available accounts vary considerably about subsequent events. Some mention a rustler rendezvous in the Summit Valley portion of Cajon Pass, whereas others say the horse thieves followed their accustomed practice of splitting the herds into more manageable numbers and taking them into various mountain and desert valleys to hide, and later to reunite somewhere on the Mojave River for the long desert drive. However, the sources concur that the thieves gathered at least three thousand head of good horses and mules through the series of well-planned raids. It is also agreed that these animals were then driven into Cajon Pass. Tiburcio Tapia, prefect of Los Angeles, immediately commenced organizing posses to go in pursuit of the stolen horses. Thirty men, led by Don Ygnacio Palomares from the family rancho in the later Pomona area, were the first in the field, with others requisitioned thereafter under threat of fine for failure to participate. To provide the necessary manpower for the various posses, Tapia eventually went so far as to free prisoners from jail.[30]

Predictably, the accounts of the horse thieves disagreed on the details of how they outmaneuvered their pursuers. One of the foremost biographers of Chief Wakara, Gustive O. Larson, recounts that the seldom-outwitted chief recognized the danger of being overtaken on the desert trails. So Wakara sent some of his men ahead with the horses while he and a few Utes hid in the willows bordering a creek—probably in Crowder or Horsethief Canyon of the upper east Cajon—where he knew Palomares and his men would stop to rest. When the unsuspecting posse dismounted to drink and lay down, the Indians made off with their horses as well, leaving the Californios on foot.[31] Another variation of the story, by fur trapper Calvin Jones, a close associate of Bill Williams, stated that as Palomares and his men pursued the horse thieves into the Mojave Desert, Williams looked back from a hill at their camp and ascertained that they had posted no guards. Jones claimed that he and Williams thereupon went back under cover of night and stampeded the mounts of their would-be apprehenders.[32]

According to Palomares, the posse encountered the horse thieves beyond the "monument," a natural landmark near Rabbit Springs in the Lucerne Valley vicinity, as they were apparently driving the stolen horses toward the Mojave River in the Daggett area. In the ensuing skirmish, in which the *changuanosos* took the offensive, Palomares lost one man killed and another wounded, with at least one Indian also being killed in the affray. The ranchero claimed his mounts were either killed or taken as they were retreating from the "Rancho de las Animas" or Ranch of Souls, said by San Bernardino historian George William Beattie to have been a *ciénaga* (marsh) south of what is now Victorville—undoubtedly the later Las Flores Ranch, near where Wakara's men allegedly stole posse horses.

Sources agree that by the time the dismounted and embarrassed Palomares men met the other posse contingents, approximately a hundred men were gathered to catch and punish the horse thieves. When they got organized, they found the tracks of the stolen animals, still estimated to be about three thousand head, had left the Mojave River heading north. On reaching Bitter Springs, the posse judged the trail sufficiently fresh to leave their excess baggage and mounts to hurry on to finally apprehend the outlaws. Some time thereafter, according to Californio accounts, they surprised the rear guard of the thieves at Resting Springs. There is no record of a fight or bloodshed, only of the rustlers abandoning saddles, clothing, and cooking gear as they fled in panic. The pursuit group went no further, mainly because they were themselves exhausted. On the posse's return, they reported seeing on the trail the carcasses of as many as half of the three thousand horses, perished for want of feed and water.[33]

Years later, in 1848, when American soldier George D. Brewerton passed through the area, he asked a mountain man guide about the innumerable bones bleaching along the desert trail and was told that Old Bill Williams had led the raid that lost the animals. As the soldier recorded the story, Williams succeeded in getting "upwards of 1500 head of mules and horses" through the desert to where they could be sold. The next year, Philip Thomp-

son, also named as being in the California raid, was met on the trail near the Big Blue River in Kansas by a party of traders, including Rufus B. Sage, one of the more reliable reporters of events in the fur trade era. Sage noted the horses "had been mostly obtained from Upper California the year previous, by a band of mountaineers . . . [who] had made a descent upon the Mexican ranchos and captured between two and three thousand head of horses and mules." The account included the pursuit by a posse, which was itself "defeated and pursued in turn."

Another variation on the theme of the 1840 raid was that of Pegleg Smith, who later boasted to visitors at his trading post on Bear River on the Oregon Trail that he had gone into "Spanish country" and got three thousand horses, but it had cost him dearly, because four close relatives of his Indian wives had been lost in the fighting, which he claimed had almost cost his own life. Smith asserted the Spaniards were more determined in that pursuit than he had ever known them to be.[34]

Some accounts of the great horse-stealing venture of 1840 mention Jim Beckwourth as being prominently associated with Wakara and Smith, but historian Clifford Walker has effectively discounted this by showing that the mountain man (who had some African-American ancestry) was still employed in Colorado and Missouri at the time.[35] Beckwourth, also a sometime chief among the Crow Indians, finally arrived in southern California in 1844. Some two years later, he launched a horse-stealing adventure that would add his name to the list of the notorious who used the Spanish Trail as a means of escape with stolen livestock. Taking advantage of California affairs disrupted by outbreak of war between the United States and Mexico, he and five other Americans "collected eighteen hundred stray horses [they] found roaming on the California ranchos," then drove them straight through for five days, until their pursuers gave up the chase. Beckwourth and his men must have made equally good time traveling almost the entire length of the Old Spanish Trail, because he encountered Gen. Stephen W. Kearny, who had just taken Santa Fe without a fight, on the Arkansas River in Colorado. On being complimented by Kearny on the quality of his horses and the high price he must have paid, Beckwourth replied the cost was mainly in "a great many miles of hard riding"—he had appropriated what he presumed were enemy mounts, because California was part of Mexico. The California-bound Kearny remarked, "Beckwourth, you are a truly wonderful man to possess so much foresight," then asked him to dispose of his loot quickly so he could serve the army as a scout, an occupation of many former mountain men.[36]

Directly as a result of the 1840 and other raids by horse thieves down through Cajon Pass, desperate Californio officials offered a land grant in the mouth of that canyon to a former English sailor, Michael White. Others, including Americans Daniel Sexton and Pauline Weaver, had received similar offers previously and declined, but White accepted. Evidence that this grant aimed to entice service as a buffer against further raids is Prefect Tiburcio Tapia's promise to furnish supplies for White's Rancho Muscupiabe so long as he occupied the land. Building a fortlike dwelling of logs and earth overlooking both Cajon Pass and the old Mojave Trail, White expressed confidence he could deter the raids by Indian horse thieves. But after suffering successive thefts of his own livestock, he abandoned the ranching venture after nine months.[37]

SETTLERS OVER THE TRAIL

A more successful program of protecting Californio livestock was offering recently arrived New Mexican families land in the San Bernardino Valley where they could not only establish homes, small farms, and herds, but could markedly enhance the manpower available for posses to pursue horse thieves in the future. These men, led by Lorenzo Trujillo, had already demonstrated skill and courage in fighting Indians, probably being themselves at least partly of Texas or New Mexico Indian ancestry. After some initial dispute and disappointment with treatment by the Lugos, the owners of the San Bernardino rancho, the New Mexicans abandoned Politana (near the present San Bernardino Valley College). They moved over to the banks of the Santa Ana River to the south, onto land donated by neighboring ranch owner Juan Bandini. There they built a truly beautiful village on both sides of the river, appropriately called Agua Mansa (Gentle Water), which survived until the terrible floods of 1862. Politana was occupied thereafter

by Cahuilla and Serrano Indians under the leadership of Chief Juan Antonio. Both local Indians and New Mexicans proved faithful defenders of the southland ranchers and their livestock.[38]

Another significant group of travelers over the Old Spanish Trail were Anglo-American settlers, some of whom had resided in New Mexico. Particularly amid the unrest after the Texan revolution, some, such as William Workman and John Rowland, concluded they would find it safer under the circumstances to migrate to California. Their party of about twenty-five, including several who had earlier intended to join the Bidwell-Bartleson party traveling the same time over a northern route branching off from the Oregon Trail, traversed the Southern Route in 1841. Their arrival initiated an increasing flood of Anglo-American migration to California by both routes that continued each year thereafter. Many settled permanently in southern California, including Workman, Rowland, and Benjamin Wilson, all later prominent there.[39] Previously mentioned Lorenzo Trujillo, along with Manuel Baca and their families, the founders of Agua Mansa, were also a part of this company. Trujillo and Wilson led at least nineteen other Latino families over the trail the following year, including other settlers of this first non-Indian village in the San Bernardino area. Former mountain men Louis Rubidoux and Isaac Christobal Slover arrived by the same route to settle in the same general vicinity in 1843.[40]

THE SLAVE TRADE

One of the more unfortunate longstanding institutions of New Spain was the forced labor the Spanish required of Native Americans. As trail historian LeRoy Hafen stated, "the principle that unbaptized and hostile Indians had few rights was early established." Although a Spanish law enacted in 1812 prohibited Indian slavery, it was clearly ignored in New Mexico. The records of such activity are relatively scarce, but the legal proceedings against the few offenders apprehended are revealing. Indian slave trade historian Lynn R. Bailey stated, "[I]f the Arze-Garcia case [involving traders apprehended returning from future Utah] can be taken as any indication of the extent of the slave traffic, it is certainly obvious that the commerce had spread by 1813 throughout the length and breadth of what is today the state of Utah." He also observed that "the Old Spanish Trail blazed in part by Friar Escalante, now became the main artery over which flowed the human commodity."[41]

Although most of this traffic in human bondage was conducted by New Mexicans selling their victims in their home province, it was far from uncommon on the California end of the road as well, both as Spanish rule ended in 1821 and thereafter. Early in the period of Mexican rule, in 1824, the California provincial governor issued a decree forbidding the Indian slave trade. But there was still considerable clandestine commerce in human property. Dr. J. H. Lyman (no relation to the author), who traveled the Old Spanish Trail in 1842, reported "'Paiuches' [Paiutes] were fair game, for the New Mexicans had captured them for slaves for years and so did the neighboring Ute." The doctor recounted how these Native Americans kidnapped from their homes "pine away and often die of grief for the loss of their natural deserts," even when surrounded by the prosperity of the California settlements. He mentioned one such Indian who refused to eat, "moaned much of the time, and finally died." The traffic to California was probably increasing at the end of the Mexican period of rule. In the 1836 census for the Los Angeles area no "Payuche" were enumerated. But the 1844 census, just four years prior to acquisition by the United States, listed nine "Payuche" Indians ranging in age from three to thirteen, indicating an increase in slaves.[42]

THE FRÉMONT-CARSON EXPEDITION

The first official American explorer to travel a major stretch of the Old Spanish Trail was John C. Frémont, returning east in 1844 from the second of his five expeditions of discovery. The Frémont party, guided by Kit Carson, entered the Mojave Desert after exiting the San Joaquin Valley through Tehachapi Pass at the south end of the Sierra Nevada. They sought the Old Spanish Trail, which headed in precisely the direction the "path marker" (Frémont) intended to go to strike the Colorado Rockies at the point he wished to cross them. They

reached the Mojave River near present Oro Grande on 20 April 1844, and lauded the roadway—such as it was—as follows: "[A] road to travel on, and the right course to go, were joyful consolations to us; and our animals enjoyed the beaten track like ourselves. Relieved from the rocks and brush, our wild mules started off at a rapid rate." Frémont continued by describing the Mojave: "[W]e reached a considerable river, timbered with cottonwood and willow, where we found a bottom of tolerable grass." The government explorer then did what many other travelers were to do at the same spot, explaining, "[A]s the animals had suffered a great deal in the last few days, I remained here all next day, to allow them the necessary repose; and it was now necessary, at every favorable place, to make a little halt." A Frémont entry several days later offers a description that might have been made more recently, saying, "[W]e had a gale of wind. We traveled down the right bank of the stream [Mojave River], over sands which are somewhat loose, and have no verdure, but are occupied by various shrubs." His description of the size of the river was that it was certainly larger than in recent times, except at flood stage, as he described "a clear bold stream, 60 feet wide, and several feet deep, had a strange appearance, running between perfectly naked banks of sand." After reporting that the drab desert scenery was "relieved by willows," he continued with notice of the dominant native trees: "the beautiful green of the sweet cottonwoods with which it is well wooded." This praise may have prompted later arborists to attach Frémont's name as species to the Linnaean genus name for the broadleaf variety of the tree, *Populus frémontii*. He concluded by noting a characteristic of virtually all the rivers of what he was first to describe as the Great Basin: "As we followed along its course, the [Mojave], instead of growing constantly larger, gradually dwindled away, as it was absorbed by the sand.[43] These reports were widely published and became the first description available to most Americans of that little-known portion of California and the adjacent region as it was about to become part of the United States.

Just as the company prepared to leave the Mojave River at what would later be called Forks in the Road, two mounted Mexicans, Andres Fuentes and Pablo Hernandez, the latter a boy, came into their camp to report

John C. Frémont exploration party, morning packing for continuation along the trail.
DRAWING BY EXPEDITION ARTIST EDWARD KERN

that their party had been attacked by Indians at Resting Springs. The two, escaping with most of the horses their small group had been driving northward, brought many of the animals back with them as far as Bitter Springs. On receiving this news, scouts Kit Carson and Alex Godoy volunteered to go in pursuit of the attackers. When the two reached Bitter Springs, they discovered Native Americans had taken the horses, so they followed the tracks into the rugged mountains. When they came to the Indian camp, some of the best animals were already butchered and cooking. Carson and Godoy charged, firing their guns and killing two Indians, and chased the others farther into the hills.

This is an unfortunate and revealing incident. The victims of the attack were from four lodges of Paiutes who lived in the area. They had doubtless found the horses straying unattended and concluded them legitimate prize to claim. As Resting Springs was some sixty miles away and the attacking force had numbered about a hundred, there is little likelihood that the Indian men whom Carson and Godoy killed had anything to do with the probable death of Fuentes and Hernandez's traveling companions. Clearly Carson and Godoy demonstrated little interest in justice and perhaps, judging partly from the fact that they scalped their victims, they had far too much inclination toward and pleasure in shedding Native American blood. Although Frémont was not a part of

the affair, no record hints that he disapproved of any of the actions. In fact he praised their exploits. The expedition later found the mutilated bodies of Hernandez's father and another man, the two women traveling with the group clearly taken elsewhere by the attackers.[44]

Word about the killings of the Bitter Springs Indians doubtless spread rapidly up the trail and may have been why the expedition was threatened and harassed along the Muddy River. And forty miles farther on, before leaving the Virgin River, something like Paiute revenge was probably exacted. A wrangler named Tabeau went back for a lame mule and did not return when expected. The alarmed Carson feared the worst, confirmed when he sighted smoke rising from a cottonwood grove. This he recognized as a signal that a blow had been struck, confirmed when they found the dead mule and a tell-tale pool of blood.[45]

The Frémont report states that thereafter the Paiutes who had so consistently followed them, disappeared. But evidence survived of a further altercation. Although the Frémont accounts do not mention it, apparently at least a small skirmish with Indians occurred somewhere near the present southwestern corner of Utah. Some ten years later Solomon Carvalho, an artist who accompanied Frémont to Utah on a later expedition, encountered on the Santa Clara River a Paiute who walked with a limp. The Indian claimed one of Frémont's men had shot him during the earlier 1844 expedition.[46] The wound may have occurred from a retaliatory shot at a distant observer, or further notice would have been made of the event. Still, it was probably sufficient to instill bitterness and ensure conflict with some future emigrant groups passing through the area.

Although documentary materials on contact between Hispanic users of the Old Spanish Trail and Native American residents along the route are not extensive, what exists indicate continuing hostility and conflict. The slave traders apparently sometimes killed adult Paiutes before kidnapping their children.[47] Attacks on Paiutes driving horses and mules across the desert demonstrate that the pattern of retaliation and forcible expropriation of property was also well established during the period of Hispanic dominance on the trail. Ewing Young's refusal to pay tribute for his company's beaver trapping on the Colorado River and the subsequent battle, the killing of Jedediah Smith's companions, along with the Carson-Frémont incidents, reveal that much initial Anglo-American contact with the Native Americans of the region was marked by ill feeling similar to that some Hispanics had displayed earlier. This situation did not improve rapidly.

SOUTHERN PAIUTE OR NUWUVI

Amazingly, almost the entire western half of the Old Spanish Trail was inhabited by the same Southern Paiute tribal group who called themselves the Nuwuvi or "Indian people." Related to Northern Paiutes, Shoshones, and Utes, they had a slightly different language and cultural identity from their neighbors. Like any people who had survived in a desert region, the Nuwuvi understood how to utilize what the land offered, and their lives were deeply involved with the cycles of nature. The history written by their descendants in 1976 stated that "most of all they knew that they loved and respected the earth and felt a deep kinship with all living things."

The Nuwuvi domain extended to the Tushar Mountains northeast of later Beaver, Utah. The Kanosh band of Native Americans just farther north were not technically included in the tribe, although they claimed some

relationship, particularly in later times. Conversely, farther east in the later Sevier and Piute Counties of central Utah, the band at Koosharem, near Fish Lake, were probably of Ute descent, but fully accepted among the Paiute tribe. Several groups of Nuwuvi lived south and even east of there, on the San Juan River, Henry Mountains, the Panguitch Lake area, Moencopi Wash, and the Kaibab Plateau, whose lands did not directly touch the Southern Route, and these groups were only slightly affected by travel on that wagon road. Similarly, farther south in Nevada the Pahrumpits of the Pahrump Valley would have to travel some thirty miles to have contact with route travelers, which they probably did fairly often. Other groups a small distance from the main road were the Shivwits north of the Colorado River in northwestern Arizona, the Matisabis of the northern Meadow Valley Wash, Nevada, and the Pahranagits farther west in what was later called the Pahranagat Valley.

The Iron County Paiutes, called Piedes by the early Mormons, and the Parrusits along the Utah segment of the Virgin River, had little impact on the travelers along the Southern Route, except perhaps for involvement in the Mountain Meadows Massacre. In contrast, the Tonequints, one of the more numerous bands situated along the Santa Clara River, were mentioned in the records of almost every company traveling through their lands. Just beyond them were the Parrusits, who lived along the Nevada section of the Virgin River and thus directly in contact with most emigrant groups. Competing with the Tonequints for the distinction of being most troublesome to emigrants, as well as the most numerous band, were the Moapas or Moapits, who lived near the Muddy River. The Kwiengomits resided in an area that included Las Vegas, Red Rock Canyon, and probably Cottonwood Springs. South of there on the trail were a few Shoshones in the Death Valley area and perhaps occasionally camped at Resting Springs and the Pegasits, a Nuwuvi band, who lived farther east near the Colorado River, but it is likely that most Native Americans contacted on the trail between Mountain Springs and Bitter Springs were Paiutes from the Pahrump Valley. There were also Chemehuevis, technically Southern Paiutes, who usually coexisted with the Mohave Indians residing primarily along the Colorado River. The Chemehuevis eventually occupied a considerable stretch of the southwestern end of the Southern Route, including along the Mojave River in the 1850s, where they were apparently just then replacing the earlier inhabitants, the desert Serrano or Vanyume. All these bands, except the Death Valley Shoshones, considered themselves one people and culture.[48]

Although some have asserted that these Southern Paiutes barely subsisted in a harsh environment, they actually adapted impressively and used a wide variety of foods. Plants such as agave, abundant in the spring when much other food was scarce, gained increased importance in the diet, and agave was the food called *yant* mentioned in several Mormon sources. Parts of this plant were roasted in pits, some still visible along the Southern Route.[49] The Nuwuvi were definitely an agricultural people from before the earliest recorded white contact,

Southern Paiute women with baskets used in one of their primary occupations of gathering food, such as grass seed.

COURTESY THE HUNTINGTON LIBRARY

cultivating corn, squash, beans, pumpkins, and sunflowers, all native to the Western Hemisphere, but long since imported to Europe. They usually planted crops in rows, using a shovel-like stick, and diverted water from nearby streams to irrigate the fields. At least one irrigation ditch extended half a mile, dug four feet deep through a gravel bed, with the diversion dam constructed of logs. Although the crops may not have been tended constantly, the Indians returned to weed after the plants sprouted, spending some of the intervening time in gathering other foods.[50] In 1849, as Mormon missionary George Q. Cannon traveled the Southern Route, he noted corn stalks, beans, squash, and other vegetables growing at an excellent Paiute village location in the upper Beaver Dam Wash. He and his fellows were clearly impressed by the example of Indian agriculture, which church members were sometimes erroneously credited with initiating.[51]

Although these Native Americans made pottery, they more fully used a variety of baskets for food gathering, storage, processing, and cooking. One of the most important was a fan-shaped, traylike basket useful in winnowing hulls from grass seed. Native Americans sometimes tossed charcoal to parch the food in the winnowing process. They then ground the seeds and stored them as flour to later mix with water for a mush or gruel. Mesquite sugar and screw beans were prevalent foods on several sections of the Southern Route, providing a nourishing food, often used for travel. Piñon (pine) nuts were another important tree food of the Paiutes, as were juniper berries. World traveler William Chandless is one of the few observers of the era who commented on the food derived from the latter source. He described a large ball called *sitcup*, "dry stuff, looking like buffalo chips, in reality made of juniper berries; it is sawdusty, and with a peculiar flavour, but still eatable," although he thought the food was likely not very nourishing.[52] The Serranos near Cajon Pass called this juniper berry food *wa'at*.

It is doubtful that much large wild game ever flourished in the vicinity of the Southern Route, although antelope were sighted occasionally in the Cottonwood Springs area, and mountain sheep beyond that point, including the Mojave River area, where deer and antelope were also hunted. All Nuwuvi apparently had the right to travel to the Kaibab plateau and forest to hunt the deer abundant there, but probably few did so with any frequency. However, small game, hunted throughout the year through large-scale rabbit drives requiring extensive cooperation, supplied a substantial proportion of the Native American diet. The Nuwuvi made large nets to snare the quarry, which was then beaten with sticks. They used the rabbit skins to make woven blankets tied about the chest as a cape as well as other items of clothing. Men commonly wore buckskin shirts, leggings, and breechcloths. Women's skirts were usually made from cliffrose bark, although they also wore dresses and shirts made of antelope and buckskin. Sandals fashioned from yucca and other fibers were preferred in the winter, with hide moccasins used in the summer. In the summer, brush shelters stood for windbreaks and sleeping. The winter season required more substantial dwelling places called *kanees*, which were of many different styles. A common type was constructed on a domelike frame of supple but sturdy branches covered with layers of bark stripped from junipers or grass or brush. Some American observers also noted huts made of old cornstalks. Smoke holes were left in the top.

Most Nuwuvi economic activities were undertaken by individual families, although larger groups gathered for hunting and celebrations. An informal council of adult men, chosen for their good reputations, knowledge, or strengths, made the decisions. In earlier times larger bands did not have one leader who held all the power but instead had several of more limited authority. These positions were not necessarily hereditary. Among the most important responsibilities of such leaders were to organize hunting and gathering and to direct the seasonal movements to different campsites. Winter was a time for telling stories. And the Indians had abundant songs and oral poetry.

They also had a rich tradition of dancing. Dances and the bigger celebrations were among the few events that brought the normally independent Nuwuvi together in large groups. The "circle" or "round" dance, "the cry," and the "bear" dance were the three major dances most Paiutes performed. The most common, the circle, could be danced at almost any time, merely depending on when the people felt the desire. This dance was primarily for entertainment and courtship among the young. It

Southern Paiutes gathered in a circle dance, apparently observed by Maj. John Wesley Powell (notice that there is no hand in the coat sleeve of man on left).
COURTESY THE HUNTINGTON LIBRARY

was usually danced around a juniper or other tree, the people holding hands while dancing clockwise, accompanied by singing led by one person.

One American emigrant observer of the Moapa dancing the circle in 1857, John Ginn, said all locked arms and circled a fire as with a loud grunt, then all leaped in unison and "every foot comes down heavily upon the ground at the same instant." They so enjoyed this dance that they sometimes kept it up for a full day. The cry dance honored and showed respect for the dead and was performed for several days at a time. In the bear dance, probably adopted later from the Utes, men and women faced each other in a circular enclosure, accompanied by the scraping of a notched stick and singing. Women chose partners, and dancing continued off and on for several days. As in many neighboring tribes, the favorite Moapa game was the hand game, played in teams, with one team shuffling objects under a blanket while the other team tried to guess their location. Wagers were commonly made on the outcomes.[53]

EARLY INDIAN CONTACTS WITH EUROPEANS AND AMERICANS

As almost always in Native American history, the coming of Europeans and Americans rather abruptly altered the lifestyle of the Southern Paiutes. Whatever wild game existed would have been quickly diminished not only by hunting but also by pasturing of cattle and draft animals on the scarce desert feed, along with frequent camping and livestock trampling at the scarce water holes. Modern Native American historians have asserted that "little is known about the specific resources [the Nuwuvi] used because Anglo settlers destroyed much of the plant and animal life of the area."[54] This is an extreme view, partly because the Anglo settlers were so late arriving, except in the Iron County area of Utah. The charge is probably more true of Hispanic and Anglo-American travelers and traders in the decades before. The same tribal historians note that "the two decades during which the pack trains traversed the Spanish Trail severely disrupted farming." This was equally true of later Anglo-American emigrants. Although some emigrant groups took great care not to allow their livestock to damage Indian crops or fields, others clearly did not. At least one, the Derr-Grewell-Hoover party of 1849, deliberately pastured their animals in a corn-and-pumpkin patch, retaliating for stolen animals. Similarly, at about the same time Thomas Wylly and some associates burned large stores of mesquite bean pods out of anger because of lost livestock. A perceptible part of the crisis precipitated by the arrival of whites was the clear decline in rabbit population, formerly a mainstay for food and clothing. One of the most telling insights is Frémont's observation that he and his party of forty fortunately got through the Spanish Trail area before any New Mexican pack train expedition coming over it that year because "a drove of several thousand horses and mules would have entirely swept away the scanty grass at the watering places." Such damage to the plant life and water holes must have caused great privation, as well as anger, among local Indians.[55]

The foreign incursions also forced the Southern Paiutes to consolidate power among fewer chiefs, who could then act more promptly and decisively than the more decentralized leadership of former times. Tutsegabits, who resided on the Santa Clara, was the undisputed head of all Southern Paiutes from Mountain Meadows through Nevada on the Southern Route throughout the entire era that trail was used as a wagon road. Fortunately, he was inclined to be fair to most emigrant groups and was, at least occasionally, notably firm in keeping his people in check when they were otherwise inclined.[56] It is clear that the thieving and cattle-wounding practices adopted in subsequent years were an attempt to exact a toll for passage through tribal lands, which when viewed from an Indian perspective was a legitimate reaction to the situation. As several contemporary western American historians, including Patricia Nelson Limerick and Elliott West, have argued, Native Americans proved as adaptable and resilient as other Americans in coping with the situations presented to them.[57]

Almost from first contact, tribal groups on the Great Plains recognized the threat to the resources essential to their way of life posed by similar travelers, and therefore demanding tribute from passing wagon trains was a natural response. More than a few emigrants reported that Native Americans requesting such payments explained their reasons for doing so. Spokesmen for various tribes emphasized that the overland trails emigrants were killing and frightening away buffalo and other wild game, overgrazing prairie grasses, exhausting the limited quantity of available timber, and depleting the water resources. Thus Overland Trail historian John Unruh quoted one pioneer saying, "[N]o people, probably, are more tenacious of what they consider their rights than the Indians."

On the main Oregon-California Trail, many travelers regarded tribute or passage payments as unwarranted "blackmail," and were particularly perturbed when fair-minded government officials advised Indians to make such demands. Yet requests for payments were actually quite nominal compared to the increasingly frequent ferry and bridge charges by other enterprising Americans. Most travelers, including those subsequently taking the Southern Route, had extensive experience with both groups, and the more objective observers understood the justification for Native Americans to use levies as they did other tolls and fees.

Southern Paiutes along the Utah to southern California road were acting in precisely the same manner for the same reasons. When such payments were not consistently forthcoming, the Nuwuvi saw no alternative to taking livestock or wounding animals to eat when the stock was left behind. This too was completely in keeping with practices of their counterparts farther north, as well as the Mohaves. There were abundant accounts of innovative and effective stealing escapades on all parts of the overland trails. Particularly along the northern Nevada portions of the California Trail, shooting arrows to kill or wound livestock was as prevalent as on the Southern Route. The preeminent chronicler of the Overland Trail, Unruh, correctly concluded that "on one point both overlanders and guidebook writers agreed: thievery and not murderous attack constituted the major threat posed by Indians."[58]

INDIAN MOBILITY

One of the truly amazing aspects of Native American life along the Old Spanish Trail and Southern Route wagon road was the Indians' mobility and geographic knowledge of areas far from a given Ute or Paiute's homeland. Illustrative of this is the family of one of the most prominent Native American leaders of the region, Kanosh. Kasheebats, a powerful Ute Indian chief, chose as one of his wives a slender, beautiful young woman who had a Spanish grandparent. She had been raised in California and, because she had a respiratory disease, always felt better spending the winter season in the warmer climate nearer her homeland. While wintering in the Mojave Desert, the young wife received the sad news that her husband had been assassinated by a disenchanted tribesman near the shores of Utah Lake. Realizing the chief had other sons who would claim tribal leadership, the grieving widow returned to Utah immediately so her own sons could vie for leadership among the Native Americans there. Her eldest son was Kanosh, who when the Mormons first arrived in the area was emerging as a highly respected head of the Pahvant band of Ute-Paiutes of Millard County, often known, in defer-

ence to him, as the Kanosh Indians. Impressively law-abiding and peace loving, Kanosh was fully familiar with the California southland. A lover of excellent horses and fluent in Spanish, he was accustomed to riding south for occasional visits, as if it were a short trip. In 1849, as some of the first Anglo-Americans made that journey, they encountered some of Kanosh's men on the Muddy River returning from a visit and perhaps horse-gathering raid. Enough of these Indians were fluent in Spanish to convince Mormon missionary Addison Pratt that more than Kanosh's mother had once lived in the California missions. Wakara, the other most famous Ute chief, gained an even broader reputation as a warrior, horse thief, and Indian slave trader and was intimately acquainted with the whole Old Spanish Trail. Wakara and Kanosh demonstrate the breadth of geographic consciousness and experience of the Native Americans residing along the trail from Utah to southern California.[59]

The fact that travelers, including Indians, were so limited by water sources and terrain on the actual route they followed may also have made those who had spent their lives near that road more familiar with localities and events transpiring far from their homes than was usually the case. Most Paiute did not yet use horses or mules for transportation, but were nevertheless amazingly mobile on foot. Partly because misfortune had so often come into their midst from afar—in the form of New Mexican slave captors, American explorer-soldiers, and sometimes murderous passing emigrants—as others had done, they devised a system of runners and signal fires to warn neighbors of the approach of outsiders long before they arrived. One observant emigrant, David Cheesman, who journeyed over the trail in 1850, noted as his wagon train moved southward that the Paiute bands "telegraphed through as [the pioneers] passed through the different villages by fires built on mountain points and answered by others in the distance."[60]

LAST PACK TRAINS
OVER SPANISH TRAIL

In late 1846, Miles Goodyear, a mountain man who operated a successful farm near present Ogden, Utah, prior to the coming of the Mormons the next year, unable to obtain a satisfactory price for his furs, took a pack train over the western half of the Old Spanish Trail to attempt a more advantageous sale at Los Angeles. His biographers assert that two years later, Goodyear drew on this experience to fashion a rough map for the Mormon Jefferson Hunt and his associates, to use on their initial trip over the Southern Route.[61]

George D. Brewerton, a young officer of the New York volunteers who had been associated with the Mormon Battalion and other United States Army troops occupying southern California after the war with Mexico was thereafter assigned to a post in the East. He engaged to travel from Los Angeles to Santa Fe over the increasingly famous Spanish Trail with Kit Carson, then becoming equally well known as he led a pack train over the route in the summer of 1848. Brewerton kept a good account of his trip later published in *Harper's Magazine*. On first encountering the Mojave Desert, he confessed temptations to back out of the trip. He quoted one of the muleteers affirming his belief that "the darned place had been on-fire and hadn't got quite cool yet." Hurrying to get ahead of the huge New Mexican mule caravan traveling northeast, probably one of the last of its kind, the narrator described it as follows: "Imagine upward of two hundred Mexicans dressed in every variety of costume, from the embroidered jacket of the wealthy Californian, with its silver bell-shaped buttons, to the scanty habiliments of the skin-clad Indian and you may form some faint idea of their dress." The military man noticed the large caravan was not well armed and could easily have been relieved of their cargo and animals. He also commented on their evening campsite, saying, "[T]he pack-saddles and bales had been taken off and carefully piled so as not only to protect them from damp, but to form a sort of barricade or fort for their owner." He continued, "From one side to the other of these little corrals of goods a Mexican blanket was stretched, under which the trader lay smoking his cigarrito, while his Mexican servant or slave—for they are little better—prepared his coffee and 'atole'."[62]

Of his own travel experience, Brewerton noted, "[O]ur daily routine of life in the desert had a sort of terrible sameness about it; we rode from fifteen to fifty miles a day, according to the distance from water, occasionally after a long drive halting for twenty-four hours,

if the scanty grass near the camping grounds would permit it, to rest and recruit our weary cattle." During such difficult stretches of travel, Brewerton observed that the men of the expedition did little of the talking and joking around the campfires common under more comfortable circumstances. Carson was said to be even more reticent than his men and extremely vigilant for signs of danger. The colonel attested that so far as watching for Indians was concerned, "[the] mule was by far the best sentry." This was a fact appreciated by several mail carriers over the same route in later years.

The daily routine commenced an hour before starting, when Carson rose from his bed to shout "Catch up," which meant prepare to start. Immediately the packing commenced. This had to be done precisely, because all understood that Carson would wait for no one and that a straggler stopping to reload a pack animal was an easy target for waiting Native Americans. When all the pack animals were aligned on the road, "the old bell-mare leading off with a gravity quite equal to the responsibility of her office," headed up the trail. On one of the numerous sandy stretches, often traveled at night, the writer described the following: "[O]ur transit [was] more like the passage of some airy spectacle where the actors were shadows instead of men." He added, "Nor is the comparison a constrained one, for our wayworn voyagers with their tangled locks and unshorn beards (rendered white as snow by the fine sand with which the air in these regions is often filled) had a weird and ghost-like look, which the gloomy scene around, with its frowning rocks and moonlit sands, tended to enhance and heighten."[63]

Near the spot on the Virgin River where Tabeau of the Frémont expedition, known to many of the present party, had been killed, Brewerton recorded "general feelings of indignation expressed by our mountaineers against the tribe who had committed the murder." Consequently when a horse guard noticed fresh Indian footprints near their *caballada* (horse herd), a squad quickly started in pursuit of the spy-scout. After some distance, Carson shouted, "[T]here he goes." The Paiute was running for his life some two hundred yards away when three of the trappers shot at him, all missing. Then a man named Lewis, armed with a long rifle, knelt, confidently took aim, and fired. The party members all recognized the Native American to have been hit in the shoulder and were amazed that he made his escape despite the wound.

When the company arrived at Little Salt Lake near present Parowan, Utah, they found Chief Wakara camped by the trail awaiting the huge Latino caravan. Even though he was at least forty miles inside of the Paiute tribal domain, he was there to collect "the yearly tribute which the tribe exact[ed] as the price of a safe-conduct through their country." If this had been the practice for most of the period of Hispanic trade over the route, it certainly explains the dearth of accounts of violence perpetrated on the caravans as they traveled through present Utah. As others would often do, Brewerton contrasted all aspects of Ute and Paiute appearance and lifestyle, and certainly, despite clear biases, there was some truth in his assertions about the superiority of the Utes. It is equally true that the Southern Paiutes would have been aware of Wakara's practice and although probably resenting it, also sought to replicate it themselves in their own way farther down the trail.[64]

That same crucial year, 1848, Orville C. Pratt, a young attorney from New York, received an assignment from the United States War Department to investigate several confidential matters in California and Oregon. At Santa Fe he received a travel log describing the Old Spanish Trail from a veteran of that route, Ben Choteau, later an Indian Territory (Oklahoma) Native American tribal leader, who had just arrived from California. This log proved a reliable guide for Pratt and his sixteen-man escort. The party started from Santa Fe in late August of 1848. The first leg of the trip proved uneventful, with some trade with Ute Indians, difficulty with pack mules, and a few quarrels among the men. When they reached the Sevier River in central Utah, a vicinity the diarist affirmed to be the best land he had ever seen, Pratt realized they had provisions for but twenty more days and were yet six hundred miles from their destination. Fortunately, they had plenty of mules that they could eat. Choteau had warned that the Paiute Indians they were approaching were notorious for their propensity to steal and wound livestock for the same purpose. Pratt resolved to avoid difficulty by increasing his guards and their vigilance.

At one point his men captured two Paiutes who were described as frightened at first and who then became

calm. Pratt's conclusion was that "these people seem greatly afraid of the Spaniards, but towards the Americans they seem better disposed." He attributed the ill feeling to the persistent brutality and threats of the slave trade. At the Muddy River, Pratt engaged some Moapa Paiutes to butcher a mule, doubtless for the party to supplement its diminishing rations.[65]

As many others would be later, Pratt was particularly disenchanted with the vicinity of Bitter Springs. He described the spring water as "the most insufferably poor kind & grass not worth mentioning." After some rain, the mid-October weather "became severely hot" with deep sand on the trek to the Mojave River. With the men's thirst, mules failing, and the provisions already short, Pratt confessed the adversities "all united to give [him] one of the severest trials of [his] life. He soon added, as he walked on blistered feet caused by worn-out boots, "never until now have I *really* known what *suffering* is." On reaching the Mojave, one of his main preoccupations was his body "literally alive with vermin." As much as he anticipated enjoying civilization, he swore that "all the far famed delights of California will be as nothing if these cursed lice stick to me." The party reached Rancho Cucamonga on 23 October after just under two months on the trail. Orville Pratt continued on to Oregon, where he served as the first justice of the territorial supreme court before returning to San Francisco to practice law.[66]

ISAAC WILLIAMS

During the first session of the California State Senate in 1850, a legislator introduced a resolution to recognize the services of Capt. John A. Sutter for extending relief to American pioneers in distress near the end of their arduous trek to California by the northern overland route. In a similar manner, Isaac Williams was honored for like generosity and care in rescuing emigrants who were virtually without food on the Mojave River toward the western terminus of their journey over the Southern Route. But the final resolution only cited Sutter's important assistance bringing new citizens to California—even though in fact the actions of Williams were at least equally helpful and laudable.

No explanation was stated for the slight, which even-

Col. Isaac Williams, proprietor of the Rancho del Chino, particularly significant for his willingness to send supply wagons to the Mojave River to help rescue provision-deprived emigrants who had just crossed the desert from Utah.

spread animosity toward him. Certainly the situation may have been an important factor in motivating his outstanding generosity over the next several years of the early American period in southern California—perhaps as a type of penance.[67] Whatever his motives, Isaac Williams was probably the most important individual in assuring success of emigration by the Southern Route between 1848 and 1850, the time of his slight by the California senate.

Williams had acquired most of the Rancho Santa Ana del Chino from his father-in-law, retired Mexican soldier Don Antonio Maria Lugo, who first applied for the land in 1834, the year the Mission San Gabriel, the former owner, became secularized. Thereafter, the son-in-law, Isaac, constructed perhaps the largest house in the entire region. Arranged in the shape of a quadrangle of about two hundred fifty feet on each side, the adobe building featured an open courtyard in the center. From here the ranch proprietor proudly lavished the hospitality he could usually well afford. There were a thousand acres of cultivated land and up to 15,000 livestock on the premises. Williams's unselfishness may also have been partly motivated by his appreciation for recovering his prosperity. During the Mexican War, he had been roughly treated by his Lugo brothers-in-law and other Hispanic neighbors, losing all household furnishings and much livestock and other movable property during the siege at his house.

Early in the U.S. occupation of the area, Williams came into contact with members of the Mormon Battalion. These soldiers had been recruited on the plains of Iowa to help fight against Mexico but had arrived on the Pacific Coast too late to do more than garrison duty. They had, incidentally, blazed another important trail across New Mexico and Arizona to California. In May 1846, some Mormon soldiers were sent to Cajon Pass to guard against the frequent Indian livestock-raiding incursions. This was something the Chino rancher had advocated for a long time. Later, while on furlough, some of these men, including their ranking officer, Jefferson Hunt, helped Williams bring in his wheat harvest. Others helped set up his gristmill, and still later some worked on an adobe wall around his domain. Discouraged after the loss of his property and the recent death of his wife, Williams offered to sell the rancho to the Mormons for an attractive

tually was duly protested. But Williams had alienated some influential southern Californians during the recent war with Mexico, and they used influence against him at Sacramento. Just before a siege on his ranch house at Chino, he diverted an appeal for help addressed to the United States Army commander at Los Angeles into the hands of his counterpart of the rival Californio-Mexican army. This might have cost the group of American former mountain men their lives as traitors, before a firing squad, except for the intervention of several Hispanic neighbors, Ygnacio Palomares and Antonio Maria Lugo, along with Californio commander Serbulo Varela. Williams's clear lack of courage on this occasion generated wide-

price. Hunt and his associates were interested but did not hold the authority to conclude such a transaction. They did promise to carry the offer to those who could. Before leaving for the Great Salt Lake region to reunite with Latter-day Saints who had just arrived there, Hunt discussed prices for cattle and other supplies he assumed might be needed by his fellow believers as they commenced colonizing what they soon called Deseret.[68]

FIRST MORMONS OVER SOUTHERN ROUTE

After traveling to Deseret-Utah by the Northern Route, Jefferson Hunt reported to the recently organized High Council of the Salt Lake Stake (diocese), then conducting affairs in the newly established Mormon settlements. Acting on his suggestion that procuring much-needed livestock and supplies could best be accomplished in southern California, they assigned eighteen other men to go with Hunt, designating Asahel A. Lathrop and Elijah K. Fuller, later one of the missionaries sent to establish Las Vegas, as the expedition leaders. Among the others who eventually became San Bernardino residents were James Hirons, A. Jackson Workman, Gilbert Hunt, John Hunt, Peter Nease, and George Garner. John Y. Green, later chosen to guide the first freight wagon train over the Southern Route, was also part of this supply-seeking journey. With no specific knowledge of the direct route to southern California, the party underestimated the time needed to make the trip, taking provisions for only thirty days. That was a mistake several other groups would make—all necessitating the same disagreeable but lifesaving adjustment made the same year at about the same place by Orville Pratt's group, of eating some of their draft or riding animals. John Hunt later asserted that "no other party of Mormon emigrants ever had to do [that]," explaining that as early as Las Vegas, they "killed and ate [their] horses." Still, the expedition struggled across the desert to a point on the Mojave River, near later Barstow, where they dispatched two of their strongest men, James Shaw and William Cornogg, to the Rancho del Chino to obtain rescue provisions. Setting a pattern followed consistently thereafter, Isaac Williams

immediately sent several of his *vaqueros* (cowboys) with beef and fresh horses to assist the company, which had continued slowly up the desert river, the first of his many rescue missions.[69]

Members of this first Mormon pack train expedition over the Southern Route were notably exhausted when they reached Chino and were particularly appreciative of the generous treatment afforded them. Williams furnished wild cows, which provided milk when properly tied down, and the famished travelers had plenty of flour for bread. The Mormons remained at the rancho through the six-week winter rainy season, gathering plant cuttings, seed, and livestock for the return trip to Utah. Finally, on 15 February 1848, they started back by the same route with 200 cows purchased at $6 per head and a few new pack animals and mares. They were offered as many bulls free as they wished to drive away, taking about forty. The expedition did not fare well with these male animals; all but one died, supposedly of thirst. Half of the cows also died, indicating they were probably pressed too hard without sufficient time to recoup at the occasional good meadows. The biographers of Miles Goodyear, Charles Kelly and Maurice Howe asserted this group took a wagon loaded with seed wheat on this return trip, but having difficulty with wild cattle and with "finding a suitable road for the wagon," they abandoned the vehicle before reaching their destination. The semisuccessful party got back to Salt Lake City in May 1848.[70]

FIRST WAGON OVER THE ROUTE

Just over a month after the Lathrop-Hunt party left for Utah, another contingent of Mormon Battalion members just released from an extended tour of garrison duty arrived at Rancho del Chino to begin assembling the "fit out" for their trip to Utah to be reunited with loved ones after some two years absence. This group took the first wagon positively known to travel over the entire Southern Route in either direction.[71] They were guided by the legendary Mormon scout Porter Rockwell, who had been in the party recently arrived from Utah. The company of thirty-five, including a woman and six-year-old boy who were the wife and son of former ranking battalion officer Capt. Daniel C. Davis, who—tired of the pressures and some dissension—declined to lead the group, started on 12 April over what until then had been a pack mule road. Although we have few details as to the exact route followed up the Cajon Pass, we know they climbed the hogback somewhere in the west Cajon rather than the more difficult east Cajon canyon that the forty-niners used.[72] No details survive of the other routes selected on stretches where a choice of pathways existed. The designated leader, Henry G. Boyle, at other times an excellent diarist, simply recorded, "[W]e had a long and arduous journey, but nothing of any note transpired on the trip."

No contemporary account mentioned coming on the remains of a packer company massacred by Indians, but someone recounted it later in the hearing of 1849 trail traveler William Lorton. That next year, while awaiting in northern Utah the time to start over the Southern Route, William Lorton reported hearing of the Boyle company discovering the remains of a "pack company," doubtless Hispanic, which had been killed, presumably by Native Americans, because they had "throats cut with stone knives." The Mormon Battalion men reportedly buried the bodies.[73]

Boyle also failed to mention the difficulties with Native Americans that travel companion John Riser noted. The latter stated that from the Santa Clara River to Little Salt Lake near later Parowan the Paiutes were "constantly hanging around our trail night and day," on one occasion stealing 11 of the company's 135 horses and mules. Some Indians were reportedly made to "pay for [their] trouble," suggesting some retaliatory gunfire. The party arrived at Salt Lake City on 5 June 1848, having inaugurated the Southern Route as a wagon road.[74]

The year 1848 was a year of transition. The Treaty of Guadalupe-Hidalgo stipulated that the so-called Mexican Cession of territory, from Colorado to the California seacoast, had become part of the United States. Symbolic of the change was the Brewerton-Carson group passing over two hundred Mexican packers along the road, returning from what would be one of the last of the annual trade excursions over the entire trail to Santa Fe.[75] That was also the year the Boyle group brought the first wagon ever over the historic trail. This event symbolized the transformation of this route into the Anglo-American

wagon highway it was to remain for the next two decades. In the first three years at least five hundred wagons and probably over three thousand emigrants traveled over that road.

Gold was discovered at Sutter's Mill on the American River 24 January 1848, as established by the diary of Henry Bigler, who traveled the Southern Route the next season. By the end of the placer mining season in the fall of the discovery year, probably some ten thousand gold seekers were working in the expanding mother lode diggings, including people arriving from Oregon, Hawaii, and Mexico. By August and September, letters from California telling of the gold discovery were being published in eastern newspapers, but most easterners did not yet believe the reports. Finally, in September, Edward Fitzgerald Beale, another later traveler over the Southern Route, brought actual specimens of the precious metal with him to the East. In his annual message to the U.S. Congress on 5 December 1848, President James K. Polk took official notice of the discovery. This served as a signal for a stampede to the gold fields.

The emigrants to California came primarily by three routes. Some sailed from eastern seaports around Cape Horn to San Francisco. Others sailed to the isthmus of Panama, traveled across, and waited to secure passage on some ocean-going vessel sailing up the Pacific Coast. Most traveled overland from Missouri up the Platte River following the same route the Oregon pioneers had been taking for a decade—at least to a departure point on the Raft River in present Idaho. There the California Trail branched southwest to follow the Humboldt River across what was later northern Nevada, then over a difficult waterless stretch to the Truckee River, which some travelers followed up through the Sierra Nevada and on to the gold fields. But those arriving at the midpoint of that journey at Salt Lake City after late July understood and were constantly reminded by others that they should hesitate to risk continuing on that route so late in the year. Just three years earlier the Donner party had met a horrible fate in the western mountains because they wrongly believed they could cross before the early winter snows closed the pass, which was forever after named for their company.

This is precisely why the new route south from Salt Lake City, essentially following the western half of the

Old Spanish Trail, held such promise. It had no forbidding mountain passes, and the entire desert route could be traveled throughout the fall and winter seasons. True, it was an indirect passageway to the gold fields, but it would get travelers close enough that they could easily arrive before the mining season began in spring. The alternative was to remain at Salt Lake City, where some suspected both commodity prices and pressures to conform with Mormon standards of behavior would be unacceptable, although some did fine with both anticipated problems.

The Old Spanish Trail as a whole was only used for some twenty years. But during that time it served an important purpose of tying together a group of Mexican provinces, which in Spain's period of rule had had almost no interaction with each other. Even after the United States acquired the entire region, segments of the trail still served similar purposes, although not so much for tying the entire region together. Certainly the western half of the roadway continued to be a major link between southern California and the vast Great Basin province. In fact, at times it proved a lifeline from the Mormon empire to the outside world. It was also a now relatively forgotten, but for a time important, wagon route to the gold mines. These early years of use impacted the regional Native Americans' lifestyle in major ways, and the extended conflict between them and other trail users persisted.

Chapter Three

The Anglo-American Road in 1849

Although the Mormons initiated the Southern Route as a wagon road, the discovery of gold in California made it significant for others as well. The extensive array of pioneer diaries for the Oregon-California Trail is well known, but it is doubtful that any emigration period or route has been more fully documented than the road from Utah to the California southland in the year 1849.[1] Historian of early trails LeRoy R. Hafen with his wife Ann W. Hafen published thirty-five accounts of various lengths in 1954 and 1961. But he had no access to several of the most detailed and insightful journals used herein. For some, including several who had intended to publish guidebooks for the route, the journey proved too painful to recommend to others. The mistakes made by wagon travelers that year markedly assisted those coming after. Despite its pitfalls, the desert passageway proved a viable and safe winter route to the gold fields.

THE PACKERS OF 1849

The excitement of the Gold Rush stimulated numerous methods of getting to the riches. Many men without families effectively packed all they required on horse and mule back. Not only could they move faster than wagons, but presumably they could also forage for livestock feed more easily. Although at least a hundred and fifty wagons and the people traveling with them waited at Utah Lake for cooler weather before embarking on the Southern Route that summer, at least two large companies of packers set out over the same route some six weeks earlier. A group from Ithaca, New York, guided as far as Salt Lake City by a mountain man named Kinney, disbanded there. Most of the members engaged a man named Charley Macintosh, of Caucasian and Cherokee ancestry, to guide them over the Southern Route. The guide and his associates reportedly engaged local Indians to travel ahead to ensure safe passage through Native

American lands, which they accomplished, and impressively. Trails historian Dale Lowell Morgan concluded this company to be the company led by I. M. Hoge of Arkansas, which arrived at Chino on 27 October 1849 with 130 men.[2]

One reason the packers chose the Southern Route was that they understood cholera raged that year on the northern trail and they assumed the alternate road would thus be safer. The Macintosh-Hoge group took the precaution of bringing a single wagon with them "for hospital purposes," which may have proved fortuitous, because some claimed that one of their companions had already contracted the dread malady. One of the four physicians among them supposedly cured the patient by "scarifying" the sick man's chest and abdomen and then rubbing him with laudanum. The man reportedly rode his own mount the next day. The party made the common mistake of carrying mining equipment they could just as easily have acquired in California. Yet they made the trip in good time, with many recording their arrival at Rancho del Chino by listing their names in Col. Isaac Williams's registry book. They reached the ranch just two days before the other packing party arrived at the same point.[3]

In contrast to the Macintosh-Hoge party, the party that James Waters led, which started several weeks later, met considerable conflict. A former mountain man associate of Kit Carson, Waters set out in September 1849 with 140 New Yorkers, equipped with pack animals. According to Ute Indians visiting emigrants camping at Utah Lake just prior to starting over the same route, the Waters packers killed six or seven Southern Paiutes near the Sevier River. The reason for the killings is not known, but if Waters held the same attitude toward Native Americans as did Carson, they would have felt they needed little pretext.

A MASSACRE OF A SMALL PACKER COMPANY?

Apparently a third group of herder-packers started over the Southern Route, by one account before the other packers. William Lorton, one of the best diarists among the waiting wagon emigrants, noted as his party was leaving that Indian messengers reported a party of Americans driving "a lot of cattle" had been attacked "on the second drive on the desert," most likely the *jornada* from the Muddy River to Las Vegas or the one just past there. Messages received by Chief Wakara and Mormon Indian interpreters indicated that the fighting lasted three days, until the last white man had been killed. The Ute runner conveying the information also mentioned the apparent Paiute justification for the deaths, asserting that "as soon as the Ams[.] see an Indian they fire on them." No other information has been discovered as to the number and identity of the victims, but there is no reason to doubt the tragedy occurred.[4]

Another trail diarist of that year, Joseph Hamelin Jr., noted that while camped in the Utah Lake area on 20 August 1849, a small group of six packers set out on foot for California over the Southern Route. Editor-historian LeRoy Hafen stated of this party that no further information had been found as to the subsequent fortunes of those men. Yet his documentary collection of accounts of overland pioneers that year also containing the Hamelin diary includes the recollections of G. C. Pearson, who asserted that while conversing with the Moapa Paiutes near the Muddy River, he learned that a "number of packers" camped nearby at the same time had "foolishly located near a fringe of willows," from which a silent and deadly ambush had been carried out, with the victims all killed and robbed. He implied his group had observed "their arms, clothing, watches, et cetera" in the possession of the Indians. The report, written forty-five years after the event, contains details subject to question, but it is entirely likely that this was the fate of the party Lorton and Hamelin had previously mentioned. Half a dozen people was not a large enough party to be safe traveling that part of the trail.[5]

Meticulous student Dale L. Morgan stated in his notes on the trail for that crucial year, "[I]t is difficult to sort out the truth from the chaff in Pearson's account of the brush with Indians at the Muddy." Yet on the ensuing page of his notes, Morgan acknowledged Addison Pratt's observation that at the lower end of the California Wash "on the side of the canyon" was a sort of barrier prepared by the Indians, saying, "[F]rom this they attacked a pack company that was the first that passed here this fall." Morgan believed the reference was to either the Waters or McIntosh-Hoge packers, but it is more likely another distinct company was killed at this point, likely in the California Wash rather than while negligently camping at the nearby Muddy River, as Pearson's account states.[6]

Evidence exists of still another packer group. In mid-October, diarist Vincent Hoover mentioned a pack mule train comprised perhaps of members of a travel company other Southern Route wagon travelers had formerly associated with on the trip to Salt Lake City. They had subsequently abandoned the Northern Route because of reports of depleted grass supplies and experience with hostile Indians and had caught up with his party near Mountain Meadows. The packers apparently only remained with the Hoover portion of the Independent party for two days before moving more rapidly along the Southern Route.[7]

INDEPENDENT
PIONEER COMPANY

The first emigrant wagon company from Utah to California over the Southern Route was called by Hafen the Gruwell-Derr train, simply because brief reminiscences by J. D. Gruwell and Peter Derr were the only participant sources he had to draw on at the time he edited his documentary history. Several more detailed diaries, particularly those of Vincent A. Hoover, Thomas Wylly, and Arthur Shearer, are now available and offer more information concerning this party.[8] The emigrant group consisted mainly of a fragment of a much larger wagon train formed at Kanesville, Iowa, in June 1849, which had stalled and disbanded at Salt Lake City after the leaders heard reports of scarce grass on the Northern Route to the gold fields west of that new Mormon stronghold. Although some of the party eventually took the Northern Route, some four dozen wagons and the accompanying emigrants concluded to take the safer all-season route southwestward. Probably on advice from local residents, perhaps someone who had traveled the road the year before, the group camped amid abundant pasturage near Utah Lake for six weeks, awaiting cooler weather on the southern deserts. By late September, after other travelers had been similarly advised from Salt Lake City church

pulpits, diarist Vincent Hoover noted that "there were a good many emigrants" gathered in that area.

These anxious travelers eventually made a choice between two guides. One, Jefferson Hunt, had been over both routes to California, including the southern road in both directions. He also had experience as a military officer. Prevailed on by fellow Masons among the emigrants, he agreed to lead the group for a fee of $10 per wagon. The alternative was a Hispanic packer named Antonio, who asked only for passage for himself and his baggage to Los Angeles. He had recently come from Santa Fe and presumably knew the western portion of the Old Spanish Trail as well. Peter Derr claimed that those who chose to engage Antonio were families with meager funds who could not afford Hunt's fee. In hindsight, they would have abundant reason to regret their decision.

This company, mainly comprised of the earlier Kanesville party, who called themselves the Independent Pioneer Company, probably hurried to depart before the Hunt-led group, partly to get to the livestock feed first, but also to avoid allegations of following the wagon captain's lead without paying for the service. Unfortunately, they neglected to organize sufficiently to maintain much discipline during the first portion of the trip, although they remedied that situation after some two hundred fifty miles en route. The half of the group in front may have been waiting for those behind to catch up before holding elections. The lead portion of this party, made up of twenty-three wagons, embarked on 27 September 1849, understanding that they were the first real emigrant wagon train to travel what was then called the "Southern Route" to Los Angeles. The first part of the journey passed over reasonably easy valley bottom terrain intersected at convenient intervals by streams of varying size coursing from the nearby mountains. But after the first hundred miles, as Hoover observed, the country traversed became increasingly desolate. The diarist certainly experienced much worse conditions before reaching the California gold fields.[9]

The guide, Antonio, was initially industrious, riding ahead to scout for water, grass, and firewood—preferably in reasonable proximity to each other. However, after the first week his failure proved an important cause of the great difficulty the group experienced before reaching the first California ranchos. On at least six occasions that month, traveling through a region later designated as Utah Territory, the livestock had to go without water and feed through the night and sometimes well into the following day. Everyone understood they faced instances farther down the trail where such "*jornadas*" would be inevitable, but later wagon companies experienced few of these before leaving the limits of modern Utah. At least once part of the group also traveled on the wrong trail for some distance before retracing their steps. Predictably, some of the draft animals soon began to show weakness and exhaustion even on a portion of the journey that proved relatively easy for other expeditions. Despite good intentions, the party failed to adequately conserve their animal resources, because they were ignorant of the trail, an ignorance that many Mormon guides could have alleviated.[10]

Actually, other reasons than poverty probably prevented part of the Independent Pioneer Company from following Jefferson Hunt. Some Latter-day Saints recognized Rev. Jacob Gruwell, a Methodist minister formerly of Montrose, Iowa, and at least one of his two brothers, Asa and Robert, to have been participants in mob activity near Nauvoo, Illinois, in burning barns and grain belonging to Latter-day Saint church members. While camped in Utah Valley, the Gruwell brothers were informed by one of their own party, himself a notorious counterfeiter, that Mormons who had suffered at their hands contemplated coming in pursuit. In August the two Gruwell men fled for their lives, leaving their families where they were. Both the Hoover and Addison Pratt diaries recount that these men traveled to California by the Northern Route and then came to southern California to reunite with their families. This left adult sons and nephews and perhaps the other brother to bring the large families—two wives and twenty-one children—southward with the Independent party. The Gruwells suffered greater privation than most others in the party, perhaps because they hesitated to deal with Mormons to purchase additional provisions necessary for the trip. Because Jefferson Hunt had been one of the most avidly bitter toward former anti-Mormon "mobocrats," the Gruwells doubtless knew better than to join his group—although Hunt later assisted their families on several occasions. It is also known that some in the party had stolen at least one yoke of oxen from a Salt Lake City farmer, and the perpetrators may have been concerned that a Mormon guide would recognize the brands or other identifying marks.[11]

Vincent Hoover was a twenty-four-year-old traveling with his physician father, Leonce Hoover, in two wagons laden with a large supply of medicines for beginning a practice in California. The unusual reticence of his diary entries concerning personal matters becomes understandable when the reader learns that he intended to publish his travel account. As Hoover's segment of the Independent Pioneer Company passed through later south-central Utah, Vincent and several associates formulated a plan not only to improve the roadway but also to compile a guidebook with the expectation of later seeking "recompense from Congress" for their efforts. Hoover's associate Purdy, equipped with a roadometer on his wagon, took the assignment to compile the actual guidebook, with Hoover recording a table of distances and presumably a narrative commentary. Another man, named Show, agreed to draw a map of the route. Certain comments in Hoover's diary are revealing, such as when some in the company discovered the good scrub oak acorns near the Santa Clara River. Hoover said, "[I]n the East you are roasting and eating chestnuts," while here they had good acorns, considered a great luxury.[12] Clearly the diarist indicated he expected a broader readership of his diaries than simply family and friends.

But because of the natural tensions generated during the journey—particularly the heated debate between those who felt constrained to hurry down the trail because of diminishing provisions, and those who believed they had to move more slowly to preserve the strength of their draft animals—the partners in the guidebook venture separated. Although he did not believe Purdy would conscientiously record the necessary distance figures, Hoover later included a distance guide log in his diary, wherever he obtained the data. There is no later reference to Show's map. It is apparent that by journey's end Vincent Hoover had become so thoroughly disillusioned with the route that he would not be likely to recommend it to anyone else, although he continued to note in his diary good camping spots and other useful information.

During a thirty-six-hour stretch of no water for the cattle in central Utah, one of the better prepared emigrants, a Dr. Hall, incurred the wrath of most of his fellows by refusing a needy woman a drink even though he carried enough water for his animals. Hoover confided that "Mr. Hall is very much censured by all in the train and left him no friends." At about the same time a man assigned his turn on guard duty refused to perform the task, provoking one fellow traveler to attempt to shoot the slacker, although Hoover dissuaded him. Just over a week later, their nerves again frayed by a lack of water for the livestock, two of the several German immigrants in the group quarreled heatedly. Finally, in mid-October, just before the rear contingent joined them, the forward party selected a judiciary committee, designating a captain, a lieutenant, and a sergeant, who immediately decided several "lawsuits" arising from quarrels within the group. Thereafter, the committee arranged guard duty and otherwise asserted more leadership and discipline. They also demanded more cooperation, which became absolutely essential as the train reached a much more demanding section of the route. Now it crossed out of the Great Basin at Mountain Meadows and afterward moved along difficult streambeds, over mountains and mesas, and across some of the most unforgiving of deserts. Despite improvement, the party members' lack of willingness to assist each other at every opportunity contrasted dramatically with some of the more successful companies that traveled the route.[13]

The first major crisis came on 22 October, at the junction of Magotsu Creek and the Santa Clara River, when several guards assigned to watch the company cattle left their posts to eat breakfast. Observant Southern Paiutes seized the moment to steal four oxen. When the teamsters finally noticed the animals missing, they sounded the alarm, and a small squad immediately gave chase—neglecting, however, to take much ammunition. After following the tracks several miles, they noticed blood on the trail, and presumed it to be from one of the animals having been wounded by arrows. Soon afterward the pursuers discovered an Indian lying on his back, and the lead man, John Hall, shot at him and missed, then struck the presumed sentry with a rifle butt. Peter Derr, next behind, then shot and killed the Indian. Hoover recorded that his associates stripped the dead man of everything he had, presumably as trophies. As the pursuit group reached the top of the hill, they saw a fire set for the purpose of cooking one of the oxen. The Paiutes fled the scene, but

no one shot at them, because the Native Americans appeared to be out of rifle range. The other animals were retrieved, although one had some twenty arrow wounds. Before leaving the area, one party member inscribed on a tree what had transpired, as a warning to companies traveling behind to be on the alert because retaliatory attacks could be expected in the vicinity.

By then late in the day the pioneer company moved only a mile and a half before camping again. Because they stopped at a just-abandoned Paiute village, they probably intended further retaliation for the lost ox. The party pastured their livestock amid the Indian corn, squash, and pumpkins, and Hoover admitted that the animals were "feasting." He noted the dwellings were fashioned primarily from corn stalks. Thereafter, the company tended more carefully to guard duty and they had no other encounters with Native Americans. They knew, however, that their movements were carefully watched and that each animal left behind would be promptly slaughtered.[14] Thomas S. Wylly, following in the rear contingent of the Independent Pioneer Company, stated, "Let an animal fall by the wayside and you might think, if the next camp were nearby, that you could return and when he had rested bring him in, and you might return and you would find his bones" where he had been butchered and eaten by awaiting Native Americans.[15]

Other difficulties were inherent in being the first wagon train to travel down the Santa Clara River canyon. The company chronicler reported they had to cut undergrowth that hindered their progress, mentioning also that in the absence of much grass, the cattle were compelled to eat leaves off the trees.[16] Hoover reported that in this segment the cattle enjoyed good feed only once in five days. This lack of pasture proved particularly unfortunate for the company, because it so sapped the strength of the draft animals. The expedition severely depleted this livestock resource even though bunchgrass and other forage species notable for their high nutritional value were not far away, mainly in the side canyons and mesas above the river bottoms. Later emigrants located and used this feed more effectively. By the time the company members became more aware of the need to conserve their animals' strength, they had entered the region of what they called "salaratus grass," actually salt grass, ranked low in food value among the forage plants found along the Southern Route—and had thus made an extremely costly error.

Wagon companies generally agreed that travel down the Santa Clara River and the pull over what was later called Utah Hill, officially the Beaver Dam Mountains, were among the four most difficult stretches of the Southern Route. Hoover explained that the party left the Santa Clara where it curved back toward the southeast, passing through "a very rocky canyon, dangerous to wagons." These segments were undoubtedly among those to which Derr was referring when he asserted that "those never having been over a mountain trail have no idea of the difficulties to be overcome to pass wagons over them." He recalled that "often they would have to leave the [Old Spanish Trail] for miles and cut their way through brush and trees in the canyons, not being able to follow over the steep and narrow mountain side." Here and in many other places the Hoover-Gruwell-Derr company blazed the trail for later wagon emigrants.

As they entered the desert on the present Utah-Arizona border, young Hoover observed changes in the flora and fauna in the transition zone from the Great Basin to adjacent desert terrain. Addison Pratt noted a week later plenty of scrub oak that bore an abundance of acorns. Members of the Independent Pioneer party roasted and ate these with relish, judging them superior to the eastern varieties. Somewhat surprised to find leaves still green on the cottonwood trees at Beaver Dam Wash, the diarist also noted what he called "Spanish bayonet," a form of yucca. Hoover mistook the abundant growth of mesquite near the later Nevada town of that name for red locust. Hoover and Pratt noticed California quail in what came to be called the Arizona Strip area, equally significant as a transitional bird habitat; Hoover even mentioned the single feather tassel protruding from the top of the head. Although Pratt sometimes earned renown as a fisherman, members of the Independent Pioneer Party proved more successful catching fish in significant quantities from the Virgin River.[17]

While the party camped along the Virgin River, a major controversy arose among Hoover's associates over whether it was wisest to remain longer to let the draft animals recuperate, or to hurry on along the trail. Proponents of the latter view were probably among those

whose supply of flour and meal was already almost gone. Placing many in the party on half rations, company leaders dispatched six men, including J. D. Gruwell and his cousin, Derr, and the discredited guide, Antonio, on foot to southern California for provisions. The Gruwells severely underestimated the distance involved, expecting to make the trip in but three days. According to Derr, it took twenty-two days to reach the California southland ranches, during which the subgroup endured severe privation.

The Hoover-Gruwell-Derr company was doubtless typical of many pioneer companies, parts of which split away and subsequently joined with others along the trail. The original forty-five wagons (Wylly claimed it was seventy) probably never traveled together for more than a few days of the entire trip, and Hoover noted small splits and reuniting at least half a dozen times. Close study of this great trek thus naturally produces an image of up to two thousand people moving along the same desolate trail over a three-month period, some going slower and others faster. Perhaps Dale L. Morgan might have charted each party's passing of certain points, as he once did with diary accounts on the Oregon-California Trail.[18]

Traversing the Virgin River bottom proved no more pleasing to these pioneers than had the recent mountain and canyon passages. They considered the water "brackish," which they attributed to the salt springs flowing into it. Numerous crossings of the river necessary within a short distance, usually over sandy bottoms—sometimes through quicksand—also greatly eroded company patience. The party remained in the area a week, after which, Hoover noted, "to the delight of all we leave the River." But conditions did not get easier, mainly because of the "hard pulling" over a succession of sand hills as they left the streambed. At the waterless camp at the foot of what was later named Mormon Mesa, they decided to drive the livestock some two miles back to the Virgin for water and salt grass.[19]

Among the most difficult challenges detailed by Hoover, Addison Pratt (then just days behind), and others was the arduous labor, after leaving the Virgin River, of surmounting the Virgin Hill onto the adjoining mesa. At the crown of this steep, three-hundred-yard incline loomed a uniformly vertical ledge of some ten feet of

The formidable Virgin Hill, unanimously rated the most difficult segment of the entire Southern Route, is six miles southwest of present-day Mesquite, Nevada, and visible just north of I-15 prior to the highway climbing up the grade onto Mormon Mesa, 2001.
COURTESY LARRY REESE

rock that the travelers had to literally chip and break through to let a roadway reach the tableland on top. Hoover said, "[W]e were compelled to work several hours rolling stone from the top of the hill before we could get up one wagon with eighteen yoke of oxen" pulling it. This was the "climax" of "bad places" on the trip until the last week, traveling through the east Cajon Pass canyon.

After preparing the roadway—a task that would immeasurably assist many other pioneers for over a decade —next morning the travelers began the exhausting work of hauling the remaining wagons up the incline. Some took only eighteen yoke of draft animals for the half-mile pull, first sandy, then rocky, but uniformly steep. At least one wagon, laden with 1,400 pounds of cargo, required thirty yoke (or pairs) of animals, usually oxen, for that purpose, and although chains broke and other people later reported the wagon wrecked, Hoover noted no serious damage done to the property belonging to Dr. Hall. Some of the group who had lagged a day behind had a wagon tongue pull out and the vehicle turn over, three men receiving bruises. This particular ordeal so exhausted some of the oxen that they too had to be helped to the top of the mesa with ropes. The animals worked the long day without feed or water. This under-

taking of supreme teamwork by all able-bodied people took until nine in the evening to get everything up the "big hill." After camping the remainder of the night, they left at daylight for the Muddy River some fifteen miles westward across the mesa. The going proved particularly slow, despite a reasonably good road, because of the poor condition of the animals, several of which were left behind and subsequently killed by ever-watchful Virgin and Muddy River Paiutes.[20]

The party deemed the Muddy River area a more pleasing camping place, despite some steep riverbanks off which a few cattle fell. The feed still consisted mostly of salt grass. The Hoover company remained four days before embarking in midafternoon across one of the most dreaded dry *jornadas*, expecting to continue through the night. After traveling up what was described as a dry creek bed, soon named the California Wash, they came out onto a hard-packed trail, which after nightfall they lost. The company appears to have been negligent in not sending out scouts to mark the way while the cattle recouped at the Muddy. This forced the group to camp without water until daylight. They carried some water and grass for their animals but took so long resting twice on the second day that they did not reach the Vegas (meadows) until after the second morning (thus two full days) of what usually thereafter took but thirty-six hours. At least five more cattle gave out and had to be left, none of which were recovered.

At this point Hoover confided the obvious, that "all [were] sick of the journey." After reaching safety at the Vegas, he candidly confessed, "[O]ne can scarcely imagine the anxiety that pervaded us all on this trying trip of the past fifty hours, not knowing whether we would be compelled to falter ere we reached water, leaving all behind." True, yet they survived the severe test, tired but well. Not so the livestock. Not one wagon in the company still possessed more than one yoke of working oxen when they reached the Vegas camp, where all had had at least two yoke, and some, three yoke, earlier on the trip.[21]

Allowing the cattle to recuperate for three days at Vegas, which was one of the ideal camps of the entire route, Hoover ventured back to seek the ox he had left on the trail. Again indicating the serious lack of group cooperation, no one in the party would agree to accompany him, even though all understood that a single person making the trip would be in danger from Indians. Unsuccessful in finding any animals, Hoover subsequently learned from other emigrants that his ox had been found slaughtered by Indians in a ravine not far from where he searched. Perhaps because the formerly balmy weather had turned cold, they cut the stay at the Vegas short. On the next leg of the journey, the oxen were very weak. Here too, ignorance of the trail forced the company to camp dry, even near an area later known as Spring Mountain, southwest of Las Vegas. Again, a well-organized group might have sent out scouts while their fellows watched the cattle at the meadows (Las Vegas). Thus they abandoned oxen almost every day as the journey continued.

By criticizing the lack of pleasing scenery where several other commentators later noted some of the best landscapes they had seen in the Cottonwood Springs area, diarist Hoover revealed his discouraged mood. After continuing on to a camp at Mountain Springs, they descended into the adjacent valley on a good road, camping that night at Stump Springs, which they mistakenly called Hernandez Springs. Because no group ever found much grass at that spot, they started early next morning,

getting to good feed in five miles. Then, following a route close to the mule trail, they crossed the large Pahrump Valley in what was later Nevada, heading straight for the next water over forty miles away. This required climbing a steep and rocky mountain rimming the northern approach to the later-named California Valley. Although subsequent companies doubtless had to negotiate the same difficult downward grade, almost none mentioned the challenging descent. The party again camped without water, grass, and wood, forcing the travelers to go as hungry as the animals, because they could not cook. After a short distance the next day, they commenced another steep, rocky climb over Emigrant Pass, which Hoover considered the second worst on the trip. The descent too was "steep and ugly." While yet on the ridge, the diarist noted that "every eye was strained in hopes of seeing grass and water," which although it could not be sighted from that point, lay not far away at what was variously called Archuleta, Hernandez, or Resting Springs—another of the best stopping places on the entire trail.[22]

As the company rested, Hoover came to the conclusion, probably too late for his associates but potentially valuable to those passing later, that livestock should not be allowed to graze on the salt grass any longer than necessary, because "the longer [they] remain on this kind of grass the weaker [the] cattle [will] become." He also noted that by then most of the company supplies of flour, meal, and other provisions were exhausted, compelling some to subsist "mostly on give out cattle." He observed that the meat "was as blue as indigo," which would hardly make eating it appealing, although necessary.[23] Lewis Granger, traveling the route soon after, recalled that by this time there was no fat on the meat, nor marrow in the bones, but only a thin jelly destitute of fatness. After a three-day rest, the company moved on and within a few miles, descended a steep hill to the Amargosa River, said to mean "bitter water."[24]

It is doubtful if the scenery here was actually better than at Cottonwood Springs, but Hoover's mood had improved, because he noted several good desert campsites and effused, "[T]he view is beautiful." However, he tempered this by adding that though scenic, he would prefer to be "among civilization" instead of on the edge of what would soon be named Death Valley. The road along the small river included several sandy stretches, thus hard pulling; and the grass continued to be impregnated and covered with alkali, yet Hoover did not regard this section as bad. The travelers located relatively good grass in the Salt Springs area, but they understood from Frémont's reports that they now approached the dreaded "desert."[25]

Then the real ordeal commenced, with Hoover reporting apprehensively that as they advanced, they found "the side of the road for miles covered with the bones of animals." These were mostly stock that had died much earlier while being driven too fast by horse thieves from the opposite direction. He confessed, "[T]o us this does not look very cheering as our cattle have had no water fit to drink since yesterday morning." The diary continued to report that the animals began to "show signs of giving out." For this reason the Hoover family left one of their wagons behind, throwing away all items except "what [was] necessary for immediate use." Thomas Wylly, in the portion of the Independent Pioneer Company traveling just behind Hoover's, recalled that at this point they "began to leave wagons as well as oxen. When two teams became too weak to pull their wagon, the owner would select the wagon they thought best, put both their effects into it, or the part they thought most valuable, [and] . . . abandon the other." He continued, "This soon became the common everyday occurrence and wagon after wagon would be left along the trail." Wylly also noted that "Along this part of the route you might almost any time see women and children dragging their weary limbs along behind the wagons to lighten the load on their tired teams that were staggering along with frothing mouths, lolling tongues, and distended eyeballs."[26]

Addison Pratt, then less than a week behind this party, noted abandoned goods all the way back at Las Vegas, reporting there that some had even "lightened their wagons of clothes and feather beds." William Lorton and Joseph Hamelin, three weeks later, offered even more detail on this. In the Stump Springs area Pratt observed half a dozen horses and cattle left to die, and at Resting Springs he mentioned wagons and more clothing abandoned by the party ahead, along with a note

confessing the distress members of the Independent Pioneer Company experienced. After a brief stop for rest, the Hoover contingent of the company made Bitter Springs in thirty-six hours. But after two full days without good water for the animals, they discovered the water there unsuitable and the party was compelled to travel a mile farther to "fair water."[27]

Bitter Springs was too close to better water at the Mojave River for even this ill-fated company to remain longer than absolutely necessary. As in many other places, matters were complicated by the water and grass not being situated close to each other. Within a day, the Hoovers and their associates again moved on, understanding they faced another long, sandy pull over Impassible Pass to the southeast, to the head of Spanish Canyon. At an early dry camp, forced on them by the weakness of the oxen, Hoover set out alone on foot in a futile effort to locate grass, water, or both. Traveling in a windstorm so severe he resorted to crawling on hands and knees, he searched in vain by moonlight, returning to his worried family thoroughly chilled.

The next day's journey, relatively easy after reaching the last summit, brought them finally to the Mojave River on the first of December 1849. The "river sinks and rises," described Hoover; they doubtless reached it at a point where it mainly ran underground through the sand. Addison Pratt's account reported holes dug by previous travelers, providing the best water they had enjoyed since Cottonwood Springs over a week previous. They also found abundant wild grapes, small but "sweet and nicely tasted," a most welcome respite from the tough, lean beef and little else that had been the diet of most for a long time. By this juncture, that was about all the remaining oxen were good for. A German emigrant named McGoon had been compelled to leave the remains of his wagon on the Bitter Springs road, driving his cattle on to the river. Another company member, John Borse, did the same. He was likely the person Pratt described as an "old Dutchman" who had gone back along the trail on foot to retrieve a chest he was reported to be dragging toward his camp on the Mojave.[28]

At the river camps, Addison Pratt and some others of the Jefferson Hunt party that had departed Utah Lake about a week after the Independent Pioneer Company finally caught up with that company, which had been traveling just ahead of them. There the Pratt group reported the split that had taken the majority of the Hunt group on a supposedly shorter route through later Death Valley. Hoover correctly anticipated that those following the cutoff would lose many of their cattle, if not their own lives. He concluded prophetically, "[C]ut offs in an unknown country are very dangerous things and too often result disastrously."[29]

In fact, some of his own company also approached disaster, particularly the two large Gruwell families. With the fathers absent for the entire journey and two of the ablest sons having gone ahead to search for provisions, the trip must have been an ordeal for the women and children. Hoover does not mention any names, but probably referred to the Gruwells when he observed, at the first Mojave camp, "children crying for bread that [was] not to be had." Pratt discovered that some of this camp had been out of "breadstuff" for six weeks. He added, "[I]t was a pitiful sight to see these poor haggard women and children." At this point, Mormon leader Charles Colson Rich, of a just-arrived party traveling without wagons, gave these sufferers a little flour. Pratt's group added a little bread, although it too was running low on such provisions. The one stroke of good fortune the Independent party had was that they reached the Mojave before snow began to fall; snow caused other travelers considerable difficulty. A week later, the snow-bound desert trail might have been more than the party's depleted strength could have endured.

While these first pioneers to cross the deserts of the Southern Route from Utah by wagon rested on the Mojave, their decimated cattle recuperated on good grass. Their difficulties with lack of food were enhanced by bitter cold weather, along with snow. They continued to barely subsist on the meager nourishment of beef from starved cattle, along with a few fish caught in the river. Hoover noted plenty of ducks in the area, but there is no record of any being killed. Addison Pratt, an excellent hunter, had recently shot several rabbits and spent at least one difficult and futile day hunting deer in the river thickets, wounding only one coyote. The group of mounted Mormon missionaries, by then two days ahead, had killed five deer along the Mojave and probably

frightened most other game out of the area. During the leisurely week, most travelers moved intermittently up the river, encountering some difficult sandy stretches of road and hard pulling. Hoover recorded that the livestock were enjoying plenty of feed and that his companions were all well and "doing first rate with the exception of no eatables." Yet as close as the party approached disaster, they had survived one of the worst of desert challenges and proved others could do the same.[30]

THE DERR-GRUWELL ORDEAL

The men who had rushed ahead of the main Independent party from the Virgin River also experienced great privation. Badly miscalculating the distance, they ran out of food after ten days, with twelve more to go before their destination at the southern California ranches. Although they had firearms, they were almost entirely unsuccessful getting game, missing good opportunities to kill a wildcat and some crows. Derr did shoot what they called a wolf, undoubtedly a coyote, which they consumed entirely. They also ate a colt they found, already nearly dead, which gave them a bad case of diarrhea. On the Mojave they tried to catch fish by using blankets, but only got a few minnows. Derr alleged that one of the Gruwell cousins proposed that they kill Antonio, their former guide, and become cannibals. To save the man, it took a firm argument that he too had the right to a chance to live.

The Gruwell fathers had an equally difficult trip over the Northern Route. On the Humboldt River of northern Nevada, at least one of their horses gave out and one sick man eventually crawled a quarter of a mile to water, returning with a canteen to save his brother. To prolong their lives, they had already been compelled to drink the blood of a recently dead ox. On arrival at San Francisco, they took a steamer to Los Angeles and traveled back with the relief party Isaac Williams dispatched to meet their families on the Mojave. Addison Pratt noted the men should have felt some chagrin on seeing their presumed antagonist, former Nauvoo, Illinois, Mormon storekeeper James Henry Rollins. This man had demonstrated no ill intent as he traveled with Rich, who had re-cently provided food to the starving Gruwell families.[31]

ASSISTANCE FROM CHINO

On 13 December 1849, a shipment of supplies, sum-moned by the Gruwells, arrived on the Mojave from Isaac Williams's Rancho del Chino. The bread-starved emigrants now had a ton of flour. Next day Hoover helped kill a "California ox," one of a goodly number that had been driven out on the Mojave to provide bet-ter beef than had been enjoyed for several months. There were also nineteen yoke of replacement oxen to bring along whatever wagons were still in use and prob-ably some that had recently been abandoned back on the trail. Although his own family had flour until the last, the company chronicler concluded the day's entry with his greatest understatement, that this assistance was "a great relief to us suffering emigrants."[32] Several subse-quent supply trains were later dispatched to help others struggling toward the ranches.

LATER PORTION OF INDEPENDENT COMPANY

The "rear detachment" of the Independent Pioneer Company also had several diarist-chroniclers, Arthur Shearer, a former postmaster of Hannibal, Missouri, who later held the same position in San Jose, California, and Thomas S. Wylly, later a gentleman residing in the south-ern states. The experiences they recounted dramatically demonstrate how different the journey could be for people with slightly more imaginative frames of refer-ence and perhaps better native judgment and good for-tune. Shearer's initial comment that the Mormons of Utah County were worse cattle thieves than the Ute In-dians may offer further explanation as to why more of the Independents did not join the larger emigrant train led by Jefferson Hunt. On several occasions during the early Utah stretch of the road, the diarist commented that a slightly different course could have saved them consider-able time and effort, demonstrating a turn of mind that might help his company avoid some hardships experi-enced by their predecessors. However, Wylly made it clear their group also suffered abundantly.

On the Santa Clara River, where the Hoover party cattle went without feed other than tree leaves for four of five days, Shearer's group made a more concerted ef-fort to locate grass. He stated that "finding feed scarce, [they] determined to stop where we could get enough for [their] animals—accordingly finding some tolerable good grass, [they] encamped early." While spending an extra day recouping the cattle, some budding prospec-tors became convinced that the area promised "gold in greatest abundance," which modern mining operations have proved was true. Yet when the time came to move on, none hesitated to do so, because the company's sup-plies were diminishing. Shearer noted pessimistically but accurately that if there were not more feed on the route than he had recently observed, "it would be dan-gerous for a large train to pass [that] way."

On encountering Virgin Hill, Shearer admitted it ap-peared "impassable." But locating no better way up and presumably realizing their preceding company mates had managed to get up at that point, they followed the trail just broken by the Hoover group. As was typical, it took all day to get the wagons up the hill, which the dia-rist estimated to average thirty to thirty-five degrees of slope, interspersed with deep sand and the "sharpest possible rock."[33]

Wylly offered important insights as well into the supreme challenge of the Virgin Hill. He reported that "All the oxen in the whole train," which with up to thirty-five wagons might well have numbered over a hundred head, "were made into two long teams," presumably mainly stretched along the west-tending road at the top of the mesa. He continued that this huge team "each al-ternately pulled one wagon to the top of the bluff, and this with greatest difficulty and with the help of all the men who were not driving the oxen. One by one all the wagons reached the top, and we now found ourselves on the high tableland too flat and open" for Native Ameri-cans to threaten livestock as they had in the past fifty miles.[34]

Actually, this company had continued to find reason to fear nearby Paiute bands. In a recent pursuit of stolen livestock, some of the pioneer men had ventured even farther down the Virgin River than the pack mule trail, which left the river at Halfway Wash, some fifteen miles southwest of where the wagons pulled away from the riverbed. Here the region's Native Americans had secreted huge stockpiles of mesquite bean pods gathered from among the abundant trees nearby. They undoubtedly considered these stores of emergency food safe, since white travelers had not previously ventured that far down the Virgin. This supply, Wylly recalled, the Indians had placed in dry well holes four or five feet in diameter, apparently reaching deep into the earth. These were filled to the top, with the pods packed tightly and covered with a sort of thatch to keep out some moisture, and over that, a cover of large flat rocks placed to form a slightly elevated cone. The members of the Independent Company, angry over the loss of their livestock, as Wylly confessed (and later regretted), "did not exhibit a proper amount of Christian charity in [their] dealings with the property of our fleeing enemies across the river." Instead, they applied the torch to numerous of these valuable food caches. The chronicler noted the mesquite beans "must have a large quantity of oil in them for they burned fiercely, the fire consuming them and following [the storage pits] down into the earth until the wells looked like veritable fiery furnaces." This, like their predecessors' killing one cattle-stealing Paiute man and then pasturing their cattle on the corn and vegetable fields of their presumed enemies, certainly enhanced the enmity already developed by the mountain men and pack mule traders of the previous era.[35]

Like all others, the small company prepared at the Muddy River for the dreaded *jornada* to Las Vegas. But much to their surprise they discovered puddled water in three different places where most others found none at all, along with good feed at least once. Shearer confessed, "[T]he desert has been the dread of the trip, [but] has proved to us much easier than many others." The group nevertheless much appreciated the Vegas, considered the best meadows on the entire route. Similarly, this rear detachment managed better than the Independents ahead of them as they departed present Nevada across the Pahrump Valley. They not only obtained water at Stump Springs but found some the next day as well, with good feed nearby on both occasions. Shearer noted the "forward company" had lost many cattle in the Resting Springs vicinity. He also recorded

that as their own provisions were becoming scarce, several companions opted to leave the wagons and livestock and head for the settlements "on foot."[36]

Perhaps the most dramatic display of good management and fortune came just prior to the most dreaded stretch of the trail from Amargosa Canyon to the Mojave River. As others following not far behind would soon do, the travelers cut grass to haul with them for times of need. They also became one of the few groups to record taking advantage of the good, fresh water from small springs along the upper northeastern wall of the Amargosa Canyon. Then too the party found good water along the sandy stretch toward Salt Springs as well as in the upper wash just beyond those springs. And in that vicinity the grass proved much better than they had been led to expect, allowing their cattle to rest where others, including those just ahead, suffered severely. Equally fortunate, in contrast to the Independent group by then some ten days ahead, Shearer's party found water near Silurian (dry) Lake, proving that it was not always completely dry. Here the party members fed their stock the grass they had carried along.

Amazingly, the party "found water frequently in holes along the stream," in the almost always dry wash heading toward Red Pass, although the water in the usually dry Red Pass Lake was frozen too hard to use. They enjoyed no better than the usual small measure of water and grass at Bitter Springs. And because of recent snow, the pull up Impassable Pass once again ranked as one of the most difficult days this detachment had experienced. However, weak as the livestock were they made the climb, which the preceding party could not have accomplished under such conditions. Shearer's account of his party's experiences contained literally none of the dire suffering noted by Vincent Hoover among his travel companions, but as previously noted, Wylly's account indicates some hardship.[37]

THE FIRST WAGONS DOWN CAJON PASS

After ten days recuperating on the Mojave River, the Hoovers and several other families embarked for the southern California ranchos. After the last crossing of the river, described as a hundred feet wide, but not swift, they started their last climb toward the mountain summit. They camped without water in a juniper grove, in present-day Hesperia. The company probably had no idea that their greatest challenge, so far as roadway was concerned, still lay ahead, but by Vincent's next journal entry they would be fully aware of that.

Making the descent from the upper ridge, Vincent boasted they had just accomplished what had never before "been performed in the annals of [the] wagon era," referring to their descending "the backbone of [the] Sierra Nevada." He was not correct on his geography, but many contemporaries considered the San Gabriel and San Bernardino Mountains intersected by Cajon Pass to be a continuation of the larger Sierra range to the northwest. Hoover explained that several teamsters unhitched all but the "wheel cattle," which were accustomed to working with the driver in turning as well as pulling. Some also "rough-locked" both hind wheels, probably tying them with chains so that the iron tires dragged and thus braked the wagons, as described in chapter 1. Hoover did neither, but drove down the steep incline at the top of the east Cajon Pass, he confessed, "with fear and trembling." Afterward he boasted that only the most "resolute" could ever have gotten down the grade and that "persons who have not wagoned much would have

thought [it] impossible for us to have got [sic] a wagon down it."

At the bottom of the hill the party reached a refreshing stream of water, but the travelers would be dismayed to discover a still more difficult stretch, the worst of the entire Southern Route, just ahead in the boulder-strewn lower stream bed. After yet another night when the livestock had but little feed, the small group was compelled to spend much of the day "fixing the canyon," which meant filling in "precipices" with smaller rocks and rolling some of the larger ones out of the intended roadway in the stream. The diarist considered it—erroneously, unless he meant this exact stretch of road—"a labor that never [had] been performed by humans before." He was certainly more accurate in asserting "the labor of the day will be remembered by [himself] as long as [he should continue] to exist." The horrible road would be recalled with equal pain and pride by other travelers who followed in ensuing days and weeks.[38]

Adding to the heart-rending chronicle of hardships and misery, rain and strong winds commenced, during a night when all deserved complete rest. The storm forced the group to go without fire and thus any cooked food. And equally unfortunate, the rain raised the level of the usually small Coyote-Crowder Creek high enough to prevent the wagons from passing over the newly im-

The rocky Coyote–Crowder Creek bed (far right) negotiated by the wagoners who traveled the Southern Route in 1849. Note remnants of the John Brown toll-road grade excavated along the slope in 1861 and later used by the first auto route, National Old Trails Highway-Route 66 through Cajon Pass, 2001.

COURTESY LARRY REESE

proved roadway. While they waited, a number of other wagons approached from behind. Addison Pratt recorded the situation thus: "[W]e were all jammed together in the narrow pass," which he described correctly as a stream bed cut "through the mountain until the perpendicular banks in some places [were] nearly one hundred feet high." He also noted that when the water level had subsided enough for the wagons to proceed, all the vehicles but his group's "had to be lifted and pried to get them up and down" over the formidable boulders. Pratt was presumably implying that his Mormon missionaries possessed sufficient manpower and perhaps a less heavy load, with no furniture to haul, to lift their wagon over the obstacles with relative ease.[39]

Sidney P. Waite, then a boy of twelve, recalled that at this time his father had to dismantle his wagon and slide the heavier pieces over the boulders on sycamore poles. Hoover felt compelled to wade down the cold and still two-foot-deep creek, presumably to steady his wagon. And inevitably, the Gruwells continued to experience more than their share of difficulty, breaking two wagon tongues and tipping over one wagon.[40]

Finally, just days before Christmas 1849, many of the thoroughly exhausted emigrants emerged from the mountains and deserts into a southern California already exhibiting what easterners considered the signs of springtime. The new growth of grass and wild oats rose several inches high, and Pratt, an avid nature lover, reported that "birds were singing as in spring." Hoover exclaimed effusively, "[T]his is one of the greatest climates in the known world," incorrectly asserting, "[I]t is eternal spring." At the popular natural campsite at the foot of the Cajon (Sycamore Grove at the present Glen Helen Park in Devore), the road forked, with the southward-tending branch going toward the Lugos's San Bernardino rancho and the Isaac Slover and Louis Rubidoux ranches, and the west trail heading for Rancho Cucamonga, San Gabriel, and Los Angeles. Some pioneers went in each direction, seeking a place where they could recuperate from accumulated ordeals.

The Hoover group traveled 14.5 miles west to the Rancho Cucamonga, overseen that year by an African American named Jackson, married to a Hispanic woman. Here they feasted on *pinole*, a cornmeal mush; tortillas; and lots of beef. The ranch also produced a large quantity of grapes, from which they made "a great deal of wine," naturally described as rich and of good flavor—as many things would be, after months of deprivation.

On the third day at the ranch, John Borse rushed into the house exclaiming his wife was dead. She had been ill for several hundred miles, suffering a great deal while crossing the desert, but had completed the trip only to succumb when comfort was at hand, tragically unable to enjoy with husband and children what they had strived so long to attain in the new country. Unfortunate though her death was, it is truly amazing that she was the only known human casualty among the Independent Pioneer Company on that mistake-fraught initial wagon trip from Utah to California.[41]

Both the Gruwell and Addison Pratt Mormon missionary companies also stopped for a time at the Rancho Cucamonga, then owned by Victor Proudhomme. The church group procured beef, corn, wheat, and wine, while some in the other party focused primarily on the wine. When drunk, some of the Gruwell people became verbally abusive to their sometime-associated packer pioneers, and several Hispanic ranch hands urged the Mormons to punish the ungrateful rowdies. Pratt informed the onlookers that the intoxicated were "not worth minding." Both groups subsequently moved to Isaac Williams's Rancho del Chino some ten miles south, where they established themselves for a longer stay, as many other recently arrived emigrants were accustomed to doing.

RANCHO DEL CHINO

In the following month one of the Gruwells operated some kind of boardinghouse on the Williams premises, perhaps working off the debt for rescue provisions. When the family first arrived, future area judge Benjamin Hayes heard them recount their immense privations on the trail and also noted their resilience, mentioning seeing some of the group conducting school in one of the wagons.[42]

Among the many priceless documents at the Henry E. Huntington Library in San Marino, California, is a register and message book kept during this period at the Rancho del Chino. It lists a goodly number of incoming emigrants who stopped there, many recounting stories of hardship on the trail, and some leaving messages for those coming later. By sending supplies to the Mojave region, Isaac Williams saved more than a few virtually from starvation. In a sense the ranch served not only as a rescue station and recuperating mission, but also as a clearinghouse for information about California and current opportunities there, otherwise essentially absent in the southern portion of the territory. The rancho also proved the best place in the southland to obtain supplies, fresh livestock, and even some clothing to replace what had worn out or been discarded on the trail. As earlier San Bernardino County historian George W. Beattie concluded, "Williams was untiring in his efforts to afford relief" to all comers. LeRoy Hafen added, "Isaac Williams was certainly the saviour of many of these destitute emigrants."

After Williams, the southern California rancher and benefactor of so many, had been eliminated from the state senate resolution lauding J. A. Sutter's similar actions in the north, he wrote a letter of protest. He detailed his numerous relief efforts performed in 1849 and 1850, saying there had been but few days during that period when he did not have emigrants receiving some sort of assistance at his ranch. He claimed that often between two and three hundred such people were on his property and that most days he had at least six and often up to twenty dinner guests at his personal table. He also stated he provided more than two hundred animals on credit, along with over $5,000 cash advanced to pioneers who promised to repay when they reached their destination. He had received only a tenth of that sum back within a year of making the loans. The rancher also provided flour and other provisions at costs below those charged at Los Angeles, and for travelers in real distress on the Mojave, such as the Gruwells, when the people had no funds he dispensed the goods without payment. There is little question some of these acts were penance for major indiscretions during the Mexican War, but the fact remains Isaac Williams performed a most essential service by ushering hundreds of newly arrived American pioneers into California by the Southern Route. The state legislature finally granted the justly deserved resolution—a hundred years after it was earned.[43]

THE HUNT-BAXTER COMPANY

The much larger company of pioneers gathering and organizing simultaneously with the Hoover-Gruwell-Derr party generally traveled just behind that group and if anything experienced an even more eventful journey. In contrast to the Hoover-Gruwell-Derr group, however, they appeared well organized and led—at least as long as they availed themselves of Jefferson Hunt's leadership. Beyond that point (of abandoning Hunt's direction) lies the chronicle of tragedies and suffering linked to the Death Valley parties who split off from the main trail in their attempt to find a shorter route through the Sierra Nevada to the gold fields—not a part of this study.[44]

William B. Lorton, a New Yorker trained as a printer, emerged as the most detailed chronicler of the experiences of this group. At Salt Lake City, Lorton, like most, but certainly not all other visitors, related well to the predominantly Mormon citizens. In Lorton's case his talent as a singer clearly enhanced his popularity. In August, after determining the necessity of waiting until autumn to travel over the Southern Route, he attended a concert organized at least partly through Brigham Young. This featured the eight-piece band of William Clayton, a prominent local musician and hymn writer, staged at John Pack's tavern, a hall 50 feet long and half that wide. After some popular "yankee" tunes by the band, by special request of President Young, Lorton sang "one of the latest 'Ethiopian' melodies, 'Dearest May,'" accompanied by a violin. This reportedly brought down thunderous applause. After an Irish number by the band, "loud cries" arose for another Lorton rendition. He performed what was probably the most popular song of the era, "Susanna."

The next day the singer attended a musical party at the home of Louisa Barnes Pratt, a former music teacher in the East, later active in Mormon San Bernardino in similar singing sessions. Lorton maintained a cordial attachment with Louisa's husband, Addison, throughout their subsequent trek to California. His singing remained popular with his company, at least until the dissension commenced when most turned onto the supposed shortcut. At the Utah County assembly grounds just prior to starting, Lorton and his fellows "stayed up till late singing negro melodies." Several weeks later, he noted they had had "a negro concert in New York boys' tent." Although at least three African Americans were among the large company, it is doubtful if they had any influence on the choice of music, which was obviously popular among many others at the time.[45]

On Sunday, 30 September 1849, at the Hobble Creek gathering grounds, after a preaching session by Lewis Granger against the use of profanity, an announcement designated a meeting to make "such regulations as would be necessary for safely pursuing the Southern Route to California." Already scribe of those proceedings, Lorton was appointed, with Granger, later a Los Angeles attorney and politician, and with Thomas M. Marshall, to draft a constitution and by-laws to present at a subsequent gathering. As John P. Reid concluded in his book on law on the emigrant trails, this was a very common procedure. After due completion of the document, probably in part drafted previously by Granger, and after "careful discussion," the company accepted the constitution.[46]

It provided for the election of a colonel who would have general command of the company and an adjutant to act as his assistant, along with serving as scribe when necessary. The constitution also split the company into seven divisions, each to elect a captain and assigned one night's guard duty per week for the duration of the journey. The colonel, adjutant, and seven captains comprised a council charged with "deciding all matters of importance on the route." They assigned another committee to raise the funds to engage Jefferson Hunt as guide. The subsequent seven divisions of 10 to 12 wagons each adopted nicknames, including San Joaquin (Sand Walking), Bug Smashers, Buckskins, Hawkeyes, Wolverines, and Jayhawkers, mostly later well known in the annals of the Death Valley experience. Each subgroup was to take the lead position in the company one day, then drop to the rear. Considering the dust raised by the 107 wagons, this proved a fair way to allow each family whatever equity there was in position within the train.[47]

The San Joaquin company appointed Adonijah S. Welch to keep an official journal of that group's trek. He first noted his division members repacking their wagon loads and adding another thickness of cotton drilling to each wagon cover. He stated this to be in preparation for resuming their "long dusty route to the San Joaquin"

Jefferson Hunt, one of the first wagon train leaders over the Southern Route, San Bernardino state legislator, and freighter over the route after the Mormon settlement was abandoned.

Valley, where some of the richest gold discoveries were reportedly being made. Actually, the divisions first traveled a few miles down the valley to what was then designated as Election Creek, later Payson, Utah. Here the new division historian noted five hundred oxen and a hundred horses grazing on the abundant grass. Meanwhile the emigrants "were generally seated in groups around large fires talking of the election which was to come off in the afternoon and discussing the merits" of the leading candidates for colonel, Alexander Ewing and Henry Baxter. After due electioneering, Baxter won, with Dr. William McCormick as adjutant. The new leader immediately urged completion of the division organizations, which naturally took into consideration many longtime friendships.[48]

While still in the preparation stage, the new council convened as a court to try a company member who had "wronged pecuniarily" two young Germans who were traveling in the same wagon. Granger presented the case, and the issue was "adjusted" in a manner satisfactory to those wronged. Even though the guide assured the company that local Indians were peaceable, after the company was formed its leaders posted the regular guard of twenty men each night. On 4 October Welch recorded, "[F]inally the train moved on in a long dusty line."[49]

Just two days later, on the Sabbath, the company laid over without traveling. Although not yet noted by any of the diarists, this layover soon proved upsetting to a goodly number of wagoners, who concluded that the progress of the huge train was too slow for their liking. On this first Sunday on the trail, those of religious inclinations could listen to three different sermons. Rev. M. Ehlers of the German Reformed persuasion spoke first, then Rev. James W. Brier, a Methodist. A German noted as a "missionary to the mines," Mr. Crow, delivered the last in his native tongue. It is difficult to determine the number of Germans in the company, but it was more than half a dozen, plus several others among the Independent Pioneer Company.[50]

At Salt Creek (later Nephi, Utah), members of the Hunt-Baxter company found a notice stating that the packers led by James Waters, who were traveling a month ahead of the Independents, had killed at least six Paiute Indians near the Sevier River, about a day's journey ahead of the current large Hunt-Baxter emigrant campsite. Someone in the Independent Pioneer Company had posted the notice and pointedly invited others to join with them for common protection. It is doubtful if any responded to these overtures or that the huge Hunt-Baxter company had reason to expect trouble from Native American sources. Indians, probably exclusively Ute, had been in the wagon camps on numerous occasions, and although pilfering and attempts at theft had occurred, the wagoners had tolerated them without incident. Later, at the Sevier, considerable trading occurred with Native Americans, along with other positive interaction, despite the Indians' continuing unsuccessful attempts to steal.

A less common facet of this emigrant train's organization was the influence of the several physicians in being able to halt travel for the benefit of sick company members. At daybreak on 11 October, two cases of illness were deemed sufficiently severe to prevent the company from moving that day. The council met and concurred in this decision. This was probably particularly galling to the impatient, because crossing the steep-banked Sevier had taken most of the previous two days, along with whatever time was expended in an emigrant trial of a man acquitted of involvement in a rape allegedly committed much farther back on the trail (before Salt Lake City). It would not be fair to judge Jefferson Hunt harshly for allowing the regular company officials to exercise their vested prerogatives, but before long some undoubtedly included him in blame for the slow progress.

Among the travelers impressed with Hunt's leadership, Jacob Y. Stover also recalled that the Mormons near Utah Lake had been good to the emigrants during their two-month stay among them. The greatest contrast between Hunt and Antonio, whom Addison Pratt called a "vagrant" Spaniard, was in the portion of the route where the latter failed to find a camping spot with the requisite necessities for at least six days. "Captain Hunt led us to wood and water and grass every night," recalled Stover. And in the daytime he took a squad of men with him out ahead of the wagons to cut down banks of streams they would cross and to clear away impeding brush along the road. Although they knew a party was traveling ahead of them, Hunt followed a better route in some places, accounting for Stover's recollections that they were the first to traverse the road.[51]

The day after the long layover at the Sevier River, the company leaders apparently attempted to make up for lost time by traveling some twenty-four miles and into the night even though—or more likely because—there was no water along that stretch of trail. Toward the end of the *jornada*, near present Holden, Utah, a beacon fire was set to pilot the teamsters struggling onward through the night. Welch wrote descriptively that as the teams approached listeners heard "in the distance the crack of the whips and the shouts of a hundred drivers." They expended an hour in forming a corral in the darkness, and midnight approached before the camp was quiet.[52] The contemporary concept of a corral did not fit the later movie version of pioneers circling the wagons for protection of emigrants from Indians. The livestock were placed inside the enclosure because of the greater fear of Indian cattle theft than any danger to the people of the wagon train.[53]

The company may have agreed to the arduous day's travel with the understanding they would rest the next day, the Sabbath. Another consideration of Colonel Baxter's was to give the sick a chance to improve, presumably better than they could on the trail. But protests immediately arose over this decision, and a company-wide meeting convened to air the matter. The colonel acknowledged a mistake in assuming that he and the council could decide the train should stop over for a day when the constitution did not so specify. He added that common custom did provide that power. Jefferson Hunt then offered what Lorton called a "stump speech" in which he stressed the need for absolute subordination to the train leaders, particularly during the coming stretch of the journey. He also mentioned the necessity to preserve livestock strength so crucial on the desert stretch ahead. This was precisely the appropriate advice so obviously missing among the Independent Pioneer Company just ahead of Hunt's group, but apparently some resented the comments. The opponents of the rest day called for a vote but were apparently defeated, because later that day Lewis Granger preached a Methodist sermon to a large audience. The episode demonstrated that the company, soon associated with struggles near and within Death Valley, was already seriously wracked by dissension. Hunt commented that even God with three hundred angels could not establish a policy that would please everybody. Here, as later in Mormon San Bernardino, Hunt's apparent pomposity sometimes tended to lose him considerable support.[54]

ALIENATION FROM HUNT

Jefferson Hunt came to believe he could save the company time in several ways that did not actually work out as planned. After passing through Fillmore, he chose to take the long line of wagons over a mountain ridge into the next valley from near Corn Creek to Dog Valley, instead of skirting several miles west around the ridge by the older pack mule route. Among the Independent Pioneer Company members traveling just ahead was Arthur Shearer, who reported "Passed over a rocky ridge" then commented "Had we known it, we could have come a shorter route by leaving the route we came after we came to this side of the ridge and bearing to the right instead of to the left," saving at least eight miles' travel. Certainly some of Hunt's huge company would have eventually recognized the same fact.[55]

Further company division and disillusionment toward Hunt developed when at the good campgrounds in Beaver Valley, the guide proposed an alternative to the known dry *jornada* on the regular route followed by the Independents south and east through the long Parowan Valley area to Buckhorn Springs just north of Paragonah. Having traveled that way twice before, Hunt knew it had no prospect of earlier water. With the assent of the council, the guide proposed to follow the Beaver River westward into the later Minersville area, then turn south across the low mountains and valley northwest of Little Salt Lake. Hunt assumed he would strike Coal Creek near present Cedar City just beyond there. While he and other scouts tried out this venture, the company wagons followed down the Beaver, then turned south where they had to camp twelve miles from water, having crossed the low mountains with no trail through the brush. Now Hunt returned to camp to announce unaccountable failure. At that crucial juncture various groups gathered around the camp to discuss the best means of extricating themselves from the crisis, some blaming Hunt and others, the council. Cephas Arms, captain of the Buckskin division, unfairly concluded at that juncture that "our guide is off the direct route and there is no disguising the fact that we are lost."[56]

Many concluded the cattle should be driven back to the Beaver River with only those wagons needed to bring back filled water casks for the people remaining in camp. Some disagreed, and forty wagons began retracing their tracks to the Beaver Valley to follow the known route. This was actually a first secession from the company prior to the outside packers bringing news of the fateful (Death Valley) cutoff route. But Hunt, backed by the council, doggedly made a second attempt to reach water by his proposed new route. This time he returned too thirsty to speak. The group then had no choice but to abandon this camp in what had been dubbed the "Valley of Errors" and to follow their associates back to Beaver, then over the Beaver–Parowan Valley road southward toward Red Creek. The experiment was an honest mistake that under other circumstances might have been more forgivable. But it cost more than a week of provisions, an observable degree of patience among a considerable number of men, and the strength of many livestock. Toward the end of this chain of events, the packers from Salt Lake City arrived with reports about a shortcut through Walker Pass to the gold fields.[57]

Even before the shortcut craze exacerbated the crisis, major discontent existed with the situation, stemming primarily from the slow progress of the giant company. Later excuses were offered involving apprehension that some members were not properly provisioned and equipped for the desert segments of either route, but it was actually the slowness of travel that appeared to be the crux of the problem. Buckskin leader Cephas Arms confessed, "[M]any are getting dissatisfied with so large a train and are determined to leave it and find their own way to California." The recollections of Adonijah Welch several months later, in a letter from Williams's Rancho del Chino, reveal the thinking perhaps typical at the time. Welch claimed that the shortcut scheme had appeal primarily because the recent experience indicated that it was "impossible that large companies should travel together on desert roads." He erroneously claimed they had spent seven weeks in "making a distance of two hundred and fifty miles" by the time the company disbanded, twice as long as it had actually taken.[58] Still, the point was well made. The small capacity of several desert water holes as well as the sparseness of the pasturelands absolutely precluded more than one hundred wagons traveling together. Perhaps Hunt couldn't admit this, because of the financial arrangements he had made, but he should have been the first to recognize this reality.

SECESSION OF THE
DEATH VALLEY PARTIES

The newly arrived pack train included some thirty Mormons under Latter-day Saints apostle Charles C. Rich and seventeen non-Mormons nominally led by an out-spoken clergyman named Orson Kirk Smith. The latter had recently spoken with an old mountain man living among the Latter-day Saints, Elijah Barney Ward, who claimed to have taken a shortcut through Walker Pass to near the California gold fields on three occasions. He reported good cattle feed and water dispersed all along this trail. Arms observed, referring to Hunt's recent shortcut mistake, "[W]ith their failure fresh in their minds, many of our company are already in favor of trying [the new route] inasmuch as it is said to be much nearer, and avoids all those deserts, so fearful which lie before us on the Spanish Trail."[59] Word of this new route spread quickly through the camps of the large Hunt-Baxter company.

Back on the main trail after the somewhat disastrous side trip, Welch reported that Capt. William H. Goddard withdrew from the company and took thirteen teams and wagons, apparently his entire division, ahead on their own. That night the scribe noted the Jayhawker division members were "dancing in grotesque attitude to the twang of an old fiddle." Although they appeared cheerful and glad to be again on the correct road, they may also have been expressing a little defiance and rebellion.[60] At least three other company members, James Martin, David Switzer, and Wiley Webster, had also moved on ahead and were camped in the Red Creek area when the main company arrived.[61]

Although no untoward incidents were recorded concerning the spread-out condition of some of the travelers, just after that time an unnamed lone rider fortunately discovered three Native Americans waiting in ambush for him. Although he saw their drawn bows, he safely distanced himself through the speed of his horse. Presumably the Indians were not mounted. The reminders of such dangers probably influenced the main company council in the following incident, among others. Convening a court, the council convicted a German doctor of stealing food from his neighbors. In the sentence passed, he was banned from coming any closer to the company than twenty rods either traveling or camping for the rest of the journey. Although it was noted that he moved ahead of them on the trail the next day, the council did not see fit to levy so harsh a penalty as sentencing him to travel entirely alone. Another company later discovered him besieged in his tent by Paiutes on the Virgin River.

That group felt sympathy and carried him along with them.[62]

At Summit Creek camp (between present Parowan and Cedar City, Utah), Welch observed a great deal of discussion about the proposed new route among company members, who were as yet undecided about what course to take. One of the primary considerations noted as influential at that juncture was the "great apprehension by those who have sufficient provisions that the deficient will be on their hands to feed in case of disaster." Even the general company leader, Henry Baxter, expressed the view that "twenty-five wagons ought to roll back to Salt Lake City from want of food and teams" that would be sufficient to properly continue the journey.

The next day Capt. Edward Doty, head of the Jayhawkers, moved on with eight wagons of his division. Capt. Cephas Arms expressed intent to do likewise the following morning with his Buckskin division. Baxter, who claimed his first obligation was membership in that smaller, older group, thereupon resigned as company colonel, to leave with his Buckskin fellows. Besides the slow progress of the large company, the other reason Arms gave for abandoning the Hunt party was the candid admission of "unwillingness of his division to incur the risk of traveling through the deserts with men who have weak teams and are short of provisions."[63] The supreme irony of this was that both the Jayhawkers and Buckskins took the supposed shorter route, and many lived to seek assistance to get themselves through the remainder of their journey, sometimes from others earlier judged to be in such poor circumstances as to not deserve their continued association or help in time of need. Such are the paradoxes of life during times of severe trial many of the disrupted Hunt-Baxter Company were about to experience.

At this juncture interest in the new route spread quickly through the wagon company, stirring up a "commotion" that diarist William Farrer suggested verged on a "rebellion." William Lorton, who followed the shortcut for a time, later recalled that "a hearsay delusion seized the camp." His diary stated that "dissension has now commenced . . . [which tended to bring out the] devil in man."[64] If historian Dale L. Morgan had published his detailed treatment of the 1849 Southern Route experience, he would have titled the chapter treating this portion of his history "A Mania for Cutoffs." During some of the deliberations, as many were deciding to take the new route, slurs were hurled at Mormons generally and Hunt in particular. When most of the company severed themselves from the guide's leadership, Hunt confided to friends the belief that because of recent threats this separation had saved his life. At a meeting before parting, some of the company called for Hunt to express his views. He stressed he had never been over the cutoff and did not know of anyone who had. He vowed he would continue to lead anyone over the known road as long as they wished to follow him. But the occupants of a hundred wagons chose to attempt the new route, only seven staying with Hunt. The former leader wished the seceders good fortune but asserted he believed they were heading for the "jaws of hell," which in a sense proved an accurate prediction.[65]

BACK TO THE MAIN ROUTE

The people who seceded from Hunt's leadership would mostly regret doing so, some facing almost unbearable hardships over pathless and sometimes impassable terrain, including the area named at that time Death Valley. The experiences of these people are well documented elsewhere and are not a part of this study.[66] However, a great number of both wagon drivers and packers eventually recognized the error of their decisions and sought successfully to relocate the tracks of Hunt's small group, thereafter making the journey with general success over the remainder of the known roadway. The first to reconsider routes was a man named C. C. Rynierson, who followed the Smith trail into present-day Nevada, then concluded it was too dangerous for his family and retraced his steps to the Hunt road. "Quite a train" of other wagons followed him.

Although this train of returnees undoubtedly included the largest portion of the seceding one hundred wagons, no diary account of the group's experiences while off the main road is known. Alexander C. Erkson later recalled a few items of information, including seeing a recently made grave of a child who may have been in a segment of the Independent party. One wise practice noted was that this group of returners made their wagons as light as possible by taking off all the boards and slats they could possibly get along without. And as some in the rear group of the Independents were already doing, Mrs. Erkson followed a practice that other prudent pioneers soon emulated, picking bunches of grass and putting them into the wagon as she walked along, collecting feed to be used between good grazing spots on the desert. It is clear from a later descriptive letter by another party member, Lewis C. Granger, that some of the so-called Rynierson company were particularly diligent in adopting this precaution. At Resting Springs the members loaded each wagon with three hundred pounds of grass and an equal amount of water for the difficult journey to the Mojave River. They probably used some of the discarded casks the Hoover party could not haul because of the weakened condition of their draft animals.

Even more fortunate for the Rynierson-Granger party was their unlikely success in procuring 600 pounds of flour while on the edge of Death Valley, when they were facing starvation. They had encountered Charles Dallas of Iowa, like Granger a former member of the Hoover-Gruwell party, at the Muddy River with seven wagons loaded with provisions he intended to sell in the gold fields. After selling a small amount of "sour" flour to the Mormon (Rich) packers, he proceeded ahead. Granger disclosed that when his company reached Las Vegas, they sent two young men ahead toward the California settlements for provisions and when they overtook Dallas, he agreed to leave the flour for them in the care of those men at Resting Springs. The straggler party, weak and emaciated by diarrhea they believed resulted from lack of proper nourishment, arrived at the common resting spot five days later. They acknowledged their good fortune to be "the indubitable evidences of Divine interposition," believing some of their number would have perished without the flour. Dallas probably recognized that he was facing the most difficult stretch of trail for his livestock, and perhaps understanding that the quality of his flour was deteriorating, sale to this needy company was better than simply discarding it on the desert.[67]

William Lorton departed from Hunt's party on good terms and moved westward away from the main trail toward what was later Enterprise, Utah. It only took a few days for Capt. William Goddard, who had been scouting

toward Nevada, to "advise all to put for the Spanish Trail" and forget the shortcut. Lorton's group was not yet ready to give up the dream, but after their animals went without water three days in the notably rough upper Meadow Valley Wash area of southeastern Nevada, their resolve weakened. They passed eleven others more determined, who in their presence pledged to "go to California or to Hell." Lorton's group commenced backtracking, "determined to make no more cutoffs." His party included a black man, Pycus Nailer, whom they knew to be mortally ill. He may have been the tall former Mississippi Riverboat steward Lorton had met at the beginning of the company trek in Utah County. This man died in Nevada on 9 November, and Lorton was constrained to reprove his fellows for quarreling over the corpse for items of Nailer's property. At least they had not left him behind, as another fragment of the old company left a man named Lawrence. Lorton's group took this man in and gave him a horse to ride.[68]

Another group of packers that went farther before seeking Hunt's proven road was led by Jacob Y. Stover. With this leader demonstrating impressive scouting ability, they relocated the Southern Route trail in the Resting Springs area. Near there the party passed a spot where forty wagons belonging to people fanatically seeking Walker Pass had been burned, reportedly so that they would not be retrieved and claimed by the Mormons. When the members of this group finally reached the Mojave River, they were again saved by Stover's good leadership, the lack of which would have proved fatal. A flash flood caused by a recent cloudburst upstream came rushing down the dry river channel where the party had camped for the night and was then traveling. Quick recognition of the crisis and decisive warnings to all travelers allowed them to scramble out of the riverbed in time to avoid the huge wall of water and debris. The Stover party was also grateful to avail themselves of an Isaac Williams supply wagon. And later, their leader waxed eloquent about the California southland, saying first it was "the loveliest place" he had ever seen, then commenting that at the foot of Cajon Pass it appeared the travelers "had passed into a new world." As several of their predecessors had, they soon drowned their bad memories in Rancho Cucamonga wine.[69]

The group of Mormon packers who had traveled

through Utah with Rev. Orson Kirk Smith also took the supposed shortcut, although ranking church leader Charles C. Rich claimed he had doubts about the decision. This group of seventeen included at least four diarists, along with others who wrote later recollections. After several weeks of struggle in the rugged terrain between the headwaters of the Beaver Dam Wash and the upper Muddy River of southeastern Nevada, Rich informed Smith that his group was no longer pursuing the "shortcut" but would seek the Hunt road to the south. The company faced death from thirst, but a rainstorm Rich reportedly had prayed for saved both man and beast. Not long after, they reunited with the Hunt party on the Muddy.

The outstanding cooperation and consideration demonstrated among the Mormon packers shows a clear contrast with many of their fellows' attitude of every man for himself. Before separation from the Smith group, one of that number became so desperate for water he offered to "pay any price for a drink" but got no offers. Henry Bigler was equally thirsty at the time, and when Rich learned of it he unhesitatingly handed over his canteen, instructing the younger man he was welcome to all he wished. Later, when Bigler's horse gave out, Rich took turns walking so that the fellow missionary would not become exhausted and worn out before the last leg of the desert crossing. Another impressive instance of cooperation noted in the group was Addison Pratt and several others riding ahead of the wagons to clear rocks from the road up the northern grade of Emigrant Pass. By the time the teams arrived, they could take their loads up what had been one of the most difficult spots for the Hoover and Shearer parties, without even adding extra draft animals to the wagons. Numerous other such instances showed sharing and brotherly concern.

Another contrast with several less cooperative and prudent groups was the Hunt company's care in sending someone out in front of the wagons to mark the proper trail—even in the snow. They too traveled at night on the dry crossings, to save their draft animals, but they always kept on the track and did not have to wait till daylight to find the proper route. An equally important purpose for this scouting was to locate the better bunchgrass feed for the livestock, which was consistently found— including places where the Hoover group had relegated

their animals to salt grass—as at the Santa Clara, Stump Springs, and Bitter Springs. The Hunt party members also took great care to cut good feed to carry with them for the most demanding *jornadas*, and even though the cattle had drunk plenty of water before starting the night journeys, the travelers filled casks to provide a smaller watering at the short feed rests en route.

There were also instances when on the systematic searches the scouts located useful water puddles on several dreaded dry crossings, such as between the Muddy and Las Vegas and between Salt Springs and Bitter Springs. Then too, this group quickly noticed the sharp, pointed stones beyond Las Vegas and stopped at the next camp to carefully shoe whatever oxen were threatened with lameness. On reaching the Mojave, the Mormon company gave much of their remaining provisions to the suffering Gruwell women and children, then promptly organized hunting parties to seek game in the thickets along the river. Although initially meeting with so little success as to be worried about food, they eventually killed and consumed five blacktailed deer in that area, which tided them through until Williams's wagon laden with provisions arrived. The Gruwell-Derr party faced starvation in that same area partly because of their own incompetence as hunters.[70]

By that time the larger group of Mormon missionaries, led by Charles C. Rich, were already at Chino, where some rented a room in one of the houses, while others pitched camp nearby. Addison Pratt noted that some of those who had split from the Hunt guidance were very reticent when they appeared on the Mojave. But a more talkative Irishman admitted to Hunt that they had frequently blamed each other for ever leaving his trail and leadership in the first place.[71]

One irony of the history of the "forty-niners" who traveled over the Southern Route was that with over two thousand avid gold seekers traveling that way during this important year of the Gold Rush, it was the less motivated Mormon prospectors who most notably searched for and first found the precious metal. Addison Pratt had the advantage of some time spent the previous year in the mother lode country, and he consistently kept his eye on the rock formations along the trail. Like some in the Shearer group, while in the Santa Clara–Utah Mountain vicinity Pratt observed what he considered "strong

Addison Pratt, Mormon missionary to Tahiti, diarist, and gold discoverer along the Southern Route in 1849.

signs of gold." Several years later, the famous "Pegleg" Smith led an expedition to the same region in search of gold.[72] Historian LeRoy Hafen, a native of that area, in the early 1950s discounted the assertions of the possibility of precious metal there, saying only copper had been discovered. But members of several parties found telling signs there, and a gold mine presently operates successfully in the vicinity.

Then, while approaching Amargosa Springs, Pratt noticed even more telling geologic signs and announced to his travel companions that if they could locate some quartz there it might well contain gold. Four men commenced a careful search and within a short time, a man named Rowan announced, "[H]ere is gold." He had found pea-sized nuggets in a 4-inch stratum of quartz in a granite ledge. This was the initial discovery of the Amargosa Mine, which thereafter intermittently produced ore in paying quantities. The Mormon discoverers felt compelled to move on to water their livestock and proceed on their missionary journey, but they clearly informed Isaac Williams and others later involved in the

mine about their discovery, perhaps in exchange for the provisions received at the end of their journey. Later, in the Spanish Canyon area between Bitter Springs and the Mojave River, some of the party prospected a little for gold while the animals were feeding during a much-needed rest break. These prospectors included Henry Bigler, who had been at Sutter's Mill and recorded the correct date of the initial gold discovery there.[73]

Another group of Mormon missionaries, traveling just days behind the first parties, found the climb up Impassable Pass even worse than usual because of the intervening snowstorm. James S. Brown recorded that their "situation was most gloomy. In mud and snow, with darkness come on, every rod of the road became more steep and difficult. The summit was two miles ahead. . . . We moved by hitches and starts and could only make three or four rods at a time." Two of the party pushed the wagon from behind, while another drove the team and a fourth member broke and marked the road through the snow in front of the rest. They understood they were stronger than their companions struggling up the incline behind them, who were in grave danger if not assisted by the partially packed pathway through the snow. Finally, Brown recalled, "[W]ith a shout of triumph, we reached the summit in two feet of snow, at eleven o'clock at night." Although all in the group would have agreed the pass was properly named Impassable, they got through the next day.

Even the best prepared pioneers were thoroughly tired of the hardships of this most arduous of desert passages. When missionary Brown reached the Mojave River, he recalled "that we felt as pleased as a man liberated from a life sentence in a dungeon, for we had reason to feel assured that we would succeed in our journey."[74] A companion, Bigler, also headed for a Polynesian mission, concluded at about the same juncture, "[S]uch tramps and fatigues as [they had just endured] will make men old before their days is [*sic*] half gone."[75] The Mormon group demonstrated the same elation at obtaining provisions from Isaac Williams's supply wagon as most others and may have overindulged themselves even more. As some of their number had gone on ahead, the remaining eight or nine men consumed 25 pounds of chopped wheat the first afternoon it was available, along with a considerable quantity of beef and probably some of the sugar and coffee noted to be in the provisions load.

They ate "very ravenously" and were consequently "much distressed in the night." Yet next morning they bought another eighteen pounds of meat for breakfast and had little left to carry on to the next campsite.[76]

At about the same time, some of the second group of the Pioneer Independent Company also made their way through the last hundred miles to civilization. Thomas Wylly recorded that "We toiled up the Mojave for four days, walking through snow in the daytime, and raking it away at night for a place to make a fire and to sleep, and on the fifth day, we crossed the pass of the San Bernardino Mountains." He continued, "Our trail led from the Mojave to those mountains and when we stood on their crest, they seemed to us the dividing line between Purgatory and Paradise. Behind us lay miles of uninhabited desert, where [the] only vegetation, the bitter sage." He then lauded that "Before us stretched from the foot of these mountains to the Pacific Ocean as beautiful a land as the eye of man could wish to rest on . . . rolling country, deliciously green."[77]

END OF THE
HOOVER JOURNEY

Predictably, Vincent Hoover and his family were among the first to move on from their temporary recuperation camps. They continued to be impressed by the climate of southern California—even as the rainy season started —partly because the new grass soon sprang up to begin the new year. At a ranch just eight miles from Chino, they bought additional corn and received beef at no cost. This did not appear unusual, because thousands of cattle were observed on the hills and any time an owner butchered one, some of the meat would spoil if not distributed among potential users. The Hispanic hospitality impressed the Hoovers, as did other aspects of the Hispanic lifestyle. On New Year's Day 1850, Vincent expressed his continuing resolve to strike it rich in the gold fields. That day they arrived at the ranch at La Puente belonging to John Rowland, an American who had found good prosperity in his time in the California southland.

The party was particularly fascinated by the remnants of the Mission San Gabriel, encountered a day or so later. They noted the old orange and olive orchards and vineyards, but also commented that they were neglected. The church featured much-admired murals on the side walls. The family camped near the mission for almost two weeks. Moving thereafter to Los Angeles, Hoover was less favorably impressed with the abundance of gamblers and saloons in that town. And when he heard a sermon there on Sunday, he assumed it might have been the first Protestant service ever in the city. Hoover noted a goodly number of American emigrants at Los Angeles anxiously awaiting the end of the winter rains so they could move on to the mother lode country.

Sketch of Mission San Gabriel by William Birdsall Lorton in his diary entry on 17 January 1850.

COURTESY THE BANCROFT LIBRARY

By April, the Hoovers had traveled into the upper Kern River area and were heading farther north.[78]

LAST OF SECEDERS
BACK ON HUNT ROAD

Leonard Babcock, another New Yorker, was among those who followed Orson Smith away from Jefferson Hunt and suffered in the wilderness of Nevada before returning in a state of short provisions to the main California trail near Mountain Meadows. His party hoped to catch up with the remnant of the Pomeroy freighter company just ahead (discussed in the following chapter) but did not succeed. At Cottonwood Springs, some men in the group gallantly decided to turn over their remaining draft animals to their companions who had wives and children to conduct over the trail. Examining the food supply, they determined they had only half enough for the estimated three weeks still left to travel. However, this was apportioned, and seventeen men prepared packs and began hiking the estimated three hundred miles remaining of the journey.

The Babcock reminiscences mentioned the usual hardships, including serious illness of the writer in the Amargosa Springs area. William H. Goddard, who had been impatient all along the route, proposed the group leave Babcock, but others promised to remain with him until he recovered. Fortunately, this was quite soon. Later, Goddard "gave out in the snow," presumably in Impassable Pass, and Babcock was among those who "urged him through." All in the group successfully reached the California ranches. At the Mojave River they encountered a Hispanic *vaquero* (cowboy), presumably one of Isaac Williams's men, who butchered a bullock and sold Babcock and his messmate eighteen pounds of meat, along with tea and sugar. As others were noted to have done after the same ordeal, he and one other consumed the entire amount in three meals.

When William Lorton and his companions struck the Hunt wagon trail they celebrated with great joy, although they understood they were far from liberated from the forbidding desert. Thereafter they lived on abandoned oxen until they caught up with some of the fellow seceders at the Muddy River. Amid the shaking

of hands came the inevitable question "[H]ow do you like horse meat?" The seceders followed by sharing all there was of a better quality of food with the Lorton group, who had been so long without. The rest of the journey was relatively uneventful, though Lorton provides the only record of a baby's death, at Resting Springs. Hearing moaning, his group soon ascertained Mrs. Mose had lost her baby, buried there in mid-December.[79]

Adonijah Welch and those with him caught up with some of Dallas's wagons. These people welcomed them with a good supper. Later Welch contracted a fever, as did former Hunt company colonel Henry Baxter, both of whom were cared for by Dr. Caleb N. Ormsby. This undoubtedly caused Welch, the former company scribe, to be even more negative about the trip when after it ended he wrote letters published in the East. After recounting the need to drive over each desert *jornada* without halting, sometimes traveling two days and a night without sleep, he commented, "[S]uch hardships were scarcely endurable to those who were well and you will imagine the sufferings of the sick." In another attempt to depict the "dreary journey," he told of an instance when extremely thirsty and his heart beating rapidly from the fever, where he had to choose between lying down in the snow or trying to struggle on ahead by drinking melted snow from oxen tracks.[80]

SUBSISTENCE DIETS

William Lorton's diary of his journey after returning to the main trail is valuable for its rare information about food on the trail at that point. Common fare was bean soup with meat from either exhausted mule or cattle. Equally common was beef soup, although he never mentioned any other ingredients. On occasion the travelers were too hungry or tired to wait for the entire cooking process and ate the meat half cooked, and Lorton admitted at least once he almost became ill doing this. When he and his travel companions were welcomed back to the trail at the Muddy River, they received a makeshift feast from their former division members. The meal consisted of rising bread, boiled fat beef, sugar biscuits, and hot coffee. The beef in the menu was in marked contrast to what Lorton usually called "carrion," by which he did not mean flesh from an already dead animal, but one so close to starvation as to be almost that undesirable. The diarist used the term consistently. Usually when an ox or cow was emaciated, they ate only the tongue, heart, and some of the meat from the rump. Sometimes the liver was also used, but at other times it appeared too deteriorated to be considered safe.

Lorton's good white horse, Maseppa, acquired by trade from an Indian while yet in Utah Valley, finally gave out at Stump Springs. Lorton put him out of his misery, then "cut out a steak for everybody said white horses eat best," presumably meaning it tasted the best of horsemeat. There was no further comment but as attached as the writer was to his mount, he would not have enjoyed the meal. At the same stop company members killed a "poor" steer and cooked up a lot of meat to carry with them over the next *jornada* to Resting Springs, during which they would find no water and little firewood. Even more extended preparations were made at Resting Springs for the most dreaded stretch of travel, including baking bread and fixing meat. He noted there were "some mince pies made in camp," a unique way to disguise the taste of the increasingly monotonous meat. After that the diarist mentioned being on quarter rations, part of which was carrion. But the group still had some flour all the way to the Mojave River.

On reaching the Mojave, Lorton stated that many, particularly the rarely mentioned women and children, were very apprehensive about the exhausted food supply. The diarist was among those who hurried upstream in search of Isaac Williams's food pack train. On New Year's Day he had only a cup of hot tea for breakfast, as he thought of his loved ones in the East eating more than they really wanted. Later that day he procured a rabbit and two fat quail, food for a better meal. When he secured some of the Williams supplies next day, he carefully noted "ten pounds of tolerable beef (not carrion)." He exclaimed, "[O]h what a supper I have of slapjacks, etc., sugar and coffee." The rest of the company, as virtually all others so served, were elated at the timely arrival of supplies from the much-appreciated "savior of pioneers" over the Southern Route.

At the end of the year William Lorton noted that eleven pack mules loaded with flour, beans, coffee, sugar,

salt, and Spanish liquor waited sixteen miles upstream from where he first struck water, probably at Forks in the Road near the present intersection of Minneola Road and Interstate 15. Unfortunately, because the Williams *vaqueros* were so terrified of the desert, they apparently relinquished control of the merchandise to members of the so-called Buckskin emigrant division, who had left Hunt's leadership and the trail but had struggled back and appeared for a time inclined to take unfair advantage and make undue profits from fellow sufferers. This situation was soon partly alleviated through general agreements regarding credit until the travelers were able to sell some of their travel outfits at the ranches.[81]

Two of Lorton's sometime traveling companions, Adonijah Welch and Cephas Arms, also offered some insights into the desert passage diet. As the former described the hardships of the route to eastern newspaper readers, he told of subsisting mostly on cattle that had become too weak to travel and eating the meat "with little or no salt." Salt would have been a much missed addition to the forced diet for many. Arms recorded toward the end of his ordeal that he and his companions had so long eaten "chew chew," which is what they called the less-than-desirable meat prepared as a kind of head cheese, that most of them suffered from diarrhea attributed to it and their "stomachs had become so weak that [they] could not eat it" any longer.[82]

GUIDEBOOKS

One member of the Rich missionary party, Joseph Caine, was sufficiently cognizant of the need for better preparation by pioneers contemplating the journey over the Southern Route that he composed a "Mormon Waybill," published at Salt Lake City in 1851 and advertised for sale for $1 per copy by late January of that year. This not only gave the mileage between each campsite along the route but also offered some description of those locations as to availability of wood, water, and animal feed or lack thereof. The now-rare document also offered considerable good advice to future emigrants, notably concerning livestock. As several of his associates had observed at the time, oxen that had traveled all the way from the Missouri River that season could not successfully complete the trip to southern California. Caine mentioned that thousands of cattle and horses had been sacrificed because emigrants in 1849 had not been aware of that fact. He advised that all livestock be exchanged at Salt Lake City prior to embarkation over the Southern Route. The waybill also pointedly cautioned that only the essentials for the trip be taken, with no wagon laden with more than eight hundred pounds total. All other items, including mining and farming equipment and clothing, could be obtained at the end of the journey. Despite the good advice it contained, so far as is known the "Mormon Way-bill" was not at all widely distributed.[83]

Accompanying Vincent Hoover's diary is his "guide," which consists of roadometer readings to the half mile from one important point on the route to the next. Almost always he measured distance from one watering place to another. He also made notations about good places to camp or lack thereof. In a few instances he also mentioned the nature of the trail and obstacles to be anticipated. The guide was detailed and accurate enough that it would have been very useful, had its compiler not become so disillusioned with the route described.[84]

H. Stickney, who traveled with the Pomeroy wagons (discussed later in this book), also made odometer notations of the distances from just south of Salt Lake City. He too described hills and creek crossings along with distances. Although not as detailed as either Hoover or Caine's, this guide too would have been useful, particularly on the first half of the route. The writer had very little to say about the trail from Las Vegas to the Williams Ranch other than distances from watering place to watering place, but then many would attest little else could be said for that segment of the road.[85]

It is apparent that by the end of the road Vincent Hoover had long since abandoned his ambition to compose a guidebook for others contemplating travel over the Southern Route. Among his last journal entries on the trip was one in which he overstated the suffering of those without food and noted that the number of give-out oxen was "almost equal to the Donner party." He then asserted that "persons who have never taken such a trip as this cannot form any idea of the suffering we are undergoing." He essentially concluded, while resting by

the Mojave River,"[W]e have taken a new route but taken it to our sorrow. The destruction on this route is immense and the suffering still greater." He further elaborated that the route was particularly trying to women, who were compelled to walk with scarcely anything to eat and children crying for bread that was not to be had. He clearly regretted his family's choice of routes and was hardly inclined to recommend it to anyone. He did later still demonstrate ambitions to publish his diary but not for the purpose of encouraging use of the Southern Route.[86]

The other most detailed diarist recounting experiences on the route during 1849, William Lorton, came to similar conclusions. Although he had initially intended to have his diary published, he now stated, "[N]o pen can describe the sufferings and fatigue endured by those coming [over] the Spanish Trail." He mentioned the deaths of thousands of oxen and horses on the desert and the hundreds of men, women, and children who struggled across those wastes without enough food. He mentioned the snow encountered on several mountains, supposedly absent from this route. He concluded, "[G]reat has been the destruction of property, and all have suffered more or less, from traveling over a country blasted by nature." Finally, as already noted, Adonijah Welch was similarly negative about the Southern Route.[87]

Yet one of Welch and Lorton's companions, Cephas Arms, took the opposite view on these matters. Although conceding the mistake of attempting to travel in so large a wagon train, he affirmed, "I am perfectly satisfied with the decision of coming through the Spanish Trail, and also that there has been far less suffering amongst us than there would have been had we gone through the northern route."[88]

The first pioneers over the Southern Route made many mistakes during the initial period of wagon use. Yet not only did almost all get successfully through to their destinations, but having the benefit of their experience inevitably made the journey easier for those coming later. Many mistakes made by the first wagon companies were never repeated by subsequent travelers over the same route. Thus the roadway proved a viable alternative to the summer-only routes.

Chapter Four

Varied Travelers

Traffic over the Salt Lake City to Los Angeles route continued to be extensive in the subsequent several years, through 1857 and to a lesser extent into 1858. Besides emigrants and gold miners, it included surveyors, mail carriers, and sheep herders, as well as the freight wagon operators mainly discussed later. Almost every group encountered Native American residents of the region. Southern Paiutes living along the Southern Route were compelled to adjust their lifestyle because of traveler incursions into their tribal lands, and they treated each passing company as they deemed necessary. With the establishment of San Bernardino, the largest number of emigrants after 1851 were Latter-day Saints, who acted increasingly more favorably toward the Native Americans than did many other travelers. The Indians duly noted the difference.

THE POMEROY FREIGHTING COMPANY

Almost two months after the main emigrant parties had commenced travel by the Southern Route, in late 1849 an early freighting venture of the Pomeroy brothers, Thaddeus and Ebeneezer, merchants and freighters from Missouri, started over the same roadway. Joseph P. Hamelin Jr., twenty-four years old, served as one of many teamsters who came with the Pomeroy wagon train to Salt Lake City in the summer of 1849. He detailed in his diary the subsequent travels of the expedition. For three months he participated as extensively in the social activities of the new Mormon metropolis as any "Gentile" (as Mormons often speak of outsiders, following biblical custom) had ever been allowed to do. In the meantime his employers were busily selling a portion of their merchandise to the local inhabitants. Then, on 3 November, the company of forty-one wagons, eighty-five men, and 480 head of livestock set off for California over the Southern Route.

The proprietors showed enough prudence to engage an experienced, but unnamed, guide for the expedition, which enabled them to generally succeed in protecting their draft animals from loss to Native Americans and in procuring the best feed and water available en route. Even in the difficult Santa Clara River area, the livestock got sufficient grass, although the men had to drive them some four miles from camp to graze through the night. However, the oxen's loads must have been too heavy, because despite notably good care, soon the number failing to pull their share rose alarmingly. The Joseph Caine "Mormon Way-bill" assessment that oxen could not successfully make the entire journey from the Missouri River to California in one season again proved accurate.[1]

As was frequently the case, the abundant and cordial social interaction on the first portion of the overland trail contrasted dramatically with the tension and impatience later on the journey, after hunger, exhaustion among the animals and fatigue among the men had taken their grave toll. The Pomeroy group carried an abundant supply of liquor, and Hamelin often noted "warm whiskey stew" being part of the supper fare. The large evening bonfires often featured card games and occasionally "stag dances." As other companies also did that year, they enjoyed such success hunting rabbits and sage hens in the future Millard County area that the game procured "actually went begging for customers to devour them." But the fun essentially faded away before the caravan reached the halfway point of the journey.

While the Pomeroy freighters struggled in the sand and mud along the Virgin River, as others in the parties ahead of them had done, some in the company became acutely aware of the rapidly diminishing supply of staple provisions. Amid a growing spirit of what Hamelin termed "mutiny," more responsible company members adopted the same solution arrived at by their predecessors, sending some ahead to Williams's Rancho del Chino "to procure relief for the train." The slowness of the ox teams as they pulled the heavily laden wagons, coupled with the severe impatience of many drivers to hurry to the California mining camps, undoubtedly exacerbated the problem. Hamelin tellingly observed, "[T]he lump of gold in view ahead has turned the brain of many who

if started afoot w[oul]d have [had] almost certain assurance of starving." Despite his realistic caution, the situation persisted, and he noted, "[M]uch dissatisfaction exists among the men and we have a very flattering prospect of a 'stampede' on Muddy." By this he meant that many of the men seemed to be planning to abandon the freight train there and move ahead independent of their employers, perhaps with some of the food, livestock, and equipment they felt entitled to. After Pomeroy offered a barrel of brandy to those who got his wagons up the Virgin Hill, some of the men spent the entire night accomplishing that task. Despite the liquor payment, Christmas on the Muddy River remained drab and did little to improve company morale.

With cooler heads prevailing but still "much dissatisfaction," the men held a meeting and resolved to ask the Pomeroys, who were clearly absent from the proceedings, to abandon twenty wagons. Besides the general slowness of ox team travel, the proposition doubtless stemmed as well from the appalling attrition rate among the oxen. Hamelin noted in his diary that for more than a week previous, they had lost up to nine head per day, leaving twenty-one along the sharp-pebbled road across Mormon Mesa, always so devastating to animal hooves. This clearly left too few strong animals per team to pull all the wagons. And as the most formidable stretches of desert loomed just ahead, an even greater prospect of livestock losses now threatened, dramatized as the train left the Muddy and proceeded up the California Wash. Hamelin described this stretch as being "over the softest road [he had] ever seen wagons rolled." In some mud holes the vehicles "popped in bed deep," meaning stuck clear past the wheel hubs. With a desperate attempt at humor, Hamelin affirmed that extricating the wagons might be "great sport for those fond of seeing oxen rolled out of the mud and [of] imitating well-diggers." He suggested that the experience might also be beneficial in the participants' future gold-mining endeavors.[2]

The ordeal resulted in the merchants agreeing to abandon what Hamelin reported to be fourteen wagons, although other accounts indicated a number as high as twenty, along with some merchandise. Some of the bull whackers' personal gear also had to be left behind. At that point a number of the Pomeroy teamsters, such as the young Mormons David Seeley and his brother-in-law

Edwin Pettit, hired at Salt Lake City, left the train. With others, they took the front wheels of discarded wagons and constructed makeshift two-wheeled carts, to be pulled by exhausted oxen. After attempting cart hauling for a distance, another employee-diarist, Albert Thurber, noted that most gave up and commenced backpacking. Joseph Hamelin and several of his companions, apparently assigned to go ahead to secure relief animals and provisions, appropriated a light carriage, accompanied by a few pack animals. But not far beyond Las Vegas Indians stole most of their animals, and almost all the party was compelled, in Hamelin's words, to try "the utensils the Almighty has furnished for pedestrian performances"— their legs and feet. A group of emigrants had also engaged to travel with the Pomeroy freighters and one, Walter Van Dyke, recorded that "all arrived well and no one had been seriously sick on the way, though subjected to many hardships."[3]

As the remaining contingent of the Pomeroy train approached Cottonwood Springs, the threat of mutiny reappeared. According to the sketchy, but credible, account of a later Southern Route veteran, William Clark, who in subsequent years associated closely with the man offering the information, C. L. Kingston, the latter reported that at least one of the company proprietors perceived a plot to steal the considerable money he carried and perhaps murder him in the process. He thereupon took a mule and some provisions and hurried ahead toward San Bernardino, leaving some twenty remaining wagons loaded with marketable goods and the coveted money in charge of his trail boss. According to the Kingston-Clark account, that man soon after buried the money near the trail in the Mountain Springs vicinity. On reaching the southern California ranches, Pomeroy procured the services of Kingston, said to have been an experienced mail carrier over that route, and the two returned to the money cache spot. There, purportedly with the assistance of a dream, they retrieved the full amount of funds, said to total $10,300.[4]

Clearly the wagon master, Hamelin, and a number of other teamsters remained committed to their agreement to travel to the California coast with what remained of the Pomeroy caravan, or, in the case of Hamelin, to fulfill other assignments. Although the diarist and the packers with him made their way to the Mojave River and

through Cajon Pass to the California southland ranches independently, they did not lose sight of their agreement to procure more draft animals and food to take back to the struggling freight wagons. After experiencing a flash flood on the desert river not long after the Stover party avoided a similar threat, the Hamelin group negotiated the mountain pass with relative ease. Members of the party expressed amazement that all preceding wagons of other groups had gotten through that area without any being left by the wayside. They made the usual stop at Rancho Cucamonga, which Hamelin remarked appeared filthier than Santa Fe. However, he appreciated the vast grasslands of the region and presumed them to be the "finest natural pasture grounds in the world." Yet despite the abundance of livestock, particularly of beef cattle, in the area, these loyal freighters had great difficulty getting fresh oxen, mules, or horses to draw the Pomeroy wagons in from the desert. They spent more than a week traveling from Louis Rubidoux's ranch in future West Riverside to the Los Angeles area some eighty miles away, visiting many ranches in search of enough draft animals.

Hamelin finally procured some mules in Los Angeles and a few extremely wild cattle farther east and began to drive some eighteen head toward Cajon Pass. After the freighters struggled with great difficulty for more than a day, Isaac Williams dispatched several *vaqueros* to help, until presumably the animals adapted to herding. But, later during a night camp in the Cajon most of the cattle got away and could not be relocated. Discouraged, ten of the party gave up the attempt to help the Pomeroy train and returned to the ranches, leaving Hamelin and one companion to carry the disappointing news back to their former associates in the Pomeroy train. However, the freighters waiting at Bitter Springs accepted Hamelin's news philosophically and remained in good spirits. The few animals brought, added to those still heroically plodding along the trail, drew the fourteen remaining wagons slowly along, some eight miles per day. A week later, on the Mojave River, another Pomeroy backpacker, Cuxall or Croxall, formerly associated with Hamelin, came into camp with ten additional cattle, at least one of which they promptly slaughtered for food. With this assistance, the Pomeroy party finally reached Rancho del Chino on Valentine's Day 1850. This expedition was thus one of the slowest ever to travel over the Southern Route.

At the end of his journey, Joseph Hamelin waxed philosophical and prophetic in his diary. He predicted that within two years, the California coastal region "would set the world in an uproar." If he included the San Francisco Bay area in this, his prediction was accurate. He further affirmed that not only would cities spring up, but perhaps "railroads [would] cause distance to be laughed at." The observant former Missourian also commented on the group of people he had encountered in the great migration, admitting astonishment at "the large proportion of intelligence which [had] wended its way to [that] distant clime. Physicians, lawyers, clergymen, and persons skilled in every branch of mechanical pursuit" had left behind "flourishing business and good salaries for an uncertainty." But those human resources, Hamelin emphasized, would make California an important addition to the United States.[5]

LATEST FORTY-NINER COMPANIES

Two other parties left the Provo, Utah, area in mid-November 1849, two months after most other pioneers, essentially placing them in the 1850 emigration group. One party contained only three wagons, led by Mormon scout Howard Egan, a later Pony Express rider and express company official. Because they had horses and mules for draft animals, the trip was faster than most and relatively uneventful. They did encounter the usual difficulty getting up the Virgin Hill, and Indian arrows wounded some cattle in the Cottonwood Springs–Blue Diamond area.[6]

The other, called the Huffaker company, included many who mixed with other parties, struggling down the California portion of the trail. Albert King Thurber, a twenty-three-year-old who had left his home in Connecticut for the gold fields in 1849, kept an insightful and detailed diary of this company. Stopping at Salt Lake City, he converted to Mormonism before heading to California by the Southern Route. At Provo, he and some thirty-one other emigrants elected Simpson D. Huffaker as captain and then started on a trip across Utah, hindered by the foot of snow already on the ground. After an otherwise uneventful trip as far as the Virgin River, one

of the company, Colwell, who had camped farther away rather than associate with Mormons, had his cattle appropriated by Indians. About a dozen of the party pursued the Paiutes into the maze of "awful gulches" characteristic of the area, without retrieving any animals. The men did discover two caches of drying meat butchered by Indians from livestock of a previous party. At the Muddy River the Thurber-Huffaker party caught up with the slow-moving Pomeroy freighter group, which had by then lost many of its draft cattle. Thurber noted thirteen wagons here burned by their drivers, and as others stated, this had been done to keep the Mormons from using them.[7]

Thurber recalled that while still in the Parowan area, his party met Capt. Orson K. Smith and thirteen others who had given up on their shortcut to California and subsisted on mule meat for twenty-three days, reportedly retracing their route to where they had left Jefferson Hunt. Several other accounts report instead that that meeting took place on the Muddy River. This contradiction is resolved by understanding that most travelers in those expeditions also called Coal Creek, running through later Cedar City, the Muddy, as well as the important Nevada stream of that name, the Muddy River. The wanderers had decided, Thurber recalled, to return to Salt Lake City but became persuaded to travel on to California, with a generous group offer to share food by then beginning to be rationed. Company member Thomas Kealy remembered, "[W]e took them in, of course, and made them as comfortable as the circumstances would permit."

Another company member, Ransom G. Moody, a New Yorker, offered greater detail on how those returning to the trail after abandoning Hunt's leadership were assimilated into the Huffaker group. While yet in the Salt Lake City area, Moody befriended Orson Smith, starting a relationship that lasted until Smith's death in 1875. Moody embarked for California later than his friend Smith set out. When they later met Smith and his half-starved companions, Moody proposed to take the entire group into his train, but his associates, after considering the provision supply, refused. The friend then suggested simply that he take Smith into his wagon, but Smith declined, preferring not to accept better treatment than his fellow sufferers. Moody then suggested that each member of the Huffaker group willing to do so take one of the

Smith party as a guest, with the understanding that should their personal provisions run short they could draw on the general supply apparently carried by the train. All reportedly agreed to this solution, and the combined company resumed their journey toward California. Thereafter, Thurber commented that "all suffered from want" of sufficient food, but with the exception of a death mentioned only by Edwin Pettit, all got through safely, albeit with the usual hardships.[8]

It is doubtful that the situation of Smith or his former companions stirred any further dissension. However, while on the Virgin River, at least some of the non-Mormon portion of the company—which the recent additions had swollen to thirty wagons, 100 men, and an unspecified number of women and children—decided to split from Huffaker and other Latter-day Saints. After both Moody and Smith declined leadership of the seceding party, they then installed as captain a man named Chalmers, less competent and not much respected. The two groups thereafter traveled separately. At the Muddy River, Chalmers asked for a small party to accompany him onto the next dreaded stretch of roadway to search for water and grass while the main body of pioneers rested and the animals recuperated their strength. None of his own group would volunteer. Moody thereon approached the Mormons camped nearby and had no trouble securing the services of several of their men for the trip.

The overnight scouting excursion proved successful in finding not only the expected bunchgrass, but more unusual, pools of water left standing on the hardpans from recent rainstorms. On returning to camp, Chalmers gave orders for his group to start over the desert immediately, obviously intending to get ahead of the Mormon travelers in Huffaker's group, assuming the newly discovered resources were insufficient for both groups. Moody reminded the party leader that some of the other company had helped him locate these resources and remained entitled to a share, and that his intended course verged on "meanness." When wagon master Chalmers proceeded with his intention anyway, Moody withdrew from the company and was welcomed again into the Latter-day Saints party. Justly, Chalmers could not again locate the grass, whereas Moody's new companions used all they needed of both feed and water.

On an even worse dry *jornada*, the Thurber-Huffaker group felt disappointed by the unpalatability of Amargosa and Salt Springs water after another water source discovered earlier by scouts dried up by the time the party arrived at the spot. In desperate need of water, the group then allowed itself to be fooled by a mirage. However, drawing on information Moody recalled from James Waters, who had learned it from fellow mountain man Old Bill Williams, the men calmly continued scouting. In an area where few would have expected it, they located a temporary pool of good rainwater in the middle of the brush. Understanding they had not discovered a permanent spring, many in the party became convinced the find must be providential. Moody fashioned a road sign from the endgate of a wagon, informing other travelers of the water just over a mile from the main roadway. Both segments of the former Huffaker party reached their destination without undue incident.[9]

On reaching the end of the desert ordeal, Thurber and some of his companions went to Isaac Slover's ranch, near present Colton, where they obtained a good meal of bread, meat, and stewed squash for $.40. It is not known if this price included the quantity of pepper-spiced spirits, *aguardiente,* that was also consumed. The group later obtained pinole from the Indians located near the San Bernardino Rancho, who concluded the travelers' playful acrobatics must be begging for food. At the Lugo ranch at San Bernardino, residents coaxed Thurber into a wrestling match with the proprietor's son and when the diarist won, they received even more food and liquor. The dance celebration staged that night may also have been part of their victory prize. The reminiscences of David Seeley and Edwin Pettit confessed this "fandango" to be "enjoyed to the utmost as a number of the dark eyed señoritas favored [them] with their presence."[10]

The Lugo host family at the San Bernardino Rancho also welcomed emigrants just arrived from the ordeal of the Southern Route. Ransom Moody and his family arrived there 8 February 1850, and Señor José del Carmen Lugo promptly butchered a beef for their use. The two families each had a daughter of about the same age and the girls soon became fast friends, as did other members of both families. At that time Moody's son fractured his leg when kicked by a horse and Lugo took him by wagon in a heavy storm forty miles to John Rowland's ranch, where a Dr. Nash, recently from Wisconsin, successfully set the bones. Lugo demonstrated such interest in Moody settling at his ranch that he offered free use of fifty cows, and presumably ownership of their calves, and all the land he wished to cultivate. This included free seed and all the *vaquero* labor and teams desired to sow and harvest the crops. Moody's expressed reason for declining the generous offer had much to do with the language barrier between the two men and the fear of future misunderstanding over the arrangement. The family later settled at San Jose, California, where they engaged primarily in flour milling.[11]

THE CHEESMAN PARTY
OF 1850

Even counting the stragglers who commenced their journey over the trail at the end of the first year, the second year of southern wagon road use apparently saw fewer emigrants to California than in 1849. However, the memoir of the journey of David W. Cheesman, traveling with ninety other wagons, probably totaling well over three hundred people, remains invaluable for its information about the emigrant experience in 1850. Cheesman was a former Indiana law student, later prominent in the infant California Republican Party, and appointed by Abraham Lincoln as director of the U.S. Mint at San Francisco. His extended family arrived in Salt Lake City in mid-August. Because his wife was approaching the end of her pregnancy, he and his father-in-law, Dr. Obed Macy, rented small residences on North Temple Street among the Mormons. While waiting, Cheesman worked cutting, hauling, and selling grass hay and generally interacting cordially with his temporary neighbors.

Some church members formerly in the Mormon Battalion had already returned from the California gold mines. One of these—Wilford Hudson, the codiscoverer of the rich California placer gold camp of Mormon Island—lived near Cheesman in Mormon bishop James A. Little's Eleventh Ward (parish). Hudson kindly afforded valuable information about watering and camping places along the Southern Route. So far as is known, he had never been over that route, but he had obviously gathered a good knowledge of it. Because Brigham

Urania Macy Cheesman, one of the amazingly few women travelers over the Southern Route for whom a photograph exists. She bore a child at Salt Lake City just prior to embarking on the most difficult portion of her journey.

Young didn't produce the promised official report of the road as an emigrant guide, probably Caine's "Mormon Way-bill," until the following year, Hudson provided the only information the currently forming pioneer group would get. At that time Elijah Barney Ward ran ads in the *Deseret News* warning travelers it was not safe to attempt the Southern Route without an experienced guide and offering the same terms Jefferson Hunt had commanded the previous year. Ward remained willing to try a shortcut to the gold fields, this time from the Mojave River through Walker Pass, which might have been a feasible route if the company still possessed sufficient provisions and animal strength. The would-be pilot intended to put the matter to a company vote at the appropriate time.[12] The new party made preliminary arrangements for Ward to lead their train. Perhaps fortunately, Ward received another call to intervene in an Indian uprising in Idaho that he was best qualified to handle, and he did not return before the emigrant party departed.

As was often the case, the pioneers of Cheesman's company sought to replenish supplies they deemed insufficient for the long journey. With so many emigrants remaining in Utah, extreme demand existed for "everything the Mormons had to sell." Items from the outside world such as coffee, tea, sugar, and soap could not be had at any price, although Cheesman eventually procured some soap from other emigrants, perhaps in exchange for hay. Flour proved particularly scarce until the wheat crop of the current season had been harvested and milled. This may have been another reason why some emigrants delayed continuing their journey until only the Southern Route remained open for them that year. Cheesman noted that Brigham Young pressured merchants to establish fair prices, appealing to his followers to not patronize them until this had been accomplished. No mention of the sometimes alleged differential charges levied on outside consumers appears in the Cheesman account, a narrative that generally conveys a positive impression of the burgeoning Mormon metropolis.[13]

The manner in which the second year's emigrants over the Southern Route conducted themselves clearly demonstrated the lessons learned from their predecessors. To better utilize the often-scarce pasture and water resources, yet still benefit from the better protection in greater numbers, the Cheesman company decided to travel and camp in smaller detached parties some distance apart. Cheesman noted that in the Utah portion of their journey they enjoyed grass in abundance and plenty of firewood virtually every night. This reflects information received from experienced travelers, including knowledge about the failure of the Hoover-Gruwell-Derr and other parties to properly find and use such resources. The group also had abundant contact with Native Americans but was cautious enough to avoid much loss of property. Hudson had warned the emigrants of localities where they needed to be particularly watchful.

One advantage of the many wagons left by preceding companies was the spare parts they provided for repairs. When Cheesman broke his left hind axle, he feared he would have to make a two-wheeled cart of his wagon. But he soon located an axle in an abandoned wagon that provided everything needed for restoring his wagon. Cheesman and his fellows, as others had before them,

Emigrant wagons in Salt Lake City staging area, a decade after the first use of such vehicles over the Southern Route.

COURTESY HISTORICAL DEPARTMENT AND ARCHIVES, CHURCH OF JESUS CHRIST OF THE LATTER-DAY SAINTS

did what they could to lessen the weight of their con-veyances. He cut off the hind end of the wagon box and removed other unnecessary items, even the end of the provisions chest. At the Santa Clara River, they also "dis-pensed of any article not absolutely essential," which undoubtedly helped preserve the strength of their draft animals. Travelers before them had also lightened their loads, but only farther down the trail—after they had es-sentially wasted away their animals' strength.[14]

The Cheesman party followed the same route as its predecessors over Utah Mountain, down the Virgin River from Beaver Dam Wash to the Virgin Hill.[15] These wag-oners encountered difficulties similar to those of the ear-lier pioneers with the latter obstacle, which Cheesman described as "too steep for cattle to get a foot-hold to pull." The party doubled and trebled the teams to haul the wagons from the ravine to the lower bench. Then the men drove the loose oxen up onto the top of the Mormon Mesa, joined all their chains together, passing them over the rim and down to be hitched to one wagon at a time while up to twenty yoke of cattle pulled each vehicle onto the tableland. Coincidentally, as with Dr. Hall of the Hoover expedition, chains breaking while hauling up Dr. Macy's heavy wagon loaded with medicine chests proved the only mishap the Cheesman group experienced. But after speeding down a short distance, the wheels on Macy's wagon cramped and tipped over, doing little damage. At two o'clock the following morning, they got the last wagon up the forbidding grade. Cheesman con-fessed they "were all worn out."

This emigrant party took the precaution of bringing ten-gallon kegs to haul water during the dry stretches. On the so-called *jornada* of death from the Muddy River to the Vegas, they also prepared by precooking food for themselves as well as storing rations of water for live-stock, later dispensed in wash basins. The Cheesman group also learned not to linger more than a day resting the animals at any given spot, including the abundant but salt grass–laden meadows at Las Vegas and Cotton-wood Springs. Thereafter, they missed Mountain Springs, but this water hole was not always reliable anyway. Some of the party went back, but Cheesman's people continued on, also bypassing Stump Springs. Here too they had enough stored water. They also drew on the emergency forage supply many had carried as their bed

ticking. Thus they arrived at Resting Springs without undue hardship—at least for the livestock.

By this time, most of the party had been walking for a hundred miles. Because snow covered the ground part of the time, many of the youngsters' feet became sore and cold so that some took turns riding in the wagons. The women continued to walk and by Resting Springs had been overcome by fatigue. Farther on the journey some younger women got into the practice of walking ahead of the teams struggling along the sandy road, then sitting down to rest and wait till the wagons caught up. Sometimes these hikers got as much as five miles ahead on the clearly visible road. Beyond Bitter Springs, as the strength of the remaining oxen diminished these heroic women gathered dry bunchgrass in their upturned skirts in order to feed the exhausted animals when they lay down. The desperate teamsters allowed the animals to rest briefly, then one of the women would hold a bunch of grass in front of the downed ox, inducing it to struggle to its feet to get the feed. They repeated the process with great frequency during the last thirty-five miles be-fore reaching the Mojave River.[16]

James Brown, Henry Bigler, William Lorton, and sev-eral other predecessors on the route had been notably solicitous of their draft animals the previous year, and the Cheesman party was also particularly sensitive in this regard. In the hottest part of the desert crossing between Salt and Bitter Springs, the company historian lost his favorite wheel ox, Bright, who dropped dead on the spot. He was not only surprised, because he re-garded the animal as most likely to survive the trip, but also genuinely saddened for days at losing the "poor faithful ox." During the same arduous stretch of trail, Dr. Macy volunteered to follow behind, urging weak animals turned out of the yoke slowly on along the road-way, oxen that others in the past would have abandoned. This allowed most of the animals to reach the Mojave River, where recuperating was eminently possible. The successful physician saved several alkali-poisoned ani-mals by administering remedies—in one case, pouring melted lard down the throat. Macy's daughter Nancy developed an uncanny understanding of the company oxen and could always tell the wranglers where the ani-mals had gone when they wandered out of sight search-ing for feed.

Crossing the Plains, *by Charles Nahl, around 1856, depicts a fallen ox such as Dr. Obed Macy cared for and Caroline Barnes Crosby and her companions coaxed to its feet with flour.*
COURTESY STANFORD UNIVERSITY

Perhaps because of the relative lack of hardships and maybe partly because of the proportionately larger number of women in the company, Cheesman's party appeared to have more than the usual amount of cordial social interaction, even near the end of the journey. From the beginning the group featured large bonfires and chats about many things, including the possibilities for mining development and the feasibility of railroad construction along the route. Many became accustomed to sitting on the ox yokes around the fire. The young single men of the party included a violinist named Burke, who willingly played for his associates most evenings. The favorite selection soon became the "Philadelphia Fireman's March," which served to signal bedtime as the fire embers died down. While on this journey, Cheesman became totally impressed with his wife's family, whom he had not known well previously, particularly his notably pleasant mother-in-law. The entire experience "cemented their affection in enduring memory."[17]

Another diarist traveling the route the same time as Cheesman and Dr. Macy was Canadian-born Washington Peck. His account of most of the distance is not particularly noteworthy, except for mentioning a travel companion named Fancher, probably later a leader of the wagon train party who were massacred at the Mountain Meadows (see chapter 6), and for referring to fellow travelers who searched for gold in the Amargosa–Salt Springs area. Of Impassable Pass, Peck recorded that "our rise was at least 150 feet per mile and much of the way the wheels sinking 1/2 the depth of the fellow [*sic*; a felloe is the circular rim segment of the wheel, into which the spokes are attached] in sand or gravel. It was so hot had to rest the animals often." This is virtually the only trail diary detailing travel down Spanish Canyon and across the next stretch, saying, "the road to the [Mojave] river is descending all the way and good except a little too much sand in places."

Early next morning, Peck noted they reached the

Mojave River, "a much desired place since it is at the end of the desert." He confessed relief on arrival there because they considered themselves through the formidable deserts. He compared the recent ordeal to a difficult ocean voyage, saying the travelers "felt like [they had survived] the dangerous and almost unknown seas when we arrive in a port." The diarist observed, significantly, that they had "crossed a desert of 260 miles with only 10 watering places intervening and part of the water salt, bitter or impregnated with alkali. The grass mostly of inferior quality and scarce." That description is the most apt summary of the challenge in maintaining animals on this exceedingly arduous road.[18]

One of the most significant facets of the 1850 emigration was its use of a better roadway down Cajon Pass. While still along the Mojave River, the Cheesman party encountered William T. B. Sanford, a freighter commissioned to deliver a steam engine to the Amargosa Mine, discovered the previous year. Understanding that such a load could not be transported up the Crowder–Coyote Canyon route the forty-niners had come down, Sanford selected an inclined ridge that intersected the upper summit "hogback," tending east–west, at approximately a right angle. Because no detailed record exists, it is not certain if Sanford then employed men to excavate a graded road up the side of this ridge, but as Sanford had the greatest need for such road improvements—which was accomplished during the five years the road was in use—it was most likely accomplished at that time. Cheesman simply recorded that Sanford's teamsters and teams whom they met on the Mojave "had rendered the canyon passable." This emigrant party became the first of thousands of people to use the new road coming downward through what proved to be the main entrance to southern California, Cajon Pass. It is certain the Mormon emigrants used the same road the next year (1851). It took "all hands, women and all" of the Cheesman group to push the wagons up a sandy twenty-foot bank to the top of the hogback from the north. There they locked the hind wheels, presumably with chains, took off all but the wheel oxen, and started down the grade with the front wheels straddling the ridge. The account stated that "for a distance of fifty or sixty feet it was so steep that the cattle and all slid down. After that the descent was gradual." Presumably by then they had reached the graded roadway down the side of the ridge to the canyon floor.

Peck offered a similarly detailed account of negotiating the hogback grade, after approaching from the north through a considerable growth of scrub oak. He noted, "Now is the steep descent to a narrow ridge being only

Excavated grade down the intersecting ridge of West Cajon Pass, probably constructed in 1850 and heavily used for half a dozen years. Photo taken in 1965 after a brush fire exposed the early wagon road.

COURTESY MOHAHUE HISTORICAL SOCIETY

2 feet wider than the wagons and the descent very steep on each side for 300 or 400 feet." The description continued, calling the approach to the grade, "a frightful looking place. We followed this ridge for 10 or 15 rods then made a very steep descent of several hundred feet into a canyon which continued to descend for miles at a very rapid rate." He reported the travelers reached water, presumably at Willow Grove (later Camp Cajon-Inman Ranch) in the afternoon. At the mouth of the canyon, he noted, they entered a "beautiful valley" well wooded with sycamore. He was equally impressed with the Rancho Cucamonga.

Like Peck and others before them, Cheesman lavished praise on the California southland. He claimed it was "a most beautiful spot," the only drawback being the winds still infamous there—now called Santa Anas. After three days camp at Sycamore Grove, the party moved on to Rancho Cucamonga, welcomed there by an Irish majordomo, Michael Snee, then employed by Proudhomme, the proprietor. Cheesman asserted, "[I]t is impossible to describe our feelings. . . . The mountains and dreary wastes and deserts were behind [them]. Here opened up the most lovely country we had ever beheld . . . [with] the climate soft and exhilarating." The next day, New Year's 1851, they drove over to Rancho del Chino to obtain provisions, after which they traveled westward to Rowland's ranch. They much admired the horsemanship and lassoing ability of the *vaqueros*.

Although the Hispanic residents of the area treated the emigrants well, a potential problem arose when some of the Californio ranchers recognized their own brands on some of the emigrant company horses. These had been stolen a few months previously by Chief Wakara and his Ute braves and subsequently sold to the emigrants in Utah. The Californios agreed to allow a jury comprised of company members to decide the case, with both sides presenting their evidence. The decisions were in favor of the former owners.

The Cheesman group intended to recoup the strength of themselves and remaining livestock, then travel by land to the gold fields. But on a brief visit to Los Angeles from their camp at San Gabriel, Cheesman encountered future mayor Stephen Foster. Foster advised them to travel to San Francisco by water, explaining the difficulty of the land trip and that the steamer *Constitution* lay at San Diego and would soon return to San Pedro to take on cargo and passengers. Steerage was said to be cheap. Grateful for the information, the young man returned to camp to discuss the matter. His father-in-law decided to remain in southern California, but most of the company hurried to San Pedro, where they obtained passage at low cost because the captain reportedly felt sorry for the ragged group. In due time they arrived at San Francisco, greeted by the literal forest of ship masts of vessels. (Many of these ships would never again leave the port, because not enough sailors could be induced to return from the gold fields.) There the company dispersed to seek the fortunes they had come west to obtain.[19]

Visiting the Mission San Gabriel with his associates, Washington Peck recorded his impressions in his diary. Repeating lavish estimates of the population of parishioners and livestock during its heyday, he observed that since then it had been "going to ruin for thirty years." Among the current few residents were two "grey-haired friars." All the fences and orchards had been ruined except for the orange orchard. Common belief that the U.S. government had assumed ownership was said to be why squatters had not more seriously damaged the premises.[20]

COMPARATIVE RESCUE MISSIONS

Although no known instances necessitated rescue on the Southern Route that season, on the routes to northern California 1850 became the most demanding year for such missions. Even before the Gold Rush, emigrants to northern California and Oregon discovered that the last leg of their overland journey was the most precarious. Besides Sutter's well-known rescue and recruitment efforts, Dr. John McLoughlin of the Hudson's Bay Company so generously offered assistance to distressed travelers as to overcome much anti-British prejudice among Americans in Oregon. And original American settler Narcissa Whitman openly criticized the generosity of her husband, Marcus, toward incoming emigrants wintering at their church mission in the Walla Walla, Washington, area. In 1849, Gen. Persifer F. Smith authorized $100,000 in emergency U.S. government funds to send supply caravans back over the northern California trails, to ensure that no straggling forty-niners met the kind of fate that haunted the Donner party.

The next year many emigrants went to extremes not to weigh themselves down by provisions, and the rescue efforts were exclusively conducted by private individuals and funds. Equally as impressive as Sutter, at least for two crucial months in 1850, Missourian William Waldo deferred his personal ambitions in order to patrol the desert west of Humboldt Sink, hauling water to fatigued overlanders and helping pull wagons in difficulty at that point. Both the Missouri and California legislatures later presented Waldo, called by one diarist an "angel of mercy," with memorials of appreciation. The California legislature also appropriated $27,000 to reimburse him for personal expenses and probably to provide a lavish and well-earned financial reward. In 1854 Waldo attempted to parlay his fame into politics, as an unsuccessful Whig candidate for governor. Another rescue hero that same year, J. Neely Johnson, in 1856 became the successful Know-Nothing candidate for California governor. In years thereafter, the state financed most rescue efforts on the Northern Routes. The Southern Route, in contrast, had no known government-sponsored rescues, which actually makes Isaac Williams's continued efforts even more impressive.[21]

Most emigrant arrivals from Utah laid over at one of the several ranchos in what was later San Bernardino County, recuperating from their extended ordeal. Some stayed for at least a month at the Williams Ranch. Thomas Kealy, a member of the Huffaker train arriving early in 1850, subsequently took employment operating the Williams gristmill. He described his employer as a "very benevolent man," who on becoming aware of their plight, offered the destitute new arrivals at his ranch flour and beef. After mentioning that many additional pioneers also arrived by way of the Gila, Arizona, route as well, Kealy attested Williams had informed him he had "given away $20,000 worth of provisions and money since the emigration first began." The same reporter affirmed his belief in the figure and further stated the rancher killed from one to three cattle every day, much of "which [was] greedily devoured by hungry emigrants, who [were] daily arriving."[22]

A MORMON COLONIZATION PARTY TO SOUTHERN CALIFORNIA

After persistent urging by former Mormon Battalion men, in 1849 and 1850 Brigham Young finally dispatched two of his quorum of twelve apostles, Amasa Mason Lyman and Charles Colson Rich, to California. He charged them with investigating possibilities for church settlements and for retrieving otherwise good Latter-day Saints who had succumbed to the enticements of the Gold Rush. On careful scrutiny, the Mormon leaders concluded a church settlement could only flourish in the California southland, far from the commotion and vices of the mother lode country. During the probe of southern California, particularly of the Rancho del Chino previously offered for sale to the Mormons, several dozen churchmen were reportedly gathered temporarily in the Los Angeles area to successfully advocate for that location.[23]

Charles Colson Rich, leader of the group of Mormon missionary-miners who packed over the Southern Route in 1849. He was also ecclesiastic co-leader of the Mormon colonization of San Bernardino from 1851 to 1858.

Although no account has been found of their return journey, a brief reference by George A. Smith and Jefferson Hunt makes clear that some of these Mormons who had investigated southern California returned to Utah Territory by the Southern Route. One important item of information relating to their trip is the report that they found no sign of Isaac H. Brown, a fellow church member who had previously embarked alone over the trail. They concluded that as his tracks ended in the vicinity of the Muddy River, he was doubtless killed there by local Indians. Rich, who had previously sold the unfortunate Brown a gun, later speculated some Paiute might yet use his own former weapon, now in Moapa hands, on him.[24]

In early 1851, Lyman and Rich were assigned by Brigham Young to lead a colonizing expedition to southern California. With no number of persons designated for the company, they commenced recruiting people they wished to be a part of the colony. Besides a large number of family and friends of each of these two apostles, an even larger number of Mormon converts from the southern United States demonstrated interest in locating in a climate warmer than Utah's. A considerable number of former Mormon Battalion members and their families also joined those preparing to embark for southern California, on what they considered a church mission.

When the group gathered in March 1851 at Payson, southeast of Utah Lake, the number approached five hundred. Brigham Young, who had come to see them off, became so angry at the large numbers he assumed were abandoning his Zion he would not even speak to them. His ranking assistant, Heber C. Kimball, urged some to reconsider and stay in Utah. But a full 437 remained determined to fulfill their callings in planting the southern California colony. This made the group the largest colonizing venture in the 1850s outside the center of Mormondom. I have argued elsewhere that President Young never again held cordial feelings toward the California colony and in time made it his business to cause its disbandment.[25]

On Sunday, 23 March, after Young, Kimball, and some dissuaded from the journey had departed, the emigrant group held an organizational meeting at the Payson fort. They elected Mormon Battalion officer Andrew Lytle captain of the entire 150-wagon company, with direct supervision over 50 wagons. Joseph Matthews and David

Andrew Lytle, former Mormon Battalion officer and captain of the 150-wagon Mormon pioneer company that founded San Bernardino in 1851. He later served as the third mayor, after Amasa Mason Lyman and Charles Colson Rich, of that municipality.

Seeley were designated as subcaptains, also of 50 wagons each. Following an impressive pattern that some (probably Jefferson Hunt) had suggested to the Cheesman party the year before, the Mormons further subdivided into groups of 10 wagons. Each of these groups, numbering 15, was headed by a man of proven leadership experience, either military, ecclesiastic, or pioneer. Thus organized, the groups soon ventured forward amid spring rains and mud, spread out at intervals of an hour apart. Because more than 1,100 head of livestock accompanied them, this staggered order was the only way to efficiently use the often small water sources and seldom abundant grass of the desert route. Yet the groups were still sufficiently close to offer mutual protection.[26]

In the same interspersed fashion the subgroups arrived several weeks later at the southernmost Mormon outposts of Iron County, Utah. There they held a church conference at which four apostles spoke. Besides Lyman and Rich, Parley P. Pratt traveled with them, along with a group of missionaries accompanying him to the South

Pacific and perhaps Chile. Apostle George A. Smith, then a resident of Iron County, also attended the conference. Along with further attempts to dissuade some from leaving Utah, most of the messages encouraged faithfulness to the Latter-day Saints religion. While assembled, the men in the emigrant group also pledged to "yoke themselves up with [Lyman and Rich] in the cause of building up the Kingdom of God" and to obey their counsel as ecclesiastical leaders in their endeavor to plant a successful colony.[27]

Soon after, on 25 April, at Iron Springs, near Cedar City, Ann Swarthout commenced a difficult childbirth labor. Her wagon train captain, Sidney Tanner, returned to his brother-in-law Amasa Lyman's group to secure the services of a church member always called "Doc" Cunningham, to help the suffering woman. She died soon after, and the later report by Lyman and Rich to Brigham Young attributed this to "improper treatment at or subsequent to her confinement." The new widower remarried several months later, while the company was yet camped at Sycamore Grove. Cunningham was never thereafter known to practice the healing arts in the ensuing years at San Bernardino. It is doubtful if such a comparably large company ever traveled over the northern overland route with but one fatality on the entire journey, as this one did over the Southern Route.[28]

Several days later, the various companies camped at the later infamous Mountain Meadows, where many engaged in final preparations for the arduous desert trek. Some brought wood from the mountains and made charcoal; others prepared a makeshift blacksmith shop. The company spent several days setting and welding iron wagon tires and other blacksmithing repairs while the cattle recouped on the good meadow grass. On Sunday, 4 May, the entire company gathered for worship services and to hear additional earnest exhortations to do right. Thereafter, the various divisions started down the Santa Clara River in their proper order and time dispersals. When Amasa Lyman's ten wagons reached a spot where Pratt's had camped the previous evening, he found a note warning the group to look out for Indians. Like their predecessors of the past two years, the Mormon pioneers found "not much feed," heavy sand, and the need to cross the Santa Clara up to five or six times each day, with some crossings "steep and deep."[29]

One of Lyman's party, Jacob Casteel, apparently befriended one of the Tonequint Indian band encountered on the lower Santa Clara. And as the company made its dry camp on Utah Hill, Lyman noted tersely, "Casteel's Piute ran off with his horse." After reaching water the next day at Beaver Dam Wash, Lyman's ten soon moved on to the Virgin River, which they crossed eight times on 9 May alone. While on the Virgin the first night, the group left nine head of cattle, with a few herders, back at Beaver Dam, presumably for better feed. Indians stole three of these animals. The next day they placed six more men on guard over the remaining cattle, but three more were nevertheless shot with arrows, though none seriously wounded. There they found a note from Charles Rich, reporting all well with his party, which had not experienced any difficulty with Indians at that location. Lyman left the note for Captain Lytle, appending the number of cattle lost and wounded belonging to his own group. Soon after, someone raised alarm about an Indian raid to drive off more livestock, but this proved false. By this time the party had become fully alerted to protect their remaining animals as they traveled through the sandy river bottoms then frequented by so many Native Americans.[30]

After experiencing the usual difficulties traveling down the Virgin River, Lyman's and William Crosby's groups of ten implemented Jefferson Hunt's suggestion to try following the river to its confluence with the Muddy. This entailed additional crossings of the stream, with even more quicksand than on the usual trail. They encountered even further difficulty struggling up the Muddy River to the old California road, which some thought to be only three miles away but was in fact far more distant. The intervening terrain proved "both sandy and mountainous, passing up and down dry canyons." Hardships experienced on this detour ensured that others would not choose to follow that route.

Lyman's diary makes clear that the groups of ten remained in their relative positions an hour's travel distance apart, arriving at the desert oasis of Las Vegas at precisely those intervals. Partly because the "road was sharp and gravely on the cattle's feet," the emigrants remained at the Vegas to shoe the oxen. As the latter portions of the company rolled up to the first watering places, presumably on the small creek or the spring at present Lorenzi Park, the emigrants who had previously occupied those grounds moved on to the larger springs, probably where the Las Vegas water works wells are now located, some distance down the trail.

On hearing that members of the Lytle company had lost some horses and cattle and perhaps in anger killed two or three Indians, Apostle Lyman felt constrained to return to the first camping place to deliver "a severe lecture on their conduct in killing Indians and abusing them as it appeared some had done." Many of the latter group also showed themselves disobedient in other ways as well and were thus chastised for their "general spirit of recklessness." This situation demonstrates an instance where the member of the Mormon hierarchy needed to assert his ecclesiastic authority when the less binding leadership of company captain Andrew Lytle had not been sufficient to maintain discipline.[31]

Amasa Lyman's chastisement of some of the party for ill treatment of Indians probably commenced a movement for more humane treatment of Native Americans along the Southern Route than other known travelers had enunciated or practiced heretofore. In a short time this treatment resulted in the Native Americans differentiating between Mormons and all other travelers. The active military alliance (of which it is doubtful Lyman ever completely approved) eventually had tragic consequences (the Mountain Meadows Massacre of emigrants, discussed fully in chapter 6).

The Mormon companies were far from immune from the harassments of Indians seeking recompense for emigrant use of trail and resources, in the form of livestock to slaughter for food. In Lyman's ten wagons almost every family lost an animal before reaching Las Vegas. Apostle Parley P. Pratt, in a preceding company, mentioned that some twenty miles beyond the Vegas, as his ten families camped for the evening, about ten o'clock they were assailed by "a shower of arrows from the savage mountain robbers." Fortunately, although some "passed near men's heads," all such missiles "fell promiscuously among men, women and children and cattle, but did no injury." This proved a rather unique instance, because human travelers were seldom even random targets for such arrows.

Pratt, who made clear in his journal he disliked the terrain he was traversing, reported they had "traveled seventy-five miles through a most horrible desert, consisting of mountain ridges and plains of naked rock and sand and gravel, and sometimes clay destitute of soil or fertility, except a few small springs and patches of grass."[32] Fellow apostle Amasa Lyman probably felt little more attachment to the area, but he made the best of what it offered, as his diary entries at Stump Springs show. He noted that water at this spring in a low point of a desert flat might be "tolerably scarce, but plenty if rightly managed for all [their] stock." After watering the animals, they drove them some three miles west of the spring to graze on better grass through the night. Meanwhile other members of the company dug a "reservoy [*sic*] to water out of the next day," in a more efficient manner than possible previously, an impressive innovation not mentioned by any other desert travelers.[33]

The Mormon companies also appreciated the relatively good grass feed and water at Resting Springs, but typically only spent one day before passing down on the Amargosa, which Lyman called Amagashi or Lye Creek. They met miners working the Amargosa mining claim and purchased sugar, coffee, tobacco, and some other provisions from them. Here too they lost cattle and were forced to abandon several wagons on the hellish stretch of road between Salt Springs and Bitter Springs. Diarist Parley Pratt mentioned that the hot weather of late May "harassed the cattle," as did the heavy (meaning soft and sandy) road. These companies also carried grass and water from Resting Springs, but depleted their supply long before they reached Bitter Springs.

During the last fourteen miles, with oxen failing, Pratt's company rested "every few minutes." Thus en route they encountered part of the subcompany traveling ahead of them "halted, and lost in slumber—every man and beast, by common consent, sank in profound slumber and probably dreaming of water and feed ahead." The Pratt group "slipped quietly past them," and reached the spring next morning finding it "about as palatable as a dose of salts." Pratt concluded that the previous two days and nights, with only the feed and water they carried with them and the company walking day and night, to be "the hardest time" he had ever seen. He credited Providence for safely delivering them "from the horrors of the desert."[34]

Amasa Lyman's group rested until sundown at Bitter Springs, then pulled over the formidable pass toward the Mojave River, compelled to leave two wagons, as Rich's group had before them. But where others previously used much of the wagon wood for fires, these vehicles were undoubtedly retrieved by men sent back while the wagon groups rested for more than a week along the desert river. At this juncture Lyman, Rich, and Joseph Matthews continued down Cajon Pass to lay out campsites for the entire company in the Sycamore Grove area in a spread-out manner that would prevent undue trampling of grass and water resources. When the large emigrant contingent arrived, they used this camping place throughout the summer while their leaders searched for the final location for their settlement.

The Mormons never actually bought the Isaac Williams Rancho del Chino, primarily because Williams changed his mind about selling. Prosperity based on beef sales in the gold fields at Gold Rush prices was the primary reason why Williams failed to honor his previous offers. The Mormon leaders had been somewhat negligent in bringing such a large group of settlers to southern California without some legal assurance of a ranch purchase. On the other hand, Amasa Lyman became convinced the Chino property did not include sufficient water or timber for optimum colony purposes and thus sought another location—eventually with success. Still, it is ironic that Williams, the man most helpful to so many of the two thousand or more emigrants who reached California by the Southern Route in the first two years, so nearly thwarted the plans of the largest single group ever, in the third year. Yet the Latter-day Saints held no grudges, as far as we know. They had considerable contact with Williams as they so impressively built the largest Anglo-American town in the California southland, San Bernardino, over the ensuing half-dozen years. It took the best efforts of all concerned to so effectively open the all-weather Southern Route to the Pacific Coast during this period.[35]

A great mystery confronting the author of this historical study is the dearth of pioneering women's diaries, particularly from the first three years of Anglo-American travel over the Southern Route. Only a few families made the trip in 1849 and proportionately more in 1850, but with more than three dozen men's accounts available, logic would dictate at least some women's views of the experience should be located. My searches thus far have proved futile. My explanations for this lack of important source material left by women are equally unsatisfying. Certainly the trip was more difficult than any other in the nation, but on other trails women proved at least as durable and resilient as their male counterparts and should have been equally capable of recording their versions of the journey. Perhaps even more perplexing is the absence of even one diary among the more than seventy-five married women known to have traveled with the initial Mormon company that founded San Bernardino in 1851. True, these people had been on the frontier more than three years already, and writing materials by then had proved extremely scarce. Only the highest church leaders, who were probably officially directed to record their actions and experiences, are known to have kept journals at this time. Still, the lack of the feminine version of the experience—which some students of the westward migration assert to be different from that of men—cannot be so discussed on the Southern Route.[36]

However, an unusual circumstance—the Utah territorial census was taken just at the moment the Mormon founders of San Bernardino embarked on their journey, and another census taken to replace the original one, considered by California officials to be inaccurate, within a year of their founding San Bernardino—allows a unique opportunity to learn more of the family structure at the time of the difficult pioneer trek than would otherwise be possible. At the time the Utah census information was recorded, at the Payson-Peteetneet emigrant camp, there were seventy-five married women under forty-five years of age. These women had 35 children listed at age one year or less, including 5 less than a month old, probably mostly born in the camp. There were 156 children between two and fifteen years old (including three belonging to widow Agnes Flake). This was almost 44 percent of the company of 437 in 150 wagons. There were thirty single men unattached to families in the group, ten wives in polygamous marriages, and nine couples presumably beyond child-bearing age. The remainder were older children still attached to families.[37]

One woman, twenty-four-year-old Ann Swarthout, died en route in childbirth as noted earlier; her child survived. In the four-month camp at Sycamore Grove at the end of the journey (present Glen Helen Park, Devore, California), at least four children were born, meaning that their mothers traveled the already hellish desert route in an advanced state of pregnancy. Three other children died during the encampment period. Recent widower Nathan Swarthout married twenty-year-old Emma Tanner just before the emigrants commenced settling the newly purchased San Bernardino rancho. During the ensuing year, at least seventeen of the original pioneer women gave birth, some doubtless becoming pregnant during the recent emigrant trek.

Thus even though the family size is not particularly large among these relatively young women (many of whom averaged eight children by the end of their bearing years), the percentage of babies under two years—in diapers and presumably receiving milk from their mother's breast—is over 70 percent, phenomenal for women at any time or place. Careful historian of women on other emigrant trails Lillian Schlissel estimates the number of pregnant women on any given journey to be around 20 percent. If one added another 20 percent for the year before and after the journey, it is doubtful if many other samples of women came close to 60 percent of their number pregnant during any three-year period.[38]

The southern roadway certainly never had as heavy traffic as the Northern Route, but in the first three years there were at least five hundred wagons, along with packers, totaling approximately five thousand people traveling the Southern Route in its initial period of use. Although its greatest long-range significance was undoubtedly as a freighting lifeline to infant Utah, this route was already serving as a safe winter emigrant passageway to the Pacific Coast from the already-settled United States.

ESTABLISHING THE MORMON CORRIDOR?

Aside from the desire to plant an exemplary colony in the middle of the seeming moral aberrations of the Golden State and to gather erring Latter-day Saints back into the church fold, the primary motivation for establishing a California settlement appears to have been because they needed an outlet from their Mormon Great Basin empire to the rest of the world. A good seaport through which both converts and manufactured goods could enter Mormondom loomed as a primary factor in the church hierarchy's interest in the Pacific Coast entryway. Not unlike the series of Franciscan missions planted along the California coast more than a generation earlier, Brigham Young and his associates envisioned a chain of settlements from San Diego through San Bernardino, then to several likely desert locations and all the way through the desert to what was then becoming Utah Territory. Thus came into existence the concept first used by Utah historian Andrew Love Neff and then church historian and general authority Milton R. Hunter, both of whom used the term "Outer Cordon," an inhabited chain of friendly posts where food, lodging, and other assistance could be offered to Mormon travelers heading toward the centers of their Zion.[39]

One of the Mormon First Presidency's most detailed letters of instruction, written by Brigham Young and his two counselors to Amasa Lyman and Charles Rich as they launched their California colonization expedition, included the direction "as fast as means and opportunity will permit, searching as far as possible on your route for the best locations for stations beyond Iron County." The church leaders' instruction "to establish location after location" back from San Bernardino to the southern Utah settlements was aimed primarily at assisting church emigration and trade. The directions also mentioned establishing a mail route along that line. The same letter recommended cultivation of semitropical plants such as cotton, olives for oil, wine grapes, sugar, and even tea. At the time President Young and his fellows were even more interested than usual in economic self-sufficiency—in all ways possible.[40]

Brigham Young and his counselors intended to open passenger and probably trade lines between Europe and the California seacoast. They understood the terrible toll of lives to cholera and other diseases seemingly endemic along emigrant routes through the Missouri River bottoms of the American Midwest. For this reason they instructed Franklin D. Richards, then in England as president of their European Mission, to "open every desirable correspondence in relation to the various routes, and rates and conveniences from Liverpool to San Diego and make an early report so that if possible the necessary preparations may be made for the next fall's emigration." At about the same time, church leaders instructed the English Latter-day Saints to "cease emigration by the usual route through the states and up the Missouri River." They were to remain in their European homes until a way was opened by either Panama or the more narrow portion of Mexico for them to travel to San Diego and thus bypass "a most sickly climate and country."[41]

Lyman and Rich also wrote to Richards in England urging the alternative Southern Route. And in the meantime, Rich, Jefferson Hunt, and others explored from San Bernardino toward San Diego to determine the feasibility of a road between the two projected entry towns. They ascertained conditions favorable for most of that distance and certainly possible for the entire journey. However, Richards did not find seagoing transportation links to English seaports over the routes desired, and consequently Brigham Young felt constrained in early 1852 to announce the prospect of the Europe-to-San Diego route "in no wise flattering." Yet even then he did not give up on such possibilities, and the next year Young directed that emigrants could "come either by way of San Diego or by way of New Orleans choosing the route that suited their convenience and desires most."[42] However, it is apparent that a careful plan for a chain of settlements along the road to California never received the consistent emphasis necessary for development. And soon the hierarchy no longer mentioned the Pacific Coast as a possible entry point to the Mormon Zion.

Besides failure to properly develop the essential shipping connections, the primary deficiency in the plan was not establishing the requested way stations across the Mojave and adjacent Nevada deserts. There were physically feasible sites for such outposts along the Mojave River; China Ranch, Resting Springs, Cottonwood Springs, and Las Vegas; and along the Muddy and Virgin rivers. But the isolation and vulnerability to Indian attack rendered permanent settlements there prohibitive at that time. No specific comments by Lyman or Rich on these matters are known to exist, but these church leaders, who had personal experience along the trail, proba-

bly realized this fact sooner than their ecclesiastic superior, Young, and that probably explains why they failed to plant the outposts as requested.

Neither Franklin Richards, engrossed in supervising Mormon missionary efforts in Europe, nor Lyman and Rich, busily planting a large church colony in California, could be expected to devote the time and attention essential to work out the details of establishing the transportation connections from Britain to California. Others soon did develop the ship lines and schedules to serve Gold Rush travelers, including an eventual railroad across Panama, enabling some to get from New York to San Francisco in five weeks for considerably less than the cost of teams and wagon. So far as is known, Mormon leaders never encouraged their people to use these facilities in their emigrations to Deseret-Utah. And given the high mortality rate of their people traveling across the plains during the decade of the 1850s, members of the Mormon hierarchy deserve some criticism for not—perhaps through a specially designated agent—following through on their original intent to promote the Southern Route for their emigrants from Europe and elsewhere.[43]

EMIGRATIONS IN 1852

In the spring of 1852 Charles C. Rich returned for a brief visit to Utah, where he had several plural-marriage families. His associates on the trip all packed their baggage on horses and mules, but he chose to take a "light wagon" drawn by four mules. On reaching the most challenging obstacle of the trip in that direction, hauling up to the summit of Cajon Pass, they partially unloaded the wagon and a dozen men carried the baggage up the grade on their backs. After that it proved relatively easy to get the wagon up the grade with the mules pulling and men pushing. There were no other incidents on the notably quick trip in either direction. Rich returned in time to accompany Lyman over the road in November of that same year.[44]

In the meantime a small company including one of the few known women diarists over the Southern Route, twenty-year-old Sarah Pratt from Jackson County, Michigan, traveled the road in the early fall of 1852. The first encounter with Indians she noted occurred on the Virgin River, where she exchanged a calf for a bow and eight arrows, which she greatly treasured. Later, while camped on the Muddy, she obtained a "case" or quiver for them. At that point Pratt noted the Native Americans to be "very troublesome [and] steal many articles from camp." She reported that one of the party frightened the Indians away, presumably threatening to use firearms. Although that season probably had considerably fewer travelers over the route than in the previous three years, Pratt mentioned two other emigrant companies camped at the Muddy while they rested there. Another group of "footmen" they encountered on the Mojave River recounted troubles with Indians in the Cottonwood Springs area, where they presumably lost their mounts or draft animals. Sarah Pratt's own impression of that same area was suggested in her comment, probably of the Red Rock Canyon cliffs, "[O]n our right was the most romantic mountain peak we have seen." She described the road north of Resting Springs as "very bad. One would think could hardly be worse," but she doubtless experienced worse ones within the next hundred miles.

On the first days of November on the Mojave River, Sarah Pratt and her associates endured the cold wind and dust common in the area at that season. Although some had considerable difficulty, including leaving wagons to pack the remainder of the distance, undoubtedly after their animals gave out, the normal patterns of trail life continued. Duck hunting persisted as a common pursuit, in which at least one woman—Pratt—joined. And the company agreed to stay on the river an extra day, occupied—by the women at least—in washing and baking, presumably in Dutch ovens. On descending the "very bad hill, sand, rocks" of Cajon Pass, one of the company shot a bear. The diarist also experimented with prickly pear (cactus) fruit in that vicinity. On reaching San Bernardino, she declined to attend church with the Latter-day Saints, but read considerably from spiritualist literature, probably not realizing how many Mormons around her at the time believed in similar practices. Sarah then engaged to teach school for a term in the Mormon community for thirty dollars per month. While there she met her future husband, storekeeper Morris Minor, origi-

nally from Hungary, whom she married the next year in northern California, where they spent the rest of their lives.[45]

Sarah Pratt, the first known woman to record any significant detail of her journey over the Southern Route, appears to have enjoyed the trip at least as much as any other diarist known. Her personal encounters with Native Americans bolster historian Lillian Schlissel's conclusion that many emigrant women overcame their fear of Indians and their menfolks' hostility toward them to establish their own mutually beneficial relationships. This conclusion must be tempered by Pratt's reports of the persistent emigrant hostility caused by Indian cattle raiding. She is also among the most lavish in her praise of the desert scenery encountered on the way. Although performing the expected womanly roles of baking and washing clothes, she also mentions a less traditional feminine avocation, duck hunting. If the record provided more detail, it would probably indicate many new skills and interests developing as well as the determination to maintain the usual family and domestic ties and traditions.[46]

When Amasa Lyman and Charles Rich set out with fourteen others from San Bernardino toward Salt Lake City in mid-November 1852, they availed themselves of the experience gained on previous desert journeys. This included the climb up Cajon Pass accomplished simply by "double teaming," meaning hitching extra draft animals to each wagon in turn and not unloading at all. As the group approached Bitter Springs, as difficult pulling up Spanish Canyon as coming from the other direction, they stopped a mile short of water to feed their animals on the best bunchgrass available before moving on to the springs. While traveling between Salt Springs and Resting Springs, the Lyman-Rich party met another company of Mormons heading for San Bernardino under the leadership of Henry G. Sherwood, a formerly prominent church leader in both Salt Lake City and Nauvoo, Illinois. While the two groups were conversing, a third contingent, thirty-eight Mormon missionaries who intended to stay at San Bernardino while raising funds to continue toward their assigned fields of labor in Asia, Latin America and the Pacific islands, also arrived at the spot, probably in Amargosa Canyon. Church leaders Lyman and

Rich seized the occasion to hold an impromptu conference at which the Apostles preached. The clerk recorded that an excellent spirit prevailed and the southbound travelers apparently went on their way rejoicing.[47]

In the Cottonwood Springs area, the northbound Mormon group encountered four men struggling to reach the gold fields but who had lost a yoke of oxen to the Indians the night before. Although showing sympathy, the company chronicler, Richard R. Hopkins, noted tellingly that "this was the effect of men laying down in an Indian country without a guard." At Las Vegas the church party came on eleven more wagons of emigrants headed for California. On the Virgin River, they also met a train of fifteen wagons, some driven by Mormons said to be of questionable commitment to their church and by some non-Mormon "Gentiles."

After noticing an absence of Native Americans at the Vegas and the Muddy, the Mormons finally began to meet some. Several miles after starting up the Virgin River, two Paiutes approached them at dusk. After feeding them, the Mormons allowed the Indians to remain for the night if they gave up their bows and arrows, repeating the practice several days later on the Santa Clara, where five Native American men approached them at dark. No negative incidents occurred either time, as a more cordial relationship between Southern Paiutes and Latter-day Saints continued to develop.

This company also was the first to mention Camp Spring on Utah Hill just over ten miles from the Santa Clara River. For those who knew how to find the watering place some distance off the main roadway and at a higher elevation, one more of the waterless night *jornadas* of the trip might thus be eliminated. After delays for preaching in the southern Utah settlements, the expedition arrived in Salt Lake City on 18 December, after just over a month on the road.[48]

EMIGRATIONS IN EARLY 1853

In the spring of 1853, another company of less-than-dedicated earlier Mormon converts, this time from Great Britain, including Welshman William Levick, headed for San Bernardino. Some probably came to perceive of the California colony as partly a haven for the disaffected who could still participate nominally in religious affairs yet reside closer to the outside world than in Brigham Young's notably strict domain. The emigrant journey remained uneventful until on reaching the Virgin River Native Americans attacked them and continued harassing the company for some distance. During this run-ning fight Scotsman James Walkinshaw sustained mortal wounds. The other travelers continued without further problems to San Bernardino.[49]

Another interesting development in the area occurred that year, later recounted by an anonymous author in a leading Latter-day Saint magazine. The writer told of a teamster, presumably Mormon, stranded on the Muddy River when local Native Americans stole his mules. In desperation, with his expedition and perhaps life in jeopardy, he drew his pistol on the Indians still in his camp, ordering them to line up, and then instructed the chief to send two good runners after the mules. The teamster threatened that if they did not return he would shoot the chief and the others. In the meantime he kept the Moapas standing in the line through the entire night. Finally, after sunrise the following morning the two returned with twenty-three exhausted animals, obviously retrieved from a long way off. Thus the innovative driver had to rest his teams before proceeding on his way. He probably kept his prisoners under guard during that time as well. Eventually, he took the Indians' ammunition and released them, then continued on his journey.[50]

In December 1853, another still-rare freighting expedition set out from Salt Lake City under the supposed leadership of Enoch and John Reese, merchants in Carson Valley and later in Salt Lake City, a trip discussed later in this book (except for their conflict with Native Americans). While traveling down the Santa Clara River, a Tonequint chief approached asking permission to enter camp, where he conversed in a friendly manner and departed. In the meantime, some packers traveling nearby shot and killed an Indian, which enraged his fellows. The chief returned to the emigrant company to report the incident, warning that many of his people were now determined to exact retribution. He expressed sorrow that he could not restrain them as well as before the killing had occurred. He affirmed he desired friendship with the Mormons but had to allow his tribesmen a chance for retaliation. In the subsequent skirmishes three travelers received wounds, including former Latter-day Saint Jaspar Wilson, who after surviving with his fellows subsequently settled at San Bernardino.[51]

THE BEALE-HEAP EXPEDITION

Edward Fitzgerald Beale was a man prominent in California history since he helped take the province from Mexico. With close ties to John C. Frémont and his father-in-law, Senator Thomas H. Benton, Beale obtained a commission from eastern promoters in May 1853 to perform a private reconnaissance of a possible central railroad route extending across New Mexico, Colorado, and Utah. Beale also became involved in establishing some of the first Indian reservations in the United States, and because of Benton's senatorial rivalries, the final assignment emphasized more reservation sites and wagon roads than railroads. The expedition included Beale's thirty-six-year-old cousin, Gwin Harris Heap, who himself claimed experience as a traveler in the deserts of Africa, and who wrote the narrative of the current trip.[52]

Falling some two months behind schedule farther east, the Beale expedition reached the main road to southern California at the small Mormon town of Paragonah on 2 August 1853. The group historian praised the excellent condition of the wagon road in southern Utah, including bridges and signposts at the crossroads indicating distances to the various settlements. Although impressed with the Latter-day Saints and the village, Heap noted the people packing up to abandon it for the larger neighboring town of Parowan because of Brigham Young's orders to evacuate small towns and "fort up" during the Wakara (Indian) War crisis then in progress farther north. The Beale group amazed the Mormons with the news that they had crossed the territory without encountering Wakara's warriors, although they had seen the tracks of a large herd of presumably stolen cattle driven past by the Utes some days previously. While the Beale group was still visiting in the area, Wakara sent a "polite message" to southern Mormon militia commander George A. Smith, chiding church members for assuming he intended to drive them from the region when he and his people intended to "confine [their] depredations to their cattle." The Ute chief encouraged

the Latter-day Saints to return to tend their crops so they would not have to abandon the region because of starvation, which the Native Americans clearly did not desire.[53]

After several days encampment at Mountain Meadows, the party headed down the Santa Clara River. Within a few miles, they encountered a party of Paiutes, "who evinced great joy at seeing [them], accosting [them] without fear." At their village, the old chief offered a peace pipe smoke as a symbol of friendship. The Indians demonstrated apprehension that the party's animals might damage their unfenced fields. Thus both groups agreed the livestock would be driven some distance back upstream to a white clover pasture and there tended exclusively by Native Americans, with expedition members understanding they could retaliate against both inhabitants and crops should any mishap occur. The cattle were returned as agreed promptly at daylight. With no remuneration mentioned in the account, this remained clearly a friendly encounter. If anything, some of the Paiutes, particularly women and children, were the ones most frightened, doubtless because of earlier raids by New Mexican slave traders. Heap discovered one naked little boy under a large basket, teeth chattering in fear. One of the Beale party, Jose Gallengo, who had boasted of participating in such forays, even then urged Beale to kill the village men and capture some women and children.

On climbing and descending Utah Hill, Heap described the Virgin as "a turbid and shallow stream, about twelve yards in breadth." Demonstrating an impressive knowledge of animal nutrition, he noted that the sweet pods of the abundant mesquite in the area served as an excellent substitute for corn and that the mules ate "greedily" on that feed. He also stated the salt grass of the vicinity "affords but little nourishment." Farther down the road at Las Vegas, Heap described the narrow stream of clear, cold water as shaded in many areas by willows, with vines covered with clusters of small but sweet grapes. The writer advocated naming the place "the diamond of the Desert," so bright did it shine in the center of the dreary waste surrounding it. The party took much-appreciated baths in the spring waters.

The semimilitary party showed itself sufficiently well organized to avoid losing livestock to Indians along what usually proved the most dangerous part of the route. This success was attributed to "keeping a strict double guard." At the Muddy River, they allowed the Moapas to approach camp in the daytime, including a young Indian who expressed desire to accompany their expedition. They named him Pite. He might have gotten the idea to join the party from observing and perhaps befriending a Delaware Indian who served as an important member of the Beale expedition. When later Las Vegas Paiutes poured a torrent of verbal abuse on the party, Pite answered, and the abusers for a moment remained "silent with astonishment at receiving a reply in their own language." No negative incident arose from the exchange.[54]

Between Mountain Springs and Stump Springs, the party discovered the remains of an American, whom they surmised from accompanying papers to have been a Mormon. He had been killed that season, by a rifle bullet in the head.[55] As they skirted the edge of Death Valley in mid-August, the expedition members faced the desert at its worst. The blazing sun heated their rifle barrels so much the men had difficulty holding them across the pommels of their saddles. They described the water at the Amargosa as "warm, fetid and nauseating." The account added that besides the almost unbearable August heat, there was a wind "laden with an unpalpable sand," which felt "as if it issued from the mouth of a furnace."

On arrival at the Mojave River, Heap rejoiced that "our troubles as regarded to scarcity of water and grass were now at an end." He described the terrain along the river as relatively flat, making comparatively easy travel on the semifinal segment of the road to the southern California settlements. The narrator lauded the willows, reeds, and mesquite bushes "interlaced with grape vines, and in some places there were beautiful groves of cottonwoods," also admiring the large sycamore trees along the river. However, he naively noted that except for the narrow ribbon of river-fed vegetation, "the land was barren and unproductive, offering no point fit for settlement." This assessment proved inaccurate but significant, because Beale had earlier considered the area a likely spot for an Indian reservation.

At one camp on the Mojave River company members found deep pools "alive with fish, principally mullets, some of which were large." Hares and partridges, probably California quail, also seemed abundant. The Delaware hunter shot several antelope, demonstrating the continuing presence of larger game as well. The party historian boasted the Native American had killed at least one specimen of each species of game encountered on the route, presumably for scientific notations. In Cajon Pass, they hoped to find the largest and fiercest quarry of all, a California grizzly, but did not. Like most of its predecessors, the party visited San Bernardino, Cucamonga, and Los Angeles, in this case ending the expedition at Fort Tejon just to the north.[56]

EARLY MAIL SYSTEM

One of the problems with having a large outpost of Mormondom some six hundred miles from church headquarters remained how to communicate between the two largest Latter-day Saint settlements then extant. After a year in southern California, an anonymous correspondent from San Bernardino to the editor of the *Deseret News*, the official LDS church newspaper at Salt Lake City, commented, "[W]e feel to be encouraged at being able to hear from you once a year." It took almost that long to receive a package of newspapers that had been routed east from Utah and then by the Isthmus of Panama to California. The writer observed that mail routed from Utah across Nevada to the San Francisco Bay area—the Northern Route—arrived at the relatively new colony in less than two months, prompting him to remark, "I have concluded that there was a possibility that communication from us [at San Bernardino] might fare better than they had last year and reach you [at Salt Lake City] without making a delay of more than one or two months on the way."[57]

The development of a more efficient mail system had by then already evolved through several crucial steps. In December 1850, the legislature of the hoped-for state of Deseret designated Feramorz Little to manage a stagecoach line through the Mormon settlements from Ogden on the north to Iron County on the south. The legislators, already anticipating a southern California colony to be established some six months later, intended to extend the line "as soon as practicable, continuing to intersect a stage road from Cajon Pass and San Diego." This company commenced operation in the spring of 1851, focusing on passengers and packages, but also undoubtedly on mail. As yet no official mail contact existed with southern California, so San Bernardino founders Amasa Lyman and Charles Rich initially sent correspondence to Brigham Young by a passing Hispanic trader caravan.[58]

In April 1851, George Chorpenning and Absalom Woodward contracted with the U.S. Postal Service to carry mails between Salt Lake City and Sacramento, California. The first winter trip took sixteen days through the Sierra Nevada because teamsters had to use wooden mauls to pack the snow on the road so teams and wagons could pass. They made two to eight miles per day in the stretches of heavy snow. In a subsequent instance in December 1851, mail carriers who had started out from Sacramento had to return there because of the snows. On another attempt, after Indians severely wounded partner Woodward, he heroically attempted to carry the mail on toward Utah. Others eventually found his body where he had died, having gone all the way across Nevada. Still another contingent of Chorpenning employees spent forty-six days in the mountains, having their horses frozen and compelled to walk the last two hundred miles.[59]

Although there would always be heroic carriers taking mail through the Sierra Nevada, Chorpenning concluded his only way to succeed was to travel by a southern approach to Utah, encountering fewer winter obstacles. He duly obtained permission from a special postal agent at San Francisco to send the mail down the coast to San Pedro and then by way of Cajon Pass over the Southern Route to Salt Lake City. Early in the process of establishing this mail route, trail veteran Jefferson Hunt, who was the Latter-day Saint representative in the California legislature and who was also widely known as the ranking officer in the earlier Mormon Battalion, secured what was undoubtedly a subcontract from Chorpenning to perform the actual carrying through his sons, foster sons, a son-in-law, and others. Usually each courier rode one horse or mule and had another to carry the mail and his equipment, although occasionally they used wagons and traveled in pairs. Some of these, including John Hunt, Sheldon Stoddard, and Jim Williams, made the overland trip up to three dozen times each.[60]

A study by Utah historian Herbert Auerbach listed eleven Indian attacks on Southern Route mail carriers between early 1853 and mid-1856, eight of which resulted in losing up to two dozen horses and mules. These incidents were spread rather evenly from the Fillmore, Utah, vicinity to Bitter Springs, California. Generally the attacks appeared to aim at acquiring livestock for food rather than taking mail carriers' lives.[61] A possible exception might have been in 1854 near Resting Springs: Native Americans there attacked Leonard S. Conger and his party with a "flurry of arrows" in which two men and three mules suffered wounds. Despite marked heroism by both Conger and fellow carrier Edward Hope, they lost a mail sack as they barely escaped with their lives from their assailants.[62]

Although not as a part of a mail-carrying expedition, one fatality was mentioned, by mail carrier Conger, but in none other of the annals of the Southern Route. He encountered a party of emigrants at Las Vegas who had just buried a woman killed in a recent skirmish with Native Americans. The mail carrier later discovered her corpse exhumed, and he reinterred it several times as he passed by on his mail excursions before the persistent antagonists allowed her remains to rest in peace.[63]

The mail carriers who traversed this forbidding desert route each month had to be as hardy and resourceful as any frontiersman in western history. Among the foremost of these was Utah resident Conger, who carried much of the Southern Route mail between 1851 and 1854. Usually traveling alone, Conger learned the water holes and scattered patches of good grass essential to maintain his mules. A favorite defensive technique of his featured sleeping in the daytime on an open stretch of desert where he and his vigilant mules could keep a lookout for approaching Indians, then traveling mostly at night through uncertain country. During one dangerous trip, Conger rode from Las Vegas more than halfway up the Santa Clara River without stopping to rest, demonstrating amazing endurance.[64]

Judging from the diary of founder Amasa Lyman, few regular events at San Bernardino were more important than the arrival of the mail. This occurred twice each month, because mail carriers on the trail from Utah to Los Angeles and their counterparts heading from California to Salt Lake City each made the entire month-long trip, on alternate schedules, instead of exchanging mail bags midway en route. The town citizens clearly appeared more active in their letter writing the few days before the mail "closed," meaning being locked into the leather mail bags to be carried over the trail probably the following day. Considering the inadequacies of other contemporary southern California mail service, the Mormon colony's connection with the outside world at this time remained much appreciated.[65]

The 1853 emigration over the Southern Route included the almost unique feature (for that road) of several groups driving sheep overland to California. Dr. Timothy Flint of Maine, not yet thirty years old, had already been in the gold fields and had concluded that more profits could be derived through a livestock drive than from mining.[66] The doctor and his herders started from a railroad terminus in Indiana in the spring with over two thousand sheep, along with some oxen, cows, and horses. En route across the plains they had occasion to assist some Mormon emigrants who experienced difficulty with Indians. This assured the Flint party of cordial treatment by other Latter-day Saints throughout their passage through Utah Territory. During a short stay at Salt Lake City, Flint and his associates purchased more oxen, paying $60 to $90 per yoke, less than demanded in the East. This proved possible because the war with Ute chief Wakara and his followers still engulfed the region. As the main Indian tactic was raiding livestock, militia officers ordered the animals gathered into the towns for safety. But this generated greater feed expense than if pastured on the open range, so many oxen had to be sold. As the company began driving over the Southern Route, Flint learned of many other such groups traveling closely together in the same direction. These included Col. William W. Hollister's train of eleven wagons, thirty drovers, and over six thousand head of sheep, just days ahead of their own party. While en route through Utah, the Flint group joined forces with a Frazier party and later several others, which allowed them to double their guard in apprehension over continuing Indian hostilities.[67]

Another contemporary emigrant company, led by Thomas Hildreth, exhibited consistent hostility toward all Native Americans. At Fillmore, Mormon bishop Anson Call urged fair treatment, informing this party's

leaders that local Indians would doubtless visit their campsite that evening. On that occasion the Pahvants (Kanosh Indians) indicated intent to trade and doubtless beg. The Hildreth group expressed willingness to allow them to remain if they gave up their bows and arrows. Then an emigrant attempted to use force to seize a bow. In the scuffle, which injured a white man, his fellows immediately opened fire, killing an old chief, Toniff, with several others wounded. Although the Mormon bishop attempted to pacify the angered Indians, the dead man's three adult sons insisted on revenge. They and a dozen willing tribesmen followed and harassed the Hildreth party for over a hundred miles, but remained unsuccessful in exacting the desired retribution.

That revenge came at the expense of a party of United States Army railroad surveyors several weeks later. While the party camped on the lower Sevier River some forty miles northwest of Fillmore, hostile Pahvants attacked the surveyors without warning. Lt. John W. Gunnison and six of his men fell in the onslaught; four others escaped. Thus one of the greatest tragedies ever in the history of that area clearly stemmed from Southern Route emigrants exerting excessive aggressiveness toward Native Americans.[68]

Dr. Flint knew of these events when he and his party arrived at Corn Creek on 7 November, just over a week after the Gunnison massacre. A Pahvant approached the group and showed them the best place to obtain water and feed. Leaving, the Indian returned with "Capt Cannuse," meaning Chief Kanosh, and a party of about a dozen other men. Next they sent for their women, all of whom the emigrants were obliged to feed. The emigrants must have felt considerable apprehension throughout this association because Flint at the time erroneously believed that one of Hildreth's men had been killed in the earlier unfortunate incident. The local Mormons could not be entirely trusted, because they would probably agree with the Pahvant version of the affair; this time, however, the Pahvant account proved correct.

Some conflict with the Latter-day Saints arose when a man named Potter of Hollister's train returned to Fillmore, reportedly to rescue two young women whose mother had married a local polygamist. He aimed to help them make their way to California and then back to a former home in Ohio. Fillmore church members thwarted the plan, alleging that Potter had seduced the girls, and thus they dispatched a posse in pursuit. After Potter first slipped away on a faster horse, his pursuers later apprehended him as he entered a canebrake through which the road passed. Possemen expressed intent to take the accused back to Salt Lake City for trial, but the combined sheep-driving parties, numbering some sixty men, concluded they "were strong enough to say no" to this procedure. Subsequent negotiations resulted in a $150 fine, which ended the matter, although considerable bitterness remained on both sides, and some of the company "got up quite a warlike feeling" and hoped to fight rather than submit to the seemingly excessive penalty payment. Although Flint and his immediate associates had been reasonably well treated during their sojourn in Mormondom, from fellow travelers he heard sufficient reports of harassment to express relief as they passed beyond the realm of church power.[69]

Another group at odds with the Latter-day Saint hierarchy included a body of Scottish converts to the church assigned to Cedar City to help establish the Iron Mission, an early manufacturing venture. After several years of good service, conflict arose when the ranking church authority, Apostle George A. Smith, ordered all extra livestock sent north, presumably for safekeeping during the still-continuing Wakara Indian War. When the Scots refused, the LDS militiamen seized one of them and held him hostage until the cattle were given up. Because of the bitterness engendered over the incident, a number of these Scottish Iron County Latter-day Saints abandoned Utah at their first opportunity. Because martial law, then in force, prevented voluntary leaving, the passing of such a sizable non-Mormon emigration party presented the ideal solution to their problem.[70] Thus, Flint reported, "[F]ive wagons of Mormons going out for California joined [their company in the Iron Springs area and] requested the privilege of traveling with us." When the newcomers' cattle proved troublesome during the night, the doctor observed that "not one of the men would go out to look after them," because they feared retaliation from the legendary "Destroying Angels," who allegedly exacted retribution on people presuming to abandon the Mormon Zion. Just a few days later, the train, by then numbering seventeen wagons of "disappointed Mormons," split off from their slow-moving

protectors, feeling sufficiently distant from retaliation to travel the trail alone.[71]

As the Flint company passed down the Santa Clara River, they "took possession" of a Paiute corn and pumpkin field, pasturing their livestock on the stripped cornstalks, but guarding the unharvested pumpkins from damage. They clearly ignored an old Indian who gestured protest. In the afternoon a dozen other Native Americans arrived and received clothing and provisions in payment for the admitted "trespassing." That night a man presumed to be a chief remained in camp under guard. At about midnight he stood before the campfire making signs to tribesmen watching from nearby ridges. When the company moved on next morning, they discovered one cow missing; Flint and a companion went back in search of it. They soon encountered Indians, who drew their bows but were deterred by the revolver already in Flint's hand. Convinced the cow was nearby, the emigrants sent for reinforcements and then headed up the likely mountain trail. Some Indians attempted to stop them but failed. Soon after, they saw other tribesmen driving the cow back toward them, pretending they had found the animal and expecting a reward, which was reluctantly offered. The next day, crossing Utah Hill, they lost additional cattle, which the Indians also returned, receiving clothing as further payment. That night the herders slaughtered a beef and offered the less desirable parts to be shared by some thirty almost-naked Native Americans at Camp Springs. The chief received the hide. Later, the same Indians returned to the camp and Flint noted them to be "dressed up in fine style in their clothing which [had obviously been] laid away in the brush," perhaps in an attempt to secure more.

Sheep driving proved a challenge throughout the trip and is not known to have been repeated in future years, presumably because of the hazards and difficulties encountered, including perhaps less-than-expected profits at the end. The men that Flint called shepherds always started down the road at daylight, undoubtedly because they moved more slowly than even the ox teams and wagons. On several occasions en route Flint noted dead sheep from the larger Hollister herd ahead of them. Concluding that poisonous plants must grow nearby, he instructed that his animals be pushed rapidly past those areas. The party still lost a few to death, but proportionately considerably less than Hollister. At the Virgin River, Flint came on his men after they had spent six hours carrying sheep individually across the stream, particularly arduous work in the November cold. As thirteen more crossings lay ahead, next day Flint took matters in hand and gently pressed the lead animals into the water, keeping the shepherds and accompanying sheep dogs quiet. Although the practice took his men some time to become accustomed to, it may have been the only way to get the sheep downstream in a reasonable time. This party, like all others, found the Virgin Hill "harder than any yet encountered on the route." But the "pebbles like rasps" on top of the mesa presented an even larger challenge not faced by emigrants without sheep. These bits of gravel proved devastating to the tender feet of many of their sheep, which had to be left along the road atop Mormon Mesa. It was probably here at the much-appreciated Mormon Mesa "Sand Grass Camp" that Hollister, traveling just ahead, observed, as he later recalled, "a thousand sheep on their knees at once, taking grass, they not being able to stand on account of the bad condition of their feet." He explained that a sheep's foot was much more tender than those of many other animals, probably a key reason he lost up to two thirds of his six thousand animals en route.[72]

Meantime, Indians continued to be troublesome and on several occasions shot cattle with arrows, although in the first instance the company sustained no loss. In the second attack, the cow shot became so "madly wild," presumably from pain, that they could not retrieve her. At that juncture the drovers encountered two Paiutes and gave chase, but in the maze of side ravines of the Virgin they easily got away. Flint admitted that the Indians dared not approach camp at night, because they understood they would be shot. No mention of sheep being wounded occurred until 4 November, when unseen Native American bowmen killed one. The next day the chronicler recorded that after the Hollister party, still ahead, lost an ox that the Indians killed, the two groups agreed that "the Indians were getting to be so troublesome that [the emigrants] concluded to declare war on them." This amounted to taking warning shots without trying to hit anyone, but to discourage closer contact. As the combined companies entered the Moapa lands, Flint noted, "Indians on bluffs proffer friendship but we

keep them out of rifle range by sending a bullet occasionally in their direction."[73]

At the Muddy River neither lame sheep nor pilfering Moapas made the area more troublesome than for most other groups, but because of the steep riverbanks and the soft bottom of the river, Flint particularly disliked the locality. About a dozen head of cattle jumped off the banks and could not get themselves out of the water. Flint and several companions had to climb into the cold river and drive the animals upstream, crossing back and forth to stay on the shallowest footings. After a cold and difficult mile, they found a place where cattle could scramble out, but some refused and had to be pulled out with ropes. The company also lost eleven more sheep on the Muddy, presumably to poisonous plants. Surprisingly, the sheep had no problem crossing the fifty-mile stretch of desert between water holes, according to the expedition leader "standing the trip finely" to Las Vegas.

The remainder of the journey appeared uneventful, although the party occasionally continued to lose livestock to Indians. Physician Flint's observations about what he called Bitterwater Springs, doubtless Bitter Springs, revealed "water very bitter but it answered very well when made into tea and could be drank clear by not stopping to taste it." He noted no deleterious effects from the spring water. From the brief record it appears the sheep experienced less difficulty than oxen or the sheep herders, some of whom he said had "such a dread of the desert that they were beside themselves imagining they would perish from thirst" before getting to the Mojave River. One problem, probably never properly resolved, related to separating out Flint sheep that had been inadvertently allowed to mingle with Hollister's larger herd.

Still on the Mojave River on Christmas Day, Flint's party feasted on wild quail shot for the occasion. They enjoyed similar fare the next few dinners, supplemented by equally abundant duck and rabbit. On New Year's Day 1854, probably at Sycamore Grove, Flint dined with Hollister, whose sister, Mrs. Brown, "made an effort in the culinary line to have a good dinner as the situation would afford." Mrs. Brown's New Year's Day dinner is an excellent example of what Lillian Schlissel, historian of women pioneers, asserts many emigrant women attempted to do. This was to "weave a fabric of accustomed design, a semblance of their usual domestic circle. Out of the disorder of traveling, the women created and held on to some order and routine." The record does not say Hollister and his sister drew on the neighboring ranchos for supplies to enhance the dinner, but that was a distinct possibility. Still, the effort is a rare glimpse—on this route at least—of what many women probably did strive to accomplish.[74]

Then, with brief stops at San Bernardino, Cucamonga, and Chino, the sheep-driving companies moved on to spend the remainder of the winter season at Los Angeles. Eventually moving the livestock on to northern California, Flint sold a thousand head for a less-than-expected $16,000, indicating that he got half his animals through. Hollister, who intended to pasture his on lands he had previously seen in central California, arrived with only a third of the 6,000 with which he had started. The successful arrival of both groups ended a unique episode in the history of the Southern Route.[75]

Not much is known about the Thomas Hildreth company traveling just ahead of the sheep herds, other than the Indian retaliation they brought down on the Gunnison party. But one young man traveling with that group, Henry C. Daulton, recorded one interesting side-light of social interaction among the company. He married Mary Jane Hildreth, the daughter of the company head, while they were yet camped near Mission San Gabriel near the end of their journey. The fact that at least one other daughter, Agnes, married another company member, Jonathan Rea, and still another, Elizabeth, married Tom Roundtree, who might have been on the journey, all presumably at San Gabriel, indicates that a great deal of courtship must have been in progress along the trail. Most companies probably had fewer eligible daughters, but this situation was probably far from unique.[76]

These crucial years after the initiation of the southern emigrant route proved significant for the relatively large volume of traffic traveling that way during portions of the year when land travel to California otherwise remained generally impossible. Warlike Native Americans largely precluded use of trails across Arizona, although a few would come that way as well. Those Southern Paiutes along the road to southern California persisted in their efforts to seek recompense for lost resources from the passing travelers, but these actions seldom, if ever, included loss of human life. Equally important was the growing friendship between Mormons and Paiutes along the Southern Route, which continued to develop thereafter.

Chapter Five

Outside Observers and
Mormon-Indian Relations

Even before the period 1854 to 1857 the manner in which Latter-day Saint travelers interacted with resident Paiutes along the Southern Route was perceptibly different from the relationships of many others who also passed through those lands. At some point cementing better relations became a conscious policy of the Latter-day Saint church hierarchy, to be carried out mainly through missionaries assigned for that and other purposes. Some of the most perceptive contemporary Gentile observers ever traveling the route noted this condition with varying degrees of apprehension, some even predicting the situation could lead to disaster. But with no known effort to counter the development of what could be accurately considered an alliance, progress in that direction continued.

THE SOUTHERN
INDIAN MISSION

Just after the April general church conference in the spring of 1854, half of the Latter-day Saints (LDS) Quorum of the Twelve Apostles set apart a group of about twenty missionaries from northern Utah assigned to open what became known as the Southern Indian Mission among the Southern Paiutes in the extreme southwestern section of the territory. These men gathered farm implements and tools along with seed in preparation for labor among the Native Americans, partly on their tribal fields and largely to show them better methods of cultivating the soil. They established a mission headquarters at Harmony, the settlement led by John D. Lee (later infamous for major involvement in the Mountain Meadows Massacre, as explained in chapter 6), near the rim of the Great Basin not many miles to the west. The missionaries also worked with earlier colonizers to develop a better irrigation water system and to cultivate more farm and garden lands. Rufus Chester Allen, described as a "youthful captain" of twenty-six, a veteran of the Mormon Battalion, headed the mission, assigned to essentially share authority in the area with Lee, who was the settlement ecclesiastic leader. Thomas D. Brown, a forty-nine-year-old Scottish merchant from Salt Lake City, selected as clerk and historian of the mission, probably also became recognized as spiritual leader of his fellows. On the first Sabbath at Harmony, Brown spoke publicly regarding the mission and its aims "of feeding, cleaning and clothing the Indians, teaching them to labor" and thereby earn the spiritual blessings that the Latter-day Saints assumed them to be entitled to as Children of Israel. He closed by observing, "[W]e need more provisions to do good among the Indians" and mentioning that the rainstorm then in progress might help them produce the necessary crops for that purpose. The missionaries may have been disappointed to learn from John D. Lee that only three hundred Paiutes lived in the general Harmony area. However, many Native Americans appeared cordial to the settlers and soon became even more receptive to the missionaries, with whom they worked cultivating and irrigating fields and cutting juniper-cedar posts for fencing.[1]

At the worship service on the second Sunday at the mission, the predominant theme discussed among the men, who firmly believed in their callings to teach and befriend the Indians, centered on revenge against the Mormons' former persecutors in Missouri. John Lott of Lehi City first mentioned the tarring and feathering of the church-founding prophet Joseph Smith, with whom the speaker claimed to have lived in Missouri. He expressed his hope of seeing "the day when the blood of martyrs will be avenged." David Lewis of Salt Lake City mentioned his brother Benjamin as among the seventeen Mormon men and boys killed in the so-called Haun's Mill Massacre in 1838 in Missouri. He also affirmed himself to be "alive to avenge his blood when the Lord will." Lewis then stated that one reason they were living among the Paiutes was to "teach them of this work," clearly meaning the avenging of loved ones killed in earlier midwestern conflicts. He advised they must treat the Native Americans as children while patiently encouraging them to give up their "savage customs."

Concluding his remarks, Lewis promised that if the missionaries were diligent in their labors, the Lord would reward them in their efforts. Reiterating that "Ephraim[2] [was] the battle ax of the Lord," he significantly revealed perhaps a major purpose of the mission and subsequent extensions of such efforts, asking, "[M]ay we not have been sent to learn and know how to use this ax with skill."[3] The ideas and desires expressed at the meeting proved far from unique among many Latter-day Saint men of that era. It reveals a current atmosphere, almost forgotten in later times, that might be best described as a "culture of revenge" pervading Mormondom of that era.[4]

So far as is known neither President Brigham Young nor any of the other members of the church hierarchy ever publicly expressed the goal of the mission as being to prepare the Indians for military or retaliatory purposes, although people in contemporary Mormon congregations widely held such sentiments. The highest church leaders' directions more specifically aimed at missionaries living among the Native Americans so that they could more effectively learn to communicate with them and teach them in their own language. Young directed the missionaries to "get to their [Indian] understanding," which probably meant to become familiar enough with their culture and thought processes to truly empathize with their feelings and actions. He essentially criticized his best available Indian interpreters, Dimick Baker Huntington and George Washington Bean, for being "deficient in understanding what they say," probably feeling that some nuances of Paiute language meaning slipped by the translators. The highest church leader specifically assigned the missionaries to "learn then their language perfectly."[5]

As the missionaries visited Chief Toquor's wickiups near the later Utah town named for him, some fifteen miles south from the mission headquarters, Thomas Brown noted better farmland abandoned on Ash Creek than what was presently being farmed. He concluded that the land, clearly cultivated in the past, had too many old corn roots in the soil, which could not be properly tilled with the wooden sticks the Indians used to work the land. Although not mentioned in the mission record, a plow was obviously needed, along with draft animals to pull it and the requisite skills to use them, as potentially taught by the missionaries.

Chief Toquor did not particularly impress the mission chronicler. However, Brown considered Toquor's son, Terab, to be much more noteworthy. John D. Lee had earlier ordained Terab a Mormon elder and sent him out to preach among his own people. Terab had journeyed all the way to the San Bernardino area of California "to tell all his brethren we [the Mormon missionaries] were come to do them good." Brown added significantly, "[A]ll the Indians on the way very favorable to the Mormons—which name is a pass word for friendship among these mountains and Indians." That is precisely what the broader mission was intended to accomplish.[6] As shown later in this book, several contemporary travelers observed this closeness of relationship, which continued to develop over the next two years. The situation certainly remained prevalent at the time of the Mountain Meadows Massacre, when Native Americans distinguished "Mormonees" (or Mormons) from "Mericats" (as Americans were designated) with the clear understanding that the latter might not be allowed to pass safely over the southern road to California. Through conversations with Moapas at the Muddy River, some of the travelers "learnt that they look upon all Americans, the Mormons excepted, as bad people, and it is this conviction that tends to make them ill-disposed to emigrants."[7]

A month after the founding of the Southern Indian Mission, a group of missionaries traveled down the Virgin River past future St. George to the Santa Clara River tributary. Here they soon met Tutsegabits, acclaimed head chief of at least six Paiute villages, whom the church men called Amos because he had already been baptized a Mormon and had consequently been given a scriptural name. The Paiute name for the area was Tonequint; the land featured several excellent wheat fields of ten acres each, as well as other field and garden plots. The Indians had a "good dam" three rods wide slanting across the river and an outlet canal almost a mile long, dug without shovels. Here too Brown recognized the great need for plows with which to improve the farming enterprise. Although Tutsegabits admitted that his people were often hungry, the Indians demonstrated real generosity in sharing their food and drink with the missionaries.

From first contact with the Tonequint band of Paiutes, the mission scribe noted that the women and children showed great fear, including adults showing fear on be-

half of their children. Although he did not say so, this reaction undoubtedly stemmed from the frequent slave-raiding expeditions that persisted in the area. After the two groups exchanged food and both sang some Mormon hymns, Brown claimed the Indian "fears gave way to confidence and love." He later recorded that when the Tonequints became aware that the Big Captain, meaning Brigham Young, had ordered Wakara "to quit stealing the squaws & children," they "rejoiced much." There were, however, still instances of parents exchanging their own children for a few meager trade goods.[8]

On the first visit to Tutsegabits's Tonequint villages, later the center of the mission, the missionaries informed the Indians, through interpreters, of their purposes. They aimed to learn the Paiute language so they could talk to the Paiutes and teach them to farm more effectively. They would include instruction using "implements," presumably plows. The resulting improvements would help the Indians obtain, by their own efforts, more food and clothing. The missionaries did not promise to provide food or clothing, but they pointed to the few Tonequints who had lived and worked among the Mormons, who had been paid partly in better clothing. This clearly conveyed the message that as the Indians learned from their teachers they would be able to acquire more for themselves. The next day, Chief Tutsegabits, also sometimes called Tsatouts, spoke to his people for most of an hour on the same objectives.

Later, the Ute chief, Sanpitch, a brother of Wakara, visited the Santa Clara area and attempted to persuade Tutsegabits and his people to resist the incursions of the Mormons and not allow them to build cabins or plant crops without paying for the land, which he asserted actually belonged to his brother Wakara. President Rufus Allen pointedly denied the Ute right to dictate in any way to the Paiutes or claim any of their lands. He stood equally forcefully while answering other allegations against the Mormons. The mission president then asked Tutsegabits if he wished the missionaries "to live among you, build houses and teach you to make food" or if they should withdraw and abandon their efforts. Chief Tutsegabits thought for a moment, then replied, "[G]o on and make houses, live among us & teach us to make food and get clothing—we have been a long time naked and often hungry & you are our friends." Brown noted

One of many Paiutes who was baptized a Mormon at a ceremony that took place in the Santa Clara area late in the Indian-mission era, perhaps 1865.

that his listeners assented in this declaration. Sanpitch accepted the decision and pursued his other purpose of trading for some local Paiute children, who still reportedly brought him up to five hundred dollars apiece on the New Mexico market.[9]

Some of the Santa Clara Indians sought baptism into the church early in the missionary visit, but this rite was deferred for the present. Brown significantly stated that "salvation to them will be increase to tools and farming implements that they may produce food for their sustenance during the whole year & have surplus wherewith to procure clothing." He noted these particular Paiutes to be "very industrious," though naturally, to white men of that day, they appeared "simple as children." In less than a month on the Santa Clara the missionaries had more than a hundred souls requesting baptism, and some of these people notably preferred to call themselves Paiute Mormons rather than simply Paiutes.[10]

Although several missionaries received assignment to

venture over the road to California as far as the Muddy River, major missionary efforts did not commence there until a year later. In early June 1855, President Allen and five associates arrived at the Muddy and received warm greeting from the Moapa Paiutes, who knew of their work among their Santa Clara neighbors. Within a few days of contact, the Mormon agents complied with supposed requests and baptized over three hundred and thirty Indians, from among more than five hundred there to witness the event.

Thomas Brown acknowledged being particularly impressed with the Moapa agricultural enterprises, saying that "[they] farm more than any others we have been among." He also noted the wheat currently being threshed with horse hooves of animals borrowed from the Mormons. Equally impressive—in marked contrast with what many other contemporary observers, including some Mormons, observed—Brown noted the Moapas' lack of greed in seeking food from their visitors. The clerk also added, significantly, "[N]or did they ever attempt to take any of our trappings, tho' they had ample opportunity." The missionaries departed with marked good feelings on both sides. This visit took place just prior to the establishment of the Las Vegas mission just beyond the adjacent "*jornada* of death" segment of the road.[11]

The first year at Harmony the missionary crops essentially failed, although other nearby farmers enjoyed greater success. Thomas Brown hardly veiled his dislike for John D. Lee, and his record makes clear others shared his sentiments. Later Lee admitted writing to his adopted father, Brigham Young, unfairly criticizing the missionaries. After this the mission clerk could not restrain himself, and recorded several pages of Lee's offenses against many of his fellow workers, pointedly confessing the belief that his presidency "militate[s] against the harmony of Harmony." Brown included in this indictment at least one instance of Lee antagonizing some of the Indians with whom the missionaries remained charged to work. It is entirely probable Lee's perceived misrule of the settlement became one of the reasons the missionaries gravitated toward Santa Clara as the primary field of their labors. When Brown returned to Tonequint a year after his mission began, in May 1855, he noted, "[W]e find the Indians there still increasing in knowledge of farming & very friendly with our brethren of the mission there."[12]

Although the mission record is fraught with entries of missionary efforts to learn the Paiute language and culture, it makes virtually no mention of actual preaching of religious doctrines. The mission purpose clearly continued to be cementing friendship and gaining the trust of the region's Native Americans, for whatever reasons. In just over a year of effort, this had been impressively accomplished among the Paiutes along the most heavily populated segment of the southern road to California. This strategy remained an essential component of the aims of some Latter-day Saints bent on retaliation for past wrongs, as would become abundantly clear in the ensuing two years.

SOLOMON CARVALHO AND OTHER 1854 TRAVELERS

In the spring of 1854, returning California miners named Atwood and Murray arrived in Utah with an account of Indians killing their companion while at Camp Springs between the Virgin and Santa Clara rivers. They stated they had left George Lamphere, formerly of Chicago, finishing breakfast as they started slowly along the trail. When the victim's horse came running by with arrows protruding, they claimed to have hurried back and found his body stripped and pierced by a dozen arrows. The man reportedly carried a watch and some quantity of gold, found missing. Even when the Los Angeles *Star* reported the incident, suspicion already pointed toward Lamphere's companions. A party that went to the murder site to investigate not only found that the local Indians denied killing the man but also discovered a serape at the place, which observers concluded murderous Native Americans would have taken. Many years later, Mormon leader Anthony W. Ivins befriended an old Paiute named Magets, who claimed to have been hiding in the rocks near the campsite and witnessed the white men kill their associate and take his gold. It is doubtful if the men were ever punished, partly because, as another traveler over the trail the following year, William Chandless, explained in his writings, white people then would hardly hold an Indian's testimony as credible. Also, Ivins alleged, the

same witness was at some point implicated in a similar killing at the spring.[13]

Solomon Carvalho, the Jewish Portuguese artist cited in chapter 1, had recently survived one of several nearly disastrous, poorly led expeditions by John C. Frémont through the western mountains in the dead of winter and had just regained his health and sixty pounds of body weight while living among the Mormons. This well-known traveler devoted particular interest to the Lamphere murder because he too intended to embark over that road. He took the precaution of joining a group of twenty-three able-bodied men who comprised another group of Mormon missionaries led by Parley P. Pratt, and thus claimed to feel as secure as he would on any other western route. For the first portion of the southward journey, Carvalho and the missionaries accompanied Brigham Young and a large contingent of Latter-day Saint

The young Portuguese Jewish artist and photographer Solomon Nunes Carvalho, a few years prior to his trip over the Southern Route, on which he made one of the most detailed descriptions of the trail ever offered.

dignitaries aiming to confer with Ute Chief Wakara to conclude the yet-unresolved Indian hostilities.

This meeting took place just off the main road between Nephi and the Sevier River. Young and his entourage brought sixteen cattle, blankets, clothing, trinkets, arms, and ammunition for the Utes. Noting that Wakara insisted on the Young group coming to him as he did when he had been invited to the church authorities' camp, the white delegation found the head chief accompanied by more than a dozen other Ute leaders. Wakara, seated on a blanket, did not rise when Young approached, but offered his hand and made room for him at his side. As the proceedings commenced, several chiefs recounted serious grievances they held against Mormons and Americans. After they finished, Wakara explained he did not wish to speak until the following day, after first communicating with his God. On smoking a peace pipe, the initial day of negotiations ended with the killing of sufficient cattle to provide fresh beef to all present. During the afternoon, the artist painted a portrait of Wakara as he also within the next week painted his much less aggressive associate Kanosh. He had already painted sev-

Portrait of Ute chief Wakara, painted by Solomon Nunes Carvalho not long before Chief Wakara's death in 1854.

COURTESY UTAH HISTORICAL SOCIETY

eral church authorities. Next day, after receiving the presents, Wakara denied any implication in the Gunnison massacre so often blamed on him, saying he had been some three hundred miles away at the time. As all present understood, rage among the Pahvants over the killing of Toniff and also, as Carvalho noted, over the general practice among many passing emigrants of wantonly killing Indians "like so many wild beasts," had brought on the massacre.

Carvalho noted, "[T]he first principle inculcated among them was life for life; it made no difference whether, in their wrath they massacred an innocent" person in exacting retribution. Without further discussion of other events and grievances, Wakara promised, "no fight Mormons or Mericats [Americans] more, if Indian kill white man again, Wakara make Indian howl." After smoking another peace pipe, the proceedings ended. Several Ute chiefs then accompanied Brigham Young's entourage farther south as a symbolic bodyguard.[14] Not long after this, President Young and his people resisted attempts to punish any Indians for the Gunnison massacre, further cementing Mormon-Indian friendship while antagonizing federal government officials on the same matter.[15]

A bridge had been erected at the Sevier crossing the previous year, but it had been either washed out in the winter floods or, as William Chandless later alleged, burned by Indians. The current travelers retrieved some of the planks and set about constructing a raft, on which they ferried forty-one wagons across. After an uneventful trip to Cedar City, on 22 May 1854 Carvalho and the missionaries proceeded down the California trail with seven teams and wagons, accompanied by a married woman heading for San Bernardino. The artist waxed eloquent about the wildflowers growing luxuriantly at the Mountain Meadows. He also noted the greater difficulty crossing the Santa Clara River in the spring than during the fall when most travelers passed that way.

Carvalho's first encounter with Paiutes occurred on the Santa Clara, where he met the man who claimed to have been crippled by a gunshot from a member of the first Frémont expedition. This Indian accused the artist of being an American, rather than a Mormon. The warrior "looked very savagely" at Carvalho, pointing to his old wound; the traveler concluded he would have been "a target for arrows" if he had revealed his recent association with Frémont. Farther down the trail on the Virgin, the group fed a small number of Paiutes. From them Carvalho procured a bow made from the horn of a bighorn sheep, covered with carefully chewed deer sinew for additional strength, along with a quiver full of steel and obsidian-tipped arrows, obtained in exchange for clothing.

The Southern Paiute lifestyle did not generally impress Carvalho, who had observed many different tribes of Native Americans, but he did credit them with being "expert thieves" and asserted that "great vigilance must be used to prevent them from robbing you before your very eyes." He considered the Moapas to be "a little higher on the scale of civilization," finding their corn and wheat fields well cultivated, with women grinding grain between stones. He also noted the Mormons heading for San Bernardino had assisted these Indians with several farm tools and that some of the bands' leaders had already been baptized into the church. The artist copied some of the Paiute language and vocabulary, already printed for church missionaries, into his own notes. Carvalho concluded concerning the Nuwuvi, "[T]hey appear friendly, and we put up with their peccadilloes [mainly stealing] for policy's sake."[16]

In the Las Vegas area, on which the European chronicler lavished one of the most detailed of all descriptions made of the locality in the entire pioneering era, Carvalho also reported on the huge volume of discarded luggage of an emigrant company traveling ten days ahead. He assumed the emigrants had thrown out articles regularly until everything they had possessed remained on the road. And in a manner similar to what he would do farther down the trail, Carvalho counted nineteen carcasses of recently dead livestock in one hour's travel. His record concluded tersely, "[W]hat a lesson to those who travel over such a country, unadvised and unprepared."

He could have said the same of the Reese company, the first freight wagon train to cross over the route, encountered on the recently initiated Kingston cutoff, which bypassed the Stump, Resting, and Salt springs, rejoining the old road midway to Bitter Springs. As the poorly led freighters had done on the previous southbound trip, the Reese party lost a great many of their draft animals, this time even though they were only a week from the Mojave River. This compelled Col. Enoch Reese to send all the way to Cedar City, Utah, for replacement animals, probably obtained at the expense of a goodly portion of the manufactured goods being hauled in the wagons. At Kingston Springs Carvalho also met and conversed with the legendary Pegleg Smith, then engaged in gold prospecting.[17] The old mountain man could have offered detailed information on the numerous weathered horse and mule bones strewn along the nearby Old Spanish Trail, because they largely resulted from the 1840 rustling foray Pegleg had participated in with Chief Wakara and others, including his own Native American in-laws.[18]

The more recently deceased animal remains most interested Carvalho as his company journeyed toward Bitter Springs. At one point he counted forty newly dead

Sketch rendered of Rabbit Hole Springs by Capt. E. Gould Bruff on the main California trail to the north, depicting the type of scene Carvalho described of dead draft animals along the trail.
COURTESY THE HUNTINGTON LIBRARY

cattle in one mile. He described the area as "a howling, barren wilderness; not a single tree or shrub for the last fifty miles," nor a sign of an animal or even insect. However, he reached the height of both eloquence and appreciation of Bitter Springs when he acknowledged God's hand in dispersing the admittedly meager life-sustaining supply of water and grass in the area, without which no overland emigrant route through the region would be possible.

As so many before him, Carvalho became truly laudatory about the Mojave River Valley, with no complaint at having to dig holes in the sand in the riverbed to obtain the "good pure water." While appreciating the shady cottonwoods in July and the good bunchgrass, his description of the "rose trees in full bloom, with hundreds of other beautiful flowers" made one wish he had been a landscape artist rather than principally a portrait painter. He continued, "[T]his is a fairy land, indeed. What a contrast to the desert of a few hours ago! Grape vines hang gracefully from the branches of lofty trees, while the air resounds with the songs of birds." After a unique description of "the whole force of the men" holding back on ropes attached to the wagons to prevent "too rapid descent" down the hogback of Cajon Pass, Carvalho reached the San Bernardino Valley without incident. Staying but three days, he traveled to Los Angeles in twelve hours on the same hardy mule with which he had crossed the desert.[19]

The group Carvalho crossed the deserts with consisted of some two dozen Mormon missionaries, mainly assigned to the Sandwich Islands. These were led by trail veteran and church apostle Parley Pratt. Several—including Simpson Molen, Edward Partridge Jr., Silas S. Smith, and Joseph F. Smith, the future head of the church, then a teenager—kept diaries, or wrote letter descriptions of the journey. Although none were as complete as Carvalho's, some additional insights were provided therein. Molen noted that on the Virgin River, the Indians exacted road tribute in the form of clothes and provisions. Pratt and several others visited what was probably the main Moapa Indian wheat farm some five miles from the California crossing and were clearly impressed with the tall crop raised without hoes or spades. They abandoned a wagon belonging to a church sister, Patton, along with some cooking utensils, clothing, and other items, at Kingston Springs. The missionaries were warmly welcomed by the San Bernardino Mormons and were duly impressed with the development of the colony. After a short stay, Lyman and Rich furnished wagons to take their brethren to Los Angeles to catch a steamer to San Francisco.[20]

SYLVESTER MOWRY'S ARMY EXPEDITION

In May 1855 Col. Edward J. Steptoe ordered a detachment of soldiers under the command of Lt. Sylvester Mowry to cross to California by the Southern Route. Certainly military aims motivated this venture, but diplomatic reasons also loomed for getting several United States Army men, including Mowry, out of Salt Lake City before hostilities erupted with the Mormons. After reportedly seducing Brigham Young's daughter-in-law, Mowry had taken up cohabiting with a teenaged Mormon girl named Tanner, who wished to go to California with him. Whether she herself went or not, a number of Mormon women did "escape" from Utah with the soldiers.[21] Mowry's party included thirty-two soldiers and an equal number of "quartermaster's employees" (presumably civilians), eighty horses, fifty mules, and seven wagons. The road through Utah impressed the commanding officer, particularly the convenient availability of water at most campsites and the wood purchasable at each town passed.

W. R. Hayes, a horse wrangler with the expedition, kept a diary of the trip. In it he recorded a seemingly unique manner of handling the extra mounts. A large rope was apparently fastened to each side of the tongue of a light wagon. To this were tied the halter ropes of each horse at twelve-foot intervals. The diarist was assigned to ride the lead horse, with another man on the wheel horse and two other hands assisting with the ropes in "bad places." Thus there were four men per string and two strings, each with twenty horses. These followed behind the dragoons but ahead of the loose-driven beef cattle. The soldiers and their associates made the entire trip in this manner.[22]

Near Fillmore Mowry heard rumors of a plot by Mormons to stampede his animals in the night, subsequently accomplished. It took two days to retrieve most of the horses and mules, successful partly with Mormon assistance, allegedly for the purpose of seeking reward funds for public use. Mowry's bitterness over the incident helped alienate his good Mormon scouts, George W. Bean and James T. S. Allred, subsequently replaced by the former mountain man and mail carrier Jim Williams, nephew of the infamous Frémont guide Bill Williams. Farther down the road the commanding officer again became angered, this time by Parowan church officials attempting to charge an exorbitant price for grain. The army purchasing agents finally obtained a better bargain at Cedar City. These and other presumed slights by members of the Church of Jesus Christ of Latter-day Saints further fueled the army officer's already abundant ill feeling toward the church and many of its adherents. He reported to United States Army superiors that similar animosity existed throughout Utah toward all employees and agents of the government, causing a "disposition to annoy and embarrass in every possible way." This proved an accurate assessment of the current and future situation, which unfortunately none of his superiors did anything about.[23]

Guide Jim Williams took the military party by way of a cutoff recently constructed by his mail contractor employer, James B. Leach, from the Cedar City settlement southwestward to Mountain Meadows. Mowry reported on the construction, which was accomplished through a congressional appropriation for a military road, from Salt Lake City to California, that Steptoe had been charged to implement. It took advantage of passing through the newly settled Pinto area and cut about fifteen miles off the travel distance.[24] The local Mormons considered the road contractors to be "spoilsmen" essentially wasting government funds, but they were not then likely to make any positive statements about either outsiders or their government.[25]

After Mountain Meadows, which the soldier described as "a beautiful level plateau, shut in by mountains, carpeted with luxuriant grass of the best varieties for grazing and divided by a perennial stream," the physical challenges of the road remained the same as others experienced, including fifteen crossings of the Virgin River in a stretch of thirty-six miles. Mowry added his vote to numerous others that "the hill leaving the Virgin

[was] one of the worst [he] ever saw."[26] Understanding these difficulties, the officer suggested, building on information provided by guide Jim Williams, that a cutoff seemed eminently feasible from somewhere near the head of the Santa Clara River west to the Muddy River skirting the edge of Mormon Mountain instead of the existing road farther south toward the middle of Mormon Mesa. This proposed route would avoid a week of Indian pilfering, the entire Virgin River, and Virgin Hill. But the federal government never implemented the suggestions, although the Utah legislature, local Mormon residents, and freighters finally established a similar road, as discussed later in chapter 9.

The soldiers doubtless experienced more personal discomfort than most travelers over the route because of the season they traversed it, May and June. It is no wonder that with the rising June heat on the desert, the army reporter considered Las Vegas the last good campsite encountered till the party reached the Mojave River. Besides poor water and grass resources, daytime temperatures reached 110 degrees Fahrenheit in the tents and on another occasion, 120 degrees, with no "shadow of a shade" in view. Beyond Resting Springs, Mowry noted, significantly, "the Pure Water Springs on the Amigosia [Amargosa]," by which he doubtless referred to the spring at present China Ranch, as an excellent water supply seldom mentioned in the pioneer or freighter sources. Wrangler Hayes mentioned part of the group at least camped at the freshwater spring. The officer also mentioned the nearby canyon of the Amargosa, where he reported more breakage to wagons than in any other place on the route, an observation Jefferson Hunt and others would agree with.

Mowry recorded aptly, "[I]n its desolation the country reminds one strongly of the Biblical curse 'from generation to generation it shall lie waste, none shall pass through it for ever and ever'" (Isaiah 34:10). Yet the army officer did lead all his men—and almost all animals—across the desert, which with their lack of experience, was a great tribute to his leadership. One historian, Carl I. Wheat, concluded that the expedition showed "a practicable route for troops." Mowry would undoubtedly have hedged this to a possible route for troops. The ambitious soldier soon applied to command the projected reconnaissance along the Colorado River as far as the Virgin

River, but the assignment went instead to his West Point classmate, Lt. Joseph C. Ives. Mowry's own sometimes-illustrious career would thereafter mainly be centered in Arizona Territory.[27]

In a separate portion of his report to S. Cooper, adjutant general of the United States Army, Mowry mentioned that his own superior, Col. Edward J. Steptoe, believed the Native Americans along the entire route traveled "had been taught that the Mormons were a superior people to the Americans, and that the Americans were the natural enemies of the Indians, while the Mormons were their friends and allies." On his own journey the lieutenant claimed to have observed much to corroborate this conclusion. He reported church missionaries working with each group of Paiutes encountered, allegedly seeking to "impress upon the Indians the belief in the inferiority and hostility of the Americans and the superiority and friendship of the Mormons." Most alarming, Mowry alleged, the Santa Clara band had been supplied with guns and ammunition. He claimed to have counted up to seventy good rifles where two years previous the Indians had only had bows and arrows. This report concerning the weapons appears exaggerated, but the matter cannot be proved either way. He proved perfectly accurate concerning the burgeoning Mormon-Indian alliance.[28]

Mowry also reported some Native Americans as being close to open hostility with the soldiers. He "talked" with all the Paiute chiefs encountered, attempting to explain to them "the true relations existing between Americans and Mormons." He also issued rations as much as possible, and a few presents. Learning that the Moapas on the Muddy River believed his expedition was approaching to attack them, the officer claimed to have entirely altered their view regarding representatives of the United States. The Mowry report concluded with the excellent suggestion that troops be sent over the trail annually to seek friendship and to demonstrate the strength of the government. He also noted that such relations with the Indians, as friends of the United States or even as neutrals, remained essential to any march to or from Salt Lake City over the Southern Route. He then pointedly warned, "[A]s enemies they cannot be too much dreaded," adding that many observers agreed that if the Indians were armed and directed by the Mormons,

war with this combined force might eventually be a distinct possibility.[29]

One of the most significant oversights in this entire era of weak national government is the fact that no superior of this young and impressively perceptive officer ever appeared to heed his warnings and there was absolutely no known response to his proposals. In light of the tragedy of the Mountain Meadows Massacre just over two years later, it can thus be cogently argued a role was played both by the federal government's sins of omission as well as those of commission by some Mormons and their Indian allies.

Garland Hurt, a thirty-five-year-old physician, became Indian agent for Utah Territory in 1854. The cornerstone of his program was establishing farms for Indians "whose lands the whites had occupied," focusing particularly on one plot of land on the Spanish Fork River. At the time the Mormons sought to win the allegiance of Native Americans to their causes, this devout Methodist, Hurt, enjoyed notable success among the Utes, "winning the friendship and loyalty of the main tribe in [the Latter-day Saints'] own back yard." U.S. government conflict with church authorities later demonstrated many Utes sided with Agent Hurt against the Mormons, whose leaders doubtless recognized those Native Americans could not be relied on as allies. However, despite promoting Indian farms in Millard and Iron counties, Hurt developed no similar relationship among the Southern Paiutes.[30]

MORMON TRAVELERS
IN LATE 1855

At the same time Lieutenant Mowry and his soldiers headed southwest over the road to California, Apostle Charles C. Rich and a half-dozen fellow Mormons also made their way the same direction on the route. One of the first notable aspects of their experience was that they took advantage of previous explorations of southern Utah that had revealed the presence of water high in the Cove Creek canyon midway between Corn Creek and Beaver River, where many other emigrant companies had been compelled to go without water. Rich's account was one of several mentioning that the government appropriation to construct a military and mail road toward California had been partly used to "greatly improve" the portion in the low mountain pass between Beaver Valley and Parowan Valley just farther south. The party passed through Cedar City before reaching Mountain Meadows, which meant they doubtless followed the new (Leach's) cutoff.[31]

At the meadows, the party caught and rode one of the army mules that Mowry's report had failed to acknowledge had been lost. The Mormons encountered the same numerous Indians along the Santa Clara as had the soldiers. Rich noted the church missionaries had recently constructed a house on tribal lands. The company made the numerous Virgin River crossings and the sandy approach to the Virgin Hill in good time and may have achieved what could be termed an easy climb up the dreaded slope, taking only forty minutes to get the entire group onto the mesa. At the Muddy, they welcomed Moapa Indians into camp, some spending the night, with no recorded negative incidents.

At Las Vegas, the Rich party met at least half of Mowry's detachment, still camped there. They also encountered the Sanford-Banning freight wagon train, discussed later, heading back the other direction to Utah. The Rich group did not camp at Cottonwood Springs but located two miles away, perhaps to avoid Indians in the night or perhaps to avoid a detour from the main wagon road if they had enough water reserves to bypass this water hole. The next morning, they reached Mountain Springs before noon and then pressed toward Kingston Springs until eleven o'clock at night. After but two hours rest, they moved on by moonlight. In the Kingston Wash area, the Mormons located good livestock feed and then took the animals two miles farther to water. Here Rich noted that the freighters they met at Las Vegas informed him they had found the body of a man named Thompson who had started over the route alone and been killed by Indians. In consequence of this, the small group "kept a strict guard" while around Kingston Springs. Other travelers later asserted that two people had been murdered at this time, but it is more likely they are combining the current death with reports of the man found dead by the Beale-Heap party near Stump Springs in the fall of 1853.

As so many had done before, the party left one wagon

on the desert near Silurian (dry) Lake, because the draft animals had become nearly exhausted. At that point Rich recorded, as noted earlier, "[W]e were about give out, both men and animals. The heat has been so intense that all had suffered in consequence, the very air seemed almost suffocating." He added, "[T]he rocks of the surrounding mountains and the sand reflected the heat with such intensity that if the air had been blown from heated ovens it seemed as if it could not have been more oppressive." They had no negative incidents at Bitter Springs and the lower Mojave, and soon thereafter they met several Mormons from San Bernardino who brought fresh draft animals and provisions—much needed and appreciated at that juncture. Before leaving the Mojave, they encountered a small group of Latter-day Saints heading for Utah, including Reuben McBride. The Rich party reached San Bernardino after just four weeks of travel, proving what could be done by a small company traveling light—even in the hot summer months.[32]

Earlier in the spring of 1855, the same Reuben McBride whom Rich met on the Mojave River had baptized a man named Nelson Paul Beebe into the LDS church at San Bernardino. Soon after, the new convert embarked for the Mormon Zion with a company of twenty-five fellow believers and fifteen wagons. This totally inexperienced traveler vividly described the beginning segment of the journey in Cajon Pass. Beebe confessed, "[T]his was all new to me to see the teams winding their way single fashion up the crooked road." When it was time to camp, Beebe observed the women cooking in Dutch ovens, producing what he judged the best meal he had ever tasted, eaten while sitting cross-legged near the fire. That night the beginner accepted assignment for several hours of guard duty. When he spread his blankets for bed at midnight, he thought briefly of "lizards, toads and bear, but weary and tired [he] soon fell asleep." Over the next few days, Beebe became a reasonably seasoned pioneer, although none of his subsequent diary entries appear particularly noteworthy except for a ten-year-old girl becoming ill, dying, and being buried at Resting Springs.[33]

Another small group traveling with the mail carriers, which must have left San Bernardino for Salt Lake City even earlier than Beebe, included John McDonald. Despite injury when a horse fell on him on the first day out of town, he remained determined to reach his mother, then alone in famine-wracked Salt Lake City. His reminiscences mention two white men murdered by Indians the night before he reached Kingston Springs. Although he may have been one of those who discovered Thompson's body, there is no real evidence of another man killed at that time, although clearly one had been shot on a more northerly stretch of the trail some two years previous. Later, on the Virgin River, the McDonald group found the Indians had barricaded the road in several places, perhaps to demand toll duties, but McDonald noted that the party finally passed by in safety.

OTHER EUROPEAN TRAVELERS AND MORE MORMONS

Another of the most valuable reports of travel over the Salt Lake City to Los Angeles wagon road was by experienced world traveler Jules Remy, a botany professor from Paris, France, accompanied by his friend, Julius Brenchley, an Englishman with a master of arts degree, in late October 1855. They started south on a "well-worn track" through Sanpete County, Utah, east of the usual road, but returned to the Southern Route near the crossing of the Sevier River. The river crossing proved extremely difficult for their wagon and mule team, not only because the bridge had not yet been replaced but also because the river current, mud, and steep banks required the utmost exertion by men and animals to cross.

Thereafter, the observers made important comments on the territorial capital at Fillmore, actually more detailed than all other travelers of the era combined. The residents, overestimated at eight hundred, enclosed their settlement within a quadrilateral wall of adobe, divided into quarters of ten acres each. The town enjoyed no church building, and all the adobe residences looked alike. Remy noted that the town's central location in the territory was its only reason for designation as the seat of government and that the federal officers who should have resided there actually lived in Salt Lake City, except when the territorial legislature sat in session. Remy and Brenchley did comment that the portion of the capitol building already completed was "very remarkable" for that vicinity's stage of development. While at Fill-

more, the travelers allowed the later-infamous federal territorial judge W. W. Drummond to sell them a horse, even though they well understood such animals were "inferior to the mule when . . . exposed to severe exertion for a long time and the poor and irregular food," which their animals would face on the trip.

As the group, including several personal servants, traveled southward, they encountered six inches of snow, which sometimes made the road difficult to follow. Although they obtained some corn from Ute Indians, Mormon settlers along the route were reluctant to offer them either provisions or lodging. Eventually, at Parowan, they learned about the scanty harvest that year and then understood that residents feared not having enough for their own families. The travelers did not attribute the treatment to "unkind feelings," although they considered the "great martinetship of the ecclesiastical officials" some distance from church headquarters to be a contributing factor.[34]

When the party reached the Santa Clara, they encountered a group of Southern Paiutes, clearly waiting for them at the roadside. The Indians wanted them to purchase beans, presented in deerskin sacks. The narrators described the winter dress of the women as a pair of rabbit skin drawers, badly sewn. They offered further description of the log hut built by the missionaries who occasionally visited, reportedly more to teach better farming techniques than anything else. When the travelers returned from a brief quail-hunting excursion, they found a far greater number of Native Americans gathering near their wagon, causing them to wonder if the intent was a friendly visit or pillage.

Apparently to intimidate the troublesome Indians, they staged a firearm target demonstration. The shots were well delivered so as to impress the Indians with a "high idea of [their] skill." But then the Paiutes held a similar demonstration of their own. The participants placed a target a hundred yards away and on a verbal signal, all shot their arrows. The observers conceded, "[N]ever had we seen such a collection of expert marksmen. Almost all the arrows, those of the children not excepted, hit the mark." They confessed that "this exhibition excited both our admiration and our alarm," although they wisely concealed the latter feeling. The Southern Paiutes had seldom been known as formidable warriors, but in fact they were clearly proficient in skills of offensive and defensive warfare. The European travelers also remained fully cognizant of the thieving tendencies of their hosts, although their company did not lose much property.

Moving along the road, the party experienced the usual difficulties with Utah Hill and the Virgin River. At the river three men traveling from the opposite direction offered to help them up a steep sand hill for a substantial quantity of sugar and coffee. The company did not feel it could spare the provisions. By transferring some of the load, including corn and oats for the animals, from the wagon to mule packs, they surmounted the obstacle on their own without undue difficulty. Still on the Virgin, they encountered Mormon leader Amasa Lyman and his company of seven wagons traveling toward Utah, with whom Remy and Brenchley had but little conversation before passing on. They also hailed two mail carriers with four mules heading toward Utah. Several days later, presumably after seeing his companion safely through Indian country, one of these men, Edward Hope, returned and requested permission to accompany them on their way back to southern California, which they were glad to grant.

At the Muddy River, they met a group of Southern Paiutes, including two chiefs who attested to being baptized Mormons. However, their demeanor appeared somewhat unsettling to the travelers. On Hope's recommendation, Remy and Brenchley offered the chiefs "a tolerably large supply of tobacco." The Indians, significantly, inquired of Hope if his companions were Mormon and were informed instead that they were "good Americans." Thus these European travelers too learned of the differentiation becoming common among the Southern Paiutes between Latter-day Saint church members and most other whites, who were generally considered "bad people." Remy concluded tellingly, "[I]t is this conviction that tends to make them ill disposed to emigrants." It could have been added that some non-Mormon travelers, although certainly not all, deserved the ill feeling harbored. The recently established Mormon outpost at Las Vegas, discussed later in this chapter, was rightly judged too limited in good soil to become a substantial settlement, but it was nevertheless recognized as a valuable stopping place for travelers.

At Cottonwood Springs, a single mail carrier from Salt Lake City, accompanied by five mounted emigrant companions and no wagons, came to their camp and spent the evening in conversation. Next day Remy and Brenchley had the luxury of switching from horse to mule teams for the pull up to Mountain Springs, which they accomplished with relative ease.[35]

As the company headed for Kingston Springs, an Indian began to follow them. Hope thought he recognized the man, from verbal descriptions, as the murderer of several Americans in the vicinity. Initially some in the group proposed to shoot him "without trial," thereby "purg[ing] the desert of a traitor and assassin." But after calmer reflection, the leaders recognized that despite appearances, they "had no right to condemn without proof." They later realized what a folly it would have been to have acted as executioner, not only because they might subsequently feel the pangs of conscience but also because they soon spotted many other Native Americans on the ridges above them "who would not have failed to avenge their brother" had the travelers fired on him. The chronicler offered no further information of importance concerning Kingston Springs, Bitter Springs, or the surrounding areas.

He did report a significant observation concerning the Mojave River vicinity, citing a German member of a U.S. government survey crew they encountered, probably Frank Lecouvreur, as authority for the observation that Indians no longer lived on the banks of that important desert waterway and thus it seemed unlikely any more would be seen on the trip. Remy and Brenchley remained at San Bernardino long enough to offer illuminating insights into life there. Their written report of the journey was soon published and probably found a larger reading audience than those by either Carvalho, who passed over the trail before them, or William Chandless, soon afterward.[36]

As previously mentioned, Amasa Lyman headed for Utah at the end of 1855. His itinerary displayed some interesting innovations stemming from his experience on repeated trips over the route. The group stopped ten miles beyond the Forks in the Road embarkation point from the Mojave River, where livestock feed grew particularly well, and rested there through the night, making the pull up Spanish Canyon in the cool of the following morning. After leaving Bitter Springs, the party passed several southbound groups driving livestock that, as always at that point, looked "rather poor." Near Salt Springs they encountered a terrible dust storm (few other emigrants ever complained about such storms, but they would have been frequent). On 3 November, the Lyman party apparently traveled a mile off the regular road to "the spring on Saleratus Creek," meaning the originating spring of Amargosa River's tributary Willow Creek, at present-day China Ranch. Lieutenant Mowry's soldiers had recently done likewise, and given the poor water elsewhere in the area it is amazing more pioneers did not avail themselves of this opportunity.

In the Cottonwood Springs vicinity, where the group spent an extra day, they met one small group of Mormons traveling south and another group of Gentiles at the Vegas heading in the same direction. Impressed with the layout and progress of the mission there (discussed later in this chapter), Lyman noted that the Native Americans appeared friendly and were working for food and clothing. At that point, the church leader commenced a practice he followed consistently thereafter, of engaging Indians to herd his livestock through the night, which they did to his satisfaction. Later, after doing the same in the Virgin River area, he confessed part of his motivation was that they did the work "for less than they would have expected of us if they had rendered [them] no service." He repeated this practice each night for a week with no losses. At the Utah settlements, the Mormon apostle, a popular speaker, naturally had to remain for the evening to preach to each congregation before moving on. He still made it to Salt Lake City in just over a month, obviously traveling some twenty miles per day. Lyman soon reported to Rich that on the trip they enjoyed good grass each day except at Bitter Springs and Salt Springs, although on the Santa Clara River they apparently had to go "some distance" from their campsites, presumably up a side canyon, to do so. He also reported satisfaction with having the Native Americans herd the livestock for "the few presents which [he] had for them."[37]

The last of the world travelers traversing the Salt Lake to Los Angeles road in this period was William Chandless, who passed over the road in late 1855 and early 1856. Naturally concerned about his safety, he could not have engaged a guide with better credentials for get-

ting him safely through Indian country than mail carrier David Savage. Probably the longest-serving Utah-based carrier, he had earned a high reputation all along the trail for his willingness to accommodate requests. Chandless commented that Savage had many of the "greatest beholden to him for some errand done or parcel brought." For this he and his companions were always offered the "best quarters" to stay in as they traveled along the corridor of settlements, although he noted that at least in winter they never slept in beds, but rolled out their own bedding in front of the fireplace. Chandless also noted "pastoral delicacies," meaning fine foods, "became more plentiful the farther south on the Utah road," where Savage may have been better known and more appreciated.

The trip through the Mormon settlements offers good insight into the situation there several years after the Wakara War. Chandless observed that although official town names had been established, such as Lehi and Nephi, the people still used the name of the creek on which the colony was planted, such as Dry Creek (Lehi) and Salt Creek (Nephi). The mail carrier faithfully visited each as he picked up and delivered letters and other items. When they arrived in Nephi at two o'clock in the morning and found the fort gate locked from the inside, Savage climbed the wall, tumbling into a snowdrift ditch on the other side. The town had reportedly been burned, including a good inn for travelers, and those accommodations had not yet been rebuilt. The former innkeeper still fed and housed the party adequately. Here Chandless learned that several travelers he had met at Salt Lake City had their feet frozen before they could reach this place. When the three-man company passed on its way, they were relieved to find an excellent bridge again spanning the Sevier River, but still had difficulty watering the mules from a hole chopped in the river ice. Traveling through the night they breakfasted at the fort-enclosed settlement of Cedar Springs, soon to be renamed Holden.

Then, without a real rest stop, they reached the territorial capital, Fillmore, featuring two inns, presumably for visiting government officials, and the already noted wing of the projected state capitol building. Brigham Young and many other dignitaries were there. Orson Pratt delivered the most impressive religious discourse the visitors heard. Plans for establishing a stagecoach line from Missouri through Salt Lake City to San Francisco was the chief subject of political conversation. After traveling on for thirty out of the next thirty-eight hours, they arrived at Parowan, again in the middle of the night, spending the remainder sleeping on the floor before a fire at the home of Savage's regular host. Next day the mail carrier was met by his notably attractive wife and several children at the fort gate at Cedar City, currently his home settlement.[38]

Here Savage discovered that his employer, James B. Leach, had sold his mail contract, so they were both consequently without a job. Nevertheless, within a few days they continued on toward California with another former Leach employee, making a total of five in the party. Savage aimed to purchase horses or mules in southern California and bring them back to Utah for sale at a higher price, one of the few profitable enterprises available during the winter months. He soon obtained reemployment by the new mail contractor. Within a year, Leach would be appointed superintendent of the El Paso, Texas, to Yuma, Arizona, wagon road, about to become part of the Butterfield stagecoach route. As they left Cedar City, they followed Leach's Cutoff, previously improved by the mail contractor. This route climbed the grade to the infant settlement of Pinto, joining the old road just a few miles from Mountain Meadows farther southwest on the Old Spanish Trail.

On leaving the last settlements in mid-January 1856, they inevitably encountered Native Americans on the Santa Clara River and beyond. Chandless's comments lend good insights into what were probably typical mail carrier practices toward the Indians. On the Virgin, Savage reportedly gave them "a great deal more" biscuits and potatoes than was warranted by their stock of provisions. The Englishman continued to complain of Savage's "hyperliberality" to the Native Americans, which generosity, he asserted, had exhausted most of their food supply. By the Mojave River the company had been reduced to one meal per day, consisting primarily of flour, which the traveler commented seemed less than desirable without proper adjuncts thereto. The journalist had earlier admitted he did not like Indians and asserted he knew of few others who did—doubtless the reason he was so critical of Savage, who on many occasions proved he really did like Native Americans. At the Muddy River,

they met the two chiefs who claimed to be Mormon. Chandless stated that although the Moapas used to be hostile, since their Mormon baptism they were friendly and "not ill mannered." Still the commentator expressed his low opinion of the Nuwuvi culture compared to the Crow and Cheyenne.

The scenery and solitude of Mountain Springs impressed Chandless, but he shared the typically uncomplimentary views that others expressed about the trail thereafter, through Kingston and Bitter Springs. Passing the latter place, the company mules strayed during feeding, and the other men searched for them in the night. This left Chandless alone in the wagon, worrying about the fact that not long before the Native Americans reportedly had killed a man near Kingston Springs. Although he kept his Colt revolver and Deane and Adams rifle "quite handy," he confessed that "the stillness was intense" until his companions returned. On completing the remainder of the journey, Chandless too offered important comments on Mormon San Bernardino. At that point he made the unique confession he had so enjoyed the journey as to be half sorry it was over. This avid traveler is the only person ever known to have expressed such sentiments after coming over the Southern Route.[39]

In fall 1856, Hans Peter Emanuel Hoth, a Mormon convert (from Schleswig, a province that had often been part of Denmark but would soon be annexed into the growing German empire), had become disenchanted with life in Utah and decided to emigrate to California over the Southern Route. He, his son, and an unnamed Danish man in a similar situation circumspectly left Salt Lake City, traveling over side roads while many Latter-day Saints were at church services. Some who knew them later encountered the group on the road but were not informed of their real intentions. When they had traveled some fifty miles, two horsemen stopped them to inquire if the Dane had paid his debt. This debt was perhaps to the Mormon church Perpetual Emigration Fund, which brought many Europeans to America, repayment of which remained such a person's first obligation in Mormondom. Detained briefly, the Dane escaped and returned to his traveling companions.

By the time the travelers reached Nephi, they had joined a larger party of emigrants, which since it included Hoth's daughter, Doris, and another married daughter, her husband and their children, must have been a pre-planned reunion, perhaps intended to occur beyond the area thought dangerous for escaping ex-Mormons. But at precisely that juncture two riders from Salt Lake City approached and demanded that Hoth and the Dane return with them presumably to answer charges of apostasy. They refused, argued some, and then, backed by their traveling companions, who intervened with pistols and sticks, convinced the would-be captors to abandon their purpose and flee for safety.[40]

At Cedar City, Utah, the company decided to expel an American woman who had proved a constant cause of conflict, leaving her with her baggage, amid protests from local authorities. Hoth also quarreled with the man he had engaged to carry him and his two children. They first contemplated remaining in Cedar City for the winter but soon began to seek an outfit with which to travel onward. However, this proved difficult, because when Latter-day Saints recognized one of their own attempting to abandon the faith, they allegedly felt pressure not to cooperate with such people. Hoth ascertained that although it "was strictly forbidden for the rest to sell anything to anybody that wanted to go to California," some Mormons "cared more for money" than for the "commands of their superiors." Thus Mormon citizens came to the travelers under cover of darkness and offered provisions, albeit at a high price.

Hoth's comments on the attitudes and situation at this southernmost Mormon town—closest to the scene of the Mountain Meadows Massacre in the ensuing year—are important contemporary insights, although naturally biased. He noted that the need to pay double what goods were usually worth naturally followed from the mandate from church leaders to, as Hoth recounted, "suppress and persecute all Gentiles, whenever there is an opportunity to do so." And this certainly included those withdrawing from the church as well as those never a part of it. The lapsed Mormon continued to observe that "love of others is unknown to them, and they only practice it on a small scale among themselves." On completing the purchase of a wagon and ox team—during which Hoth complained, "[E]very one I dealt with sought to cheat me"—his family prepared to leave with eight other wagons that he mentioned also contained apostate Mormons moving to California. That night sev-

eral people attempted to steal the oxen, as the son discovered just in time, overtaking one of the thieves and giving him a "thorough beating across the back." The next day they got away from what the diarist termed "this devilish place," taking the Leach Cutoff.[41]

Like most other emigrants, Hoth's party did not rest comfortably in the known Indian country along the Santa Clara River. Their fears proved well founded when a party of forty armed Native Americans rushed toward them with much whooping and general noise. The Southern Paiutes demanded clothing, and each company member offered them some. But the Indians insisted on more, forcibly stripping the men of all their outer clothing, and even taking more when some men tried to put on other pants and shirts. The antagonists also required and obtained gunpowder and blankets. The emigrants drove on in their underwear, glad to have saved their provisions, livestock, and lives. A similar proceeding recurred at the Muddy River, where they were surrounded by about sixty Moapa men, women, and children demanding provisions, clothes, and two cows. The emigrants resisted and offered what they thought they could spare. But the Native Americans clearly disagreed and drove off ten cows. When the chief appeared, the besieged travelers offered him a pistol, some gunpowder, and two knives, after which the cattle were returned. Thereupon the pioneers quickly set out on their next desert *jornada*, unprepared though they were.

The remainder of the trip was uneventful, except for an amazingly friendly encounter with the Las Vegas—area Indians, including participating with them in celebrating a "war festival." At journey's end the group rested temporarily at San Bernardino. There they sought financial assistance from the German-Jewish merchants of the settlement rather than from members of the dominant (Mormon) church. Thereafter they moved completely away from any Mormon influence.[42]

COMPARING EMIGRANT TRAILS

With the last of the known 1856 companies completing their journey, what could be termed the middle phase of emigration over the Southern Route to California essentially came to a close. Never again as much used as in the first three years of 1849–51, the trail had still seen substantial traffic each year. Mormon San Bernardino reached its peak of over three thousand people, almost all of whom had traveled at least once over the route. A reasonable estimate is that the Mormons accounted for about a third of all who used the wagon roadway during the initial eight years. Considering the lack of major problems with Indians and the absence of any reported disease—in comparison with a relative abundance of both on other routes—clearly it was unfortunate the passageway was not more frequently used by travelers heading for the Pacific Coast. It was particularly unfortunate for Latter-day Saints, whose leaders almost adopted the route as the primary entryway for up to twenty-five thousand additional souls. Naturally a few deaths stemmed from illness along the Southern Route, as there would have been among any group at the time even when not traveling, but the total number mentioned from all causes in the considerable documentation related to this roadway totals less than twenty-five, including ten Native Americans.

As John D. Unruh Jr., the fine historian of the Oregon–northern California routes, concluded, recollections by Overland Trail emigration veterans of deaths from Indian attack became grossly overstated. He endeavored to establish a more accurate death rate based on the somewhat sketchy and sometimes contradictory documentary evidence. He concluded that 1852 emigrant Charles Moore's 1904 total of 800 deaths, offered in a speech at a meeting of the Oregon Pioneer Association, was more than twice too large. According to Unruh's best assessment, deaths to emigrants from Indian attack on the main overland trails between 1848 and 1860 totaled 330, with Native Americans suffering at least 432 deaths at emigrant hands in the same period.[43] This is certainly a different view from the general image conveyed by popular literature, movies, and television.

Although no agency gathered valid mortality figures on the northern overland trail, one contemporary, Sarah Wisner, calculated that between 1842 and 1859, 30,000 people died on the plains trails. Some observers claimed that during the Gold Rush era there was an average of a grave every 200 feet on the Platt River portion of the route. A more conservative figure for the entire length of the Oregon-California Trail was 20,000 deaths in 2,000

miles, or an average of ten graves to each mile. Assuming just over a third of a million people traveled by that route, the average was thus one death for every seventeen persons who embarked on the journey. While there were many fatalities from accidents, particularly gunshot and drownings, most deaths resulted from disease and illness. Although emigrants suffered and died from the same gamut of contagious diseases that afflicted their contemporaries, all these paled to insignificance compared to the greatest killer, Asiatic cholera.

This cholera plague proved particularly virulent during several peak years of the Gold Rush and Mormon emigrations. In 1849, most cholera victims died on the Mississippi and Missouri rivers, aboard steamboats, and along the river bottom trails. An observer named McCollum was quoted by Platte River Road historian Merrill J. Mattes as saying, "[T]he road from Independence [Missouri] to Fort Laramie [was] a graveyard." McCollum estimated the number of burials as between 1500 and 2000, which Mattes calculates would make an overall mortality rate of 6 percent. Some large wagon trains lost two thirds of their members, and some wagons were abandoned because all of the owning family had succumbed. Although there were fewer emigrants, the following year, 1850, was almost equally costly, with contemporary estimates ranging from 1000 to 5000 deaths. If an average figure between these extremes is accepted, that would make four graves per mile all the way to Laramie, offering full credence to the contemporary assertion of Abraham Sortore that along the Platte Route he was "scarcely out of sight of grave diggers." In 1851 cholera casualties were mercifully light, but the following year the plague resumed its rampant toll. Ezra Meeker noted that some of the South Platte Trail resembled a battlefield, with the dead lying at times "in rows of fifties or more." Although cholera persisted throughout the decade of the 1850s, the trail epidemic passed its peak by 1853. It had certainly cast a terrible pall over the entire overland emigrant experience. The decimation wreaked by the cholera epidemic, along with the more ordinary disease and accidental deaths, transformed the northern trail to California into what Mattes correctly stated "took on the resemblance of an elongated cemetery." However, no part of the southern branch of the Pacific highway heading toward Los Angeles and the Pacific was anything close to that deadly.

Resting Springs appears to have had some half-dozen emigrant graves during this period, approximately a third of the total for the entire route.[44] The route was clearly more healthful because of the lack of swamps and rivers.

These crucial years after the initiation of the southern emigrant route remained significant for the relatively large volume of traffic traveling that way during portions of the year when land travel to California was otherwise generally impossible because of snow in the Sierra. Native American hostilities, mainly with Apaches, largely precluded use of trails across Arizona, although a few emigrants came that way as well.[45] Southern Paiutes along the road to southern California persisted in their efforts to profit from the passing travelers, but their behavior seldom included loss of human life. Equally important at that juncture loomed the growing friendship between Mormons and Native Americans along the Southern Route.

THE LAS VEGAS MISSION

At the April 1855 Conference of the Church of Jesus Christ of Latter-day Saints, as missionaries received calls to preach the Mormon gospel to many nations of the world, the church leaders designated several new groups to go among Native Americans of the Great Basin, including thirty men to establish a mission at Las Vegas. If locating amid the largest concentration of Paiutes in the region had been the prime motive, either the Moapas along the Muddy River or the Tonequints along the Santa Clara, with whom other church missionaries had already commenced such efforts, would have been a better choice, partly because better agricultural potential existed in both those locations. On learning the destination of missionaries passing along the Santa Clara River, some Indians chided that the Las Vegas mission location seemed too hot for comfort part of the year and the missionaries should remain with them.[46]

Obviously, one of President Brigham Young's main objectives was to establish something of a way station approximately halfway between San Bernardino and the southern Utah settlements. He had mentioned that goal to Amasa Lyman and Charles L. Rich when they were first assigned to plant a colony in southern California in 1851, but perhaps because they better understood the thieving tendencies of the Las Vegas and other bands of Paiutes, they had not complied with that assignment. Although that particular objective was not mentioned in 1855, the impetus for the mission project still came from church headquarters, where that aim had been harbored most firmly.

A major aspect of the Las Vegas assignment was to promote whatever degree of economic self-sufficiency was possible for Native Americans in that area. As elsewhere, this would be primarily cultivating crops as an example to the Paiutes and helping them master more advanced agricultural techniques. The people who called themselves Nuwuvi repeatedly expressed desire to generate a more adequate food supply than any of their cultivated fields currently produced. Another purpose of the mission clearly was to gain friendship and support from Native Americans, who had been mistreated by some passing government and emigrant trains and sometimes almost came to regard "every man who wore a white skin as their enemy." Cedar City stake (diocese) leader Isaac C. Haight enunciated a related purpose: to prevent the Native Americans "from committing hostilities, both upon the mail and upon Americans," including killing the cattle and horses of the travelers. Ironically, this local ecclesiastic later functioned as a key participant in the decision to violate this policy at Mountain Meadows, resulting in the massacre there. The mission temporarily improved the safety of those passing over the trail, as well as provided people at hand who could intervene in the Indians' behalf in case of misunderstanding. As the missionaries left for their assignment, they were charged with setting an example of sobriety and industry for their "Lamanite" brethren.[47]

After considering several possible locations, mission head William Bringhurst selected a site where the Vegas Creek coursed down a gentle slope several miles east of the main springs. Here the Mormons built an adobe fort 150 feet square, with garden plots closest in and larger fields on the lower flatland, both accessible to irrigation by the stream. There is evidence Native Americans had previously cultivated land along the creek and near several of the springs in the area. But the agricultural tradition had probably not been as extensively established at Las Vegas as at Santa Clara, Moapa, or Indian Springs

William Bringhurst, chosen head of the Las Vegas Native American Mission, although he was probably not sufficiently flexible to balance the several demands of the position successfully.

George Washington Bean, a Latter-day Saint missionary to the Las Vegas and other Indians, who came closer to mastering their language than any other missionary.

some forty miles to the northwest. Among the initial matters of business was assembling some of the chiefs from throughout the area and entering an agreement granting permission to make a settlement on their lands. The Mormons promised to treat the Native Americans well, with the Indians making a similar reciprocal agreement.[48]

Some missionaries immediately recognized that because of sand and alkali-impregnated soil, the amount of land well suited for cultivation would be limited at best. The better-drained garden plots had more production potential than the lower five-acre plots assigned to individual missionaries primarily for wheat and corn. John Steele saw his crops "come up beautifully," but despite his exertions to bring to maturity what he had planted, "saleratus killed it." Neither Steele, Lorenzo Brown, nor mission counselor William Covert believed that the grain and other crops raised the first season were sufficient to maintain operation until the ensuing harvest. Missionary

Lorenzo Brown later lamented, "[T]he land is filled with saleratus. To all appearance there will not be one half enough grain to support the mission. Things look rather disheartning [sic]." Bringhurst remained more optimistic about the grain supply. The difference of opinion probably centered on how much could be shared with the Indians.[49]

This may well have been one of the greatest failings of the several contemporary Mormon Indian mission undertakings—the inability to properly reward Native Americans demonstrably willing to do whatever the missionaries required of them.[50] During any other period, an Indian mission with as much prospect for success as the Las Vegas venture would likely have received necessary assistance from church headquarters. However, in 1855 and 1856 Utah citizens experienced serious famine and hunger—a fact Brigham Young and his supporters preferred to remain relatively unknown, both at that time and later. Ravages of drought, grasshoppers, and crickets helped cause food shortages that had motivated some Mormon emigrants then passing through Las Vegas to flee Utah to avoid hunger. Individual missionaries also seemed hard-pressed to continue their dedicated efforts when reports arrived that their families were destitute and the local bishops, with responsibility for supporting the families of missionaries, had few resources with which to accomplish that assignment.

Meanwhile, the Indians demonstrated their desire and ability to work as farmers, willing to labor hard all day for two squash—which became essentially the main means of exchange among the Native American laborers. Yet with so little land yet in production, the Paiutes had insufficient opportunity for meaningful employment. George W. Bean, probably the missionary closest to the Nuwuvi, spoke to the Las Vegas congregation in July 1856, expressing regret that "they did not have sufficient provisions and grain to deal out to the Indians and put them to labor as many of them desired." Others agreed with him, including President Bringhurst, who added that "if he only had food to deal out to them, he would have fifty of them at work at the present time." John Steele had already confessed to Mormon general church authority George A. Smith that the grain would not "hold up" because the Native Americans were so "uncommonly friendly" it was "impossible to refrain from giving some of it to them." And most tellingly of all, Bean had earlier communicated to Smith that "if we only had plenty to feed [the Southern Paiutes] for their labor, we could govern and control them to the very letter."

The missionaries initially boasted of no known pilfering by the Indians, but it was only a matter of time before items, including grain and vegetables, began disappearing in the night. In the first autumn of the mission, counselor William Covert asked one of the more effective interpreters, James T. S. Allred, to preach to the local Indians, warning them they must abandon the practices of "lying and stealing and learn to be honest and industrious." Bringhurst attempted to work through the Indian leadership structure to discipline offenders as he tried to alleviate the situation. There was clearly a difference of opinion as to how serious an offense stealing was, and the chiefs were often hesitant to punish offenders physically. Yet Native American leaders also desired continued cordial relations with the missionaries

and strove to accommodate them as much as possible. Brigham Young too admonished the Mormons to be patient and essentially lenient with their charges, and few instances of corporal punishment actually occurred at Las Vegas. More often scolding by the chiefs and banishing individual offenders from the fort premises for an extended period served as punishments.

Part of the stealing problem throughout the era stemmed from the fact that most Native Americans doubtless believed they were entitled to share the goods of people who essentially trespassed on their domain. Even one of the chiefs narrowly missed getting caught at such stealing. The greater problems persisted: Resources were simply not sufficient for everyone, and the Indians remained grossly deficient in food supply. On several occasions the chiefs protested they could not restrain stealing—or punish it when their people were on the verge of starvation. This proved correct. An almost inherent promise and essential obligation of any mission should have been to alleviate such conditions.

During the winter before the second growing season, President Bringhurst and others located a separate Indian farm on a "little stream two miles north of the fort," probably at what was later called Keil Ranch. In late March, Chief Toshearump and other Indians returned from the mountains "for the purpose of farming." The missionaries gathered teams and plowed the Indian fields, reporting their Native American associates "much pleased" with the prospects. They were "anxious to raise their provisions instead of hunting, etc." The latter food-procuring methods had not recently been effective because they were "poor and hungry at that time," apparently their usual state. Steele had earlier observed to Apostle George A. Smith that he "did not blame the Indians for stealing anything to eat," because the only thing he could see the barren country offering them was mesquite and lizards.[51] Yet without a larger water source for irrigation, this location was bound to eventually prove a disappointment.

Although the missionaries spent part of their time learning the Paiute language and sometimes working with Native Americans in the fields, as elsewhere, they appeared to do little actual proselytizing among them. They sometimes invited the Southern Paiutes to attend the regular worship services held within the fort. The

Indians were noted to be "interested and anxious to understand the nature of the proceedings." Brigham Young instructed that should some express desire to be baptized, it would be permissible to usher them into formal church membership without complete knowledge, since Young noted that according to church teachings all could better understand spiritual matters by having conferred on them the right to the constant companionship of the Holy Ghost, to which only full-fledged Latter-day Saints were supposedly entitled. By the first winter, many Indians expressed willingness to become church members. Bringhurst meanwhile departed on a six-week trip to San Bernardino to obtain mules, ordering that no baptisms should take place until he returned. This delay caused difficulty with some impatient Indians, one missionary complaining, "[I]t is all we can do to obey orders." Finally on a Sabbath in early November 1856, seventy Southern Paiutes gathered. George W. Bean, the best missionary interpreter, explained as best he could the nature of the obligation the applicants undertook. The Paiutes listened with great attention. Fifty-six individuals promised to "set aside evil practices" and were baptized, with at least another hundred doing likewise sometime thereafter.

Although William Bringhurst occasionally appeared overly arbitrary, his leadership of the mission seemed more than adequate. He had a genuine commitment to assisting the Indians and to keeping the men he was charged to lead focused on their duties. On several occasions, he summoned before him men who had proved overly critical or unproductive, chastised them, and elicited promises from them to do better in the future. John Steele candidly confessed just months after the initial planting of the mission that Brother William L. Covert, chosen first counselor, was "a great deal better liked as a president than Bro. William Bringhurst." Yet the man designated to head the mission generally proved an acceptable leader and might have succeeded in his assignment had he been given clearer written directives by the highest church authorities.[52]

The Las Vegas Mission served as an important stopping place for a variety of travelers passing through in 1855 and 1856, including Lieutenant Mowry's soldiers and European travelers Remy, Brenchly, and Chandless. Most frequent and appreciated of these were the regular mail carriers. This postal service stood as the missionar-

ies' only real contact with their loved ones in Deseret-Utah. In mid-August 1855, when David Savage arrived with mail from California, the mission record reported that President Bringhurst "prepared the mail from the camp," which consisted of checking the postage on some sixty letters being sent to Utah. Three days later, the southbound post brought a similar amount of mail to the missionaries. Obviously the Vegas residents continued sending and receiving letters by way of San Francisco as well, because they were equally engaged in letter writing before the southbound mail left for San Bernardino and beyond. At the end of the first year, official papers arrived establishing a post office at Las Vegas, which simply meant that a designated person possessed a key to the mail sacks, instead of the carriers contriving some other means of sending and receiving mail from there. Not long thereafter, a near crisis occurred when William Vance, a "new hand at the business," broke the mail key before he opened the leather bag, but with "some difficulty" they obtained their mail.

On his initial trip to the mission John Steele recognized what he considered a natural spot for a well on the edge of the dry lake midway between the Muddy River and the Vegas. Mail contractor James Leach offered a hundred dollars to assist the effort to dig the well, with two of his mail carriers, Leonard Conger and Edward Hope, each offering $20 for that purpose. However, though attempted, such a remedy to the dreaded *jornada* never came to fruition, at least in the pioneering era. Steele noted in 1855 that he found the main California road, presumably in Utah, "in many places is greatly improved" since he had last traversed it in 1853. This was accomplished through the congressional appropriation for a mail and military road.[53]

Less than a year into the Las Vegas mission venture, John Steele organized a party to investigate reports of nearby lead deposits. Within a month of that investigation, Nathaniel V. Jones, who had previous ore-milling experience, was dispatched to the settlement specifically designated to head up a lead-mining and processing operation. Neither Jones nor Steele was impressed with the first mine location, but an Indian named Colorado informed Steele of another lead-bearing formation not far from the California emigrant road. This proved to be a promising location. But President Bringhurst unfortunately did not consider the letter Jones brought from

Brigham Young clear enough to relinquish mission men and supplies for mining purposes. With hindsight, the highest church authority could well have worded his instructions more strongly or even better, sent the requisite supplies, which the mission could hardly spare. As it was, the frustrated Jones, without much assistance, investigated and determined that local resources were inadequate for construction of a smelting works. Thus in September 1856, he left for Salt Lake City. After verbal reports to Brigham Young of Bringhurst's lack of cooperation, the latter's dismissal became automatic. Jones returned to Las Vegas with documents not just replacing Bringhurst with original missionary Samuel Thompson as head of the mission, but disfellowshipping the former mission president for unnamed offenses clearly relating to failure to properly back the mining venture.[54]

Equipped with a horse-powered bellows, furnace and hearth components, and other lead-refining apparatus from Utah, Jones erected a furnace of adobe and fire brick and by Christmas had the mining and milling process fully operational. A crew set about cutting wood for charcoal. The mineral deposit, situated about four miles from the emigrant road near Mountain Springs, the site of the later Potosi mining camp, lay several rods wide and up to four feet thick. The vein outcrop loomed high on the mountain slope, inaccessible until construction of a footpath almost half a mile long, first used by Indian ore packers, then mules. The furnace processed some nine thousand pounds of ore in the first season, with a yield of 20 to 30 percent lead. Some asserted that the sulfur content caused some of the molten metal to burn in the smelting process, netting a disappointingly low yield. One of the experienced smelter operators, Isaac Grundy, attributed part of the problem to the presence of a considerable proportion of silver, which later proved true. Although some deemed it more costly to operate the furnace than the product might be worth, the enterprise continued, partly to fulfill the demand for lead in Mormondom. And perhaps mainly because of the mine, the mission effort persisted as well, albeit with a smaller staff of missionaries.[55]

Nathaniel Jones wrote from the lead mines to Brigham Young in September 1856 to complain that the mission appeared unable to supply the provisions needed for his crew. The church leader instructed him to secure what he needed at Cedar City, hauling lead there on his

upward trips. Although Jones showed inclination to lay out a supposedly better wagon road, Young urged him for the present to stick to producing more lead. A few weeks later, President Young, writing to missionary Miles Anderson, revealed his regard for the mining operation when he stated that "if the finding of the immense lead mine was the only good resulting from the [Las Vegas] mission, it would amply justify all that has been done."[56]

Yet Brigham Young added that the "good influence" that continued to be exerted among the area Native Americans stood as another notable accomplishment of the mission. In early October 1856, the church president sent a letter addressed directly to the Las Vegas Indians. He assured them that if they did not understand anything—presumably about policies of the missionaries close at hand—he offered permission to send someone to see his chief Indian interpreter, Dimick B. Huntington or to directly visit him (Young). He pledged that they would mutually arrive at solutions and understanding of whatever the issue.[57] This appears to be a response to Paiute complaints about local missionaries, but no further details have been found.

At the beginning of 1857, Brigham Young continued to be anxious to support Jones's lead production. He requested Cedar City bishop Phillip Klingensmith, another later participant in the Mountain Meadows Massacre, to send some men and cattle to bolster the mining operation. He also informed new Las Vegas mission leader Samuel Thompson that he hoped they could raise sufficient produce for themselves and "some to spare to Bro. Jones" so he wouldn't have to send all the way to Utah for needed provisions. President Young commended the missionary approach of meeting the Paiutes in their own wickiups and expressed hope the Mormons could "conciliate the Indians and protect the stock," presumably their own and those of the miners.

Unfortunately, just as Thompson received this communication, he sent one to Young reporting "uneasy feelings" among the Las Vegas Native Americans toward the Mormon mission. For this reason the church leader quickly relayed permission for those assigned there "to leave the Las Vegas Fort to solitude and the Indians." He hoped they could explain their departure in a manner that might generate some regret among the Paiutes, expressly so that at some later time another attempt at missionary work might be undertaken. Young tellingly observed that because the mission post appeared unable to sustain the personnel assigned there, it "became an expense to the Kingdom," and, alluding to the adopted beehive symbol of Mormondom, the venture "at present seems not to add any honey to the hive." A permanent mission clearly did not then appear to be of primary importance. In a sense this seems a heartless act—after raising Indian hopes and implying promises of a continued presence and assistance—then closing the mission precipitately and semipermanently. The mining operation was terminated at the same time, although it may have been briefly revived the next year. Thompson offered some supplies to the Indians as his men withdrew and reported to Brigham Young that some Native Americans regretted their leaving. He stressed that the Paiutes "understood it is partly their actions that caused the mission disbandment."[58] When Apostle Amasa Lyman passed Las Vegas some five months later, he discovered the fort to be "a desolation." He concluded the entire mission demise to be "a sad monument of the folly of poor, short-sighted, selfish men who [could] sacrifice the interests of a Kingdom and people on the altar of personal selfishness."[59]

Later, in the crisis following the Mountain Meadows Massacre, missionaries were temporarily reassigned to reside among the Indians at the Muddy River and Las Vegas. But in late September 1858, the Latter-day Saint mission leaders then centered at Santa Clara, in the Utah Territory, decided to again disband the Las Vegas and Muddy Missions, at least for the near future. The specific reason offered again focused on "the thieving disposition of the Indians at these places." The report continued that although some Indians there admittedly demonstrated willingness to work, most "would steal everything they could get their eyes upon and the chiefs had no control over them." Yet as argued previously, the fault was more directly the failure to provide the promised farm produce, a main purpose of the mission. Adequate crop production may have been impossible at the Las Vegas location. If a successful agricultural mission was the primary purpose, church leaders would have been far better served if they had more carefully selected a location, perhaps choosing the Moapa Valley along the lower Muddy River, where Latter-day Saint and other farmers later proved notably successful.[60]

MORMON OUTER CORRIDOR— NEVER MATERIALIZED

Closing the Las Vegas mission signaled the final demise of any plan for assisting Mormon emigrants over the Southern Route from California to Utah. That had never been a stated purpose of the mission, but it had been

Portion of the Las Vegas Fort–residential area was doubtless also later used by the Gass Ranch operation and others. Some of the structure still stands amid other buildings recently constructed, ca. early 1900s.

COURTESY LDS CHURCH ARCHIVES, SALT LAKE CITY, UTAH

discussed during the time San Bernardino became established earlier in the decade. Although no doubt exists about the early hopes of Brigham Young and his associates to establish a series of way stations between the Pacific Coast and their burgeoning Zion, those hopes waned too quickly. Like other outermost posts of the initially projected Mormon empire, as Mormon historian Eugene E. Campbell has concluded, the entire scheme appeared "executed in a haphazard manner, and abandoned without the usual heroic effort that characterized Mormon enterprise." Campbell's analysis of relevant documents reveals no systematic plan to maintain any semblance of an "outer cordon." That conclusion is certainly borne out by my recent study of Mormon San Bernardino. In light of President Young's persistent negative feeling toward California in general and San Bernardino in particular, as demonstrated by critical statements by the church leader every year of its existence, the author (Lyman) has no doubt that by the mid-1850s all serious considerations involving a corridor of Mormon settlements to the Pacific Coast had been abandoned.[61]

Because of the tremendous transportation demands of the California Gold Rush, a railroad was completed across the Isthmus of Panama in 1855. Reliable steamship transportation did not always await passengers on the Pacific Coast side to take them to California, but if connections properly coincided, a traveler could get from New York City to San Francisco in five weeks, at a much smaller expense than traveling by covered wagon across the plains.[62] And President Young's original view of San Diego being the best southern California seaport proved entirely valid. With a nucleus of Mormon settlers there as well as at the major stronghold at San Bernardino, the potential to develop the original way station concept remained entirely favorable.

In the summer of 1856, numerous enthusiastic Mormon emigrants gathered at Iowa City, Iowa, to make the handcart trek to Salt Lake Valley. Many proved successful in this, but the companies of James G. Willie and Edward Martin, compelled to wait for their handcarts to be finished, did not begin the trip until late July. Some knowledgeable and experienced travelers advised them to delay departure until the next season, but their eagerness to gather to Zion and perhaps some assurance of divine protection for the faithful induced them to take the

chance. Early winter snowstorms in Wyoming caused almost unbelievable hardship and suffering, with more than two hundred losing their lives and countless others, the use of limbs. It remains the worst tragedy—so far as actual death rate—in the history of American overland emigration.[63]

If the all-season route from California had been in use—as it would have been if the matter had been properly pursued—this tragedy along with a vast number of other lives lost to the continuing cholera epidemic might well have been averted. The almost fatality-free Southern Route was used by a relatively few Mormon converts from Australia and the South Pacific, with some who elected to travel that way later choosing instead to remain in the southern California Mormon colony. The roadway continued to be much more heavily used by southbound emigrants, including an increasing number apparently abandoning Brigham Young's strictly ruled empire. Perhaps that was a reason for him changing his mind about improving the route through convenient way stations. Still, not more fully utilizing the all-season, disease-free Southern Route stands as a major failing that must be at least partially attributed to the highest church leaders, including Brigham Young, who accepted no responsibility for the handcart disaster. The very idea of an "outer cordon" offers too much credit for planning and foresight, which were never actually present among the Mormon hierarchy, who perhaps generally have been too highly praised as great colonizers.[64]

Continuing to be an effective alternative route to California, the road from Utah to Los Angeles was temporarily improved through the establishment of an important way station at Las Vegas. The genuine missionary concern for uplifting the Lamanites—the Indians—spiritually and temporally had been demonstrated, although the southern Nevada mission succumbed essentially from lack of productivity, poor leadership, and insufficient support from church headquarters. Another purpose for this station remained the less enlightened motive of the Mormons for cementing relations with Native Americans along the crucial central portion of the trail, perhaps to help them close that route to outside traffic. Several travelers passing through the region during this era noted with apprehension the burgeoning alliance and its negative implications for non–Latter-day Saint citizens.

Chapter Six

Conflict with the
Federal Government—and Tragedy

There is no denying the magnitude of the tragedy of the Mountain Meadows Massacre, unquestionably the most important event in the history of the southern transportation route to California. That horrible affair has been debated and analyzed for over one hundred forty years. Yet nothing more effectively illuminates many of these events than the chain of circumstances developing along the trail through southern Utah that converged to make this monstrous mass murder almost inevitable. Unfortunately, the Latter-day Saints leaders, and many of their people during this crisis period, regarded as enemies almost all non–Mormon American citizens residing beyond their intermontane realm.

The fateful mixture of circumstances culminating in the massacre includes the Mormons' cordial relationship with virtually all the region's Native Americans, which by the time of the massacre was a literal military alliance. The fanatic religious fervor that the Mormon Reformation generated in the last half of the previous year, 1856,

continued to resonate strongly through the southern Utah settlements. Equally important, just a few months before the mass killings, the residents of Mormondom discovered that a large contingent of the United States Army had been dispatched in their direction. Some Mormons believed the soldiers were being mobilized to forcibly impose the much hated will of outsiders on the region, and others suspected that should the soldiers actually enter Utah, even more drastic punishments were inevitable against the Mormon leaders. Furthermore, several companies of emigrants, including some from hated Missouri and others from Arkansas, now entered the region wracked by the brewing fanaticism. The latter were from a state where the citizen image had recently been tarnished by the murder there of one of the most popular Latter-day Saint apostles, Parley P. Pratt. Perhaps the most difficult aspect for a modern reader to fathom or empathize with is the Mormons' unbelievably bitter resentments over events of the preceding two

decades in Missouri and Illinois and their fervent desire—even sense of religious obligation—to exact revenge. These elements will be discussed here in more
detail than a better understood historic episode would
merit, so that a modern reader can appreciate the com-
plexity of these circumstances along the subject trail.

VALUED ALLIANCE

Even before any hints that the Las Vegas mission would
end, Brigham Young asked the missionaries to become
acquainted with the chiefs and principal men of all the
Indian bands in the region. Mojaves from the Colorado
River and Indians from several days' journey north and
west in Nevada, presumably Northern Paiutes, had visited at the mission, expressing friendship and interest in
further association with the Mormons. Church leaders
fully encouraged this relationship. Some missionaries
continued to appreciate the secular benefit of this relationship. John Steele, head of the Las Vegas mission militia unit, significantly mentioned in a letter to Apostle
George A. Smith that if Providence blessed their efforts
with the success they were striving for, "[W]e can have
1000 brave warriors on hand in a short time to help quell
the eruption that might take place in the principalities."[1]
Relationships with federal officials were already deteriorating, and as noted in the previous chapter, some Mormons had long recognized and spoken of Native Americans as "battle axes of the Lord," who could be brought
into a military action by Mormons, who had firmly established a reputation for friendship toward Indians. As
noted, many Indians along the Southern Route had long
since begun to differentiate between "Mormonees" and
"Mericats," with positive and negative connotations, re-
spectively. The Indian alliance being now virtually assured, many Mormons awaited the proper moment to retaliate for past "Mericat" injustice to Latter-day Saints.

CULTURE OF VIOLENCE

Perhaps the factor most crucial to understanding the
tragic events of this period along the Southern Route and
throughout Mormondom was the fervent belief among

Latter-day Saints at the time in the efficacy of violent
punishment for sinners and for enemies of God's faithful.
This tenet of doctrine can only be understood by review-
ing the horrible history of mob violence against the
Saints in Missouri and Illinois in the 1830s and 1840s.[2] An
associated aspect was the Mormons' marked awareness
that the federal government had been unwilling to protect the persecuted Mormon citizens. Because they had
inherited this legacy of suffering and injustice and because they knew the founding Mormon prophet, Joseph
Smith, had condoned some organized retaliation against
known enemies back in the Midwest, Mormon leaders in
the far west of Deseret-Utah acted similarly.

Bolstered by doctrinally based sermons stressing punishment for those who acted in ways not approved by
church leaders, Mormons developed what D. Michael
Quinn, a leading historian of the church hierarchy, has
called "a culture of violence." He states, "L.D.S. leaders
publicly and privately encouraged Mormons to consider
it their religious right to kill antagonistic outsiders, common criminals, L.D.S. apostates and even faithful Mormons who committed sins 'worthy of death.'" Equally
significant was that although the sometimes-drastic punishments meted out in keeping with such preachings and
doctrines often occurred without prior approval of the
church general authorities, it is relatively clear that they
condoned almost all such actions after the fact.[3] Eventually a few scapegoats might be chastised for these ex-
cesses, but there is no real record of Mormon church
leaders punishing religious fanaticism.

This vengefulness cannot be rationalized by arguing
that the American frontier was an inherently lawless
environment, because the Mormon settlements had
promptly established an orderly system of government.
Although many church members then and later lamented
the violence, it was part of the heritage of the church in
its initial half-century, and this fact does much to illumi-
nate the (to a modern reader) perplexing developments
discussed herein. Doubtless the approach of federal
troops exacerbated the beliefs and actions of the period.
Certainly this culture of violence and revenge explains
some aspects of the hatred and fanaticism that were visible in southern Utah at the time of the Mountain Meadows Massacre that might otherwise baffle even observers
with the most sophisticated knowledge of history.

MORMON REFORMATION

The first great historian of the Mountain Meadows Massacre, Juanita Brooks, stated that even in the name of war, mass murder is a highly complex act "requiring the creation of a mass mind and powerful psychic contagion of great intensity." She was correct that to a large extent in Utah in the mid-1850s such fervor stemmed from the so-called Mormon Reformation. The fanatical Jedediah M. Grant, counselor to Brigham Young in the First Presidency of the Church of Jesus Christ of Latter-day Saints, set the tone for this intensity. President Young, who sensed a decline in spiritual fervor after almost a decade in the Great Basin, allowed Grant unlimited sway in attempting to regenerate such dedication.

On 4 July 1856, as citizens of the temporary territorial capital at Fillmore celebrated Independence Day, Jedediah Grant rode into their midst, having been on his horse most of three days coming from Salt Lake City. The only report of his subsequent speech states that "he addressed the [militia] battalion in a brief and spirited style, manifesting a noble, patriotic spirit, and causing the blood of '76 to thrill in our veins." This did nothing to chill the spirit of the celebration.

However, later in the year Brigham Young visited Fillmore and made a speech full of chastisement. He informed those present he "should no longer dwell among a people filled with contention, covetousness, pride and iniquity" and warned his listeners to abandon their sins or the unrighteous would forever be separated from the righteous. When he asked for a standing vote of those who would henceforth obey all the gospel principles, everyone reportedly responded in the affirmative. Although no hint refers to the extent of sins allegedly prevalent in the community, the majority promptly submitted to rebaptism. Some also reported that a few families reconsidered the situation at this juncture and quietly moved on to California.[4]

Even a year later, after Apostle George A. Smith visited the southern Utah area, as discussed later herein, he boasted, "I am perfectly aware that in all the settlements I visited in the south, [Fillmore included] one single sentence is enough to put every man in motion; in fact, a word is enough to set in motion every man, or to set a

torch to every building, where safety of this people is jeopardized." D. Michael Quinn, among others, stated there was strong evidence of blood atonement at the time, particularly in southern Utah, presumably of sinners discovered during this fervent revival which included a "catechism" of detailed questions about personal behavior.[5]

Another aspect of the vengeful atmosphere then pervasive in Mormondom involved the patriarchal blessings that were traditionally given church adults as a guide for their lives. In 1854, Iron County patriarch Elisha H. Groves blessed William H. Dame thus: "[T]hou shalt be called to act at the head of a portion of thy brethren and of the Lamanites in the redemption of Zion and the avenging of the blood of the prophets upon this earth." Phillip Klingensmith received similar guidance just three months before he took part in the Mountain Meadows Massacre. Others with such prediction-promises were ordered by Dame and his associates to take part in the same affair.[6]

INVASION AND
SIEGE MENTALITY

In the absence of specific statements by President James Buchanan, historians will always speculate on his true motives for sending the troops west. One major issue was whether the Mormon leaders had the right to use the local courts to circumvent the function of the federal territorial courts and thus undercut the essential power of the officials appointed from outside. Brigham Young and his associates in the Utah-Deseret legislature fervently asserted they had such rights. Utah historian Donald R. Moorman has suggested the president was seeking to use force to prevent the self-destruction of the Republic, using Utah as "a testing ground" to reassert federal control over a region that some claimed was at least semi-independent from the Union.[7]

Another student of the same period, Eugene E. Campbell, observed that the president and his cabinet assumed the Mormons would welcome invading soldiers, believing a large portion of the population "would wish nothing more than to escape from the cruelties of

Mormondom."[8] Indeed, a careful examination of the California newspapers for the year indicates that a great many Utah residents did avail themselves of the opportunity to leave the territory, something difficult to do during the previous two years of famine and martial law related to the Wakara War prior to that.[9] Yet whatever Buchanan's reasons, the federal government seriously miscalculated the number of Latter-day Saints willing to offer their lives and property to resist the imminent invasion.

Just after the Fancher emigrant party, which would be murdered at the Mountain Meadows, passed through Salt Lake City, as church authorities were laying the southeast cornerstone of the just-started Salt Lake Temple on 13 August 1857, Brigham Young expressed hope in his dedicatory prayer that their enemies "not have power to come into these valleys to disturb us but may we conquer our enemies and that they may be destroyed." In the same prayer the church leader besought that the "hearts of the Lamanites would be turned" toward the Mormons so that they could serve "as a wall of defense round about us."[10] Although many might wonder how such items could appropriately fit in a prayer, their inclusion pointedly illustrates the current preoccupations of Brigham Young and many of his followers.

On 16 August Brigham Young delivered a discourse at the Tabernacle. He started by rhetorically posing the question of how long the Latter-day Saints had been left without outside oppression, then answered by saying that the previous decade had been by far the longest such period ever in the history of the church. He reminded his listeners of the explicit Mormon doctrine that trial and opposition were essential in order for the saints (all the members) to be perfected. Without it they had no opportunity to demonstrate either faith or willingness to sacrifice for the Kingdom of God. The church leader (whom Mormons regarded as a prophet) also stated that such circumstances tended to expose people without sufficient commitment to be included among church members in good standing, and he gently warned those so inclined to "leave while [they] can go in peace" rather than later be cut "down like cucumbers on the ground." Then he suggested to the faithful that even burning all they had built rather than have it fall into en-

emy hands was nothing compared to the privileges of gaining eternal blessings with the other full-fledged saints. At each point in the sermon where the church leader called for a verbal commitment to follow his lead in the various aspects of resistance, the congregation voiced appropriate loud assent.

In the same discourse Brigham Young assured those present that he had striven to maintain peace between the region's Native Americans and emigrants passing through, despite supposedly numerous acts of violence committed by the latter against the former. He then pointedly warned that if the anticipated war commenced with U.S. troops, all travel by the nation's citizens through his domain must be halted. "To accomplish this," Young asserted he only needed to say a word to the Indians and they would "use [the emigrants] up." At that juncture he significantly affirmed he would no longer restrain the Native Americans but leave them alone to do as they pleased. Brigham Young certainly implemented that policy in precisely that manner in the ensuing weeks.[11]

In the United States Army investigations subsequent to the Mountain Meadows Massacre, Maj. James H. Carleton learned of this sermon from Judge John Cradlebaugh, probably the most outspoken critic of Brigham Young among the federal government officials assigned during the era to Utah Territory. Carleton raised the point that "turning the Indians loose upon" the emigrants came just at the point when the "rich" Fancher train had entered the Salt Lake Valley "and was now fairly entrapped." The army officers termed the sermon a "letter of marque to these land pirates who listen[ed] to him as to an oracle." His report stated that from the moment of the sermon, the emigrants were "considered the authorized, if not legal prey of the inhabitants." He also concluded that the "hint thus shrewdly given was not long in being acted upon."[12]

PUNISHMENT POLICY
IMPLEMENTED

Another revealing insight into the directions given southern Utah ecclesiastic leaders by those ranking above them at Salt Lake City is a letter from the church First Presidency in early February of 1857 to Bishop Aaron Johnson at Springville. This letter informed of two men just released from short terms in the territorial prison, perhaps earlier than some believed they deserved, who were then waiting at Garland Hurt's Spanish Fork Indian farm to join an emigration to southern California. The communication suggested they might be inclined to steal horses from church members for their purposes. The presidency instructed the bishop to assemble a few men to scrutinize the situation and be prepared "to act in case of emergency." The message clearly instructed that if the men in question conducted themselves in a lawful manner, they should be allowed to proceed safely along the trail. But if they again misbehaved, the (unsigned) orders stated, in veiled but meaningful words, "[W]e shall regret to hear a favorable report." Then, implying that federal court officials may have earlier accused Mormon law enforcers of unjustly detaining the men, the instructions continued, "We do not expect there would be [later] prosecutions for false imprisonment or tale bearers left for witnesses." This policy would be sufficiently clear to Johnson, whom the correspondents asserted knew "these things." He was also cautioned to "have a few men that can be brought on hand and make no noise about it," also to keep the communication from church headquarters "safe."

Three days later several other local church leaders, including Lewis Brunson of Fillmore, William Dame of Parowan, and Isaac Haight of Cedar City received similar directives to have "a few trusty men ready in case of need to pursue, retake & and punish." Their instructions also appear to encourage that the men should not be brought back for another trial, likewise saying, "[W]e do not suppose there would be any prosecution for false imprisonment, or tales for witnesses." The fate of these two men is unknown, but such a policy might match the subsequent fate of some of the Aiken brothers, and Aaron Johnson doubtless soon played a similar role in the demise of William and Beetson Parrish at Springville. And Haight was also involved in some aspects of the Peltro-Tobin incident, which with the Parrish-Potter murders will be discussed shortly. The policy clearly stands as a general guideline for local Mormon officials along the Southern Route who might need to make quick decisions regarding major offenders without immediate direction from church headquarters.[13]

THE PELTRO-TOBIN AND PARRISH ATTACKS AND THE PRESS

In the spring of 1857, before the newspapers raised alarm at the seemingly hostile and inflammatory rhetoric emanating from the published sermons of Brigham Young and his associates, an incident of emigrant attack or harassment on the Southern Route had already been well publicized. Col. J. C. Peltro, previously employed surveying a military road from Fort Leavenworth to Salt Lake City, had completed his duties and was on his way to California to make his report. He was accompanied by another soldier, Sgt. John Tobin, who had come to Utah with the earlier Stansbury survey expedition and during his stay became a Mormon, courted Brigham Young's daughter, and went on a church mission. When Alice Young chose someone else, he married the daughter of another prominent church leader, Charles C. Rich. It may have appeared to some Latter-day Saints, recently aroused to a high pitch of religious fervor by the Mormon Reformation, that Tobin was abandoning his wife and his faith, a view with which his father-in-law in California agreed. At the time some believed this to be legitimate grounds for severe punishment.

For whatever reasons, unknown persons fired on the party of four as they camped for the night at a spot on the Santa Clara River, thereafter known as Tobin Point, near present Gunlock, Utah. Three of the men in the group were wounded in a hail of bullets, Tobin most seriously injured by a slug striking his left cheekbone dangerously close to the eye. The party also lost six valuable horses. Peltro later reported sixty to seventy gunshots fired, mostly hitting the baggage that had been placed in such a position that it protected the sleepers. An investigation next morning, presumably of the footprints, convinced the colonel the attack had been perpetrated by eight white men. Local church leader Isaac Haight admitted he and other Mormons were in the area at the time but blamed the incident on a party of "Mapaches." It is known that church enforcers of discipline maintained a corps of agents assigned to leave Cedar City and "to go on the road; to find out who trailed [to California] and their circumstances." As the injured parties started back toward Painter (Pinto) Creek, established not long before as a small Latter-day Saints settlement, they met the California-bound mail carriers, who agreed to assist them on the journey to their original destination. Tobin suffered considerably, but he made the trip. He was placed in the care of leading San Bernardino apostate Mormon Dr. Woodville M. Andrews, even though Tobin's father-in-law, Rich, was also in town. Later Brigham Young ordered Haight to return some of the stolen horses through mail carriers to Tobin and Peltro in California. The account of this incident, along with other negative reports emanating from Utah, helped predispose outsiders to believe the worst about the Mormons and their treatment of non-Mormons passing through their midst.[14]

Soon after, the New York *Times* drew on an anonymous Utah letter to their editor recounting not only the details of the Tobin-Peltro incident but an even more tragic event shortly thereafter, involving the murder of an apostate Mormon and his son. William Parrish and his son Beetson were killed at Springville in central Utah as they reportedly started for California over the Southern Route. William Parrish had experienced difficulty retrieving property he had "consecrated" to the local church authorities before his contemplated move. He had also been blocked from going to Salt Lake City to appeal to President Young.[15]

The *Times* report, four front-page columns of anti-Mormon fact and embellishment, alleged the Latter-day Saint hierarchy had quietly decreed no disaffected church members would be allowed to leave Utah Territory to spread negative stories, and cited the two attacks as proof. Some months later as the army invasion appeared imminent, such restrictive orders became a reality. On 5 August 1857, Brigham Young issued a proclamation that not only forbade any armed force from entering the territory but also required that "no person shall be allowed to pass or repass into or through or from this territory without a permit from the proper officer." The policy thus enunciated was already being enforced, a tyrannical decree for those who no longer desired to remain in Mormondom.[16]

The same New York *Times* item also recounted the difficulties of Thomas S. Williams, whose death along

the Southern Route three years later will be discussed in chapter 8, as he sought to leave Utah in 1857. He had abandoned his formerly held faith in the dominant church and reportedly encountered threats to his life. The newspaper article was probably written by John E. Page, a young missionary who had recently apostatized—left the faith. Accompanying these lurid details were several stories of women compelled to join polygamous marriages against their will and a letter from former Utah judge W. W. Drummond to the *Times*, also published on the front page, answering Mormon denials of his recent allegations to U.S. Attorney General Jeremiah S. Black. The New York newspaper editorialized, expressing regret that such "outrages, usurpations and disregard of the law" could yet recur in Utah, expressing hope that in the swelling tide of hostile public sentiment President James Buchanan would "give immediate and practical attention" to the long-standing problem of the defiant and seemingly lawless Mormons. Drummond actually predicted a change in territorial governors and the dispatching of troops.[17] This influential newspaper coverage may well have pressured the president into these subsequent moves more than has previously been recognized.[18]

Certainly Brigham Young's conflict with virtually all non-Mormon territorial officials, along with the bombastic statements he and fellow church leaders made concerning them, the approaching army, and the attitude expressed toward the government in general did nothing to assuage an explosive situation. Admittedly, such rhetoric was an effective method of arousing the Mormons to the armed resistance that the church hierarchy presumed might be necessary. Many of the church leaders' speeches were published verbatim in the West Coast press. The California newspapers may have been in the forefront of reflecting the mounting public apprehension over the situation in Utah, including the violent incidents on the emigrant road to southern California.

The Los Angeles *Star* was still mentioning the Tobin-Peltro attack when it reported "another massacre" in the territory, detailing the Parrish murders. Technically the Springville killings were the first trail-related fatalities, but it is doubtful if anyone challenged the assertion that the Tobin-Peltro incident also fit the category of a massacre. A growing number of non-Mormon citizens would have agreed with the *Star* statement that "these outrages are of so frequent occurrence that it behooves the local authorities to take steps to bring the perpetrators to punishment." Yet in the absence of federal intervention and little cooperation demonstrated by the territorial governor, no participants were ever apprehended. There would also have been widespread outside approval of the Los Angeles newspaper editor calling for the "heavy arm of the law" to be brought to bear in the region through the president's drastic action of sending one of the largest contingents of the United States Army ever yet assembled to assert federal authority in Mormondom.[19]

BRIGHAM YOUNG'S INVOLVEMENT IN INDIAN HOSTILITIES?

In the late summer of 1857, not long after Brigham Young learned of the approach of the United States Army toward Utah, presumably to punish him and his followers, he wrote to one of his most trusted Indian missionaries, Jacob Hamblin, advising an even closer relationship with the Native Americans. Indicating the gloomy outlook then current, the church leader directed that "they must learn that they have either got to help us or the United States will kill us both." This communication was the first mention of what was soon a widely held outlook and policy, although in fact there may never have been an actual threat to the Southern Paiutes—if they remained neutral. Within a month, Hamblin brought more than a dozen Indians, including several chiefs, with him to Salt Lake City to confer personally with Brigham Young. The message they were given would not likely have been any different from that contained in Young's recent letter to Hamblin.[20]

Some have attempted to link Young to subsequent events through focusing on the instruction conveyed by messenger James Haslam from Cedar City church leaders at the time of the initial Paiute attack on the Fancher wagon train at Mountain Meadows. Such attempts have been far from conclusive. The church leader-governor's implication in the murders in fact centers on the message apparently conveyed in his presence more than a week before the fateful southern Utah incidents. Dimick Baker Huntington, a forty-nine-year-old Mormon Battal-

ion veteran, had become one of President Young's most trusted Indian agents. He had been dispatched to investigate and if possible pacify the situation after the Gunnison massacre, and there were other similarly sensitive assignments. On 1 September 1857 he accompanied the Native Americans brought to Salt Lake City by Hamblin, including doubtless the most influential Indian leaders along the emigrant route south of the Sevier River, to an interview with Brigham Young. Kanosh, the head of all Millard County Pauvants, was there, accompanied by eleven others of his band. Ammon, Wakara's brother and leader of most Indians residing in the Beaver River area, brought a wife with him. Tutsoygubbit (Tutsegabits), the undisputed head chief of all Paiutes from Mountain Meadows south past Las Vegas, was accompanied by Youngwad (also referred to as Youngweids or Youngquick), who may have been a chief among the Piedes residing near Harmony. Apostle Wilford Woodruff, usually an accurate diarist, observed that Tutsegabits had "with him [some] of the Indians of Harmony." According to the interpreter, these Indians had come in order to learn more about the impending army invasion, of which Huntington had recently noted other chiefs from farther north were greatly frightened, perhaps partly through his reports.[21]

According to Huntington's journal, in the presence of the highest church authority and doubtless at his direction the interpreter gave the Native Americans residing along the road "all the cattle that had gone to Cal[ifornia by] the south rout [*sic*]." Huntington noted the Indian reaction in his diary, saying, "[I]t made them open their eyes." The Indians retorted that the Mormon leaders had previously instructed them "not to steal." The interpreter conceded this was true but went on to explain—linking emigrants with the invading army and the federal government—"now they have come to fight us & you for when they kill us they will kill you." To this Native American spokesmen replied that "they was [*sic*] afraid to fight the American," but affirmed that if they could engage sufficient other tribesmen and allies, they "might fight." The reference to the cattle that had gone by the south route clearly referred to those possessed by all the emigrant parties currently traveling through southern Utah. It certainly had to be understood in the interview that the owners would not likely give up their livestock without conflict, although probably no one as-sumed this policy would lead to more than a few scat-tered skirmishes or deaths. Young probably did not real-ize how many emigrants were then traversing southern Utah. As will be discussed later, these instructions sig-nificantly amplify the meaning of the directive Brigham Young sent by Haslam to Iron County church and militia leaders during the Mountain Meadows crisis.[22]

As clear as Dimick Huntington's diary account ap-pears to make President Young's interview with Native American leaders, a countervailing source raises ques-tion as to whether the highest church leader was actually present when Huntington allegedly gave the fateful instructions. The best corroboration is the "Historian's Office Journal" that George A. Smith apparently super-vised, which states that on 1 September 1857 "Tutse-gabits, Kanosh and Ammon had an interview with Prest. B. Y. [in] the evening." Wilford Woodruff's journal has Jacob Hamblin present instead of Huntington when the chiefs met with Brigham Young, with some disagree-ment on dates of the occurrence. However, it remains extremely doubtful if Huntington or Hamblin would of-fer any such extreme instructions without the expressed approval of the highest church authority. Similarly, Woodruff's journal appears to show that some of the Na-tive Americans did not immediately return to southern Utah and thus may not have been there at the time of the subsequent Mountain Meadows Massacre. Hamblin returned south during the time of the massacre, yet Woodruff has him present at Tutsegabits's subsequent ordination to the Mormon priesthood on 16 September, indicating a possible return trip during the week after that horrible event. Ammon was noted by P. M. Warn to be in the Beaver area immediately after the massacre, al-though no one ever implicated him in the murders.[23]

FEDERAL GOVERNMENT PRESENCE
ALONG THE SOUTHERN ROUTE

In the previous year, Brigham Young, acting as ex officio territorial superintendent of Indian affairs, worked with federal Indian agents separate from Garland Hurt to further promote agricultural development among the Southern Paiutes. Maj. George W. Armstrong visited

southern Utah as far as the Santa Clara River in the fall of 1856. This visit apparently included distribution of farm implements and tools. Governor Young subse-quently wrote to Armstrong and his Indian commis-sioner superiors, recommending more equipment and gifts to encourage what he reported to be a vastly ex-panding interest in establishing irrigated fields and crop cultivation.

Just at the time of the Mountain Meadows Massacre, Brigham Young wrote to James W. Denver, commis-sioner of Indian affairs, to complain of the hostile attacks by emigrants on Indians along the travel routes and also to urge keeping the invading troops well away from the Paiutes. Although there are no known hostile incidents between Southern Paiutes and U.S. Army personnel since John C. Frémont's expedition in the mid-1840s, Young asserted that "it is a prevalent fact that where there are the most of these [soldiers], we may expect to find the greatest amount of hostile Indians and the least security to persons and property." Although these letters were sufficiently cordial and described an entirely pa-cific policy, current actions severely refuted the written reports. And President Young's comments earlier in the year to southern settlement leaders reveals his assump-tion that the government Indian policy aimed to disrupt the cordial Mormon-Paiute relationships. He thus di-rected his local officials "to conciliate the feelings of the Indians and thereby thwart the purposes of our enemies, who seek to stir them up against us."[24]

In almost a decade of supposed U.S. government control over the region, only Indian agent Armstrong and Lt. Sylvester Mowry's military expedition in 1855, along with a little road building that year, served as countervailing influence among Southern Paiutes, con-trasted with the abundant contact with followers of the Church of Jesus Christ of Latter-day Saints. Within this vacuum the Mormon policy developed unchecked, ce-menting a friendship that became virtually a military alliance. Mowry perceptively reported more than two years prior to the Mountain Meadows Massacre that this was happening and that the consequences might be dis-astrous. The federal government made no known re-sponse to the situation. The young army officer con-ferred with some Paiute chiefs and attempted to explain that federal government officials were not the murderous villains they were sometimes portrayed to be. Nor were all Americans enemies to the Indians. But as this view was not further reinforced, the Mormon policy prevailed of convincing the Paiutes that any military force approaching to confront the Mormons was also an enemy of the region's Native Americans. And this policy of uniting the two threatened groups to resist anticipated oppression was effectively implemented. Although the Mormons' past experience generated real fear of occupation by a hostile force, there was no real threat to Native Americans along the Southern Route. As had been the case farther north among the Utes, any Indian agent loyal to the federal government who visited more than once might have been able to convince several reasonable Paiute leaders of that fact. But as no such agent did in fact visit, the "battle axes of the Lord" were soon unleashed with terrible effect.

THE FANCHER PARTY
AND ASSOCIATES

One of many emigrant companies formed in the Mississippi Valley in the spring of each year to head west over the various trails was the ill-fated Fancher party. In May, it started across Arkansas under the leadership of Alexander Fancher, a veteran of two previous trips to California, at least one over the Southern Route. John T. Baker served as second in command. The company grew to forty wagons, with a thousand head of cattle and several hundred horses, including some blooded animals. With a total wealth allegedly approaching seventy thousand dollars, it was certainly one of the richest emigrant companies of the era. The conduct of the company appeared markedly exemplary, with no profanity permitted and with a regular morning and evening prayer circle.

Unfortunately, a group of self-proclaimed "Missouri Wildcats" later joined the train and their aggressive, sometimes violent, behavior along the trail, including poisoning springs prior to reaching Utah, should have prompted expulsion from the group. But it did not. Fancher did have his people camp some distance from their unruly companions as observed by Latter-day Saint Eli Kelsey, who traveled the last leg of the journey to Salt Lake City with the combined company. He noticed a particular bent of hostility toward Mormons, "swearing vengeance against the saints and generally making a nuisance out of themselves." Particularly after learning that Utah residents would not sell the company needed food and supplies, the "wildcats" became increasingly hostile and offensive. They reportedly expressed gladness the troops were approaching and even allegedly affirmed the wish they could remain and help kill every Mormon in the territory.

Some students of the Mountain Meadows Massacre who have recently completed or are completing extensive works for publication argue both that there were actually no Missouri Wildcats and that it was in fact the later Dukes-Turner party, comprised partly of Missourians, which committed the offenses that most angered Utah residents. However, William Clark, who traveled just behind that company and later spent time with members of the party in California, recorded that the Dukes-Turner group strived expressly to prevent conflict with local residents as they traversed through Utah. True, this may have been self-justification after the massacre proved the stupidity of generating local hostility. However, whatever actions aroused the Mormons against passing emigrants almost certainly occurred before the latter company entered that volatile southern Utah area.[25]

Although information is extremely sketchy about the "Missouri Wildcats," the existence of such a group cannot be totally discounted without further evidence. The supreme injustice regarding the troublemakers, whoever they were, appears to be that they moved on down the trail out of Mountain Meadows while their more lawfully inclined fellows stopped there to recoup their livestock—and suffered the ultimate punishment at least partly for the misdeeds of others.

Despite continued assertions to the contrary, there is little doubt that many stories later recounted to bolster the case that misdeeds by the passing emigrants partially justified the massacre are fabrications formulated later. These include the following: that at Beaver a teamster boasted of having participated in the Haun's Mill Massacre, and later, another Fancher company member claimed to possess the gun that killed Joseph Smith. Some of the most frequently cited statements were first recorded by Joseph A. Ray, of Fillmore, who was actually on a mission at the time and thus was not a particularly reliable witness. Historian Donald Moorman has concluded that "a half-dozen Mormon journals and numerous affidavits, never intended for public view, confirm" some such reports. But careful analysis finds virtually all such accounts to be highly questionable.[26]

The San Francisco *Alta California* conceded amid bitter denunciation of the subsequent massacre of the Fancher party, "[T]heir conduct was said to be reckless and they would commit little acts of annoyance for the purpose of provoking the Saints." Accuracy demands differentiation between the Arkansas emigrants and their Missourian traveling associates. On being denied opportunity to purchase provisions one last time at Cedar City, the Missourians supposedly rode into the center of the settlement and reportedly fired indiscriminately among the citizens, wounding several.[27] Yet it appears that if such an incident took place and some had actually been seriously injured, Utah residents would more often have cited this offense as some justification for the subsequent murders. Indeed probably no capital crimes were committed by any emigrants that season.[28]

The incident most often cited as outraging both Indians and Mormons against the broader Fancher party was the poisoning of a spring or portion of Corn Creek near Kanosh, Millard County. Others have correctly argued that the amount of chemical necessary to poison such a large body of water would not likely have been carried by emigrants. A young Fillmore resident, Proctor Robison, died shortly after skinning a cow found dead in the area. However, a careful study of the surrounding circumstances by a relative, Jolene A. Robison, has determined not only that he succumbed two weeks after the emigrant party passed by but that his symptoms were consistent with what would happen to someone who skinned an animal that had died of anthrax, known to be common at the time and likely present in the area, since contemporary reports mention a number of other animal carcasses in the vicinity.[29]

Recent scholarship has also refuted the claims, including some by Brigham Young, that the murdered party included many Missourians so much hated by the Mormons for persecutions perpetrated on them there in the 1830s. The supremely unfortunate Fancher-Baker Company consisted entirely of citizens from Arkansas.

However, just that year an incident in that state, the murder of popular church apostle Parley P. Pratt, had greatly angered many Mormons. Reverend Hector H. McLean was infuriated by the fact the church leader, who married his former wife in polygamy, had previously been acquitted of implication with the woman in kidnapping her and McLean's children away from McLean's care. The angry father shot Pratt from his horse and then killed him as he lay helpless in the road. The woman in question subsequently resided at Salt Lake City, and when the Fancher party passed through she reportedly recognized one or more of the emigrants as having been present at the murder of her apostle-husband. The truth of this allegation also needs to be ascertained more precisely.[30]

It is doubtful if any emigrant misdeeds loomed as particularly prominent as a motivating factor for the massacre. Several new developments converged with the already-existing emotional state aroused by apprehension concerning the invading army, doctrines of revenge, and fervor aroused by the religious reformation. One new ingredient in the disastrous mix was Brigham Young's public announcement on 16 August that he would no longer restrain local Native Americans from attacking passing emigrants. Another was his conference with key southern Utah Indian leaders on 1 September in which he offered their tribesmen the cattle then in the region being driven over the Southern Route. The timing of these announcements, along with George A. Smith recently informing the Paiutes that the invading soldiers would treat them as enemies as well as the Latter-day Saints, appears to have made the subsequent attack on the first and best-stocked wagon company of the season virtually inevitable.

SOUTHERN UTAH FANATICISM

It is possible that many in southern Utah were even more inclined to follow seemingly unreasonable decrees from ecclesiastic leaders than some others in more densely populated areas might have been disposed to do. During the Wakara War of 1853, which hardly threatened the extreme southern settlements, militia leader Apostle George A. Smith forcibly implemented an order to take all "surplus cattle" north even without the consent of their owners, who often asserted the cattle thus seized were not surplus at all. Those who resisted this "compulsory consecration" were incarcerated, put in chains, and allegedly threatened with decapitation. Although this generated considerable bitterness toward church authorities, including the previously mentioned Scottish converts who soon after left for California, many others accepted and helped implement the clearly unfair policy.[31]

Another episode revealing the situation there just prior to the Mountain Meadows Massacre relates to William Leany, an older man residing at Parowan who recognized among the Fancher party (which was not allowed to pass directly through the town) the son of a man who had earlier rescued him from a mob while on a Mormon mission near Paris, Tennessee. After a visit, Leany gave the young man some food and wished him a safe journey to California. Not long thereafter, Leany was summoned from his house "by one of the local police," and so severely beaten for having rendered "aid and comfort to the enemy" that he never fully recovered from his injuries.[32]

Southern Utah whites would long afterward argue that, so fully outnumbered in the region, they needed to maintain the goodwill of the Indians, which might be jeopardized by attempting to hold them back when aroused to fight. That was certainly the message of San Bernardino correspondent J. Ward Christian, who answered a letter of inquiry from a California judge friendly to the Mormons, Benjamin Hayes, for information on the situation in southern Utah less than a month after the Mountain Meadows Massacre. He argued it required a most judicious policy to sustain the settlers there because they were so heavily outnumbered by Native American inhabitants of the area. Estimating that two hundred white families resided between Fillmore and Parowan, he reported there were some eleven hundred Indians in that same area. Although he did not have a figure for residents at Cedar City and Harmony farther south, the number would not have exceeded another hundred families, compared to several hundred Paiute-Piedes. He drew on the best estimate of mail carrier Edward Hope to state there were up to seven hundred in the Tonequint and perhaps the Shivwits bands near the

Santa Clara River, with at least three hundred more along each of the next two rivers, the Virgin and the Muddy.[33] George A. Smith later wrote to Brigham Young in justification for the emigrant murders, falsely implying it was an Indian affair, "for the [Iron County] citizens to have attacked and killed the Indians in defense of the emigrants would have been little else than suicide" because of . . . [the Iron County people] being so severely outnumbered by the Native Americans in the region.[34]

John D. Lee, widely believed to have been instrumental in inciting the Indians, later claimed that when he first arrived at the Paiute camp, presumably near Mountain Meadows, he found them in a "frenzy of excitement," threatening to kill him unless he agreed to lead them. Although this may well have been true, he was the leading Mormon-Indian farmer in the area and doubtless played a key role in the initial process of arousing the Paiutes. Somewhere in the alliance-enlistment process, incidentally, the Native Americans allegedly had been "promised that the Gentile bullets could not harm them while they were fighting with the 'Lord's Army.'"[35]

One of the most fervent expounders of the Mormon Reformation doctrines, Apostle George A. Smith, was still in command of all of southern Utah's militia. On a crucial late summer visit to the southern settlements, he combined his ecclesiastic role, in which he delivered "fiery sermons about resisting the U.S. Army and taking vengeance on anti-Mormons," with what was perhaps his primary objective: to deliver orders from Brigham Young to the militia commanders in the southern military districts. These orders were to "instruct the Indians that our enemies are also their enemies."[36] On his trip south, the church leader actually camped near the Fancher party at Cove Creek and could easily have granted them a safe passage permit if he had been so inclined. When Smith reached Parowan, he observed the "Iron Battalion" (which he had earlier helped organize) conducting drills and inspections in preparation, reportedly because they were "under the impression that their country was about to be invaded by an army from the United States," presumably from the direction of the southern California road. Indeed, one of the other allegations against the Fancher-Missouri party was that they threatened to help lead "some four or five hundred dragoons" over the Frémont trail from southern California.

So far as has been determined, no actual report of any such movement came from California at that time.[37]

When Smith returned to Salt Lake City the next month, he stated to a local congregation that church members in Parowan, over whom he had long presided, "wish that their enemies might come and give them a chance to fight and take vengeance for the cruelties that had been inflicted upon us in the states." He well knew that among the people he referred to were some who had lost loved ones at the Haun's Mill Massacre in Missouri. Whether Apostle Smith was aware of the fact or not, by the time he delivered this sermon some of the men of whom he spoke had already acted on the feelings he attributed to them.[38]

Two days after the emigrant company arrived at Cedar City, the local church high council convened to deliberate what action to take regarding their offenses. One resolution proposed treating them as enemies of war and acting accordingly; another, to allow the train to pass on to California unmolested. The solution adopted focused on laying the case before Brigham Young for decision, dispatching James Haslam next day by horseback. Cedar City stake (diocese) president Isaac C. Haight then summoned Indian farmer John D. Lee, assigned as the chief intermediary between local Native Americans and white church members, and after explaining the situation, ordered him to engage some Paiutes to surround the emigrant camp and immobilize them until the policy directive arrived from Salt Lake City. Lee promptly enlisted Native Americans from Cedar City and Harmony, sending Indian missionaries Samuel Knight and Dudley Leavitt to Santa Clara to recruit more warriors.[39]

MOUNTAIN MEADOWS MASSACRE

On the fateful Tuesday, 8 September 1857, the attack commenced on the Fancher train of at least two dozen wagons and approximately one hundred forty persons. Led by Paiute chiefs, who some reports say included Tutsegabits, just before daybreak the aroused Indians and probably some Mormons disguised as Indians opened fire from the nearby arroyo, and others reportedly charged yelling and shooting down the slope of a nearby hill. The emigrant cattle herders caught away

from their wagons were the main victims of the first onslaught. Taken totally by surprise, the pioneer men seized their arms and returned fire, which reportedly killed three Indians and wounded several others.[40] According to Anthony W. Ivins, who in the next generation knew the local Native Americans extremely well, two chiefs were slain in this early offensive. Although it is not possible to positively establish the Fancher party casualties suffered in the initial attack, Lee later claimed seven men were killed and three others seriously wounded. Thereafter, some of the Paiutes reportedly became disgusted that the promised divine protection had proven false, and in the ensuing days they were not nearly so inclined to make another frontal assault. Instead they remained concealed and shot at any who exposed themselves outside the barricade that the Fancher party had hastily erected. This situation continued for the next two days.[41]

During this semirespite from pitched fighting, emigrant leaders dispatched a three-man party toward Cedar City with petitions for help. However, they were attacked at Leach Springs, allegedly by a squad of Mormon militiamen. One of the emigrants, William Aden, a recent addition to the Fancher party, who had resided in Utah for six months, was killed and the others escaped into the darkness with minor wounds. These survivors were hunted down by cooperative Indians and killed en route to California.[42] Some observers have concluded that the deaths made inevitable further Mormon participation in perpetrating the Mountain Meadows Massacre. It was presumably after this that some militia leaders concluded that all adults in the company must die and cruel plans were formulated to implement that policy.[43]

John D. Lee, who, disguised as an Indian reportedly participated in the first attack, warned Haight by messenger that he feared the Indians would turn against the Saints if the emigrant resistance was not promptly overcome. Regarding the matter a military problem, the church leader ordered out the Iron County militia. He then traveled to Parowan to confer with his military superior, Col. William H. Dame. After midnight on 10 September, the ranking officers of the Iron County militia initially decided to allow the besieged emigrants to move on in peace, providing they were willing to offer the Native Americans all their livestock, presumably ex-

Photo of the Mountain Meadows Massacre site over half a century later, by Frank A. Beckwith. Some of the attack was launched from the hill labeled 5, with orders to attack allegedly given from behind the hill by Major Higbee. Several nonparticipant eyewitnesses were on the hill labeled 3. Many women and children were attacked beyond the ranch area labeled 7. The men were mainly attacked farther west around the hill, as shown in left foreground.

cept those needed to continue their travels. But in a subsequent meeting among Haight, Dame, and another man, possibly Maj. John Higbee, also Haight's counselor in the stake presidency, the decision was reversed. Apparently fearing that reports by the survivors in California might implicate the Mormons, these highest military leaders concluded the entire company must be destroyed. Juanita Brooks, the first careful historian of these events, cites Charles Adams, then a boy holding the horses the Cedar City officers were about to mount, as claiming that Higbee reminded the others of the high council decision to await Brigham Young's orders. He attested Dame answered, "I don't care what the council decided. My orders are that the emigrants must be done away with." These orders were soon conveyed to the militiamen gathered in the Cedar City fort, eventually numbering from fifty to fifty-five men, including a few volunteers who were less official militia and several who

were notably unwilling to actively participate. Higbee was the company commander, and Philip Klingensmith, a bishop at Cedar City, second in command.[44]

The man designated to carry out the specifics of Dame's written directions was John D. Lee. When the militiamen arrived near the siege scene at Mountain Meadows, Major Higbee handed them the orders, which Lee later testified were "to decoy the emigrants from their position and kill all of them that could talk." On reading the paper, Lee recalled he dropped it on the ground, saying he could not do that. He claimed to have then gone off by himself and shed tears, somewhat corroborated by his Indian name from then on being Yauguts, or "crybaby." Finally he accepted the reality of the order of what had to be done.

Significantly, Higbee's later recollections disagree with Lee on the nature of Dame's orders. He asserted that the military superior instructed Lee to compromise

John D. Lee, Mormon, Indian farming supervisor, and a full participant in the Mountain Meadows Massacre, was later a proprietor of several southwestern Utah stopping places serving freighters and other travelers headed over the Southern Route.

with the Indians by letting them take all the stock, go home, and allow the pioneers to leave with no further incident. Higbee recalled that Dame expressed hope that the Indian farmer, Lee, could save the company and if not, at least "save wimen [*sic*] and children at all hazards." Brooks has suggested this contradictory version might have been part of a later attempt to clear Dame from responsibility, which in fact was essentially accomplished for a time. The truth of the matter may never be fully established. Both versions, seemingly inaccurately, stressed fear of the Southern Paiutes should the emigrants go free. Higbee claimed to have asked Lee what the Indians thought of the current solution of taking the

cattle, to which Lee replied he had earlier informed the warriors the Mormons were at war with the Americans and had sent for them to assist in their fight. Now after some of the Paiutes had been killed, the rest were not disposed to take livestock only and return to their villages. He warned Higbee that if he and his men showed inclination to side with the besieged emigrants, the Indians threatened, "[W]e will fight you as well as them if you don't help us to get them out of their fort." Lee stated he and Klingensmith concluded they had to at least make a pretext of helping accomplish the Native American wishes.[45]

A messenger, William Bateman, carrying a white flag, approached the besieged wagon train members and was admitted into their camp. He falsely explained to Captain Fancher and his associates that the Mormons too feared the Indians and that the militia unit was willing to escort the emigrants through the hostile lines. Fancher replied to Major Higbee that his people would seriously consider the proposition. Although it may seem improbable that these people would put their trust in others they had reason to distrust so completely, they were probably running low on ammunition and, according to Lee, forty-six company members had been wounded in the previous attacks. They probably had no other choice except certain death at Indian hands as the siege ended. Lee recalled that when he reached the Fancher party enclosure, the emigrants "welcomed him as their deliverer" and agreed to accept the terms offered. These terms were to lay down their arms and walk with Lee toward Cedar City, with the children carried in one wagon and the wounded and some women in another.[46]

The emigrant men were lined up behind the wagons, each escorted by a militiaman. After walking on the main road for some distance, as the children's wagon passed out of sight around a knoll, Higbee ordered his men to halt and open fire on the emigrants. Nephi Johnson later testified "at the signal quite a number of the posse failed to kill his man, for the reason that they did not approve of the killing." Other accounts state that men not killed immediately ran back among the women and children, probably condemning them as well. Whoever dispatched those remaining, all accounts agree it was all over within a half hour. Approximately one hundred twenty people were slain; only some seventeen younger children were spared. The event stands as one of the largest mass murders in U.S. history, with but little excuse except for a large degree of long-generated fanaticism and mass hysteria.[47]

As Juanita Brooks has concluded, "[W]hatever the details, the fact remains that the entire company was betrayed and murdered, an ugly fact that will not be downed." She continued, asserting correctly, "[T]here is not justification enough for the death of a single individual." And once it was over, the participants were mainly "shocked and horrified at what had been done," but they swore each other to secrecy on the matter and essentially attempted to blame the massacre on the Native Americans. To a large extent the highest church leaders tried to do the same.[48]

It may be impossible for people who have never been immersed in a pervasive environment of bitterness toward past oppressors to understand the mentality of a people who have. A recent rough analogy might be Slobodan Milosevic's Serb fanatics and similar ones involved with the terrorist attacks of 11 September 2001, who have been imbued with a cultural barrage of negative images—including in popular music, children's stories, legends, poetry, and religious doctrines—about atrocities at the hands of others in earlier times. In each case murder of innocent people has been the result—justified by the perpetrators in a manner that cannot seem rational to those uninitiated into the milieu of bitterness. How can outsiders fathom the psychological depths of emotions unleashed by an opportunity to wreak vengeance on people who are at least symbols of what has so long been the object of hatred? In the final analysis, people so far removed from the frenzied moment may never completely grasp how such a thing as the Mountain Meadows Massacre could occur. There are but few parallels to it in this country, although at least three massacres of Native Americans by white soldiers involve numbers of deaths surpassing this lamentable affair. It has also happened elsewhere under similar circumstances. The entire episode demonstrates that besides a culture of violence, a people can obviously develop and embrace a related culture of paranoia, hatred, and revenge.

RECRIMINATIONS

Despite the strict oath of secrecy among Mormon participants, considerable information eventually leaked out about the massacre. Francis Marion Lyman, who as a teenager spent the most harrowing night of his life passing the scene of the murders within days of their occurrence, continued a lifelong interest in the affair. Almost four decades later, as a senior LDS church apostle, he had occasion to converse with several participants then residing in the Virgin and Muddy River communities of Nevada. At St. Joseph, George Adair informed him that only a few white men did much killing. But he alleged that three—John M. Higbee, Josel White, and John D. Lee—each killed up to a dozen persons. Nephi Johnson of Bunkerville, the participant who first interested young Juanita Brooks in the massacre, denied Adair's allegations about Higbee and White but admitted that "white men did most of the killing."[49]

The Native Americans often declined to accept the brunt of responsibility for the massacre. Federal Indian agent Garland Hurt sent his personal servant, Ute Pete, to the area to ascertain firsthand what had happened. He was informed by Piede participants that although they had taken part in the massacre, "the Mormons persuaded them into it," explaining that some ten days earlier John D. Lee had come to their village and informed them that "Americans were very bad people and always made a rule to kill Indians whenever they had a chance." Jackson, a Santa Clara subchief, who reportedly had lost a brother in the battle, was apparently the Indian most inclined to discuss the incident.

Maj. James H. Carleton, who investigated the massacre within a year and a half, quoted the Tonequint leader as stating that the Indians received few spoils from the attack. Similarly, the army officer cited Moapa band spokesmen complaining that the Mormons blamed the killings on them and then they asked, "[W]here are the wagons, the cattle, the clothing, the rifles and other property belonging to the train?" The army officer answered that these items would be found among the church members. To Chief Jackson was also attributed the allegation, in the words of Carleton's subsequent report, "that orders came down in a letter from Brigham Young that the emigrants were to be killed." Carleton added that Touche (always thereafter known as Tosho), chief of the Virgin River Paiutes, specified that the letter was sent by a man named Huntingdon (Huntington), an Indian interpreter.[50] Although there is no direct corroboration of this, the known attitudes and actions of Dimick B. Huntington clearly point to the possibility of such correspondence. It is also possible some Indians misunderstood the source of the policy their superior, Tutsegabits, apparently received personally from Brigham Young through Huntington.[51]

Relatively little is known about Tutsegabits other than that for a decade he was widely acknowledged to be the head chief over at least six Paiute villages. With the possible exception of leaders of the Harmony band, he was the only Paiute chief who attended the Salt Lake City conference with Brigham Young who may have helped carry out the policy approved at that time. Yet some knowledgeable students argue he did not return from Salt Lake City in time to be a massacre participant.[52] It is equally possible that at some point about a week after the massacre, Tutsegabits returned to Salt Lake City and was ordained an elder in the Latter-day Saints priesthood. There was no known implication that this ordination was at all related to his willingness to help implement any desired policy. Nor was there any hesitance to withhold the presumed honors of church authority because of any activities in which he had recently been a participant. He later served as a missionary for the church among other Native Americans, including the Navajos.[53]

THE YOUNG-HASLAM MESSAGE

When James Haslam reached Brigham Young after an amazingly quick horseback ride of almost three hundred miles, he received orders directing the southern Utah leaders as follows: "In regard to emigrating trains passing through our settlements we must not interfere with them until they are first notified to keep away. You must not meddle with them. The Indians we expect will do as they please, but you should try and preserve good feelings with them [Paiutes]. . . . Let them [the emigrants] go in peace."[54] This has usually been cited as evidence that Brigham Young was against the violence. But knowl-

edge of his earlier directive, either directly or through his interpreter, to the Native American leaders of the region argues he essentially approved—indeed, encouraged—their actions. And given that church authorities made absolutely no effort to chastise or punish any of the participants, the massacre could hardly have been so displeasing to them. It is difficult to disagree with historian R. Kent Fielding, negative though he usually is toward Brigham Young, when he stated the church leader's "message to Isaac Haight was a clear order that the Indians should not be punished for what they had done." Young granted the right of the Indians to "do as they please[d]," which, according to his earlier instructions, included cattle stealing and had to imply some killing.[55]

CALIFORNIA REACTION TO THE MASSACRE

The first notice of the Mountain Meadows Massacre to reach southern California was from San Bernardino residents and mail carriers William Matthews and Sidney Tanner and two non-Mormons they agreed to bring with them just days after the fateful murders. George Powers of Arkansas and P. M. Warn of New York offered reasonably accurate affidavits of their experiences in Utah, widely published in the California newspapers. At the Tonequint–Santa Clara villages, Chief Jackson and his warriors recognized Warn as an American and although Matthews and Tanner denied it, arguing their associates to be Latter-day Saints, the Indians reportedly grew restive and threatening toward him and Powers. Fortunately for the travelers, they had enlisted a missionary to the Indians, Ira Hatch, to accompany them through the Virgin and Muddy river areas. Tanner was quoted as asserting he would not venture down that dangerous segment of the trail without Hatch, who was notably influential among the Paiutes.

A most damaging portion of Warn's affidavit was the clearly cordial relationship observed between the Mormons and the otherwise-hostile Indians. At Las Vegas, the chief reportedly asked Hatch whether any word had been sent from Brigham Young about whether he was yet ready to fight their common enemies. The chief claimed he and his warriors were ready, that he had poisoned his arrows and was properly prepared. It is entirely likely that while the Cedar City–Harmony Paiutes, and some of those from the Santa Clara, Virgin, and Muddy river areas, had been involved in the earlier killings, these Las Vegas–area warriors had not participated in the Mountain Meadows Massacre and were then anxious to get their own opportunities to loot and perhaps kill.

The initial notice of a "rumored massacre" on the trail, published in California, was in the Los Angeles *Star* the first week of October. It stated that twenty-five families comprising some ninety-five individuals had been cruelly murdered and that only the younger children had been spared. The *Star* expressed reluctance to give credence to the initial reports until further information was available. Additional details were forthcoming in the following issue, which reported that in fact over one hundred had been killed at Mountain Meadows. At that time, the newspaper concluded it to be "the foulest massacre . . . ever perpetrated on the route and . . . call[ed] loudly for the active interposition of the government," demanding in addition that "the authorities inflict a terrible retribution on those concerned."

Attached to this second newspaper notice was a letter from J. Ward Christian, the non-Mormon recently moved to San Bernardino, and already married into one of the prominent church families there. Christian drew on the reports of Matthews and Tanner, who had been in Utah when the emigrant train crossed the territory. He recounted the rumor that someone in the party had poisoned an ox carcass and also a nearby water hole, for the purpose of killing Indians. This he denounced as senseless, because it endangered not only that emigrant train but also subsequent ones. Christian correctly concluded that whatever the details of the circumstances and causes, the catastrophe would be attributed to the Mormon people.[56]

As soon as notice of the massacre arrived at San Bernardino, many others also recognized that it was likely to affect them in unfortunate ways. Young Francis Lyman confided to his father, Amasa, "[T]here is considerable sentiment in this place and Los Angeles on account of the murder of that company of emigrants at the Mountain Meadows," asserting he would not be surprised "if it raised a beef with us . . ." in California. Stake

(diocese) President William J. Cox confided essentially the same to Brigham Young, saying that "the apostates [were] doing all they can to make the citizens believe that the Mormons [were] accessory to the murder." Cox predicted that such reports "no doubt will give us some trouble at this place."[57]

The focal point of public outrage over the massacre was a citizen's meeting held at a circus pavilion near the Los Angeles plaza. Here the proceedings featured the written depositions of Powers and Warn dictated to Los Angeles *Star* correspondent W. A. Wallace, who was usually friendly to the Latter-day Saints. Both accounts first noted the hostile mood of both Mormons and Indians, not only toward the invading army that they both expected to fight but also toward travelers, to whom the Mormons essentially refused to sell supplies. Powers stated that on his approach to Salt Lake City, he observed both church militiamen and well-armed Indians awaiting orders from Mormon authorities concerning resistance to the approaching U.S. troops. And he claimed to have observed, in Cedar City, a wagon loaded with clothing and driven by a white man accompanied by jubilant Indians driving cattle he asserted belonged to the murdered emigrants. The New Yorker also recounted a conversation with a Native American in the Beaver area, some forty miles from where the latter's neighbors were supposedly poisoned through the intentionally prepared dead ox, which reportedly had been central in arousing the Indians to hostility. Warn stated that the well-known chief Ammon denied that anyone had died from poisoning. This suggested the alleged poisoning incident provided absolutely no justification for the massacre.

Certainly the most significant part of the testimony, so far as San Bernardino was concerned, was Powers's report of the reaction he perceived among citizens there to the news of the massacre. He recounted that whereas one Mormon traveling companion, Sidney Tanner, appeared to deeply regret the affair, the other, William Matthews, "rejoiced greatly at the massacre and considered it the beginning of long-delayed vengeance," presumably on the perpetrators of crimes against the Mormons in Missouri two decades previously. The witness also stated that at San Bernardino he had heard "many people express gratification at the massacre," specifically mentioning former California state assemblyman Jefferson Hunt, who was quoted as saying, "[T]he Hand of the Lord was in it whether done by whites or redskins, it was right! The prophesies [of vengeance] concerning Missouri were being fulfilled." The witnesses also mentioned in their statements that their Mormon associates had cautioned them not to say much about what they had seen. Most of the resolutions subsequently focused on the "persistent and systematic robberies and murders on the Utah to California trail," with Brigham Young blamed for each and calling for government action not only to bring the perpetrators to justice but also to make the route safe for all travelers.[58]

When the San Francisco *Alta California* published first notice of the Mountain Meadows Massacre, it also editorialized, "[W]e were prepared to expect such deeds, and more of them, because everyone who comes from Salt Lake repeats the imprecations that are breathed out" against presumed enemies of the Mormon church. The next month the paper further denounced the tenor of the speeches that church leaders continued to deliver. The *Alta* editors specifically contended, of Brigham Young's rhetoric, "[T]here is a vein of ferocious denunciation of Americans running through those discourses that chills the blood, and taken in connection with the recent massacres and outrages, clearly establishes not only his complicity in them, but his determination to destroy all that comes in his power." The editor concluded that a true civil war then existed—"a war of religious fanaticism." Many of his readers would have agreed, and Californians in general were truly alarmed over recent developments in Utah. But until these comments in the *Alta California* in mid-November, people in the San Francisco Bay area did not link the California Mormons with this escalating ill feeling.

The editor of the San Francisco *Daily Evening Bulletin* bitterly affirmed, "[T]he blood of American citizens cries for vengeance, [and] virtue, Christianity and decency require that the blood of incestuous miscreants who have perpetrated this atrocity be broken and dispersed." He continued that not only should the Latter-day Saints be relegated to the fires of hell but also "once the general detestation and hatred pervading the whole country is given legal countenance and direction, a crusade will start against Utah which will crush out this beastly heresy forever." The editor then asserted that if

the government proved incapable of resolving the problem, "from this state alone, thousands of volunteers could be drawn, who would ask no better employment than the extermination of the Mormons at the call of the government."[59] Many California newspapers made similar claims regarding the availability of willing volunteers for a retaliatory invasion from that direction. The Los Angeles *Star* even published a travel log to show how easy such a campaign would be using the Southern Route. Mormon leaders, justly concerned about the possibility of this becoming a reality, did what they could to counter that thrust.

CALIFORNIA ARMS PROCUREMENT

Even before news of the Mountain Meadows Massacre reached California, newspapers throughout the state reported on the inclination of Mormons everywhere to defy the national government and prepare to defend their church leaders and fellow believers in the Salt Lake Valley. Members of the San Bernardino stake presidency had been directed by Brigham Young to procure guns and ammunition in the "Golden State," along with teams, wagons, and other items useful in the resistance. Thereafter, missionaries and businessmen from the San Francisco Bay area brought large quantities of the desired items with them to the center of California Mormondom at San Bernardino. These materials were often carried surreptitiously up Cajon Pass to emigrants already prepared to make the desert crossing northeastward to the Utah war zone. Local church leaders understood the alarm with which their growing number of enemies in California regarded the role of the San Bernardino colony as an arsenal for the presumed Utah rebels, and acted with great circumspection. Trail veteran Edwin Pettit of San Bernardino recalled that during the crisis the town marshal summoned him to accompany him in a light spring wagon on a night trip up Cajon Pass, to "carry ammunition and firearms to deliver to those who were [heading for] Salt Lake." He wondered why he had been selected for the undertaking, but it was undoubtedly because he was not among those church opponents were watching in an effort to prevent just such a mission.[60]

The regional newspapers attempted to arouse the citizenry to prevent these shipments. In mid-November 1857, the *Alta California* asserted, "[P]rudence demands that a military force be stationed at the Cajon Pass to prevent the transportation of munitions and supplies to the enemy camp." But the paper lamented that "arms and ammunition continue to be forwarded from San Bernardino." An *Alta* reporter asserted that recently a mail carrier had taken 500 revolvers to Utah. The paper also alleged that "purchase of powder, pistols and duck for tents have been made to a considerable extent in this city [San Francisco] and forwarded to San Bernardino," where they were sent under heavy guard. Similarly, the *Star* stated that the 1,200 people estimated to have left for Utah by late December 1857 "took with them not less than from ten to fifteen tons of pow[d]er, two or three thousand guns, revolvers, &c, and other warlike articles in proportion." These estimates were likely exaggerated, and the Californians did little except talk to halt the flow of munitions that had made the San Bernardino outpost indispensable up to that time.[61]

THE DUKES-TURNER COMPANY

Although the Mountain Meadows Massacre discredited Mormondom and discouraged emigrant travel over the Southern Route for some time, other emigrant trains already in the southern portion of Utah had no choice but to complete their journey—if they were more fortunate than the party traveling just ahead of them. The biggest threat to these, because even fanatical Mormons had had more than their fill of killing, was that the Indians were just now becoming fully aroused. As Juanita Brooks described, "having once been stirred up to kill and loot," they virtually "knew no restraint." She commented, "The Natives, however, thought the war with the Mericats was just getting well underway, a war which might yield much loot for them." Thus every other company on the road was now in jeopardy, whatever their origins or past actions. Because Native Americans regarded every passing emigrant train with equal hostility, to expect the warriors to abandon such an exhilarating policy after only one major episode would be difficult.[62]

At the time of the Mountain Meadows Massacre, an emigrant train led by men named William C. Dukes and Nicholas Turner encountered difficulty while approaching Beaver, some eighty miles to the north. One of the local militia leaders, Philo T. Farnsworth, was informed by an Indian that his fellows were planning to attack the emigrants. Farnsworth promptly warned the train captain, who confessed that his people, who had doubtless heard of the Indian attack on the party ahead, were so "demoralized" they would hardly act even in this crisis. On 9 September, with the assistance of the militia, the emigrants were brought into Beaver, but not before Indians had attempted to run off their cattle and an emigrant guard had shot one of the raiders. The Native Americans sought revenge. They later wounded Turner and another man, Collins, right within the limits of the town. Farnsworth thereafter removed the belligerents from Beaver—the Indians sent back to their camp and the emigrants moving on toward Parowan under militia escort, still justifiably afraid of Paiute attack.[63]

Beyond Iron County the company hired Mormon guides to pilot them over a new route by way of Black Ridge east of the Pine Valley Mountains, instead of west through Mountain Meadows. They were thus the first emigrant train to use the route later followed by the Arrowhead Highway, U.S. Highway 91, and Interstate 15 through later St. George. This group apparently moved very slowly because of the large number of cattle they were driving and doubtless also because of the steep mountain incline at Black Ridge later called "Peter's Leap," where the wagons may have been lowered by ropes.

When the new head of the Latter-day Saints Southern Indian Mission, Jacob Hamblin, who had had no part in the Mountain Meadows Massacre, returned to southern Utah soon thereafter, he learned that hostile Native Americans were following the Dukes-Turner company with intent to perpetrate another massacre. Hamblin immediately dispatched two fellow missionaries, Dudley Leavitt and Sam Knight, to catch up with the company and prevent any further Indian attacks. The missionaries were soon convinced it was impossible to save both the emigrants and their livestock. Hamblin had instructed his men to do the best they could, and two days later Leavitt returned to report the Indians had robbed the

Jacob Hamblin, president of the Southern Indian Mission of the Latter-day Saints, successfully sought to restrain aroused Native Americans from further violence after the Mountain Meadows Massacre.

party of some three hundred head of cattle. Hamblin's earliest biographer, James A. Little, later explained that "finding it altogether impossible to control the Indians," the missionaries reached a compromise on the matter. "The Indians agreed to only take the loose stock of the company and not to meddle with the teams and wagons and not to make any effort to take their [the emigrants'] lives." The attack came by moonlight some seven miles west of the Muddy River crossing, toward the end of the so-called California Wash.

Since the Dukes party had engaged eight Mormons to guide them through the notably difficult portion of the route, the emigrants were particularly angry, because they assumed that the church members were fully involved in the cattle thefts. Later reports from the area at the time attested that some of the livestock were driven

back toward Utah by riders of mounts that had horse-shoes, presumably not by Indians.[64] Members of the pioneer company apparently never knew how close they came to death or how their white guides had done their best under difficult circumstances. Missionary Leavitt later stated he had taken his life in his hands to ask the Muddy River Indians, painted and dressed for war, not to harm the wagon train. He said he had risked this because his ecclesiastic superior Hamblin, whom he greatly respected, had assigned him to do so. In fact, the fifty-four adults and forty-six children narrowly escaped the fate of the Fancher party, ironically probably saved by some of the same men who had participated in that earlier tragic affair and who, under direction from higher church authorities, had doubtless initially aroused the Moapa Paiute band and their neighbors to war. Reports were that Hamblin later retrieved some of the animals not already slaughtered and delivered these to an agent representing members of the Dukes-Turner party. This did nothing to assuage the bitterness of that group, some members of which remained in San Bernardino for the expressed purpose of punishing other Mormons for what they had suffered.[65]

Utah historian Will Bagley, in his popular recent study of the Mountain Meadows Massacre, argues that Jacob Hamblin and his Latter-day Saint Indian missionary associates conspired from the outset to steal the Dukes-Turner company cattle. This is one of the several instances where I strongly disagree, even though both used essentially the same source materials. Where Bagley concluded that Mormon leaders, including Hamblin, "made sure the emigrants left Deseret with nothing but their lives, wagons, and teams," I believe to have left that region at all at that explosive time was a major accomplishment and tribute to Hamblin and his men. I will concede that Hamblin and other Indian missionaries probably ended up with some of the stolen cattle, although they also helped return some to their owners.[66]

JACOB HAMBLIN

As historian D. Michael Quinn has argued, most early Mormons avoided violence and were saddened by the news of such incidents.[67] Jacob Hamblin was certainly one of these. He had emerged as one of the Mormon Indian agents most trusted by both Native Americans and Mormon church leaders. During his formative years in that endeavor he once defied a military superior in Tooele County in order to prevent killing of Indians he had promised to protect. He was later one of the original missionaries in the Southern Indian Mission, eventually replacing Rufus C. Allen as head of that effort, by then centered at Santa Clara, where Hamblin's imposing stone home still stands as a famous landmark. Early in his ministry among the Tonequint Paiutes he blessed a sick Indian woman who was miraculously healed. That was the beginning of his legendary reputation among Native Americans of the region. Several Indians who opposed him also died mysteriously of illness, which enhanced his standing as a man of supernatural power.[68]

Hamblin had camped near the Fancher party on Corn Creek as he traveled to Salt Lake City to take another wife. On his return to the same area, he heard some vague information about their deaths from leading perpetrator John D. Lee, whom he had good reason to distrust. He heard more as he ventured south. Too exhausted to go himself, he sent his fellow missionaries to save the Dukes-Turner party. Because his home was then near Mountain Meadows, he witnessed the ghastly murder scene before the victims were properly buried. Stating this experience to be impossible to describe, he affirmed, "[T]he gloom that seemed to diffuse itself through the air and cast a shade over the hills and vales was dismal in the extreme." His former cattle range, the meadows, would never seem the same again to Jacob and many others familiar with the area and with the recent events transpiring there.

Southern Utah church officials soon received letters from President Brigham Young, carried by other emigrants whom the church leader instructed should be assisted safely through the dangerous stretch of road. Repeatedly Hamblin and his associates risked their lives to carry out these assignments. Jacob Hamblin was perplexed to learn that two of the missionaries from Cedar City stationed among the Moapas at the Muddy River swore they had been sent to "kill off and take the spoil" of a company he had just ushered through. He explained he had recent instructions from Brigham Young to protect the people, but they continued to assert that

"there was [sic] secret instructions that had been taken." The mission president concluded that evidently a "local conspiracy existed among a few fanatics to destroy the caravans that were going through to California." He believed these conspirators "had been misled and given secret instructions telling them what to do, and they had taken steps to carry out the evil plan" but had been thwarted.[69] Among the Cedar City residents then at the Muddy were Perry Liston and Jeheil McConnell, probably the men that Hamblin noted were persisting in their violent inclinations.[70]

OTHER EMIGRANT GROUPS THREATENED

About the time of the Mountain Meadows Massacre, a small party of emigrant men, including William Clark, the future mayor of Ames, Iowa, passed along the pioneer route from the Platte River toward Salt Lake City. While circling around contingents of Col. Albert Sidney Johnston's invading soldiers, Mormon militiamen apprehended the travelers and interrogated them about the rival army's strength. They wisely replied that although they themselves were simply teamsters, they assumed the invading federal force to be low on provisions because Mormon scouts had successfully destroyed wagon trains laden with essential supplies. Clark befriended Bill Hickman, allegedly one of Brigham Young's secret corps of "Danites" charged with enforcing discipline through threats and violence against backsliding church members and outside opponents. This acquaintanceship, and hinting that Clark and some associates might be interested in becoming LDS church members, secured them passes to travel safely within and through Utah Territory. At Salt Lake City, Clark also met Jim "Griff" Williams, the mail carrier over the Southern Route, who reported difficulty getting through the Nevada–southern Utah sector safely on his recent trip north.

Williams told Clark that he intended to return over the route in the company of church leader Amasa Lyman, who reportedly disapproved of the murders at Mountain Meadows and of any other violence recently advocated in the region. Mail carrier David Savage, noted to be particularly friendly with the aroused Indians, would also be in the small company heading south toward Los Angeles. Clark experienced difficulty getting from Provo to Cedar City because of a band of Native Americans, whom Clark's small group of "Gentiles" assumed were waiting to kill and rob them before they joined those who would be influential in protecting them. The Clark party understood that several Aiken brothers had been killed in the Salt Creek–Sevier River vicinity just a week earlier.[71]

By remaining an extra day with a sympathetic Spanish Fork bishop and his wife, the small group outwaited the Indians and passed safely through. They met Savage at his newly established home at what would soon be Holden, traveling with him to Cedar City where Savage, Clark, and their associates joined Williams and others intending to travel with Lyman. Apostle Lyman had gone ahead to Santa Clara expressly to arrange for safe passage for all party members, including non-Mormons. To assist with this, Lyman engaged Ira Hatch to interpret for him as he spoke to the Paiutes summoned to hear him. Lyman not only appealed for safety but also directed each Paiute chief to send similar word to the next band down the trail. After these precautions, the company passed through the Mountain Meadows area, camping at a spring four miles from the massacre site. The travelers were instructed to remain close to their wagons and not look around, but Clark counted eighteen unburied skeletons, mostly women and children, with hair still on the skulls. Part of the reason he confessed this sufficient to "make a man's blood run cold" was that he understood some of the perpetrators of the crimes were accompanying his train.[72]

Veteran church leader Amasa Lyman was apparently becoming increasingly disenchanted with some of Brigham Young's policies, including stress on the culture of violence.[73] After the horrible chain of events of this period, and after a mission to England in which he preached views concerning the Atonement of Christ clearly not in keeping with Latter-day Saints doctrine, Amasa Lyman resided in Fillmore, not far from many participants in the massacre. According to newspaperman John Isaac, who had been closely associated with him during the period, Lyman "heard so many confessions from those who had been forced by the leaders to imbue their hands in the blood of the innocent, and he

Amasa M. Lyman, perhaps the Mormon general authority least supportive of the doctrine of vengeance for past injustices toward church members, which was influential in bringing about the Mountain Meadows Massacre. While he was committed to defending the Southern Route from invasion by potential enemies, Lyman also helped protect passing travelers who might otherwise have been in jeopardy in the southern region.

had seen so much wretchedness of mind among those, that he encouraged them to make a full confession of their crime and take the consequences." Although none dared do so in any public manner, this may be the source from which some of the affidavits and individual accounts of the Mountain Meadows Massacre apparently later contained in the LDS church archives stemmed. Isaac claimed that some of the first information eventually leading to territorial court proceedings against John D. Lee may also have stemmed from this influence. Since Brigham Young and most of his associates continued to discourage mention of the entire matter, Lyman was again in conflict with his superiors. Yet he clearly continued the practice of assisting participants to unburden their consciences, and this may have been another breaking point between him and his longtime close associates in the church hierarchy, from whom he eventually severed ties.[74]

At the Muddy River, the Savage-Clark group encountered Mormon missionaries Perry Liston and Jeheil McConnell, the latter of whom attempted to explain how difficult it had been to keep the Indians from killing the mail carrier, Williams, on his recent upward trip. At that point a young Paiute man stepped forward to contradict that account, saying it had been McConnell who had wished the non-Mormon Williams killed. According to Clark's observations, the Moapas liked Williams, whom they called Poshupa because of his heavy eyebrows and who was said to have been consistently generous on his mail trips, offering food and tobacco. The embarrassed McConnell walked away without replying. The Clark-Savage party passed safely through the dangerous area, and the remainder of their journey was uneventful. Although no corroboration exists of the details of Clark's account, there is no reason to discount any part of it, negative though it may be toward McConnell.[75]

Williams's interaction with the Moapa missionary McConnell and the earlier exchange Jacob Hamblin had had with the same McConnell illustrates the persistence of somewhat contradictory policies and aims enunciated among Mormon leaders and missionaries in regard to Native Americans in the region. Clearly some wished to arouse hostility toward all non-Mormons passing through the area, even encouraging violence. The situation stemmed from the sometimes-changing individual inclinations of those charged to carry out such instructions. There is no evidence Brigham Young persisted in encouraging violence, but sufficient orders had earlier emanated from church headquarters that it proved difficult to curb the continuing import. This continuation could have been quickly thwarted through another visit from George A. Smith or Young.

But the record is equally clear that some LDS brethren held a long-standing opposite frame of reference, notably Amasa M. Lyman, Jacob Hamblin, and Chief Kanosh. These men persistently opposed the violence and used their influence to ensure the safety of all passing along the Southern Route, often with difficulty. Nevertheless, there was at least one additional failure to ensure safe emigrant passage, as discussed slightly later herein.

An irony concerning Jim Williams's reported difficulties is that earlier the same year he had helped another pioneer company, of English Mormon converts, travel through the same region. These people had become disillusioned with the church as they observed it in Zion and regarded themselves as virtually escaping from Utah. Encountering Williams and his family at the Santa Clara, they traveled south with him and credited him with getting them safely through the danger zone, partly, it was said, because he had lived among Indians and understood their language. Historians are not certain where or with whom he lived, but he or perhaps his uncle, Old Bill Williams, at some point occupied some type of homestead near Cottonwood Springs (Blue Diamond) and that vicinity continued to occasionally be referred to as the Williams ranch or camp.[76]

THE HUNTINGTON–HORACE CLARK PARTY AND GINN ACCOUNT

Another emigrant party passing the Mountain Meadows site some ten weeks after the massacre enjoyed the official protection of Brigham Young. On 2 November 1857 he wrote to Isaac Haight and John D. Lee to explain that former Salt Lake City merchant William Bell and a Mr. Ray, recently an employee of the Gilbert and Gerrish express company, had requested his assistance in engaging protective guides, for which they were willing to pay well. Young suggested Ira Hatch, if Hamblin could not accompany the group. He also ordered that an Indian chief, preferably Tutsegabits, be engaged to accompany them through the most threatening area. Hamblin and Kanosh filled these guide roles. Young reported that William D. Huntington, like his brother Dimick a seasoned trail veteran, currently employed by the freighting company of Livingston and Kinkead, headed the party, assisted by future trail ore freighter Horace Clark.[77] Equipped with five light spring wagons each drawn by four good mules, this party could thus move with greater speed than most traveling over the Southern Route. One of Huntington's wives accompanied him, along with at least one other unnamed Mormon. Four non-Mormon men, one other woman, and perhaps a boy, Heber Huntington, son of the leader and later a Victor Valley way station operator, also traveled in the company.

Party member Enoch Parrish, cousin and nephew of the men killed earlier in the year at Springville, like his less fortunate relatives had been thwarted in his first attempt to embark for southern California. In his case he did not hold a "travel permit" required by Utah civil and religious leaders. After some delay, Enoch and his travel companions obtained the proper pass, although some southern Utah officials were still pessimistic about their chances of safely getting past the still-hostile Native Americans. At some point, presumably in southern Utah, Parrish and Horace Clark were attacked in the night, while encamped. Leaving some equipment behind, the men hitched up their wagon and quickly moved on. After daylight another wagon overtook them and the two fellow travelers advised them to stop and await arrival of a larger group of emigrants known to be approaching. The reason given was "the Indians which is [*sic*] very excited on account of some immigrants [*sic*] which has marred their peace. Killing some of them." The unnamed informants continued to assert the opinion that the Native Americans had by then obtained some revenge through killing and robbing. They also mentioned that "one or two whites" had at some point been captured by the Paiutes. There is no other known reference to this situation, which was recorded by Parrish apparently as his party reached the Santa Clara River.[78]

Forty-six years later, one of the non-Mormons, John L. Ginn, recorded his experiences. An important episode he recounted involved the Pahvant Indians as the party passed through southeastern Millard County a hundred miles from Mountain Meadows. Chief Kanosh had been engaged to accompany the group to Iron County, including through his own tribal domain. Perhaps as a test of some of his warriors he had good reason to distrust, he rode his horse on the opposite side of the covered wagons, out of the line of sight of any fellow tribesmen watching from vantage points near their village. When a party of Pahvant warriors charged toward the emigrants, Kanosh rushed out to halt the attack, saying that Brigham Young had approved of these people passing safely by. Parashot (Parashant), described by Ginn as "an old patriarch of the tribe" and known to have been in favor of the Gunnison massacre four years previously, made an impassioned plea to kill the emigrants. Kanosh met this direct challenge by calling for a division of the tribesmen into those who would obey him and those persisting in advocating the killing. About two-thirds sided with Kanosh, who was by this time glowering at Parashant, probably a long-time antagonist. Chief Kanosh warned those inclined to fight that if they did so, it would be a battle to extermination, and that if he, the emigrants, and the loyal Indians won, not a single opponent would be left alive. Parashant asserted he had fourteen grown sons and that his family alone could accomplish his purpose. Kanosh thereon instructed his own brother Hunkitter, called "Shot" for his marksmanship, to kill anyone who presumed to leave the residential area before he returned. That ended the confrontation and fully demonstrated the loyalty of Kanosh to what he perceived to be the policy of the Mormon leaders, at least when it involved pacific actions.[79]

Arguably the most impressive Native American leader of his generation in the southern Utah region, particularly in his commitment to maintaining peace,

Pahvant chief Kanosh, champion of peace between southern Utah Native Americans and all others who might be in their domain. He was a full partner in the fervent efforts to curb further bloodshed after the Mountain Meadows Massacre.

Kanosh certainly risked his life in his confrontation with Parashant, carrying out what he considered Brigham Young's current policy. The fact that none of his band participated in the Mountain Meadows Massacre, despite his presence at the earlier crucial Salt Lake City interview, is evidence he made his own decisions in such matters.[80]

After an uneventful trip as far as the Santa Clara River, they encountered about a hundred and fifty Indians. Ginn admitted he antagonized some of them by warning his fellows to carefully watch the wagons, to prevent the Tonequint band members from stealing from them. Thereafter some of the Indians who understood his words acted menacingly. At that point, a chief, probably Tutsegabits, arrived and after quietly observing the situation, chastised his people for working themselves into a high state of excitement just because someone alleged they might steal. He chided that the Indians knew they would in fact take anything they could get their hands on, whether useful or not. He then ordered the Native Americans to leave the camp before they had been fed, saying their behavior did not merit even that benefit. The chief demonstrated decisive authority, because, as Ginn reported, they left, although "you can scarcely run a hungry Indian out of camp at meal time even with a gun."

Fortunately for the emigrant company, they enlisted Jacob Hamblin to bring them through the next segment of road past the still-hostile Paiutes along that way. As they approached the Muddy River, near where the Dukes train had recently been threatened and lost its cattle, Hamblin went on ahead. Ginn claimed that up to five hundred armed tribesmen had made preparations to attack and kill them all before they reached the river. But Hamblin convinced the Moapa chiefs, Isaac and Thomas, to let the company pass by. Ginn claimed to have observed, from atop the adjacent hills, native runners darting through the brush and then groups of other Indians rising up and taking the roadway to the ford of the Muddy. Later the company fed the entire group of Moapas gathered there.[81]

That evening the emigrants observed and listened to a program of love ballads and dances, accompanied by low chants in monotone harmony, with loud grunts in unison. The large body of dancers circled the fire with

locked arms, leaping simultaneously into the air and every foot coming down heavily at the same instant. These dances were enjoyed for a long duration. Then someone requested demonstration of a war dance, with which the Moapas complied. However, in the midst of the proceedings, there were seemingly menacing glances, particularly at the non-Mormons in the party. Hamblin felt constrained to explain that no one with whom the Paiutes were not "thoroughly friendly" could witness such a ceremony "with total safety."

Later, Chief Thomas noticed that as many as one hundred thirty of his Indians were missing from the camp. He recognized they were among those who had not been pleased with his decision to allow the emigrants to pass, and after speaking to Hamblin on the matter, he sent runners to warn them not to act on their desires. Thereafter, the pioneer company set out for Las Vegas, where they camped in the abandoned mission-fort. Next day they were essentially surrounded, presumably by Paiutes from both Vegas and the Muddy. Hamblin determined that the hostile Indians were simply waiting for the chief of the Vegas band to give the proper signal for attack. Fortunately, the missionary understood that his fellow worker, Ira Hatch, was expected momentarily and that he had great influence with that chief.

Hamblin's initial efforts to inquire about his sometime companion elicited statements first that Hatch had been killed, then that he had already left the area. But through sheer good luck Hamblin discovered fellow missionary Hatch in a wickiup, sleeping after a harrowing experience among the Mojave Indians and then traveling all night to reach the Las Vegas village. The Las Vegas chief, it soon became clear, was simply waiting for Hatch to leave the area before he ordered the attack on the other emigrants. As Ira Hatch sought to negotiate for the safety of the party, however, his promises of gifts made little impact, because if the owners were killed *all* their possessions would be in Indian hands. Finally the missionary reportedly offered to use his influence with Mormon authorities and others to elevate the Las Vegas chief to the status of Tutsegabits's successor as leader of all Paiutes south of the Great Basin rim. Whether the promise was ever fulfilled, it settled the emigrants' fate favorably. The Indians allowed them to complete the journey. Hamblin traveled with the company all the way to the

Mojave River, where friendly Mormons warned that members of the Turner-Dukes party remained in San Bernardino and would surely lynch him for a supposed role in their losing cattle to the Paiutes. The grateful emigrants paid Hamblin $300 for his services.[82]

ANOTHER MASSACRE

Despite all the heroic efforts to quell the Native American excitement for attack and plunder, at some point, probably later, one Indian massacre of undetermined magnitude was not averted. Mormon missionary Thales T. Haskell's journal has an entry concerning a scene he came on that has never otherwise been noted. Somewhere in the area southwest of Las Vegas on the California road, he observed fires burning "the wreckage of an emigrant train," including, on closer examination, the charred bodies of the victims. He surmised the fire had been set to "destroy what evidence they could of the savage deed."

This apparently took place in early 1860 after Haskell and his associates had completed a Mormon mission led by Jacob Hamblin among Arizona Native Americans. He and others received reports of Nevada Paiutes "ready to attack a small party of emigrants who were on their way to southern California and who by this time were well out past the Las Vegas Springs." With eight others, Haskell hurried to the scene to "if possible, persuade the Indians to change their savage plans." It was too late.

He recorded that "the struggle had evidently been a desperate one. Many arrows were left sticking in the ground and remains of the camp." They noticed a child's shoe, but found no child's body or other clothing, thus surmising it had been carried away by the raiding party. After burying the dead, probably in the vicinity of Cottonwood Springs-Blue Diamond, the group took a round-about course homeward for the expressed purpose of determining which band or tribe was "guilty of the awful deed." But the Native Americans encountered were so "saucy and mean [that they] learned little about it."[83] Given the prevailing hostility, that so many people made the dangerous desert passage safely is a significant accomplishment of some dedicated, and often unappreciated, missionaries to the Indians.

THE MORMON EXODUS FROM SAN BERNARDINO

As most post–Mountain Meadows Massacre parties that had survived passage through Deseret-Utah crossed the so-called ninety-five-mile desert approaching the settled portion of southern California, they encountered numerous Mormons who had just abandoned San Bernardino and were en route back to Utah. Although the colony could probably have survived the hostile reaction to news of the recent massacre, cattle theft, and other occurrences, Brigham Young had long wanted the settlement to be disbanded or at least the faithful there called back to Zion, and now he could act on that wish. As soon as the committed Latter-day Saints residing there recognized that his desires were partly to test their faithfulness, they virtually abandoned six years of farm and home development. Many sold for less than a third what their property was deemed to be worth. Some simply traded their California holdings for an outfit sufficient to return to Utah.

Louisa Barnes Pratt, who believed the San Bernardino Latter-day Saints community was the best she had ever seen, was quickly reconciled to the need to sacrifice. Still, she likened the disbandment to "a great shipwreck at sea, where all is sacrificed." Forced to delay her own departure and hoping to persuade a reluctant husband, trail veteran Addison Pratt, to leave California, she observed, "[A] great company started, a hundred teams, all strong and reliable. It was a grand sight, all white covered large wagons." She noted that another company was nearly ready, not quite so large, which included one of her married daughters, along with Louisa's sister Caroline and her family. The plan was to get beyond the "tremendous mountain to pass over," meaning the Cajon, then strengthen the livestock on the lush natural feed along the Mojave River before starting across the deserts in the dead of winter.[84]

One of the most impressive women in Mormon San Bernardino was Sister Pratt's sister, Caroline Barnes Crosby, who kept an even more complete diary of her two-year sojourn there. When the family concluded to leave, they traded perhaps the most admired house in the town for a wagon, oxen, and some provisions—without her recording a word of complaint. In the first two days on the Cajon Pass road, a soldier and an elderly Mormon woman they passed both commented positively on their wagon, the latter calling it "as comfortable as a house." In fact, on the journey Caroline occasionally slept in the bed inside as her husband and son drove the vehicle along the road. At an early juncture she noted, she "regulated the wagon, which [she] found topsey turvey," which it would doubtless be many other days as well. Her subsequent journey along the trail and her extended stay at Las Vegas is recounted in chapter 8 in this book.[85]

THREATENED INVASIONS
FROM CALIFORNIA

In the meantime, both the Mormon leaders and some of their opponents in southern California focused considerable interest on efforts currently under way to explore the lower Colorado River, with special attention to the feasibility of navigating the waterway with steamboats. Although the church hierarchy was then apprehensive that steam riverboat transportation might be used to make a military invasion of Utah Territory from the southwest, they had actually helped stimulate interest in such an enterprise. Several years earlier, during more peaceful times, Amasa Lyman had appealed to western United States Army commander John E. Wool for explo-

ration of the river at government expense. Largely as a result of the process commenced at that time, the federal government built a stern-wheel riverboat drawing only two feet of water, capable of negotiating rapids and swift currents expected on the Colorado. Lt. Joseph C. Ives and a crew experienced in the topographic surveys of the region gathered at Yuma, where the steamboat, shippped from Philadelphia in pieces, was being assembled. As the crisis between the Latter-day Saints and the federal government heightened early in 1858, the Los Angeles *Star* editor, Henry Hamilton, speculated that the current object of the Ives expedition was to "select a site for a military depot," in view of the contemplated movement against the Mormons in the spring.[86]

At the same time that the Los Angeles newspaper discussed the possibilities of a military invasion of Utah assisted by steamboats, its writers were also advocating a volunteer military mission overland to aid the United States Army approaching from the East in what it presumed to describe as war with the Mormons. The *Star* published freighter W. T. B. Sanford's detailed description of the route, stressing the ease with which a large force of soldiers could be transported to Utah. In mid-January 1858, Los Angeles citizens learned that Major Smith, recently appointed commander of the Western Division but now in the East, had been called to the nation's capital to consult "on the expediency of equipping an expedition to California" to assist Gen. Albert Sid-

Lt. William C. Ives's steamboat, Explorer, *on the Colorado River in 1858.*

ney Johnston's invasion. Los Angeles newspaperman Hamilton argued that it was "only by using southern California as a base that the [Utah] rebellion could be speedily suppressed." The *Star* reported that Secretary of War John B. Floyd was not then in favor of employing California volunteers, as the newspaper had been urging, but the same Washington, D.C., dispatch stressed that other military officials were yet considering the possibilities of using willing southern California citizens in an expedition against the Mormons.[87]

COLONEL KANE'S MISSION

Fortunately, the crisis was quickly diffused by the arrival of an unofficial emissary who had recently conferred with U.S. president James Buchanan. Col. Thomas L. Kane, an old friend of the Mormons and of Buchanan, hurried to California from the East by ocean steamer to Mexico and then across to the Pacific. He arrived at San Bernardino after a difficult month's journey from Washington, D.C. His anxiety to get to the Utah Mormon settlements aroused suspicion and caused him to be detained for questioning by opponents of the church, led by recently arrived former Mormon attorney William Pickett, then becoming a leading anti-Mormon spokesman in the region. But upon examining Kane's papers, including a "passport" from President Buchanan, they released him and by the time they reconsidered, he had made his way through Cajon Pass and rushed over the desert road toward Utah.

Although Kane had received the considerate attention of Alden and Caroline Jackson at San Bernardino, including bed covers hastily made by Caroline, the emissary was not in good health when he embarked on the difficult desert passage. He was probably even more ill by the time the young men to whom he had offered a good compensation to get him over the trail quickly (George Clark, John Mayfield, and Joseph Tanner) brought him into Lyman's camp at Cottonwood Springs. Lyman's new daughter-in-law Rhoda, and other emigrant women gathered at the camp, greatly revived Kane through "home cooking" and additional winter clothing fashioned from a buffalo robe.[88] Accompanied by Lyman, he found the second leg of the journey as uneventful as February wagon travel through Utah could be. On his arrival at Salt Lake City, as has been well documented and recounted elsewhere, Kane's intervention in the so-called Utah War markedly soothed a potentially explosive situation, ultimately resolved without bloodshed. An interesting side note important in the history of the Southern Route was that the future prominent Utah merchant and political rebel William S. Godbe and a companion, Thomas Copley, sent to San Bernardino to retrieve Colonel Kane's baggage, reportedly made the journey in record time. They covered the 1,300-mile round-trip in twenty-four days and three hours.[89]

GUARDING THE
CALIFORNIA ROAD

In hurrying the special intermediary, Thomas L. Kane, toward his destination, Apostle Lyman postponed, temporarily, his major assignment to guard the southern California approaches to the centers of the Mormon kingdom. He and his associates were aware the California press had encouraged that volunteers be sent to bolster the federal military force invading from the East.[90] San Bernardino stake (diocese) president Cox reported early in the crisis that dispatches had been received from San Diego friends about such an expedition. Later, Lyman reported that the Indians of the Vegas–Muddy River region believed "Americat" soldiers intended to move up the big river to kill them and their Mormon associates. He rightly complained the Native Americans had been too much aroused by other LDS brethren. But he also was concerned about the possible implications of the military approach he had actually helped stimulate during more peaceful times by initially requesting the river exploration.[91]

The contemporary California newspapers reported the movements of Lt. Joseph C. Ives and the steamboat activity on the Colorado. Just as Lyman's report made its way toward Salt Lake City, the *Alta California* noted appeals for additional troops from the San Francisco Presidio, to bolster Ives's numbers. The newspaper surmised that the reinforcements were desired because of the close proximity of their explorations to the presumably hostile "territory of the Mormons." Led by old

San Bernardino neighbor Pauline Weaver, Ives took his steamboat *Explorer* upstream as far as El Dorado Canyon, and some in this party went by skiff as far as the Las Vegas Wash. From there the explorers established connection with the Utah-to-California road some twenty-five miles to the north. With this, Ives reported he had found a "passable line of communications," making military invasion by way of the Colorado River eminently feasible.[92]

Southern Utah residents, particularly the missionaries to the Indians Jacob Hamblin and Thales Haskell, were also convinced a river invasion of federal troops into their midst was a real threat. On Hamblin's initiative, Dudley Leavitt and Ira Hatch began to reconnoiter the progress of the Ives expedition. After attempting to establish friendly relations with the equally concerned Mohave Indians, these men posed as escaping Mormon apostates on their way to California, actually boarding the steamboat at Cottonwood Valley in a bold attempt to ascertain the strength and intentions of the army expedition. Ives was suspicious of the potential enemies and later ascertained the men to be spies when, on their departure, they headed back toward Utah, not California.[93]

Returning along the Southern Route toward Utah in mid-January 1858, Lyman continued the significant process of testing the friendship of the Paiute chief Tosho, who emerged as most important in helping maintain peace on the segment of the trail southwest of where Tutsegabits held direct sway. Lyman left Chief Tosho a store of grain to protect until his return. The church leader, who had initiated the peaceful accommodation process with these Native Americans over seven years previously, did this not only to cache a convenient store of food but also "in order to prove Tosho and find out whether he can be trusted." The Lyman group also received Paiute assistance negotiating Virgin Hill, Indians packing much of the wagon cargo up the grade on their backs, for which the Native Americans were paid in crackers. In the ensuing decade Tosho was to play a most significant role promoting the peace process in the region.[94]

Thereafter, Amasa Lyman led a company of citizen soldiers, comprised mainly of his former San Bernardino neighbors, to establish observation posts to monitor the approach of troops. He also made a Mormon reconnais-sance of the supposed army road from the Colorado River to the main trail, presumably along the Virgin River, and determined it to be much more difficult than Ives had reported. This news was welcome, but it would have arrived at church headquarters about the same time as other notices disclosing that the government had rejected all plans for movements on Utah from the California trail, dissipating that portion of the general threat to Mormondom.

On this expedition, Lyman made a significant exploration of the desert region near the Colorado River, including reinforcing a cordial alliance with the Mohave Indians. Then, led by Indian guides, the party traveled the new government road from the Colorado River to the sink of the Mojave River, finally intersecting with the familiar California-to-Utah road near Kingston Springs. Soon thereafter, Lyman returned to Salt Lake City, where as the crisis subsided he attended several of the crucial negotiations conferences then amicably resolving the long-brewing conflict with the U.S. government.[95]

As he returned toward California, Amasa Lyman met many of the former San Bernardino residents in a large number of small wagon companies heading toward Utah. He and Brigham Young had earlier recruited some who had already reached southern Utah and some longer-term residents there to take wagons to California to assist those with less resources for the move, if they desired, to comply with church leaders' requests. In more peaceful times Lyman would have disagreed with the policy of disbandment and although he would have been disheartened to see his colony abandoned, this was hardly a time to oppose President Young's policies. Such journeys in the dead of winter were not easy, and several infants died. Most of the evacuees relocated in the southern Utah settlements. The demise of the California Latter-day Saints city was another casualty of the so-called Mormon War.[96]

MIXED INTENTIONS

There is no doubt, in light of the earlier tragedy-ridden history of the Church of Jesus Christ of Latter-day Saints, that many Utah residents felt truly threatened by the approach of federal troops. However, this situation probably posed no danger to Southern Paiutes, and any messages to the contrary sent them from Mormon leaders or missionaries must be regarded as falsehoods conveyed for purposes of arousing Native Americans to assist them in resisting the government forces. Although this policy was understandable, its wisdom must be severely questioned. Even without the benefit of historical hindsight, the alliance essentially ensured that a tragedy such as the Mountain Meadows Massacre would become eminently more probable and that the Indians, once aroused, would be far more difficult to control.

As territorial governor, Brigham Young should have ensured protection and safety to all citizens traveling through his domain. Moreover, his encouragement, direct or not, of Southern Paiutes to acts of violence, was culpable. The church and territorial leader has never been sufficiently condemned in regard to both actions. Young of all people should have realized that such an event as a mass murder could not be long covered from public view, and yet it essentially was, for a considerable period—at least so far as apprehension and punishment of perpetrators was concerned. The crisis of the approaching army stemmed at least in part from the questionable treatment by the territorial governor of most non-Mormon fellow government officials and the clearly inflammatory rhetoric of the highest church leaders at that time. The so-called Great Colonizer was fortunate indeed that these collective lapses of good judgment and ethics did not result in far more disastrous retaliatory consequences for Mormondom that would also have justly

ruined his positive historic reputation—which amazingly still generally prevails.

Certainly the Mormon role in inciting the Southern Paiutes to acts of violence and theft grossly distorted the record of fatality and property loss along the Southern Route from what had been the case in the past or what could otherwise have been expected under more normal circumstances. But the tragedy did occur, and it is amazing the repercussions therefrom never more severely affected the dominant population of Utah. It might have been much worse except for subsequent attempts to protect emigrant groups passing through the area after the massacre, attempts that sometimes demonstrated heroism by individual Mormons as well as by some Native Americans.

The federal government may well have had a good reason for dispatching an army to Utah, but if so there should have been some kind of campaign of explanation and reassurance preceding it. And speaking of misgovernment on the national level, the failure to heed the precise warnings of Lt. Sylvester Mowry has also never been properly criticized.

Illuminating the Mountain Meadows Massacre through the context of events and circumstances developing along the trail lends insights not usually offered to that most unfortunate incident. Today, we cannot fully gauge the intensity of the hatred and compulsion for revenge that prevailed among many Latter-day Saints of that time and place, although it is important to attempt to empathize in that regard.

Chapter Seven

Freighting from the Pacific Coast to Utah

Although there was almost no freighting over the Southern Route in the first half-dozen years of its use, for more than a decade thereafter, from 1855 to 1868, it was one of the busiest freight routes in the West. In fact, one of the foremost western historians, John Walton Caughey, asserted some years ago that it became "a most important route for freighters as well as emigrants until the completion of the Central Pacific and Union Pacific railroads in 1869 restored the preference for the old western (or central) route."[1] The claim for emigration may be somewhat overstated, but a good case can be made that Caughey was likely correct that the route was very important for freighting. Despite the absence of specific data concerning actual numbers of wagons or freight tonnage, anecdotal material and related history of the route substantiate Caughey's assertion. That the road was so disease free and usable in the winter months loomed perhaps even more crucial for freighting than for emigration.

If Brigham Young ever realistically dreamed of economic self-sufficiency for his Great Basin kingdom, it hardly had a chance of fruition in the first fifteen years, because of the vast influx of merchandise brought in through various unusual circumstances almost from the time of first settlement. He and his fellow Mormon leaders strove mightily to dissuade their people from the attractions of being among the first to arrive in the California gold fields, with President Young's first counselor, Heber C. Kimball, predicting in 1848 "that the commodities, known among the brethren as 'states goods,' would be as cheap in Salt Lake City as in New York." Some California-bound wagon trains thereafter arrived at the Mormon metropolis laden with valuable merchandise and livestock that their owners expected to sell at Gold Rush prices. But these travelers were dismayed to learn that other trains had recently passed through with similar goods and that the California markets were presumably already well stocked. Some, too, had become more cognizant of the difficulty of pulling the heavy loads over the high Sierra Nevada passes. The emigrants therefore were often glad to exchange the expensive merchandise for foodstuffs and trade the fine, but exhausted, livestock for fresh draft animals at whatever terms they could get so far out on the trail.[2] Whatever the other effects of the Gold Rush migration through Utah and its infusion of extra manufactured goods from the outside world, it certainly kept a goodly number of Latter-day Saints from adapting to doing without important comforts of life.

The Gold Rush not only made outside goods available in Mormondom in large quantities but also greatly stimulated food prices. True, occasional differentials probably arose between what Mormons charged fellow believers and what they charged "outsiders"—perhaps even encouraged by the church hierarchy. In 1850, flour sold for $1 per pound; sugar, $2 for three pounds. Prices were even higher in the Gold Rush country, so there was no chance goods would be coming from that quarter, and the Southern Route was not yet established for freighting. Still, Great Basin appetites for goods manufactured beyond the region remained strong, with some consumers inclined to procure the merchandise at any price demanded, whenever the opportunity arose. Even before the Gold Rush subsided, many Utah-Deseret residents, including Mormon leaders, recognized that in many ways the best route for contact with the outside world was southward toward the southern California coast. That had been a consideration in planting the colony at San Bernardino, with its leaders directed to improve roadways and trade routes from the seacoast. However, the church never really pushed for the establishment of additional settlements to serve as way stations along the route.

THE FIRST FREIGHTING EXPEDITION

The first known freighting expedition from Salt Lake City to southern California was that of Mormon merchants John and Enoch Reese, which set off with twenty-four essentially empty wagons and eighty to ninety draft animals on 12 December 1853. The so-called Reeses' Train aimed to procure dry goods and groceries for sale to Utah settlers. Indications show the venture had at least tacit approval from the church hierarchy, including the fact that the designated "pilot" was John Young Green, nephew of Brigham Young. The Reeses also had an order from the official church newspaper, *Deseret News*, to obtain a supply of newsprint paper.

However, the expedition proved ill fated from the beginning, largely because it lacked adequate leadership and discipline, which most subsequent freighting endeavors had enjoyed. The company held no formal organizational meeting to establish regulations before the trip commenced, and the teamsters were later noted to be "acting independently." Also, the company began to run out of provisions just over halfway to their destination, showing lack of proper preparation. Actually, the Reeses had trusted too much their pilot's recommendation for what he considered a sufficient supply of foodstuffs. Although John Green had been over the route previously, his leadership never played a positive role in the expedition. At least two men and up to sixty animals lost their lives, along with the merchants' loss of up to $20,000 on the venture.

Another crucial mistake was not maintaining good relations with Native Americans along the road. As previously recounted, while traveling down the Santa Clara River the company experienced some kind of trouble with Indians, and in retaliation associated packers killed one of that Indian band. The Indians then sought revenge through an ambush in which they wounded three emigrant men in the rear wagons with arrows—not an auspicious beginning for freighting on the route.[3]

By the time the group reached the Muddy River, they realized their meat supply was about depleted, as were their tea, coffee, and sugar. Thus as the teamsters began to subsist on flour and occasional mule meat, the proprietor Reese brothers hurried ahead toward southern California to obtain more provisions. If either Reese had been able to assert any authority at this point, he should have stayed with the train, because by the time it reached Cottonwood Springs, what was termed a mutiny was at hand. Green attempted to resolve the problem by taking eight wagons and some of the people who had engaged as passengers for the trip to go on ahead. The remaining teamsters were to stay with the draft animals until they recovered enough strength to continue or until the Reeses sent back extra draft animals. At that campsite a further difficulty occurred: A large quantity of money, left in Green's charge, disappeared. This was "uncurrent money," probably "Great Salt Lake Pure Gold" pieces, which were being shipped to the San Francisco mint for recoining. The thief, clearly a member of the party, was not apprehended. It was assumed the culprit had buried the money for future retrieval. However, John Reese later returned to the spot and, supposedly assisted by a dream, located most of the coins, which he took back to Los Angeles for purchasing additional trade goods.[4]

After the split of the company, Green and his group had to leave two of their wagons before reaching Bitter Springs, with another left at that waterhole. There Green also abandoned this group to make their way as best they could with the remaining wagons while he moved on ahead toward San Bernardino. The men left behind with the exhausted livestock further divided, with some taking their ration of flour and starting down the trail on foot. These "packers" experienced untold hardships, including four driven by extreme hunger to eat mistletoe berries, from which two died and the others only recovered after a long illness. Those remaining with the animals also, after a time, attempted to move on from the separating point at Resting Springs. Eight or ten horses died within a few days, and Indians killed or drove off a dozen others. When the provisions were exhausted, the group subsisted for almost a week on horse meat. By the time rescue came, only about thirty animals remained, with up to sixty lost. Those staying with the wagons, including most of the paying passengers, reached the Mojave River without further incident. Thereafter they had better feed and water for their draft animals, some of which were still slaughtered for food. When word arrived of a supply wagon near at hand, it naturally evoked cheers from the company as its members discarded their remaining supply of mule meat in preparation for something more palatable. The rest of the journey proved relatively uneventful. The entire trek took forty-eight days.

Enoch Reese, one of the first to attempt a freighting venture over the Southern Route, with far too many mishaps to avoid serious losses.

The anonymous chronicler of the expedition emphasized the problems of improper preparation before the company embarked for California but acknowledged that the Reeses exerted themselves to the utmost when in the middle of the route they realized their men faced starvation. No such positive words were offered for "pilot" John Y. Green, who grossly underestimated the provisions needed, and certainly the Reeses were remiss in trusting him with any part of the leadership of their train. In fact, the reporter of the journey, who signed his article in the Los Angles *Star* "J. C.," concluded that one key to the expedition success might have been "paying their pilot to remain at home."[5]

After obtaining the desired goods, mostly from San Francisco, the Reeses headed back for Utah over the same trail. Undoubtedly they experienced great difficulty at the summit grade atop Cajon Pass, with the teamsters compelled to pack much of the freight up the hogback on their own backs. They thereafter helped pioneer the cutoff by way of Kingston Springs, although mail carriers had also doubtless commenced going that way. This return journey proved difficult as well. The artist Solomon Carvalho met the freighters on the road and noted, "They were in a most distressed state." Again the draft animals gave out after just over a week on the road, essentially proving they were compelled to pull loads too heavy for the sandy roads. The Reeses had to send ahead to Cedar City to get fresh animals to bring in the heavily laden wagons. They disposed of some merchandise at the Iron County settlements, probably partly in payment for the stock procured to finish the journey, then took the remainder to Salt Lake City for sale. The failures of the expedition at least temporarily dampened hopes of a successful overland trade with the southern California coast. Seeking to shift blame for the lack of success, Enoch Reese informed Brigham Young that Mormons in the San Bernardino colony had not proved as helpful as they might have been, but this could not have been a major factor in the failure of the expedition.[6]

SEAPORT AND ROADWAY IMPROVEMENT

A key phase of the Southern Route freighting process was purchasing goods at San Francisco and then shipping them by the semiregular coastal steamers down the coast to San Pedro. The latter place was not a real harbor until dredged and a breakwater built, years later. The ocean-going craft had to anchor beyond the surf to be downloaded into smaller boats called "lighters," used to transport the cargo to shore. A few wharves and storage warehouses served the infant shipping industry. Even though the Reese train comprised the only significant overland trade expedition, in June 1854 the Los Angeles *Star* predicted optimistically that "San Pedro is to be the permanent depot for the Territory of Utah. . . . Vessels have already cleared from foreign ports for San Pedro with emigrants and merchandise for San Bernardino and Salt Lake."[7]

One source of difficulty on the Reese expedition was a portion of the road at each end of the route that greatly

needed improvement before freight wagon trains could pass successfully. Soon after the Reeses' struggle, efforts were launched to resolve that problem. In 1854, Congress appropriated $25,000 for the Utah end of the road, expressly for military and mail route improvement to the coast by the Southern Route, but such improvements would be equally useful to freighters. When Lt. Edward J. Steptoe, designated to oversee the project, advertised for bids to accomplish the various improvements, he indicated specific interest in building a road from the head of the Santa Clara River down that stream and across Utah Hill over the nearby stretch of desert to the Muddy River. Such a road would permanently bypass the almost-impassable Virgin River bottoms, many troublesome Native Americans, and the Virgin Hill pull. It is difficult to ascertain what contracts were fulfilled, but probably none of the funds were expended on this segment of the road. Brigham Young wanted all the funds expended within the settled stretch of Utah, from Parowan north, but did not get his way. Some criticism was naturally voiced in the usually biased Mormon newspapers that little had actually been accomplished, the money allegedly having been funneled into the pockets of favorite "spoilsmen." Yet San Bernardino Mormon leaders Amasa M. Lyman and Charles C. Rich noted significant improvement of the low mountain pass between Beaver and Parowan Valley and attributed it directly to the federal appropriation. After a visit home to Parowan, Las Vegas missionary John Steele observed that the main California road had been greatly improved in many places since he had last traveled it. And most important, many freight wagons subsequently transversed the desert portion of the route with no reports of difficulties with the road other than the inherent vastness of the expanses.[8]

Despite the improvements made on the route, the Leach Cutoff might still fit the category of a spoilsman scheme. It followed convenient westerly tending canyons from Cedar City along present State Highway 56 almost to the soon-to-be-infamous Mountain Meadows. Observation today indicates a distance reduction of at least fifteen miles over the earlier road, which headed west from the present Enoch area just north of Cedar City and then turned south, skirting the eastern edge

Canyon where the Sanford Cutoff, constructed in 1855, exited from near the western end of the T-shaped Cajon Pass, 2001. In the absence of old road ruts elsewhere in the area, it is evident the current road is the same grade as the earlier one created for the first freight wagons heading northeast over the Southern Route.
COURTESY LARRY REESE

of the huge Escalante Valley toward the meadows. The question is, How much actual grading and excavation were performed for the funds expended? Evidence suggests that Col. James B. Leach slighted such work later when he obtained "a pretty fat appropriation from congress" to improve a segment of the newly established Butterfield stagecoach road in southern Arizona, without in fact then doing much improving. Newspaperman Waterson L. Ormsby, who traveled the route at the time and became its first historian, reported that some of the roadway must have been "a terrible one indeed" before the construction, because afterward it was still very poor. In fact, Ormsby stated, some of the Leach-improved road had already been bypassed in the first month of stagecoach use.[9]

Not long after the congressional action on behalf of the Utah road, San Bernadino Mormon assemblyman Jefferson Hunt introduced a bill in the California legislature to improve the road at the southern end of the route. Although continuing sectional rivalries in the state caused some opposition to improving the Southern Route, eventually the bill passed "for constructing a wagon road from San Pedro through the Cajon Pass to the state line in the direction of the Salt Lake Valley." As always when given a chance, the Los Angeles *Star* editorialized concerning the all-weather advantages of this route and

chided northern Californians for seeking lavish funds for roads that could only be used part of the year. The *Star* also mentioned that the Mormons were cognizant of the advantages of the Southern Route and were prepared to use it to the fullest extent practicable.[10]

Even before the California funds became available, former Santa Fe trader William T. B. Sanford, brother-in-law of the emerging southern California freighting magnate Phineas Banning, took the initiative to improve the most needed stretch of road approaching the southland in Cajon Pass. Having hauled a large steam engine up the steep "hogback" he had excavated in 1850, Sanford was aware of the difficulties. Thereafter he doubtless discovered a better possible road grade just a mile farther west, where an arroyo intersected the main ridge of the T-shaped pass. Grading a roadway up the side of that draw could offer a more gradual incline, enabling heavy freight wagons to be hauled up the pass with less difficulty. Sanford and Banning likely took the initiative to improve the road, in anticipation of being reimbursed when state funds became available. There is some indication that neither they nor the northern California road builders seeking even larger appropriations ever received the state funds, but Sanford and his associates nevertheless profited from the improvements, as did the entire region. The *Southern Californian*, which in April 1855 announced the Salt Lake road was "completely free of obstacles," did not pay sufficient respect to the desert expanses, but the vastly improved segment thereafter known as the Sanford grade did facilitate better use of the route for extensive freighting for years to come.[11]

EARLY SUCCESSFUL FREIGHTING VENTURES

The first to use the newly improved road were the Mormon merchants J. Henry Rollins and Richard R. Hopkins, probably representing the former's brother-in-law, Amasa Lyman, as well. In the spring of 1855, they took three wagons loaded with a "handsome assortment of goods" up Cajon Pass and on to Utah without untoward incident. Rollins later recalled they "sold the things enroute," stopping at each of the merchandise-hungry Mormon settlements along the so-called Mormon corridor. They disposed of the remaining goods at the Salt Lake City mercantile firm of William Hooper and Thomas Williams, after which the successful traders returned to California.[12]

Just weeks after Hopkins and Rollins departed for Utah, the Alexander and Banning company sent Sanford with a far larger trade train over the same route. Alexander was a former Utah resident, and Phineas Banning had previously conferred with San Bernardino Mormon leader Amasa Lyman about the possibilities of opening commerce with the Utah communities. The partners had received nothing but encouragement for the venture. The Los Angeles entrepreneur dispatched 15 ten-mule teams, each pulling a wagon loaded with two tons of merchandise, over the road Sanford had recently improved. Wagon master Sanford carried a letter of introduction from Lyman addressed to the "Saints" in Utah. This venture fully inaugurated the trade between Los Angeles and Salt Lake City.

The Sanford train was certainly better led than the Reese group, but nevertheless met its own challenges en route, as all would over so long and difficult a road. It took thirty-two mules hitched to each wagon—in turns—to get them up the Sanford grade. Even then the pull was not entirely without mishap, as a wagon axle broke in the process. The party handled the difficulty, however, and

was soon on its way slowly down the Mojave River. A week later, at Bitter Springs, Sanford's teamsters found plenty of essential grass feed for the livestock. However, in that vicinity they also lost twenty pair of harness and two tea chests to pilfering Indians. All except a little tea were subsequently retrieved when abandoned by the thieves, who probably found the items useless. People who encountered the train at the Vegas noted it was doing well, although Apostle Charles Rich was not as optimistic about its welcome in Utah as Amasa Lyman had assured.[13]

More than a week later, probably after crossing Beaver Dam Wash and Utah Hill, Sanford recognized the poor condition of his livestock and had them driven without wagons some thirty miles to the headwaters of the Santa Clara River to recoup their strength. This showed an impressive degree of care for the crucial animals and a wise solution to the problem, assuming the wagons were left well guarded, as they surely were in the midst of the Tonequint Paiute tribal lands. After good grazing at Mountain Meadows, what would have been an arduous stretch for weak animals became much easier.[14]

The merchandise brought to Salt Lake City was valued at $20,000, and eager local residents purchased all that was offered. Brigham Young, however, was not particularly pleased to see such profits going into non-Mormon coffers. The *Star* later alleged that some Mormon officials even cautioned their people from the pulpit against trading so freely with the Californians, obviously to little avail. Part of President Young's motives may have been related to his plans for the BY [Brigham Young] Express and Carrying Company, organized about that time to haul freight and passengers from the Missouri River to Mormondom. Young secured some contracts, manpower, and equipment, but because of subsequent conflicts with the federal government this enterprise never got off the ground.[15]

Although Sanford did not receive a cordial welcome from church leaders in Utah, the journey must have been profitable or it would not have been repeated the following year, 1856. However, further opposition was engendered among the church hierarchy when Sanford allegedly tried to sell his considerable supply of liquor. The merchant petitioned the Salt Lake City Council for a license to sell the merchandise. Although church lead-

Heavily loaded freight wagons in Salt Lake City during the era when the Southern Route was in frequent use. The city was the hub of extensive freight wagon transport in all directions in the early 1860s, although more for incoming than outgoing merchandise.

COURTESY UTAH STATE HISTORI-
CAL SOCIETY

ers certainly dominated this body, debate still transpired before the council asked Sanford to withdraw the petition, which he did. The trader may have erred in attempting to sell within the city instead of more circumspectly outside. At the end of the previous year Jim Williams, former mountain man and sometime mail carrier over the Southern Route, had brought a similar load of liquor, probably by pack mule train, from southern California and had apparently sold his merchandise without undue incident. Even some Latter-day Saints had learned it was easier to get forgiveness than permission from the ecclesiastic authorities of Mormondom. After this incident, Banning claimed, Brigham Young essentially forced his company out of the Utah trade.[16] But by that time, with proven feasibility of the freight route and the need for overland trade demonstrated to both Mormon and non-Mormon, an increasing commerce continued over the route at least until replaced by the Central–Union Pacific Railroad in 1869.

YEARS OF FAMINE IN UTAH

In 1856 Sanford's timing was not good for selling an item such as liquor. Utah was then suffering its second consecutive year of virtual famine. The territory's agricul-

tural prospects in 1856 were devastated by the recurring curse of insect infestation. Grasshoppers, reinforced by crickets, destroyed the young sprouts of early crops. The church newspaper, *Deseret News*, reported people apprehensively scrutinizing "the movements of the depredators, destroying them, laying new plans for their destruction, and taking advantage of such localities as they [had] vacated." The account did not veil the prevalent discouraged expectations that farmers would have little to harvest in the fall, confessing that "both classes of these devouring insects [were] still constantly hatching out [reproducing]."

The primary source of expected relief from anticipated famine was the Mormon colony in southern California. The same newspaper article detailing the plague also suggested that although eight hundred miles was a long way to haul wheat, there was "no nearer place than San Bernardino from which to procure it." At that time Utah readers had just learned of the bright prospects for a bumper harvest for their California brethren. They were not informed of rust damage in California dispelling such hopes until early the following month, and destroying any chances of assistance from that quarter.[17]

As usual, Brigham Young was unflappable. Probably as a joke, he speculated that the Lord had sent the insects "in lieu of Gentile soldiers or a more severe ordeal."

Perhaps in the same mood the church leader stated to Lyman that if the grasshoppers "continue their ravages perhaps we may have to take up our line of march to your point in order to save ourselves from threatened starvation." Even in jest this is an amazing statement for Brigham Young to make in light of his often-expressed negative comments about San Bernardino.[18]

The destruction of such a large proportion of the Utah crops in both 1855 and 1856 was a source of some embarrassment to the church authorities. On 1 June 1855, Young advised Lyman and Rich that in light of Utah food prospects, he wished them to "husband [their] grain well, store it and take good care of it" and not allow it to be sold to speculators at any price until he had given further direction. Soon after the meager Utah harvest, Young confided to Rich, "[W]e never seriously contemplated being dependent on California," although he lamented that impression had been allowed to be spread abroad. During the ensuing winter season, as word reached California of considerable hunger and want at the center of Mormondom, the Latter-day Saints colonists in San Bernardino commenced efforts to alleviate the suffering. Mormon newspaper spokesman at San Francisco, George Q. Cannon, first denied the existence of a crisis, contending that the Mormon system of taking care of those in need already exceeded that of any other society. But as reports of hunger persisted, confirmed by the southern California Mormons appealing to outsiders for commodities they could transport to the needy, the condition was finally acknowledged. However, just as the San Bernardino brethren were about to embark on their errand of mercy with the proffered food, the Utah mail carriers brought word that conditions had improved, so they canceled the supply expedition. Later, Young expressed appreciation for the concern expressed by the California Saints but firmly asserted there had been little real suffering.[19]

PLANS FOR EXPRESS AND FREIGHTING COMPANIES

Even at the inception of overland trade by the Southern Route, promises of government freight contracts, perhaps including mail, may have provided some encouragement. The large Adams Express Company of San Francisco was at least preparing to run some wagon outfits over the road. But the company was a notable casualty of the California financial slump of 1854, which probably prevented it from ever doing more than discuss the venture. Thereafter, the more financially stable Wells, Fargo and Company appears to have encouraged one of their popular agents, Abel Gilbert, also associated in some way with mail contractor George Chorpenning, to establish a freight line from Salt Lake City to Los Angeles, connected to the Wells, Fargo system in southern California. In 1855 the Salt Lake City freighting company of Gilbert and Gerrish began to flourish in that area. Because it is known that this company carried mail first by horse saddlebags, then at least sometimes by wagon between Utah and southern California, probably the partners became the employers of the Mormon mail carriers from both ends of the line. Doubtless they also hauled some freight during the last several years the Latter-day Saints occupied San Bernardino.[20]

The *Southern Californian* was then particularly lavish in its praise and optimism toward several express and freighting companies who announced their intent to use that road. Former employees of the defunct Adams and Company organized the Pacific Express Company, and the California Stage Company actually bought a group of "splendid coaches" and livestock for use on runs from Los Angeles to San Bernardino and from there to Salt Lake City. The newspaper stated, "[T]he movements are significant of the future importance of the business relations [of Los Angeles] destined to bind us in interest to the immense territory occupied by our Mormon brethren" at the other end of the trail. However, the Kern River gold rush apparently diverted the stagecoaches, and no evidence shows the promotions ever went as far as any runs over the route.[21]

Actually, any company that had to make the long trip from Utah to San Bernardino, or even the shorter ones within the southern California region, whether it had a full paying load or not, would be hard pressed to compete with the freelance operations by a large number of the San Bernardino men. These men launched hauling ventures between planting and harvesting their crops and during the winter seasons. Several dozen different individuals are documented as engaged at times in freighting, particularly hauling lumber from the local mountain sawmills to Los Angeles. Sometimes freighting trips were a means of paying LDS tithes by delivering what others had paid in kind to outside markets. And during their six-year sojourn in southern California, a considerable number of Mormons also made at least one hauling trip back to Utah. Already possessed of the necessary outfit for the enterprise, all they needed was the load, which on their part-time basis they could contract for at lower rates than could those who had to maintain a regular freighting service. Thus one of the foremost students of freighting on the Southern Route, Ray Reeder, has asserted there were probably more nonprofessional freighters who traveled it than drove over other routes, which is probably true if these Mormon teamsters are included. But because they owned the teams and equipment and worked for all the profits derived, they probably served the purposes as well as any others. After moving back to Utah, many former southern Californians continued in this hauling trade. After the Mormon exodus from San Bernardino, that city became an extremely busy trading and freighting center, with several regular companies involved in all aspects of the business.[22]

TRADING ENDEAVORS BY RETURNING SAN BERNARDINO MORMONS

When Brigham Young essentially provoked federal officials into requesting that President James Buchanan send the United States Army to Utah to assert government authority over the Mormons, the general course of events was altered in several ways. The Mormon militia was initially impressively successful in disrupting army supply lines, to the point where the largest military force gathered in the nation up to that time nearly faced starvation. Eventually, however, a huge number of federal government–financed freighting expeditions, including some over the Southern Route, flooded Utah with outside trade goods. In the long run the seemingly hostile invasion led to the disbandment of Mormon San Bernardino, but in the meantime the California community served as an essential supply-gathering station for the Utah Mormon resistance to the invading force.

Among the two thousand Mormons who demonstrated their obedience by selling their San Bernardino property at a low rate and heading for Utah were some

who brought with them a considerable quantity of trade goods. Although many useful articles were abandoned or sold for far less than the real value at San Bernardino, after six years of reasonable prosperity many returnees owned manufactured items that were of great value in isolated Utah and some of these found their way to the territory. James Henry Rollins, who had been in the process of acquiring merchandise to open a new store in San Bernardino, brought five wagonloads of goods with him to Utah. Because he settled in the southern portion of the territory, eventually Minersville, he probably avoided any conflict with Mormon authorities, who were then sensitive about such matters. Besides, a great need for outside merchandise was clearly evident in that area.

Fellow returnee to the southern area Louisa Barnes Pratt noted how "great was the poverty of the people at Cedar City." She recorded that every day her house was thronged with women "wanting to buy groceries, cloth and everything [she] had." The good diarist and seamstress recalled she had never seen a "poorer dressed congregation than assembled every Sabbath Day in [the Cedar City] House of Worship." But she also noted a visible change in just three months, which she attributed to the volume of goods brought from California by the returning San Bernardino Mormons, which were exchanged for provisions the new arrivals needed to subsist through the remainder of the winter and spring. Pratt's sister Caroline received a good cow in exchange for sixty-six yards of various fabrics, five pounds of sugar, four canisters of powder and three boxes of matches. Thus both the returning emigrants and the established southern Utah settlers mutually benefited.[23]

Others, particularly the original San Bernardino stake president, David Seeley, were less fortunate, because they sought to sell their supply of trade goods farther north. There Seeley immediately became embroiled with local church officials over means of payment for the merchandise. When Brigham Young heard that Seeley refused to take the newly issued paper currency for his goods, or even the extralegal valley gold coins, he ordered Pleasant Grove bishop Henson Walker to tell Seeley "to clear out; he had gone to California to get gold and he ought to be contented with the gold there, and not come [to Utah] to take the gold and silver from [that] community." Obviously Young was sensitive to anyone questioning the value of his local currency.

In a subsequent interview held to clarify the situation, Seeley found Young still infuriated. In a revealing outburst of anger, Young informed Seeley that "if he had lived his religion and been in the line of duty, he would not have gone to California, then come back [to Utah] and bring a few goods and try to sell them at exorbitant prices and depreciate the currency." The California brother attempted to explain he thought he was "in the line of his duty in going to California," further pleading that he had not come to speculate but had borrowed the money for the goods at the interest rate of 5 percent per month and would be hard pressed to make any profit. The church leader replied Seeley could prove his good intentions by taking currency in place of the $70 in gold he had already obtained through his previous sales. After more of what his brother later termed a "heated argument," Brigham Young gave Seeley the counsel that when he came into a settlement "in the Kingdom of God," he should go to the leading LDS authorities there and ask them what he could do to advance the Mormon kingdom. He thus strongly implied that such acts of independence and private enterprise were to be condemned at that time. No record exists of David Seeley's reaction, but undoubtedly he felt falsely accused. He soon returned to California, where he and his family prospered for the rest of their lives.[24]

Seeley had been unfortunate to find Young at one of the moments when Young was attempting to assert some economic independence for the Mormons. This mood passed rather quickly, and Brigham soon apparently condoned the flourishing trade developing between his domain and southern California. Any dreams of economic self-sufficiency needed to await the time when Mormondom was better prepared to meet the demands for home-manufactured goods yet only partially ingrained among the Latter-day Saints.

THADDEUS KENDERDINE WITH A LATE-1850s FREIGHTING EXPEDITION

At the end of 1858, one of the few known diarists traveling with a freight wagon company over the Southern Route chronicled some of his experiences. Thaddeus Kenderdine and some twenty companions arranged at Salt Lake City with a large group of Mormon freighters to travel with them to southern California. Stopping at Fillmore, the chronicler offered further insights into life at the territorial capital. Many in his traveling party anticipated a drink of the liquor, reputedly available in the territory, affectionately called "Mormon lightning." However, they were dismayed to learn that Fillmore was the only territorial capital in the nation that prohibited the sale of any intoxicating beverages within its limits. The chronicler lamented that "a miserable species of beer was the strongest available article to be had for love or money." Pumpkin pies, he said, were the "staple productions of Fillmore." The visitors consumed both pies and beer in copious quantities before they moved down the trail.[25]

Before reaching the Santa Clara Paiutes, the designated captain, trail veteran, and former San Bernardino resident Sidney Tanner carefully outlined to the 150 members of the company the behavior essential to prevent conflict with Native Americans along the crucial stretch of roadway ahead. This included posting a double mounted guard each night, including one to watch the camp and the other, the draft animals. The diarist regarded the Paiute demands for food as "impudent" and reported one of the Tonequint chiefs enraged that so large a caravan attempted to pass through his domains without paying what was termed "the usual toll." The Mormon guides calmly satisfied the demands with presents of flour and clothing. Despite a generally negative view of the Native Americans, Kenderdine considered the Paiutes "the best natured" Indians he had met in all his travels. This he attributed at least partly to a clearly discernible friendship with the Mormon freighters. Certainly an essential part of this feeling was the care exhibited in feeding each group they met, making three large kettles of a form of "hasty pudding," a mixture of boiled water and flour, for the large group awaiting the company at the Muddy River.

At that time there was yet another near-miss of tragedy in the area just over a year after the Mountain Meadows Massacre. A group of eight travelers had become impatient with the rate of speed of the larger body and rashly decided to move ahead of them from the Virgin River crossings. When the main party arrived at the Muddy, they discovered their former companions completely under the subjugation of Moapa Indians, who had already robbed them of all their goods, including weapons. Kenderdine noted the men were not only humiliated but close to terrified at the prospect of their fate. No doubt the party would not have finished their journey had the larger group, including people friendly to the Native Americans, not intervened in their behalf.

From the beginning of the trip, the company enjoyed a good deal of cordial social interaction, including occasional musical cotillions, featuring a "well-played" violin and sometimes, dancing among clumps of sagebrush—with no female partners. More than one of the Moapa men was persuaded to join in the activities. These relaxed and compatible relationships contrasted strongly with the situation later in the journey, as party members became aware of their seriously depleted provisions and the rapidly declining strength of their draft animals. By that time, the diarist noted that joking was no longer appreciated; "wearied looks, irritable tempers and listlessness abounded among [their] half-starved company." He confessed their campfires were "no longer redolent with the uproarious merriment and practical joking which characterized those of the forepart of [their] journey." At the successful completion of the trip, Kenderdine commented significantly on how much San Bernardino had declined since the departure, earlier in the year, of most of the founding Mormon citizens.[26]

FREIGHTING AFTER THE MORMON WAR

The two Mormons who probably did most to legitimize the overland freighting business through their status and relationships with both Latter-day Saint leaders and California merchants were early southern trail guide and former California assemblyman Jefferson Hunt and recent San Bernardino rancho coproprietor Ebenezer Hanks. Both engaged extensively in the enterprise in 1858 and thereafter. Hunt arrived in Los Angeles from Utah in mid-March of 1858 and reported plenty of money on hand in Salt Lake City, with great demand for goods from the outside world. Hunt naturally encountered numerous small freighters en route northward and reported them all to be in good condition, as was the road traveled. The best-known Latter-day Saint in Cali-

fornia, outside of sometime Mormon Sam Brannan, Hunt was the highest-ranked church member in the Mormon Battalion and was later the first state legislator from San Bernardino County. Hunt returned to the southland in March 1859, then traveled by stagecoach, steamboat, and probably railroad, to St. Louis and on to Washington, D.C., apparently for further negotiations with federal officials after the recent conflict in Utah. He returned to California by way of Utah in mid-February 1860 and a month later took a large wagon train of merchandise over the Southern Route to Salt Lake City. Hunt probably passed Bitter Springs just before his former associate in the Mormon Battalion, Salt Lake City merchant and freighter Thomas Williams, was killed there (discussed in chapter 8).[27]

Hanks had also been in the California southland earlier, in November 1858, and reported great numbers of work oxen available in the Salt Lake area at low prices, as were beef cattle. He visited southern California to complete the sale of a sawmill in the San Bernardino Mountains to Los Angeles merchant Felix Bachman. Thereafter the two men became partners in freighting over the Southern Route, commencing with one of the first postconflict wagon trains to Utah. Hanks returned to Los Angeles in early April 1859 to reiterate that recent loads of goods found a ready market in Mormondom. His partner's relative Ben Bachman remained in Utah at that time, perhaps to procure draft animals or some of the numerous good wagons left there over the years by gold seekers. Sanford and Banning had earlier procured some of their best freight outfits in the same manner.[28]

UNITED STATES ARMY IN UTAH GENERATES FREIGHTING BOOM

After the Mormon War, in early May 1858, the Los Angeles *Star* published a note from well-known express company operator Abel Gilbert reporting his cordial reception in Utah as he traveled through that country with the regular mail carriers, probably to investigate restoring his interrupted express trade. He noted, significantly, that the Indians along the Southern Route were "all peaceably disposed." Thereafter, the newspaper item added, the non-Mormon businessman had a favorable interview with Brigham Young prior to starting for the main army post at Camp Floyd, undoubtedly to procure government freighting contracts. This news certainly stimulated the burgeoning Los Angeles freighting trade. By November the *Deseret News* reported that southern California merchants were able to supply the needs of the Utah area when all other routes were closed by winter weather. Southland businessmen clearly capitalized on their advantage, shipping more than $180,000 in goods to Camp Floyd by early April 1859, besides what they shipped to nonmilitary consumers.[29]

In January 1859 at least sixty freight wagons left for Salt Lake City from Los Angeles, with the same number the next month, reportedly with goods valued at $60,000 to $70,000. At that time some predicted that within a month's time a hundred tons of additional merchandise would be shipped. Judging by the earlier loads of two tons per wagon, the amount far exceeded that, because in March, merchants sent another 150 loaded outfits to the Mormon city over the Southern Route—making a phenomenal total of at least 270 wagons in just three months. During this period the *Star* reported that previous traders "had done well in that market," with plenty of spending money seemingly available in Utah. The newspaper reiterated the advantage southland merchants had in that wagons from the Missouri River and northern California could not yet travel over their snow-filled roads to the lucrative market.[30]

Los Angeles had only recently emerged from being a predominantly Hispanic ranching center. Several Anglo-American merchants established themselves in an adobe building stretching 300 feet along Los Angeles Street. Among these was John Goller, who had arrived in the area over the Southern Route and got his start as a blacksmith partly by gathering iron from abandoned wagons out on that trail, from which he fashioned useful articles for sale. Associated with a partner, John J. Tomlinson, Goller was among those sending large shipments to Utah in early 1859. M. G. Jones was another who entered enthusiastically into the Utah trade. Felix Bachman arrived in 1853, took several partners into Bachman and Company, and within a few years had built the largest mercantile establishment in town. He too became fully involved in freighting to Salt Lake City. Harris Newmark, a merchant who chronicled much regional history, in-

cluding mercantile and freighting, claimed that after the early years his own firm gained preeminence in the Utah trade.

Certainly the still-few Utah merchants were also engaged in procuring goods and hauling them to their places of business. And the smaller itinerant Mormon freighters, often familiar with the route from earlier experience as pioneers, were employed by various merchants from both ends of the road. Historian Newmark recalled that in February 1859 "Mormon wagons arrived overland almost daily."[31] Beaver, Utah, resident Marcus L. Sheperd, recently of San Bernardino, became one of many involved in this trade. Similarly, Sidney Tanner was already a veteran of freighting over the Southern Route.

Early in the summer of 1860, several freight wagon trains again arrived at Salt Lake City, by both California routes, filling orders of local merchants who, notwithstanding the "enormous amounts of dry goods and gro-

Lafeyette Shepherd, one of the most frequent independent freighters over the Southern Route, starting while he was still a resident of San Bernardino and continuing long after he moved to Beaver, Utah.

Sidney Tanner, prominent freight wagon operator while he was a citizen of San Bernardino. Tanner carried several groups of travelers through hostile territory in 1857–58 and continued to be active in trade over the route, usually in partnership with Shepherd.

ceries which [had] been brought into the territory," were reportedly by no means overstocked. More goods arrived in the summer via trains from San Francisco, as well as more from Los Angeles. That autumn, Ebenezer Hanks returned to California after another successful trade expedition associated with the Bachmans. He again reported a number of other trains returning from equally lucrative ventures. That year considerable difficulty arose with Native Americans on the Mojave Desert (discussed in a later chapter). And the ensuing spring Ben Bachman returned with less positive news: a dull demand for merchandise and scarce money. Since the Utah army outpost, by then named Camp Crittenden, was now about to be disbanded as the American Civil War got under way, with the post equipment declared surplus to be sold to the highest bidders, it is entirely likely the Mormons appeared less willing to trade at that juncture, because they

were awaiting the windfalls of the government surplus auction.[32]

It is unlikely the Bachmans were discouraged with trade with the Mormon settlements. Rival merchant Newmark noted that in 1861 the Bachman firm led the opposition to raising freight rates. The prevailing price at that time was $0.25 per pound from Los Angeles to Salt Lake City. However, partly under pressure from his wife, who apparently wished to relocate to San Francisco, the leading southland mercantile firm disbanded in 1864, with Bachman receiving real estate in payment for debts, which he subsequently liquidated at "ridiculously low prices." Thereafter, the Newmark firm gained preeminence in the Utah trade. In this they were greatly aided by close association with the Mormon leaders, to whom they offered credit when they were short of funds. Newmark asserted that it was not long before his firm was "brought into constant communication with Brigham Young and through his influence monopolized the Salt Lake business."[33]

OX AND MULE TRAINS AND DRIVERS

Naturally, as the volume of freight carried overland increased, so did the size of the loads. Wagons manufactured in the West, including the Studebaker works at Placerville, California, catered to the demand and specifications required. The cost of a good freight wagon ran from $500 to $1500 each, depending on the type. Those safely negotiating the Cajon Pass or Virgin Hill grades required powerful brakes. And often wagons were fitted with shoes and rough locks for such occasions. Shoes were a type of iron skid placed under the rear wheels before descending steep grades, the wheels chained stationary and thus the friction with the ground markedly slowing descent. When ascending, chock blocks or "hill holders," triangular wooden blocks, were dragged directly behind the wheels, which on a steep incline would stop the wagons from rolling backward when the draft animals stopped to rest on the upward grade.

Although many oxen were still used for emigrant trains and for freighting on other routes, mules were the

Large wagon driven over the Southern Route by the Hancock family during the middle period of Mormon occupation of San Bernardino, mid-1850s. Notice the size of the wheels, the brake mechanism, and the skids attached to the wheels when tied for slowing down on declining steep grades.

COURTESY SAN BERNARDINO
COUNTY MUSEUM AND LARRY
REESE

unanimous favorites on the Southern Route because of their durability, as they could subsist on the desert feed and inconsistent and often saline water, as well as because of their pulling ability. A good pair of mules could command a price of $500 to $1000.

As freight outfits, both wagons, harness, and mules became more expensive, owners hesitated to entrust their property to just any driver. It was particularly important to have a seasoned professional in charge of the entire wagon train. Although several observers mentioned that a higher percentage of amateur teamsters was working on the Southern Route than any other trail, most of these were nevertheless experienced—even if they did farm in the summer and freight only in the winter season and looked, as one California observer described, "like substantial farmers and patriarchs—which no doubt, they were." Some were in fact Utah settlers simply traveling to Los Angeles to obtain supplies for their own use and for close associates, using an average-sized farm wagon pulled by four to six mules, perhaps some borrowed for a couple of usually slack winter months. But more than a dozen former San Bernardino residents, veterans of the road, were consistent winter freighters and were probably as professional as any traveling that route. In fact, during the heyday of overland freighting to Utah,

many of the full-time professional freighters took one trip from the Mormon capital to the Missouri River in the spring and summer and took another from Utah to southern California during the fall and winter, usually aiming to be back at Salt Lake City by the time in April when many Mormons gathered there for general church conference—and to do the most important shopping for the year. Thus the Utah winter-only freighters actually made as many trips over the Southern Route as the full-time freighters.[34]

Like many professions, gradations of status differentiated among teamsters, with skills now almost forgotten commanding admiration toward expert bull whackers and mule skinners—meaning simply the drivers of those teams. Although fascinated by the teamsters, outside observers probably indulged from a distance, because of various abhorrent odors. Close proximity to their draft animals may have been partly responsible; another cause was the teamsters' widespread phobia of water for washing or bathing purposes. Some teamsters were reported to sit by the campfire regaling their sympathetic fellows "with the most frightful stories of the evil effects of washing."

Equally infamous was their vocabulary of profanity acquired and practiced to a high type of eloquence, particularly during difficulties such as a "mud hole stick" or a spell of balkiness of one of the animals in his team. A San Francisco *Alta California* writer noted toward the end of the Southern Route era that observers were nearly unanimous in their contention that few anywhere could equal the "originality, quality, and quantity" of the "strong expression" of California teamsters when they "cut loose." The bull whacker was said to swear in an almost steady stream but was reportedly well surpassed by the mule skinner. His oaths were longer and delivered with expression evidencing months of rehearsal. The *Alta* reporter concluded, "[O]ne would think [the mule skinner's] entire life had been spent in the study and practice of uttering fast and complicated ejaculations, not all together polite." These men had truly elevated swearing to an art.[35]

Perhaps more important to the mule skinner's success than profane eloquence was his skill with the whip. This essential tool was a twenty-foot rawhide "black snake" lash with a short handle, oiled and pliable, sometimes with wire added in weak places to give it strength and spring according to the preference of its user. There were as many variations of design as there were teamsters, but most had a piece of buckskin at the end some six inches long and half an inch wide, which was the portion that would strike the animal's flesh if desired, even tearing it if the driver was inclined. Usually the crack of a whip was all that was needed to motivate a lagging animal to greater efforts. Good drivers were usually careful not to abuse or injure the animals they were so dependent on for crossing the desert, which was almost impossible without a healthy team. In fact, drivers were particularly valuable if they possessed some skill in caring for sick mules. Many wagon jockey boxes contained various liquors and other remedies for this purpose. Numerous nights were spent caring for sick animals so that the mule could take its place in the team when needed.

The mule skinner usually drove from eight to twelve mules, which he knew and understood better than most people today might be aware is possible. Each mule had a name to which it responded, and each had unique qualities, positive and negative, that the driver well understood. As with most professionals, mule drivers knew teaming and talked it to fellow teamsters to the exclu-

sion of most other subjects. According to the San Francisco *Alta California* reporter, they could extol the merits of their animals by the hour, pointing out peculiar characteristics in a "detail that appears singular to one unacquainted with this class of men." The newspaperman continued that the teamster spoke to the animals in a sort of paternal way, remonstrating and chiding them when wrong, also applauding and praising them when doing well. He concluded, "[I]t is a fact well worth the observation of those who extend the power of thought to the brute creation that the animals in the big teams of California and Nevada, seem endowed with a thorough knowledge of the human voice, for, as it is modulated so they act."

As in any era and with most jobs, some would find driving teams over the vast desert expanses less than exciting. En route from Utah to San Bernardino, Mormon missionary Hosea Stout penned his impressions in a terse but vivid manner: "Up hill, road not very good. Weak teams. Dull music. 'Hack, whack, gee up, whack, whack, roll on, trot a little, walk a little, the sound of the grinding is low.' More than half the company is out of provisions & horses failing and has to be taken out of the teams. Bait our teams a while then roll on. My mare is given out and has to be beaten along." When this diarist resumed his regular employment of attorney at law, he was doubtless grateful not to be a career teamster. However, compensation for teamster employment was relatively good at the time. Drivers handling the largest wagon outfits often commanded pay of $75 to $100, plus expenses, and sometimes netted $175 monthly, with those driving smaller wagons getting $50–$75 per month.[36]

Mule skinner Bill Streeper, a veteran of the Southern Route, recalled that the six mules used on what he called the Los Angeles trail would each come right up to him when called by name. He also asserted that mules were at least as smart as horses. In fact, although he never credited the animals for contributing to his safety when on the Southern Route, he did later when he carried "heavy mail" by pack mule over the same route then used by the more famous Pony Express. The mule he rode would often sense when hostile Indians were nearby and warn him by twitching its ears. Several close calls occurred in

1860 when some of his fellows were being attacked; Streeper credited his mules with his own safe passage through dangerous territory.[37]

One writer in the Sacramento *Union* asserted not only that mules had been grossly misrepresented as stubborn, but also that they were so "quiet, gentle, obedient, energetic, powerful, they make you respect and almost love them." When teamed in numbers greater than could practically be hitched to a wagon tongue, they were carefully situated in pairs along a central chain. The animals placed next to the wagon were called *wheelers* and those at the end of the tongue, *pointers*. Those situated in tandem along the tongue ahead of the wheelers were all termed *swing teams*, numbered in pairs. The foremost mules, on the swing chain ahead of the tongue, called the *leaders*, were well-trained animals in which each freighter took particular pride because they were so much depended on for the proper handling of the entire team. Each pair forward from the pointers were hitched to doubletrees attached to the swing chain, which was fastened to the front axle of the wagon. Well-trained mules instinctively stepped over this chain as soon as it pressed against their legs during a turn. This maneuver was necessary to prevent the lead teams from pulling other teams and the wagon into the turn prematurely.[38]

Driving a team of up to six animals was relatively easy, with a separate rein attached to each animal's bit, as so often shown in pictures of stagecoaches. With more draft animal teams the matter was certainly more complicated. Bull whackers drove oxen simply with voice commands of *gee* and *haw* and the whip to give direction, not using reins at all. The great majority of large mule and horse teams used a "jerk line." Although teamsters had various ways to rig this line, most hooked a single strap into the outside bit of the near leader and led it back through the outside hame rings (or special spreader rings) on the successive animals on the same side all the way to the mule skinner's hands as he sat on that side of the wagon seat or, at times, astride the near wheeler. Usually a jerk on the line meant a turn to the right and a steady pull signaled the leaders should turn left. Each animal on the "off" side was tied to the inside hame of its near teammate by a tie strap. The off leader was even more rigidly attached, by a rigid distance pole from the near teammate's hame to its own bit, which thus directed its head when the signal was given to turn that way.

Freighters on the Southern Route generally did not use the Conestoga wagon with sloping ends and large overhead canvas cover, which was so famous at the time as the preferred conveyance for more than a generation of western pioneer emigrants. Eastern-made wagons were deemed too small for western commerce and could not withstand the wood shrinkage and cracking inherent in the arid desert climate. It was largely this need that motivated John M. Studebaker to commence his immensely successful manufacture of wagons at Placerville,

Large mule team and wagons near the railroad at Daggett, California, in the 1870s.
COURTESY THE HUNTINGTON LIBRARY

California. The wagons most desired for transporting goods on the Southern Route had a bed 40 to 48 inches in width, with sides sloping slightly outward, some 4 feet tall, 16 to 20 feet in length. Some of these wagons hauled as much as fifteen tons of merchandise, but could not be loaded that heavily for the grades and sandy crossings of the Southern Route.[39]

As freighting continued to evolve, trailing wagons were hitched to the larger front one. Observers such as Dr. Marcus Jones, a Utah mining expert, recorded that some "claimed a much greater load can be hauled in several wagons by the same team than to have the whole load in one wagon." This, he explained, was true because the load was distributed over a larger area and "only a part of it goes into a rut at the same time, or into a mud hole or against an obstruction of any kind." Besides, he argued, on a hill the extra wagons could be unhitched and single wagons more easily hauled up the grade one at a time. Wider iron wagon tires were another innovation said to prevent sinking so deep in soft road materials, making the haul easier, and were particularly effective on the Southern Route. Any wagons attached to the lead one were called "back actions"; the last of as many as four was the "rear action." These trailers usually had short tongues, enabling relatively small turning circles. On routes like the desert road from Utah to southern California, experienced teamsters became accustomed to hauling hay, grain, and water with them for their animals when acceptable provender was not available. The wagon carrying this, sometimes a simple farm wagon, was called a "tender." It was also the custom among such freighters to hide caches of animal feed on the desert in hopes Indians would not disturb it before it was used for the more heavily laden vehicles and thus the more greatly needed animal energy of the return trip.[40]

Although oxen were never the preferred draft animals for freight wagons on the Southern Route, some ox teams were used in the beginning, until the sparse feed and water of the desert crossing proved their ineffectiveness there. Certainly enough ox-drawn emigrant wagons traveled the route to merit discussion of the process—in contrast to mule and horse teams. One veteran of travel over the Southern Route in both directions was William H. Jackson, a young painter and Civil War veteran later nationally famous as photographer of

Yellowstone Park and the Colorado Rockies. Jackson vividly recorded his initiation as a bull whacker with a freight train heading to Salt Lake City from the Missouri River in 1866. Fifty wagons were coupled in pairs, each requiring six yoke, or twelve oxen, for pulling the load. Most of the oxen provided were semiwild Texas longhorns, mixed with just enough broken and experienced animals to make up manageable teams. The wagon boss pointed out to each driver the animals he was to yoke to his wagon, starting with the wheelers, who were the first in line hitched to the wagon tongue and ending with the leaders, the brains of the team, who set the pace and direction for the rest. Behind them were the swing, three yoke of unbroken riff-raff, controlled to some extent by the pointers hitched next to the wheelers, who were the main animals relied on in some emergency situations.

It was relatively easy for the beginning ox driver to catch the tame designated wheelers from the crowded corral and, by watching experienced hands, he succeeded in placing the heavy wooden yoke and bow around their necks and leading them to the wagon. Then, after being told which longhorn was intended for his off leader, the young easterner's challenge really commenced. As he later wrote, "I trailed him around for some time, maneuvering for an opportunity to clap on the bow under his neck—almost succeeding on the first attempt, but when he found out what I was up to he became wary and gave me a lovely chase, dashing into the most crowded part of the corral while I kept up the pursuit encumbered with a heavy yoke, besides being knocked around, squeezed and stepped on most plentifully." At that point he finally got the bow and yoke connected. However, there was another long chase with only the bow to catch the near leader. This featured being kicked head over heels among the surging bulls, dust, and manure before finally getting them securely yoked. The other four yoke, never before in such service, were even more difficult. After the lengthy catch-and-yoke battle, Jackson described the next intricate process: Beginning with the leaders, the other four yoke "were added successively, connecting each pair with heavy chains running from yoke to yoke." Then, after the wheelers were hitched in place with the tongue pointing outward, "the long string of the five yoke had to be maneuvered out of the crowded corral and around

Drawing possibly based on artist William Henry Jackson's own initiation as an ox team harnesser and driver. He was heading West to seek his fortune, not long after being mustered out of the Union army at the end of the Civil War.

COURTESY OREGON TRAIL MEMORIAL ASSOCIATION, SCOTTS BLUFF, NEBRASKA

to their place in a line so precisely that the driver could hook the pointers' chains on to the end of the tongue while this movement was under way." Certainly this was not an easy task for a beginner. On one occasion Jackson's oxen became entangled with other teams and needed considerable assistance to get them properly extricated. The artist-photographer got better at the hitching job with each passing day, but as many of the other twenty-four bull drivers were also inexperienced, the first session of getting the ox teams properly yoked took eight hours, beginning at daylight.

Jackson greatly appreciated assistance from the two wagon masters as his team and wagons were directed onto the road behind the preceding wagons, but there he was left to his own devices. Things went well for a time, but the wagons soon came to a hill steep enough to require a "chain lock" to prevent the hind wheels from turning in making the descent. Jackson yelled, "Whoa," and the wheelers held back, but the leaders and the rest of the team pulled all the harder. As he kept up the "whoa"ing, the bulls kept on going, acting almost like runaway horses. Jackson ran after them yelling with all his might, expecting at every moment "to see the wagons go tumbling over in a heap." Fortunately this didn't happen. Still not adept with either the whip or authoritative commands, Jackson confessed that his driving was

more "herding than driving," meaning that if he wished to turn in a certain direction, he "would get over on the opposite side and shoo them over." But soon the days of exhausting work made a real bull whacker out of the eastern dude.[41]

MAIL SERVICE AFTER THE MID-1850S

The federal government mail service to southern California was seldom adequate during the 1850s, partly because the more populous northern California representatives did not press the matter and partly because sectional rivalries on the national level disrupted service. The most horrible illustration of the ineffectual mail system was at the beginning of 1855; for example, a convicted murderer had his execution stayed by judicial authority in the north, but the stay documents did not arrive in Los Angeles in time to save him. The San Diego *Herald* published a February letter from a Mormon at St. Louis advising midwestern church members to send their correspondence through Panama to San Diego and thence on to Utah, because snow blocked the westbound routes. Still, the letter writer understood that the mail-carrying ships would go first to San Francisco and that mail would return to San Diego by way of notoriously unreliable coastal steamboats. The Mormons regularly joined other southern Californians in petitioning for bimonthly mail service. If anything, Utah was in a worse situation. One correspondent from Salt Lake City to the San Francisco *Alta California* reported, "[W]e are entirely shut out for the balance of the winter from any communication by the eastern route and have to rely upon California for all of our news."[42]

The 1856 session of Congress almost passed an appropriation for an overland mail system from the Missouri River to San Francisco. An even better-funded bill did pass the following year, leaving the route and precise terminus undetermined. Part of the motivation for these initiatives, particularly by California senator William Gwin, was to break the ocean mail service and Panama Railroad monopoly on mail carrying. His fellow senator from California, John Weller, particularly desired the system to promote military posts and thereby a safer way west for emigrants. The law also specified suitable conveyance for passengers as well as security of mails. It left the selection of mail contractor and route to the discretion of the U.S. postmaster general, who happened to be from Tennessee.

Some bidders favored a northern route through Salt Lake City, but a company headed by John Butterfield and including William G. Fargo preferred a St. Louis eastern terminus. The postmaster general, seeking to answer the numerous critics who said a more northern route was preferable for emigration, argued the impossibility of mail delivery by that route during the snow season. He also dismissed the Beale route through Albuquerque as unsafe. The prescribed route swept in a giant semicircle from the railhead town of Tipton, Missouri, to Fort Smith, Arkansas, westward through El Paso, Texas, and Yuma, Arizona, to Los Angeles. The roadway then headed north through the San Joaquin Valley and over Pacheco Pass to its western terminus at San Francisco. It was opened with much fanfare 15 September 1858, taking under the prescribed twenty-five days travel each way. Within less than two years, more overland mail came by the Butterfield line than via the rival ocean steamers. Yet northern critics never ceased attempting to get the route shifted to their advantage.[43]

Largely through the outcry over location of the first overland mail route, other shorter routes were not entirely eliminated. Mail contracts over the Utah-to-southern California route were renewed through congressional action in 1860 and 1861 just prior to the outbreak of the Civil War. But matters remained in flux for the duration of that great conflict. In May 1861, a large detachment of men employed by the war-dismantled Butterfield Overland Mail Company, with about a hundred horses, left for Salt Lake City over the Southern Route. This venture was presumably intended to reestablish service from Missouri through northern Utah and Nevada to San Francisco, with other employees from further out on the route to follow soon. Still, there was optimism that the postmaster general would recognize the value of carrying at least winter mail over the Southern Route. In 1869, after completion of the transcontinental railroad, a similar crew of displaced former employees and horses of the Overland Route again traveled to southern California seeking employment on shorter stagecoach and freight routes. Despite the proliferation of railroad lines, the pressing demand for stagecoach and freight lines from the railroad stations to the outlying areas would long continue.[44]

ROAD IMPROVEMENTS AT THE SOUTHERN CALIFORNIA END OF THE TRAIL

The same year as the Carleton military campaign against Indians on the Mojave Desert, namely 1860, discussed hereinafter, also saw the beginning of the greatest gold rush in southern California history. The California Mormons had done extensive prospecting and mining between 1852 and 1858, successful not only in extracting ore but also in deliberately preventing any resultant rush excitement among "outsiders." This changed in late 1860 when a series of rich prospects was discovered throughout the area later named Holcomb Valley. Among the first but certainly not the first to find these rich locations were William F. Holcomb, a longtime prospector who may have struggled over the Southern Route in 1849, netting several negative comments from diarists of the route, and his hunting partner and earlier Old Spanish Trail veteran-guide, Ben Choteau. It did not take long for word to spread, and by summer there was a full-fledged rush to the valley.[45]

Most miners and freighters who arrived at the mushrooming mountain camps came directly from the San Bernardino Valley up the very steep and difficult Santa Ana River Canyon. Goods arriving on pack mules by that route commanded high prices even for a mining camp. For this reason, the Holcomb Valley inhabitants soon seized on the route used by the earlier Mormon miners, which went up Cajon Pass through what was later Victor Valley and into the mining district from the northwest. They raised $1,500 and engaged resident blacksmith Jed Van Dusen to construct a wagon road from the Cajon summit eastward across what would later be Hesperia and south Apple Valley and up the relatively gradual canyon slopes into the west end of Holcomb Valley. In early June, the Los Angeles *Star* reported that "Van Dusen [had] a strong force working on the road to connect with the one being constructed through Cajon Pass."

Meantime, those hauling freight through the Cajon area had long dreaded the final climb over the hogback at the rim of the pass. The Sanford Cutoff markedly eased the grade in 1855, but the sandy road immediately to the north was still inadequate for the heavy loads that would be hauled to the new Holcomb Valley mining camps. In early April the Los Angeles *Star* agitated for a better road, reporting that many teamsters compelled to use the road were offering a toll of $5 per load to anyone who would "cut down the mountain and make a turnpike road of it." Within a month the paper reported selection of a committee that included several of the most prominent men in the southland, with direct personal interest in the improvements. One was freighting company official W. T. B. Sanford, probably already contracted to transport a heavy steam boiler to the mining camp, and Francis Mellus, brother of the Los Angeles mayor, who had bought that equipment. These and other men visited the area and recommended either more extensive excavations of the existing roadway in the western Cajon Pass or, preferably, avoiding that wing of the pass completely by grading a new road up the rocky creek bed in the east wing of

the pass. They estimated that the cost of either would be much less than earlier anticipated, and they divulged that the funds necessary had already been raised, presumably by private subscription.

These interests were probably not even aware of the enterprise that ultimately constructed the road. A San Bernardino partnership had been formed, with Judge Henry Willis drafting the proper application to the state legislature for a toll road franchise through the Cajon Pass. George L. Tucker, one of three men who had profited most from the Mormon abandonment of the area several years previously, was probably mainly a silent financial backer. The prime mover both in construction and operation was John Brown, a former mountain fur trapper and sometime partner of Kit Carson. Brown had resided in San Bernardino since 1852 and played an important and varied role in the development of the Mojave Desert region during the ensuing decade. After the franchise was granted, on 17 April 1861, Brown pressed the work on the east Cajon roadway energetically, with between thirty and forty men employed there in early summer. By mid-June, it was open to teams and wagons. The San Bernardino County Board of Supervisors later in the summer agreed the proprietors could charge a dollar per wagon trip, with corresponding prices for other categories of customers. In August the 8,000-pound "monster boiler" owned by Mellus and hauled by Sanford arrived in Holcomb Valley, a tremendous feat of freighting that proved the road to be "very good."[46]

CONTINUED FREIGHTING DURING AND AFTER THE CIVIL WAR

The Civil War era may have stimulated even greater amounts of trade over the Southern Route, although not as much mention of desert transportation appears in the vastly altered Los Angeles *Star* of the war years (whose editor was eventually imprisoned partly for his pro-Confederacy leanings). No evidence suggests that the volume of goods freighted to Salt Lake City declined or that the demand there did not remain equally high. Byron Grant Pugh, a careful student of the southern freight route, concluded from the source materials he had examined that the year 1862 "must have been one of the busiest on the trail." He noted a dozen wagons loaded at San Pedro heading for Salt Lake City the first week of the new year. A week later, nine large wagons hauling merchandise for Salt Lake City merchant W. W. Jennings, captained by Sidney Tanner and hauled at the low rate of $.18 per pound, also started over the route. Two weeks later, six heavily laden wagons departed, also loaded with goods shipped south by Bachman and Hanks from San Francisco. The unprecedented rains of that time may have posed some mud and trail washout problems but probably improved the new growth of grass on the deserts enough to offset any obstacles presented. The first week in February, Walter Dodge—another former San Bernardino resident and more recently of Utah's Dixie—led a train away from California carrying eighty tons of freight costing about $30,000. Late that same month two large trains from Utah, one of sixty wagons, arrived to haul loads back over the trail. At that time the Los Angeles *Star* editorialized on the importance of the Southern Route from the California southland to Salt Lake City, commenting that even San Francisco businessmen conceded its essential role in conveying their freight during the periods when more direct roads for them were impassable.[47]

In late April 1863, tragedy struck at San Pedro, affecting, among others, the family most prominent in that area: Banning and Sanford. During a storm, a steamer that Phineas Banning used as a tug and passenger transport to the larger coastal steamers exploded when cold water entered the superheated boilers. This killed William T. B. Sanford outright and severely injured his wife, a sister of Phineas Banning. Both Banning and his wife were also injured, as were some thirteen others; at least twenty-six persons were killed in the mishap, and only seven escaped unharmed. Thus ended the life of Sanford, the man most instrumental in opening the Cajon Pass as a freighting road to the outside world.[48]

Silas Cox, a San Bernardino Mormon freighter, veteran of sixteen trips over the Southern Route, boasted several skirmishes with Native Americans—all on other trails in Nevada and Idaho in which the attackers got the worst of the matter. In late 1863 Cox encountered an emigrant company of over ten wagons and up to fifty

people stopped at "Sand Grass Camp" between the Virgin and Muddy Rivers. He noticed a greater number of Native Americans in the camp than most freighters deemed safe. On discussing the matter with the company captain, Cox discovered the travelers had the Virgin River Paiute chief Tosho tied under guard at one of the wagons, to ensure the good behavior of his tribesmen. The chief confirmed that the situation was entirely cordial and that Tosho's central purpose was securing lots to eat for his fellows. The freighter Cox engaged several Indians to herd his own teams through the night, after which the band leader was released and his people withdrew from camp, much to the relief of some company women. This practice apparently continued to develop, because four years later the same Paiute leader agreed to similar practices of allowing Paiute hostages to be retained at Fort Mojave, on the Colorado River, to ensure the continued good behavior of fellow tribesmen.[49]

Farther down the trail on the same freight expedition, at Kingston Springs, Cox and his brother-in-law, Tap Dotson, met another small emigrant company. Most of the group remained at the water hole an extra day, but the Hamilton family indicated intent to press on toward Bitter Springs with their two wagons. After his own arrival there almost a day later, Cox watched for signs of the wagons as his livestock grazed. When they did not arrive in a reasonable time, he took six mules, a light wagon, and a barrel of water back over the trail. He found them seven miles back in the Red Pass area, "completely given out and the folks were perishing for water." After administering to the needs of the family and their animals, Cox assisted them on to the springs. When he met Hamilton at Los Angeles several years later, the man acknowledged Silas had probably saved his family's life.[50]

By 1863 the Utah Cotton Mission had become established in the St. George, Utah, area. It eventually expanded southwest into present Nevada as well. The initial families assigned there experienced several trying years attempting to procure provisions in exchange for the cotton they produced. The difficulty appeared to be that cotton manufacturing was supposed to take place farther north in Utah's longer-established settlements, but entrepreneurs there seemed hesitant to pay the necessary price for the cotton. The desperate growers thereupon sold some of their cotton to California brokers.

Silas Cox, early cattle wrangler along the Mojave River, who later drove freight wagons and sheep over the Southern Route. On one occasion, he rescued a small wagon company from probable death of thirst not far before Bitter Springs.

With a market price as high as $1.90 per pound in New York during a period of scarcity induced by the Civil War, these brokers could not only afford to freight the product across the desert of the Southern Route but also could ship it by sea around South America to its destination and still make a good profit.

Reports of these transactions greatly disturbed Brigham Young, who promptly sent a letter offering to pay for any cotton presented—though presumably not for so high a price. Yet despite all the efforts to prevent more cotton from leaving the territory by the Southern Route, some still made its way to California. Of the twenty-eight tons of Dixie (Utah) cotton produced in 1863, half was still on hand the ensuing winter. Some was purchased locally by Utah merchant William S. Godbe, who brought goods over the Southern Route from California

to exchange with Dixie brethren, presumably with his own financial interests benefiting more than theirs. After that some of the growers, whose provision supply was almost depleted, did not hesitate to send at least eleven thousand pounds of cotton to southern California for sale. The Los Angeles *Star* noted the arrival of the large train of six- and eight-mule-team wagons loaded with Utah cotton, significant as one of the first loads of marketable freight ever brought in that direction over the trail.[51]

The cotton problem was partially resolved the following year by Latter-day Saints authorities deciding to locate a cotton-manufacturing establishment in the heart of the growing region. Brigham Young directed that the cotton machinery in operation at Parley's Canyon near Salt Lake City be dismantled and taken to Washington, near St. George, to help instill enthusiasm among a dedicated people who had sufficient reasons to be discouraged with the prospects of their cotton mission. This, along with other hardships of the time, and the end of the Civil War again making inexpensive cotton from the southern states available in northern markets, probably prevented much future cotton hauling over the Southern Route.[52]

In the summer of 1864, two young southern Utah men, William Wright and David Ott, were dispatched to San Pedro to haul a threshing machine back to Utah's Dixie in time for the fall harvest. This was one of the very few freighting expeditions on the Southern Route attempted during the hottest portion of the year. The down trip, with grain carried for the six draft horses and two kegs of water to tide them across the dry stretches, was uneventful. But on the return journey with the heavy load, food supplies diminishing amid terrible heat most of the way, the men almost perished between Las Vegas and Santa Clara. Although they reached the latter Mormon settlement and received the food, shade, and rest essential to revive them, their animals could not successfully complete the trip without assistance from fresh teams. Promoters would for years call the Southern Route an all-season roadway from the Intermountain West to the Pacific Coast, but those who ventured over it between June and September were risking more than just extreme discomfort.[53]

Further insight into the freighting industry at that time is provided by the reminiscences of a cowhand assigned to tend a large herd of cattle on the pastures along the Mojave River during a devastating southern California drought in 1864. J. R. Pleasants, working for former veterans of the Old Spanish Trail—southland ranchers William Workman, John Rowland, and William Wolfskill—noted the great number of freight wagons traveling near the river. He also mentioned the practice of the incoming teamsters camping on the Mojave meadows for extended periods while their animals regained strength on free grass and water during the time their employer was purchasing and gathering the cargo for the return trip. It was certainly an ideal spot for such purposes, better than any available closer in to the southland settlements. The cowboy noted that there was never a lack of good company along the Mojave, because so many freighters stopped there.[54]

CHANGING ATTITUDES OF THE MORMON HIERARCHY

Even before the transcontinental railroad totally obliterated any prospects of Mormon economic independence and self-sufficiency, LDS authorities tacitly conceded trade with the outside world was inevitable. In a message published in the official church organ, the *Deseret News*, in October 1865, Mormon leaders stated that those who had labored so diligently to develop Utah were the ones who should benefit most from the trade taking place in that vicinity. There was no good reason, the newspaper item stated, for "outside speculators coming [to Utah] by express train" to reap "the choicest of the harvest which others have sown and tended," with those outsiders taking their profits elsewhere to spend and invest. Specifically appealing for some Mormon citizens to "follow freighting as a business," the newspaper writer, who would never have made any statement not approved by the church hierarchy, asked, "[I]f there is money and other advantages to be obtained in the freighting trade, why should not our own people have those advantages and the means be made to conduce to the welfare and wealth of the citizens of the territory, instead of to strangers, who have no further interest here than to make and carry off the dimes?"

Plenty of citizens in Utah, the article further stated,

were capable of undertaking the freighting business, concluding that "all or nearly all the carrying trade connected with this territory" should be controlled by those citizens. By that time this aim was already partly accomplished, but the heyday of overland freighting was almost over. Essentially, Brigham Young's temporary change in attitude came too late for his people to garner a very high proportion of the freighting profits of the era. The Mormons would probably control transportation even less in the railroad era already close at hand, although freighting from rail centers to outlying areas would continue for many years, with individual Mormons playing an important role.[55]

END OF THE OVERLAND FREIGHTING ERA

Historical source materials for 1865 and 1866 are not good; nevertheless, judging by the still frequent mention of freight trains heading for Utah, Idaho, and Montana from southern California in these years, traffic likely continued unabated. A good insight into the tremendous volume of traffic making the journey all the way from Los Angeles to Salt Lake City in 1866 is offered by the report of Joseph Bull, an employee of the *Deseret News* dispatched to San Francisco for paper and other supplies. Bull returned over the Southern Route with Truman Swarthout, another former San Bernardino resident turned freighter, and noted meeting the mule train of Salt Lake merchant William Godbe, in charge of well-known Mormon freighter Capt. Billy Streeper, at Mountain Springs. Not long after, they met the train of other Mormon teamsters, namely Kimball, Pack, and Shirtliff, consisting of some twenty-five wagons. Three days later, they came on Worley's train at the dry lake between Las Vegas and the Muddy River. And not long thereafter, they encountered Crosby and Fuller's mule train, and finally, Capt. Jefferson Hunt's train on the Virgin.[56]

For several years thereafter, the annual trips sometimes started earlier than previously, as when the initial freight journey of the winter season of 1867–68 commenced in early October instead of after the first of the new year. The San Bernardino *Guardian* observed that many expected a particularly good trade season over the route that year. Later the same newspaper noted that many of the team and wagon owners over the route were local men who had been all the way to the Missouri River that year. The "usual number" of freight trains was also reported active in February 1868.[57]

A SHEEP HERD IN THE OTHER DIRECTION

Early in 1867, Silas Cox and his father, Andrew Jackson Cox, purchased 2,000 sheep in southern California at a price of $1 a head, and with two other men began herding them over the Southern Route toward Salt Lake City. The drive proceeded without incident until near Kingston Springs, where something—presumably coyotes—stampeded the flock, which ran some fifteen miles back across the desert. By hauling water by wagon from the springs, the men saved the sheep, which then required several days rest at Kingston Springs. Unfortunately, as they finally left for Mountain Springs the weather turned hot and many of the animals proved unable to continue across the desert *jornada*. Over a third of the sheep died, the carcasses of which still lay where abandoned next time Silas Cox passed that way. After resting longer at Cottonwood Springs, which Cox called Williams Ranch, the herders moved the survivors on through to northern Utah without further incident. Unable to secure a fair price there, they proceeded on to Montana in the late spring. They sold the sheep for $10 per head, making a considerable profit despite the animals lost on the desert.[58]

WILLIAM H. JACKSON OVER THE TRAIL—IN BOTH DIRECTIONS

One of the most illuminating diary accounts of travel over the Southern Route in the later years is that by William Henry Jackson, the Civil War veteran and soon-to-be famous photographer mentioned earlier, who traveled it in both directions in 1866 and 1867. After his bullwhacking experiences traveling to Salt Lake City, he spent several months there helping a Mormon construct an adobe barn. In early December, the restless traveler inquired among the emigrant camps temporarily located

in the city and discovered, significantly, that trains were starting over the Southern Route "almost every day." He learned that many trains would take an additional passenger for thirty to thirty-five dollars for the entire trip, if he carried and cooked his own food. He chose the company headed by Ed Webb of Los Angeles, which embarked 19 December 1866.

Jackson's journey through Utah was notable for the clearly enjoyable aspects of the trip. Some of his group attended community dances along the route some half-dozen times, as well as numerous singing sessions among the company in the evenings around the campfire, sometimes featuring a companion playing a fiddle and another, the "bones," which were doubtless sticks used to keep time to the music. The longtime landscape artist also noted that he painted numerous mountain and Mormon town scenes along the road. When the party encountered the persistent beggars among the Moapa band of Paiutes near the Muddy River, as had several preceding travelers, William traded an old shirt and blanket for a bow and arrows and was pleased with his acquisitions.

Like several other travel groups of the 1860s, the Webb-Jackson train continued straight south from Cedar City down the difficult grade at Black Ridge and on through the new settlements of Utah's Dixie. The party rejoined the old route at Utah Hill, called Conger Hill by the diarist. Jackson and his companions slept each night in a covered wagon and also spent much of the trip riding in and driving that vehicle, often playing card games en route. On the Utah Hill segment, traveled in one day all the way to Beaver Dam, the passenger complained tersely, "[T]raveled very fast. Riding no pleasure—jolted about most awfully." The remainder of the trip was uneventful, the highlight, as usual, being the winery and store at Rancho Cucamonga, where the much-treasured beverage could be obtained for $1.50 a gallon. Jackson noted that towns such as El Monte appeared "dilapidated" compared to the Mormon communities observed earlier in his journey. Unsuccessful in obtaining passage to San Francisco, Jackson worked through the spring digging ditches and ranching near Mission San Fernando.[59]

In the late spring of 1867, Jackson signed on as a wrangler with a half-dozen others driving a herd of horses northeastward from Los Angeles over the Southern Route. After a slow drive up the Cajon, interrupted one night when a bear stampeded the herd, the group commenced the "tedious and dusty" stretch to the Mojave River. When within a couple of miles of water, the horses stampeded for it, with the herders' mounts accompanying in the rush to quench their thirst. As others before them, primarily going the other direction, the wranglers moved their stock slowly along the river to spots where grass and water were easily available, building the animals' strength for the desert crossing. Some of the horses were also shod en route, to withstand the sharp rocks of the trail. One difference between this and previous diary accounts was that by this time numerous ranches were established along the Mojave River, although farther down several had been recently burned by marauding Indians.

The trail boss clearly understood his business, as he concluded to do much of the herding at night, particularly through the formidable desert stretch skirting Death Valley. He also knew where to find the best bunchgrass before reaching Bitter Springs and in other crucial locations. Again, at the desert water holes, the herders attempted to hold some of the stock back so smaller numbers could drink at any given moment. This ploy was usually unsuccessful. Jackson noted that the crowded animals "managed to get about as much mud as water." One challenge for the herders was getting sufficient sleep in the heat of the day for the night driving. It was mid-May and often stiflingly hot on the shadeless desert. Jackson, later a photographer of natural scenery, commented how much greener the desert plants were and how many were in bloom compared to his southwestward trip through the region in December. Another challenge of herding horses across the forbidding wastelands was footsore animals attempting to head up each sandy wash encountered rather than on the harder-packed and sometimes rocky main trail. And more than once a serious stampede was narrowly averted when a rider raced to reach the head of the horse herd and turn the leaders into a circle until they calmed down.

At Kingston Springs the group found no indication of Indians recently in the area, but suffered considerably from high winds, which stirred up much dust and sand. Jackson was understandably "disgusted with Kingston Springs." He stated it was the "most disagreeable place [he] was ever in." Soon after, with the tired, hungry

horses struggling up the grade to Mountain Springs, the diarist recorded, "[I]t was a difficult job to drive them. There was enough swearing done to make everything look blue." At Cottonwood Springs, the group encountered several Native Americans, with whom they had cordial interaction. One of the Indians repaired the bow Jackson had acquired on the downward trip. As had most other travelers, the wranglers considered the Vegas springs nothing less than "splendid." The ranch there was noted to be in full operation at the time they passed, which would have been during the initial phase of Octavius Gass's long occupancy, discussed later in this book. As the wranglers had done on the Mojave, they borrowed a corral to hold some of the horses while they lassoed them for reshoeing.

On the *jornada* between Vegas and the Muddy River, the horse herders passed a "big train," doubtless of freight wagons. They had seen another such company at Kingston Springs, indicating the road was still quite busy in the summer of 1867. An occupational hazard of the trip was that one or two of the hands had to stay with the herd even when the others were trying to relax, which added to a serious accumulated lack of real rest. Near the Muddy, Jackson confessed he had dozed off while on horseback more than a hundred times, although never falling from his mount. The diarist recognized some of the Moapa Indians he had encountered previously, reporting they were "as great beggars as ever and fully as dirty."

Just as the sheep herders had discovered more than a dozen years before, the road over Mormon Mesa was good for wagons, but "very hard" on horses' hooves, with Jackson noting the animals were "getting very tender footed" on the sharp rocks. Even without a wagon, Jackson and his horse had considerable difficulty getting down the Virgin Hill grade. At the Virgin River, the herders recognized an urgent need to hurry because threatened rains would raise the water level at the many fording spots. They mostly succeeded in making the crossings, although several riders and their horses encountered quicksand and the mounts rolled over the men in the water. Eventually they discovered better traveling south of the river, up on the benchlands where wagons could not go. By the time the herders reached the Santa Clara River, the boss had difficulty getting any

The later-famous landscape photographer William Henry Jackson made this sketch of Cottonwood Springs (present-day Blue Diamond, Nevada) and of the horses he and his fellow wranglers were driving northeast in May 1867. The lack of characteristic trees and other vegetation may be explained by an earlier diarist's mention of at least one grass fire in the area.

COURTESY OREGON TRAIL MEMORIAL ASSOCIATION, SCOTTS BLUFF, NEBRASKA

of his men "to go on herd." It had been an arduous trip, not improved in the least by the "vexatious time" they had crossing the high water on the Santa Clara.

As almost all other travelers before them, Jackson and his associates observed an abundance of Native Americans in the Tonequint–Santa Clara vicinity. However, there was one notable difference this time, in that some of the Indians were mounted on horses, which in earlier years they had been more inclined to eat than to ride. Another contrast to earlier years was the relatively new settlement farther down the Santa Clara, still only a dozen houses and some long-famous peach orchards. As with Jackson's earlier traveling companions, this party also chose to travel through St. George rather than by way of Mountain Meadows, stopping at the larger settlement to get some blacksmithing repairs. Subsequent travel through the towns along the Utah segment of the road found the people cordial, and the trip uneventful. Jackson returned east and launched a photography career that made him nationally famous.[60]

In 1868, former mail carrier over the Southern Route Leonard Conger contracted to deliver a herd of cattle from Utah to southern California over the old trail. When he and his wranglers were more than halfway to their destination, at Kingston Springs, they were surrounded by a band of Native Americans five times their own number. The chief spokesman, who knew a little English, as-

serted that the surrounding country belonged to the Indians and not to the *hikos*, as white men were called, particularly the mountain sheep, rabbits, quail—all native game. After continued conversation, the speaker declared the local water and grass also did not belong to the white men, although their cattle were consuming it. The demand for tribute was obvious. Conger agreed to butcher and distribute three head of beef, which the domain proprietors conceded was acceptable payment.[61]

It was the seemingly senseless killing of merchant Frank Woolley, discussed in the next chapter, that most dramatically signaled the end of the overland freight trade to Utah from southern California. The need for manufactured goods from the outside world had never abated, and in 1868 the Southern Utah Cooperative Mercantile Association was established to secure such goods. This was actually the first time the Utah Dixie residents amassed sufficient capital to import the merchandise essential to commence real mercantile trade. The all-weather Southern Route was particularly desirable to those living in the extreme southwestern corner of Utah and with the railroad still some four hundred miles away, Los Angeles was just about as close. On 1 February 1869, teams and wagons were dispatched to the Wilmington seaport to be loaded with goods that the recently appointed purchasing agent, Woolley, had had shipped from San Francisco.[62] But after his well-publicized murder a month later, freight would arrive in northern Utah by rail and be shipped by wagon to Dixie and elsewhere. The transcontinental railroad was completed two months after the Woolley murder. Those two events dramatically signaled the close of overland freighting on the Southern Route. Extensive hauling ventures would still head out partway from each terminus of the historic old trail, particularly to mining camps. But almost no more expeditions all the way along the roadway would be attempted thereafter. Overland journeys on the Southern Route would remain rare indeed until after the turn of the twentieth century, when another railroad was built essentially following the old emigrant and freighting trail.[61]

CONCLUSIONS

Despite a shortage of freighting records related to the Southern Route, what can be learned of the less-consistent transportation ventures persuasively indicates it served as a vital supply source of goods from the outside world, which were in great demand in the burgeoning Mormon empire. This trade succeeded—sometimes in spite of Brigham Young's expressed desires to the contrary. Historians have long recognized that the settlements established in what became northern Utah were an important rest and resupply center for emigrants passing over the more heavily traveled routes from Missouri to California and Oregon. It is equally clear that the Mormon inhabitants also enjoyed great advantage from their close proximity to these major overland trails because of the markets the freighters provided for food, livestock, and services. This advantage included the favorable exchange they received in payment: usually exhausted but good strains of livestock and heavy excess baggage and wagons. Almost all this activity took place during the summer months each year, because the weather in both east–west directions from Salt Lake City precluded overland transportation during other seasons.

That is why the six-hundred-mile-long lifeline roadway between Mormondom and southern California was so much more important than has heretofore been recognized. For more than half of each year, at least from 1855 to 1869, that route delivered a truly massive amount of the goods produced in the shops and factories of the outside world to eager customers of the Utah area. It thus served as a crucial supply source for burgeoning Utah. John W. Caughey's assertion that the Southern Route was among the most important wagon roads is indeed highly plausible.

Chapter Eight

Continued Emigration, Early Mojave Settlement, and Conflict with Native Americans in California

After the immediate reverberations of the Mountain Meadows Massacre subsided, the Mormon exodus from and to San Bernardino continued. A few other emigrant parties also passed along the route. And although relations between the region's Native Americans and Latter-day Saints remained generally good, even church travelers subsequently confronted more persistent Paiute begging and demands for land- and road-use tolls. At the other end of the trail, permanent settlement by whites began. Many white southern California residents became more vocal in advocating severe chastisement of desert Indians and after several deaths of citizens along the roadway to Utah, California-based contingents of the United States Army commenced delivering the desired punishments and temporarily established several outposts on the Southern Route. Later in the decade whites murdered three Native American youths near the headwaters of the Mojave River. Primarily in retaliation, Paiutes killed four white men, in the same area. Thus the

long and unfortunate heritage of ill–will between Native Americans and white Americans continued through the 1860s.

CROSBY-HUNT AND OTHER NORTHBOUND PIONEERS

When Caroline Barnes Crosby and her family arrived on the upper Cajon, the same older woman who had befriended her a few days earlier, as they had left San Bernardino, offered Caroline Crosby tea and sweet cake and was "remarkably polite and kind," a consideration that remained a hallmark among fellow believers throughout the Mormon exodus to Utah. An even better example of this was the Crosbys' wait at the bottom of the Cajon Pass summit ridge for other evacuees, to ask for their teams' help in hauling the wagon up the trail; Jonathan Crosby had found the hill impossible to negotiate without assistance. Caroline's description of the passageway as "very steep and worn by wagons" better fits the old road up the hogback than the three-year-old Sanford grade a mile farther west. It is entirely likely many Mormon teamsters sharing each other's yokes of oxen, as the Crosbys soon did, used the same roadway on which they had entered the Cajon a half-dozen years before. The two evening camps above the Willow Grove water supply were possible because in January 1858 patches of snow were scattered along the trail at the upper elevations, which the Crosbys and others melted in buckets for themselves and their animals. After a day of waiting, the William D. Huntington and Montgomery Button wagons came by and the drivers promised that on reaching the top of the pass they would return to assist the Crosby wagon. The experienced teamsters, using mules rather than oxen, got up the grade "without any hesitation." But even with their added teams, the Crosbys had to unload some of their lighter, loose items, which all hands carried up that night after dinner. Thus passed Caroline's fifty-first birthday, with her family obediently "pursuing [their] course to the valleys of the saints." She concluded, "[T]he Lord only knows what we may be called to pass through"; she could only assume the journey ahead would be difficult.[1]

The following morning the Crosbys traveled a dozen-mile stretch without feed or water for their livestock until reaching the Mojave River just after sunset. The first campers they encountered enjoyed blazing fires, inviting to travelers. Next day they moved downstream to where they found Caroline's niece, Lois Hunt, and the extended family of Lois's husband John. Dinner was almost ready; the new arrivals "soon joined them round a hearty meal of cornbread and beans." The ensuing evening Indians attempted to steal the livestock, and it took the Mormon men all night and into the next day to round up the scattered animals. Thereafter, a Native American approached their camp and was welcomed, although some travelers compared his moccasin prints with those of the would-be rustlers, determining to their satisfaction the visitor to be from a different tribe. Although the group intended to await the arrival of Caroline's sister, Louisa Barnes Pratt, the men became sufficiently apprehensive about Indian theft of livestock to

move on sooner, even though it meant sharing the extra weight of Pratt's load of flour, which they had brought up the pass for her.[2]

At about the same time, the family of James Henry Rollins, minus the father, also camped along the Mojave. One day the seventeen-year-old son, John Henry, determined to get the family teams and wagon moving down the river road before the remainder of their company was ready. As they passed a large rock at the side of the trail, "two big Indians jumped out from behind it, all painted and with head bands, feathers and bows and arrows." One of the Native Americans grasped the lead mules and cramped the wagon wheels, while the other drew an arrow in his bow. The young mule driver was preparing to use his long whip, when his pregnant mother shouted, "[D]on't touch them or they will kill every one of us." At that crucial juncture the other wagons rolled into view and the Indians ran off. That night Emeline Rollins went into labor and the child died, complications probably resulting from the recent frightful experience. She remained ill most of the way to Utah.[3]

In mid-January 1858 the Crosby-Hunt party departed the Mojave River camps and set off across the desert. Leaving the separation point (Forks in the Road) at eight o'clock in the morning, they traveled over "heavy roads" until sunset. After supper and a short rest, they started up Spanish Canyon, where the men doubled their teams and asked the women to walk alongside up the sandy wash. The travelers reached the summit well after dark and built a bonfire as a beacon for those following behind. They then traveled on until midnight, rested at a dry camp, and at 6 A.M. continued down the sandy grade toward Bitter Springs. After two hours they stopped for breakfast and allowed the cattle to graze and rest. The party reached the springs at noon. Here Caroline observed that the water appeared red, but she had anticipated this and brewed tea from water carried from the Mojave River. During the rest stop, she wrote a note to her sister, Louisa, presumably traveling several days behind, and as many travelers were accustomed to do, left it on a bush. This means of communication was sometimes effective along the pioneer trail, but Louisa Pratt's diary makes no mention of ever seeing the missive.

The company moved on at seven the next morning

along one of the most desolate stretches of the trail. Later Caroline considered Silurian (dry) Lake "a great curiosity" because it appeared larger and flatter than anticipated. She noticed a kind of well along the trail at the lake bed that contained dirty ice, which party members melted for the livestock. Despite the frozen well water, the afternoon became uncomfortably warm and the white clay along the road caused eye inflammation among some of the group. Partly because of the fatigue of their oxen, the company did not reach Salt Springs until four the following afternoon. The travelers deemed the water there too mineralized for human consumption. Caroline tried brewing tea with it—but it made her sick.

Beyond the springs the next day, Caroline Crosby judged the road the worst she had ever seen, doubtless speaking of the sand in the Dumont Dunes vicinity. Although sometimes the women rode, here they had to walk as the teams struggled along the banks of the Amargosa River. They found the stream level sufficiently high that they did not consider the water dangerous for the livestock as many others often did when the mineral content was less diluted. As noted before, the road in Amargosa Canyon was made particularly difficult by rocks, sand, and mud. One exhausted ox laid down and could only be coaxed back to his feet by an offering of flour and meal. Several breakdowns occurred to wagon tongue, axletree, and wheels. But despite the challenges, all the travelers were reported to be in good spirits and grateful they had remained safe and healthy.

The company stayed in camp on the Amargosa River while Jefferson Hunt's sons, formerly frequent travelers in the area as mail carriers, sought to retrieve goods from an emergency supply cache. They discovered that someone else had taken the main provisions, and they returned with only a keg of vinegar. Noting the sculpted rocky cliffs on all sides, Caroline commented on the "romantic" scenery of the area, "of grand and majestic appearance." The only other known female diarist yet recording experiences on the route, Sarah Pratt, had earlier used the same term for scenery just a short distance from the spot.[4]

Several days of rain, uncommon in that area, had left mud that reached up to the wagon hubs on the trail. This naturally exhausted the oxen and frustrated and discour-

aged the teamsters. Mormon teamwork proved effective in getting through the quagmire, which Caroline observed to be the hardest time they had seen on the journey. Women and children trudged through the mud and water, and when they reached camp, they could locate so little firewood that small comfort could be derived from the campfires. One terse diary entry described "children crying, mothers fretting."

The weather improved as they reached Resting Springs late on 25 January. They remained there two days to rest and repair the wagons. The women washed clothes and baked. Caroline mentioned at the time an Indian farm nearby where Native Americans raised quite a variety of vegetables. After their rest, the group moved on over Emigrant Pass to a dry camp with only a little brush for firewood. At four o'clock the following afternoon they reached Stump Springs, just across the boundary of what was still part of New Mexico Territory. The next day, the diarist mentioned John Hunt eating his dinner with Cottonwood Springs–area Native Americans, demonstrating a long-standing friendship that would dramatically contrast with his feelings on a subsequent trip through the area in 1862.[5]

Meanwhile Louisa Pratt finally reached the Mojave River and was much disappointed to discover her family had moved out ahead of her. She traveled with the company of Bishop Nathan Tenney, a small group that moved slowly, partly because the captain also had the responsibility of driving a herd of goats to Utah. Because her husband, Addison, refused to return to Utah, Sister Pratt employed a good teamster, "kind and obliging, but terribly afraid of Indians." Another company member was a Mormon convert from Australia, Ann Stanley Taylor. Her daughter, Rhoda, so captivated Francis Lyman, then a young teamster assisting the emigrant group from San Pedro to San Bernardino, they soon married, even though the mother had advised against it. The newlyweds were now traveling ahead of her, on the only honeymoon they were to have. Sister Taylor also had a son who had decided to return to Australia. Thus the two women, Pratt and Taylor, walked together for days "and wept as [they] crossed the barren desert, thinking of the loved ones behind us, and of those who had gone before."[6]

THE CROSBYS' EXTENDED
STAY AT LAS VEGAS

When Caroline Crosby and her small company arrived at the Las Vegas fort 1 February 1858, they discovered it to be "in a dilapidated state having been partly destroyed by the Indians." A single Latter-day Saint missionary, Benjamin Hulse, had been assigned to reside among the local Paiutes and help pacify them until the last of the evacuees from the California Mormon colony passed through the vicinity. As soon as the travelers arrived, Indians surrounded them begging for bread. Hulse advised the Mormons not to offer much at any given time and to let him distribute it for them. The travelers, doubtless unaware of the recent inclination of these Native Americans to kill passing emigrants, appreciated the counsel from Hulse, because they had little experience with Indians. Most of the pioneer company moved on within a few days, but the Crosbys remained to further strengthen their draft animals and to await Caroline's sister, Louisa Pratt. This gave the diarist good opportunity to observe rather closely the Las Vegas Paiutes and their visitors from other bands and tribes.

The Indians became increasingly annoying through their persistent "teasing [the Mormons] for food." After losing an ox from a nearby pasture and cloth and a carpetbag full of valuables through slits cut in the wagon cover during the night, the group moved their outfit inside the fort for further protection. After other pioneers lost two horses the following week, the chief of the Las Vegas Indians explained there was a nearby band of marauders who lived primarily by stealing and robbery. This may well be true, but there is no other known reference to a separate village of thieves, and most local Native Americans remained notorious for similar tendencies. In fact, reports of persistent thievery twice loomed as the primary consideration in the disbandment of the Las Vegas Mission.[7]

The Crosbys were grateful when another emigrant company arrived and offered temporary respite from the begging, as the Indians tested the generosity of the other group. On one occasion after the attempted theft of a baby diaper, the chief sought to justify the actions of his people, asserting that the Mormons should provide all his people with clothing. His immediate ground for this assertion was that the Paiutes had to spend so much time in the cold mountains obtaining food that they needed warmer clothing. The chief may also have been blaming emigrant traffic through the area for the scarcity of food supplies closer at hand. Although the chief did not specify why providing clothing was the responsibility of the Latter-day Saints, there are several possible lines of thinking. First, the church had promised to establish a mission, which according to general practice included the prospect of a greater abundance of food and clothing. Or the chief may have been alluding to some presumed reciprocal agreement including food and clothing in exchange for Indian participation in the presumed military alliance with the Mormons. Another possibility would be the Indians' continued disappointment at not having the expected opportunities to loot wagon trains, as perhaps promised.

Missionary Hulse tried to reason with the Vegas chief about why he should not expect such gifts and refused to appeal to the emigrants for additional corn. He apparently sought to encourage the Indian leader to persuade his people to more conscientiously cultivate the fields the Mormons had helped develop for their use. The missionary certainly proved kind and sympathetic with the circumstances of the Native Americans. When shortly thereafter further livestock were stolen, Hulse exhorted the emigrants not to display hatred or enmity toward his charges but encouraged the Mormons to remember the "low and degraded condition" of these people, whom they considered descendants of *Book of Mormon* Lamanites, and to try to set good examples for them at all times. As had been the case throughout church contact in the area for over seven years, the policy recommended was to whip or punish offenders if necessary, but in no case should Indians be killed for stealing.[8]

At that time Amasa Lyman's party passed through the Las Vegas area with Dr. Osborne, the mysterious companion who later proved to be Col. Thomas L. Kane, unofficial emissary to the Latter-day Saints from President James Buchanan. While resting there, this longtime friend of the Mormons visited with Caroline Crosby. He commented that her camp, which featured the bedroom-like wagon in which she slept as comfortably as at home and her stove, which was set out on the ground and closed off from general view by the wagon and hanging blankets, appeared quite a contrast with the rougher manner in which he had been accustomed to camping with his male associates on the trail. Particularly on seeing her and perhaps several other women sitting by the stove ironing clean white clothes, he asserted he would almost as likely have expected to see his own mother somewhere on the trail. Although not mentioned, it is just as probable that this excellent housewife also produced the same array of bread, pies, and cakes for her husband and son as they had been accustomed to at home.[9]

When the Crosbys finally moved on toward Utah, Hulse accompanied them on a temporary respite from his mission to visit his family at Pinto, not far from Mountain Meadows. At the Muddy River, a dozen Moapa Paiutes followed them, "continually asking for food." The party, low on provisions themselves, traded corn and flour for *shorts*, the coarse meal, germ, and bran by-products of flour milling. Caroline described these Native Americans as "very rough and wild." Hulse attempted to reason with them and discovered they were angry at the Mormon leaders, having heard Brigham Young had allegedly called some of their chiefs "good for nothing." There is also evidence that several missionaries recently in the area had courted young Indian women, thus alienating other suitors. The Paiutes continued to beg hard, and although the small company felt obliged to feed them twice in a day, the Indians still stole what they could. Hulse was so discouraged with the Moapas he expressed hesitance to come back among them to resume his mission. That night the emigrant party left and traveled four miles by moonlight, clearly seeking to get away "before [their] visitors returned." Although the Mormon company exercised good patience with their Lamanite brethren, the six-week sojourn in their midst had been exceedingly trying.

The Native Americans encountered by the Crosby-Hulse group on the lower Virgin River were described as "very civil," and farther upstream an Indian referred to as "young chief Amasa" and his companion "conducted themselves remarkably well" among the emigrant camp, with the men sleeping soundly through the night without posting guards. On departure, the two Indians obtained a letter of recommendation to Bishop Nathan Tenney, who was then at Las Vegas with Caroline's sister,

Louisa. Thus they were warmly welcomed by the latter emigrants.[10]

THE TENNEY-PRATT PARTY

After the required rest days at the Vegas, Tenney and Sister Pratt's wagons pulled out for the Muddy. On the first night of travel, Louisa lost a large ox to Indian thievery. It might have been possible to retrieve the ox if her timid teamster had not hesitated to pursue the culprits into a canyon, even though he and his companion were well armed. This forced a single ox to pull the wagon, which it did for some distance, then fell dead. In desperation, they dispatched the Indian Amasa with a letter to former San Bernardino bishop William Crosby, then residing at the new Mormon settlement at Santa Clara. The faithful Paiute never stopped to sleep until he reached his destination. Meantime the party felt compelled to bury most items of the Pratt wagon load in a "vault" dug near the road, presumably somewhere on what would eventually be named Mormon Mesa. Although they feared the Native Americans might see the light by which they dug in the night and loot the cache, it proved the best means of securing the property while the group struggled up the trail. When on the Virgin, Chief Isaac became aware of the plight of the company, particularly the lack of provisions, and camped with them through the night to prevent his tribesmen from begging or stealing. When Amasa, the Paiute, returned with Bishop Crosby's son driving an extra team and bringing provisions, he received rewards of appreciation fully expected after such service. Besides getting a suit of clothes, he was invited to eat dinner with the rest of the group.[11]

These Virgin River Paiutes had never been as prominently mentioned in the emigrant accounts as the Moapa and Tonequint bands on either side of them on the trail, but at this time their leader was emerging as particularly impressive. The chief some Mormons called Isaac is probably the same others knew as Tosho. Just the previous December one of his band had stolen a pistol from passing Latter-day Saints, and when the chief discovered the theft he overtook the group, which had passed on up the river, returned the pistol, then traveled with them for some distance. Tosho asserted he had not stolen anything from the Mormons, nor from the Mericats, and pledged he would not mistreat the church members in the future. He admitted some hostility to some passing non-Mormon groups, because some had earlier killed a number of his men. It was clear from the reported exchange that the chief thought the Latter-day Saint leaders had the power to help maintain good health among the Indian people.[12]

MISSIONARY PROBLEMS WITH INDIANS AND ARMY FREIGHTERS

Later in 1858, missionary Ira Hatch was assigned to reside among the Moapa Paiutes to help maintain peace with other passing emigrants. Living in an abandoned wagon, Hatch had difficulty protecting his own meager provisions supply from pilfering Indians, who justified their action by arguing he could more effectively beg food from passing Americans than they could. Some of the more troublesome Native Americans even made veiled threats as he maintained his lonely vigil watching for approaching wagon trains. When church apostles Ezra T. Benson and Orson Pratt came through returning from foreign missions, they concluded Hatch's position to be sufficiently perilous to order Indian mission leader Jacob Hamblin to send Thales Haskell to assist him. After several additional months, the travel season ended and the two returned to the Santa Clara. Their reports about the poor conduct of the Muddy River Paiutes probably led to the formal early closure of that branch of the Indian mission in the fall of 1858.[13]

The next year, 1859, teamsters traveling from Camp Floyd to California by both main routes proved among the most lawless individuals in the annals of the West. Members of one group who had hired a guide, Gilbert Hunt, son of Jefferson Hunt, to lead them over the Southern Route, cut his throat while he slept, to steal the money he had been paid for the trip. The mistreatment of Northern Paiutes on the Northern Route helped bring about the Indian war in Nevada in the following year, 1860. More than occasionally these teamsters also fought with each other, including an incident at Salt Springs on the Southern Route where two men quarreled over a blanket, one receiving a knife wound that proved fatal.[14]

According to a sketchy report recorded in the LDS church historian's office letter press copybook, Native Americans along the Southern Route killed seven of these discharged teamsters and had thereafter stolen horses and killed cattle belonging to the settlers of the new Santa Clara settlement. When Jacob Hamblin (who had been absent in Arizona) returned, it appeared war with some Southern Paiutes might be imminent. But Hamblin promptly traveled to Las Vegas and conferred with the restless Indians—who returned the stolen horses and otherwise manifested a "good spirit." The missionary blamed the whites involved as much as the Native Americans for the recent ill feelings.[15]

ANOTHER MORMON EXODUS— TO CALIFORNIA

It is impossible to confirm the Los Angeles *Star* allegation that early in 1858 several companies of Mormons who had recently moved to the Utah Zion were already reconsidering and returning to San Bernardino. But whether that was true so early or not, a large southbound traffic soon developed in that and the ensuing several years, much of which originated in Utah.

Later that year an emigration originating in Kansas, of about one hundred men, also crossed by the Southern Route. In June, an item in the new Los Angeles newspaper the *Southern Vineyard* reported "quite a number of the [former] San Bernardino people regret the day they left California and it is no more than probable that some will shortly begin to migrate to distant parts, probably California." The next month mail carrier Daniel Taft led a group back to San Bernardino that was reportedly "greatly disappointed with Mormon affairs in Utah." The *Star* asserted "about a hundred Mormons had arrived back at San Bernardino" by that time, with eleven more wagons arriving the next month and thirty-two more individuals a few weeks later. Both the *Star* and San Francisco *Alta California* may have been correct that the presence of federal troops in Mormon Utah had emboldened people who had earlier decided to leave but had not dared to act until then.[16] This was certainly true of the so-called English train of a dozen former Mormon convert families leaving in full disillusionment that season. They had been unable to flee Utah earlier because of two years of famine as well as because of Mormon military restrictions. The church daily historical journal noted in mid-November that several hundred had recently passed through Cedar City heading for California, concluding with the slight overstatement that "a large portion of the brethren, who came from California last winter, have returned." Still other companies of former Utahans and citizens of San Bernardino were moving to southern California in 1859. And in early 1860 the *Star* reported that "San Bernardino County was experiencing an increase in population due to the fact that a large number of families from Utah had arrived during the past few weeks." However, examination of the 1860 San Bernardino census indicates at least as many first-time Mormon arrivals there as former residents returned.[17]

OTHER SOLDIERS OVER THE SOUTHERN ROUTE

Early in 1859, an unnamed Camp Floyd soldier who later wrote under the pseudonym "Utah" suffered an arm wound in a skirmish with Ute Indians and fought another battle to prevent the army surgeon from amputating the limb. Three days later, with the compound fracture poorly bandaged, the man was mustered out of the service holding a severance paycheck on a St. Louis bank. A Mormon cashed the draft for a typically exorbitant 50 percent commission. The wounded man then made his way to Fillmore in hopes of engaging passage from there to California. But after most of his money and possessions were stolen, he held less hope for an easy ride to the coast. Finally, at Santa Clara, he met a cattle drover who agreed to take him along for whatever service he could render with his right arm still in a sling.

This ex-soldier's comments on the Southern Paiutes along the trail are a significant commentary on their relations with non-Mormon travelers in the later years. He called them "inveterate thieves," capable of "pilfering" with "a skillfulness that will do credit to a London pickpocket." He observed an Indian lift a large knife from the belt of his associate while in the process of testifying that he never stole. As others such as Hans Peter Hoth had earlier discovered, these Native Americans were

"numerous and well-armed" and were prone to "bully and browbeat small parties, taking what they want, despite all remonstrance." The Indians were reportedly much more courteous and submissive when the traveler group was larger and on guard.

On the Mojave River the cattle wranglers encountered an emigrant party who had lost their mules to thieving Paiutes. The cattlemen loaned sufficient cows to pull the pioneer wagons the rest of the way to San Bernardino. They also observed Lt. Edward Beale's experiments with camels as he headed back for Yuma, working on his army assignment to determine the animals' effectiveness on the desert trails. The party reached their destination at Los Angeles without untoward incident. By that time the former soldier had healed sufficiently to write at least one long report to friends about his journey experiences.[18]

In the spring of 1859, Maj. James H. Carleton, United States Army, received orders from his California commander to travel to southern Utah to help investigate the Mountain Meadows Massacre as well as to properly bury human remains still visible there. He interviewed several people close to the unfortunate events, including militia colonel William Dame, missionaries Dudley Leavitt and Jacob Hamblin, along with the latter's wife and Indian foster son, Albert. The first two attested to the intense hostility and excitement then current among the Native Americans. Specifically referring to the Dukes-Turner party, Leavitt testified that "all hell" could not stop the Paiutes from killing—or at least robbing the livestock of the company—as well as complete inability to restrain the Mountain Meadows killings. As previously stated, the extremely biased army officer also conferred with Santa Clara Paiute Chief Jackson, who reiterated that the orders for the main attack had come by letter from Brigham Young, delivered by an Indian interpreter named Huntington.

Carleton quoted another Native American leader, from the Muddy River, as complaining that the Mormons attributed the massacre to his people, but asked, "[W]here [were] the wagons, the cattle, the clothing, the rifles and other property belonging to the train?" implying that these items remained mainly in the possession of non-Indians.[19] This significant question revealed lingering resentments among at least a portion of the Moapa band, thereafter particularly troublesome to most whites traveling through their domain. The ambitious investigating army officer (who next year attacked the Indians of the Mojave Desert and in the Civil War led Union troops to reconquer Arizona and New Mexico) made a biased and not entirely accurate report to the assistant adjutant general of the United States Army stationed at San Francisco, Maj. W. W. Mackall. This report, eventually published in the Los Angeles *Star* and elsewhere, encouraged the widespread anti-Mormon sentiment still prevailing in the region and beyond.[20]

INDIAN RELATIONS AT THE SOUTHERN END OF THE ROAD

Serrano Indian residents at several rancheria-villages situated along the Mojave River had been visited and aspects of their lifestyle noted by Old Spanish Trail founders Padre Francisco Garcés (in 1776) and Jedediah Smith (in 1826–27). These Native Americans occasionally proved formidable opponents to the Spaniards during the late mission period, sometimes in alliance with the Mojaves from the Colorado River area.[21] But no instances of hostile attack by these people on Anglo-American pioneers are recorded during the entire subsequent era. By 1848, a considerable number of desert Serranos had been persuaded to relocate to the San Gabriel and San Fernando missions, and many probably died there of diseases for which they had no immunity prior to or soon after secularization in 1834. The first of several major smallpox epidemics also ravaged the future San Bernardino County region, doubtless claiming desert victims as well as those more carefully observed in the areas of Hispanic and Anglo-American settlement. The numerous diarists traveling along the Mojave River during the American period make virtually no comments even about semipermanent Serrano residences in that vicinity, although archaeologists and ethnologists have determined longer residence of those peoples some fifteen and more miles distance from the main traveled route in the Bowen Ranch and Lucerne Valley areas, as well as in places even farther from the trail.[22]

When Edward F. Beale led his expedition over the

Southern Route in 1853–54 he was searching in part for locales in which to establish some of the nation's first Indian reservations. He intended to examine the Mojave River vicinity for that purpose, but on arrival there, the party encountered no Native Americans. Company leaders were also unimpressed with the "barren and unproductive" land back from the river, erroneously concluding that the area offered "no point fit for settlement," apparently also for an Indian reservation.[23] Several years later as world travelers Jules Remy and Julius Brenchley approached the final segment of their journey, they met a German engineer associated with one of the several Army Corps of Engineers survey parties operating in the Mojave Desert region. The surveyor, probably Frank Lecouvreur, known to have been in the area at the time, assured them "that the Indians had disappeared from the banks of the Mojave, and that it was not at all likely [the party] should fall in with any of them."[24] The former residents had in fact withdrawn from the best residence locations in the region, presumably because of the perceived danger of remaining in such close proximity to the numerous travelers over what had become a major thoroughfare. There may have been some hostile encouragement for the move by the more aggressive Southern Paiutes, including the Chemehuevi, who became increasingly more frequent visitors and at least temporary residents along the river, but this hostility was never recorded in the known written sources.

The lack of emigrant observations of Indian villages does not necessarily mean Native Americans were never encountered along the Mohave. In fact, some time prior to 1856 there may have occurred one of the most unfortunate events ever recorded along the river, although compelling evidence suggests it is in fact apocryphal. Six passing emigrants encamped across the river from where what was described as a Mohave woman was seen cooking over a fire. One of the party had boasted that prior to finishing the journey he would kill an Indian. His associates teased him, saying that he was perhaps in the last day of proximity to Native Americans, upon which he seized his rifle and replied he would save himself from losing the wager. Although his companions begged him not to fire and offered to call off the bet, he took aim and killed the woman.

Within half an hour many angry Mohave warriors quietly surrounded the emigrant camp, only revealing themselves when they suddenly stampeded the mounts of their presumed adversaries. Then, instead of attacking indiscriminately, the Indians sent an emissary to demand the surrender of the murderer and, to his credit, the guilty man gave himself up so as not to further endanger his comrades. After his seizure, the Indians returned the stampeded horses, allowing the other men to depart freely. Not so the prisoner. As English traveler William Chandless described the horrible retribution, "[O]n the spot where the squaw fell, they flayed him alive and buried her, wrapped in the skin of her murderer." There is an excellent chance that Chandless, an otherwise careful observer, thus unwittingly passed on an often-told Gold Rush–era story that has no foundation in fact.[25] Whether the event actually occurred or not, the account of this worst of tortures, published within the decade in England, could only have prejudiced many white southern Californians even more against Native Americans in the region.

Despite the reestablishment of peace between the Utah Latter-day Saints and the U.S. government after the so-called Mormon War, enough anti-Mormon sentiment persisted in southern California for consistently hostile press articles to help keep public opinion aroused through the long-used tactic of linking LDS and Indian threats. In mid-September 1858, a correspondent reported large numbers of Paiute, Mojave, and Navajo Indians—an unlikely set of allies—"congregated on the Mojave River, busily engaged in making bows and arrows and other implements of war." The writer alleged that the warriors were under orders from the Mormons to "kill all the whites on the San Bernardino ranch." It was implied that such threats to the safety of the citizens could not occur if the government would fulfill its responsibility and establish military posts in the area.[26]

In late 1858, Aaron G. Lane established a ranch and way station on the west bank of the Mojave River at what had long been known as the upper or last crossing, near future Oro Grande. Lane, a veteran of the war with Mexico and the California Gold Rush, thus became the first permanent resident of what would become known as the Victor Valley. Settlement did not get off to an auspicious start, because in May of that first year Indians attacked him and presumably some employees. The newspaper account stated they were "overpowered," which more likely meant driven from the location than captured, with the houses and surrounding premises not burned but ransacked, "dispossessing the occupants of all their worldly goods." The Los Angeles *Star,* consistently hos-

Original log structures built by Aaron Lane at his way station at the last crossing of the Mojave River (heading south, near present-day Adelanto, California), by photographer Rudolph D'Heureuse, 1863.
COURTESY THE BANCROFT LIBRARY

tile to Native Americans, chided, "[S]urely it is high time that our government should adopt some efficient means to prevent these Indian outrages, that are daily being committed in our midst and afford that protection to our citizens which is guaranteed to them by the Constitution of this country."[27]

The newspaper appeals probably had little impact on military decision making. However, the Mohave Indian attack on the first pioneer company to attempt using Beale's road across Arizona to the Needles, California, area prompted the dispatch of 500 soldiers, under Maj. William Hoffman, to the Colorado River. When the troops arrived in April 1859, they so completely overawed the Mohaves that they capitulated without a fight. The Indians did make an unsuccessful attack later, after most of the soldiers had been withdrawn, leaving a smaller garrison at the newly established Fort Mojave. It was assumed the new outpost would be supplied by steamboats up the Colorado, but those rumors proved unreliable. Los Angeles–area quartermaster and later Civil War hero Winfield Scott Hancock decided to send the supplies overland. Whether the numerous freight wagon contingents originated at Los Angeles or Fort Tejon forty miles to the north, all companies converged at the Mojave River and followed it through Afton Canyon to the so-called Mojave Road eastward across the desert to the fort on the Colorado River. This was an extensive boost to the sagging southern California economy, with the government employing up to fifty men and expending some $2,000 per month.

Captain Lane recognized enough potential for profits that he saw fit to reoccupy his Mojave River station. Several San Bernardino–based Mormons also attempted to establish ranches along the Mojave River in 1860. These included Silas Cox, Billy Margetson, and members of the interrelated Bemis and Hancock families. However, they soon abandoned the attempt at permanent settlement because of continued Indian hostilities.[28]

THE WILBURN KILLING

Problems with Native Americans on the Mojave really commenced on 23 January 1860, when a wrangler herding cattle belonging to Los Angeles merchant Felix Bachman in the present Hodge area, long called Cottonwoods, was ambushed while searching for stolen stock. Robert Wilburn acted as range boss of a group of cowhands, none of whom were longtime residents of the San Bernardino area. When more than twenty head of cattle and several horses went missing, Wilburn accepted his responsibility for recovering the animals. Later observers surmised that he discovered a dead ox, recently slaughtered for food and, noticing footprints, was investigating further when pierced by three arrows. He was not yet dead when his companions found him, but soon expired. The funeral held, probably in the Los Angeles area, was reported as "largely attended."

It is impossible to ascertain who the perpetrators of the Wilburn murder were, but many contemporaries professed to be able to differentiate among the various Indian tribes' arrows and moccasin footprints. The sources make no mention of anyone seeing the attackers or following their escape trail for any distance, but some concluded that the perpetrators were "Pah-Utes" (Paiutes) from either the Las Vegas area or the region farther northeast along the Santa Clara River. Indians from that vicinity were noted in the same news reports to have been in southern California at the time. These bands were said to still be closely associated with the nearby Mormons, and more than a few southland citizens surmised that some of those Mormons were implicated not only in Wilburn's death but also in similar killings soon thereafter farther out on the trail, near Bitter Springs.[29]

During the first week in April 1860, a rough mountain man named Joaquin Johnston, attracted by availability of government funds to Camp Floyd, Utah Territory, from California, and a U.S. marshal named Kirk, both came to the Mormon town of Holden, a hundred miles south of the army post, and inquired after an Indian about eighteen years old then residing with former mail carrier David Savage. When the young man showed himself, Johnston pointed his pistol at him saying, "[Y]ou are my prisoner." When Savage intervened, the men produced a writ for the Native American's arrest for the murder of Wilburn, a document later presumed fraudulent. The Indian protested his innocence, and Savage recalled the man claimed he had been ill for some five months prior to his coming to Holden. The accused agreed to go to Camp Floyd for trial, being assured of protection by the marshal.

A few days later, reports reached the area that Kirk and Johnston had subsequently boasted of killing the Indian, supposedly when he was escaping. Savage took several fellow Mormons to the location of the affair, the Sevier Bridge. Reading the footprint record there, along with gunpowder burns on the skin of the victim, whose body was found farther downstream, it became clear he had been shot from close range, not when escaping. The body was penetrated by four bullet wounds, after which the Indian was scalped before both perpetrators pitched his body into the river. Johnston later admitted he sent the revenge trophy to Wilburn's orphans in California.[30] Most likely this was the murder of an innocent man, although he may have been implicated in the distant killing of the range boss by some other Native Americans, possibly through individual arrow markings.

THE WILLIAMS-JACKMAN MURDERS

The second fatal Mojave Desert attack occurred on 18 March 1860, on the trail from Salt Lake to California, near Bitter Springs. Thomas Williams, among Utah's first and most independent-minded merchants, was traveling to California to procure goods to stock a new store. He was leading a train of fourteen wagons southward to transport much-needed manufactured goods back to sell in Utah, despite Brigham Young's preference that the Mormons go without whatever they couldn't produce themselves. While thus en route to Bitter Springs, the party encountered four supposedly friendly local Paiutes, who offered to show Williams where to find water and better forage for his animals. Taking only his brother-in-law, Jehu (Parmeno) Jackman, the merchant trustingly accompanied the Native Americans to a spot south of the springs, where there was more abundant grass, and, being satisfied with the location, they turned back toward the springs to await the coming wagons. On the way, the brother-in-law became suspicious of their companions and turned his horse to warn Williams. Just at that instant

each was struck by several arrows. Jackman fell wounded from his horse and was eventually pierced by seven arrows, two passing entirely through him. Williams remained on his mount, which bore him back to the wagon train, where he soon died. The alarmed freighters started in search of Jackman, whom they found yet alive. Burying Williams at Bitter Springs, the teamsters carried Jackman by wagon all the way to Lane's Station, where he was cared for as well as possible under the circumstances. Even in the initial newspaper notice of the attack, no hope of his recovery was held out. He lingered for a month and finally died at San Bernardino.[31]

Williams had been a true friend of many Native Americans, knowing seven Indian dialects and sometimes dressing and riding with them in such a manner that his own wife reportedly had difficulty distinguishing him from one of the Indians. Once, finding a baby girl still strapped in the traditional manner to the back of her dead mother at the scene of a major Indian battle, Williams took the child home to be raised by his wife and an older daughter. Family tradition, along with some anti-Mormon literature, has since maintained that Williams died because some white people at Salt Lake City ordered his demise. However, although he had engaged in a four-year series of clashes with members of the church hierarchy, no evidence links the killings to Mormon influence. Given past actions, it would be unusual for Indians residing closer to Utah to kill someone known to be friendly to their people, particularly a Latter-day Saint—although it is possible.[32]

Adding to the public outrage among southern Californians, after details of these murders were announced, in a rare extra edition of the Los Angeles *Star*, were the subsequent reports by soldiers accompanying Gen. Albert Sidney Johnston, a future Confederate army general, later killed at Shiloh, traveling to California after a two-year tour of duty in Utah. On arrival at Bitter Springs a few days after Williams's death, they discovered his body disinterred, stripped, and exposed to the ravages of weather and animals. The *Star*, which reflected as well as molded public opinion, detailed the atrocities, then concluded "a severe castigation should be dealt out to these Indians." It further implied that the Mormons, presumed by the biased reports of Johnston as well as by the newspaper editor to be behind the killings, should also be exposed and punished.[33]

Although the war with the Northern Paiutes of northern Nevada did not erupt until more than a month after these southern California killings, Indian discontent and hostility had been mounting for some time throughout the greater region. Many of the freighters just released from government service at Camp Floyd-Crittenden, Utah, were among the most ruthless people ever gathered in the West, and some of them traveled over both Northern and Southern Routes to the Pacific Coast, on the way committing atrocities against Native Americans and occasionally against their own fellows. Moreover, the silver stampede to Washoe County, Nevada, clearly signaled to Native Americans in that area that a substantial portion of their traditional homeland had been permanently lost. In two engagements of the later May war, at least seventy-eight white men and more than a hundred sixty Indians were killed. After that still other attacks and skirmishes erupted along the Pony Express route. Evidence shows Southern Paiutes and Utes of Utah and Nevada understood the problems and often sympathized with the plight and actions of their northern brethren.[34]

CARLETON'S PUNITIVE CAMPAIGN

The Mojave Desert murders directly prompted some of southern California's most prominent citizens to petition California governor John G. Downey urging establishment of a military post somewhere on the Salt Lake Road. The petitioners argued that it was "the duty of the federal government to assist in developing the resources of this part of California by affording protection" to travelers on this important emigrant highway. They further urged the governor to bolster their similar requests to the military officials in the region, which he did. Addressing his letter to Gen. Newman S. Clarke, commander of the Pacific Division of the United States Army, Downey explained, "[T]he recent outrages committed by Indians in that region and the murder of several of our most worthy and enterprising citizens, induces me to apply to you for the relief so urgently demanded."[35]

Results were immediate. As promptly as possible,

General Clarke assigned Maj. James H. Carleton to lead a company of eighty men from Fort Tejon to the Mojave River, to establish a chain of military posts for protecting travelers on the roads in the area. Carleton was also ordered to go to the Bitter Springs area and "chastise" whatever Indians were found in that vicinity, "then give them to understand that they have been punished for their recent murder and that the punishment will be certain for future offenses and of increasing severity." The order did not specify that the perpetrators of the murders be the only Indians punished. Dennis G. Casebier has well documented and recounted Carleton's effective but indiscriminate execution of these orders. The execution included the construction of Camp Cady some ten miles north of the junction of the Mojave and Salt Lake roads, along with less elaborate redoubts at Bitter Springs some thirty-five miles out on the latter route, and Soda Springs, the same distance northeast on the Mojave Road. As the soldiers literally combed the deserts seeking Indians to punish, they encountered two bands who engaged them in battle, with at least five Indians being killed. Despite criticism of the tactic both at the time and since, the soldiers hung two of the bodies at a place near where Williams had been buried, and carried the severed heads of the other three to the same location, displayed as a gruesome warning to offending Native Americans. While the soldiers continued their search in all directions, from Las Vegas to Death Valley on the north and west, to the San Bernardino Mountains and Marl Springs on the south and east, most Indians retreated farther into later Nevada, kept careful watch through scouts, and stayed well out of the way.[36]

Carleton's orders and their execution appear overly harsh, but they were in keeping with contemporary military policy. Sending expeditions out onto the emigrant trails to cow Native Americans was not a new tactic for the United States Army. In 1845, Gen. Stephen W. Kearney advocated that approach to impress and, when necessary, "chastise" Indians. In subsequent years, as the California and Oregon trails became so heavily traveled, many military posts were established along the routes. Between 1848 and 1861 soldiers and Indians fought 206 engagements, many of which were relief or punishment forays from the nearest fort after emigrants reported Native American misdeeds.

The United States Army out-post Camp Cady (along the Mojave River twenty miles north of present-day Barstow), by photographer Rudolph D'Heureuse, 1863.
COURTESY THE BANCROFT LIBRARY

When in Wyoming in 1854, Lt. John L. Grattan unwisely refused to accept Sioux Indian offers of repayment for a butchered stray cow and instead attempted to severely punish the offending tribesmen with a force of but twenty-eight men, his rashness led to tragedy. Although initially the Sioux chiefs restrained their warriors from returning fire, when the army officer ordered another volley in which a chief was mortally wounded, all the soldiers and their interpreters were killed and mutilated. Some Indian Bureau officials hesitated to retaliate, because the attack had not been premeditated, but Brig. Gen. William S. Harney was "hot for war." The following year at Ash Hollow, Nebraska, the general, who was already notoriously hostile to most Indians, led 600 soldiers into battle. They killed at least eighty-six Native Americans, mostly women and children. Only six of his men were killed, and an equal number wounded.

Meanwhile, just one day after the Grattan massacre, Indians killed nineteen westbound overland emigrants near Fort Boise, Idaho. A military force under Maj. Granville Haller sallied forth from Fort Dalles to rescue other presumably threatened pioneers. But again, retribution had to wait until the following year, when Haller and 150 soldiers held council with 200 assembled Indians. With four of the Indians implicated in the earlier Idaho massacre, the soldiers seized three and killed the other as he tried to escape. After a prompt trial and conviction, the soldiers hanged the accused Indians over the graves of the emigrant victims, then buried them at the foot of the gallows.

Similar orders were promulgated in another incident, closer to the time of the Carleton campaign. In 1859 word came of an attack on the Shepherd emigrant train. The Indians had killed at least five men, severely abused a woman and child, and stolen thirty-five horses and other property. Lt. E. Gay was immediately dispatched from Camp Floyd-Crittenden to the Hudspeth Cutoff portion of the Idaho–California road. There his detachment engaged in battle, killing about twenty Native Americans. At that time, the officer's orders, along with orders sent to other such units, were that if punitive measures became necessary, the Indians needed "to feel the power of the government." This fear was exactly what Major Carleton sought to instill on the Mojave Desert.[37]

Failing to locate other Native Americans in several weeks of search, Carleton released an Indian woman captured at one of the early encounters, instructing her to go to her people and tell them that if they approached to confer under a flag of truce they would not be harmed. Finally, on 2 July 1860, the day before the soldiers were to abandon Camp Cady and return to Fort Tejon, Paiute chiefs, including representatives reportedly from later Nevada and Utah, along with two dozen other warriors, appeared and were welcomed into camp. After smoking peace pipes, Carleton informed the Indians why the retaliatory campaign had been launched—because Americans had been killed on the desert when they had done no harm. The officer explained he had no choice but to act thus, because they had not been able to directly apprehend the guilty parties. The Paiutes reportedly agreed and implied that some of the dead tribesmen had indeed been among the culprits. They promised thereafter to themselves punish with death Indians who committed such crimes against unoffending white travelers. The major affirmed that although the military was powerful in comparison to the Indians, the soldiers had no desire to further harm them "if they would be friendly and not molest the white men who might come into their country, either in their persons or property." The Native Americans thereupon accepted the invitation to camp adjacent to the fort and spent the remaining day in friendly interaction with the troopers.[38]

Drawing on information from participating soldiers as well as the negative comments of the Mormon organ *Deseret News*, the Los Angeles *Star* reported that at the "big talk" Indian conference with Major Carleton, eight "head chiefs" had attended. The chiefs represented distant bands from the Vegas, Muddy River, Santa Clara, and Colorado River, as well as those from the closer proximities of the Providence Mountains and the area along the California portion of the Salt Lake Road. These Native American leaders were described as "perfectly humble and abject," promising good behavior and simply begging for the lives of their people. One *Star* account alleged that these Indians denied implication in the Williams, Jackman, and Wilburn murders, saying that Utah Native Americans had pursued the victims on Mormon direction. But it is doubtful if this information stemmed as much from the Native Americans as from the bias of the California newspapermen and military reporters.[39]

As troops withdrew from the Mojave River area, they not only promised that soldiers would return but assured that if the Indians behaved well in the meantime, they would be properly rewarded. In his official report at the end of his campaign, Major Carleton recommended such rewards. However, as so often in San Bernardino County and elsewhere, the government failed to follow up on promises that would have cost little compared to the consequences of negligence or indifference. That fall, the Indians did gather on the Mojave River and sent word through passing express train drivers that they had complied with the terms previously agreed on. By the time Carleton heard of this, he had so often been criticized for allowing the distasteful display of the dead Indians that he reportedly declared to his superiors, "I am not a volunteer for the position of commander of any body of troops that may be sent to council with, or to fight the Pah-Utes." No troops were dispatched to the region that fall, and the Indians reportedly concluded Carleton was "afraid to come among them again." Thus the somewhat ruthless, but effective, campaign against the desert Indians proved essentially futile, with the recently "cowed" Native Americans newly infused with confidence. With a perceptibly changed demeanor, some threatened to attack the freight wagon contractor who commonly traversed the road supplying Fort Mojave, the next time he and his teamsters passed by. Capt. W. S. Hancock (who three years later would be enjoying acclaim for his exploits helping lead the Union army to victory at Gettysburg) recognized that Paiute-Chemehuevi Indians had rarely been seen previously near the roadway along the Mojave River from the abandoned Camp Cady southward to its headwaters. Thereafter they frequented that area with far greater consistency, sometimes reportedly exhibiting hostile inclinations. Thus was completed the almost undocumented transition from desert Serrano residency along the Mojave River to occupation by the Southern Paiutes.[40]

FURTHER EMIGRANT JOURNEYS DURING THE CIVIL WAR

Whereas most wagon traffic since 1858 had been freighters, some small parties still traveled the Southern Route. In 1862, John Hunt, who as a longtime mail carrier had probably traversed the roadway as often as anyone else, brought his mother-in-law (Louisa Pratt) and other family members with him on a visit from Utah back to San Bernardino, where Hunt had three married sisters still residing. Louisa's husband, trail veteran Addison Pratt, also still lived in California. The journeys in both directions were essentially uneventful, except for an episode at Mountain Springs on the return trip. The men of the small company decided to follow Amasa Lyman's old policy of protecting their livestock by hiring Native Americans to guard them through the night. However, they neglected to keep at least one of the tribesmen with them in camp as security. In the morning, when the livestock was not returned, the men started toward the pastureland and soon came to a campfire where the Hunt party's pet mare was being roasted. When the only Indian present jumped up and ran, the formerly friendly Hunt angrily fired pistol shots at him, to no effect. Fortunately, the travelers located the remaining animals grazing without herdsmen. The party promptly moved down the mountain "not with much brotherly love for the red men."[41]

Another small company of emigrants traveling the trail in late 1864 included a third woman known to have kept a reasonably detailed diary of her journey over the Southern Route. This was English-born Sarah Jane Rousseau, wife of physician James A. Rousseau, whose family hailed from Iowa and Kentucky. The small company left the New Harmony area of southern Utah on 1 November 1864, and after passing a newly erected monument to the memory of the victims at Mountain Meadows, where the diarist reflected much misinformation about the still-vivid tragic occurrences there, the travelers entered a stretch of what she called "the hundred miles of Indian country." The group was well informed on what that situation entailed, posting extra guards each night. Although the travelers had little contact with the Santa Clara Paiutes, Sarah Jane knew they were fond of eating horseflesh and would "steal anything they can lay their hands on." She confessed being quite afraid of these potential adversaries. At a stop at Camp Springs on Utah Hill, a Native American chief informed the party they must each offer something for traveling through Indian country to remunerate them for using Paiute water and grass. Without argument, company members paid in flour. Thereafter, at least four

nights in the ensuing week, they engaged Native Americans for pay to herd the livestock through the night while some of the band were fed and remained in camp with the emigrants in a status, Sarah Rousseau noted candidly, "as prisoners." The one instance where the Indians who had been accompanying the party left, while on the Virgin River, proved the only night when cattle went missing. The diarist attributed the company's relatively good relations with the Paiutes to the fact that their guide, a Mr. Hatten, had "passed [the party] off" as Mormons.

While on the *jornada* from the Muddy River to Las Vegas, James Rousseau became ill and could not assist his wife when stranded while traveling in a separate carriage. He remained sick during the several days the company camped at the Vegas. Throughout that time he drew medicine from the store he carried on the trip to administer to others. He recovered sufficiently to continue the journey but was far from robust in health. Sarah Jane described herself as "almost helpless" yet much improved in physical condition since the journey commenced. Earlier she had termed her condition as "entirely helpless" and believed her improved condition to be the direct result of the pioneering experience. Although it cannot be positively determined whether the trip itself either improved Sarah Jane's health or undermined her husband's, the hardships encountered, including depleted funds and provisions and lack of cooperation from many of their traveling companions, clearly discouraged both.

One unacknowledged aspect of the problem was that the family had attempted to haul too much baggage, in two separate conveyances. Their horses showed definite symptoms of real exhaustion even before reaching Las Vegas. At Mountain Springs the animals gave out sufficiently that they had to abandon the carriage Sarah Jane had enjoyed thus far on the trip and buy an old wagon to accompany the larger one already used. The three children—fifteen-year-old Elizabeth; John James, two years younger; and another brother, even younger—already had to walk most of the way, which neither parent was able to do. At Resting Springs, the family felt constrained to continue, because they were almost out of food for themselves and their horses. This appeared to anger others in the company who remained there because some were too ill to travel at that time. While struggling across the ensuing difficult desert stretch, three of the Rousseau horses gave out entirely and had to be unhitched and driven ahead by the sons to find life-saving feed near Bitter Springs. At that point two travel companions, Charlie Copeley and Richard Curtis, hurried ahead on foot to the Mojave River to obtain a fresh team and some provisions.

While the Rousseaus remained stranded on the desert, the remainder of their former company approached but essentially snubbed them. Their erstwhile companions camped a small distance away and ate their meal, without either offering the couple any or even speaking to them. The families of the group had never been particularly close, partly, as Sarah Jane surmised, because Mr. Earp (father of the soon-to-be-famous gunfighters) was inclined to be a divisive influence among many party members. The Rousseaus were particularly disconsolate because their three favorite horses were virtually starving to death while members of the emigrant party possessed extra grain they would not share even to save the animals. Earlier, James Rousseau had asked one of the party, J. C. Curtis, to carry his wife and daughter in his vehicle, but Curtis had replied he was too heavily loaded to undertake the extra burden. Now Curtis approached the doctor and volunteered to take the two women the rest of the way, but Sarah Jane stubbornly declined. This situation might have been disastrous had not the relief team and supplies returned within two days. The rescuers hurried particularly fast on hearing that the stranded travelers might be in danger if Indians learned they were so few. This assistance impressively contrasted with the notable lack of similar help from company members throughout much of the desert crossing.[42]

Interestingly, the Rousseaus selected a slightly different route from Bitter Springs to the then-abandoned army fort of Camp Cady. On finally reaching the Mojave River, the weary travelers found problems mainly over. During that leg of their journey, they encountered people more cooperative than the ones they had previously traveled with. The diarist recorded at that point, "[W]e have been treated very kindly since we came here," meaning to the lower Mojave River. First they met an old rancher, head of the family then residing at or near Camp Cady. He offered grain for the livestock and

a mule if they needed one to help pull the wagons to San Bernardino. The rancher's offer was made partly in exchange for Dr. Rousseau promising to bring the animal back later, along with supplies from the settlements. Farther upstream at what was becoming known as Forks in the Road, a family named Allcorn requested the physician's services for their son, although the doctor determined that the young man was too close to death to be helped. Farther up the Mojave they encountered a Prussian named Jacobi, who lived alone at a ranch located in the future Barstow area. Still another ranch was operated by the Nicholsons, including three children, at Point of Rocks. Sarah Jane Rousseau was one of several contemporaries who noted that the woman of the place was often intoxicated. As the previously discussed cowhand J. E. Pleasants noted that year, many extra draft animals were being pastured by freighters waiting for their wagon bosses to secure full loads for another trip across the desert. It was therefore easy to borrow enough teams to easily pull the wagons to San Bernardino. There, after some investigation, the family elected to settle indefinitely.[43]

Another small emigrant company from Missouri also chose the "California Road" toward Los Angeles in the fall of 1865. Ruth Shackleford, traveling with her husband and at least four children, her brother-in-law and his family, and several other close friends, kept a good diary of the trip. Besides noting several roadway alterations along the route, her record is most notable for the large amount of sickness and death in her company, unusual compared to most accounts of journeys over the road. Two company members succumbed and were buried along the busier main trail while still in Wyoming. When they left Salt Lake City, both Shackleford parents and half their children were ill. However, it was the sister-in-law, Ann Gatewood, who next died, reportedly of mountain fever. She was buried at Fillmore.

The diarist was too weak to leave her wagon to attend the burial. Ruth suffered frequent headaches, made worse by the jolting of the wagon. But she continued to improve, whereas her little nephew got progressively worse. At Parowan they secured the services of an "old lady doctor," probably one of Amasa Lyman's wives, Paulina Phelps Lyman, who became legendary as a midwife there. The boy lived until the party reached the Virgin River. They carried his coffin several days farther to the Muddy River so his grave could be dug sufficiently deep to be protected from coyotes.[44]

As the pioneers crossed Utah, they exchanged their cattle and oxen for horses and mules in Provo, Fillmore, and Beaver. Despite illness, they occasionally attempted to lift spirits by singing together in the evening in one of the wagons. At Corn Creek, the Santa Clara, Camp Springs, and the Muddy River, as many Indians were begging as ever, but the emigrants were generous, particularly with flour, and had no problems.

The company chose the newer route by way of Black Ridge and bypassing the still-infamous Mountain Meadows. This ensured following some of the worst roads they had encountered on the entire trip. Ruth commented, "[N]o one can imagine how bad they are." This was partly because of heavy sand and partly the steep incline later known as Peter's Leap, where wagons were frequently lowered with ropes. After passing the burgeoning new towns of St. George and Santa Clara, the small company struggled in the Utah Hill area—perhaps no more than others but with more detail in their narrative. Near the summit the party chose to travel the road along the dry creek bed rather than climb over the adjacent ridge and down the steep, shale-strewn descent slope. On this segment, Ruth wrote, "[W]e started up the creek over the rock," probably meaning around the rock formations at the mountain divide. It is truly that kind of terrain. At Camp Spring, high to the west, the travelers found the rocks covered with names of people who had previously camped there.[45]

Although this was about the time the freighting road was constructed west from the main emigrant road on the downward grade of Utah Hill, the Shackleford company stayed with the old road and experienced the usual hardships along the Virgin River. Ruth called Virgin Hill "the awfulest hill you ever did hear of." From her descriptions, the passageway had apparently eroded and gotten even more difficult than in the earlier years. On the Muddy, the group apparently traveled downstream more than most other parties before heading over the desert *jornada* to the Vegas.

The rest of the trip was uneventful until Bitter Springs, which they called Soda Camp, where they noticed that the redoubt built after the murder of Thomas

Williams was occupied by several soldiers assigned from Camp Cady, which had been reoccupied in April 1865. When they got to the Mojave River, the Shacklefords lost a niece to sickness, Annie, the daughter of the earlier deceased Ann Gatewood. At Fish Ponds way station farther upstream, one of the company's horse teams gave out, but fortunately a freighter loaned them a mule team to get them on to San Bernardino. The party camped at the upper toll station in Cajon Pass and then enjoyed the good road cut along the side of the canyon. They paid their toll at the lower John Brown toll station. None of the party was particularly impressed with the residents of San Bernardino, and after a short stay they moved on to Los Angeles, where many remained. Before long, the Shacklefords went eastward to Texas.[46]

Some emigrant travelers were still arriving by the all-season Southern Route later in the decade of the 1860s. In October 1867, the San Bernardino *Guardian* mentioned "a large emigration from the [United] States sojourning in the city" (San Bernardino). And the next May, the same newspaper noted that former area resident Tom Burdick had just reached San Bernardino in six days travel from St. George. Longtime San Bernardino attorney and resident Alden A. M. Jackson and his musically talented wife Carolyn were just then moving to St. George over the same route.[47]

CIVIL WAR–ERA INDIAN RELATIONS

One week after the Civil War erupted, the Los Angeles *Star* began to persistently urge moving the troops now stationed at Fort Mojave on the Colorado River to the Las Vegas area.[48] The same newspaper had also reported the need for troops closer to home. In May 1861 Col. William Mayfield, owner of one of the Potosi mines in Nevada, lost six of his draft animals while camping at the Fish Ponds. A saddle mule and two horses were shot and three other mules run off, allegedly by Native Americans, whose footprints following the mules were soon recognized. This stranded the wagon train until the colonel could obtain more animals from the mining camp. Thereafter, the *Star* consistently attributed a series of livestock thefts from southern California ranches to white rustlers from Utah headquartered on the Mojave River. In October, a Los Angeles posse supposedly discovered where the gang had camped before they presumably departed northward over the trail. However, within a month a San Bernardino correspondent to the same newspaper reported that up to seven of the rustlers had been apprehended in California and sent to San Quentin Prison, and at least forty horses had been retrieved. The *Star* persistently called for an army post in the vicinity of San Bernardino to quell all such activity.[49] In March 1862, the paper again noted that the Indians in the Mojave area were "becoming troublesome." Troops were stationed at San Bernardino that year, but they fought no engagements and were soon transferred.[50]

THE LOS FLORES RANCH KILLINGS

Soon after the end of the Civil War, an incoming wagon train brought four sick or hungry young Paiute boys, probably from Nevada, each placed in separate San Bernardino homes. One boy lived with the Jimmy James family on the north bank of the Santa Ana River near the site of what was later Norton Air Force Base. One Sunday morning the James boys and their Indian foster brother went rabbit hunting in the river bottom with the family shotgun. There they encountered the Thomas brothers, similarly engaged and armed. This family was one of those originally from Texas via El Monte, notorious for tough, "short-tempered residents who were quick to violence" and also far from open-minded on questions of race. While the Indian was carrying the James gun and John Thomas holding theirs, the youths began exchanging comments, which, as sometimes happens, erupted into an argument between John and the Paiute. The hot-tempered Texas boy lost control and raised his gun to threaten his opponent. The Native American, with no understanding of the gestures of bluff, acted instinctively against what he perceived to be a deadly threat and pulled his own trigger, killing John Thomas. It was an unfortunate incident, but the inquest could conclude no other than accidental death.

Yet the resentment naturally continued to smolder among the Thomas family. The tragedy escalated when

in late February 1866, two of the dead boy's brothers, Mark and Jeff, and two like-minded men, Jake Buchanan and Thomas Enrufty, volunteered to take the four Indian boys back to their tribal homelands. The citizens of San Bernardino should not have allowed such a thing, for what might have been obvious reasons in a less-biased place. Further suspicion should have been raised when the group did not go by way of the well-traveled Brown toll road but instead chose the steep route up Devil's Canyon and onto the old Mojave Trail. On the way down Sawpit Canyon, the Indian who had shot John Thomas became suspicious, waited for his chance, and ducked into the heavy timber to escape. The other Indians were taken down the mountain slope to the lower end of what was then called the Dunlap Ranch, where they were coldly murdered. The vengeful killers then severed the heads and stuck them on poles before returning to the San Bernardino Valley, where during the entire era no questions were known to have been asked, nor any press notice given of the atrocity.

Perhaps the saddest commentary on San Bernardino at the time, certainly reflective of the widespread attitude toward Indians, was the killing (discussed next) of Ed Parrish, Pratt Whiteside, and Nephi Bemis. These three, among the county's most promising young men, died just one month later on approximately the same spot where the young Indians had died. This was clearly retaliatory. Yet there was no known implication of the Thomas brothers and their friends in the deaths until more than a third of a century later.[51]

The meadowlands near the headwaters of the west fork of the Mojave River had long been recognized as excellent cattle range. By 1866, the brothers-in-law Ed Parrish and E. K. Dunlap had been running cattle there, in at least some seasons, for more than six years. By the time of the fateful incidents there, a ranch headquarters had been erected, including two houses, some corrals, substantial haystacks, and at least some surrounding fence. The property had recently been overseen by a man named Anderson, described as "a shiftless fellow" and a "boaster," who prior to his discharge found two skulls of Indians reportedly killed in "one of the encounters thereabouts," doubtless actually from the murders of the previous month. He fastened them to the posts of the front ranch gate, commenting that he knew the story of the skulls and that "any Indian prowling near him would meet the same fate."[52]

During the early spring, Parrish, Dunlap, and several other southland ranchers contracted to have a substantial combined herd of their cattle driven by local cowboys all the way to the western Montana mining camps for sale there. Thus by mid-March the brothers-in-law had organized a roundup of their own semiwild cattle from throughout the Summit Valley rangelands. For this purpose they engaged several local cowhands, including J. W. Gillette, Nephi Bemis, Pratt Whiteside, a discharged soldier named Porter, a Hispanic *vaquero* named Antonio, a boy named Reeves, and an old cook, Strickland. On the way to the ranch from Cajon Pass, Dunlap directed Gillette and Antonio to ride north and eastward through some of the excellent grasslands, there to begin pushing cattle toward the Mojave River. En route they noticed a "soft trail full of moccasin tracks," which Antonio deduced to be those of about a dozen Chemehuevi he considered "very bad Indians" from the Big Rock Creek area to the west, presumably heading for the Mojave River forks several miles eastward. At supper at the ranch that evening, Gillette mentioned their discovery, but none of the men appeared particularly concerned. The most frequent resident of the area, Parrish, essentially ridiculed the idea of danger to themselves or the livestock. The rancher suggested that if the Indians appeared, which he did not much anticipate, he would satisfy their wants by simply butchering a beef and giving them all they could eat or carry.

Next morning the roundup commenced in earnest, with several hands assigned to hold the easily gathered cattle in a close bunch, while three outriders performed the difficult work of extricating the more wild cattle from the heavy chaparral where they instinctively hid at such times. Because the thick undergrowth was so difficult to ride horses through with anything protruding, the cowboys left their accustomed sidearms at the ranch house. Whiteside alone was carrying his own revolver, intending to shoot a vicious cow should he encounter her again. At midday, Gillette took some newly gathered cattle to the main herd. There because his mule was exhausted, he exchanged places with Whiteside, who joined Bemis and Parrish searching through the brush. The wind was blowing so hard that Gillette dismounted

and huddled near the ground to avoid the stinging airborne grains of sand and the cold. Antonio loped his horse around the herd to report that he and another cowhand had heard what they believed was a shot too loud to be Whiteside's pistol, and thinking of the Indians, he asked if he should investigate. Just then they noticed a riderless horse running toward the ranch house, and soon afterward, another broke from the trees. The conferring cowboys each went after one of the terrified animals, and on catching them near the ranch headquarters, noticed blood on the saddles and a rifle shot wound in the hindquarters of one.

Immediately recognizing that their companions had been attacked by Indians, they rushed to the ranch house and reported to the stunned Dunlap, who had remained in bed ill that day. Gathering what firearms were at hand, four mounted men and the others in a wagon headed for where they presumed the victims to be. The search eventually located the bodies, each stripped of their clothing and shot through the neck in the same spot, making it clear that as the three cowboys wove their way northward through the brush of a small ravine, they had been fired on from ambush on the left, with the shots so close together they sounded like a single one. Bemis and Parrish had evidently clung to their saddles temporarily, then fallen dead. Whiteside was knocked from his mount by the impact of the bullet but had had sufficient strength to climb the hill to fight his foes. Apparently Whiteside received another wound from a pistol shot while apparently wounding an Indian in the groin, as indicated by the blood and by the footprints on the trail, which showed that one assailant thereafter dragged his leg. The attackers crushed Whiteside's face with a large stone as he fought bravely to the death.

Returning to the ranch with the corpses, the survivors spent a harrowing night expecting another attack. Next day they made the sad journey to San Bernardino, where Parrish had a wife and several children and Bemis, at least a wife. At the time of his demise, Whiteside was reportedly engaged to marry. Coincidentally, all three victims were from Latter-day Saint families long in the area. After the cowboys left the ranch, the buildings and haystacks were burned to the ground. The day after the corpses were brought to San Bernardino, a joint funeral was held, including a 104-vehicle procession to the burial, said by John Brown to have been the largest in the county's history. The county sheriff and "a large force" of local men went in pursuit of the attackers, reportedly catching up with them. They killed two Indians and supposedly recovered several "trinkets" identifying them as the band who had struck the cowboys at Los Flores Ranch.[53]

REESTABLISHMENT OF A MILITARY PRESENCE ON THE MOJAVE DESERT

Camp Cady had been reoccupied by soldiers in 1865, but there was almost no communication or coordination between the military and local civilians. In fact, San Bernardino citizens still felt considerable dissatisfaction that the presence of troops offered them so little benefit. In early 1866, the garrison was too short of horses for much patrol duty beyond the immediate area, and a high-ranking military inspector, who recently visited there, reported the region had no use for the post, because "the country for miles around [was] not of such a character to induce any sane man to settle." This led to orders again closing the outpost.

Yet Camp Cady was still being manned when Parrish, Bemis, and Whiteside were killed near the opposite end of the Mojave River, although news of its abandonment nearly coincided with first notice of the upper Mojave murders. This probably caused the best early historian of San Bernardino County, George W. Beattie, who drew much of his source material from interviews with long-time area residents, to erroneously blame the massacre on the fact that the military had already withdrawn from the area.[54] Whatever the actual connection between the two events, after the cowboy deaths numerous parties appealed for the reestablishment of soldiers in the area.

The California newspapers were most vocal in this agitation. In mid-April, the Los Angeles *News* complained, without specifics, that in the brief absence of the military, "a considerable number of livestock [had] been stolen by Indians, and it [was] considered unsafe for small parties to travel the road almost anywhere from San Bernardino to Fort Mojave." A week later, the San Francisco *Alta California* reported that while one of the wran-

glers of a large livestock herd being driven over the Salt Lake Road to Montana was scouting ahead for a camp location, Indians presumably ambushed him, and when his companions arrived they discovered his lifeless body. The fact that there were no similar news items in southern California papers raises the distinct probability that this report was false, although it certainly bolstered the general demand that troops immediately reoccupy Camp Cady or some other Mojave River locality.

The Los Angeles *News* noted that as the troops were being removed, Native Americans demonstrated more signs of hostility, seriously threatening travel on the wagon road toward Salt Lake City. Then, aiming pointed criticism at the commanding general of the California military department, the newspaper writer stated that "if Gen. [Irwin] McDowell had purposely sought to injure the trade of this section of the state he could not have chosen a more effectual way of doing so than to remove the protection from one of the principal thoroughfares of trade." Naturally the newspaperman added his voice to the others requesting restoration of troops to the desert region.[55]

Whatever the accuracy of the reports, Gen. Irwin Mc-Dowell, commander of the Pacific Division of the United States Army, immediately directed a contingent of some twenty soldiers to move back into Camp Cady as soon as practicable. The first month after reestablishing the fort, several incidents involving Indians occurred in the desert region. A government express rider and his single soldier escort were attacked near Soda Lake, some thirty miles from Cady, and two civilian prospectors were killed in separate attacks in the new Macedonia mining district farther to the northeast. In late July 1866, a settler named Crow, located on the lower Mojave River nine miles south of Camp Cady, demonstrated his utter contempt for a band of passing Native Americans not only through verbal abuse but finally by firing his rifle at them. Then, fearing retaliation, he took his family to a more secure location thirty miles farther upstream and on his return, requested military protection. Several soldiers accompanied him to his ranch, which (predictably) they found looted in his absence, presumably by Indians. While the troopers were still with Crow, other passing emigrant trains also requested protection, and the commander complied. This left only eight men at the fort.

Thus shorthanded, on 29 July sentries sighted a band of some three dozen Indians passing along the river trail opposite Camp Cady. Commanding officer Lt. James R. Hardenburg, probably mistakenly determined them to be hostile. With amazingly poor judgment for four years of experience, the lieutenant led a six-man patrol out of the fort, supposedly for a surprise attack on the presumed enemy. The Indians, compelled to defend themselves, soundly defeated the vastly outnumbered soldiers, killing three and severely wounding another, whose life was spared through the notably chivalrous act of one of the Native Americans. The so-called Battle of Camp Cady resulted in additional troops being assigned there, but no further fighting occurred in the ensuing months. Soon thereafter, federal postal officials authorized a major mail route along the Mojave Road, connecting the increasingly important Prescott, Arizona, mining region with the outside world. This promptly led to additional military outposts being established eastward along that road.[56]

In the late 1860s, when these military outposts of the desert flourished, the traffic in freight from Los Angeles by way of Cajon Pass was great. An observer in mid-February 1867 one day counted not less than forty-three teams and wagons outbound between San Bernardino and Lane's Crossing. A large percentage of the freight volume was feed for livestock, including for cavalry horses and army draft animals. Barley, which cost $.02 per pound at the San Pedro–Wilmington seaport cost $.15 per pound by the time it was delivered to Camp Rock Spring midway to the Colorado River from the Mojave. Hay, freighted largely by Phineas Banning's company, was similarly costly. There was doubtless favoritism and manipulation in securing supply and freighting contracts, but with the excellent agricultural productivity of the San Bernardino Valley, it was ridiculous to freight livestock feed from the seacoast. True, the local merchants would have to combine efforts of smaller producers and secure the requisite hay-baling equipment, but both John Brown and longtime merchant Marcus Katz promptly accomplished this and probably undercut some outside contract bidders.[57]

The continuing military activity seemingly had little effect on the civilians of the upper Mojave River or San Bernardino area. Although the army purchased some livestock feed and supplies from them, there was little other contact. The San Bernardino newspaper, the *Guardian*, reflected considerable ill feeling among county citizens toward at least those in command at Camp Cady. The army officers had supposedly ignored several Indian attacks. One of the most critical earlier newspaper editorials was 16 February 1867, which alleged that the Native Americans had held a council camp within thirty or forty miles of Camp Cady, a situation virtually unknown to the soldiers until civilians told them. The editor implied that the gathering was dangerous to local inhabitants, then charged it appeared futile to request assistance from the army post. Reflecting an attitude consistently expressed throughout the southland during this era, the news article concluded that travel through the area was "too important to be jeopardized by these pests of the frontier."[58]

In early March 1867, Paiutes burned the way station at Point of Rocks between later Victorville and Barstow. The next month, farther out on the main Southern Route–Salt Lake road at Kingston Springs a Paiute raiding party numbering around sixty, the largest ever recorded along the Southern Route outside of the Mountain Meadows affair, attacked a freight wagon train. This train, owned by a man named Butler, was hauling goods and equipment to the new Pahranagat mining district in southern Nevada. The teamsters circled their wagons for fortification, and none were killed by the assailants, who were apparently more interested in the livestock, forty-two of which they successfully drove away. Some men made their way back to San Bernardino to obtain more draft animals, while their fellows stayed to guard the freight wagons. Apparently no army force intervened in this episode.

The San Bernardino *Guardian* lamented that some government officials appeared inclined to make peace with the seemingly hostile Native Americans. With reference to adjoining newspaper columns recounting the recent attack on the mail carrier at Marl Springs, the editorial sarcastically suggested that under such unwise policies perhaps the mail rider, who fired back in self-defense, "will be brought to grief for his cruelty in killing the Indians and not permitting himself to be killed." He should, the paper likewise commented, at least be court-martialed for his offense, if not dismissed from the service.[59] Local animosity toward the desert-stationed military also failed to diminish. Later in the summer of 1867, soldiers burned the house of a neighboring rancher, Z. F. Deane, who had apparently cheated them in liquor transactions. San Bernardino officials arrested five soldiers and brought them to the county jail. When the highest ranking Army officer in the West, Gen. Irwin McDowell, passed down the Mojave River sometime later, new Camp Cady commander Lt. Manuel Eyre defended the men. This stance ultimately led to his dismissal from the service, which did nothing to assuage local anger. And in October, just as the additional garrisons were being established at Soda and Marl Springs and eventually Pah-Ute Springs along the Mojave Road, Indians surprised three people accompanying a mail carriage through Afton Canyon. Army surgeon Dr. Merril E. Shaw suffered a shot through the neck by a Paiute arrow, after which the teamster outran the unmounted attackers and reached the Soda Lake redoubt safely. The wounded man lived to pen a last letter to his father in New York before expiring the next day.[60]

In late November 1867, Brevt. Lt. Col. William R. Price extended and formalized a fifteen-year practice, probably unique to travel over the western wagon routes. This featured six specifically named Southern Paiute chiefs, who led bands comprising an estimated five hundred persons, situated from Las Vegas to Santa Clara, each offering one of their tribesmen as a hostage to assure the "good conduct of the band and the security of the whites in their neighbourhood." Those held would be "responsible for depredations of any kind committed by any of his band." American travelers were likewise required "not to make any unprovoked attack upon [the Paiutes] but to report [at Camp Mojave] any occurrence that may warrant the interference of the military authority." The willing captives would be fed and "provided for" while at Camp Mojave, where the significant treaty was signed. Price gave each of the signatories a paper they could show, indicating the terms of the agreement. Tosho, chief of the Virgin River band, who had previously emerged as a stalwart in maintaining peace between the emigrants and his people, and who had also occasionally served cheerfully as voluntary "prisoner" while his fellows enjoyed the generous hospitality of passing emigrants, appeared to act as spokesman for the

Brevet Lt. Col. William Redwood Price, who negotiated a unique treaty with Southern Paiute chiefs at Fort Mojave in which they offered hostages to be held at the fort in order to assure the good behavior of their entire participating bands of Native Americans.
COURTESY GOFFS SCHOOL MOHAVE DESERT ARCHIVES, ESSEX, CALIFORNIA

Paiutes in this significant pact entered 22 November 1867. Price confidently reported relations were thus sufficiently cordial that "no case of disturbance" would arise on either side.[61]

As effective as the Price-Tosho treaty at Camp Mojave proved for quelling violence in the East Mojave area and the Salt Lake Trail north of Las Vegas, it appeared to have little effect on Native American behavior along the trail in California. In the winter of 1868, several other Mojave ranches were destroyed by fire, again raising suspicion toward Native Americans, who definitely harassed mail carriers and another freight train owned by C. F. Roe heading for Camp Cady during that time. Several months later, as a result of rumors about the presence of Indians supposedly from outside the region, Captain Hamilton, then commander of the troops at Camp Cady, dispatched a detachment to pursue the invaders. But although the soldiers supposedly located the trail, they could not apprehend their presumed adversaries.[62] In early 1868, the mail road was rerouted farther south on the pretext of being a less costly road to Arizona, and the recently established intermediate Mojave Road posts between Cady and the Colorado River were promptly vacated. Thus that historic route east fell into disuse about the same time as the far more heavily used Southern Route from Utah to southern California was also about to be essentially abandoned by through traffic.

Probably more to the liking of many southland readers than any recent accounts of military actions against local Native Americans was a report that appeared in the Los Angeles *Star* in early March 1869. In this account a correspondent using the name "Prospector" boasted to have stalked, with two companions, a half-dozen Indians, whom the whites alleged were in the habit of stealing cattle that were being driven toward Utah. Attacking a half-dozen Native Americans at what was called Lovejoy's Spring some twenty miles northeast of Big Rock Creek, on the southern edge of what would soon be known as Antelope Valley, Prospector and his fellows opened fire, later claiming to have killed four or five unsuspecting Indians. One of the assailants was later severely wounded by a rifle shot from an unseen Native American adversary as they were leaving the scene. The column-long account concluded "hoping [the *Star* readers were] not uneasy about our shooting good Indians."[63] This event occurred the same month as Franklin Woolley was subsequently killed, less than forty miles away.

Franklin B. Woolley, an upcoming young Utah businessman who was killed by Paiute Indians at Las Flores Ranch in retaliation for previous murders of Native Americans at that spot, near the headwaters of the Mojave River in March 1869.

THE FRANK WOOLLEY MURDER

In March 1869, a seemingly senseless killing of a passing merchant by Indians in the Dunlap (future Las Flores) Ranch area essentially signaled the end of the overland freight trade to Utah. Franklin B. Woolley was among the most promising young men in Mormondom, having served as Salt Lake County recorder and on the stake (diocese) high council there before being assigned to help Apostle Erastus Snow in settling Utah's Dixie region. Despite heroic attempts at self-sufficiency, the need for manufactured goods from the eastern United States continued, and in 1868 the Southern Utah Cooperative Mercantile Association was established to secure such goods. The all-weather Southern Route was particularly desirable to those residing in the extreme southwestern corner of Utah. On 1 February 1869, teams and wagons were dispatched to the Wilmington seaport to be loaded with the goods that recently appointed purchasing agent Woolley had had shipped from San Francisco.

The slow return trip was uneventful until the night of 16 March, when while camped probably at Lane's Crossing, three draft horses that Frank Woolley had recently purchased strayed away and could not be found in a search the following day. Concluding the animals had returned to San Bernardino, he sent the wagons on down river while he started on a mule after the missing horses. Frank Woolley spent the first night at either the upper toll station, by then operated by James Fears, or at Martin's station at the foot of Cajon Pass. Next day, while visiting the seller of the horses, a Mr. Thorne, at San Bernardino, who had not seen them, they decided the missing animals might have returned to their pasture of the previous summer at Dunlap's ranch. Securing directions, Frank started back, again staying the night at either Martin's place or that of Fears. Reaching the ranch meadowlands next day, he apparently searched extensively, but unsuccessfully. Then, because of a rainstorm, he decided to spend a night there, taking a cabin door and placing it over him as he slept in a nearby haystack. According to the silent evidence of the footprints, Frank Woolley was awakened next morning to find himself surrounded by some twenty Indians, who engaged in a war dance. At some point in this terrifying ordeal, he was either allowed to pass through the circle or made a desperate break for safety and was immediately killed by arrows.

After waiting three days at the Mojave Forks Station, on 20 March, the other teamsters concluded they needed to embark across the desert before their provisions were depleted. Young Edwin D. Woolley alone resolved to remain, but the following day he became too apprehensive to wait longer and started back up the Mojave in search for his missing brother. When he reached Burton's Station, at present Victorville, operated by Charles and William Burton (whom, also being Latter-day Saints, the Woolleys may have known previously in Utah or elsewhere), Edwin inquired of any word about Frank. Mrs. Burton burst into tears and went into the house, leaving one of the freighters standing nearby to inform Edwin of his brother's fate.

When the searcher for the missing horses failed to return to either Fears's or Burton's station, men from each place, William Gregory and Charles Girard, had started toward the upper Mojave River rangelands to search for him. They had soon found nine horses that Girard had pastured there, slaughtered by Indians, and finally had found Frank's body, stripped of clothing and mutilated by coyotes, as well as his mule with its throat cut. The remains had been taken down Cajon Pass to Martin's Station and buried. Girard later accompanied Frank Woolley's brother Edwin there and helped disinter the wooden casket. The body was then taken to San Bernardino, where it was placed in a sealed zinc coffin purchased

George Martin Station below the mouth of Cajon Pass (near present-day Devore, California), by photographer Rudolph D'Heureuse, 1863.

with borrowed funds. Thereafter, the surviving Woolley crossed the deserts with his wagon, accompanying a freighting party led by a Mr. Murphy, whom he met en route. On arrival at St. George, after appropriate funeral services Frank Woolley was reinterred, and his loss much mourned by his family and by citizens throughout Utah.

A significant insight into the cause of Frank Woolley's death was offered by later St. George historian and prominent Mormon church leader Anthony W. Ivins, who recalled that not long before, three Indians had been killed in the same vicinity and decapitated, their heads placed on fence posts. Ivins asserted that "because of this barbarous act members of the Paiute tribe had declared that white men should never again occupy the place, and had made Franklin B. Woolley the innocent victim of their revenge." Ivins and his associates were much more likely than anyone residing in San Bernardino County during the ensuing years to be on sufficiently friendly terms with knowledgeable Paiutes to hear the Indian explanation for the killings. At this point there is no reason to doubt the accuracy of Ivins's explanation. Thus the senseless act of some ruthless San Bernardino citizens cost not three but at least seven lives. County historian George W. Beattie considered the Woolley killing the last of a tragic era, and he is correct so far as documented deaths are concerned.[64]

One of the most unconscionable distortions of fact I have ever witnessed was perpetrated on the reading public by a Las Vegas newspaper writer and sometime serious historian, John Townley, in a 1970 article published by the Las Vegas *Sun*. He embellished the facts of the Woolley murder with a titillating but preposterous account of the purchasing agent Woolley returning home with an unspent $20,000 in gold in his saddlebags, which disappeared at the time of his demise. Supposedly such treasure still exists somewhere in the Mojave River headwaters area and, based on that apocryphal report, some are still seeking it.[65]

With completion of the transcontinental railroad and the murder of popular young Frank Woolley, emigrant and freight wagon use of the overland route from Salt Lake City to southern California essentially came to an end. It had served well for a full two decades, allowing travel when all other routes were as dangerous as that which had cost the lives of half the Donner party in 1846. Although certainly some killing attended its use, one of the most amazing facts about the Southern Route was the relative lack of deaths, other than the externally motivated tragedy of the Mountain Meadows Massacre. Although it is impossible to really document the volume of emigrants who entered California over the road, some twenty thousand can be estimated with reasonable certainty between 1849 and 1869. And the all-season roadway was even more important as a freight-carrying lifeline back the other way to Utah and Nevada.

Chapter Nine

Later Developments at Each End of the Southern Route

The Southern Route remained unique in that a four-hundred-mile stretch of mainly unsettled desert continued to loom threateningly in the middle of the important roadway even after many other former frontier sectors were well settled. However, in a manner similar to most other emigrant and freight wagon routes, both ends of the trail between Utah and southern California became more inhabited, and at those ends the conveniences for travelers much improved. It would never be as fully developed as on the main route from South Pass to the Pacific Coast where, as historian John D. Unruh has described, after a decade "there were, literally, hundreds of supportive facilities en route. Rarely did the emigrant travel more than twenty-five or thirty miles without encountering at least one habitation." He added that certainly "the presence of sizeable numbers of permanent or semi-permanent residents at periodic trail locations proved comforting to the long distance traveler." After a similar period of use, the Southern Route travelers also enjoyed some such outposts and scattered residents extending about a hundred miles out from either end of the road. This still left the almost impassible expanse of desert, continuing to make the route the most difficult overland road in American history.[1]

CONTINUED FREIGHTING OVER THE SOUTHERN END OF THE ROAD

The opening of the Brown and Van Deusen roads from San Bernardino to Holcomb Valley by way of Cajon Pass promised rapid development for the rangelands long known to be available along the Mojave River. At the beginning of 1861 the Los Angeles *Star* received word that some forty families had settled along the river. This development, probably grossly exaggerated, was lauded as positive particularly because it reduced the unsettled area between southern California and Utah by a distance the newspaper erroneously asserted was considerably less than two hundred miles; actually the distance was about four hundred miles. Still, the road improvement appreciably enhanced freight traffic onto the Mojave Desert, where numerous mining camps were springing up. The *Star* effusively reported that this road was becoming the "great thoroughfare for Los Angeles and San Bernardino to the great gold and silver fields" of the far-flung desert regions. The newspaper used the term "lifeline," which to a large extent that portion of the Southern Route indeed became.[2]

Although much of the booming mining region of Arizona had been most effectively reached by way of Cajon Pass and the Mojave River road, just after the major 1862 floods a supposedly shorter and safer road was constructed south of the San Bernardino Mountains. Young Bill Bradshaw marked out and publicized a roadway from water hole to water hole through later Riverside County farther south. The discovery of mines in the La Paz, Ehrenbergh, and Wickenberg, Arizona, areas helped bolster claims for the superiority of the Bradshaw road. Selection of the Mojave Road to the Colorado River and the subsequent establishment of army posts along that route had been accomplished partly through political manipulation and closing of that road, and outposts probably occurred partly in the same manner.[3]

Yet sometimes the water supply along the Bradshaw route proved inadequate and the Indians, uncooperative. Thus throughout the decade of the 1860s and beyond, there were always teamsters who preferred the route through the Cajon Pass and down the Mojave River. In August 1862 the *Star*, always an advocate of the entire Southern Route, noted a goodly number of wagons had persisted in going that way even when en route to the Colorado River, believing it was the best overall route.[4] Certainly the Mojave River road continued to be the main winter thoroughfare of goods shipped from San Francisco by way of San Pedro to Salt Lake City, with the Los Angeles *Star* consistently boosting it as the best route for mail as well as freight. Another boost to the old Southern Route was the discovery of mineral wealth in the Bannock district of Montana. In early 1864, merchants dispatched a train of forty wagons from Los Angeles toward the new camps, followed by many others soon

thereafter. Cattle herds were also driven over the trail in the next several years.[5]

AMARGOSA MINE

While crossing the deserts near Death Valley, several diarists described the ruins of the works at the Amargosa Mine, discovered on the first downward journey by Addison Pratt and other members of the Jefferson Hunt company in 1849 at Amargosa Springs. After this Mormon discovery party let the location be known, perhaps in exchange for the hospitality of Isaac Williams's rancho, considerable competition arose to claim and develop the property. "Wash" Peck, whose company passed the mine in late November 1850, reported two companies had been formed that expected to commence mining and milling operations within days. He assumed the prospect must be rich to "pay for working in [such a] place." W. T. B. Sanford had been engaged to haul a large steam engine out to the spot in 1850, as noted earlier, but the machinery never worked well, because the mineral content of the local water used in the boiler was too high. When Latter-day Saint leader Amasa M. Lyman's party passed that way on its initial journey to southern California in 1851, some members purchased sugar, coffee, and other provisions from the miners then working there. Another Mormon emigrant that year, John Henry Rollins, noted that as his party moved up the Mojave River in June he found a pouch and belt containing ore specimens, which he later determined to have been left by Milton Sublette, then operating the mine. The next January, the San Francisco *Alta California* reported one of the employees at the mine had been shot with arrows and severely wounded when attacked by ten Indians within two hundred yards of the mine. The few other miners then present launched a counterattack, although no further casualties were reported on either side. The next year Native Americans stole mining tools and destroyed machinery. Soon thereafter, the company suspended operations.[6]

Various interests worked the mine intermittently during the ensuing decade. In the fall of 1863 the property was reportedly owned principally by San Francisco investors who sent an experienced Washoe district mine manager to make the improvements essential for "fast and efficient working of the mine." But the optimism proved ephemeral. In early December 1864 diarist Sarah Jane Rousseau recorded that she and her companions found the mine premises a "dilapidated looking place, four houses beside a quartz mill." It was clear to her that a great deal of money had been expended in the quest for gold. She noted the operation had been essentially destroyed by Indians just two months earlier, and three of the employees killed. She observed, "[T]he destruction of things seem [*sic*] a pity, stoves, buckets, iron and all that is needed for such a mill." This company also folded, soon thereafter.[7]

Another report on the mine in 1870 mentioned it had been "exceedingly rich" during several periods in which it had operated. High freighting costs, along with difficulties with Native Americans, were the cause of persistent cessation of mining and milling activities. At that time, lower wage levels and improved roads, along with "better behavior" from local Indians, stimulated renewed activity at Amargosa Springs, with "astonishing results" expected but apparently not accomplished.[8] At about the same time, similar operations were established at relatively close Tecopa and Resting Springs, also along the overland emigrant-freight road, continuing the pattern of boom-and-bust cycles.

POTOSI MINING ACTIVITY

In August 1860 a Colorado Mining Company prospecting party organized at Marysville, California, made its way from the Washoe mining district to the old Mormon lead mine just off the California emigrant road some four miles from Mountain Springs, not far within the boundaries of the about-to-be-created Nevada Territory. Interested in well-circulated reports of the Mormon mine, they soon discovered that the ore the Latter-day Saints had found "too hard to melt" was indeed largely silver "of the richest kind." The party returned to Washoe, then traveled individually to southern California, where they quietly assembled outfits to reestablish mining operations at what was soon named Potosi, presumably after similarly rich ore at the more famous Bolivian or Mexican mines both of the same name. The next week a

letter from J. A. Talbott, a former Amazon River explorer as well as a Calaveras County miner, explained the company had sent forty men to the American Potosi area and had already discovered four new leads besides the old Mormon lode, which they expected would make the mining district the richest in the region. Company members wisely distributed presents to a delegation of forty Native Americans in hopes that would enable the miners to work the mine in peace. There were still a few Indian difficulties until the population of the mining camp became sufficiently large to discourage Paiute incursions. Captain Allen, an officer of the Colorado Company, returned to Los Angeles for the materials to erect a reduction furnace.

Two weeks later several other mining companies, with up to eighty men, were prospecting in the area amid rampant optimism. One report noted of the Stephens company's ore, "[T]he metal has so much lead, that they have no need to stamp the ore; consequently it will not take much time or labor to bring it to market." The usual number of veteran miners attested no other place in the United States was so rich in lead, besides the value of the silver contained in the ores. The Potosi townsite had been laid out on more level land less than a mile from the mines and materials ordered for a store and saloon.

Company official A. Hardpending took ore samples from the various prospect holes to San Francisco for assaying, and most observers understood the results would determine whether a major mining rush would ensue. Before the assays were completed, many experienced miners proclaimed the Potosi galena (lead ore) to be extremely rich. Another news item mentioned a strike forty miles north in the Charleston district and a new discovery twenty miles south of the original mine. The assay reports for Potosi were all that had been hoped, and soon three other companies were preparing to either mine or mill in that area. In early May, reports from what was apparently initially organized as the Galena Mining District of New Mexico Territory were still optimistic. Three new mines, the Colorado company's San Antonio, along with the Jayhawk and the Mayfield, were established along what appeared to be a well-defined vein, appearing even richer than anticipated. Some found a thread of pure silver an inch and a half wide. Nevertheless, only sixty miners were at work at the time; others were heading back to the still-booming gold-mining center at Holcomb Valley in the San Bernardino Mountains or leaving for the newly discovered Colorado River mines.[9]

Some Potosi-based miners had periodically engaged in prospecting along the Colorado River. One reported "good gold prospects from gravel deposits" on the adjacent Gila River. Still, Potosi prospects remained equally promising, with some assays termed "remarkably good." Capt. J. W. Gleason, one of what would be southern Nevada's first mining camp's first promoters, was reportedly bringing men with sufficient supplies to maintain mining and prospecting through the ensuing winter of 1861–62. Gleason reported to the Los Angeles *Star* that several families were among those moving to Potosi. In early October, men from the mining camp told of finding the bodies of four prospectors, presumably from northern California, in the Death Valley area. They also discovered the remains of one who had left their own camp in late July with insufficient water to get himself across the desert stretches. He was found with a self-inflicted gunshot wound to the head some fifteen miles from Bitter Springs. His acquaintances assumed this resulted from a temporary insanity "produced by want of water."

By the late fall of 1861, there was apparently already a slump in Potosi mining activity. A Mr. Hill was then reported to have purchased "delinquent shares" of stock in the Colorado company's San Antonio lode, sufficient to give him controlling interest in the property. He naturally aimed to "recommence the operation of the company," seeking to "prosecute the work" of mining and milling with renewed vigor. But no subsequent newspaper reports show Potosi activity in the immediate future, so the attractions of other mining camps and the particularly difficult winter must have stifled further activity by both miners and investors.[10]

Another brief news item in the Los Angeles *Star*, presumably also reported by Potosi miners visiting southern California, stated that an unspecified number of settlers, doubtless including Mormon merchant William Knapp and perhaps the first non-Mormon semipermanent residents there, spent the 1861 season at Las Vegas. They reportedly raised "luxuriant" crops of several kinds. Unfortunately, this did not benefit the growers or the Potosi miners, who were probably the intended market for the produce because in the words of the newspaper, which was always biased against Native Americans, "the rascally Indians carried away the produce," presumably as fast as it ripened.[11]

UTAH'S DIXIE COLONIES EXPERIENCE OUTSIDE TRADE

With the establishment of the first settlements in Utah's Dixie on the Virgin River and Ash Creek, and later on the Muddy River, freight wagon train operators could obtain much-needed livestock feed, provisions, and liquor in exchange for some of the trade goods they were hauling as well as cash. John D. Lee, who operated well-stocked public lodging houses at Washington and Harmony, recorded numerous transactions with passing teamsters, typically receiving $10 to $13 in gold for one night's meals and rooms for a half-dozen patrons. Sometimes, as in January 1859, a train of thirty wagons stopped and the employees involved purchased $120 worth of feed, liquor, and other refreshments. On another occasion the same year, Lee had a beef slaughtered to feed seventy-five teamsters en route for California, each with ten-mule teams and wagons. At about the same time, Lewis Newell and Harley Swartout, probably still residents of San Bernardino, arrived from California for an overnight stay with Lee, and on the following day they opened their stock of goods and sold the eager people of Harmony $300 worth of goods, much of which Lee purchased.[12]

LITTLE-KNOWN MILITARY PRESENCE IN SOUTHWESTERN UTAH

In late February 1859, three United States Army officers approached John D. Lee about purchasing grain to help maintain a proposed military post in the Santa Clara vicinity, reportedly at the behest of Gen. Albert S. Johnston. The stated purpose was to watch for deserters, presumably from Camp Floyd, and to "keep down the Indians." No sources indicate that this outpost was ever

established, but if it was it probably did not last long, because the supporting post was closed about a year later.
However, just over four years thereafter, during the last
year of the Civil War, Mormon freighter Josiah Rogerson, accompanying a wagon train to Las Vegas led by former mail carrier John Louder, noted encountering some
sixteen Union soldiers at Camp Springs in the Beaver
Dam Mountains–Utah Hill vicinity. The presence of
this unit, probably dispatched by Col. Patrick Edward
Connor's command at Salt Lake City to guard the crucial passageway to California, has not previously been
noted in the historical literature. Although the length of
the soldiers' stay is unknown, apparently they damaged
the spring by attempting to dig it out to improve the
flow. The Mormon freighters purchased provisions from
the military men both going and coming, partly in exchange for a small quantity of liquor. Both groups enjoyed friendly relations with the local Paiute bands led
by Jackson, Isaac, and Thomas. Again, there is no evidence the military outpost was anything but temporary,
but it is amazing that any manpower was then thus expended at such a locality.[13]

COLORADO RIVER NAVIGATION

In the summer of 1861 a San Francisco company advertised intent to use steamboat transportation on the Colorado River to deliver freight to Salt Lake City at a reduced rate over what then prevailed overland. The going
wagon hauling price was still $.25 per pound, said to total
around $100,000 per year. The steamer-assisted shipping
could reportedly deliver the goods to Salt Lake City for
$.15 per pound. Although this venture never actually
went into operation, it foreshadowed considerable further pursuit of river shipping later in the decade.[14] In the
peak year of Colorado River freight promotion, 1864, one
of the companies promising service included overland
freight operators Jefferson Hunt and Ebenezer Hanks in
connection with R. E. Raimond of San Francisco. Five
riverboats were then competing for Colorado River shipping, and their promotional efforts helped arouse Mormon interest in the possible advantages of using the
river.[15]

The 1864 season was particularly trying for those

Mormon pioneers seeking to fulfill their mission assignment to establish cotton production in southwestern
Utah. In June floods washed out dams, after which crops
withered from lack of irrigation. Amid much discussion
in Utah that season, the St. George High Council of the
LDS church recommended exploration of a route to the
Colorado River in June 1864. The intense summer heat
demanded full attention to the Dixie crops, delaying the
search. At the church general conference in October,
Apostle Erastus Snow similarly urged the highest LDS
leaders to recognize and act on the need for river reconnaissance. The Mormon hierarchy was sympathetic,
and before the conference ended a hundred "men of
wealth," primarily from northern Utah, enlisted to become involved in the Dixie mission affairs. Later that
month they organized the Deseret Mercantile Association, headed by Horace S. Eldridge, who that year profited greatly from regular freighting over the Southern
Route, with sale of stock sufficient to promote exploration of the Colorado River as high up as navigable and
to establish wagon trade from the head of that navigation
to Utah and beyond. The company members agreed to
build a warehouse at that point and talked of sending a
cargo of goods to demonstrate feasibility of the route.
Seasoned pioneer Anson Call was chosen to select the
warehouse site and supervise construction. He left for
his new assignments in mid-November.[16]

Just at that time, at another St. George–area church
conference, the presiding area ecclesiastical official, Erastus Snow, read a recent letter from William H. Hardy,
founder of the primary town involved with the new trade
methods, proposing Mormon commerce with California
by way of the Colorado River. He listed his prices on
some staple articles, including flour at $10 per hundred
pounds, bacon, $.17 per pound, and general merchandise
at a "small advance on San Francisco prices." He pledged
to convey any freight from San Francisco to Hardyville
for $.03 to $.04 per pound. At that time Snow proposed to
select a group to make further explorations toward the
Colorado, to find a road to the head of navigation and also
to more specifically arrange with Hardy concerning the
propositions offered. Before this group got under way, it
was combined with Anson Call's expedition.[17]

Call, in St. George by 24 November 1864 and assisted
by Jacob Hamblin and several other Dixie residents,

soon commenced exploring the area between St. George and the Colorado River. He was sufficiently impressed with Beaver Dam Wash to report it could sustain fifty families and demonstrated even more optimism about the Muddy River area, stating 200 to 300 people could live there. The Call expedition traveled to the confluence of the Virgin and Muddy rivers and along the combined stream for twelve miles to a location called Echo Wash, then thirteen miles up the wash and across a summit into what became known as Callville Wash and southwest to the Colorado River ten miles farther down.

The spot designated as Callville was above the mouth of Black—later Boulder—Canyon. They placed the warehouse a quarter mile downstream from the wash on the north bank of the river, where Call assumed water could be diverted from a point farther upstream to irrigate some two hundred acres. The venture leader visited Hardyville and promptly ordered building materials essential to erect the warehouse. He also engaged masons to lay up the rock walls for the storage facility, and with tenders and Indian water carriers, they commenced construction of the structure, which was 30 feet wide and 75 feet long and probably cost over $15,000.[18]

At the end of 1864, Brigham Young wrote to Utah territorial delegate to Congress John F. Kinney, asking him to seek a government subsidy for the navigation venture. Young also attempted to gain further control over the entire region by seeking to induce Congress to alter the Utah-Nevada border two degrees in Utah's favor. This effort was blocked by both senators of the new state of Nevada and the delegate from Arizona, whose territory then held actual jurisdiction over the area. This attempt came back to haunt Utah and Young as Kinney complained that the proposal essentially established a precedent "opening the way for clipping off Utah." Much of the same area in question was soon granted to Nevada, including jurisdiction over several just-established Mormon colonies.[19]

By early 1865, President Brigham Young was sufficiently committed to the water route to announce, "I indulge the hope . . . that before long the way will be open for our emigrants to come by way of the Colorado River." It was further specified that church authorities were again contemplating directing emigrants from Europe to travel by way of Panama and the Gulf of California, to the

Colorado, to be conveyed more efficiently thence to the Utah-Zion region than ever before.[20] Young's close associate George Q. Cannon affirmed that the new road would be opened that winter and that "supplies for the territory would come by that route for the next year." He disclosed that Brigham Young was "much impressed with the importance of communication being opened by that route," because he did not believe the roads from the east could be depended on during wartime.[21]

The discussion of greatly increased freight traffic naturally excited many Dixie residents and convinced some their communities were about to become a central hub of a large transportation network. One particularly optimistic venturer, William E. Branch, erected a St. George hotel in anticipation of the influx of travelers. There were in fact extra trains of freight wagons from Hardyville routed through southwestern Utah. And for a time James W. Parker maintained a mail rider route from St. George to Hardyville. But the entire boom soon subsided, because of changes resulting from the end of the Civil War.[22]

Later in 1864, one of the Colorado River freighting company heads, Sam Adams, persuaded Capt. Thomas E. Trueworthy to take the steamboat *Esmeralda* to Callville with all the goods that had been ordered up to that time. En route the crew heard that Call had returned to Utah for a visit, perhaps not learning that he had designated others to receive the freight. Adams and Trueworthy concluded from erroneous reports that Callville had been abandoned, and they thus turned back downstream with their cargo. Both Adams and Trueworthy thereupon journeyed overland to Salt Lake City to bolster interest in the Colorado transportation venture, holding a public meeting in one of the ward (parish) meetinghouses. Much enthusiasm still prevailed among many, but no further financial support proved forthcoming.

In retrospect it is clear that the Colorado River freight route endeavor had already passed its peak of opportunity. The Civil War ended precisely at the time of the Salt Lake City meeting. And even before that news reached Utah, Judge Elias Smith, who presided at the public meeting, observed that whether the steam navigation enterprise on the Colorado succeeded or failed, the "Iron Horse," meaning the recently begun transcontinental railroad, would soon fulfill most of the West's transportation needs. In the meantime, travel and freighting from the Midwest soon resumed unimpeded. Thus the Colorado steamboat venture—so far as Utah was concerned—was essentially stillborn.[23]

Unfortunately, Call neglected the important detail of promptly securing ownership of the lands he had chosen for the warehouse and settlement. Before church officials were aware of the problem, non-Mormon W. A. Cowan, assisted by James Ferry, claimed the property for their own purposes. That was not the only blunder, because no river steamboat had ever pushed as far upstream as Callville. And although merchant William B. Hardy poled a barge to that point to deliver the ordered building materials, the first two steamboats intent on reaching the warehouse turned back short of that destination. It was October 1866, after the Mormons had essentially abandoned the venture, before the *Esmeralda*, towing a barge, steamed to Callville to unload a cargo of over a hundred tons. Although Mormon settlers were still in the vicinity, they were too poor financially to be good customers for the merchandise, which was still in the warehouse as the ensuing year commenced. Thereafter, prosperous Salt Lake City merchants bought the stock of goods and hauled it to northern Utah.[24]

COLONIZING ALONG THE VIRGIN AND MUDDY RIVERS

Several Virgin and Muddy River settlements were originally conceived as freight way stations for the Colorado River trade, but later they took on a separate identity as Mormon agricultural communities. Thus despite the failure of the steamboat freighting enterprise, interest in that project helped stimulate Mormon settlement of the region. At the time Anson Call embarked on his exploration to the Colorado, Thomas S. Smith overtook him en route and helped improve part of the roadway up the hill from the Muddy onto Mormon Mesa, a project never adequately completed. Smith founded St. Thomas south and west of the Muddy's confluence with the Virgin. New colonists thereupon built shelters, cleared land, and planted crops. At about the same time, Henry W. Miller and another party of Mormons settled at Beaver Dam Wash and soon cleared land there for crops as well. In

May 1865 Brigham Young assigned Warren Foote, with still another group, to colonize St. Joseph north of St. Thomas along the east bank of the Muddy, near where Logandale would be later. West Point, farther upstream, was settled around 1868, and Overton, near St. Joseph, a year later. In 1868 President Young dispatched another expedition to explore the Vegas Wash junction with the Colorado, and a small settlement named Junction City was planted there. The Utah territorial legislature optimistically organized Rio Virgin County to govern the area, formerly Pah-Ute County, Arizona, and later Clark County, Nevada.

The Muddy settlements were always isolated, with the road to St. George by way of Mormon Mesa still regarded as "a nightmare." Travel down the Virgin was equally terrible, because of the numerous necessary crossings and quicksand threatening at many points. Longtime resident in the area Ute W. Perkins recalled sometimes having to cross the river thirty-two times en route to the lower Muddy settlements. And if the wagon got stuck, as often happened, little could be done but cut the draft animals free from the harness to fight their way to the bank. As for the wagon, it would have to be unloaded piece by piece; then, with brush under the wheels of the lightened vehicle, it could usually be retrieved through much arduous labor. On at least one occasion, however, a wagon laden with heavy mining equipment literally sank out of sight there. Church official Joseph W. Young reported that a thousand pounds was a big load for a span of mules in the Virgin River area, and even then muleteers often had to double the team in several places. Besides reporting much property destroyed, he also noted several lives lost when wagons were upset while fording the stream.[25] The influx of Mormon settlers did stimulate some local freighting over that segment of the Southern Route, but most citizens there were generally too impoverished to be consistent customers.

THE CUTOFF ROAD ACROSS MORMON MESA

As early as 1855, sometime mail carrier Jim Williams pointed out to interested observers the practicability of bypassing the Virgin River fords, the dreaded Virgin Hill, and much conflict with Native Americans along the Santa Clara and Virgin rivers. Lt. Col. Edward J. Steptoe, in charge of improving the road for mail and military use, suggested this practicability in his advertisements for contracts to construct a road from a "sideling" hill within nine miles of the rim of the Great Basin, making a cutoff from near the Santa Clara to the Muddy. As guide for Lt. Sylvester Mowry, Steptoe's subordinate, and his troops later that year, Williams easily convinced Steptoe and Mowry of the desirability of the proposed route and Mowry included the recommendations in his military reports. His version of this "cutoff" was from the head of the Santa Clara to the Muddy River, essentially skirting the foot of Mormon Mountain rather than traveling the old road midway out on the Mormon Mesa several miles south of the new route. The report stated (understated) that the bypassed segment was "one of the most trying portions of the route," and thus would be a great improvement of the roadway to southern California.[26]

Like the rest of Mowry's report, no action was taken on this recommendation for more than a decade. Then the Utah legislature appropriated $800 to establish the freight road, doubtless with urging from fellow citizens of the new Muddy settlements, which were still presumed to be situated in Utah Territory. This road cut west from the old pioneer road soon after starting the descent of Utah Hill, at a spot long known as Castle Cliff, crossing Beaver Dam Wash some twelve miles farther upstream, where Apostle Erastus Snow assigned the digging of Mormon Well. Although this was the only water before reaching the Muddy River, freighters were by this time well equipped with water barrels with which to carry what their livestock required for the trip. This shortcut was easily worth the effort, because the route completely avoided the obstacles of the old road, although as one family sadly discovered, it could be disastrous for the unprepared (discussed in the next section). In April 1868 a Utah newspaper mentioned that "quite a number of small freight trains had passed through St. George the previous week on their way north from California." Yet the new roadway was not long used even by local freighters, because by the time it was built there were no longer many flourishing Nevada mining camps that could not be more easily reached by another route more closely connected to the railroad.[27]

THE DAVIDSON TRAGEDY

One of the saddest tragedies on the Southern Route was the death from thirst of James Davidson, his wife, and twelve-year-old son in early June 1869. Davidson, a Mormon convert from Scotland, was an expert machinist. When the cotton mill was established at Washington in late 1866, he received the call to superintend the installation of the machinery. Why the family had gone to St. Thomas is not precisely known, although it was likely to visit their daughter who lived there, married to B. F. Paddock. On 9 June, they started with a group of other travelers to return to St. George in a light spring wagon drawn by a single horse. Within a few miles, the iron tire on one of the wheels "ran off," compelling them to stop for repairs. The son-in-law fixed the vehicle and warned the family not to attempt crossing the thirty-mile stretch of desert alone. They did not reach St. Joseph until the following day, and discovered that the rest of their party had left without them. They remained in town that night, but next day the family started alone over the road with only a keg of water and a canteen. Unfortunately, some three-quarters of the distance across the forbidding expanse one of the wheels again broke.

Unable to continue with the wagon, the parents sent their son on the horse with the water containers to get assistance while they waited under a blanket stretched between two Joshua trees. The boy may have lost his bearings for a time and strayed from the road, although his body was subsequently found near it. Meanwhile, George Jarvis, William Webb, and John Lloyd had been sent to clean and deepen the Mormon Well in the Beaver Dam Wash. While thus engaged, the Davidson horse approached for water and after drinking was fed and tied up. Toward the following evening, when the horse owner never appeared to claim him, Webb rode out on the trail to investigate. He discovered the bloated remains of the boy not far from the water he desperately needed. Observers later determined he had passed several water pockets in the rocks not far from the road, but it would have taken a more experienced person to locate the life-saving substance. Soon after, Lorenzo Young traveled the same road toward the Muddy River, having already learned of the death of the unidentified youth. Some five miles past the new grave, the traveler discovered the bodies of the parents lying together on the bed they had fashioned under their meager shade. The three graves are marked on what is now an untraveled portion of the mesa. Their story, published in several books on the region, is a sad testament to the perils of the formidable desert route—for those not properly prepared, or fatally unlucky. These are the only nonprospector travelers known to have succumbed to thirst on the Southern Route during the entire period of use. The family's sad fate demonstrates the fine line between life and death on the desert and in a sense is a vivid example of how well prepared the thousands of predecessor trail users had been.[28]

NEVADA STRUGGLES, STRAINED INDIAN RELATIONS, AND ABANDONMENT

All the Mormon settlements in what became Nevada struggled with severe poverty, disease, and the elements. Floods, a major problem in nearby Dixie, virtually destroyed Millersburg on the Beaver Dam Wash, compelling those settlers to move mainly to the lower Muddy settlements. West Point, on the upper Muddy, also suffered floods and was soon abandoned. A number of area residents fell victim to malaria and the flux. Flies and mosquitoes were also particularly oppressive. And with few real shade trees, the summer heat was probably more intense than in any other Mormon settlement of that time.

Despite earlier Paiute expressions of desire for the Mormons to settle among them, it is doubtful if relations with Native Americans on the lower Virgin River or the Muddy were ever very cordial even during the early period of settlement there. Within a year of the founding of St. Thomas, settlers became so angered by thieving Indians they agreed to mete out five lashes with the whip for the first stealing offense, with the punishment doubling with each succeeding infraction. Two of the local Paiutes defied these policies, essentially declaring they would steal as long as they lived. One was eventually sent to St. George, presumably to jail, and the other was shot while fleeing his impending hanging. At about the

same time at St. Joseph, innovative Indians constructed a bridge across the Muddy, then stole over a dozen oxen and almost that many horses and mules. After driving the animals across the bridge, they dismantled the structure so the posse giving chase could not use it. The livestock were herded into the desert where water had been strategically secreted for their use. The pursuing Mormons were poorly mounted, because most of their good horses and mules had been taken, and when they ran out of water, they were compelled to turn back, never retrieving the stolen animals.

Cattle were also lost along the rivers when they became mired in quicksand, and it was not uncommon for Native Americans to drive foraging animals into the water and bogs, in order to retrieve meat from the animals given up by their owners when found dead. In the summer of 1869, Bishop James Leithead noted Indians admitted they had killed or drowned at least sixteen head of cattle at St. Thomas, most of which had been pushed off the riverbanks. He also reported wheat stolen and tribesmen strongly objecting to any punishment to offenders. Eventually that year, Leithead and others caught an Indian in the act of stealing a cow and informed his fellows that thereafter repayment would not be accepted; instead, if caught the thief would be put to death. This growing sense of alienation had to be a factor in the decision by some Mormons to abandon the settlements.[29]

Even at the most promising spot for Mormon missionary activity, among the Tonequint band of Paiutes on the Santa Clara River, in the nearby corner of Utah, progress toward making the Indians good Latter-day Saints proved largely futile. As regional historian Melvin T. Smith has asserted, even the fervent efforts of the missionaries failed to permanently instill "Mormon souls" into the Lamanites. Jacob Hamblin had earlier listened in patient discouragement as Chief Tutsegabits admitted with all sincerity that his people "cannot be good, must be Paiutes." He pleaded that the missionaries would continue to be kind and assist them, and he affirmed the possibility that perhaps some of the younger generation "will be good, but we want to follow our old customs." Despite the natural, but to the churchmen, disheartening, inclination of the Indians to maintain the old lifestyle, portions of which were clearly discouraged by the missionaries, LDS efforts persisted among these people.[30]

As the Dixie region became the cotton mission, emphasis on the Southern Indian Mission apparently waned. Jacob Hamblin was transferred to Kanab and was not replaced with someone of equal influence and commitment. The Tonequints doubtless recognized that they were now losing in the quest for use of the area resources and acted accordingly.

In 1866, at the behest of Nevada politicians, the U.S. Congress took one full degree of territory from western Utah and Arizona and added it to Nevada. Without consent by the residents of that area, the towns on the Muddy and Virgin rivers were thus placed in a state the citizens perceived as hostile to their interests. In 1870 a federal government survey proved all the Mormon colonies were well within Nevada boundaries, and the officials of that state immediately pressured for tax payment, including what had formerly been paid to Utah and Arizona. After appealing to appropriate entities, and even proposing creation of a new Mormon county to be named Las Vegas, to no avail, LDS authorities began to consider abandoning the affected area and releasing the people from their missions there if they desired to leave.[31]

Brigham Young and his high church associates expressed regret "that so many of the settlers on the Muddy [thought] it necessary to spend their summers in the north," doubtless because of the unrelenting heat of the southern Nevada desert summers as well as because of the endemic malaria along the rivers and hordes of houseflies. Yet as Dixie historian Andrew Karl Larson has pointed out, neither stake nor general LDS authorities displayed any willingness to travel around that area during the hot season. President Young did promise a visit later in the fall of 1870, which he apparently started to fulfill. According to some accounts, however, once he took a hard look at the desolate-appearing lands, he ordered his driver, Charles Savage, "turn north Charley," which meant to reverse directions and head back to St. George. Soon thereafter, Bishop James Leithead informed Erastus Snow he had just visited all the Muddy River settlements and discerned a widespread "spirit of uncertainty and doubt as to the permanency of the Muddy Mission." He specifically stated the people believed "since the [abortive] visit of Prest. B. Young that there [was apparently] little or no interest for the future of the country" among high church officials.[32]

The bishop reported at that point many still wished to remain, but the message was clear: Settlers were disappointed by the apparent lack of high church commitment toward the venture so many had devoted years to accomplishing. No doubt Brigham Young was discouraged over developments concerning the Nevada state line and tax matters, which meant he would have less control over the area than he desired. However, the future success of the settlements when other Mormons moved back into the area in the following decade proved that accommodation could be made and the Virgin and Muddy colonies could succeed. The best evidence of such possibilities was already at hand. In the spring of 1870, Amos M. Musser reported that seven crops of fully mature alfalfa hay were being harvested each year at St. Thomas, more than twice what most Utah farms could produce.[33]

Nevertheless, President Young, under further pressure from Nevada tax collection officials, soon granted releases to those assigned to colonize the Muddy, if the majority voted to leave. The subsequent ballot was 123 in favor of disbanding, with but 5 for remaining at that time. One of the best historians of the colonization venture, young graduate student Melvin T. Smith, then under the scrutiny of Brigham Young University officials who, among others, had essentially deified Brigham Young, cautiously concluded, "[I]t is well that Brigham Young, the colonizer, passed other tests."[34] Indeed, those boasting about the greatness of Young could find little in his connection with the Muddy River Mission to bolster that view of the church leader.

THE LAS VEGAS ARMY OUTPOST AND GASS RANCH

During the first year of the Civil War, the abandoned Las Vegas mission served as a decoy to cover the real intentions of the United States Army, which was moving from southern California toward Confederate-influenced positions in Arizona and New Mexico. The Los Angeles *Star* had consistently advocated that establishing a military post at the old Las Vegas ranch would help deter Confederate sympathizers in the region from traveling that road to assist in the rebellion. The newspaper editor also argued that protecting emigrants and (as hoped) the soon-to-be-rerouted mails made the post a necessity.[35]

Late in 1861 James H. Carleton, now a colonel and still headquartered near Los Angeles, issued a circular indicating new troop assignments. Four companies were to establish a post at the old Mormon stockade to be named Fort Baker, after popular Oregon colonel Edward D. Baker, who had been killed early in the war. Several California newspapers thereafter mentioned how anxious Carleton was to protect the road to Salt Lake City. A report in March 1862 mentioned a large shipment of army supplies on their way to Fort Baker. Yet in fact no California-based military activity at all took place in the Las Vegas vicinity during that period. All the announcements were part of a clever cover-up for Carleton's actual objective. The freight addressed to Fort Baker was actually shipped to Fort Yuma, to be carried farther east in support of Carleton's "California Column," which played a crucial role in securing the greater New Mexico region for the Union cause and possibly in helping prevent the opening of a Confederate seaport at San Diego.[36]

Perhaps attracted by the recent Potosi strike, prospectors were also reported scouring the canyons near the Colorado River, and in 1861 a group headed by mountain man Johnnie Moss, led to the spot by hungry Indians, discovered gold outcrops in the steep walls of El Dorado Canyon about twenty-five miles downstream from present Hoover Dam. Up to forty prospectors may have been in on the first strikes, with Moss and Joseph W. Good (for whom the town of Goodsprings was later named) as the most notable. After a quiet start, a considerable rush to the area ensued between 1863 and 1866.

Octavius D. Gass, an Ohio-born forty-niner who had spent much of the previous decade in southern California, joined the rush to El Dorado Canyon in 1862. Not enjoying much success, in 1865 he and partners Nat Lewis and Louis Cole occupied the old Mormon fort in the Las Vegas Valley, cultivating fields and reconstructing dilapidated buildings. For a time Mormon Albert Knapp

Johnnie Moss, an intrepid mountaineer who claimed to have led the non-Mormon locators to the Potosi mines in 1860, is here photographed with Paiute chief Tercherum, who perhaps was one of the Indians who reportedly led him to the ore discoveries at El Dorado Canyon. Paiutes led white prospectors to the four major mining strikes within eighty miles of Las Vegas in the late 1860s.
COURTESY THE BANCROFT LIBRARY

operated a store at the old fort and held title to some of the property. In 1860, Knapp sold to his brother William, who continued serving the still-numerous travelers.[37] As his sometime partner James H. Ferry had done at Callville, Gass took the precaution of acquiring the land from the government, first securing a full section at the fort and then half a section at the spring. Within a decade, Gass either bought out his associates or they simply moved away. In early 1872, Octavius married Mary Virginia Simpson, whom he courted while she lived with her sister's family at St. Thomas some sixty miles away. The couple had six children during the decade they remained at the ranch.

Achieving an impressive degree of self-sufficiency in a farming and cattle-ranching operation, often with the assistance of Indian labor and some Mormon cowhands, profits were derived from serving passing travelers on the still-busy Southern Route passageway to southern California. The Gass family sold milk, vegetables, and fresh beef at reasonable prices to weary and appreciative emigrant customers camped along the creek as their animals recovered on the nearby grass. The station also offered blacksmith repair, including shoeing animals for the next section of road west, known to be tough on hooves. The commodious Gass house included a dining room featuring a 20-foot table where ranch hands and other visitors enjoyed the good food prepared by a Chinese cook, Lee. Besides grain, the other main crop on the hundred and fifty acres of cultivated land was pink Mexican beans, gathered and threshed by a large crew of local Paiutes, mainly paid in food, clothing, and other supplies. Consistently good relations benefited both the Indians and the Gass couple, who learned the Paiute language. The ranchers butchered beef twice each week during seasons when there were customers, including miners and soldiers at El Dorado Canyon willing to pay well for the meat and other provisions. Besides what was used at the ranch, beef was made into jerky. The Las Vegas proprietor also continued to sell clothing and merchandise, ordered mostly from San Bernardino.[38]

The same year Octavius Gass moved to Las Vegas, his former associates at El Dorado Canyon elected him to represent them in the Arizona territorial legislature at Prescott. There he helped draft the law to create Pah-Ute County, Arizona, in late December 1865. This included about the same area later comprised of Clark County, Nevada, with Callville as the county seat. Gass was also appointed postmaster there, serving through his partner, Ferry, for almost two years. Clearly popular with fellow lawmakers, Gass was selected to preside in the upper house of the Arizona legislature in 1867. By then, Congress had altered the boundaries of the area, placing most of the new county in Nevada. Gass and Mormon associate Andrew Gibbons continued to sit at Prescott in 1868 while their fellows unsuccessfully protested the boundary change, eventually casting the controversial votes to move the territorial capital to Tucson.[39]

Late in 1866 a group of Arizona citizens convening at Prescott adopted resolutions declaring the Paiute Indians farther west to be hostile and requested the territorial governor, Richard C. McCormick, to seek a greater military presence in that region. As the territorial legislature was then in session, O. D. Gass was probably present or would have been available with more accurate information—if he had been inclined to offer it. Few frontiersmen at the time, particularly merchants, would not favor an army outpost in their realm of business activity, not only for added protection but for the opportunity to prosper from supply contracts. The governor promptly headed for San Francisco over the Mojave Road, receiving a similar petition from Hardyville citizens en route. Civil War veteran Gen. Irwin McDowell was quick to dispatch seventy men of Company D of the United States Infantry, then stationed at Camp Cady, to establish a post at El Dorado Canyon.[40]

In historical hindsight, the entire episode appears the epitome of self-interest and inefficient military bureaucracy. When the troops arrived at the assigned canyon location, only three non-Indians were still living there. The mining camp had essentially been abandoned, as Gass doubtless knew, before the request for the military outpost. Besides, the Southern Paiutes had never caused any problem in the vicinity other than perhaps some begging and stealing. The officer first in charge of the post was Lt. James R. Hardenbergh, who never overcame the ignominy of the recent poorly led skirmish and defeat by Paiutes at Camp Cady. John E. Yard, already cleared for promotion to major, was too ill to travel to the camp when it first opened, but he took charge soon thereafter. With no Indian threat and not much else to do besides constructing shelters from whatever natural materials could be found, the officers soon determined it advisable to divide their troops and establish small branch posts at Callville and Cottonwood Island, where some of their cattle were to be pastured.

Within two months of Camp El Dorado being established, in response to further requests from Octavius Gass and his associates, Captain Yard also ordered creation of an army camp at the Las Vegas Ranch. Although the Vegas residents probably had other motives than fear of local Native Americans, the justification expressed by army officers later that summer stated "the resident white man became alarmed as the roving Indians who were well armed [and] were very bold and making threats to avenge on these men the wrongs and losses sustained by them at the hands of some Mormons who had passed over the road." Although possibly this assertion was based on fact, no record is known of any such outrages or resultant threats by Las Vegas Indians. However achieved, the presence of soldiers at the ranch was certainly welcomed and their location there made more sense than did stationing them at any remaining post on the upper section of the Colorado River.

Lt. Charles H. Shepard, veteran of a New York cavalry unit during the Civil War, took command of Camp El Dorado in June 1867. Like all others, he was not impressed with the spot and promptly embraced the idea of having the post headquarters moved to Las Vegas, a much more desirable place for several reasons. Scurvy was a frequent problem in desert commands, as well as at sea, and the known solution was the fresh vegetables available at the Gass ranch. Besides, as a source of needed goods the supply on a well-used freight wagon road was much more likely than the mostly talked-of Colorado River steamboats. Forage and firewood, still another drawback at El Dorado, were not a problem at Las Vegas. Unfortunately, the letter of request was channeled through Fort Mojave, where Maj. William R. Price had already received authorization to recall Shepard's command to offer garrison support duty while he took his cavalry on an offensive foray against the recently troublesome Halapai Indians farther east. Although Shepard did not relish the back-up role, he soon prepared to comply with the orders of his superior officer.[41]

When the ever vigilant Gass heard of these developments, he hurried to Fort Mojave and warned Major Price that he considered his neighboring Paiutes to be hostile, as did his associate Ferry at Callville, both (probably falsely) asserting fear of trouble should the troops be withdrawn. Most Camp El Dorado soldiers had already commenced marching toward Camp Mojave on 24 August, leaving but a small detachment under Lieutenant Hardenbergh to guard the remaining quartermaster stores. But Gass's appeal caused an about-face by Major Price, who assured the still politically powerful Las Vegas ranch proprietor that he never intended to abandon either Callville or Las Vegas. The first relief

parties sent back to those places were from the old Company D, but soon the troops there would be from Company K Fourteenth Infantry, also from Camp Cady.

That autumn Price's resolve was further bolstered by a formal petition from the Arizona territorial legislature—of which Gass was still leader—that a company of cavalry be stationed at Las Vegas. The request cited the distance from other settlements and military posts from which aid could be dispatched in the event of Indian attack, also reporting "the very threatening attitude of the Indians during the past six months." There was also a claim that freight wagon trains from southern California bound for Utah and Montana had been robbed of animals, with those and other travelers supposedly sustaining losses estimated at $12,500. The petition requested cavalry because presumably foot soldiers could not properly protect the area, even though the reportedly threatening Paiutes were also unmounted.

In response to these requests, in November 1867, Las Vegas received a detail of one corporal and six privates, with Callville and El Dorado each getting the same size garrison. A few months later an army inspector, Capt. Charles A. Whittier, analyzed the outposts and reported of Las Vegas that the soldiers there were the only guards on the entire middle section of the long desert road. He remarked sarcastically that they seemed "to have sufficed just as no troops had before." Although he did not say so in his report, the inspector doubtless understood the self-serving nature of proprietor Gass's requests for troop presence near his ranch.

Yet army officers too had to justify their presence in an area seemingly with little strategic value. Thus after Whittier's report resulted in orders from headquarters that the Las Vegas and El Dorado outposts be abandoned, Major Price successfully resisted by reporting that he had effectively quelled Paiute warlike tendencies through negotiations that included agreement to keep several warriors at his camp as "hostages," thereby ensuring the good conduct of nearby bands. He also asserted that previously the Indians had committed depredations against the new Mormon settlements on the Muddy River. Price affirmed suspicion that some Paiute warriors had joined with their frequent trade partners among the Halapais in some of the recent attacks along the extension of the Mojave Road through Arizona. The cavalry officer mentioned taking several Paiute chiefs with him on his recent patrol into Arizona and claimed this had generated hostility between the tribes, which tension he argued it was essential to maintain. This, Price stated, could only be accomplished by maintaining a military presence in the area. Although the military units providing the personnel changed, the Las Vegas installation thus continued to function. The Callville outpost was again disbanded in the spring of 1868.[42]

Gass and his ranch employees had experienced a little trouble with Native Americans, probably Northern Paiutes, visiting from more distant locations, but no record exists of anything but cordial relations with the two hundred Southern Paiutes who consistently resided in the Las Vegas Valley. In fact many of these Indians continued to work for Gass at least part of each year. It can actually be argued that sometimes the soldiers stationed at Vegas were more troublesome than the Indians. And on at least one occasion the Paiutes helped solve the problem. Pvt. Clark Bixby deserted from the Soda Lake (Hancock Redoubt) post, taking a horse and equipment. The Camp Cady commander quickly dispatched word to Las Vegas for the soldiers to be on the lookout for the deserter. When Bixby arrived there, his former associates were waiting. Perhaps because he was mounted and the other soldiers were not, they engaged several Indians to assist in capturing him, along with his horse and equipment. The deserter was returned for punishment to Camp Cady.

The most notable instance of soldier misbehavior was a drunken brawl in early July 1868. Later investigation determined the entire military contingent then at Las Vegas, a corporal and seven privates, had "had liquor and were nearly all drunk" on a hot Sunday afternoon in a mud hut at the ranch. A thirty-one-year-old soldier named Richard W. Barron reportedly bit an associate, Private Connolly, on the ear, and the latter consequently shot him in the head with a shotgun. The accused murderer was transferred to Camp Cady, where he escaped from the guardhouse and was never again apprehended by military officials.

The military detachments remained at their Nevada posts for the remainder of 1868, and Gass doubtless gar-

nered some profits from their presence, as well as whatever security they afforded. In February 1869, orders arrived from Fort Mojave to reduce the number of men stationed at Las Vegas and El Dorado Canyon to three each. That May, Company K also received orders to report to San Francisco, an action signaling the end of both outposts, which were permanently closed in the early summer. The Gass family remained at Las Vegas in relative safety until 1882, when the longtime owner Gass failed to repay a loan for which the ranch was collateral and thus lost the property to Archibald Stewart. The Gass family moved to the San Bernardino area in California, and the Stewarts, or at least Archibald's widow and children, occupied the property until the railroad arrived, after the turn of the twentieth century.[43]

UTAH'S ADJUSTMENT TO THE COMING OF THE RAILROADS

After the transcontinental railroad was completed in northern Utah in May 1869, a branch line was soon extended southward through Salt Lake City to York, in Juab County, near the center of the territory. That became a shipping point from which the St. George area received much of its goods. From there a consistent stream of freight wagons and stagecoaches followed the Southern Route beyond Kanosh, where many branched to the west to carry their loads mainly to Pioche, then the primary booming southern Nevada mining camp. Peddler-freighters from virtually all the Mormon towns within a hundred twenty miles of the mining district also hauled a large quantity of provisions, lumber, and other items into the neighboring state. In 1879, the Utah Southern Extension Railroad was completed to the Utah mining camp of Frisco, some thirty miles east of Beaver on the Southern Route. Thereafter, Frisco was the shipping point into the still-active southern Nevada camps. Because none of these camps were particularly close to the old southern wagon route, it fell permanently into disuse. Eventually it was partly replaced by the San Pedro, Los Angeles, and Salt Lake City Railroad, which extended and rebuilt the Utah Southern Railroad in 1904–5.[44]

NEVADA PROSPECTORS
KILLED BY INDIANS

It is doubtful if the presence of soldiers in the area could have prevented the loss of several lives within three years after the troops withdrew from Las Vegas. In the spring of 1870, Indians attacked two men, as they headed north some fifteen miles beyond the Gass ranch. A German, named Fritz, was killed and his companion, an Irishman, fled for his life and after much suffering made his way back to Las Vegas. The assailants were presumed to be Moapa Paiutes, which seemed to indicate that the treaty between Major Price and Chief Tosho may have lapsed. Fort Mojave, where Paiute hostages had been held by terms of the agreement, had also been abandoned. However, Tosho's commitment to peace may actually have continued.

The San Bernardino *Guardian* reported in the spring of 1870 that miners in the Yellow Pine District demanded that a chief called by the paper Tecoha, possibly Tosho, help apprehend the murderers of the German. The chief delivered up "Piute Jack," termed a

"notorious scoundrel who had always been the chief instigator if not the actual murderer of many white men." At a subsequent "miner's trial," the accused was condemned to be shot, which sentence was promptly carried out. In 1872 a former San Bernardino resident, William Kirk, apparently died of thirst on a desert road between Mountain Springs and the Colorado River. At about the same time travelers discovered the body of another German prospector on the same road, near Ivanpah, presumably dead from the same cause.[45] The fates of all these travelers over the Southern Route illustrate its status and continued limitations in its final phase.

CALIFORNIA WAY STATIONS

Despite the death of young Franklin Woolley, the California end of the Southern Route commenced to flourish with more localized transportation activity. John Brown's toll station continued to function at a wide spot above the narrows once so difficult for Gold Rush–bound emigrants in 1849. After losing some revenue to stockmen driving

Upper John Brown toll station in Coyote-Crowder Canyon (just south of present highway 138 in Cajon Pass), by photographer Rudolph D'Heureuse, 1863.

COURTESY THE BANCROFT LIBRARY

their herds around this location through the west Cajon, Brown built an even more elaborate toll station several miles down the pass at its narrowest point, at what was later called Blue Cut. Life at the lower station was seldom dull. A daughter, Louisa Brown, recalled that deserting soldiers from desert posts were pursued and shot somewhere not far below the station. A familiar sight, she said, was the passing of "Hi Jolly," the Turkish camel driver and mail carrier. The upper station continued dispensing liquid refreshment at its barroom selling brandy and wine brought in considerable quantities from Dr. Benjamin Barton's San Bernardino mission district vineyards and winery.[46]

In the latter years of the decade, this so-called Canyon Station operated under the management of Jim Fears. Mrs. Naomi Fears gained a reputation as a masterful cook, particularly of the common fare at her table, venison steak, easily procured nearby. Sleeping accommodations were offered for both man and animal amid a persuasive motivation to pay and thus avoid sleeping outdoors in the Cajon, still dangerous because of numerous California grizzly bears prowling there at night. The later proprietors of the lower toll station, Tay and Lawrence, subsequently constructed a more substantial building, including a large sleeping area.[47]

By the early 1870s several other way stations were operating down the Mojave River from Aaron Lane's, near present Oro Grande, including one seven miles away at Point of Rocks, near present Helendale. This last was then kept by an older English couple named Saunders. At least one visitor there noted the substantial cornfield, which the proprietors proudly boasted set at rest all doubts about the productivity of the desert lands, when properly irrigated. At this station the road veered away from the sandy river bottom, turning up a wash and onto the benchlands east of the Mojave. From there it was nine miles to the Cottonwoods station near present Hodge. Cottonwoods was sporadically occupied during the previous decade, but permanently operated in the 1870s, when it was considered, at least by some, to be "the station par excellence of the Mojave River." At this time the Frank Lightfoot family operated the station, and Mrs. Lightfoot's reputation as a cook equaled that of Mrs. Fears'. Here too there was apparently some type of lounge for guests spending the evening in smoking and talking, if not drinking, and plenty of beds in a "nice large, cool room." This and all other Mojave way stations also offered feed and bedding facilities for the livestock and opportunities to grease and make small repairs to wagons and harness, making them a type of combination

Nicholson family's way station, built in 1861, at Point of Rocks (near present-day Helendale, California), by photographer Rudolph D'Heureuse, 1863.
COURTESY THE BANCROFT LIBRARY

restaurant, motel, and service station for their generation.[48]

Another important station near present Daggett was established by Lafayette Meacham, who had earlier kept a store at Camp Cady. When he left that situation, he located some fifteen miles up the Mojave River at a place soon dubbed Fish Ponds because one pond there was full of chub. Meacham served the continuing needs of travelers over that challenging stretch of road. He also contracted to supply hay to the Camp Cady post. Although at first he had neither machinery for cutting nor hauling, Meacham and his sons cut the gayote grass with a butcher knife and pulled the sand grass by hand, stuffing both into sacks set at the side of the road for passing soldiers to carry to the fort. With the hay selling for $80 per ton, it was not long before Meacham expanded his operation, purchasing not only one of the first mowing machines in the region but also the draft animals and wagons he needed for easier harvest and delivery. As he expanded his harvesting to the tall grass meadows both sides of the Upper Mojave Narrows of the later Victorville area, some of the teamsters he employed to haul the hay broke or improved a road straight from the latter area to the Daggett vicinity.

This route was vastly enhanced by former mail car-

rier Sheldon Stoddard digging a well midway, and at some point someone constructed corrals and shacks there, making the necessary overnight stay by teamsters and their outfits much easier. Some wagon masters began choosing to bypass Lane's station and the longer river route to take this shortcut, which usually reduced their total journey by at least a day. The Stoddard's Well route probably enhanced the importance of the Mormon Crossing station serving the teams and drivers as they left the Mojave River at what would later be Victorville. Situated on the west side of the river where the road forked between the routes toward Lane's to the west and Stoddard's Well to the northeast, the earliest known occupants, the Burtons, left after a brother was killed and was replaced by John J. Atkinson and his wife. Here too, the woman of the house was often praised for her culinary skills.[49]

Yet another station was located at the forks of the road, where those heading for Resting Springs, the Ivanpah and neighboring mining camps, and Utah separated from those heading for the Colorado River and Arizona. This station was first operated by Hieronymous Hartman. In 1871 this recent emigrant from Germany, who had served for a time in the army at Camp Cady and married the relative of one of the officers there, took his bride with him to embark on civilian life as a way station proprietor. His special skills as a blacksmith were probably particularly welcomed by those approaching the river after the long desert crossing from whichever branch of the road they were on. Although the Mojave River did not often flow on the surface that far downstream, good water was easily procured by digging a few feet in the channel. This was much appreciated by all incoming travelers. The Hartmans at first maintained a garden by hand carrying buckets of water several hours every day, but after one season this arduous task was undoubtedly abandoned.[50]

FREIGHTING TO DESERT MINING CAMPS FROM THE SOUTH END OF THE ROAD

Without any question, the key to the continued massive amount of freight activity and the general prosperity of both the Mojave River and San Bernardino Valleys was the abundance of good new mining strikes and the rapid development of at least half a dozen booming mining districts within the desert regions of San Bernardino County in the 1870s and early 1880s. This also included increasing trade to similar districts in Inyo and Kern counties and in Arizona and Nevada. The first of these, after Holcomb Valley, which boomed several times, was in late 1863 at Macedonia Mountain, ten miles north of Camp Rock Spring in the East Mojave area. Several other ore locations, including Silver Mountain to the south, led to the establishment of a half-dozen mines that year and the creation of the Rock Springs–Macedonia mining district. This is precisely when sometime photographer Rudolph de Heureuse was dispatched over the Southern Route and out on the Mojave Road to investigate mining claims for San Francisco investors. Besides taking the first known photographs of several important sites along the Southern Route (included in these chapters), he served as the first deputy recorder of the mining district, as well as one of the primary assayers of the various ores. Unfortunately, the district was soon closed because of Indian troubles and remained so until soldiers returned to the area after the Civil War.[51]

The Clark Mountain district, not far from the Kingston cutoff on Salt Lake Road and the California boundary with Nevada, was located in 1868, with the assistance of an Indian—one of four major early mining district discoveries of the southern Nevada region so commenced.[52] Soon a heavy freight traffic developed between the principal mining town of Ivanpah and San Bernardino. For the first several years, during which about three hundred miners were reported active in the district, high-grade silver ore placed in sacks was hauled by way of the Mojave River and San Bernardino, to be shipped first by sea and later by railroad to smelters at San Francisco. Horace Clark, a pioneer over the Southern Route in 1857, became the primary operator of a flourishing freight wagon trade over the desolate, but profitable, route from the Clark district to San Bernardino. One newspaper item in 1873, not atypically, mentioned 12,000 pounds of ore thus shipped in one freighting trip. Lower-grade ores were reduced locally by Mexican and Native American workmen using the ancient *arrastra* method for pulverizing ore-bearing rock and then treating it with quicksilver (mercury).[53]

Not much later, similar rich strikes were made in the neighboring Providence Mountain area, formerly the Macedonia Mining District. After 1872, this was known as New York Mountains Mining District. The promise of both the Clark and New York Mountains claims prompted leading mining men Matt Pelan and Dr. Winchester to purchase machinery for a fifteen-stamp mill, five tons of which were transported by wagon over the old road to the booming area, where it was soon placed in operation. Thereafter, the freight hauled back to San Bernardino and beyond was primarily bullion, the precious concentrate derived from reducing the far greater volume of ore produced in both camps but still needing further refining at San Francisco. Newspaper items often mentioned shipments of thousands of dollars worth of silver bullion carried by Horace Clark's incoming mule train, kept constantly busy hauling foodstuffs and other supplies to the camps. These districts maintained amazingly consistent production through the entire decade.[54]

In the early summer of 1868, the Los Angeles *Star* had focused on the Pahranagat Valley, Nevada, mining camp in a column-long article. The main camp, Hico, about four hundred fifty miles from Los Angeles and eighty miles from the Mormon settlements on the Muddy River, and some forty miles north of the main overland road, was said to consist of about forty cabins and a good mill. During the earlier boom days reportedly four hundred people had been in the area and at other mills operating in nearby Silver Canyon, but these mills were now closed and many of the people had already departed for other camps. Freight wagon trains from southern California thereafter made substantial profits from goods transported there over the Southern Route. And several herds of cattle from the Mojave River ranches and others nearby were driven over the route to be consumed by the miners there.[55] Earlier the nearby Mormon farmers produced a goodly proportion of the provisions needed at Pahranagat, but more recently, goods from there had "become rather scarce at the mines." This may have been because of resentment over the boundary changes and seeming demonstrations of hostility from Nevada tax collectors.

The area east and south of Pahranagat Valley had been a matter of heated congressional debate in 1864 and 1865. Representatives of the infant state of Nevada sought additional territory in those directions, arguing on dubious grounds that the area was valuable for mining and Nevada was a mining state. Spokesmen for both Utah and Arizona territories could not prevent the land grab, even though Hico and its environs were already safely within the existing state boundaries.[56]

SUGGESTIONS OF DESERT RAILROADS

In the spring of 1869, the Los Angeles *Star* editorialized optimistically that many of the estimated 70,000 people attracted to Hamilton and other nearby White Pine, Nevada, mining camps considerably north of Pahranagat and Pioche would eventually become discouraged and gravitate not only into prospecting adjacent areas but also into agricultural endeavors supporting the mining camps. No evidence suggests the newspapermen understood the extreme limits on easily irrigable land in that sector of what had for five years been the state of Nevada, but most of the "agricultural resources" the *Star* hoped would be developed would likely be in California, which in fact often fed such burgeoning camps. However, with the completion of the transconti-

nental railroad just two months later, some provisions would soon originate from Utah and points east as well, freighted more easily from the Central Pacific roadway to the Nevada camps than could be done over the more lengthy wagon route from southern California.

Prior to completion of the railroad, San Bernardino merchants Wolff and Folks sent a train of wagons toward White Pine. But the demand for their goods proved so great at Pahranagat, which reportedly then had "money plenty," that the merchandise was disposed of at the closer camp and the wagons returned from a shorter trip. Great as the company profits were from that venture, the San Bernardino *Guardian* editorial several months later advocating a permanent stage line to Pahranagat was unrealistic because the Nevada railroad stations north of the mining region were considerably closer and would soon adequately serve both that camp and White Pine.[57]

In fact, by the time the transcontinental railroad was completed, Gen. George H. Thomas had ordered Lt. George M. Wheeler to survey and report on agricultural, grazing, and mineral resources in the vast region of southeastern Nevada. He was also to determine the best route for a railroad from the main Central Pacific Railroad line to the Colorado River via the White Pine mining district. In 1869–70, army engineer Wheeler traveled along the southern wagon route from Stump Springs northwest through Las Vegas to the Mormon town of St. Thomas. Then, heading farther east, he commented that the area between St. George and the Colorado River was certainly not fit for a railroad because of the deep canyons with high, blufflike walls. In 1872 Wheeler returned to the field, approaching the Colorado through southern Utah. Although speculation and surveys continued for several more decades, no such railroad materialized before 1905.[58]

Another flurry of railroad excitement at the time centered at the southern end of the Southern Route. In 1868, the entire nation anticipated completion of the first transcontinental railroad then being laid in both directions from California and Nebraska. This historic development was distant from southern California but influenced that region in several ways. Although the coming of the railroad to the Pacific Coast essentially ended overland wagon transportation from Utah to California, many in the southland fervently hoped not only for ties through branch lines to the Central Pacific to the north, but also for their own transcontinental line, projected to be built along the thirty-fifth parallel route to southern California.

In August 1868, San Bernardino citizens held a series of mass meetings to consider the proposal of Anaheim, California, Mayor Max Strobel and his associates of a railroad from the envisioned seaport at Anaheim Landing, near present Seal Beach, to San Bernardino. Many prominent San Bernardino–area businessmen and political figures affirmed personal financial support, although their resolution to ask the county government to assist with a subsidy of some $5,000 per mile of track laid was certainly unrealistic. The San Bernardino *Guardian* consistently supported the scheme, arguing that the seaport was actually superior to San Pedro-Wilmington. Well-known western financial men Samuel Brannan and Ben Holladay purchased the Abel Stearns rancho, through which the proposed railroad would run, and were also reported to be substantially involved in the railway construction venture, which for a time appeared destined for timely completion. The railroad was undoubtedly expected to connect with other lines. These lines included the Atlantic and Pacific Railroad, which was authorized to reach the coast by the route following the thirty-fifth parallel across New Mexico and Arizona, and the Utah Central, which anticipated entrance into southern California from the northeast. The Utah Central, when built, was likely to partially follow the old southern wagon road.[59]

While the Anaheim-to-San Bernardino project was still seeking financial support locally and beyond, promoter Strobel, a German emigrant with the military title of major, became simultaneously involved in a real estate project in the desert above Cajon Pass. He knew the area well, having delivered cattle on contract to the army post at Fort Mojave as recently as the previous August. He purchased 8,737 acres at a cost of $1.25 per acre for the contiguous sections of land that would later be Hesperia. It is clear that Strobel was acting for fellow California Germans, who incorporated the 35th Parallel Land Association, probably aiming at subdivision and sale of the property after the arrival of the railroad over that route. According to the universally accepted government railroad surveys, the second transcontinental railroad would have to enter southern California through those lands and Cajon Pass.

Unfortunately, the Atlantic and Pacific Railroad ran into major financial difficulties and misunderstandings over land claims in Indian Territory (later the state of Oklahoma) and would not actually reach connection with the West Coast for more than a dozen additional years. Also, a financial panic caused partly by overextension of American railroads gripped California and the nation by the middle of the 1870s. Still another factor probably contributing to the failure to secure sufficient financial support for the Anaheim-to-San Bernardino project was the superior claim of San Diego, which had a real seaport and which was also seeking support at San Bernardino and in the East as the southern California terminus for the second transcontinental railroad.

While the southern California railroad excitement was still current, the Los Angeles *Star* speculated that the ultimate intent of the promoters was to reach at least to the Colorado River, fully tapping the Arizona trade, which steamboat transportation had failed to satisfy. The newspaper editors also suggested that a less-expensive narrow-gauge railroad could easily be extended from San Bernardino to the Clark Mining District on the Nevada border. So far as is known, no investors were ever seriously engaged in this endeavor, presumably because the freight wagons were adequately serving the immediate needs of the region, at least for the time being.[60]

FREIGHTING STIMULUS TO SOUTHERN CALIFORNIA ECONOMIC GROWTH

The Mojave wagon route to the Colorado still continued to be used in the early 1870s, with one caravan of thirty 12-mule-team wagons carrying 200,000 pounds of freight toward Prescott in mid-1873. Finally, in 1875, because of politics, greater frequency of Indian attacks on the rival Bradshaw road, and decline of the mining camps near the Colorado River, the California and Arizona Stage Company changed its primary route back to the Mojave River. San Bernardino newspapermen gloated that the river route "knocks off every opponent ever started against it," presumably because of the general superiority of the road and service along it, as reported by knowledgeable freighters and other travelers.[61]

The greatest beneficiaries of this era of vast mining booms—besides the financiers who eventually purchased and developed many of the best claims—were the merchants who supplied the camps with food and supplies for the men and feed for the considerable number of animals engaged in a variety of ways in the mining operation as well as in transport. Several of these were centered at San Bernardino, notably the firm of Meyerstein and Company established in 1870. With the foresight and ambition to send agents not only to the camps of the California desert, but also into Arizona, the company prospered sufficiently to be able to divide its local center of operation into two stores, one for groceries and the other reputedly with the greatest variety of dry goods in the county. Usually they engaged local men with good freighting experience and allowed them to profitably operate the transportation end of the enterprise. They also depended partly on such men for merchandising at the camps, although Julius Meyerstein was noted to make a number of trips there as well. For a time in the early 1870s his firm held the contract to supply much of the merchandise to the boomtown of Panamint in the Death Valley area, regularly hauling two hundred tons of freight each month. Other local merchants such as Wolffe and Folks were similarly engaged, although on a lesser scale.[62]

San Bernardino County newspapermen smugly called their area "the granary and storehouse of the region," but more candid observers would concede the considerable reciprocal prosperity enjoyed by farmers, freighters, harness makers, liverymen, hotel and way station operators, and many others of their community stemmed directly from the mining boom. On one Saturday in 1873, thirty-six mining camp–bound teams and wagons were counted on Third Street in the heart of the San Bernardino business district. And two years later, on a similar day, twenty teams embarked for Ivanpah, Coso, Panamint, and Arizona, as well as to the camps closer in. At that time the San Bernardino *Times-Index* editor reminded his readers that "the prosperity of San Bernardino lies in her mining resources," and a newspaper competitor at about the same time boasted that San Bernardino should be called the "mineral county" of California.[63]

Although on a far lesser scale in population as well as wealth derived, the increasing number of residents along the Mojave River also profited considerably from the truly immense volume of freighting traffic passing through the area in both directions. Besides the food and feed purchased and consumed by those along the route, virtually all the primary product of the growing number of area beef ranches was also marketed at the mines. Certainly the closest camps consumed most, but the Bemis family and others also drove cattle all the way to

Loaded freight wagons in the booming commercial center of San Bernardino, probably in the 1870s.

COURTESY SAN BERNARDINO MUSEUM

the mining camps of Pioche and Pahranagat, Nevada, for successful sale, although rancher and county clerk Frank McKenny met with far less profit in a similar venture to Utah.

In mid-March 1874, the *Guardian* noted that Heber "Pete" Huntington, who had moved to California from Utah with his parents William and Caroline over the Southern Route in 1857, purchased and was keeping the old Atkinson-McKenney station on the Mojave. Weeks later, the same newspaper announced the new proprietor also had bought the Fish Ponds station formerly owned by the Meachams, which he intended to operate through a "deputy." The paper lavished special praise on Huntington's "accomplished lady," who, it was said, would attend to the wants of the traveling public in such a manner that "nothing shall be wanting to their accommodation and comfort." Another laudatory note assured splendid satisfaction from a reporter who had "often tried Mrs. Huntington's epicurean cuisine." The newspaper ads boasted "excellent accommodations for the traveling public."[64] The family appears to have operated the station for several years at good profits to themselves and satisfaction to a steady flow of customers. What was later to be Victorville was for a time indicated on maps as Huntington.

OUTLAW ACTIVITY NEAR THE SOUTHERN END OF THE ROAD

There had always been interest in mining in the Death Valley area just west of the Southern Route to California, including the Amargosa and other mines almost on the road. Often the best shipping routes used the southwest portion of the historic trail, sometimes branching off as that to the Panamint district did and heading north from the Cottonwoods station. Not long after this road was established, a Hispanic bandit named Cleovaro Chavez, a former lieutenant of the then recently notorious Tiburcio Vasquez, made his appearance in the area. In May 1875, the Chavez gang robbed the proprietor of a newly established way station between Point of Rocks and Cottonwoods, taking a rifle, shotgun, and $80 in gold. Chavez then looked at his victim and exclaimed, "I know you," to which the station operator bravely replied,

"[W]ell if you know me, you had better return me my horses, as it is by them I make a living." The sympathetic robber retorted, "Sí, Señor, there your horses; I'm Chavez, not take all from poor man. Rich man—Carnjo!" The bandit then tipped his hat chivalrously and left without the horses.[65]

Half a year later the Chavez gang reappeared at Willow Springs station midway between the Mojave River and Panamint. Responding to a rumor that one of the express wagon passengers soon to pass was carrying $15,000 on his person, the outlaws commandeered the station, tying up the operator, Mr. Riley. During the ensuing three days, a teamster, two foot travelers, and an Indian approached the station and were each relieved of their valuable property and detained so they could not warn the main intended victim. When the express finally arrived without any passengers, the outlaws robbed the driver, Mr. Mowray, of $127.50 in cash, but on his appeal they returned $7.50. Similarly, when Chavez threatened to take the draft horses, the teamster observed the animals were too poor to do the gang any good, and the gang agreed. Besides these semblances of fairness, Chavez was also reportedly very considerate of the station operator's wife, Mrs. Riley, even paying her for cooking for his men during the extended ordeal.[66]

It is amazing that there were not more incidents recorded of robbery on the desert roads branching from the Mojave River, considering the vast wealth being transported through the region, unwisely publicized in the San Bernardino press. But the only other such incident is of someone following veteran freighter Horace Clark over the road from Ivanpah and while he was staying at Cottonwood Station, taking four bars of bullion from the wagon, leaving the other fifteen undisturbed. When the theft was discovered, the culprits were tracked to the river, where all trace of them disappeared. Mine owner John McFarlane offered a substantial reward for recovery of the loot, but no report hints that it was ever collected.[67]

Mining camps were notoriously transitory, and the vast deserts intersected by the Southern Route from Utah to California had been strewn with innumerable ghost towns since the first decade of the road. Yet sufficient mines remained in operation for some freight operations to continue prospering, providing a service essential to maintaining the lifeline from the Pacific Coast sources of food and supplies and virtually everything else essential for life of man and animal in the camps. Although neighboring states and territories by then had other sources of supply, the volume of wagon freight to the far-flung California desert mining camps still remained extensive.

CLOSE OF THE ERA

In 1883, the long-delayed Atlantic and Pacific Railroad finally bridged the Colorado River and penetrated toward southern California population centers. Although Collis P. Huntington attempted to maintain the Central Pacific monopoly in the southland, what soon became the Atchison, Topeka, and Santa Fe Railroad, including the old Atlantic and Pacific, extended a railroad from National City, south of San Diego to join its main lines at Barstow. This permanently broke the earlier railroad's stranglehold on overland transportation, and there was soon a rate war that did much to bolster southern California growth and development.[68] With new railroad-located distribution stations at Barstow, Mojave, and Victorville, local freighting and stagecoach transport companies continued to flourish for many years (eventually replaced by automobiles and trucks), still serving to tie desert and mountain people to supplies from the outside world. In the later years, settlement and development along hundred-mile stretches on either end of the Southern Route markedly improved conveniences for travelers over that road, even though far fewer journeys went all the way through the deserts, because the transcontinental railroad had been completed. Transportation links to Colorado River steamboats proved disappointing, but that transportation interest in the area helped lead to semipermanent settlement along the Virgin and Muddy rivers. A great volume of transportation still flowed to and from the far-flung mining camps of the greater region, often via segments of the historic old roadway from each end. Even when the railroad approached fairly close to the region, team-drawn freighting and passenger transportation continued to flourish from the railroad centers to the destinations away from the railway lines.

Chapter Ten

Summary and Conclusions

The transportation route from Salt Lake City to Los Angeles led through some of the most forbidding deserts any American pioneers were ever compelled to cross, and because so little water could be found en route, it was actually the most challenging of all well-used emigrant and freight roads. Yet grass and water, however meager the supply, were distributed in such a manner as to allow a reasonably heavy flow of wagon traffic across the roadway for two decades, and of pack mule trains for about the same period previous to that. The road was particularly valuable because it was open all winter, when virtually all routes farther north were snowed in.

The pack mule trail from Santa Fe-Taos to San Gabriel-Los Angeles, opened primarily by Spaniards linking Spanish towns, was the western segment of the first trade route from the Pacific Coast to the United States. The designation "old" is relative but also reasonably apt in relation to other roads in the Far West. Mexican California received manufactured goods and pro-

vided mules, which markedly improved the quality and supply of those animals in Missouri and elsewhere. The trail proved particularly useful as a conduit for transporting livestock stolen in California to northern and eastern markets. Tragically, a trade in Indian slaves flourished at both ends of the Old Spanish Trail. This was just one aspect of the negative long-term relationship of trail travelers with the Native Americans who resided along the route.

The mule trains, often a mile long while under way, not only consumed and destroyed a massive amount of animal feed probably formerly used by wild game, but also affected the water holes in major ways, including trampling much natural vegetation and frightening away wildlife. Later observers can only surmise the effect of these developments on the Native American lifestyle, but it must have been extensive, and doubtless meant that Indians could access a lesser supply of a number of previously used foods and clothing materials. At an early juncture Indians along the trail and their neighbors formulated the concept they probably had heard that whites practiced elsewhere of levying use fees for travel and sustenance provided in their domain. This was evident in the late 1820s when a Mohave chief used sign language pointing to the beaver pelts in the pack saddles and the Colorado River from which they were taken, then pointing to a horse he required as reimbursement. When the trappers refused, violence ensued, reportedly costing the chief his life. Often thereafter the Indians made fewer requests, but they exacted tribute nevertheless, by wounding livestock that the emigrants and freighters subsequently abandoned to be eaten by awaiting Indians, and they stole a massive amount of animals and property. By the end of the era of major trail use, Southern Paiutes had better developed their ability to communicate with the continuing users through their domain. The Paiutes could then more fully articulate their policy and its justification, which had probably not really changed throughout the entire period. Native American spokesmen now specifically stated they were asking for reimbursement for expended resources and trail use.

As the Southern Route became a wagon road with the Gold Rush in 1849, up to five thousand emigrants traveled the road during that initial year. Many of these had exhausted their livestock and depleted their provision supplies, thus suffering great privation and making slow progress. This was the case with many of those who preceded the people who attempted a supposed shortcut to the gold fields through the region of Death Valley, as well as those who made that area infamous. Nevertheless, virtually all travelers who stayed on the main trail or returned to it got through successfully and fully established its practicability. However, as noted earlier, several travelers who had at first intended to publish guidebooks of the route became so disenchanted after their difficulties there that they could never bring themselves to recommend the Southern Route. The suffering and depleted resources in 1849, the first year of wagon travel, make clear that the rescue missions Isaac Williams sponsored were just as significant as the many similar efforts on other routes. Rancho del Chino and neighboring California southland ranches were likewise important as rest havens for weary travelers.

The reported experiences of that first year's wagon travelers markedly improved the preparation of those who followed over that route, and it is doubtful if all the pioneers over the route in later years combined suffered as much as did those in that first year of the Gold Rush, 1849. As noted, one practice learned from the initial year was to exchange depleted and exhausted draft animals at Salt Lake City for animals in better condition to pull across the deserts and mountains of the final segment of the journey. The early pioneers also learned to avoid the poor nourishment of salt grass as livestock feed, even if better varieties of grass grew some distance off the main road. Later pioneer companies naturally carried better supplies of provisions and water, and did not set out burdened with so many other inessential items. Such excess baggage was mainly left on the trail the first year—but only after most livestock were worn out hauling the extra weight. Also, after the first year many pioneers clearly avoided traveling in large groups, because water and pasture were too limited for larger numbers of animals. Subsequent travelers avoided the worst portion of the 1849 trail—down the east Cajon Pass—by using a newly constructed grade down the west Cajon. Although impossible to measure, it appears that the social tension so prevalent among the emigrants during the desert crossings in the first year was also less noticeable in succeeding years, perhaps because proportionately more women were present later.

With the major Mormon migration starting in 1851, a more decisive leadership was demonstrated by ranking Mormon leader Amasa M. Lyman curbing growing conflict between Indians and Latter-day Saints and introducing a more cordial relationship between the two groups. When Lyman and fellow San Bernardino leader Charles C. Rich returned to Utah in 1852, they allowed Native Americans in their camp and soon paid them to herd livestock through the night for pay, a policy that halted much animal wounding and stealing. Certainly this situation was not universal; members of some Mormon companies violated policies of humane and non-violent treatment of Southern Paiutes. Some non-Mormon companies during the early years, notably the Beale-Heap group, also enjoyed markedly cordial relationships with Native Americans throughout their journey. By early 1853 reported conflicts had increased between non-Mormon companies and soldiers with both Latter-day Saints and neighboring Indians. At that time a number of disaffected Mormons began "escaping" from Utah over that route. In 1856, Mormon apostate Hans Peter Hoth experienced rather harsh treatment at the hands of Native Americans as his party traveled southward.

One of the most amazing situations on the trail is that in well over a hundred through trips by mail carriers there was no known human fatality. Native Americans wounded some carriers and killed and stole their animals and occasionally some mail, but it is doubtful if there is any comparable record along any other similar expanse so heavily inhabited by Native Americans. This peaceful transit was accomplished largely through the mail carriers demonstrating marked generosity, carrying and dispensing extra food and tobacco and developing cordial personal relationships with many Southern Paiutes along the way. English traveler William Chandless, admittedly no friend of Native Americans, pointedly complained about his mail carrier companion David Savage's "hyperliberality" to Indians. The carriers' generous behavior probably kept travelers such as Chandless alive.

Southern Route mortality rates as a whole were amazingly low throughout the era. No drownings occurred as were common on the main northern trails, nor were there any of the vastly more numerous deaths from cholera. Perhaps half a dozen deaths of whites occurred at Indian hands (before the Mountain Meadows Massacre, which was in fact an aberration from normal trail conditions) and probably only a dozen others, including infant deaths, took place during the first seven years of Anglo-American travel over the road. This is a dramatic contrast with the main Oregon-California Trail, which some observers considered one elongated cemetery.

Despite the numerous accounts of travel over the desert route, surprisingly few mentions are made of the daily routine on the journey. This is characteristic of travel on other routes as well, but the Southern Route posed so many unique challenges that historians would much appreciate more detail about ordinary daily tasks and procedures. No diarist ever mentioned the necessary waits for small springs and seeps to fill adjacent watering holes for each animal to drink enough to continue. Doubtless at some places this process would have taken many hours. Many diarists refer to the need to drive cattle off the trail to find better feed. In the many areas of sparse brush, wood for cooking fires would also have been particularly difficult to gather. Emigrants on some other trails burned dry buffalo chips (dung) when wood proved scarce. Diarists mention Southern Route emigrants going without cooking fires and thus without much food even when very near to abundant stands of mesquite—which was probably too thorny for tired travelers to cope with. And speaking of food, it is doubtful if any other American pioneers ever ate so much horse and mule meat for subsistence as did the forty-niners on the Southern Route!

Combining draft teams to pull wagons up challenging grades was common on many pioneer trails, but the Virgin Hill climb onto Mormon Mesa garnered votes from virtually every diarist experiencing it as one of the most difficult pulls in the annals of American pioneering. Although frequently journals note soft footing on several segments of the road, demanding heavy pulls, few refer to the clouds of dust frequently complained of on other roads. Yet probably no contemporary travelers faced more dust than those traveling across the Mojave and adjacent deserts.

With the establishment of the Latter-day Saint Indian Mission in southern Utah in 1854, positive relations between these groups continued to develop. Although no evidence has been found of any official charge from LDS leaders to foster a military alliance, comments by Mormon missionaries make abundantly clear that was part of their intent. They also sought, of course, to improve material conditions by teaching better farming techniques. The message reportedly disseminated by Indian convert Terab, son of Chief Toquor, along the Southern Route all the way to San Bernardino, stressed Paiute friendship toward Mormons and noted church members' superiority to other Americans, or Mericats. Several astute observers, including Solomon Carvalho, recognized the Indians' differentiation made between Mormons and other travelers, with a certain hostility toward the latter contrasting the marked cordiality toward the former. Jules Remy's Mormon guide attempted to pass him and his companions off as "good Americans," so Remy too recognized that non-Mormons were generally regarded as "bad people." Lt. Sylvester Mowry noted that Indians currently employed the term "enemies" for the non-Mormons and "allies" for the LDS churchmen. Given his observations, he warned about the alliance and commented on how effective the united Mormon-Indian forces might be if war with the federal government broke out in the Southern Route region. He appealed for at least annual demonstrations of United States military strength along the road to help quell the ardor of these potential foes. But tragically, the federal government made no response to his recommendations. It was not a time of great national leadership.

It can be cogently argued that at the time no place in the United States was so distant from the visible presence or even interest of the nation's government officials than the expanses traversed by the Southern Route to California. Even a decade later, Maj. John W. Powell was virtually penetrating the unknown in his Colorado River voyage through the edge of the same vast region. This negligence looms as a factor enabling the horrible Mountain Meadows Massacre and underlies the failure of federal officials to bring the perpetrators to justice.

The Las Vegas LDS mission continued to generate strong ties of friendship between church members and Native Americans in that vicinity. But in other aspects it was a decided failure. The location for the endeavor was ill conceived if agricultural production was a prime consideration—as it should have been if Indian temporal welfare was a major factor. Even the promise, through the missionary presence, of the greater availability of food and clothing—which was a standard assumption for such undertakings—proved to be a rather cruel falsehood, despite Southern Paiutes initially demonstrating their willingness to labor for what they received. Failure to achieve true self-sufficiency in producing food essential for maintenance of the mission, and the increasing tendency of Las Vegas Valley Paiutes to simply take their share of crop harvests, were the key factors in the demise of the enterprise. Poor leadership also looms as a major cause of failure. In a larger sense, however, the entire venture proved abortive because the the church hierarchy was unwilling to support the effort with extra provisions needed. Of course, such support may have been impossible at that time of near famine in Utah.

The Las Vegas mission served temporarily as a haven for travelers approximately midway over the vast desert

expanses between Salt Lake City and southern California. There are no records of goods sold, sick people cared for, or besieged travelers rescued, but it served, as it always had, as a favorite resting spot for weary and often-discouraged pioneers. It could have been an important component of the proposed "cordon"—the occasionally mentioned series of Mormon settlements, each to be situated perhaps a day's journey apart, all the way from Mormondom to the Pacific Coast. But the church hierarchy never elected to make that endeavor a priority.

The early efforts to establish ocean-going ship connections from Great Britain to San Diego also lapsed. If some traffic manager-agent had been assigned to work out the essential arrangements for Mormon converts to travel over the proposed route, success could likely have been ensured. It was not long before American gold seekers would travel from New York City to San Francisco, crossing over the Isthmus of Panama, in some five weeks, and by the mid-1850s a railroad over Panama linked the two ocean segments of that route. But no evidence suggests that Brigham Young and his associates ever encouraged use of such transport once it was in place.

There is abundant basis for concluding church leaders, particularly Young, became disenchanted with their San Bernardino colony, presumed to serve as a haven for disaffected and "worldly" Latter-day Saints. This fear may have emerged as a reason they did not follow through on earlier plans to use the substantial southern California settlement as the foundation for the way station network. It might have enticed even more church members away from the Mormon Zion. Or perhaps the desert experience of many emigrants and the Las Vegas missionaries convinced the church leaders that although certain physical locations were feasible, only truly substantial colonies could survive possible Indian threats in such isolated places. The church leaders were clearly unwilling to devote the required resources and manpower to that cause.

The failure to use the considerable all-season benefits of the Southern Route can be regarded as a major error of omission by LDS leaders. The greatest loss of life and other instances of suffering in the entire annals of western emigration occurred among Latter-day Saint converts from Britain attempting to walk to Zion pushing handcarts over the main Great Plains routes in 1856, caught in deadly blizzards in Wyoming. When Mormon deaths to cholera and other illnesses endemic in the river bottoms of the Great Plains are added, the failure not to more seriously pursue use of the alternative, safer, and more cost-efficient Southern Route to Salt Lake City appears to be negligence of major proportions.

Consideration of conditions and developments along the Southern Route to California greatly amplifies understanding of the events leading to the Mountain Meadows Massacre and of the circumstances its victims and other emigrant companies confronted as they attempted to pass through southern Utah during the fateful autumn of 1857. Among the foremost of these circumstances was the full-fledged alliance with the region's Native Americans that Mormons developed partly with the intention of drawing on these Indians, the "battle axes of the Lord," whenever the necessity arose. This alliance proved an integral component of what has been termed the "culture of violence" in which many survivors of earlier mob activity in Missouri and Illinois anxiously awaited opportunity for revenge to fulfill what they came to regard as a religious obligation to avenge past wrongs through inciting war against unbelieving outsiders, whether the actual parties were guilty of those wrongs or not.

The Mormon Reformation also heightened the religious fervor of the time to fanatic pitch. Preaching throughout Mormondom, particularly in southern Utah, aroused a good number of otherwise reasonable people to perform acts of retribution and punishment, in the name of religious obligation and military necessity, that would otherwise have remained improbable. This arousal was possible partly because of Mormon awareness of past injustice at the hands of vested governmental and military authorities but also consequent anticipation of similar injustice at the hands of invading forces of the United States Army presumably sent to quell the supposed Mormon rebellion and to punish church adherents.

Another component of the explosive situation out of which the Mountain Meadows Massacre erupted was that the members of the Fancher-Baker wagon company hailed from Arkansas, where popular Latter-day Saint leader Parley P. Pratt had recently been killed, presumably with the assent of many citizens. And perhaps more

important, the emigrants may have allowed a reckless group of so-called Missouri wildcats to travel through Utah with them. The reported misdeeds and utterances of these semirenegades tended to arouse the local Mormon citizenry and their leaders against the entire company, to the point of violence.

A final circumstance virtually pronounced a death sentence on at least some adults of the Fancher train and potentially members of other companies. This was an interview President Brigham Young held with Southern Paiute leaders at his headquarters in Salt Lake City on the first day of September 1857. The church leader had recently proclaimed he would no longer restrain Indian hands in their inclination to "use up" passing emigrants, which Young boasted could be accomplished any time he gave them word. Through interpreter Dimick B. Huntington, the head of the LDS church reportedly offered the Paiute chiefs permission to take the cattle of all emigrant companies then passing through southern Utah. When the Indians protested they had been taught not to take what was not theirs, they were erroneously informed that non-Mormon emigrants then in the region might be there partly to assist the United States Army to destroy both Mormons and Native Americans. Everyone understood that the cattle offered could not be taken without bitter fighting. Young later sent word to the Iron County militia officers that the Indians would do as they pleased and it was important to maintain good relations with them. Thus Young had more insight into Paiute motives than the militia, although the wording has often been interpreted to absolve Young of direct implication in the matter.

Yet the militia leaders also played a major role in making the decision. Uncertain of how to deal with the offending intruder-travelers, the militia officers called on Indian agent John D. Lee to enlist Paiute warriors to forcibly detain the emigrants at Mountain Meadows until they learned from church headquarters what Young wanted the militia to do. But before the messenger returned, the two highest local military officials apparently decided to order their soldiers to see that no adults left the area to spread negative reports about the Mormons. Thus Mormon militiamen and Paiute Indians murdered approximately one hundred twenty non-Mormon emigrants.

After this worst mass murder of non–Native Americans in the history of the West—if not the nation—the Mormon participants, shocked by the atrocities, swore each other to secrecy and sought to blame most of the affair on the Indians they had enlisted and initially aroused to assist them. Some Paiutes resented such allegations and pointedly asked who had ended up with most of the loot from the notably prosperous victims. There was, however, no known hint of such disloyalty from the head chief, Tutsegabits. He was ordained an elder in the LDS church.

It is doubtful if any event in Mormon history generated more hostility among other Americans than the Mountain Meadows Massacre. Fanned by semiaccurate newspaper reports, this ill will spread like wildfire throughout California, where church members had formerly been well received and respected for a full decade. According to some Mormon reports, Pacific Coast citizens already posed a threat to their counterparts in Utah because of the emigrants killed at Mountain Meadows, and their associates had earlier threatened to raise volunteer troops in California and lead them back over the southern trail to help the army punish Mormon residents there. Numerous Golden State newspaper columns continued to discuss the possibility of this invasion for several months after the massacre.

In fact, the so-called Mormon rebels received substantial reinforcements from California as the largest church colony outside Salt Lake City, San Bernardino, disbanded. Over two thousand hurried back to Utah to help resist the expected onslaught from the invading U.S. military forces. They brought a huge supply of war material and other useful goods with them for the anticipated conflict. Fortunately, Col. Thomas L. Kane, a friend of President James Buchanan, also traveled over the Southern Route and eventually proved instrumental in obtaining a peaceful accommodation between Mormon leaders and the invading military and newly appointed Utah territorial officials. In the meantime, a contingent of seasoned Southern Route Mormon pioneers and Mormon Indian missionaries performed important semimilitary service guarding the desert approach from southern California, to prevent what some considered a real threat of invasion from that direction.

One of the least-known aspects of Southern Route history is the intervention of Mormon Indian missionaries and others to prevent the several other pioneer companies already in the vicinity from suffering the same fate as the Fancher party. In the first case, involving the Dukes-Turner party, several missionaries apparently risked their lives in efforts to persuade Moapa Paiutes to simply take the livestock not being used to pull wagons instead of killing the company members and taking all their property.

New head of the Southern Indian Mission, Jacob Hamblin, not a participant in the events transpiring near his ranch at Mountain Meadows, played a significant role in restoring peace in the region despite the inclination of some other missionaries and Native Americans to continue the killing and looting. In this he was assisted by church apostle Amasa M. Lyman and Pauvant Indian chief Kanosh, who proved more obedient to Brigham Young's order to protect emigrants than to earlier encouragement to take their cattle. The source documents indicate contradictory policies emanating from church leaders during the period, which continued to render the situation in southern Utah and beyond extremely volatile.

Perhaps because of Brigham Young's emphasis on self-sufficiency, historians of Utah have never fully considered the huge volume of freight that entered that territory from California and the Midwest—consistently for over a dozen years from 1855 until 1869. In a sense, the transcontinental railroad could hardly have ended economic isolation, because that "isolation" never really existed. Extensive wagon freighting operations had functioned throughout much of the previous two decades. Although historians probably cannot establish precisely which road was most heavily used for incoming freight, a massive amount of freight was hauled over the Southern Route from California to Utah during the entire period. For example, in the first three months of 1859 at least 270 wagons, probably not counting trailers, embarked from Los Angeles for Utah. The mercantile and freighting businesses of southern California prospered so mightily from this extensive overland trade that the transfusion of Utah wealth into the California southland economy and the growth stimulated by the large amount of goods demanded contributed significantly to the economic growth of the California southland as it was maturing as a new Anglo-American province. And although it added less to the growth of infant southern Nevada, still the Southern Route was a lifeline to some of the southernmost mining camps of that area as Silver State settlements struggled for permanence.

Over the years of continued American contact with Native Americans along the Southern Route, the never-abundant food supply must have seriously declined. In 1859, Indian agent Jacob Forney reported less game present near the Southern Paiutes than in most Native American hunting grounds—undoubtedly less than there had been in previous years. He described some of the tribe as "destitute" and thus more prone to stealing. Just before that time Caroline Crosby had noted a Las Vegas Paiute chief demanding extra clothing from the Mormons and partly implying that because the Indians then needed to spend more time in the mountains gathering food—a changed pattern of food procuring—the additional clothes were necessary for warmth not required at the more accustomed lower elevations.

An associated situation was the long-standing practice of exacting a toll of stolen animals and other items from passing emigrants and freighters. As reality and widely understood prior practice demanded, many whites learned it was less costly to voluntarily pay "the usual toll" rather than suffer the predictable alternative methods of extracting payment. As Paiute language facility in English improved, payment demands were more fully articulated. Sarah Rousseau in 1864 recorded Tonequint band leaders near the Santa Clara River required remuneration for "using Paiute water and grass." This use fee could easily be understood by most fair-minded Americans, although some obviously hesitated to grant such concessions to Indians. Four years later, seasoned trail traveler Leonard Conger was confronted by a large band of Native Americans at Kingston Springs. The chief spokesman asserted that the surrounding lands, along with the mountain sheep, rabbits, quail, and other native game, belonged to his people, not to "hiko" (white men). He also included the water and grass as possessions the Conger party's cattle had no right to consume without proper payment. The former mail carrier nego-

tiated a settlement of three cattle butchered as the fee for resources used.

The other practice that Southern Route travelers used well was to employ Native Americans to herd their livestock through the night. The originator of the policy, Mormon leader Amasa Lyman, admitted it was the most cost-effective method of getting through the hundred-fifty-mile gauntlet of Indian tribute demands. Many of these arrangements included emigrants retaining a hostage in their camp to ensure good behavior from his fellows. One of those cheerfully held, as noted by Silas Cox in 1863, was Tosho, chief of the Virgin River band of Paiutes. It is doubtful if such accommodations were common on any other emigrant route. It was but a small step from this practice to a formal agreement late in the period of roadway use when Lt. Col. William R. Price entered a written compact with Tosho featuring the same basic practice. According to the treaty concluded 22 November 1867 at Camp Mojave, the Paiute spokesman offered to allow a Paiute prisoner to be held at the army outpost, to ensure the continued good behavior of his tribesmen. The army officer also encouraged white travelers to refrain from unprovoked attacks and to appeal to the military whenever need arose.

Equally significant was the willingness of Tosho and some other Paiute subchiefs, after the soldiers had been withdrawn from the region, to help punish those guilty of wrongdoing toward passing travelers. When the German prospector Fritz was killed between Las Vegas and the Muddy River in 1870, residents of the nearby mining district demanded assistance in bringing the murderers to justice. A local chief, probably Tosho, and his associates complied by delivering a known renegade named "Paiute Jack" over to the summary justice then common in American mining camps. Deaths along the trail never ceased totally, but the fact that there were so few looms as an amazing aspect of the history of the Southern Route. Had the roadway continued in frequent use, it is likely that the relatively excellent relations between the two races would have persisted.

The Southern Route to California is significant beyond any previous recognition as a continuing avenue for late-season emigration to the Pacific Coast. Although the percentage of the total emigration to the West Coast was small—probably no more than twenty thousand total, out of hundreds of thousands—it doubtless saved the lives of a goodly number who might otherwise have risked taking a route more dangerous during questionable times of year. Although documentation of the experience of pioneers over this route is now adequate, travel on this road has never previously been given full historical attention. Now these heroic people who followed the most difficult of roads west may get their due.

Notes

Preface

1. Anthony W. Ivins, "Traveling Over Forgotten Trails: The Old Spanish Trail," *Improvement Era* 26, no. 9 (July 1923): 771. As discussed briefly in chapter 7 herein, many full-time Southern Route freighter wagons traveled all the way to the Missouri River every summer—a segment of the great central road beyond the scope of this study.

2. Ralph P. Bieber, *Southern Trails to California in 1849* (Glendale, Calif.: Arthur H. Clark, 1937); Harlan Hague, *The Road to California: The Search for a South Overland Route, 1540–1848* (Glendale, Calif.: Arthur H. Clark, 1978); Patricia A. Etter, *To California on the Southern Route, 1849: A History and Annotated Bibliography* (Spokane, Wash.: Arthur H. Clark, 1998). All deal with various routes across Mexico, Texas, New Mexico, and Arizona, but except for some discussion by Hague of the Old Spanish Trail, not with the road from the Salt Lake City area to southern California.

3. See [Edward] Leo Lyman and Larry Reese, *The Arduous Road: Salt Lake to Los Angeles, The Most Difficult Wagon Road in American History* (Victorville, Calif.: Lyman Historical Research and Publishing, 2001), vi, for further discussion of the choice of the name for the roadway in question.

4. Dale L[owell] Morgan, "The Significance and Value of the Overland Journal," presented at the Western History Association conference at Santa Fe, New Mexico, in 1961, copy in Dale Lowell Morgan Papers, microfilm reel 55, 257–67, The Bancroft Library, University of California, Berkeley.

5. Ray M. Reeder, "The Mormon Trail: A History of the Salt Lake to Los Angeles Route to 1869," unpublished doctoral dissertation, Brigham Young University, 1966, 102.

6. I concede that until Interstate 15 was completed through the Virgin Narrows of the Arizona Strip, there was a greater total mileage similar to the pioneer route. See studies of the later transportation eras on the same route: Edward Leo Lyman, "From the City of Angels to the City of the Saints: The Struggle to Build a Railroad From Los Angeles to Salt Lake City," *California History* 70, no. 1 (spring 1991): 76–93; Edward Leo Lyman, "The Arrowhead Trails Highway: The Beginnings of Utah's Other Route to the Pacific Coast," *Utah Historical Quarterly* 67, no. 3 (summer 1999): 242–64; Edward Leo Lyman, "The Arrowhead Trails Highway: California's Predecessor to Interstate 15," *Southern California Quarterly* 81, no. 3 (fall 1999): 315–40.

7. Harold Austin Steiner, *The Old Spanish Trail Across the Mojave Desert: A History and Guide* (Las Vegas, Nev.: Haldor, 1996, reprint 1999), does differentiate somewhat between the two eras and variant trails, photographing several two-track ruts. C. Gregory Crampton and Steven K. Madsen, *In Search of the Spanish Trail: Santa Fe to Los Angeles, 1829–1848* (Salt Lake City: Gibbs Smith, 1994), stops short of the Anglo-American period but offers several photos of the trail showing two-track ruts, presumably indicating that in those spots the two roads are the same.

8. As many "rut nuts" well understand, there is a special thrill discovering and retracing pioneer trails. I have experienced this on many occasions in a variety of locales along the route. One of the first I shared with members of Victorville Boy Scout Troop 856 when on a hike in Cajon Pass we first discovered the man-improved grade down from the hogback summit (pictured in chapter 4 herein). Another was the discovery with

Cliff Walker of the distinct two-track wagon track both sides of the summit of a Utah Hill grade. And in late October 1999, in company with Glen Shaw and Neal Johns, discovering and following a five-mile section of distinct but virtually untraveled (for a century and a quarter) road approaching Resting Springs, California, not far from the Nevada border. My coauthor on *Arduous Road*, Larry Reese, and I shared the rediscovery of portions of the road at the Sevier River crossing, Black Mountain passageway south of the Beaver River and Antelope Springs, all in Utah, along with portions of the road near the Virgin Hill, the Muddy River ford and road from there to Las Vegas in Nevada, and the trail approaching Point of Rocks in southern California. He was also involved with myself, Walker, and Emmett Harder in making important discoveries in the north end of California Valley, California. Lavoid Leavitt showed Reese and me much that was almost lost to the present generation of the freight wagon road from the southwestern corner of Utah, through a small portion of northwestern Arizona and into Nevada. See Lyman and Reese, *Arduous Road*, 33, 40–41, 46, 50–51, 55–66, 71–74, 90–91, 94.

9. Such a history is one of my next projects, already commenced through a series of three articles (see note 6) on the Arrowhead Trails Highway recently published in *Utah Historical Quarterly*, *Nevada Historical Society Quarterly* and *Southern California Quarterly*.

Chapter One.
Contemporary Impressions Along the Southern Route

1. The exception to this statement is a hundred-page guidebook that I and photographer Larry Reese published for use with a wagon train reenactment of travel over the route, in the fall of 2001. It includes numerous modern photographs of portions of the actual roadway remnants and is cited in these endnotes. That small guidebook has none of the detail and interpretive comment contained in this book but is an excellent companion volume for careful study of the Southern Route. [Edward] Leo Lyman and Larry Reese, *The Arduous Road: Salt Lake to Los Angeles, The Most Difficult Wagon Road in American History* (Victorville, Calif.: Lyman Historical Research and Publishing, 2001), is available from the authors.

2. Lt. Sylvester Mowry to Col. S. Cooper, 23 July 1855, National Archives, Washington, D.C.; William Birdsall Lorton Journal, 1, 2, 3, 9 October 1849, The Bancroft Library, University of California, Berkeley. Eminent scholar Dale Lowell Morgan combined travel companion Adonijah S. Welch's diary fragments 30 September–5 November 1849 with the most illu-

minating Lorton journal as a "good supplement"; see Welch, 6, 9 October 1849, in Morgan typescript, microfilm pages 1374–1506, Morgan Papers. See also Lyman and Reese, *Arduous Road*, 26–32.

3. Lorton Journal, Welch fragments 9, 10 October 1849; Lyman and Reese, *Arduous Road*, 32–33.

4. William Chandless, *Visit to Salt Lake: Being a Journey Across the Plains and a Residence in the Mormon Settlements* (London: Smith, Elder, 1857; reprint, New York: AMS Press, 1971), 270–72.

5. Jules Remy, *Journey to Great Salt Lake City*, 2 vols. (London: W. Jeffs, 1861), 334; Chandless, *Visit to Salt Lake*, 99, 274–77.

6. Solomon N[unes] Carvalho, *Incidents of Travel and Adventure in the Far West; with Col. Frémont's Last Expedition* (New York: Derby & Jackson, 1857; reprint, Philadelphia: Jewish Society of America, 1954), 269–71; Mark Sibley Severance Journal, 28 September 1872, page 3 of typescript in private manuscript collection, copy in possession of Edward Leo Lyman. See also Lyman and Reese, *Arduous Road*, 34–43.

7. Carvalho, *Incidents of Travel*, 140; Stephen Bonsal, *Edward Fitzgerald Beale: A Pioneer in the Path of Empire, 1822–1903* (New York: Putnam's, 1912), 140.

8. *Deseret News*, 30 May 1855.

9. Carvalho, *Incidents of Travel*, 283; Lyman and Reese, *Arduous Road*, 43–49.

10. Washington Peck Diary, 14 November 1850, Oregon California Trails Association Collection, Mattes Library, National Frontier Trails Center, Independence, Missouri.

11. Addison Pratt Diary, in *Journals of Forty-niners: Salt Lake to Los Angeles*, ed. LeRoy R. Hafen and Ann W. Hafen (Glendale, Calif.: Arthur H. Clark, 1954), 81–84; "Journal of Thomas Morris," 10–12 December 1849, Utah State Historical Society, Salt Lake City; Lyman and Reese, *Arduous Road*, 49–55.

12. Vincent Hoover Diary, 26 October–4 November 1849, The Huntington Library, San Marino, California; Addison Pratt Diary, in Hafen and Hafen, *Journals of Forty-niners*, 81–87; Lyman and Reese, *Arduous Road*, 55–58.

13. Peck Diary, 15, 16 November 1850; Thomas Flint, "Diary of Dr. Thomas Flint: California to Maine and Return, 1850–1855," ed. Walter Westergaard, *Annual Publications, Historical Society of Southern California* (1923), 115; Bonsal, *Edward Fitzgerald Beale*, 155–57; Lyman and Reese, *Arduous Road*, 59–65.

14. Carvalho, *Incidents of Travel*, 295–96; Lyman and Reese, *Arduous Road*, 66–68.

15. Addison Pratt Diary in Hafen and Hafen, *Journals of Forty-niners*, 91–92; Remy, *Journey to Great Salt Lake City*, vol. 1, 423.

16. Chandless, *Visit to Salt Lake*, 295.

17. Peck Diary, 28 November 1850; Charles C. Rich Diary, in Hafen and Hafen, *Journals of Forty-niners*, 190; Amasa Mason Lyman Journal, 30 May 1851, Historical Department and Archives, Church of Jesus Christ of Latter-day Saints, Salt Lake City, Utah [hereafter abbreviated as HDA]—Amasa Lyman is the great-great-grandfather of Edward Leo Lyman; Lyman and Reese, *Arduous Road*, 68–70.

18. William Farrer Diary, in *Journals of Forty-niners: Salt Lake to Los Angeles*, ed. LeRoy R. Hafen and Ann W. Hafen (Glendale, Calif.: Arthur H. Clark, 1954), 214; Lyman and Reese, *Arduous Road*, 71–75.

19. Caroline Barnes Crosby Journal, 14–28 January 1858, Utah State Historical Society, Salt Lake City.

20. Addison Pratt Diary, in Hafen and Hafen, *Journals of Forty-niners*, 95; Lynn R. Bailey, "Lt. Sylvester Mowry's Report on His March in 1855 From Salt Lake City to Fort Tejon," *Arizona and the West* 7, no. 4 (winter 1965): 340–41; Lieutenant Sylvester Mowry to Colonel S. Cooper, 23 July 1855, copy in Utah Writers' Project Papers, Utah State Historical Society, Salt Lake City, Utah; original in National Archives, Washington, D.C.

21. Sarah Pratt Journal, in Kenneth L. Holmes, ed. and comp., *Covered Wagon Women*, vol. 4 (Glendale, Calif.: Arthur H. Clark, 1985), 201; Crosby Journal, 20 January 1858; Lorton Journal, 16 December 1849; Hoover Diary, 27 November 1849; Lyman and Reese, *Arduous Road*, 76–79.

22. David W. Cheesman, "By Ox Team From Salt Lake to Los Angeles, 1850: A Memoir by David W. Cheesman," ed. Mary E. Foy, *Historical Society of Southern California* 14 (1930): 296; "Mormon Way-Bill," in Hafen and Hafen, *Journals of Forty-niners*, 322; Addison Pratt Diary, in Hafen and Hafen, *Journals of Forty-niners*, 96; Lyman and Reese, *Arduous Road*, 80–82.

23. "Map of a Reconnaissance of the Snow Mountain (N.W. of Camp Cady, California) made by 1st Lt. B. F. Davis, 1st Dragoons U.S.A.," in Dennis G. Casebier, *Carleton's Pah-Ute Campaign* (Norco, Calif.: Privately printed, 1972).

24. Chandless, *Visit to Salt Lake*, 296; Remy, *Journey to Great Salt Lake City*, vol. 1, 431–32; Carvalho, *Incidents of Travel*, 298; William Clark, "A Trip Across the Plains in 1857," *The Iowa Journal of History and Politics* 20, no. 2 (April 1922): 220–22.

25. Lieutenant Sylvester Mowry to Colonel S. Cooper, 23 July 1855; Charles C[olson] Rich Journal, 31 May 1855, HDA.

26. Parley P. Pratt, *Autobiography* (Salt Lake City: Deseret Book Company, 1938; paper, 1976), 379; Lyman and Reese, *Arduous Road*, 82–87.

27. Carvalho, *Incidents of Travel*, 302–3; Lorton Journal, 27 December 1849. Caroline Barnes Crosby left a letter for her sis-

ter Louisa Barnes Pratt at Bitter Springs; see Crosby Journal, 17 January 1858. One feature of this alternate road is the recently rediscovered grave of an emigrant mother buried along the way in the 1870s.

28. Hoover Diary, 1 December 1849; Peck Diary, 4, 5, 12, 14 December 1850. Longtime desert explorer Emmett Harder at the end of 1999 discovered old fireplaces probably used as beacon fires, which were known to have assisted travelers struggling up Impassable Pass and Spanish Canyon from both directions.

29. James S. Brown Account, in Hafen and Hafen, *Journals of Forty-niners*, 125–26.

30. Peck Diary, 4, 5, 12, 14 December 1850; James S. Brown Account, in Hafen and Hafen, *Journals of Forty-niners*, 126–27; Parley P. Pratt, *Autobiography*, 380; Lyman and Reese, *Arduous Road*, 87–89.

31. Bonsal, *Edward Fitzgerald Beale*, 162.

32. Addison Pratt Diary, in Hafen and Hafen, *Journals of Forty-niners*, 102–3.

33. Carvalho, *Incidents of Travel*, 304–5.

34. Bonsal, *Edward Fitzgerald Beale*, 164. The Mormons probably took advantage of the initiative of W. T. B. Sanford, who apparently made the necessary grade excavations in the west Cajon in 1850. See also Lyman and Reese, *Arduous Road*, 90–93.

35. Hoover Diary, 15, 16, 18, 19 December 1849.

36. Addison Pratt Diary, in Hafen and Hafen, *Journals of Forty-niners*, 106–7.

37. Sarah Pratt Journal, 5–6 November 1853, in Holmes, *Covered Wagon Women*, vol. 4, 203.

38. Cheesman, "By Ox Team," 301.

39. Carvalho, *Incidents of Travel*, 306; Lyman and Reese, *Arduous Road*, 93–95.

40. Cheesman, "By Ox Team," 301–2.

41. Lorton Journal, 16 January 1850; Lyman and Reese, *Arduous Road*, 95–97.

42. Hoover Diary, 1–31 January 1850; Lorton Journal, 16 January 1850.

Chapter Two.
The Old Spanish Trail—
Highway of Diversity

1. David J. Weber, "Introduction," in LeRoy R. Hafen and Ann W. Hafen, *Old Spanish Trail: Santa Fe to Los Angeles, With Extracts From Contemporary Records and Including Diaries of Antonio Armijo and Orville Pratt* (Glendale, Calif.: Arthur H. Clark, 1954; reprint, Lincoln: University of Nebraska Press, 1993), 11–17, 79.

Ann Woodbury Hafen, whose husband was LeRoy Hafen, assisted with final proofreading and manuscript preparation, but all references to scholarly work are to LeRoy Hafen alone.

2. Clifford J. Walker, *Back Door to California: The Story of the Mojave River Trail* (Barstow, Calif.: Mojave River Valley Museum Association, 1986), ix–x.

3. Herbert Eugene Bolton, ed., *Font's Complete Diary: A Chronicle of the Founding of San Francisco* (Berkeley: University of California Press, 1933), 118, 121. Font displayed less than admiration in describing Garcés as well suited for his lifework, saying he was like an Indian himself, "phlegmatic in everything." Font said his fellow friar sat with the Indians around the fire, with his legs crossed, musing two or three hours or more, "oblivious to everything else, talking with them with much serenity and deliberation." The describing diarist also mentioned that "although the foods of the Indians are as nasty and dirty as those outlandish people themselves, the father eats them with great gusto and says that they are good for the stomach and very fine." Padre Font concluded that God had created Padre Garcés "solely for the purpose of seeking out these unhappy, ignorant, and rustic people."

4. Joseph Sanchez, *Explorers, Traders, and Slavers: Forging the Old Spanish Trail, 1678–1850* (Salt Lake City: University of Utah Press, 1997), 45–48.

5. Sanchez, *Explorers, Traders and Slavers*, 47. Desert Serranos had *kikas*, or weak chiefs, for nominal leaders of individual rancherias or villages. Acorns were a staple of the diet of most California Indians.

6. Padre Francisco Garcés Diary, trans. Bob Black, in Walker, *Back Door to California*, 249–59; Edward Leo Lyman, "Outmaneuvering the Octopus: Atchison, Topeka and Santa Fe," *California History* 67 (June 1988): 94–100; Edward Leo Lyman, "The Arrowhead Trails Highway: California's Predecessor to Interstate 15," *Southern California Quarterly* 81, no. 3 (fall 1999): 315–40.

7. Walker, *Back Door to California*, 77–80; Sanchez, *Explorers, Traders and Slavers*, 46–52.

8. Herbert E. Bolton, *Pageant in the Wilderness: The Story of the Escalante Expedition to the Interior Basin, 1776* (Salt Lake City: Utah State Historical Society, 1951): 185–205. Ted J. Warner, ed., *The Dominguez Escalante Expedition to the Interior Basin, 1776* (Provo, Utah: Brigham Young University Press, 1976; reprint, Salt Lake City: University of Utah Press, 1995), 74–101.

9. Sanchez, *Explorers, Traders, and Slavers*, 51, 57–58, 63, 71, 74.

10. Dale L[owell] Morgan, *Jedediah Smith and the Opening of the West* (Indianapolis: Bobbs-Merrill, 1953; paper, Lincoln: University of Nebraska Press, 1964), 47–255.

11. George R. Brooks, *The Southwest Expedition of Jedediah S. Smith: His Personal Account of the Journey to California, 1826–1827* (Glendale, Calif.: Arthur H. Clark, 1977; paper, Lincoln: University of Nebraska Press, 1989), 64–77.

12. Hafen and Hafen, *Old Spanish Trail*, 119; Harold Austin Steiner, *The Old Spanish Trail Across the Mojave Desert: A History and Guide* (Las Vegas: Haldor, 1996; reprint, 1999); C. Gregory Crampton and Steven K. Madsen, *In Search of the Spanish Trail: Santa Fe to Los Angeles, 1829–1848* (Salt Lake City: Gibbs Smith, 1994). The former of these two is clearly the more detailed and accurate on the western segment of the route.

13. Morgan, *Jedediah Smith*, 210–13.

14. Richard Batson, *James Pattie's West: The Dream and the Reality* (Norman: University of Oklahoma Press, 1984), 175–77.

15. Reuben Gold Thwaites, *Early Western Travels, 1746–1846: A Series of Annotated Reprints of Some of the Best and Rarest Contemporary Volumes of Travel, Descriptive of the Aborigines and Social and Economic Conditions in the Middle and Far West During the Period of Early American Settlement*, vol. 28 (Cleveland: Arthur H. Clark, 1905), 133–35; Hafen and Hafen, *Old Spanish Trail*, 122–25.

16. Maurice S. Sullivan, *The Travels of Jedediah Smith: A Documentary Outline, Including the Journal of the Great Pathfinder* (Santa Ana, Calif.: Fine Arts Press, 1934), 167, note 54, tells of a company of about one hundred reported trapping in the region. See also Hafen and Hafen, *Old Spanish Trail*, 120–22.

17. Sullivan, *Travels of Jedediah Smith*, 31; Morgan, *Jedediah Smith*, 338.

18. Morgan, *Jedediah Smith*, 238–69, 329–30.

19. Hafen and Hafen, *Old Spanish Trail*, 138–39; Walker, *Back Door to California*, 104.

20. Hafen and Hafen, *Old Spanish Trail*, 135–36. As mentioned later herein, Smith returned to the Virgin River area in 1854 to search for gold he apparently discovered on this trip.

21. Sanchez, *Explorers, Traders, and Slavers*, 104.

22. Antonio Armijo Diary, in Hafen and Hafen, *Old Spanish Trail*, 156–70; Elizabeth von Till Warren, "Armijo's Trace Revisited: A New Interpretation of the Impact of the Antonio Armijo Route of 1829–1830," unpublished master's thesis, University of Nevada, Las Vegas, 1974, 31–34, argues persuasively for the Duck Creek route, then asserts the expedition traveled farther south and east than most people, including the Hafens, have assumed. Because most later pack mule trains did go by way of Las Vegas Springs, Cottonwood Springs, and Mountain Springs, it hardly matters exactly which way Armijo went.

23. Walker, *Back Door to California*, 107–8.

24. Iris Higbie Wilson, *William Wolfskill* (Glendale, Calif.: Arthur H. Clark, 1965), 59–67.

25. Wilson, *William Wolfskill*, 72–80, including citation of Warner, "Historical Sketch of Los Angeles County," 53.

26. Hafen and Hafen, *Old Spanish Trail*, 172–73, including George F. Ruxton, *Ruxton of the Rockies* (Norman: University of Oklahoma Press, 1950), 172–73.

27. Hafen and Hafen, *Old Spanish Trail*, 179.

28. Walker, *Back Door to California*, 123.

29. Hafen and Hafen, *Old Spanish Trail*, 180–81.

30. Hafen and Hafen, *Old Spanish Trail*, 236–40.

31. Gustive O. Larson, "Wakara, Ute Chief," in *The Mountain Men and the Fur Trade of the Far West*, vol. 2, ed. LeRoy R. Hafen and Ann W. Hafen (Glendale, Calif.: Arthur H. Clark, 1965), 339–44.

32. Frederic E. Voelker, "William Sherley (Old Bill) Williams," Hafen and Hafen, *Mountain Men*, vol. 8 (Glendale, Calif.: Arthur H. Clark, 1971), 381–82; Harvey L. Carter, "Calvin Jones," in Hafen and Hafen, *Mountain Men*, vol. 6, 207–8.

33. George William Beattie and Helen Pruitt Beattie, *Heritage of the Valley: San Bernardino's First Century* (Oakland, Calif.: Biobooks, 1951), 141–43.

34. George Douglas Brewerton, *Overland with Kit Carson: A Narrative of the Old Spanish Trail in '48* (New York: Coward-McCann, 1930), 70–77; Hafen and Hafen, *Old Spanish Trail*, including Sage quote, 239–42; [Rufus B. Sage], *Scenes in the Rocky Mountains* (Philadelphia: Carey and Hart, 1846), 51.

35. Walker, *Back Door to California*, 129.

36. Hafen and Hafen, *Old Spanish Trail*, 246.

37. Beattie and Beattie, *Heritage of a Valley*, 58.

38. Leonard B. Waitman, "The Watch-dogs of San Bernardino Valley: Chief Juan Antonio and Lorenzo Trujillo," *San Bernardino Museum Quarterly* (winter 1991): 1–26. See also Joyce Carter Vicery, *Defending Eden: New Mexican Pioneers in Southern California, 1830–1890* (Riverside: University of California at Riverside and the Riverside Museum Press, 1977), 9–66.

39. Donald E. Rowland, *John Rowland and William Workman: Southern California Pioneers of 1841* (Spokane, Wash.: Arthur H. Clark, 1999), 13–34.

40. Hafen and Hafen, *Old Spanish Trail*, 202–8, 216.

41. L[ynn] R. Bailey, *Indian Slave Trade in the Southwest* (Los Angeles: Westernlore Press, 1973), 145–47.

42. Walker, *Back Door to California*, 118–19; Sondra Jones, "'Redeeming the Indian': The Enslavement of Indian Children in New Mexico and Utah," *Utah Historical Quarterly* 67 (summer 1999): 220–41.

43. Donald Jackson and Mary Lee Spence, *The Expeditions of John Charles Frémont I* (Urbana: University of Illinois Press, 1970), 675–76.

44. Walker, *Back Door to California*, 134–35.

45. Allan Nevins, *Frémont: Pathmarker of the West* (New York: Appleton-Century, 1939), 182.

46. Solomon N[unes] Carvalho, *Incidents of Travel and Adventure in the Far West; With Col. Frémont's Last Expedition* (New York: Derby & Jackson, 1857; reprint, Philadelphia: Jewish Society of America, 1954), 284.

47. Stephen Bonsal, *Edward Fitzgerald Beale: A Pioneer in the Path of Empire, 1822–1903* (New York: Putnam's, 1912), 150–51, cites Gwin Harris Heap, the chronicler of Beale's expedition, noting in regard to the slave trade that "one of our men, Jose Gallengo, who was an old hand at this species of man-hunting, related to us, with evident gusto, numerous anecdotes on this subject; and as we approached the [Paiute] village [on the Santa Clara] he rode up to Lieut. Beale, and eagerly proposed to him that we should 'charge on it like h-l, kill the mans and maybe catch some of the little boys and gals.'"

48. Winona Holmes et al., Inter-Tribal Council of Nevada, *Nuwuvi: A Southern Paiute History* (Salt Lake City: Inter-Tribal Council of Nevada, 1976), 5–15; Martha C. Knack, *Boundaries Between: The Southern Paiutes, 1775–1995* (Lincoln, Nebraska: University of Nebraska Press, 2001), 30–94.

49. Joan S. Schneider, Elizabeth J. Lawlor, and Deborah L. Dozier, "Roasting Pits and Agave in the Mojave Desert: Archaeological, Ethnobotanical, and Ethnographic Data," *San Bernardino County Museum Quarterly* 43, nos. 1 and 2 (winter and spring 1996): 29–33.

50. Holmes, *Nuwuvi*, 5–15.

51. George Q. Cannon Narrative, in Hafen and Hafen, *Journals of Forty-niners*, 240.

52. William Chandless, *Visit to Salt Lake: Being a Journey Across the Plains and a Residence in the Mormon Settlements* (London: Smith, Elder, 1857), 291; William Duncan Strong, *Aboriginal Society in Southern California*, in *University of California Publications in American Archaeology and Ethnology*, vol. 26, A. L. Kroeber and R. H. Lowie, eds. (Berkeley: University of California Press, 1929), 5–40.

53. Holmes, *Nuwuvi*, 11–20; John L. Ginn, "Mormon and Indian Wars: The Mountain Meadows Massacre and Other Tragedies and Transactions Incident to the Mormon Rebellion of 1857, Together With the Personal Recollections of a Civilian Who Witnessed Many of the Thrilling Scenes Described," manuscript copy, Historical Department, Church of Jesus Christ of Latter-day Saints, Salt Lake City, Utah, 52. Ginn copy also in Dale Lowell Morgan Papers, The Bancroft Library, Berkeley, California.

54. Holmes, *Nuwuvi*, 11.

55. Vincent A. Hoover Diary, 22, 23 October 1849, The Huntington Library, San Marino, California; Thomas S. Wylly, "Westward Ho—in 1849: Memoirs of Captain Thomas S. Wylly," The Bancroft Library, University of California, Berkeley, 55–81; John Charles Frémont, *Narratives of Exploration and*

Adventure, ed. Allan Nevins (New York: Longman's, Green, 1956), 399; Holmes, *Nuwuvi,* 41.

56. The best example of this is given in chapter 6, "Conflict With the Federal Government—and Tragedy," and footnote 80 in chapter 6.

57. Patricia Nelson Limerick, *The Legacy of Conquest: The Unbroken Past of the American West* (New York: Norton, 1987), 180–81, 190–92; Elliott West, "A Longer, Grimmer, But More Interesting Story," in *Trails: Toward a New Western History,* ed. Patricia Nelson Limerick, Clyde A. Milner II, and Charles E. Rankin (Lawrence: University Press of Kansas, 1991), 108–10.

58. John D. Unruh Jr., *The Plains Across: The Overland Emigrants and the Trans-Mississippi West, 1840–60* (Urbana: University of Illinois Press, 1979; paper, 1982), 127–29, 132, 139, 142–43; J[ames] S. Holliday, *The World Rushed In: The California Gold Rush Experience* (New York: Simon & Schuster, 1981), 241–42, 278.

59. Lee Reay, *Lambs in the Meadow* (Provo, Utah: Meadow Lane Publications, 1979), 46–48. Addison Pratt Diary, in Hafen and Hafen, *Journals of Forty-niners,* 89.

60. David W. Cheesman, "By Ox Team From Salt Lake to Los Angeles, 1850: A Memoir by David W. Cheesman," ed. Mary E. Foy, *Historical Society of Southern California* 14 (1930): 289.

61. Charles Kelly and Maurice L. Howe, *Miles Goodyear* (Salt Lake City: Western Printing, 1937), 55–56, 60, 89–90.

62. Brewerton, *Overland With Kit Carson,* 56–60.

63. Brewerton, *Overland With Kit Carson,* 64–69.

64. Brewerton, *Overland With Kit Carson,* 97–101.

65. "The Journal of Orville C. Pratt," published in Hafen and Hafen, *Old Spanish Trail,* 341–53; Choteau's Log, in Hafen and Hafen, *Old Spanish Trail,* 365–66.

66. "Journal of Orville C. Pratt," in Hafen and Hafen, *Old Spanish Trail,* 356–58.

67. *Journal of the Senate of the State of California, 1850,* 8, 10 January 1850, 76, 84; *Journal of the Senate of the State of California,* 12 January 1942, Senate Resolution no. 24, 117, remarks of Sen. Ralph E. Swing in support of resolution concerning Isaac Williams; Beattie and Beattie, *Heritage of the Valley,* 131–33; Neal Harlow, *California Conquered: The Annexation of a Mexican Province, 1846–1850* (Berkeley: University of California Press, 1982), 164–65; see also other instances of Williams's generosity at end of present chapter and in the following two.

68. Edward Leo Lyman, "Larger Than Texas: Proposals to Combine California and Mormon Deseret as One State," California History 80 (spring 2001): 19–25; Effie Mona Mack, *Nevada, a History of the State From the Earliest Times Through the Civil War* (Glendale, Calif.: Arthur H. Clark, 1936), 194, asserted that a few Mormon Battalion members traveled to the Salt Lake Valley by the Southern Route in 1847, something no one else has stated.

69. Milton Reed Hunter, "Brigham Young the Colonizer," unpublished doctoral dissertation, University of California, Berkeley, 1937, 38.

70. Kelly and Howe, *Miles Goodyear,* 55–56, 60, 89–90.

71. Henry G. Boyle Diary, 7 March 1848, Harold B. Lee Library, Brigham Young University, Provo, Utah; Hafen and Hafen, *Old Spanish Trail,* 198–99, cite several documents indicating an emigrant wagon from New Mexico to southern California in 1837.

72. Thomas Morris ("Journal of Thomas Morris," typescript, Utah State Historical Society, Salt Lake City, Utah, entry March 1850), when traveling with the Pomeroy freight wagon train discussed later, stated, "[W]e passed over the mountain a little right of this [Coyote–Crowder Creek canyon] in 1847" (meaning 1848). He recalled his previous journey through Cajon Pass with the Boyle-Davis group had been "comfortable," which the creek bed road of the forty-niners was not. Morris questioned the wisdom of anyone following the creek bed, saying, "[T]his exceeds all the road for taking wagons over the rocks."

73. Boyle Diary, 21 March, 5 June 1848; Daniel Tyler, *A Concise History of the Mormon Battalion in the Mexican War, 1846–1847* (Glorieta, N.M.: Printed privately; reprint, 1969), 331, states, "On the 14th of March, 1848, the company's time of enlistment having overrun nearly two months, it was disbanded at San Diego. These veterans drew their pay the day following and, on the 21st, a company of twenty-five men, with H. G. Boyle as Captain (Captain Daniel C. Davis having declined a 'third term'), started for Salt Lake Valley." William Birdsall Lorton Journal, 20 August 1849, The Bancroft Library, University of California, Berkeley.

74. John Riser, "Mormon Battalion Memoir," two pages typed obtained by Lyman from Will Bagley. A more brief one-paragraph "Biography," 1887, is in The Bancroft Library, University of California, Berkeley. See also Norma B. Ricketts, *The Mormon Battalion: U.S. Army of the West, 1846–1848* (Logan: Utah State University Press, 1996), 265, 346.

75. Brewerton, *Overland With Kit Carson,* 58–59.

Chapter Three.
The Anglo-American Road in 1849

1. Because the northern overland routes carried such vastly greater numbers, this argument implies documentation proportionate to total numbers over each trail.

2. W. C. Randolph, assigned as one of two rear guards to bring along spent livestock, noted encounters with numerous Native Americans. He asserted he befriended a Paiute chief, Scott, to whom he confided that the travelers wanted no trouble with Indians. He stated they "appointed a messenger to go one day before [their party] to notify all the Indians along the route that we were friendly, and would treat with them" (W. C. Randolph, "Statement," in *Supplement to the Journals of Forty-niners: Salt Lake to Los Angeles,* ed. LeRoy R. Hafen and Ann W. Hafen [Glendale, Calif.: Arthur H. Clark, 1961], 21). H. S. Brown, later a San Francisco judge, recalled strict orders "not to interfere with [Indian] crops to the extent of an ear of corn" as they passed through the Paiute country. He also claimed he composed a treaty with the Southern Paiutes, who sent runners ahead to inform other related bands. He attested that as a result of these efforts "they never molested us in any way, nor attempted to steal from us so much as a knife or a cup" (H. S. Brown, "Account," in *The Far West and Rockies: General Analytical Index to the Fifteen Volume Series and Supplement to the Journals of Forty-niners, Salt Lake to Los Angeles,* vol. 15, ed. LeRoy R. Hafen and Ann W. Hafen (Glendale, Calif.: Arthur H. Clark, 1961), 24–26.

3. "Charles V. Stuart's Trip," in Hafen and Hafen, *Supplement to the Journals of Forty-niners,* 17–19; Randolph, "Statement," in Hafen and Hafen, *Supplement to the Journals of Forty-niners,* 21; H. S. Brown, "Account," in Hafen and Hafen, *Supplement to the Journals of Forty-niners,* 24–26.

4. John Brown Jr. and James Boyd, *History of San Bernardino and Riverside Counties,* vol. 2 (Chicago: Lewis, 1922), 676; Vincent A. Hoover Diary, 27 September 1849, The Huntington Library, San Marino, California; William Birdsall Lorton Journal, in Dale Lowell Morgan Papers, The Bancroft Library, University of California, Berkeley, California, 2 September 1849, 189.

5. Joseph P. Hamelin Jr. Diary, in Hafen and Hafen, *Supplement to the Journals of Forty-niners,* 79; G. C. Pearson Recollections, in Hafen and Hafen, *Supplement to the Journals of Forty-niners,* 46, 48–49.

6. Dale Lowell Morgan Papers, microfilm pages 1130–31, The Bancroft Library, University of California, Berkeley; Addison Pratt Diary, in Hafen and Hafen, *Journals of Forty-niners,* 89, for Pratt statement on Indian barricade.

7. Hoover Diary, 17, 18 October 1849.

8. As stated in the preface, prominent historian Dale Lowell Morgan displayed a strong interest in the Hoover and several related diaries and was editing the former with Eleanor Towles Harris for publication through the California Historical Society. He was similarly preparing the Lorton Journal for publication by Alfred A. Knopf. Unfortunately, his health deteriorated just at that time, and so far as can be determined the project was never carried out. There are two versions of the Hoover Diary at The Huntington Library, deposited there by donor Guy C. Earl in 1964. One is a rougher, pencil version and the other, in the same type of small leather pocket diary, is in pen and is far more legible. Morgan concluded, and I concur, that the second version was also made while still on the journey, based on the added minute details not in the original that would probably have been forgotten if it had been copied at any later time. See Dale Lowell Morgan to Eleanor T. Harris, 24 January 1969, Dale Lowell Morgan Papers, The Bancroft Library, University of California, Berkeley. See also Mr. Shearer's Journal, in *Supplement to the Journals of Forty-niners,* 31–41; Thomas S. Wylly, "Westward Ho—in 1849: Memoirs of Captain Thomas S. Wylly," The Bancroft Library, University of California, Berkeley, 55–81.

9. Hoover Diary, 26, 27 September 1849. This study uses Hoover's more polished second version throughout, unless otherwise noted; Hafen and Hafen, Peter Derr Experiences, *Journals of Forty-niners,* 51.

10. Hoover Diary, 1, 3, 12, 14, 18, 21 October 1849.

11. The Hoover Diary, 16 December 1849, makes it clear LeRoy Hafen was mistaken in assuming the elder Gruwells followed the Southern Route. See also John D. Unruh Jr., *The Plains Across: The Overland Emigrations and the Trans-Mississippi West, 1840–60* (Urbana: University of Illinois Press, 1979; paper, 1982), 282; Unruh asserts that "Mormon threats against Missouri and Illinois 'mobocrats' [passing as emigrants] were legion." Unruh also said, "Mormons went out of their way to locate overlanders who had participated in the turbulent struggles of the 1830's and 1840's."

12. Hoover Diary (original), ed. Dale Lowell Morgan, copy in Dale Lowell Morgan Papers, The Bancroft Library, University of California, Berkeley, 5, 20 October 1849. Another reason for Hoover's reticence on personal matters is that apparently his wife left him, taking their two children, while his pioneer company was still on the Mississippi River (see Hoover Diary, 28 April 1849).

13. Hoover Diary, 9, 12, 14, 16 October 1849; see original Morgan edition for first two days.

14. Hoover Diary, 22, 23 October 1849; J. D. Gruwell has a differing account of killing the Indian. See J. D. Gruwell's account in Hafen and Hafen, *Journals of Forty-niners,* 54.

15. Wylly, "Memoirs," 58. The diarist added that while the draft animals were grazing near camp "let one get for only a moment out of rifle range and he journied no farther. He would be filled with Digger [the most derogatory term designating Paiutes] arrows. That was all they wanted; you had to leave him,

and they ate him. They had no other use for any animal." Actually, local Paiutes would have horses for mounts within a generation.

16. Hoover Diary, 22, 23, 24 October 1849.

17. Hoover Diary, 27, 28, 29 October 1849; Addison Pratt Diary, in Hafen and Hafen, *Journals of Forty-niners*, 82–84.

18. Morgan, "Notes on the Journey, Salt Lake to Los Angeles," 2–3, Dale Lowell Morgan Papers (microfilm pages 838–41); Shearer Journal, 14 October 1849, notes that even his rear contingent of the Independent Company split in two at the Beaver Valley. See Hafen and Hafen, *Supplement to Journals*, 33–34. Wylly, "Memoirs," 54, also noted selection of a wagon captain named Hooker. Dale Lowell Morgan, ed., *The Overland Diary of James Avery Pritchard: From Kentucky to California in 1849* (Denver: Old West Publishing, 1959), 14–17, sought to study "the Gold Rush as an aggregate of human experience, distilled from the absolutely contemporary record." For me, the main contribution of his work was that it for the first time brought the overland diaries relating to the main California trail "under scholarly discipline. With a chronologically arranged chart and an alphabetically arranged list of diaries, each complementing the other, every known diary . . . during the first year of the Gold Rush has been reported." This included a table of 100 forty-niner diarists passing way points along the California Trail. He probably had something like that in mind for his ultimate work on the Southern Route.

19. Hoover Diary, 29, 30 October, 3, 4 November 1849.

20. Hoover Diary, 5 November 1849; Addison Pratt Diary, in Hafen and Hafen, *Journals of Forty-niners*, 87. Addison Pratt was falsely informed that the Hall wagon had been broken into pieces after a rush down the slope at "lightning speed." See also [Edward] Leo Lyman and Larry Reese, *The Arduous Road: Salt Lake to Los Angeles, The Most Difficult Wagon Road in American History* (Victorville, Calif.: Lyman Historical Research and Publishing, 2001), 52–59.

21. Hoover Diary, 9, 10, 11 November 1849.

22. Hoover Diary, 14, 15, 20, 21, 22, 23 November 1849; Lyman and Reese, *Arduous Road*, 70–75.

23. Hoover Diary, 24, 25 November 1849. This condition of the meat would exist when insufficient red blood cells were in the circulatory system, caused by a buildup of lactic acid in the bloodstream prohibiting adequate oxygen supply.

24. Lewis Granger, "Letter," in Hafen and Hafen, *Supplement to Journals of Forty-niners*, 62. These were certainly abnormal animal conditions, doubtless brought about by near starvation.

25. Hoover Diary, 27, 28, 29 November 1849; Lyman and Reese, *Arduous Road*, 76–81.

26. Wylly, "Memoirs," 62.

27. Lorton Journal, 26 November 1849; Addison Pratt Diary, in Hafen and Hafen, *Journals of Forty-niners*, 91, 94; Hoover Diary, 30 November 1849; Hamelin Journal, in Hafen and Hafen, *Supplement to the Journals of Forty-niners*, 88.

28. Wylly, "Memoirs," 62.

29. Hoover Diary, 1, 2, 3, 4 December 1849; Addison Pratt Diary, in Hafen and Hafen, *Journals of Forty-niners*, 99.

30. Hoover Diary, 3 December 1849. There could be suspicion the diarist added these observations in his later rewrite of the entries, but they are in the original diary books as well.

31. Hoover Diary, 7, 9 December 1849; Charles C. Rich Diary in Hafen and Hafen, *Journals of Forty-niners*, 191; Addison Pratt Diary, in Hafen and Hafen, *Journals of Forty-niners*, 101–5.

32. Hoover Diary, 10, 12, 16 December 1849.

33. Hoover Diary, 10, 12 December 1849; Addison Pratt Diary, in Hafen and Hafen, *Journals of Forty-niners*, 103–5.

33. Arthur Shearer Journal, in Hafen and Hafen, *Supplement to the Journals of Forty-niners*, 33, 35–37. Benjamin I. Hayes, later district judge in southern California, copied Shearer's diary into his notes while they were both camped at Isaac Williams's Rancho del Chino early in 1850.

34. Wylly, "Memoirs," 64.

35. Wylly, "Memoirs," 79–81.

36. Shearer Journal, in Hafen and Hafen, *Supplement to the Journals of Forty-niners*, 38–39; Wylly, "Memoirs," 52.

37. Shearer Journal, in Hafen and Hafen, *Supplement to the Journals of Forty-niners*, 39–40.

38. Hoover Diary, 14–19 December 1849.

39. Hoover Diary, 14, 15, 16 December 1849; Addison Pratt Diary, in Hafen and Hafen, *Journals of Forty-niners*, 106–7; Lyman and Reese, *Arduous Road*, 93–94.

40. Hoover Diary, 19, 21 December 1849; Sidney P. Waite Sketch, in Hafen and Hafen, *Journals of Forty-niners*, 129.

41. Hoover Diary, 20–23 December 1849.

42. Hoover Diary, 19, 21, 23 December 1849; Addison Pratt Diary, in Hafen and Hafen, *Journals of Forty-niners*, 56, 107–8. It is entirely likely that the Mormon party of Addison Pratt exchanged knowledge of the Amargosa Springs gold mine for provisions. Williams was definitely involved in the early phase of the mine development.

43. George William Beattie and Helen Pruitt Beattie, *Heritage of the Valley: San Bernardino's First Century* (Oakland, Calif.: Biobooks, 1951), 129, 131–33; Thomas Kealy Letter, in Hafen and Hafen, *Supplement to the Journals of Forty-niners*, 107.

44. See note 66 of this chapter for Death Valley accounts.

45. Lorton Journal, 21, 22 August, 2, 11 October 1849, The Bancroft Library, University of California, Berkeley.

46. Dale Lowell Morgan notes explain that the Adonijah Welch record "is preserved only as a fragment," but Morgan incorporated the remaining comments into his typescript of William Lorton's excellent daily journal account of the same company trip. Dale Lowell Morgan Papers, The Bancroft Library, University of California at Berkeley; Welch Journal, 30 September 1849, The Bancroft Library; John Phillip Reid, *The Law and the Elephant: Property and Social Behavior on the Overland Trail* (San Marino, Calif.: The Huntington Library, 1980; paper, 1997), 140–41, 168, 180, 205.

47. William Lewis Manley, *Death Valley in '49: An Important Chapter of California History* (San Jose, Calif.: Pacific Tree and Vine Company, 1894; reprint, New York: Wallace Hubbard, 1929), 104. William L. Manley's later recollections hint that the company organization may have been structured to somewhat curb the absolute power Jefferson Hunt had already declared he deemed necessary for success. Manley reported that Captain Hunt said it was necessary to have some sort of system about the move and that before the company moved it must organize and adopt rules and laws that must be obeyed. Hunt said the members must move like an army, and that he was to be a dictator in all things except that in case of necessity a majority of the train could rule otherwise. It was thought best to get together and try out one day, then go into camp and organize.

48. Welch Journal, 30 September, 1, 3 October 1849.

49. Welch Journal, 4 October 1849.

50. Welch Journal, 7 October 1849.

51. Stover Narrative, in Hafen and Hafen, *Journals of Forty-niners*, 276.

52. Welch Journal, 12 October 1849.

53. Lyman and Reese, *Arduous Road*, 33–35; J[ames] S. Holliday, *The World Rushed In: The California Gold Rush Experience* (New York: Simon & Schuster, 1981), 119. Diarist William Swain noted just a few months earlier as his emigrant train started from Missouri "[L]ast night our wagons were formed in what is called a corral. Into that space . . . we drove the cattle and set watches upon them. . . . The watches were continued until half past four this morning, when the cattle were let out and herded. This is a custom we shall keep all the way through."

54. Lorton Journal, 14 October 1847; in Holliday, *World Rushed In*, 167. William Swain notes similar dissension when his company concluded to take a day off near Fort Laramie to celebrate Independence Day. Edward Leo Lyman, *San Bernardino: The Rise and Fall of a California Community* (Salt Lake City: Signature Books, 1996), 380–81.

55. Arthur Shearer Journal, 11, 14 October 1849, in Hafen and Hafen, *Supplement to the Journals of Forty-niners*, 33–34.

56. John Cumming, ed., *The Long Road to California: The Journal of Cephas Arms Supplemented with Letters by Traveling Companions on the Overland Trail in 1849* (Mount Pleasant, Mich.: Private Press of John Cumming, 1985), 99.

57. Lorton Journal, 20, 21, 24, 25 October 1849; Welch Journal, 23, 24 October 1849. Jefferson Hunt suffered tremendously as he sought the closer water source.

58. Cumming, *Long Road,* 101, and Welch to Milwaukee *Daily Sentinel and Gazette,* 1 March 1850, both in Cumming, *Long Road,* 119–21.

59. Cumming, *Long Road,* 100; George Q. Cannon Narrative, in Hafen and Hafen, *Journals of Forty-niners,* 225–31.

60. William Lewis Manley, *The Jayhawkers' Oath and Other Sketches,* select. and ed. Arthur Woodward (Los Angeles: Warren F. Lewis, 1949), 25. Although Manley denied they were a "secret order," the Jayhawkers were as firmly bound together as such a group. They regarded almost everybody outside their own group as strangers. Thus they considered it "safer and better to have a binding code to go by, and an agreement to stand by each other under all circumstances and fight if compelled to, together, until the last drop of blood should be spilled." They also underwent an initiation ceremony.

61. The Welch Journal, 26, 27 October 1849, indicates that the latter three men may have been scouting for water under Jefferson Hunt's direction. The journal mentions them finding Antelope Springs on the edge of the Escalante Valley to the southwest before backtracking to meet the company. They then subsisted on rabbits and came back with horses nearly spent. This being the case, Hunt was searching too far west to find Coal Creek, which was some twenty-five miles south of the last emigrant camp.

62. Welch Journal, 28, 29 October 1849. Cephas Arms, after his return from what he called "the dangerous experiment" of the shortcut, was among those encountering "the Dutchman." They made him throw away all but his provisions and clothing, which he did reluctantly. Arms jokingly suggested that perhaps he preferred to remain among his Indian "friends," presumably to practice homeopathy. See Cumming, *Long Road,* 108–9; also Lorton Journal, 1 December 1849.

63. Welch Journal, 29 October 1849.

64. Lorton Journal, 29 October 1849; William B. Lorton, *Over the Salt Lake Trail in the Fall of '49* (Los Angeles: Privately printed, 1957), 1. The same account also reported some unhappy with Hunt having the company rest on the Sabbath.

65. Addison Pratt's diary entry for 29 October 1849 stated, "Bro. Hunt came to me and told me that his life was at stake as there was a party that intended to kill him if their cattle died in crossing the deserts and he thought there was but one way to escape and that was to have the company voluntarily take the in-

tended cut off and leave a few wagons of us to go where we were of a mind to." See Addison Pratt Diary, in Hafen and Hafen, *Journals of Forty-niners*, 76–78.

66. Manley, *Death Valley in '49;* Lorenzo D. Stephens, *Life Sketches of a Jayhawker of '49* (San Jose: Nolta Brothers, 1916); Margaret Long, *The Shadow of the Arrow* (Caldwell, Idaho: Caxton Printers, 1941); Addison Pratt Diary, in Hafen and Hafen, *Journals of Forty-niners*, 75–80.

67. LeRoy Hafen, ed., *Letters of Lewis Granger: Reports of the Journey From Salt Lake to Los Angeles in 1849, and of Conditions in Southern California in the Early Fifties* (Los Angeles: Glen Dawson, 1959), 18–19.

68. Hafen and Hafen, *Journals of Forty-niners*, Alexander C. Erkson Account, 132–35; Lorton Journal, 9, 24 November 1849.

69. Stover Narrative, in Hafen and Hafen, *Journals of Forty-niners*, 281–82, 284–85.

70. William Farrer Diary, in Hafen and Hafen, *Journals of Forty-niners*, 204–18; Cannon Narrative, in Hafen and Hafen, *Journals of Forty-niners*, 234–68. For a more extensive edition of one of the best accounts, see Michael N. Landon, *To California in '49: The Journals of George Q. Cannon*, vol. 1 (Salt Lake City: Deseret Book Company, 1999). Addison Pratt Diary, in Hafen and Hafen, *Journals of Forty-niners*, 94, 96, 98; Bigler Journal, in Hafen and Hafen, *Journals of Forty-niners*, 155–56, 166–69; Rich Diary, in Hafen and Hafen, *Journals of Forty-niners*, 187.

71. Addison Pratt Diary, in Hafen and Hafen, *Journals of Forty-niners*, 105.

72. San Francisco *Alta California*, 11, 26 April 1854; Alfred Glen Humpherys, "Thomas L. (Peg-leg) Smith," in *The Mountain Men and the Fur Trade of the Far West*, ed. LeRoy R. Hafen and Ann W. Hafen, vol. 4 (Glendale, Calif.: Arthur H. Clark, 1966), 329.

73. Addison Pratt Diary, in Hafen and Hafen, *Journals of Forty-niners*, 83, 96, 169; Bigler Journal, in Hafen and Hafen, *Journals of Forty-niners*, 169. It is understood that Williams was never successful with this claim as others of his era were. But he still had the information and claim first. Morgan notes (microfilm page 1016), Dale Lowell Morgan Papers, The Bancroft Library, University of California, Berkeley, entitled "relief mission," 3, mention another gold mine near Bitter Springs discovered by Dr. McCormick and later worked by J. Earle, an emigrant who came west by the Gila route. He reportedly mined about three thousand dollars worth of ore, which was just about as much as his expenses.

74. James S. Brown's Account, in Hafen and Hafen, *Journals of Forty-niners*, 125–27.

75. Bigler Journal, in Hafen and Hafen, *Journals of Forty-niners*, 170.

76. Hafen and Hafen, *Journals of Forty-niners*, James H. Rollins Recollection, 266–68.

77. Wylly, "Memoirs," 67.

78. Leonard Babcock's Recollections, in Hafen and Hafen, *Supplement to the Journals of Forty-niners*, 65–68.

79. Lorton Journal, 29 November, 13 December 1849; Lorton Journal, including Welch Fragments, pages 250–54 of Morgan Papers including letters printed in the Milwaukee *Sentinel and Gazette*, 19 April, 25 September 1850. See also Cumming, *Long Road*, 123. Adonijah S. Welch, who was later elected U.S. senator from Michigan and president of what became Iowa State University, was ill with what the attending physician assumed was mountain fever, as was Welch's close companion, former company leader Henry Baxter, later a Union army brigadier general.

80. Lorton Journal, 24, 26, 28 November, 3, 10, 14, 25, 31 December 1849, 1, 2 January 1850. See also Lorton to New York *Sun*, 8 May 1850, copy in Dale Lowell Morgan Papers. Lorton later moved back to New York, where he sold some of the early domestic sewing machines. He also served in a militia unit that helped suppress the terrible antidraft riots in July 1863.

81. Lorton Journal, 29, 31 December 1849, 2 January 1850.

82. Cumming, Long Road, Welch letter, 96, and Arms, 116.

83. Joseph Cain, Mormon Waybill, in Hafen and Hafen, *Journals of Forty-niners*, 321–24.

84. Morgan Notes, 1–11, in Dale Lowell Morgan Papers, copied from Benjamin I. Hayes Notes in The Bancroft Library, who had copied from Stickney's original while both were at Williams Ranch early in 1850 Morgan Notes, 14–28, for Hoover Guide.

85. H. Stickney, "Stickney's Log," 44–51, typescript in Dale L. Morgan Papers, The Bancroft Library, University of California, Berkeley.

86. Hoover Diary, 3, 4 December 1849.

87. Lorton Journal, 16 January 1850.

88. Cumming, *Long Road*, 97.

Chapter Four:
Varied Travelers

1. Joseph P. Hamelin Jr. Journal, in *Supplement to the Journals of Forty-niners: Salt Lake to Los Angeles*, ed. LeRoy R. Hafen and Ann W. Hafen (Glendale, Calif.: Arthur H. Clark, 1961), 79–87; Joseph Cain, "Mormon Waybill," in *Journals of the Forty-niners: Salt Lake to Los Angeles*, ed. LeRoy R. Hafen and Ann W. Hafen (Glendale, Calif.: Arthur H. Clark, 1954), 323. William Birdsall Lorton Journal, 13 August 1849, The Bancroft Library, University of California, Berkeley, states Pomeroy had been accused of

hostility to the Mormons in Missouri, but a hearing on the matter proved that he had in fact been friendly. However, Thomas Morris, "Journal of Thomas Morris," Utah State Historical Society, Salt Lake City, 14 November 1850, states that when Pomeroy consented to burning one of his own wagons near Beaver, he "manifested secret dislike to the Mormons."

2. Hamelin Journal, in Hafen and Hafen, *Supplement to the Journals of Forty-niners*, 82–90; Lorton Journal, 13 August 1849. Lorton states that the teamsters did in fact mutiny and that Pomeroy solicited and obtained protection from Howard Egan's small Mormon company, discussed later in this chapter. Thomas Morris, who mentioned the liquor incentive in his 23–25 December entry, stated Egan only stayed with the company a week from 29 November to 7 December.

3. Hamelin Journal, in Hafen and Hafen, *Supplement to the Journals of Forty-niners*, 82, 89–91; Edwin Pettit Biography in Hafen and Hafen, *Journals of Forty-niners*, 295, 303–5; Walter Van Dyke Account, in Hafen and Hafen, 303–5.

4. William Clark, "A Trip Across the Plains in 1857," *Journal of Iowa History and Politics* 20, no. 2 (April 1922): 220–21.

5. Hamelin Journal, in Hafen and Hafen, *Supplement to the Journals of Forty-niners*, 93–97, 100–1.

6. Howard Egan Diary, in Hafen and Hafen, *Journals of Forty-niners*, 313–15.

7. Hamelin Journal, in Hafen and Hafen, *Supplement to the Journals of Forty-niners*, 85, 104–6, 109; "Journal and Diary of Albert King Thurber," in *Treasures of Pioneer History*, vol. 3, ed. Kate B. Carter (Salt Lake City: Daughters of Utah Pioneers, 1954), 775–76.

8. Pettit Biography, in Hafen and Hafen, *Journals of Forty-niners*, 295, states that "one man belonging to our company died crossing the desert." John Phillip Reid, *The Law and the Elephant: Property and Social Behavior on the Overland Trail* (San Marino, Calif.: The Huntington Library, 1980; paper, 1997), 136–40, makes clear that having the company own property and supplies was not uncommon.

9. Ransom G. Moody, "Reminiscent Account," in Hafen and Hafen, *Supplement to the Journals of Forty-niners*, 110–13.

10. Hafen and Hafen, *Journals of Forty-niners*, 296–97, 295–96; Thurber Journal, in Carter, *Treasures of Pioneer History*, 775–76; David Seeley Sketch, in Hafen and Hafen, *Supplement to the Journals of Forty-niners*, 297.

11. Ransom G. Moody Account, in Hafen and Hafen, *Supplement to the Journals of Forty-niners*, 108–10, 111–15.

12. *Deseret News*, 7 September 1850, 16 March 1854. The latter contains a report of John C. Frémont taking a course similar to what Ward and Joseph Redford Walker probably advocated, skirting north of Death Valley and cutting through the Sierra not far from the gold fields. It would have been a feasible route if so much negative publicity had not been attached to the proposal.

13. David W. Cheesman, "By Ox Team From Salt Lake to Los Angeles, 1850: A Memoir by David W. Cheesman," ed. Mary E. Foy, *Historical Society of Southern California* (1930): 271–85.

14. Cheesman, in Foy, "By Ox Team," 286–93.

15. I (Lyman) previously misread the documents and believed the group followed the Santa Clara to its confluence with the Virgin in the Virgin River Gorge, which would have made an even more difficult climb out of that gorge. I so stated—mistakenly—in at least one published account: See Edward Leo Lyman, *San Bernardino: The Rise and Fall of a California Community* (Salt Lake City: Signature Books, 1996), 32.

16. Cheesman, in Foy, "By Ox Team," 293–98.

17. Cheesman, in Foy, "By Ox Team," 9, 289, 293–98, 305–6. An Internet search for the "Philadelphia Fireman's March" yielded nothing, but there is a record, Desto/CMS Records, New York, New York LCCN: 75-750633, which includes a "Philadelphia Fireman's Cotillion."

18. Washington Peck Diary, Oregon California Trails Association Collection, National Frontier Trails Center, Mattes Library, Independence, Missouri, 4, 5, 12, 14 December 1850.

19. Peck Diary, 21, 22, 24 December 1850; Cheesman, in Foy, "By Ox Team," 301–2, 307.

20. Peck Diary, 27 December 1850.

21. John D. Unruh Jr., *The Plains Across: The Overland Emigrants and the Trans-Mississippi West, 1840–60* (Urbana: University of Illinois Press, 1979; paper, 1982), 285–86, 302, 305, 311, 315, 318.

22. Thomas Kealy Letter, in Hafen and Hafen, *Supplement to the Journals of Forty-niners*, 107.

23. Lyman, *San Bernardino*, 27.

24. "Journal History of the Church of Jesus Christ of Latter-day Saints," Historical Department and Archives, Church of Jesus Christ of the Latter-day Saints, Salt Lake City, Utah (hereinafter HDA), 1 February 1851.

25. Lyman, *San Bernardino*, 39, 378–79, 389–92, 400–401.

26. Brigham Young instituted the pattern of subdivided emigrant companies on the original Mormon trek west.

27. Lyman, *San Bernardino*, 41–42.

28. Amasa M. Lyman Journal, 25 April 1851, copy in HDA; Amasa M. Lyman and Charles C. Rich to President Young and Council, 30 July 1851, Brigham Young Papers, HDA.

29. Amasa M. Lyman Journal, 4–6 May 1851.

30. Amasa M. Lyman Journal, 8–12 May 1851.

31. Amasa M. Lyman Journal, 13–15, 19, 21, 22, 24 May 1851.

32. Parley P[arker] Pratt Jr., ed., *Autobiography of Parley Parker*

Pratt (Salt Lake City: Deseret Book Company, 1938; paper, 1976), 178.

33. Amasa M. Lyman Journal, 30 May 1851.

34. Parley Pratt, *Autobiography*, 379–80.

35. Lyman, *San Bernardino*, 46–83.

36. Lillian Schlissel, *Women's Diaries of the Westward Journey* (New York: Shocken Books, 1982; reprint, 1992), 7–158.

37. Utah Territorial Manuscript Census, Utah County, 1850, actually taken in March 1851; List of those willing to be counseled by A. Lyman and C. C. Rich, HDA; A List of Names Destined for Southern California, HDA.

38. California State Manuscript Census, Los Angeles County, 1852 (San Bernardino County census was created the following year); Lyman, *San Bernardino*, 51.

39. Milton R. Hunter, "The Mormon Corridor," *Pacific Historical Review* 8 (1939): 179–200; Andrew Love Neff, *History of Utah, 1847–1869*, ed. Leland H. Creer (Salt Lake City: Deseret News Press, 1940), 217–20.

40. Brigham Young, Heber C. Kimball, and Willard Richards to Amasa M. Lyman and Charles C. Rich, 17 March 1851, First Presidency Papers, HDA; "Journal History of the Church of Jesus Christ of Latter-day Saints," 5 March 1850, HDA.

41. *Millennial Star* (Liverpool, England) 12 (1851): 214.

42. *Millennial Star* 15 (1851): 116.

43. See discussion of Mormon Corridor in chapter 5.

44. Andrew Jensen, "History of San Bernardino Branch," 22–24 March 1852, HDA.

45. Sarah Pratt Diary, in *Covered Wagon Women: Diaries and Letters from the Western Trails, 1840–1890*, vol. 4, ed. Kenneth L. Holmes (Glendale, Calif: Arthur H. Clark, 1985), 198–201, 205.

46. Schlissel, *Women's Diaries*, 13.

47. "Journal History," 21, 24 November 1852, HDA; Nathan Tanner Diaries, 23 November 1852, HDA.

48. Amasa M. Lyman, Charles C. Rich and company, Richard R. Hopkins, clerk, "Journal of Expedition," 16 November to 19 December 1852, HDA, 27, 30–31 November, 3 December 1852.

49. Luther A. Ingersol, *Ingersol's Century Annals of San Bernardino County, 1769 to 1904* (Los Angeles: Privately printed, 1904), 660–61. It is not known if the dead man's brother, Robert, was also in that party or one passing through soon after, but he was a San Bernardino storekeeper for years thereafter.

50. Newaygo, "Saving a Wagon Train," *Juvenile Instructor* 21 (1886): 140–41.

51. Enoch Reese to Brigham Young, 6 February 1854, Brigham Young Papers, HDA; Bushrod W. Wilson Journal, original in Daughters of Utah Pioneers Museum, Salt Lake City, Utah.

52. Gerald Thompson, *Edward F. Beale and the American West* (University of New Mexico Press: Albuquerque, 1983), 60.

53. Stephen Bonsal, *Edward Fitzgerald Beale: A Pioneer in the Path of Empire, 1822–1903* (New York: Putnam's, 1912), 138–43. This may be the only record of the Wakara communication, which greatly amplifies the Indian viewpoint regarding the Wakara Indian War.

54. Bonsal, *Edward Fitzgerald Beale*, 150–52, 153, 156, 158–59.

55. It is not known who the person was, but I (Lyman) recall some reference by San Bernardino citizens at the time of an insane man refusing to remain with his party and meeting this fate at unknown hands.

56. Bonsal, *Edward Fitzgerald Beale*, 162–65.

57. "Journal History," 20 July 1852.

58. Ralph L. McBride, "Utah Mail Service Before the Coming of the Railroad, 1869," unpublished master's thesis, Brigham Young University, 1957, 17–19.

59. McBride, "Utah Mail Service," 22–23; John M. Townley, "Stalking Horse for the Pony Express: The Chorpenning Mail Contracts Between California and Utah, 1851–1860," *Arizona and the West* 24, no. 3 (autumn 1982): 229–44.

60. Juanita Brooks, ed., *Journal of the Southern Indian Mission: Diary of Thomas D. Brown* (Logan: Utah State University Press, 1972), 82, also lists David Savage, Leonard Conger, John Louder, and Ed Hope.

61. McBride, "Utah Mail Service," 23–24, 26, 28, 32, 35; Herbert S. Auerbach, "Map Showing the Several Mail Routes through the Indian Country from 1858 to 1861 and Indian Depredations Committed upon Mail Trains," *Utah Historical Quarterly* (1941): 56; Townley, "The Chorpenning Mail Contracts," 229–40.

62. *Deseret News*, 17 August 1854, for letter from San Bernardino resident William Hyde detailing the Resting Springs Indian attack on the mail carriers. See also Amasa M. Lyman Journal, 11 August 1854. Ray Reeder, "The Mormon Trail: A History of the Salt Lake to Los Angeles Route to 1869," unpublished doctoral dissertation, Brigham Young University, 1966, 314, mistakenly identifies George Lamphere, murdered by his traveling companions at Camp Springs on Utah Hill, as a mail carrier. See more details on this in the next chapter of this book.

63. Anthony W. Ivins, "Traveling Over Forgotten Trails: The Old Spanish Trail," *Improvement Era* 26, no. 9 (July 1923): 778; Caroline Barnes Crosby Diary, 24 January 1858, Utah State Historical Society, Salt Lake City, Utah. At Resting Springs, Crosby stated, "I understand that Charles Bills' mother was buried near here, and twice dug up by the Indians, but buried again by the mail carriers." Wherever the location, this is doubtless the same occurrence.

64. Ivins, "Traveling Over Forgotten Trails: The Old Spanish Trail," 774–78.

65. Amasa M. Lyman Journal, 10, 30, 31 July, 6, 27, 30 August, 25, 30 October, 2, 14 November, 16, 19 December 1853, 4, 11, 12, 21, 30 April, 1, 12, 25, 26 May, 13, 15 November 1854.

66. This was not the first year sheep were driven over the trail. David Cheesman noted that in late 1850 a herd of between six and seven thousand animals was being driven toward southern California. Some of the leaders of the Fancher party later killed at Mountain Meadows were apparently involved with livestock drives over the route in this early period. See Cheesman, in Foy, "By Ox Team," 293.

67. Thomas Flint, "Diary of Dr. Thomas Flint: California to Maine and Return, 1851–1855," ed. Walter Westergaard, *Annual Publications Historical Society of Southern California*, 1923, 53–106.

68. Edward Leo Lyman and Linda King Newell, *A History of Millard County* (Salt Lake City: Utah State Historical Society, 1999), 67–70; Robert Kent Fielding, *The Unsolicited Chronicler: An Account of the Gunnison Massacre, Its Causes and Consequences, Utah Territory, 1847–1859* (Brookline, Mass.: Paradigm Publications, 1993), 145–67, is the most detailed account, but is seriously skewed as to conclusions—attempting to blame Brigham Young for the tragedy. Henry C. Daulton of the Hildreth company claimed the wounded man later had his arm amputated, presumably because of a poisoned arrow wound. See Lucille H. Desmond, "Henry Clay Daulton I," *The Madera County Historian* 9, no. 3 (July 1969): 1–5.

69. Flint Diary, 106.

70. Alexander Kier Jr., "Statement," Kier folder, George William Beattie and Helen Pruitt Beattie Papers, The Huntington Library, San Marino, California.

71. Flint Diary, 107–9; Lyman, *San Bernardino*, 110–12; Brooks, *Journal of the Southern Indian Mission*, 70–71; Janet B. Seegmiller, *History of Iron County: Community Above Self* (Salt Lake City: Utah State Historical Society, 1998), 60–62.

72. Flint Diary, 110–14; Col. [William] W. Hollister, "Statement of a Few Facts on California from 1852 to 1860," gathered by Hubert H. Bancroft, interviewer, 1878, The Bancroft Library, Berkeley, California. The interviewee claims several Native Americans were probably killed in skirmishes near the Virgin River–Mormon Mesa area.

73. Flint Diary, 112, 114–15, entries of 29, 31 October, 4, 5, 9 November 1853.

74. Schlissel, *Women's Diaries*, 14.

75. Flint Diary, 116, 119–23, entries of 6, 13, 14, 16 November, 25, 27 December 1853; Hollister, "Statement."

76. Desmond, "Henry Clay Daulton I," 2–3.

Chapter Five.
Outside Observers and
Mormon-Indian Relations

1. *Thomas D. Brown*, in *Journal of the Southern Indian Mission: Diary of Thomas D. Brown*, ed. Juanita Brooks (Logan: Utah State University Press, 1972), 3–4, 19–21. Latter-day Saints church members believe the *Book of Mormon* is a record of God's dealings with Israelite immigrants from the Middle East to ancient America, some of the descendants of whom were the Lamanites, or modern Native Americans.

2. The speaker may have erroneously referred to the Indians as descendants of Ephraim, when most Mormons would consider them to be of the tribe of Manasseh.

3. Brown, in Brooks, *Journal of the Southern Indian Mission*, 25.

4. D. Michael Quinn, *The Mormon Hierarchy: Extensions of Power* (Salt Lake City: Signature Books, 1997), 248–51, includes discussion of Mormon songs mentioning retaliation for past wrongs the author recalls singing as a youth in the church.

5. Brown, in Brooks, *Journal of the Southern Indian Mission*, 30.

6. Brown in Brooks, *Journal of the Southern Indian Mission*, 21, 27, 49.

7. Los Angeles *Star*, 10, 17 October 1857; Jules Remy, *A Journey to Great Salt Lake City* (London: W. Jeffs, 1861), 408, states that at the Muddy River "the Indians inquired of [mail carrier Edward] Hope if [Remy, Brenchley, and their employees] were Mormons; he replied that [they] were good Americans, under which name they confound all whites, whatever be their country."

8. Brown, in Brooks, *Journal of the Southern Indian Mission*, 52–54, 68, 104–5. See pages listed in note 9 for parents trading children.

9. Brown, in Brooks, *Journal of the Southern Indian Mission*, 56, 59, 99–100, 104–5.

10. Brown, in Brooks, *Journal of the Southern Indian Mission*, 68, 74.

11. Brown, in Brooks, *Journal of the Southern Indian Mission*, 130, 169.

12. Brown, in Brooks, *Journal of the Southern Indian Mission*, 128.

13. Solomon Nunes Carvalho, *Incidents of Travel and Adventure in the Far West; With Col. Frémont's Last Expedition* (New York: Derby & Jackson, 1857; reprint, Philadelphia: Jewish Society of America, 1954), 242; Los Angeles *Star*, 6 May 1854; Anthony W. Ivins, "Traveling Over Forgotten Trails: The Old Spanish Trail," *Improvement Era* 26, no. 9 (July 1923): 776. The other death at the springs may well have been one of the escapees from Mountain Meadows Massacre; see note 42.

14. Carvalho, *Incidents of Travel*, 253, 256–61, 263.

15. Robert Kent Fielding, *The Unsolicited Chronicler: An Account of the Gunnison Massacre, Its Causes and Consequences, Utah Territory, 1847–1859* (Brookline, Mass.: Paradigm Publications, 1993), 271–72, 281.

16. Carvalho, *Incidents of Travel*, 281, 293, 290–91, 293.

17. Carvalho, *Incidents of Travel*, 295, 298.

18. Alfred Glen Humpherys, "Thomas L. (Peg-leg) Smith," *The Mountain Men and the Fur Trade of the Far West*, vol. 4, ed. LeRoy R. Hafen and Ann W. Hafen (Glendale, Calif.: Arthur H. Clark, 1966), 329, asserts Smith returned to Los Angeles after a failed gold hunt with some of Frémont's expedition. These had all left the area long before the Smith journey—except for Carvalho, who spent several additional months in Utah recovering from his ordeal with Frémont.

19. Carvalho, *Incidents of Travel*, 295, 298, 300, 302–4, 306–7.

20. Scott G. Kenney, "Early Trials of Joseph F. Smith," copy of unpublished chapter of Joseph F. Smith biography. Copy of chapter in author's possession (Edward Leo Lyman).

21. Edward Leo Lyman, *San Bernardino: The Rise and Fall of a California Community* (Salt Lake City: Signature Books, 1996), 161–63.

22. W. R. Hayes, "Diary," 1–4 May 1855, The Bancroft Library, University of California, Berkeley.

23. Lynn R. Bailey, "Lt. Sylvester Mowry's Report on His March in 1855 from Salt Lake City to Fort Tejon," *Arizona and the West* 7, no. 4 (winter 1965): 329–32. Lieutenant Sylvester Mowry to Col. S. Cooper, 23 July 1855, copy Utah Writers' Project, WPA, Utah State Historical Society, Salt Lake City; original National Archives, Washington, D.C. See conclusions regarding this in next chapter.

24. The Leach Cutoff apparently followed present State Highway 58, which has a Leach Canyon through the Harmony Mountains. The older route followed the Old Spanish Trail from Enoch to Iron Springs to Antelope Springs. See [Edward] Leo Lyman and Larry Reese, *The Arduous Road: Salt Lake to Los Angeles, The Most Difficult Wagon Road in American History* (Victorville, Calif.: Lyman Historical Research and Publishing, 2001), 45–47.

25. Ray M. Reeder, "The Mormon Trail: A History of the Salt Lake to Los Angeles Route to 1869," unpublished doctoral dissertation, 1966, Brigham Young University, 189, states that Steptoe informed Secretary of War Jefferson Davis that $100,000 was needed to build a satisfactory road, but no such project was funded; John Steele Diary, 10 June 1855, copy in Harold B. Lee Library, Brigham Young University, Provo, Utah. See also W. Turrentine Jackson, *Wagon Roads West: A Study of Federal Surveys and Construction in the Trans-Mississippi West,*

1846–1869 (New Haven, Conn.: Yale University Press, 1965), 143.

26. It is entirely probable that both the Beale-Heap and Mowry expeditions, essentially without wagons, followed the Old Spanish Trail route some dozen miles farther down the Virgin River, then pulled up onto the Mormon Mesa by way of Halfway Wash, rather than the more difficult Virgin Hill. See Lyman and Reese, *Arduous Road*, v–vi, 55–59.

27. Bailey, "Lt. Sylvester Mowry's Report," 333–46; Carl I. Wheat, *Mapping the Trans-Mississippi West*, vol. 4 (San Francisco: Institute of Historical Cartography, 1957), 31; Hayes Diary, 31 May 1855.

28. A circumstantial evidence case can be made that these particular Native Americans still depended little on rifles. About the same time, Jules Remy and his associates essentially challenged the Tonequints to a shooting match, with the latter demonstrating amazing skill with bows and arrows, instead of choosing rifles, which they would have done if they possessed them. See Remy, *A Journey to Great Salt Lake City*, 388–90. When Solomon Carvalho expressed astonishment that arms and ammunition were being furnished to Indians in 1854, Brigham Young explained that being so close to the emigrant roads, many possessed arms already. "And as it was the object of the Mormons to protect, as much as possible, their people from the aggressions of Indians, and also from the continual descent upon their towns—begging for food, and stealing when it was not given, he thought it more advisable to furnish them with the means of shooting their own game." See Carvalho, *Incidents of Travel*, 256.

29. Lt. Sylvester Mowry to Col. S. Cooper, 23 July 1855.

30. David L. Bigler, *Forgotten Kingdom: The Mormon Theocracy in the American West, 1847–1896* (Logan: Utah State University Press, 1998), 100–101, 148–49.

31. Charles Colson Rich Journal, 15 May–10 June 1855, copy in George William Beattie and Helen Pruitt Beattie Papers, The Huntington Library, San Marino, California; Amasa M. Lyman Journal, 28 October, 19 November 1855, Historical Department, Church of Jesus Christ of Latter-day Saints, Salt Lake City, Utah (hereinafter HDA), states the same thing. John Steele mentioned the same year that the road had been much improved since he last journeyed over it. John Steele Diary, 10 June 1855, copy in Brigham Young University Library, Provo, Utah. See also Lyman and Reese, *Arduous Road*, 40–43, 47–48.

32. Rich Journal, 30 May–4 June 1855.

33. Nelson Paul Beebe, "Life and Diary," copy in HDA.

34. Remy, *Journey to Great Salt Lake City*, 334, 349, 362, 375.

35. Remy, *Journey to Great Salt Lake City*, 388, 407–8, 412–13, 426–27.

36. Remy, *Journey to Great Salt Lake City*, 430–31, 443.

37. Amasa Mason Lyman Journal, 25 October–30 November 1855; Amasa Lyman to Charles C. Rich, 15 December 1855, Rich Papers, HDA; "Journal History of the Church of Jesus Christ of Latter-day Saints," 1 November–1 December 1855, HDA.

38. William Chandless, *Visit to Salt Lake: Being a Journey Across the Plains and a Residence in the Mormon Settlements* (London: Smith, Elder, 1857), 266, 269–70; Edwina Jo Snow, "William Chandless: British Overlander, Mormon Observer and Amazon Explorer," *Utah Historical Quarterly* 54, no. 2 (spring 1986): 116–36.

39. Chandless, *Visit to Salt Lake*, 298, 302.

40. Hans Peter Emanuel Hoth Journal, 14, 18, 19, 20 September 1856, The Bancroft Library, Berkeley, California.

41. Hoth Journal, 2, 3, 6 October 1856.

42. Hoth Journal, 15, 21 October 1856.

43. John D. Unruh Jr., *The Plains Across: The Overland Emigrants and the Trans-Mississippi West, 1840–60* (Urbana: University of Illinois Press, 1979), 127–58.

44. Merrill J. Mattes, *The Great Platte River Road: The Covered Wagon Mainline Via Fort Kearny to Fort Laramie* (Lincoln: University of Nebraska Press, 1969; paper, 1987), 82–93.

45. Ralph P. Bieber, *Southern Trails to California in 1849* (Glendale, Calif.: Arthur H. Clark, 1937); Harlan Hague, *The Road to California: The Search for a South Overland Route, 1540–1848* Glendale, Calif.: Arthur H. Clark, 1978); Patricia A. Etter, *To California on the Southern Route, 1849: A History and Annotated Bibliography* (Spokane, Wash.: Arthur H. Clark, 1998).

46. John Steele Journal, 3 June 1855, copy in Harold B. Lee Library, Brigham Young University, Provo, Utah.

47. Andrew Jensen, comp., "History of the Las Vegas Mission," *Nevada State Historical Society Papers, 1925–1926* (Reno: Nevada State Historical Society, 1926), 119–31.

48. Jensen, "History of the Las Vegas Mission," 119–46. Second-ranking Latter-day Saints leader Heber C. Kimball wrote to his son William that many of the missionaries chosen for the Indian missions were men noted to be loitering around Salt Lake City court sessions who were believed to be good men, "but they need to learn a lesson." The fact that some understood their assignment was partly a punishment probably did nothing for dedication of the missionaries. See Eugene E. Campbell, *Establishing Zion: The Mormon Church in the American West, 1847–1869* (Salt Lake City: Signature Books, 1988), 86. See also Stanley W. Paher, *Las Vegas: As It Began—As It Grew* (Las Vegas: Nevada Publications, 1971), for reproduction of fort layout sketch; Lyman and Reese, *Arduous Road*, 65–68.

49. John Steele to George A. Smith, 1 October 1855, in Jensen, "History of the Las Vegas Mission," 168–70; Lorenzo Brown Journal, 1823–1900, vol. 1, 17 June 1856, typescript, Harold B. Lee Library, Brigham Young University, Provo, Utah.

50. Campbell, *Establishing Zion*, 119–33.

51. Jensen, "History of the Las Vegas Mission," 170, 188, 227, 267, entries 25 December 1855, 19, 23, 31 March 1856, including letters from John Steele to George A. Smith, 1 October 1855 and G. W. Bean to George A. Smith, 1 December 1855; Lorenzo Brown Journal, 17, 20 June 1856, Harold B. Lee Library, Brigham Young University, Provo, Utah.

52. Jensen, "History of the Las Vegas Mission," 30 July, 30 December 1855, 24 February, 20 July 1856; John Steele Diary, 20 September 1855, copy in Harold B. Lee Library, Brigham Young University, Provo, Utah.

53. Jensen, "History of the Las Vegas Mission," 151, 269; Steele Diary, 10 June 1855.

54. Jensen, "History of the Las Vegas Mission," 271–73; John Steele Diary, May 1856. Disfellowshipment is ecclesiastic discipline short of excommunication, where the person loses all but actual church membership.

55. Paher, *Las Vegas*, 30.

56. Brigham Young to Nathaniel V. Jones, 3 September 1856; Brigham Young to Miles Anderson, 4 October 1856, Brigham Young Papers, HDA, both copied by Weber State University professor Donald Moorman when he had rather unrestricted access to the LDS Church Archives, in Donald Moorman Papers, Weber State University, Ogden, Utah.

57. Brigham Young to the Piedes at Las Vegas, 8 October 1856, Moorman Papers, Weber State University, Ogden, Utah.

58. Brigham Young to Samuel Thompson, 7 January, 4 February, 20 March 1857; Brigham Young to Phillip K. Smith, 7 January 1857; all Brigham Young Papers, HDA, copies in Moorman Papers, Weber State University, Ogden, Utah.

59. Amasa M. Lyman Journal, 9 May 1857, HDA.

60. Samuel Thompson to Brigham Young, 20 March 1857, Brigham Young Papers, HDA; Jensen, "History of the Las Vegas Mission," 167, 281; Wesley R. Law, "Mormon Indians Missions—1855," unpublished master of science thesis, Brigham Young University, 1959, 79.

61. Eugene E. Campbell, "Brigham Young's Outer Cordon—A Reappraisal," *Utah Historical Quarterly* 41, no. 3 (summer 1983): 220–53; Lyman, *San Bernardino*.

62. John Haskell Kemble, *The Panama Route, 1848–1869* (Berkeley: University of California Press, 1943), 71, 74.

63. LeRoy R. Hafen and Ann W. Hafen, *Handcarts to Zion, 1856–1860* (Glendale, Calif.: Arthur H. Clark, 1960), 53–141; Bigler, *Forgotten Kingdom*, 103–20, including Brigham Young's curse on anyone who blamed him for the disaster.

64. Campbell, *Establishing Zion*, 87–91.

Chapter Six.
Conflict with the Federal Government—and Tragedy

1. John Steele Journal, 3 June 1855, copy in Harold B. Lee Library, Brigham Young University, Provo, Utah; Andrew Jensen, comp., "A History of the Las Vegas Mission," 4, 19 August 1856, *Nevada State Historical Society Papers* (Reno: Nevada State Historical Society, 1926), 119–31.

2. James B. Allen and Glen M. Leonard, *The Story of the Latter-day Saints* (Salt Lake City: Deseret Book Company, 1976), 124–34, 181–83, 190–98, 211–15. Even earlier in Kirtland, similar conflict arose. One perceptive student of the situation stated the Mormons "never perceived that their quest for social and political control might have influenced others negatively. In their minds the strife and contention that pluralism had engendered imperiled not only Kirtland [their Ohio city] but the nation as well. . . . The Mormon mind was a millennial mind, longing for peace and tranquility but convinced that war and destruction would come first." To a large extent, after ten years in Utah Territory this outlook had not really changed. See Marvin S. Hill, *Quest for Refuge: The Mormon Flight From American Pluralism* (Salt Lake City: Signature Books, 1989), 67.

3. D. Michael Quinn, *The Mormon Hierarchy: Extensions of Power* (Salt Lake City: Signature Books, 1997), 241–61.

4. "Journal History of the Church of Jesus Christ of Latter-day Saints," 4 July 1856, Historical Department and Archives of the Church of Jesus Christ of the Latter-day Saints (hereinafter HDA), Salt Lake City, Utah; Stella H. Day and Sebrina C. Ekins, *One Hundred Years of History of Millard County [Milestones of Millard]* (Springville, Utah: Art City Publishing—Daughters Utah Pioneers of Millard County, 1951), 18, lists those leaving the community at the time as William Bickmore, Robert Lasenby, Jacob and William Benn, and William Parkes.

5. *Deseret News*, 23 September 1857, quoted in Juanita Brooks, *The Mountain Meadows Massacre* (Palo Alto, Calif.: Stanford University Press, 1950; reprint, University of Oklahoma Press, 1962), 39. Page 12 lists the catechism, page 29 quotes G. A. Smith's boast. Blood atonement, a doctrine and practice often denied by later church spokesmen, assumes that certain serious offenses fall beyond Jesus Christ's atonement for the world's sins and that such persons must have their own blood shed if they are to have any hope for redemption. For Brigham Young sermon statements on blood atonement, see also *Journal of Discourses*, vol. 4 (Liverpool: Latter-day Saints Booksellers' Depot, 1855–1886), 53, 219–20.

6. Quinn, *Mormon Hierarchy: Extensions*, 248, 21 September 1856, 8 February 1857.

7. Donald R. Moorman, with Gene A. Sessions, *Camp Floyd and the Mormons: The Utah War* (Salt Lake City: University of Utah Press, 1992), 10–11, 17.

8. Eugene E. Campbell, *Establishing Zion: The Mormon Church in the American West, 1847–1869* (Salt Lake City: Signature Books, 1988), 234; Norman F. Furniss, *The Mormon Conflict, 1850–1859* (New Haven, Conn.: Yale University Press, 1960), 66–69, 93; Will Bagley, *Blood of the Prophets: Brigham Young and the Massacre at Mountain Meadows* (Norman: University of Oklahoma Press, 2002), 73–75, 79.

9. A large group of disenchanted Mormons headed east in October 1856, and the next spring Thomas Williams and other "apostate scruff" went the same direction. *Millennial Star*, 10 January 1857, Juanita Brooks, ed. *On the Mormon Frontier: The Diary of Hosea Stout, 1844–1861*, vol. 2 (Salt Lake City: University of Utah Press, 1964); 625; Los Angeles *Star*, 16 January 1858, stated, "[W]e have heard a rumor that several companies of Mormons, who had but recently started for Salt Lake, had reconsidered the matter, and returned to San Bernardino." Los Angeles *Southern Vineyard*, 12 June 1858, reported that "quite a number of the [former] San Bernardino people regret the day they left California and it is no more than probable that some of them will shortly begin to migrate to distant parts, probably California." In July mail carrier Daniel Taft brought back a group reportedly "greatly disappointed with Mormon affairs in Utah." It was also reported "about a hundred Mormons had arrived back at San Bernardino by that time, with more coming in the fall. See Los Angeles *Star*, 25 September, 20 November, 25 December 1858, 19 March, 9 April, 30 May, 18 June 1859, 7 January, 15 December 1860. Also Edward Leo Lyman, *San Bernardino: The Rise and Fall of a California Community* (Salt Lake City: Signature Books, 1996), 413–15. It is evident that the presence of federal troops in Utah encouraged the out-migrations not always possible previously. San Francisco *Daily Alta California*, 29 May 1859, reported that Utah governor Alfred Cumming published a note from Gen. Albert Sidney Johnston stating that "If persons desirous of emigrating from this Territory would assemble at a given time and place, with their families, trains, stock, etc., complete protection, by a special escort, could be given them; and should I be notified by any considerable number, of such intention, I will furnish the force for their protection." Bagley, *Blood of the Prophets*, 203, reports that fifty-six men and thirty-three women accepted the governor's proposal.

10. "Journal History," 13 August 1857.

11. Brigham Young Discourse, Tabernacle, 16 August 1857, reported by George D. Watt, HDA. See also Bagley, *Blood of the Prophets*, 138–39.

12. James H. Carleton, *"Special Report: The Mountain Meadows Massacre," to Maj. W. W. Mackall, Assistant Adjutant General, United*

States Army, San Francisco, California (Spokane, Wash.: Arthur H. Clark, 1995), 25. A letter of marque was legal permission to loot enemy ships at sea.

13. Unsigned letter from Latter-day Saints' First Presidency's office to Bishop Aaron Johnson, 3 February 1857; Unsigned to Bishop Lewis Brunson and Presidents William H. Dame and Isaac C. Haight, 6 February 1857, President's Office Journal, HDA; Thomas B. H. Stenhouse, *The Rocky Mountain Saints: A Full and Complete History of the Mormons, from the First Vision of Joseph Smith to the Last Courtship of Brigham Young* (New York: D. Appleton, 1873), 464, attributes the letter to Johnson directly to Brigham Young and otherwise corroborates its contents.

14. Robert Kent Fielding, *The Unsolicited Chronicler: An Account of the Gunnison Massacre* (Brookline, Mass.: Paradigm Press, 1993), 358, asserts Tobin had been sifted out of Mormondom by the Mormon Reformation. Los Angeles *Star*, 7 March 1857; Andrew Jensen, "San Bernardino Branch History," 24 March 1857, HDA, notes that Stake (diocese) Clerk Richard R. Hopkins reported the infamous "destroying angel" (alleged murderer for the church) Porter Rockwell had been sighted in the area, presumably to finish the work others had failed to accomplish. Indian agent Garland Hurt specifically blamed Brigham Young Jr. for the Tobin incident, in his letter to Superintendent Forney, Docs., 10:71:88, no. 956, Fiche 2 (microfiche). See also letter from John C. Chatterley to Andrew Jensen, 18 September 1919, cited in Moorman, with Sessions, *Camp Floyd and the Mormons*, 125, 301. Brigham Young to Isaac C. Haight, 4 April 1857, Brigham Young Office Journal, HDA. Some observers believe the two unnamed men in the Peltro-Tobin attack were the former jail inmates the earlier letters referred to.

15. New York *Times*, 20 May 1857; Marionette Parrish, "Account," in Alexander Kier Folder, George William Beattie and Helen Pruitt Beattie Papers, The Huntington Library, San Marino, California, recounts that on the fateful night her uncle William and his two sons were walking single file through a cane thicket, followed by "Duff" Potter, who apparently knew of the planned attack. The elder Parrish insisted Potter not walk last, and was subsequently shot with William and Beetson after Potter changed position. Orrin Parrish, who was then trailing behind, was not shot and subsequently escaped. Within days of the Parrish killings, the incident was discussed in a sermon in Big Cottonwood Ward, Salt Lake Valley, some forty miles away. One listener later wrote he was "glad to hear that the Law of God has been put in force in Springville on some men who deserved it." See Winslow Farr Jr. Diary, HDA, quoted in Paul Peterson, "The Mormon Reformation," unpublished doctoral dissertation, Brigham Young University, 1981, 195. Church historian William Hartly, in his book *My Best for the Kingdom*, called

these the "Parrish-Potter religious murders" (quoted in Quinn, *Mormon Hierarchy: Extensions*, 243).

16. Fielding, *Unsolicited Chronicler*, 392, 395. Travel restrictions had clearly been imposed during the Wakara War of 1853 as well. A significant tie exists between the Parrish murders and the previously cited letter from Brigham Young's office to the Springville bishop, Aaron Johnson. Joseph Bartholomew in 1859 attested to having been summoned to Johnson's home for a meeting about 1 March 1857. He affirmed that "at the meeting the conversation was about the Parrishes and about persons at the Indian farm [Spanish Fork]. The meeting was called to enter into arrangements to find out what these persons expected to do. Bishop Johnson made a remark however that some of us would yet 'see the red stuff run.'" The affidavit then stated the bishop claimed that "he had a letter." Although the record did not state who the letter was from, it was likely the unsigned one from the First Presidency office. A similar allusion in both the letter and the meeting was Bartholomew quoting someone at the meeting: "Dead men tell no tales." Affidavit obtained by Springville historian Rell Francis from Wayne Bartholomew of the Bartholemew family 9 August 1991, copy in author's possession (Edward Leo Lyman).

17. New York *Times*, 20 May 1857; Moorman, *Camp Floyd and the Mormons*, 12. For a time Drummond apparently hoped to be appointed Utah governor.

18. New York *Times*, 20 May 1857; John Hyde, a well-known Mormon apostate, author of *Mormonism, Its Leaders and Designs* (New York: W. P. Feteridge, 1857), is a likely source of the anonymous *Times* article. See Fielding, *Unsolicited Chronicler*, 356, 358, 361, who also cites Utah Expedition Documents, 35th Cong. lst Sess. House Ex. Docs. 10:71–88 no. 956.

19. Los Angeles *Star*, 9, 30 May 1857.

20. Brigham Young to Jacob Hamblin, 4 August 1857, Brigham Young Office Journal, HDA, copy in Donald Moorman Papers, Weber State University Library, Ogden, Utah. Mission leader Allen was told his release related to his sick mother, but in fact Young needed a stronger person, Hamblin, leading the mission to the Indians.

21. Dimick Baker Huntington Journal, 18 August, 1 September 1857, HDA; Scott G. Kenney, *Wilford Woodruff Journals*, vol. 5 (Midvale, Utah: Signature Books, 1985), 80, 88.

22. Huntington Journal, 1 September 1857 entry states, "Kanosh the Pahvant Chief, Ammon & wife (Wakara's Brother) & 11 Pahvants came in to see B & D & find out about the soldiers. Tutseygubbit [*sic*] a Piede Chief over 6 Piede Bands, Youngwuds another Piede Chief & I gave them all the cattle that had gone to Cal the south rout [*sic*]. It made them open their eyes. They sayed that you have told us not to steal so I have but now they have come to fight us & and you for when

they kill us they will kill you. They sayd they was afraid to fight the Americans & so would raise [friends] and we might fight." Not long previous, Huntington had visited northern Utah Indians who were known to have stolen emigrant horses and mules. The chief asked if Brigham Young was angry about this, and Huntington replied that he was not. Fielding, *Unsolicited Chronicler*, 401.

23. "Historian's Office Journal," 1 September 1857, HDA, 30; Kenney, *Wilford Woodruff Journals*, vol. 5, 1–16 September 1857, 88–92. Woodruff often wrote up his journal from notes some time after the events he recounts, and he sometimes gets dates mixed. For Warn statement, see Los Angeles *Star,* 17 October 1857.

24. Brigham Young to Maj. George W. Armstrong, 14 March 1857; Young to George W. Manypenny, Commissioner, Washington, D.C., 31 March 1857; Young to James W. Denver, Commissioner of Indian Affairs, 12 September 1857, 6 January 1858; Young to bishops and presidents (Lewis Brunson, Fillmore; William H. Dame, Parowan; and Isaac C. Haight, Cedar City), 6 February 1857, all in President's Office Journal, HDA. There had been a group of emigrants "from Missouri" on the northern Nevada segment of the California trail who boasted to passing Mormons they had killed "10 or so" Indians a day or two previously. "Journal History," 12 August 1857, cited in Fielding, *Unsolicited Chronicler,* 418.

25. In his book *Blood of the Prophets*, Will Bagley argues that since William Dukes and at least eight other men of his party were from Missouri, they "may well have been" the Missouri Wildcats. And Lawrence Coates, a careful scholar of the Mountain Meadows Massacre, in *The Fancher Party Before the Mountain Meadows Massacre* (Rexburg, Idaho: Privately printed, 1992), 13–49, argues there were actually no "Missouri Wildcats" with the Fancher party but that up to half the Dukes-Turner company, traveling not far behind, hailed from Missouri. Either may yet conclusively prove their case. But so far even without conclusive documentation of the Wildcats the possibility of such a group cannot be totally dismissed. William Clark, in "A Trip Across the Plains in 1857," *Iowa Journal of History and Politics* 22, no. 2 (April 1922): 218, states, of the Dukes party, "They had been very careful not to arouse the Mormons."

26. Moorman, *Camp Floyd and the Mormons*, 127–28, 302, note 28; Brooks, *Mountain Meadows Massacre*, 56, cites Cedar City historian William R. Palmer recalling as a young man having older area resident Ed Parry tell him on many occasions he had overheard an emigrant assert he had the gun that killed Old Joe Smith. See also Bagley, *Blood of the Prophets,* 117, where the author observes, "Given the mood of the Utahns, a confrontation in Cedar City seems possible. Yet would men with families act

so recklessly and provoke people who were known to be intolerant of outsiders?"

27. San Francisco *Bulletin*, 24 March 1877, a much later article cited by Moorman, *Camp Floyd and the Mormons*, 302, note 28.

28. Moorman, *Camp Floyd and the Mormons*, 128, 131.

29. Jolene Ashman Robison, *Almon Robison, Utah Pioneer: Man of Mystique and Tragedy* (Lawrence, Kan.: Richard A. Robison, 1995), 82. The well-developed Mormon version of the situation, expressed in 1859 by Jacob Hamblin to Maj. J. H. Carleton, started with the poisoning of a spring at Corn Creek, which caused "considerable excitement" among both white and Indian residents of the area. Eighteen cattle had supposedly died from the water and six Pahvants poisoned from eating the meat. Hamblin stated the Robison [*sic*] boy had been buried the day before he [Hamblin] passed, poisoned in "trying out" the tallow of the dead cattle. See Carleton, "Special Report," 12–13.

30. Coates, *The Fancher Party*, 13–49; Hoffman Birney, *Zealots of Zion* (Philadelphia: Penn, 1931), 141–43; Bagley, *Blood of the Prophets*, 68–71, 81, 89, 98, 265–66, 269, attempted to make a case that Brigham Young retaliated against the Fancher party for Parley P. Pratt's murder. The case still has holes.

31. Juanita Brooks, ed., *Journal of the Southern Indian Mission: Diary of Thomas D. Brown* (Logan: Utah State University Press, 1972), 70–71. For more on Scottish escapees, see also chapter 4 in this book, as well as notes 66 and 67 in chapter 4.

32. Moorman, *Camp Floyd and the Mormons*, 129–30; Brooks, *Mountain Meadows Massacre*, 31–59, contains an entire chapter on the "Zealous South."

33. J. Ward Christian to Hon. Benj. F. Hayes, 25 October 1857, Benjamin Hayes, "Scrapbooks," vol. 94, The Bancroft Library, University of California, Berkeley, California.

34. "Journal History," 11 September 1857, published letter, perhaps composed for public consumption, dated 17 August 1858.

35. Frank Beckwith, "Shameful Friday: A Critical Study at the Mountain Meadows Massacre," 49, manuscript, The Huntington Library, San Marino, California.

36. Fielding, *Unsolicited Chronicler,* 401, 410, 417, 419.

37. *Journal History*, 31 August, 11 September, 31 October 1857.

38. Quinn, *Mormon Hierarchy: Extensions*, 251, cites church historian's office journal, 8–26 August 1857, HDA, and Brooks, *Mountain Meadows Massacre*, 36–40. Parowan bishop Tarleton Lewis had been wounded at Haun's Mill and survived only because the mob thought he was dead.

39. Moorman, *Camp Floyd and the Mormons*, 131.

40. There is some persuasive evidence suggesting that this

initial attack of the cattle herders took place farther down the trail at Kane Springs, where old-timers recall that trench-redoubt remnants were visible for years thereafter. This subject demands further investigation.

41. Brooks, *Mountain Meadows Massacre*, 56–57, 70; Beckwith, "Shameful Friday," 49; Anthony W. Ivins, "Traveling Over Forgotten Trails: The Old Spanish Trail," *Improvement Era* 26, 775. Maj. J. H. Carleton's record of Jacob Hamblin's version of the initial attack is as follows: "The Indians have often told me that they made an attack on the emigrants between daylight and sunrise as the men were standing around the campfires, killing and wounding fifteen at the first discharge, which was delivered from the ravine near the spring close to the wagons and from a hill to the west. That the emigrants immediately corralled their wagon and threw up an intrenchment [*sic*] to shelter themselves from the balls. When I first saw the ditch it was about four feet deep and the bank about two feet high. The Indians say they then run off the stock but kept parties at the spring to prevent the emigrants from getting to the water, the emigrants firing upon them every time they showed themselves, and they returning the fire. This was kept up for six or seven days. The Indians say that they had lost but one man killed and three or four wounded." See Carleton, "Special Report," 14–15.

42. Moorman, *Camp Floyd and the Mormons*, 134–35.

43. According to Charles P. Lyford, *The Mormon Problem: An Appeal to the American People* (New York: Phillips & Hunt, 1886), cited in Brooks, *Mountain Meadows Massacre*, 97–100, but considered by her unreliable, one escaping man was caught asleep on Utah Hill between the Santa Clara and Virgin Rivers, where he was killed by Chief Jackson, who reportedly later showed the writer the spot and the human remains. The other two messengers of mercy traveled forty miles down the Virgin where they too were overtaken by Indians, surrounded, and one killed. Some say the other escaped and traveled past Las Vegas to Cottonwood Springs. There he encountered two brothers named Young, alleged horse thieves, who convinced him the desert stretch ahead was too much for a single traveler in his weakened condition. He concluded to turn around and go with them toward Salt Lake City. But on the Muddy, some of the Moapas who had participated in Mountain Meadows recognized the man and demanded he be killed, which was accomplished, although the Young brothers escaped.

44. Brooks, *Mountain Meadows Massacre*, 80; Beckwith, in "Shameful Friday," 23–25, recounts the story of William Hawley who, when he refused to assist in the killing, was chained to a wagon wheel and forced to witness the killings. Author (Lyman) recalls this newspaperman as a white-haired man with a goatee who had gathered secondhand accounts from the

founders of West Millard County, Utah, about their fathers' participation in the Mountain Meadows Massacre.

45. Brooks, *Mountain Meadows Massacre*, 86–91.

46. Brooks, *Mountain Meadows Massacre*, 79–82; Moorman, *Camp Floyd and the Mormons*, 135–36.

47. Brooks, *Mountain Meadows Massacre*, 74, 87. Barre Toelken, folklorist at Utah State University, sang a ballad about the Mountain Meadows Massacre at the Western Historical Association conference at Portland, Oregon, 10 October 1999. He obtained the song from an old resident of Blanding, Utah, who received it from his father, who was contemporary at least with John D. Lee's execution. In this source, Brigham Young, through his Destroying Angels, bears the brunt of the responsibility. Also, a recent novel by Diane Noble, *The Veil* (Colorado Springs, Colo.: Waterbrook Press, 1998) is, within the limits of her literary license and "Christian fiction" bias, historically accurate and well worth reading as a way to grasp the emotions and fanaticism of these momentous events.

48. Beckwith, "Shameful Friday," 14, 22, for interview with Josiah Gibbs, who played marbles with a boy, Charley Fancher, who asserted his parents were killed by Indians, but when the Indians washed themselves they were white; Brooks, *Mountain Meadows Massacre*, 108; Bagley, *Blood of the Prophets*, 158, 173, 227.

49. Francis Marion Lyman Journal, 19, 21 September 1895, HDA, now restricted from scholarly examination. Good typed notes in my possession (Edward Leo Lyman). Amasa Mason Lyman was my great-great-grandfather. Francis Marion Lyman was his son through another plural wife, Louisa Maria Tanner, from author's own family line of descent. Josel White's first name may be a nickname or a typographic error for Joel. Indian missionary Thomas D. Brown lists Sam White as among his associates.

50. Carleton, "Special Report," 25–26, 29–30; Bagley, *Blood of the Prophets*, 147, asserts, but hardly proves, that there were apostate Mormons among those killed in the massacre.

51. Moorman, *Camp Floyd and the Mormons*, 139, 304, notes 73 and 74; Beckwith, "Shameful Friday," 113.

52. There is no evidence that Kanosh or any of his band participated in the Mountain Meadows Massacre. Ammon and the Beaver Indians also appear to have been entirely uninvolved in that affair, although their chief was back home before emigrants Powers and Warn passed by just after the massacre. Indian agent Jacob Forney Report, 5 May 1859, stated the Paiutes were divided into ten bands, each comprised of from sixty to one hundred fifty, presumably adult men, residing from Beaver, Utah Territory, to California. He added that while all the bands had subchiefs, they all regarded Tutsegabits as the principal Southern Paiute chief. Some students of this era, including Larry

Coates of Ricks College, believe Tutsegabits remained in Salt Lake City until after his ordination, which is entirely possible.

53. Bagley, *Blood of the Prophets*, 170, 416, note 69, cites good evidence that Tutsegabits returned to Salt Lake City after the massacre. Fielding, *Unsolicited Chronicler*, 418, note 13, also discusses the ordination of Tutsegabits. William R. Palmer, *Forgotten Chapters of History* (Logan: Utah State University Press), vol. 3, no. 65 (1978): 3 (transcript of radio broadcast, Cedar City, Utah, 1952), on Tutsegabits's missions.

54. Brooks, *Mountain Meadows Massacre*, 63, cites LDS "Church Letter Book," no. 3, 827–28, HDA.

55. Fielding, *Unsolicited Chronicler*, 405; Robert Glass Cleland and Juanita Brooks, eds., *A Mormon Chronicle: The Diaries of John D. Lee, 1848–1876*, vol. 1 (San Marino, Calif.: The Huntington Library, 1955), 314, recorded that on 31 May 1861 the host and adopted son quoted his guest, Brigham Young, as stating of the massacre almost four years after its occurrence that the "company that was used up at the Mountain Meadows were the fathers, mothe[rs], bros, sisters & connections of those that murdered the prophets; they merited their fate & the only thing that ever troubled him was the lives of the women & children, but that under the circumstances [this] could not be avoided." Young went on to say that those who "wanted to betray the brethren [who had participated in the affair] into the hands of their enemies, will be burned & go to hell."

56. Los Angeles *Star*, 3, 10 October 1857.

57. Hopkins-Jensen, 1, 3 October 1857; F[rancis] M[arion] Lyman to A[masa] M[ason] Lyman, 4 October 1857, William J. Cox to A[masa] M. Lyman, 7 October 1857, both in Amasa M. Lyman Papers, HDA.

58. Los Angeles *Star*, 10, 17 October 1857. The editor concluded that the testimony of Warn and Powers exhibited "a deplorable picture of the working of Mormonism which, if correct show the leaders of this sect to be actuated by the most atrocious designs towards their fellow-citizens of the Union."

59. San Francisco *Alta California*, 12 October, 12 November 1857; San Francisco *Daily Evening Bulletin*, 12, 17 October 1857.

60. Henry G. Boyle Diary, 11, 12 November 1857, Harold B. Lee Library, Brigham Young University; Caroline Barnes Crosby Diary, 6 December 1857, Utah State Historical Society, Salt Lake City; *Autobiography of Edwin Pettit* (Salt Lake City: Arrow Press, no date), 8.

61. San Francisco *Alta California*, 12 November 1857; Los Angeles *Star*, 26 December 1857.

62. Brooks, *Mountain Meadows Massacre*, 113, 119.

63. Jesse N. Smith Journal, 9 September 1857, HDA, states, "another company of emigrants having been attacked by the Indians at Beaver, Silas [his brother] went over with some men to assist them." Cited in Brooks, *Mountain Meadows Massacre*, 72.

64. Church historian Brigham H. Roberts, *A Comprehensive History of the Church of Jesus Christ of Latter-day Saints, Century I*, vol. 4 (Salt Lake City: Deseret News Press, 1930), 170–71, stated that the Indians informed the missionaries "to mind their own business, or their lives would not be saved." Roberts also quotes Jacob Hamblin, *Personal Narrative of His Personal Experiences, as a Frontiersman, Missionary to the Indians and Explorer*, ed. James A. Little (Salt Lake City: Juvenile Instructor Office, 1881), as reporting, "I talked with the principal Indians engaged in this affair, and they agreed that the stock not killed should be given up. I wrote to the owners in California, and they sent their agent, Mr. Lane, with whom I went to the Muddy, and the stock was delivered to him as the Indians had agreed." Hamblin informed Major Carleton he and his missionary associates recovered between seventy-five and one hundred head of the two hundred eighty cattle lost. But then the Indians demanded and stole another forty head before they were delivered to Lane. See Carleton, "Special Report," 15.

65. Philo T. Farnsworth, "Sketch," The Bancroft Library, Berkeley, California, cited in Brooks, *Mountain Meadows Massacre*, 18, 23, 115–16, 121; Brooks also cites James A. Little, *Jacob Hamblin: Personal Narrative*, 46. Hartt Wixom, *Hamblin: A Modern Look at the Frontier Life and Legend of Jacob Hamblin* (Springville, Utah: Cedar Fort Incorporated, 1996), 135, cites Brooks's biography of Dudley Leavitt. See Lyman, *San Bernardino*, 367, 388, for Dukes party bitterness in California.

66. Bagley, *Blood of the Prophets*, 164–70, 173.

67. Quinn, *Mormon Hierarchy: Extensions*, 261.

68. Pearson H. Corbett, *Jacob Hamblin: The Peacemaker* (Salt Lake City: Deseret Book Company, Utah, 1968), 43, 98–101.

69. Corbett, *Jacob Hamblin*, 123–24.

70. Liston later boasted, "I never disobeyed any of my superiors in office in the church, nor have [I] ever spoken a saucy word to any of them, which is a great comfort to me" ("Sketch of Commodore Perry Liston Autobiography," Utah State Historical Society, Salt Lake City).

71. Clark, "Across the Plains," 199-210; Harold Schindler, *Orrin Porter Rockwell: Man of God, Son of Thunder* (Salt Lake City: University of Utah Press, 1966), 272–77.

72. Clark, "Across the Plains," 211–19.

73. Within four months after the massacre, Lyman delivered a sermon to the Cedar City congregation, which doubtless included many of the participants in the recent atrocious military action. In it he courageously (or rashly) elaborated at "some length" on the idea that violent retaliation and revenge against outsiders for past wrongs was not a proper course of action. He delivered another series of discourses on the same subject at several southern Utah communities a year later. See Iron County Stake Records, William R. Palmer Notes, Southern Utah

University Library, Cedar City, Utah; Lee Diaries, in Cleland and Brooks, *A Mormon Chronicle* (San Marino, Calif.: The Huntington Library, 1955), vol. 1, 201–2, entries for 14, 16 March 1859.

74. Moorman, *Camp Floyd and the Mormons*, 302–4, contains many endnotes citing affidavits and notes from an HDA file entitled "Mountain Meadows Massacre File." San Bernardino *Times*, 9 February 1877, in which editor John Isaac, an earlier founder of the Salt Lake *Tribune* and Godbeite associate of Amasa Lyman, published the latter's obituary including the following statement: "[I]t was returning into southern Utah [from Salt Lake City] that he learned the whole of the facts attending that wholesale and inhuman butchery of one hundred and twenty men, women and children by the Mormon militia and their Indian allies. The home of the Apostle Lyman was, after his return from San Bernardino, right among those who had murdered immigrants and he heard so many confessions from those who had been forced by the leaders to imbrue their hands in the blood of the innocent that, and he had seen so much wretchedness of mind among those, that he encouraged them to make a full confession of their crime and take the consequences. It was probably more due to Lyman's quiet influence—for he dared not publicly speak—than to any other man's efforts that the facts of the Mountain Meadows Massacre were ever known to the public and during the first steps taken by the courts to fathom the depths of this great crime and national disgrace, Lyman labored faithfully everywhere, encouraging the guilty to unbosom themselves." See Bagley, *Blood of the Prophets*, 155, 159, for oaths of secrecy, and pages 260–61 for participants harrowed by guilt.

75. Clark, "Across the Plains," 163–220.

76. *Illustrated History of Southern California* (Chicago: Lewis Publishing Co., 1890), 541; Lyman, *San Bernardino*, 356–58; Thaddeus S. Kenderdine, *A California Tramp and Later Footprints* (Doylestown, Penn.: Doylestown Publishing, 1898), 165–66, mentioned reaching the Cottonwood Springs area, which freighter Sidney Tanner apparently called Williams Ranch, after Old Bill, who sometimes pastured livestock stolen from Californios at this ideal spot—just beyond the reach of their posses.

77. Brigham Young to Isaac Haight and John D. Lee, 2 November 1857, Brigham Young Office Journal, HDA.

78. O. W. Willits, comp., *The Story of Oak Glen and the Yucaipa Valley* (Yucaipa, Calif.: Cobb's Printing, 1971), 24, drawing from entries in the "Diary of Enoch Parrish," 7, 23 September, 9 November 1857. The reputed possessor grandson of the complete diary, residing not far from Los Angeles International Airport, slammed the door in my (Edward Leo Lyman) face on at least three occasions in as many years as I sought access to this potentially fabulous (and now presumably lost) historical source.

79. John L. Ginn, "Mormon and Indian Wars: The Mountain Meadows Massacre and Other Tragedies and Transactions Incident to the Mormon Rebellion of 1857, Together with the Personal Recollections of a Civilian who Witnessed Many of the Thrilling Scenes Described," manuscript copy, HDA; copy also in The Bancroft Library, Berkeley, California. This is not the first time Kanosh had risked his life in the pursuit of peace and cooperation with Mormon policy as he understood it. Trail traveler Solomon Carvalho learned that in 1853, after the Gunnison massacre, Kanosh went to the perpetrators' camp to retrieve stolen property to return to American officials. Some of the participants were "exasperated at his interference, and several arrows were aimed at him to kill him. His indomitable courage alone saved him." He ultimately succeeded in retrieving most of the property. See Solomon Carvalho, *Incidents of Travel and Adventure in the Far West: With Col. Frémont's Last Expedition* (New York: Derby & Jackson, 1857; reprint, Philadelphia: Jewish Society of America, 1954), 264.

80. In 1859, Indian agent to Utah Territory Jacob Forney concluded, "After strict inquiry I cannot learn that even one Pah-vant Indian was present at the massacre." Indian interpreter Nephi Johnson agreed with that statement. Brooks, *Mountain Meadows Massacre*, 255; Bagley, *Blood of the Prophets*, 124. Historian Bagley makes a good case that Chief Kanosh misled Col. Thomas L. Kane into believing the Fancher party mistreated his fellow Native Americans sufficiently to have essentially deserved some of their fate (Bagley, 197-99). Others assert this to be a gross misinterpretation of the source material. Still, the Pahvant chief was generally an honest and independent Indian leader—and never a simple tool of Brigham Young.

81. Brooks, *Mountain Meadows Massacre*, 120–21, 128–29, citing Ginn, "Mormon and Indian Wars"; Ginn, "Mormon and Indian Wars," 52–56; Paul Bailey, *Jacob Hamblin: Buckskin Apostle* (Los Angeles: Westernlore Press, 1948), 176.

82. Ginn, "Morman and Indian Wars," 55–60; Bailey, *Jacob Hamblin*, 178.

83. Albert E. Smith, assembler, *Thales Hastings Haskell: Pioneer, Scout, Explorer, Indian Missionary, 1847–1909* (Salt Lake City: Privately printed, 1964), 32.

84. Kate B. Carter, ed., *Heart Throbs of the West*, vol. 8 (Salt Lake City: Daughters of Utah Pioneers, 1947), 327; S. George Ellsworth, ed., *The History of Louisa Barnes Pratt: A Mormon Missionary Widow and Pioneer* (Logan: Utah State University Press, 1998), 259–60; Lyman, *San Bernardino*, 390–94.

85. Crosby Diary, 1–4 January 1858; Carter, *Heart Throbs of the West*, vol. 8, 324–28.

86. Los Angeles *Star*, 5 December 1857, 23 January 1858; Lyman, *San Bernardino*, 141.

87. Los Angeles *Star*, 19 December 1857, 16 January 1858;

William B. Rice, Los Angeles *Star, 1851–1864: The Beginnings of Journalism in Southern California* (Berkeley: University of California Press, 1947), 195.

88. Ebenezer Hanks to Brigham Young, 6 February 1858, Thomas L. Kane Papers, HDA, cited in Moorman, *Camp Floyd and the Mormons*, 34; Los Angeles *Star,* 13 February 1858; San Francisco *Alta California,* 10 March 1858.

89. Albert L. Zobell Jr., *Sentinel in the East: A Biography of Thomas L. Kane* (Salt Lake City: Nicholas G. Morgan, 1965), 110–18; Zobell, *Sentinel,* 47–53; Furniss, *Mormon Conflict,* 176–203; Moorman, *Camp Floyd and the Mormons,* 35–42; Campbell, *Establishing Zion,* 244–48; *Deseret News,* 9 June 1858, for Godbe-Copley trip.

90. San Francisco *Bulletin,* 27 October 1857; Los Angeles *Star,* 12, 19 December 1857, 16 January 1858; San Francisco *Alta California,* 5 December 1857; Young to Amasa M. Lyman, 4 February 1858, Brigham Young Papers, HDA.

91. Melvin T. Smith, "Colorado River Exploration and the Mormon War," *Utah Historical Quarterly* 38 (summer 1970), 207–23; Amasa M. Lyman to Brigham Young, 25 December 1857, 20 January 1858, Brigham Young Papers, HDA; San Diego *Herald,* 10 October 1857; San Francisco *Alta California,* 25 January 1858.

92. Cox to Young, 7 September 1857, Brigham Young Papers, HDA; Cox and Crosby to Young, 1 October 1857, Brigham Young Papers, HDA; Lyman to Young, 25 December 1857, Brigham Young Papers, HDA, 20 January 1858, Brigham Young Papers; San Diego *Herald,* 10 October 1857; Los Angeles *Star,* 5, 12 December 1857, 23 January 1858; San Francisco *Alta California,* 25 January 1858; Smith, "Colorado River Exploration," 207–23.

93. Smith, "Colorado River Exploration, 207–23; Clifford L. Stout, *Search for Sanctuary: Brigham Young and the White Mountain Expedition* (Salt Lake City: University of Utah Press, 1984), 40; San Diego *Herald,* 8 May 1858.

94. Amasa M. Lyman Journal, 18 January 1858, HDA.

95. Amasa M. Lyman Journal, 15 April–6 May 1858, HDA; Los Angeles *Star,* 16 January 1858.

96. Lyman Journal, 14–29 January 1858, HDA; Lyman, *San Bernardino,* 410–20.

Chapter Seven.
Freighting from the
Pacific Coast to Utah

1. John W. Caughey, "Southwest From Salt Lake in 1849," *Pacific Historical Review* 6 (1937): 164.

2. Hubert Howe Bancroft, *History of Utah* (San Francisco: Hubert Howe Bancroft, 1889; reprint, Salt Lake City: Bookcraft, 1964), 299.

3. William B. Rice, "Early Freighting on the Salt Lake—San Bernardino Trail," *Pacific Historical Review* 11, no. 1 (March 1942): 75–77; Enoch Reese to Brigham Young, 6 February 1854, Brigham Young Papers, Historical Department and Archives, Church of Jesus Christ of Latter-day Saints, Salt Lake City, Utah (hereinafter HDA), stated he had "put in the wagons the amount of provisions that our pilot said would answer, but they gave out some 300 miles short of the California settlements." See chapter 4 for details of Indian attack.

4. Rice, "Early Freighting," 78. This story is strikingly similar to that of the Pomeroys in chapter 4.

5. Rice, "Early Freighting," 77–80.

6. Enoch Reese to Brigham Young, 6 February 1854, Brigham Young Papers, HDA.

7. Los Angeles *Star,* 17 June 1854.

8. *Deseret News,* 30 May 1855; Ray M. Reeder, "The Mormon Trail: A History of the Salt Lake to Los Angeles Route to 1869," unpublished doctoral dissertation, Brigham Young University, 1966, 189, states Steptoe informed Secretary of War Jefferson Davis that $100,000 was needed to build a satisfactory road, but no such project was funded; Charles C. Rich Journal, 15 May–10 June 1855; Amasa M. Lyman Diary, 28 October, 19 November 1855; John Steele Diary, 10 June 1855, copy in Harold B. Lee Library, Brigham Young University, Provo, Utah. See also W. Turrentine Jackson, *Wagon Roads West: A Study of Federal Surveys and Construction in the Trans-Mississippi West, 1846–1869,* reprint (New Haven, Conn.: Yale University Press, 1965), 143.

9. Waterson L. Ormsby, *The Butterfield Overland Mail* (San Marino, Calif.: The Huntington Library, 1942), 78–79, 104; [Edward] Leo Lyman and Larry Reese, *The Arduous Road: Salt Lake to Los Angeles, The Most Difficult Wagon Road in American History* (Victorville, Calif.: Lyman Historical Research, 2001), 45–48.

10. Los Angeles *Star,* 5 May 1855.

11. Byron Grant Pugh, "History of Utah–California Wagon Freighting," unpublished master's thesis, University of California, Berkeley, 1949, 28–30; Sacramento *Union,* 26 December 1854; Jefferson Hunt to Rich, 7 March 1855, Charles Colson Rich Papers, HDA; *California State Assembly Proceedings,* 4 April 1855, 608; Los Angeles *Star,* 28 April 1857.

12. Pugh, "Wagon Freighting," 44–45; Mary Osborne and Melissa Lee Haybourne, "A Life Sketch of James Henry Rollins," undated manuscript, HDA.

13. Los Angeles *Star,* 18 April 1855; Charles C. Rich Diary, quoted in Pugh, "Wagon Freighting," 47.

14. Los Angeles *Star,* 2, 30 June 1855.

15. Los Angeles *Star,* 8 September 1855; Maymie Krythe, *Phineas Banning, 1830–1885* (San Francisco: California Historical Society, 1957), 72–75; Leonard J. Arrington, *Great Basin Kingdom: Economic History of the Latter-day Saints, 1830–1900* (Cam-

bridge, Mass.: Harvard University Press, 1958; reprint, Lincoln: University of Nebraska Press, 1970), 162–70, alleges that rival freight and mail contractors did nothing to smooth relations between the Mormons and the government, perhaps for their own benefit.

16. Pugh, "Wagon Freighting," 45–48; Los Angeles *Southern California*, 1 April 1855; Los Angeles *Star*, 14, 18, 28 April 1855, 19 December 1857; Blanche Christie, "Phineas Banning: With Special Reference to the Development of Transportation in Southern California," unpublished master's thesis, University of Southern California, 1932, 17.

17. *Deseret News*, 6 June 1855, in "Journal History of the Church of Jesus Christ of Latter-day Saints," 6 June 1855, HDA.

18. Young to Lyman, 1 June 1855, Amasa M. Lyman Papers, HDA.

19. Young to Lyman and Rich, 1 June 1855, Amasa M. Lyman Papers; Young to Rich, 28 September 1855, 28 May 1856, Rich Papers, HDA; Los Angeles *Star*, 29 March 1855; San Francisco *Alta California*, 26 May 1856; San Francisco *Western Standard*, 5 April, 17 May 1856.

20. Los Angeles *Southern Californian*, 2 November 1854, 18 January 1855; Los Angeles *Star*, 21 April 1855; Maurice Newmark and Marco Newmark, eds., *Sixty Years in Southern California, 1853–1913, Containing the Reminiscences of Harris Newmark* (Los Angeles: Zeitlin & Ver Brugge, 1916; reprint, 1970), 155.

21. Los Angeles *Southern Californian*, 8 February, 14, 28 March, 18 April 1855.

22. Reeder, "The Mormon Trail," 262–63.

23. John Henry Rollins Sketch, HDA; S. George Ellsworth, ed., *The History of Louisa Barnes Pratt: A Mormon Missionary Widow and Pioneer* (Logan: Utah State University Press, 1998), 269; Louisa Barnes Pratt Diary, in *Heart Throbs of the West*, vol. 8, ed. Kate B. Carter (Salt Lake City: Daughters of Utah Pioneers, 1947), 331; Caroline Barnes Crosby Diary, 8 April 1856, Utah State Historical Society, Salt Lake City.

24. "Journal History," 10, 20 May 1858; David Randolph Seeley to George William Beattie, 7 April 1937, George William Beattie and Helen Pruitt Beattie Papers, The Huntington Library, San Marino, California. Young may also have been angry that there were indications, such as Seeley's wife remaining in California, that the former church leader did not intend to remain in Utah, which the president considered an offense.

25. Thaddeus S. Kenderdine, *A California Tramp and Later Footprints* (Doylestown, Penn.: Doylestown Publishing, 1898), 141–82.

26. Kenderdine, *California Tramp*, 141–82.

27. Los Angeles *Star*, 19 March 1859, 18 February, 31 March 1860.

28. Los Angeles *Star*, 20 November 1858, 9 April 1859.

29. Los Angeles *Star*, 8 May 1858; *Deseret News*, 24 November, 1858; Thomas G. Alexander and Leonard J. Arrington, "Camp in the Sagebrush: Camp Floyd, Utah, 1858–1861," *Utah Historical Quarterly* 34 (winter 1966): 3–21.

30. Los Angeles *Star*, 2 April 1859; Reeder, "Morman Trail," 249.

31. Harris Newmark, in Newmark and Newmark, *Sixty Years*, 61, 66, 242, 290, 345.

32. Los Angeles *Star*, 9 June, 20 October 1860, 13 April 1861.

33. Harris Newmark, in Newmark and Newmark, *Sixty Years*, 290, 332, 345; Los Angeles *Star*, 3 August 1861.

34. "Bancroft Scrapbooks," vol. 5, The Bancroft Library, University of California, Berkeley, 12, quoted in Pugh, "Wagon Freighting," 106–9, 116; Anthony W. Ivins, "Traveling Over Forgotten Trails: The Old Spanish Trail," *Improvement Era* 26 (July 1923): 774.

35. San Francisco *Alta California*, 13 July 1870.

36. *Alta California*, 13 July 1870; Reeder, "Mormon Trail," 220; Juanita Brooks, *On the Mormon Frontier: The Diary of Hosea Stout, 1844–1861*, vol. 2 (Salt Lake City: University of Utah Press, 1964), 464.

37. Howard R. Driggs, *The Pony Express Goes Through: An American Saga Told by Its Heroes* (New York: Frederick A. Stokes, 1935), 121, 123–27.

38. Sacramento *Daily Union*, 16 June 1858; Kate B. Carter, ed., *Heart Throbs of the West*, vol. 10 (Salt Lake City: Daughters of Utah Pioneers, 1948), 89, 93. To better enable turning, swing teams were often hitched to a swing chain by means of single-trees and stretchers instead of doubletrees. Thus each mule was hitched to its own singletree, which was kept in place by hardwood sticks about the size of a short pitchfork handle, to prevent tangling. This allowed the animals away from the turn to pull ahead longer while those on the turn side began pulling in that direction.

39. Pugh, "Wagon Freighting," 106; Reeder, "Mormon Trail," 264.

40. Pugh, "Wagon Freighting," 11–16; Dr. Marcus Jones, Utah Report, in United States Government, *Report on the Internal Commerce of the United States for the Year 1890*, Commerce and Navigation series, vol. 2, ed. S. G. Brock (Washington, D.C.: U.S. Government Printing Office, 1891), 852–53; Ivins, "Old Spanish Trail," 772.

41. LeRoy R. Hafen and Ann W. Hafen, eds., *The Diaries of William Henry Jackson: Frontier Photographer to California and Return, 1866–67; and the Hayden Surveys to the Central Rockies, 1873, and the Utes and Cliff Dwellings, 1874* (Glendale, Calif.: Arthur H. Clark, 1959), 35–40.

42. San Diego *Herald*, 27 January, 6 June 1855, 29 March

1856; Los Angeles *Star*, 5 March 1856; San Francisco *Alta California*, 9 February 1856.

43. LeRoy R. Hafen, "The Butterfield's Overland Mail," *California Historical Society Quarterly* 11, no. 3 (October 1923): 211–22; Los Angeles *Star*, 23 October 1858; Oscar Osburn Winther, *Via Western Express & Stagecoach* (Palo Alto, Calif.: Stanford University Press, 1945), 105–19.

44. Los Angeles *Star*, 11, 13 May 1861, 2 October 1869.

45. Edward Leo Lyman *San Bernardino: The Rise and Fall of a California Community* (Salt Lake City: Signature Books, 1996), 237–41; Arthur Shearer, "Journal," 10 November 1849, The Bancroft Library, University of California, Berkeley; Thomas S. Wylly, "Westward Ho—in 1849: Memoirs of Captain Thomas S. Wylly," Bancroft Library, University of California, Berkeley, 68–79, for Holcomb's difficulties en route to California. However, it is still possible there were two men of the same name.

46. Los Angeles *Star*, 6, 20 April, 1, 8 June, 31 August 1861.

47. Pugh, "Wagon Freighting," 57, which cited San Bernardino *Patriot*, 11 January 1862, Los Angeles *Star*, 23 January 1862, Benjamin Hayes, "Scrapbooks," vol. 5, The Bancroft Library, University of California, 79; Los Angeles *Southern News*, 28 February 1862; Los Angeles *Star*, 1 January 1863.

48. Los Angeles *Star*, 19 August 1863.

49. Silas C. Cox, "Autobiographical Sketch," typescript, San Bernardino County Library, San Bernardino, California, 15–16; Dennis G. Casebier, *Camp Rock Spring, California* (Norco, Calif.: Tales of the Mojave Road Publishing, 1973), 64.

50. Cox, "Autobiographical Sketch," 16–17.

51. Andrew Karl Larson, *I Was Called to Dixie, the Virgin River Basin: Unique Experiences in Mormon Pioneering* (St. George, Utah: Dixie College Foundation, 1961; 3rd reprint, 1992), 1188–90; Los Angeles *Star*, 13 February 1864.

52. Larson, *I Was Called to Dixie*, 191–94.

53. Kate B. Carter, ed., *Heart Throbs*, vol. 10 (Salt Lake City: Daughters of Utah Pioneers, 1947), 77.

54. J. E. Pleasants, "Ranging on the Mojave River in 1864," in Automobile Club of Southern California, *Touring Topics* (March 1930), 193–95.

55. "Journal History," 9 October 1865, actually a scrapbook entry from *Deseret News* of that date. Brigham Young's most concerted effort for self-sufficiency and hostility to outside merchants was made probably just a couple years later, about the time the railroad came to Utah.

56. "Journal History," 28 February 1866.

57. San Bernardino *Guardian*, 5 October, 14 December 1867, 29 February, 4 April, 6 May 1868.

58. Cox, "Autobiographical Sketch," 21–22; Richard D. Thompson, ed., "Silas C. Cox: Daniel Boone of the West," *San*

Bernardino County Museum Association Quarterly 22, no. 1 (fall 1974): 20–24.

59. Hafen and Hafen, *Diaries of William Henry Jackson*, 92, 98, 102, 108–12, 115–19.

60. Hafen and Hafen, *Diaries of William Henry Jackson*, 108–12, 115–19.

61. George E. Perkins, *Pioneers of the Western Desert* (Los Angeles: Wetzel, no date), 15–17.

62. Larson, "I Was Called to Dixie," 255.

Chapter Eight.
Continued Emigration, Early Mojave Settlement, and Conflict with Native Americans in California

1. Caroline Barnes Crosby Diary, 2–5 January 1858, copy in Utah State Historical Society, Salt Lake City (currently being prepared for publication by Utah State University Press, Edward Leo Lyman and Susan Payne, editors).

2. Crosby Diary, 8–12 January 1858.

3. Melissa Keziah Rollins Heybourne, "Autobiographical Sketch, John Henry Rollins," copy in Historical Department and Archives, Church of Jesus Christ of the Latter-day Saints, Salt Lake City, Utah (hereinafter HDA).

4. Crosby Diary, 14–21 January 1858; [Edward] Leo Lyman and Larry Reese, *The Arduous Road: Salt Lake to Los Angeles, The Most Difficult Wagon Road in American History* (Victorville, Calif.: Lyman Historical Research and Publishing, 2001), 76–79.

5. Crosby Diary, 14–28 January 1858; this portion of the text has been published in [Edward] Leo Lyman and Cliff Walker, "Water Holes to California: Emigrant Travel Over the Most Difficult Portion of the Southern Route From Utah to California," *San Bernardino County Museum Quarterly* 44, no. 2 (spring 1997): 64–65.

6. S. George Ellsworth, ed., *The History of Louisa Barnes Pratt: Mormon Missionary Widow and Pioneer* (Logan: Utah State University Press, 1998), 264–65; Louisa Barnes Pratt, "Journal," in *Heart Throbs of the West*, vol. 8, ed. Kate B. Carter, 328; Anthony W. Ivins, "Traveling Over Forgotten Trails: The Old Spanish Trail," *Improvement Era* 26, no. 9 (July 1923): 782, 784.

7. Crosby Journal, 1, 7, 9, 11, 13, 15 February 1858.

8. Crosby Diary, 18, 20, 22 February 1858.

9. Crosby Diary, 14, 15 February 1858.

10. Crosby Diary, 25–27 February 1858; see note 54 in this chapter and text mention for courtship of Indian women. See also Juanita Brooks, "Indian Relations on Mormon Frontier," *Utah Historical Quarterly* 12, nos. 1–2 (January–April 1944): note 27.

11. Ellsworth, *History of Louisa Barnes Pratt*, 266–67; Louisa Barnes Pratt, "Journal," in Carter, *Hear Throbs of the West*, vol. 8, 329–30. The Mormons were accustomed to using biblical names for local Paiutes who had been baptized.

12. "Journal History of the Church of Jesus Christ of Latter-day Saints," 12 December 1857, HDA.

13. "Journal History," 27 May 1870.

14. "Journal History," 31 October 1858; Los Angeles *Star*, 5 March 1859.

15. Historian's Office Letterpress Copybook, 18 December 1858 (probably supposed to be 1859), HDA.

16. Los Angeles *Southern Vineyard*, 12 June, 14 August 1858; Los Angeles *Star*, 25 September, 3 October, 20, 25 November, 25 December 1858; San Francisco *Alta California*, 16 January, 12 July, 3 September, 25 November, 25 October 1858, 29 May 1869; "Journal History," 10 November 1858, HDA; United States Census, San Bernardino County, California, 1860, manuscript, family listings.

17. Los Angeles *Star*, 7 January 1860; Edward Leo Lyman, *San Bernardino: The Rise and Fall of a California Community* (Salt Lake City: Signature Books, 1996), 414–19.

18. Harold D. Langley, ed., *To Utah With the Dragoons and Glimpses of Life in Arizona and California, 1858–1859* (Salt Lake City: University of Utah Press, 1974), 136–41.

19. See note 49 in chapter 6.

20. Los Angeles *Star*, 22 June 1861, "The Mountain Meadows Massacre: A Special Report by J. H. Carleton [to W. W. Mackall, May 25,] 1859," (reprinted Spokane, Wash.: Arthur H. Clark, 1995).

21. Edward Leo Lyman, "History of the Victor Valley," chapter of manuscript not yet complete, copy on file at Victor Valley College Library, Victorville, California.

22. Dell Alcorn, *Juniper Flats Archeology: An Area of Critical Environmental Concern in Western Mojave Desert* (New York: McGraw-Hill, 1996); David D. Earle, "Indians of the Upper Mojave River and Victor Valley: The Historic Period," paper and videotape commissioned by Victor Valley College lecture series, delivered September 1991, copies in Victor Valley College Library, cited John P. Harrington Papers, 1907–1957, vol. 3, Smithsonian Institution, Washington, D.C., quoting one of Harrington's interviewees, Thomas, as saying, "the viruelas [smallpox] came 3 times (4 or 5 times according to Thomas) and killed all the Serranos. The people tried to run away but died on the road and the coyote ate them—men, women and children. . . . Before these epidemics the Serrano were very numerous."

23. Stephen Bonsal, *Edward Fitzgerald Beale: A Pioneer in the Path of Empire, 1822–1903* (New York: Putnam's, 1912), 148, 162.

24. Jules Remy, *A Journey to Great Salt Lake City* (London: W.

Jeffs, 1861), 413; Frank Lecouvreur, *From East Prussia to the Golden Gate: Letters and Diary of a California Pioneer*, trans. Julius C. Behnke (New York: Angelina Book Concern, 1906), 307–8.

25. William Chandless, *A Visit to Salt Lake: Being a Journey Across the Plains and a Residence in the Mormon Settlements* (London: Smith, Elder, 1857; reprint New York: AMS Press, 1971, 283–84. There is no corroborating documentation for this incident, and in fact an excellent scholar noted the same type of accounts in connection with the Oregon-California Trail far to the north. John D. Unruh Jr., *The Plains Across: The Overland Emigrants and the Trans-Mississippi West, 1840–60* (Urbana: University of Illinois Press, 1979; paper, 1982), 188, refers to "possibly mythical" stories he noticed appearing in numerous reminiscent travel accounts, which are strikingly similar (without the geographic details) to the one Chandless recounted. It is entirely likely this otherwise excellent English observer was misled into believing this probably false account.

26. Los Angeles *Star*, 19 September 1858.

27. Los Angeles *Star*, 10 May 1859; Richard D. Thompson and Kathryn L. Thompson, *Pioneer of the Mojave: The Life and Times of Aaron G. Lane* (Apple Valley, Calif.: Desert Knolls Press, 1995), 51–62.

28. Lyman, "Victor Valley."

29. Los Angeles *Star*, 28 January 1860.

30. Los Angeles *Star*, 28 January 1860; "Journal History," citing a small Salt Lake City newspaper named the *Mountaineer*, 21 April 1860.

31. Los Angeles *Star*, 31 March, 19, 28 April 1860.

32. Williams's wife, Albina, testified to veterans pension officials, "I am sure the Mormon leaders hired the Indians to kill my husband." On another occasion she affirmed to persons in the same government department "from the relations existing between the Mormon church and my husband at that time I have not the shadow of a doubt but what he lost his live [*sic*] through the instigation of the Mormon church." A brother, William A. Williams, who was on the freighting trip at the time, was just as certain the church hierarchy played *no* role in the deaths. A few years later it was reported in the San Bernardino *Guardian*, 14 December 1867, that a "renegade band of Amargosas" was active in the vicinity.

33. Los Angeles *Star*, 31 March 1860.

34. Russell R. Elliott, *History of Nevada* (Lincoln: University of Nebraska Press, 1973), 92–94; *Deseret News*, 30 May 1860, speculated that Native American unrest in Nevada resulted from ill treatment of Indians by desperados, including a group of gamblers from Camp Floyd and reports of deaths of Indians in the California gold fields. See also *Deseret News*, 6, 20, 27 June 1860. Other *News* articles (11 July and 29 August 1860) reported

on well-known Ute Indian chief Peteetneet, who had visited
Ruby Valley, Nevada, after the fighting and observed, "[T]he
soldiers found it anything but fun to fight well-armed Indians
when ensconced behind rocks and trees."

35. Dennis G. Casebier, *Carleton's Pah-Ute Campaign* (Norco,
Calif.: Privately printed, 1972), 10.

36. Casebier, *Carleton's Pah-Ute Campaign*, 10–39; *Deseret
News*, 13 June 1860, contains a critical account by San Bernardino resident Calisher, one of a dozen Jewish merchants there,
and Elijah K. Fuller, a Mormon who had formerly been one of
the missionaries stationed among the Indians at Las Vegas,
deeply lamenting these army actions, reportedly much more
costly in Indian lives than the official reports indicated.

37. Unruh, *The Plains Across*, 153, 171–74.

38. Casebier, *Carleton's Pah-Ute Campaign*, 43–44; Los Angeles *Star*, 14, 28 April, 12 May 1860.

39. Casebier, *Carleton's Pah-Ute Campaign*, 48–49.

40. Casebier, *Carleton's Pah-Ute Campaign*, 48–49; Dennis G.
Casebier, *The Battle of Camp Cady* (Norco, Calif.: Privately
printed, 1972), 28, note 7; Los Angeles *Star*, 31 March, 19 April
1860.

41. Louisa Barnes Pratt, "Journal," in Carter, *Heart Throbs of
the West*, vol. 8, 351.

42. Gerald A. Smith, ed., "Rousseau Diary: Across the
Desert to California From Salt Lake City to San Bernardino in
1864," *Quarterly of San Bernardino County Museum Association* 6,
no. 2 (winter 1958): 1–15.

43. Smith, "Rousseau Diary," 15–17. Much additional infor-
mation on the inhabitants in the Mojave River area at the time
may be gained from Henry P. Walker, "Soldier in the California
Column: The Diary of John W. Teal (1864)," *Arizona and the
West* 13, no. 1 (spring 1971), excerpted in Clifford J. Walker, *Back
Door to California: The Story of the Mojave River Trail* (Barstow,
Calif.: Mojave River Valley Museum Association, 1986), 277–80.
See also Ray M. Reeder, "The Mormon Trail: A History of the
Salt Lake to Los Angeles Route to 1869," unpublished doctoral
dissertation, 1966, Brigham Young University; page 407 is an ap-
pendix containing material drawn from notes the Brigham
Young University graduate student borrowed from his professor,
LeRoy R. Hafen, who had interviewed the late judge Dix Van
Dyke of Daggett. The longtime desert historian Van Dyke had
in turn interviewed Southern Route freighter Silas Cox, who
told him about some of the way station operators. He stated the
location of the "Grapevine Station (to be across [the Mojave]
from Barstow about where the #91 highway dips into the river
bottom)." Jacobi operated a mail station (probably for the Utah
mail carriers) and hauled loose hay from the Brown ranch (now
Verde Ranch) above Victorville. He described the next station,

Fish Ponds, as four miles up river from Daggett. He asserted
there was a cool-weather alternate route following the present
Highway 91 for four miles west of Yermo and then paralleling it
about a mile north and on the north side of Lead Mountain and
through the pass in the hills near the river, rather than following
the sandy river bed.

44. Ruth Shackleford, "To California by the Mormon Trail,
1865," in *Covered Wagon Women: Diaries & Letters From the Western
Trails, 1840–1890*, vol. 9, ed. and comp. Kenneth L. Holmes
(Spokane, Wash.: Arthur H. Clark, 1990), 141–45.

45. Shackleford, "To California," 141–44.

46. Shackleford, "To California," 146–50; Casebier, *Battle of
Camp Cady*, 4.

47. San Bernardino *Guardian*, 5 October, 14 December 1867,
29 February, 4 April, 6 May 1868.

48. Los Angeles *Star*, 20 April, 21 December 1861, 11 January, 12 July 1862.

49. Thompson and Thompson, *Pioneers of the Mojave*, 64–66,
74, has Mormon renegade Lot Huntington involved in these
thefts, which he was for a time. However, the diary of John D.
Lee asserts that Huntington, Indian interpreter Dimick Huntington's son, and three associates stole 150 government mules
from Camp Floyd and drove them to southern California, assuming Mormon law enforcement authorities did not care who
harassed their enemies among the military personnel. Instead,
the infamous sometime–Mormon lawman Porter Rockwell went
in pursuit. He arrested Lot Huntington and several others and
took them back to Utah. After further offenses, the alleged
Danite enforcer, Rockwell, finally shot and killed Lot Huntington (at an undetermined date but presumably in 1859).

50. Los Angeles *Star*, 4 May, 13 July, 3 August, 14, 28 September, 12 October 1861, 1 March 1862; Thompson and Thompson, *Pioneer of the Mojave*, 63–80. See also Harold Schindler, *Orrin
Porter Rockwell: Man of God, Son of Thunder* (Salt Lake City: University of Utah Press, 1966), 313–14.

51. Foremost San Bernardino County's newspaperman-his-
torian Burr Belden discovered a manuscript, at the Randsburg
Branch of the Kern County Museum, that recounted the story
of the killings. Albert B. Clyde was a pioneer in San Bernardino
who had been told the story by a neighbor, James F. Pike.
Belden published an article based on the account, under the
heading "Rabbit Hunt May Have Triggered Indian War," in the
San Bernardino *Sun*, 20 March 1966; the manuscript was later
edited by another fine San Bernardino historian, Arda M. Haenszel, and published under the title "History of Pioneer Days, by
J. F. Pike, as told to A. B. Clyde," in *Heritage Tales*, vol. 7, a publication of the City of San Bernardino History and Pioneer Society, 1985.

52. J. W. Gillette, "Some Indian Experience," *History of Southern California Annual* (1904), 158–63; J. W. Gillette to Mrs. H. E. Parrish, 31 March 1866, copy in George William Beattie and Helen Pruitt Beattie Papers, The Huntington Library, San Marino, California.

53. Gillette, "Indian Experiences," 163–64; John Brown Jr. Diary, 25–29 March 1866, copy in Beattie Papers, states, "Mr. Dunlap came. Men were murdered by about fifteen Indians, as their tracks show. But few men are on their track yet, but more are expected soon." There were two similar forays against Mojave Desert Indians during the following year, in which up to eleven more Native Americans were killed. In each of these there were also supposedly items retrieved proving those Indians too were among the murderers of the three cowhands on the upper Mojave. See Lyman, "History of Victor Valley," 116–19.

54. George William Beattie and Helen Pruitt Beattie, *Heritage of the Valley* (Oakland, Calif.: Biobooks, 1951), 420.

55. Los Angeles *News*, 13 April 1866; San Francisco *Alta California*, 20 April 1866; Casebier, *Battle at Camp Cady*, 6–7. Gillette, the almost-witness of the Las Flores murders, was a participant in a cattle drive to Montana at that time, probably the one reported. If there had been an Indian killing of one of his companions en route, or even one in a neighboring company, he probably would have mentioned it in the same reminiscences as of the former affair.

56. Casebier, *Battle at Camp Cady*, 15–16; Dennis G. Casebier, *Camp Rock Spring, California* (Norco, Calif.: Tales of the Mojave Road Publishing, 1973), 63–64.

57. Casebier, *Camp Rock Spring*, 45; Los Angeles *Star*, 29 January 1867; San Bernardino *Guardian*, 16 April 1870.

58. San Bernardino *Guardian*, 16 February 1867.

59. San Bernardino *Guardian*, 22, 30 April 1867.

60. Casebier, *Camp Rock Spring*, 82–84. A report from the treaty talks at Camp Mojave that fall stated Shaw's assailants were "renegade Amargosas," presumably Shoshone rather than Paiute.

61. San Bernardino *Guardian*, 14 December 1867; letter dated Camp Mojave, Arizona Territory, 24 November 1867, from William Redwood Price, Brvt. Lt. Col. 8th U.S. Cavalry to Maj. J. P. Sherburne, A.A.G. [Assistant Adjutant General] Dept. of California. Cited in Casebier, *Camp Rock Spring*, 64. Copy in possession of Edward Leo Lyman, courtesy Dennis G. Casebier, Mojave Desert Archives, Goffs Schoolhouse, Essex, California. The report implies the Paiutes declined to gather at a reservation among the Mojave Indians along the Colorado River, preferring the treaty instead. They also agreed to "have no intercourse with the hostile tribes [presumably in Arizona]." Among the fifty Paiutes who gathered at Camp Mojave were Chiefs Techerib [Toshearump of Las Vegas], Baramutto, Tanocke, Toucho [Tosho], Ta-Che-abit, and Espagnoe. See also San Bernardino *Guardian*, 14 December 1867, which states only three Paiutes were detained at the fort.

62. San Bernardino *Guardian*, 9 November, 19 December 1868; Casebier, *Camp Rock Spring*, 24.

63. Los Angeles *Star*, 27 February, 6 March 1869.

64. *Desert Evening News*, 20 March 1869; "Journal History," 20 March 1869; San Bernardino *Guardian*, 27 March, 8 May 1869; Anthony W. Ivins, "Traveling Over Forgotten Trails: Indian Revenge and a Brother's Devotion," *Improvement Era* 19 (May 1916): 603–7. Ivins led out in encouraging local citizens to show generosity to residents of what would during the era become the Shivwits Paiute reservation, and although some have alleged he gained special land concessions in related matters, the Indians trusted and respected him. He certainly secured information about Woolley's death that no one else in California could have obtained. Beattie and Beattie, *Heritage of a Valley*, 421.

65. Las Vegas *Sun*, 1 November 1970. On author's (Edward Leo Lyman) urging, historian Will Bagley, an acquaintance of the man in question, now deceased, asked Townley about the article. He replied essentially that the piece was simply a "treasure story"—which he was known to fabricate occasionally as a journalist. He had previously been director of the Nevada Historical Society and written good history, but he certainly duped many Mojave River residents with this story.

Chapter Nine.
Later Developments at Each End of the Southern Route

1. John D. Unruh Jr., *The Plains Across: The Overland Emigrants and the Trans-Mississippi West, 1840–60* (Urbana: University of Illinois Press, 1979; paper, 1982), 245, 248. When referring to the upper end of the trail, I mean Utah's Dixie. If Salt Lake City had been that terminus, there would have been some four hundred miles with developed conveniences for travelers in the latter period of Southern Route use. For an evaluation of the difficulty of the road, see [Edward] Leo Lyman and Larry Reese, *The Arduous Road: Salt Lake to Los Angeles, the Most Difficult Wagon Road in American History* (Victorville, Calif.: Lyman Historical Research and Publishing, 2001), 4.

2. Los Angeles *Star*, 4 February 1861.

3. J. Wilson McKenney, "Gold Builds a Road," *Desert Magazine* 1, no. 1 (December 1937): 8–9, 24.

4. Los Angeles *Star*, 19 August 1862.

5. Los Angeles *Star*, 3 January 1863, 13 February 1864.

6. Amasa M. Lyman Journal, 5 June 1851, Historical Department and Archives, Church of Jesus Christ of Latter-day Saints, Salt Lake City, Utah (hereinafter HDA); Heybourne, "Sketch, John Henry Rollins," HDA; Washington Peck Diary, Oregon California National Frontier Trails Center, Mattes Library, Independence, Missouri, 28 November, 7 December 1850; San Francisco *Alta California*, 29 January 1852; Ray M. Reeder, "The Mormon Trail: A History of the Salt Lake to Los Angeles Route to 1869," unpublished doctoral dissertation, Brigham Young University, 1966, 336–37.

7. Los Angeles *Star*, 10 October 1863; Gerald A. Smith, ed., "Rousseau Diary: Across the Desert to California From Salt Lake City to San Bernardino in 1864," *Quarterly of San Bernardino County Museum Association* 6 (4 December 1964): 2.

8. San Bernardino *Guardian*, 23 July 1870.

9. Los Angeles *Star*, 5, 12, 26 January, 9 February, 9, 23 March, 4 May 1861.

10. Los Angeles *Star*, 2 November 1861.

11. Los Angeles *Star*, 3 August, 5 October 1861; Stanley W. Paher, *Las Vegas: As It Began—As It Grew* (Las Vegas: Nevada Publications, 1971), 32–33.

12. Larson, *I Was Called to Dixie*, 249–50; Juanita Brooks, *John D. Lee: Zealot—Pioneer Builder—Scapegoat* (Glendale, Calif.: Arthur H. Clark, 1962).

13. Lee, John D., *A Mormon Chronicle: The Diaries of John D. Lee, 1848-1876*, vol. 1, ed. Robert Glass Cleland and Juanita Brooks (San Marino, Calif.: The Huntington Library, 1955), 198, 26 February 1859; Josiah Rogerson Journal, 31 May–10 July 1864, HDA.

14. Los Angeles *Star*, 3 August 1861. Brigham Young had been interested in Colorado River transportation to Utah even in 1851 and again in 1855. See Melvin T. Smith, "The Colorado River: Its History in the Lower Canyons Area," unpublished doctoral dissertation, Brigham Young University, 1972, 242–43, 247.

15. San Francisco *Evening Bulletin*, 16 January 1864, cited in Smith, "The Colorado River," 264. Francis H. Leavitt, "Steam Navigation on the Colorado River," *California Historical Society Quarterly* 22 (March 1943): 15.

16. James G. Bleak, "Annals of the Southern Mission," Book A, 147, copy in Family History Center, Church of Jesus Christ of Latter-day Saints, St. George, Utah. See Edward W. Tullidge, *History of Salt Lake City* (Salt Lake City: Star Printing, 1886), 65–82, for the sizable profits made by Eldridge and William Jennings trading over the Southern Route in 1864.

17. Bleak, "Annals of the Southern Mission," 172–74.

18. Smith, "The Colorado River," 270–74, 278–79; Salt Lake City *Daily Telegraph*, 16 January 1865, published Call's report.

19. Brigham Young to Judge J. F. Kinney, HDA, 23 December

1864; and Judge J. F. Kinney to Brigham Young, HDA, 23 February 1865.

20. Bleak, "Annals of the Southern Mission," 174.

21. *Millennial Star* 27 (21 January 1865): 41; (2 February 1865): 78.

22. *Deseret News*, 23 April 1865; Smith, "Colorado River," 299.

23. Smith, "Colorado River," 286–87.

24. Smith, "Colorado River," 270–71, 299; Melvin T. Smith, "Mormon Exploration in the Lower Colorado River Area," in *The Mormon Role in the Settlement of the West*, ed. Richard H. Jackson, Charles Redd Monographs no. 9 (Provo, Utah: Brigham Young University Press), 41, 49, note 63, stated that "a search of Mojave County (Arizona Territory) records revealed that William Cowan had filed on 160 acres at the landing on May 5, 1865, some eleven days before Call filed on his land."

25. Larson, *I Was Called to Dixie*, 140–45; Kate B. Carter, ed., *Heart Throbs of the West*, vol. 10 (Salt Lake City: Daughters of Utah Pioneers, 1948), 75.

26. Lt. Sylvester Mowry to Col. S. Cooper, Adj. Gen. U.S. Army, 23 July 1855, copy at Utah State Historical Society, Salt Lake City, Utah; *Deseret News*, 14 December 1854.

27. *Deseret News*, 23 April 1865; "Journal History of the Church of Jesus Christ of Latter-day Saints," HDA, 19 January 1866, 15, 19 March, 27 April 1868. The March entries in the "Journal History" assert that Erastus Snow procured another appropriation from the territorial legislature amounting to $1,500, "For the altering and improving the road between Beaver Dam Wash and the Valley of the Muddy. . . ." "Scrapbook Notes, Beaver Dam," Desert Valley Museum, Mesquite, Nevada, 1, stated, "[T]he water often failed at Beaver Dam Wash during the dry season so President Snow had a well dug there to guarantee it for the travelers. It wasn't a spring, but went down 30 feet like a cistern. Users would have to dip the water up with buckets." Bill Vincent, "Glendale to St. George on the Mormon Trail, Las Vegas *Review-Journal*, 21 November, 26 December 1976. See also Lyman and Reese, *Arduous Road*, 59–64, for more on freight roads, including much information contributed by modern road historian Lavoid Leavitt.

28. Israel Bennion, "Before the Arrowhead Trail," *Improvement Era* 29, no. 6 (April 1926): 543–44; Andrew Karl Larson, *The Red Hills of November: A Pioneer Biography of Utah's Cotton Towns* (Salt Lake City: Deseret News Press, 1957), 127–29.

29. Larson, *I Was Called to Dixie*, 146–48; "Journal History," 13 March 1866.

30. Pearson H. Corbett, *Jacob Hamblin: The Peacemaker* (Salt Lake City: Deseret Book Company, 1968), 107. Tutsegabits remained faithful to the church himself. Historian of the Paiutes William R. Palmer reported that Tutsegabits was "sent out alone to preach among the Navajos and other tribes across the

Colorado." It is also possible his fervor waned, perhaps as a result of subsequent deteriorating relationships with some Mormons. William R. Palmer, *Forgotten Chapters of History,* vol. 3 (Logan: Merrill Library, Utah State University, 1978), 3; Smith, "Mormon Exploration," 32.

31. Larson, *I Was Called to Dixie,* 149–52. See earlier in chapter for a discussion of Brigham Young's role in stimulating this unfortunate occurrence. Jane Percy Kowalewski, "Strange Bedfellows: Mormon and Miners in Southern Nevada," unpublished master's thesis, University of Nevada, Las Vegas, 1984, 22–70.

32. Brigham Young to the bishops and others on the Muddy, 17 September 1870, James Leithead to Erastus Snow, 24 November 1870, both in James G. Bleak, "Annals of the Southern Mission," Book B, 75, 81; Bennion, "Before the Arrowhead Trail," 544, states that after seeing several barren mesas and groves of gray mesquite, "[W]ell might Brigham Young doubt his own prophetic vision when in 1869 he drove down to the edge of the Mojave Desert with white top carriage and 'spanking bays.' Long and earnestly he looked southward. Then turning to his boon companion, the late C. R. Savage, he said simply 'Turn north, Charley.'" Savage's journal mentions being in the area that year, but makes no mention of such an event. Other sources state that he did visit in the area.

33. Amos Milton Musser to *Deseret News,* 28 March 1870; Larson, *I Was Called to Dixie,* 143, also gives a good idea of the productive capacity of the Muddy settlements before their demise.

34. Smith, "Colorado River," 311–16.

35. Los Angeles *Star,* 21 December 1861, 11 January 1862.

36. San Francisco *Alta California,* 5 March 1862.

37. Sam P. Davis, *History of Nevada,* vol. 1 (Reno: Elm Publishing, 1913), 219.

38. Paher, *Las Vegas,* 38–46; Luther A. Ingersol, *Ingersol's Century Annals of San Bernardino County, 1769 to 1904* (Los Angeles: Privately printed, 1904), 694, for Gass biographical sketch.

39. Paher, *Las Vegas,* 50–51; Don Fufkin, "The Lost County of Pah-Ute," *Arizoniana: The Journal of Arizona History* 5, no. 2 (1964): 1–11.

40. Dennis G. Casebier, *Camp El Dorado, Arizona Territory: Soldiers, Steamboats, and Miners on the Upper Colorado River* (Tempe: Arizona Historical Foundation, 1970), 22–25.

41. Casebier, *Camp El Dorado,* 30–33.

42. Casebier, *Camp El Dorado,* 63–65; San Bernardino *Guardian,* 14 December 1867.

43. Casebier, *Camp El Dorado,* 52–61.

44. Edward Leo Lyman, "From the City of Angels to the City of Saints: The Struggle to Build a Railroad From Los Angeles to Salt Lake City," *California History: The Magazine of the California Historical Society* 70, no. 1 (spring 1991): 76–93, in-

cludes discussion of earlier efforts to construct railroads through this region. For outlaw activity led by Ben Tasker along the Utah border near Pioche, see Edward Leo Lyman, "History of Millard County" (the uncut, long version), typescript copies in Great Basin Museum and Delta Public Library, both Delta, Utah.

45. San Bernardino *Guardian,* 23 April, 14 May 1870, 13 July 1872. Admittedly, this chief could also be Tecopa.

46. Louisa Brown Waters, "Trail Blazers of Cajon Pass," *Westways* 31 (January 1931): 8–9; John Brown Jr. Diary, George William Beattie and Helen Pruitt Beattie Papers, The Huntington Library, San Marino, California.

47. *Guardian,* 17 January, 9 September 1871; Thaddeus S. Kenderdine, *A California Tramp and Later Footprints* (Doylestown, Penn.: Doylestown Publishing, 1898), 179, reported in 1858 spending a night at the upper end of the Cajon Pass in a locality "badly infested by grizzlies, the whereabouts of which were made manifest by the restlessness of our animals, which were neighing, braying and scampering hither and thither through the night." Area ranch hand Silas Cox had been chased by a mother bear in the same area.

48. San Bernardino *Guardian,* 9, 16, 23, 30 September 1871; Lyman and Reese, *Arduous Road,* 89–96.

49. G. Frank Meacham, "The Discovery and Location of the Silver King Mine in Calico Mountain" (undated, but doubtless published early 1969 as a final segment of *Pioneer Cabin News* by San Bernardino Society of California Pioneers, ed. Harold B. Meacham, G. Frank's son, who died in March 1969). This publication series has been followed by *Heritage Tales;* both are available in libraries in San Bernardino County. San Bernardino *Sun,* 13 November 1938. Fred Holladay—"The Stoddard Boys," *Heritage Tales* (San Bernardino: San Bernardino Society of California Pioneers, 1988) 11, 44–47, drawing on a March 1970 *Los Angeles Westerners Brand Book* article by grandson R. Jackson Stoddard, asserts that the Stoddard Well was dug by brother Arvin rather than Sheldon. I have found no evidence that Arvin was still residing in the California southland during the time in question.

50. San Bernardino *Guardian,* 16 September 1871; Ingersol, *Ingersol's Century Annals,* 835, for Hartman biographical sketch.

51. Los Angeles *Star,* 19 December 1863.

52. As mentioned earlier herein, the predecessor of Potosi was started when a Native American named Colorado informed Mormon missionary John Steele of the ore deposit near the California Road (see figure in chapter 5). Johnnie Moss's discovery at El Dorado Canyon had a similar beginning (see figure in chapter 9). The fourth such instance was a Paiute named Moentich initially showing some of the ore deposits of the Paranagat Valley to another Mormon missionary to the Indians, Ira Hatch,

thus quickly stimulating the mining rush to that locality. See "Journal History," 6 July 1866 (recounting developments of the previous 6 January). See also notes 53, 54 below.

53. San Bernardino *Guardian*, 2 July, 13 August 1870, 30 September 1871, 11 May 1872, 10 May, 27 September, 4 October 1873; Larry M. Vredenburgh, Gary L. Shumway, and Russell D. Hartill, *Desert Fever: An Overview of Mining in the California Desert* (Conoga Park, Calif.: Living West Press, 1981), 96–106; Alan Hensher, "Ivanpah—Pioneer Mojave Desert Town," *Heritage Tales* (San Bernardino: San Bernardino Society of California Pioneers) 7 (1984): 37–58.

54. San Bernardino *Guardian*, 17 May 1873.

55. Los Angeles *Star*, 20 June 1868.

56. Russell R. Elliott, *History of Nevada* (Lincoln: University of Nebraska Press, 1973), 108–9.

57. Los Angeles *Star*, 27 March, 17 April, 17 July 1869; San Bernardino *Guardian*, 12 June 1869.

58. Los Angeles *Star*, 17 July 1869; George M. Wheeler, Corps of Engineers, *Preliminary Report Concerning Explorations and Survey Principally in Nevada and Arizona, 1871* (Washington, D.C.: U.S. Government Printing Office, 1872), 84–85; Mark Severance Diary, 13 October–30 November 1872, as assistant to Wheeler on expedition, copy in my possession (Lyman). See also William H. Goetzman, *Exploration and Empire: The Explorer and the Scientist in the Winning of the American West* (New York: Vintage Books, 1966), 467–85; Richard A. Bartlett, *Great Surveys of the American West* (Norman: University of Oklahoma Press, 1962; reprint, 1989), 339–49; Lyman, "From the City of Angels," 81–93.

59. San Bernardino *Guardian*, 8, 13, 22, 29 August, 5, 12, 19 September, 3 October 1868, 22 June 1872.

60. Los Angeles *Star*, 6 August, 17 November 1870.

61. *Guardian*, 29 April, 12 June, 11 November 1871, 17 May 1873, 29 May 1875.

62. *San Bernardino Guardian*, 8 November 1873, 2, 18 November 1874; Ingersol, *Annals of San Bernardino County*, 248; Neill G. Wilson, *Silver Stampede: The Career of Death Valley's Hell-Camp, Old Panamint* (New York: Macmillan, 1937), 116–19, 123–29.

63. *Guardian*, 7 June, 4 October 1873, 7 February 1874; San Bernardino *Times Index*, 22 November 1875.

64. Los Angeles *Star*, 22 July 1865; San Bernardino *Guardian*, 14 March, 5, 26 December 1874. When the way station was later put up for sale, advertisements listed fourteen rooms in the establishment.

65. San Bernardino *Guardian*, 22 May 1875; Joseph Henry Jackson, *Bad Company: The Story of California's Legendary and Actual Stage-robbers, Bandits, Highwaymen and Outlaws From the Fifties to the Eighties* (New York: Harcourt, Brace, 1939; reprint, Lincoln: University of Nebraska Press, 1977), 308, 312–13, 320.

66. San Bernardino *Guardian*, 17, 18 November 1875. Chavez was reportedly killed within the year, in Arizona.

67. *Guardian*, 17, 18 November, 16 December 1875; Lyman, "History of Millard County," typescript, 235–37, for episode involving Utah outlaw Ben Tasker, who preyed on freighters outside of Pioche, Nevada, at the same time.

68. Keith L. Bryant Jr., *History of the Atchison, Topeka & Santa Fe Railway* (Lincoln: University of Nebraska Press, 1974), 87–103; Edward Leo Lyman, "Outmaneuvering the Octopus: Atchison, Topeka and Santa Fe," *California History* 67, no. 2 (June 1988), 94–107.

Bibliography

Books

Alcorn, Dell. *Juniper Flats Archeology: An Area of Critical Environmental Concern in Western Mojave Desert*. New York: McGraw-Hill, 1996.

Allen, James B., and Glen M. Leonard. *The Story of the Latter-day Saints*. Salt Lake City: Deseret Book Company, 1976.

Arrington, Leonard James. *Great Basin Kingdom: Economic History of the Latter-day Saints, 1830–1900*. Cambridge, Mass.: Harvard University Press, 1958; reprint, Lincoln: University of Nebraska Press, 1970.

Bagley, Will. *Blood of the Prophets: Brigham Young and the Massacre at Mountain Meadows*. Norman: University of Oklahoma Press, 2002.

Bailey, L[ynn] R. *Indian Slave Trade in the Southwest*. Los Angeles: Westernlore Press, 1973.

Bailey, Paul. *Jacob Hamblin, Buckskin Apostle*. Los Angeles: Westernlore Press, 1948.

Bancroft, Hubert Howe. *History of Utah*. San Francisco: Hubert Howe Bancroft, 1889; reprint, Salt Lake City: Bookcraft, 1964.

Bartlett, Richard A. *Great Surveys of the American West*. Norman: University of Oklahoma Press, 1962; reprint, 1989.

Bateman, Richard. *James Pattie's West: The Dream and the Reality*. Norman: University of Oklahoma Press, 1984.

Beattie, George William, and Helen Pruitt Beattie. *Heritage of the Valley: San Bernardino's First Century*. Oakland, Calif.: Biobooks, 1951.

Bieber, Ralph P. *Southern Trails to California in 1849*. Glendale, Calif.: Arthur H. Clark, 1937.

Bigler, David L. *Forgotten Kingdom: The Mormon Theocracy in the American West, 1847–1896*. Logan: Utah State University Press, 1998.

Birney, Hoffman. *Zealots of Zion*. Philadelphia: Penn Publishing, 1931.

Bolton, Herbert E., ed. *Font's Complete Diary: A Chronicle of the Founding of San Francisco*. Berkeley: University of California Press, 1933.

———. *Pageant in the Wilderness: The Story of the Escalante Expedition to the Interior Basin, 1776*. Salt Lake City: Utah State Historical Society, 1951.

Bonsal, Stephen. *Edward Fitzgerald Beale: A Pioneer in the Path of Empire, 1822–1903*. New York: Putnam's, 1912.

Brewerton, George Douglas. *Overland with Kit Carson: A Narrative of the Old Spanish Trail in '48*. New York: Coward-McCann, 1930.

Brooks, George R. *The Southwest Expedition of Jedediah S. Smith: His Personal Account of the Journey to California, 1826–1827*. Glendale, Calif.: Arthur H. Clark, 1977; paper, Lincoln: University of Nebraska Press, 1989.

Brooks, Juanita. *John D. Lee: Zealot—Pioneer Builder—Scapegoat*. Glendale, Calif.: Arthur H. Clark, 1962.

———. ed. *Journal of the Southern Indian Mission: Diary of Thomas D. Brown*. Logan: Utah State University Press, 1972.

———. *The Mountain Meadows Massacre*. Palo Alto, California, 1950; reprint, Norman: University of Oklahoma Press, 1962.

———, ed. *On the Mormon Frontier: The Diary of Hosea Stout, 1844–1861*, 2 vols. Salt Lake City: University of Utah Press, 1964.

Brown, John, Jr., and James Boyd. *History of San Bernardino and Riverside Counties,* 3 vols. Chicago: Lewis, 1922.

Bryant, Keith L., Jr. *History of the Atchison, Topeka & Santa Fe Railway.* Lincoln: University of Nebraska Press, 1974.

Campbell, Eugene E. *Establishing Zion: The Mormon Church in the American West, 1847–1869.* Salt Lake City: Signature Books, 1988.

"The Mountain Meadows Massacre: A Special Report by J. H. Carleton [to W. W. Mackall, May 25,] 1859." Reprinted Spokane, Wash.: Arthur H. Clark, 1995.

Carter, Kate B., ed. *Heart Throbs of the West,* 10 vols. Salt Lake City: Daughters of Utah Pioneers, 1947–1949.

Carvalho, Solomon N[unes]. *Incidents of Travel and Adventure in the Far West: With Col. Frémont's Last Expedition.* New York: Derby & Jackson, 1857; reprint, Philadelphia: Jewish Society of America, 1954.

Casebier, Dennis G. *Camp El Dorado, Arizona Territory: Soldiers, Steamboats, and Miners on the Upper Colorado River.* Tempe: Arizona Historical Foundation, 1970.

———. *The Battle of Camp Cady.* Norco, Calif.: Privately printed, 1972.

———. *Carleton's Pah-Ute Campaign.* Norco, Calif.: Privately printed, 1972.

———. *Camp Rock Spring, California.* Norco, Calif.: Tales of the Mojave Road Publishing, 1973.

Chandless, William. *Visit to Salt Lake: Being a Journey Across the Plains and a Residence in the Mormon Settlements.* London: Smith, Elder, 1857; reprint, New York: AMS Press, 1971.

Cleland, Robert Glass, and Juanita Brooks, eds. *A Mormon Chronicle: The Diaries of John D. Lee, 1848–1876.* San Marino, Calif.: The Huntington Libary, 1955.

Coates, Lawrence G. *The Fancher Party Before the Mountain Meadows Massacre.* Rexburg, Idaho: Privately printed, 1992.

Corbett, Pearson H. *Jacob Hamblin: The Peacemaker.* Salt Lake City: Deseret Book Company, 1968.

Crampton, C. Gregory, and Steven K. Madsen. *In Search of the Spanish Trail: Santa Fe to Los Angeles, 1829–1848.* Salt Lake City: Gibbs Smith, 1994.

Cumming, John, ed. *The Long Road to California: The Journal of Cephas Arms Supplemented With Letters by Traveling Companions on the Overland Trail in 1849.* Mount Pleasant, Mich.: Private Press of John Cumming, 1985.

Dale, Harrison Clifford. *The Ashley-Smith Explorations and the Discovery of the Central Route to the Pacific, 1822–1829.* Glendale, Calif.: Arthur H. Clark, 1941.

Davis, Sam P. *History of Nevada,* vol. 1. Reno: Elm Publishing, 1913.

Day, Stella H., and Sebrina C. Ekins. *One Hundred Years of History of Millard County [Milestones of Millard].* Springville, Utah: Art City Publishing-Daughters Utah Pioneers of Millard County, 1951.

Driggs, Howard R. *The Pony Express Goes Through: An American Saga Told by Its Heroes.* New York: Frederick A. Stokes, 1935.

Elliott, Russell R. *History of Nevada.* Lincoln: University of Nebraska Press, 1973.

Ellsworth, S. George, ed. *The History of Louisa Barnes Pratt: Mormon Missionary Widow and Pioneer.* Logan: Utah State University Press, 1998.

———, ed. *The Journals of Addison Pratt.* Salt Lake City: University of Utah Press, 1990.

Etter, Patricia A. *To California on the Southern Route, 1849: A History and Annotated Bibliography.* Spokane, Wash.: Arthur H. Clark, 1998.

Fielding, Robert Kent. *The Unsolicited Chronicler: An Account of the Gunnison Massacre, Its Causes and Consequences, Utah Territory, 1847–1859.* Brookline, Mass.: Paradigm Press, 1993.

Frémont, John Charles. *Narratives of Exploration and Adventure,* ed. Allan Nevins. New York: Longman's, Green, 1956.

Furniss, Norman F. *The Mormon Conflict, 1850–1859.* New Haven, Conn.: Yale University Press, 1960.

Goetzman, William H. *Exploration and Empire: The Explorer and the Scientist in the Winning of the American West.* New York: Vintage Books, 1966.

Hafen, LeRoy, ed. *Letters of Lewis Granger: Reports of the Journey From Salt Lake to Los Angeles in 1849, and of Conditions in Southern California in the Early Fifties.* Los Angeles: Glen Dawson, 1959.

Hafen, LeRoy R., and Ann W. Hafen. *Handcarts to Zion, 1856–1860.* Glendale, Calif.: Arthur H. Clark, 1960.

Hafen, LeRoy R., and Ann W. Hafen, eds. *Journals of Forty-niners: Salt Lake to Los Angeles: With Diaries and Contemporary Records of Sheldon Young, James S. Brown, Jacob Y. Stover, Charles C. Rich, Addison Pratt, Howard Egan, Henry W. Bigler, and Others.* Glendale, Calif.: Arthur H. Clark, 1954.

———. *The Diaries of William Henry Jackson: Frontier Photographer to California and Return, 1866–67; and the Hayden Surveys to the Central Rockies, 1873, and the Utes and Cliff Dwellings, 1874.* The Far West and the Rockies Historical Series, 1820–1875, no. 10. Glendale, Calif.: Arthur H. Clark, 1959.

———. *The Far West and Rockies: General Analytical Index to the Fifteen Volume Series and Supplement to the Journals of Forty-niners, Salt Lake to Los Angeles.* Glendale, Calif.: Arthur H. Clark, 1961.

———. *The Mountain Men and the Fur Trade of the Far West,* 10 vols. Glendale, Calif.: Arthur H. Clark, 1965–1972.

Hafen, LeRoy R., and Ann W. Hafen. *The Old Spanish Trail: Santa Fe to Los Angeles, With Extracts From Contemporary Records and Including Diaries of Antonio Armijo and Orville*

Pratt. Glendale, Calif.: Arthur H. Clark, 1954; paper, Lincoln: University of Nebraska Press, 1993.

Hague, Harlan. *The Road to California: The Search for a South Overland Route, 1540–1848.* Glendale, Calif.: Arthur H. Clark, 1978.

Harlow, Neal. *California Conquered: The Annexation of a Mexican Province, 1846–1850.* Berkeley: University of California Press, 1982.

Hill, Marvin S. *Quest for Refuge: The Mormon Flight From American Pluralism.* Salt Lake City: Signature Books, 1989.

Holliday, J[ames] S. *The World Rushed In: The California Gold Rush Experience.* New York: Simon & Schuster, 1981.

Holmes, Kenneth L., ed. and comp. *Covered Wagon Women: Diaries & Letters from the Western Trails, 1840–1890,* 9 vols. Spokane, Wash.: Arthur H. Clark, 1985–1990.

Holmes, Winona, et al. *Nuwuvi: A Southern Paiute History.* Salt Lake City: Inter-Tribal Council of Nevada, 1976.

Hyde, John. *Mormonism, Its Leaders and Designs.* New York: W.P. Feteridge, 1857.

Illustrated History of Southern California. Chicago: Lewis Publishing Co., 1890.

Ingersol, Luther A. *Ingersol's Century Annals of San Bernardino County, 1769 to 1904.* Los Angeles: Privately printed, 1904.

Jackson, Donald, and Mary Lee Spence. *The Expeditions of John Charles Frémont,* 3 vols. Urbana: University of Illinois Press, 1970–84.

Jackson, Joseph Henry. *Bad Company: The Story of California's Legendary and Actual Stage-robbers, Bandits, Highwaymen and Outlaws From the Fifties to the Eighties.* New York: Harcourt, Brace, 1939; reprint, Lincoln: University of Nebraska, 1977.

Jackson, W. Turrentine. *Wagon Roads West: A Study of Federal Surveys and Construction in the Trans-Mississippi West, 1846–1869.* New Haven, Conn.: Yale University Press, 1965; paper, Lincoln: University of Nebraska Press, 1979.

Jensen, Andrew, comp. *History of Las Vegas Mission.* Nevada State Historical Society Papers. Reno: Nevada State Historical Society, 1926.

Journal of Discourses, by Brigham Young, His Two Counselors and the Twelve Apostles, vol. 4. Liverpool: Latter-day Saint Booksellers Depot, 1857.

Kelly, Charles, and Maurice L. Howe. *Miles Goodyear.* Salt Lake City: Western Printing, 1937.

Kemble, John Haskell. *The Panama Route, 1848–1869.* Berkeley: University of California Press, 1943.

Kenderdine, Thaddeus S. *A California Tramp and Later Footprints.* Doylestown, Penn.: Doylestown Publishing, 1898.

Kenney, Scott G. *Wilford Woodruff Journals,* 9 vols. Midvale, Utah: Signature Books, 1985.

Knack, Martha C. *Boundaries Between: The Southern Paiutes,* 1775–1995. Lincoln, Nebraska: University of Nebraska Press, 2001.

Krythe, Maymie. *Phineas Banning, 1839–1885.* San Francisco: California Historical Society, 1957.

Landon, Michael N., ed. *To California in '49: The Journals of George Q. Cannon,* vol. 1. Salt Lake City: Deseret Book Company, 1999.

Langley, Harold D., ed. *To Utah With the Dragoons and Glimpses of Life in Arizona and California, 1858–1859.* Salt Lake City: University of Utah Press, 1974.

Larson, Andrew Karl. *The Red Hills of November: A Pioneer Biography of Utah's Cotton Towns.* Salt Lake City: Deseret News Press, 1957.

———. *I Was Called to Dixie, the Virgin River Basin: Unique Experiences in Mormon Pioneering.* St. George, Utah: Dixie College Foundation, 1961; 3rd printing, 1992.

Lecouvreur, Frank. *From East Prussia to the Golden Gate,* trans. Julius C. Behnke. New York: Angelina Book Concern, 1906.

Limerick, Patricia Nelson. *The Legacy of Conquest: The Unbroken Past of the American West.* New York: Norton, 1987.

Limerick, Patricia Nelson, Clyde A. Milner II, and Charles E. Rankin, eds. *Trails: Toward a New Western History.* Lawrence: University Press of Kansas.

Little, James A. *Jacob Hamblin: Personal Narrative of His Personal Experiences, as a Frontiersman, Missionary to the Indians and Explorer.* Salt Lake City: Juvenile Instructor Office, 1881.

Long, Margaret. *The Shadow of the Arrow.* Caldwell, Idaho: Caxton Printers, 1941.

Lorton, William B. *Over the Salt Lake Trail in the Fall of '49.* Los Angeles: Privately printed, 1957.

Lyford, Charles P. *The Mormon Problem: An Appeal to the American People.* New York: Phillips & Hunt, 1886.

Lyman, Edward Leo. *San Bernardino: The Rise and Fall of a California Community.* Salt Lake City: Signature Books, 1996.

Lyman, Edward Leo, and Linda King Newell. *A History of Millard County.* Salt Lake City: Utah State Historical Society, 1999.

Lyman, [Edward] Leo, and Larry Reese. *The Arduous Road: Salt Lake to Los Angeles, The Most Difficult Wagon Road in American History.* Victorville, Calif.: Lyman Historical Research and Publishing, 2001.

Mack, Effie Mona. *Nevada, A History of the State From the Earliest Times Through the Civil War.* Glendale, Calif.: Arthur H. Clark, 1936.

Manley, William Lewis. *Death Valley in '49: An Important Chapter of California History.* San Jose, Calif.: Pacific Tree and Vine Company, 1894; reprint, New York: Wallace Hubbard, 1929.

———. *The Jayhawkers' Oath and Other Sketches.* Los Angeles: Warren F. Lewis, 1949.

Mattes, Merrill J. *The Great Platte River Road: The Covered Wagon Mainline Via Fort Kearny to Fort Laramie.* Lincoln: University of Nebraska Press, 1969; paper, 1987.

Morgan, Dale Lowell. *Jedediah Smith and the Opening of the West.* Indianapolis: Bobbs-Merrill, 1953; reprint, Lincoln: University of Nebraska Press, 1964.

———, ed. *The Overland Diary of James Avery Prichard: From Kentucky to California in 1849.* Denver: Old West Publishing, 1959.

Moorman, Donald R., with Gene A. Sessions. *Camp Floyd and the Mormons: The Utah War.* Salt Lake City: University of Utah Press, 1992.

Neff, Andrew Love. *History of Utah, 1847–1869.* Salt Lake City: Deseret News Press, 1940.

Nevins, Allan. *Fremont: Pathmarker of the West.* New York: Appleton-Century, 1939.

Newmark, Maurice, and Marco Newmark, eds. *Sixty Years in Southern California, 1853–1913, Containing the Reminiscences of Harris Newmark.* Los Angeles: Zeitlin & Ver Brugge, 1916; reprint, 1970.

Noble, Diane. *The Veil.* Colorado Springs, Colo.: Waterbrook Press, 1998.

Ormsby, Waterson L. *The Butterfield Overland Mail.* San Marino, Calif.: The Huntington Libary, 1942.

Paher, Stanley W. *Las Vegas: As It Began—As It Grew.* Las Vegas: Nevada Publications, 1971.

Palmer, William R. *Forgotten Chapters of History,* 5 vols. Logan: Merrill Library, Utah State University, 1978.

Pattie, James Ohio. *The Personal Narrative of James Ohio Pattie. Early Western Travels, 1748–1846: A Series of Annotated Reprints of Some of the Best and Rarest Contemporary Volumes of Travel, Descriptive of the Aborigines and Social and Economic Conditions in the Middle and Far West During the Period of Early American Settlement,* ed. Reuben Gold Thwaites. Cleveland, Ohio: Arthur H. Clark, 1905.

Perkins, George E. *Pioneers of the Western Desert.* Los Angeles: Wetzel Publishing, no date.

Pettit, Edwin. *Autobiography of Edwin Pettit.* Salt Lake City: Arrow Press, no date.

Pratt, Parley P[arker], Jr. *Autobiography of Parley P. Pratt.* Salt Lake City: Deseret Book Company, 1938; paper, 1976.

Quinn, D. Michael. *The Mormon Hierarchy: Extensions of Power.* Salt Lake City: Signature Books, 1997.

Reay, Lee. *Lambs in the Meadow.* Provo, Utah: Meadow Lane Publications, 1979.

Reid, John Phillip. *The Law for the Elephant: Property and Social Behavior on the Overland Trail.* San Marino, Calif.: The Huntington Libary, 1980; paper, 1997.

Remy, Jules. *A Journey to Great Salt Lake City,* 2 vols. London: W. Jeffs, 1861.

Rice, William B. *Los Angeles Star, 1851–1864: The Beginnings of Journalism in Southern California.* Berkeley: University of California Press, 1947.

Ricketts, Norma B. *The Mormon Battalion: U.S. Army of the West, 1846–1848.* Logan: Utah State University, 1996.

Roberts, Brigham H. *A Comprehensive History of the Church of Jesus Christ of Latter-day Saints, Century I,* vol. 4. Salt Lake City: Deseret News Press, 1930.

Robison, Jolene Ashman. *Almon Robison, Utah Pioneer: Man of Mystique and Tragedy.* Lawrence, Kan.: Richard A. Robison, 1995.

Rowland, Donald E. *John Rowland and William Workman: Southern California Pioneers of 1841.* Spokane, Wash.: Arthur H. Clark, 1999.

[Sage, Rufus B.]. *Scenes in the Rocky Mountains.* Philadelphia: Carey & Hart, 1846.

Sanchez, Joseph P. *Explorers, Traders, and Slavers: Forging the Old Spanish Trail, 1678–1850.* Salt Lake City: University of Utah Press, 1997.

Schindler, Harold. *Orrin Porter Rockwell: Man of God, Son of Thunder.* Salt Lake City: University of Utah Press, 1960.

Schlissel, Lillian. *Women's Diaries of the Westward Journey.* New York: Shocken Books, 1982; reprint, 1992.

Seegmiller, Janet Burton. *History of Iron County: Community Above Self.* Salt Lake City: Utah State Historical Society, 1998.

Senter, W. Riley. *Crossing the Continent to the California Gold Fields.* Exeter, Calif.: Privately printed, 1938.

Smith, Albert E., assembler. *Thales Hastings Haskell: Pioneer, Scout, Explorer, Indian Missionary, 1847–1909.* Salt Lake City: Privately published, 1964.

Steiner, Harold Austin. *The Old Spanish Trail Across the Mojave Desert: A History and Guide.* Las Vegas: Haldor, 1996; reprint, 1999.

Stephens, Lorenzo D. *Life Sketches of a Jayhawker of '49.* San Jose, Calif.: Nolta Brothers, 1916.

Stenhouse, Thomas B. H. *The Rocky Mountain Saints: A Full and Complete History of the Mormons from the First Vision of Joseph Smith to the Last Courtship of Brigham Young.* New York: D. Appleton, 1873.

Stout, Clifford L. *Search for Sanctuary: Brigham Young and the White Mountain Expedition.* Salt Lake City: University of Utah Press, 1984.

Strong, William Duncan. *Aboriginal Society in Southern California.* In *University of California Publications in American Archaeology and Ethnology,* vol. 26. Ed. A. L. Kroeber and R. H. Lowie. Berkeley: University of California Press, 1929.

Sullivan, Maurice S. *The Travels of Jedediah Smith: A Documentary Outline, Including the Journal of the Great Pathfinder.* Santa Ana, Calif.: Fine Arts Press, 1934.

Thompson, Gerald. *Edward F. Beale and the American West.* Albuquerque: University of New Mexico Press, 1983.

Thompson, Richard D., and Kathryn L. Thompson. *Pioneer of the Mojave: The Life and Times of Aaron G. Lane.* Apple Valley, Calif.: Desert Knolls Press, 1995.

Tullidge, Edward W. *History of Salt Lake City.* Salt Lake City: Star Printing, 1886.

Tyler, Daniel. *A Concise History of the Mormon Battalion in the Mexican War, 1846–1847.* Privately printed, 1881; reprint, Glorieta, N.M.: Rio Grande Press, 1969.

Unruh, John D., Jr. *The Plains Across: The Overland Emigrants and the Trans-Mississippi West, 1840–60.* Urbana: University of Illinois Press, 1979; paper, 1982.

Vicery, Joyce Carter. *Defending Eden: New Mexican Pioneers in Southern California, 1830–1890.* Riverside: University of California at Riverside and the Riverside Museum Press, 1977.

Vredenburgh, Larry M., Gary L. Shumway, and Russell D. Hartill. *Desert Fever: An Overview of Mining in the California Desert.* Conoga Park, Calif.: Living West Press, 1981.

Walker, Clifford J. *Back Door to California: The Story of the Mojave River Trail.* Barstow, Calif.: Mojave River Valley Museum Association, 1986.

Warner, Ted J., ed. *The Dominguez Escalante Expedition to the Interior Basin, 1776.* Provo, Utah: Brigham Young University Press, 1976.

Wheat, Carl I. *Mapping the Trans-Mississippi West,* 5 vols. San Francisco: Institute of Historical Cartography, 1957.

Willits, O. W., comp. *The Story of Oak Glen and the Yucaipa Valley.* Yucaipa, Calif.: Cobb's Printing, 1971.

Wilson, Iris Higbie. *William Wolfskill.* Glendale, Calif.: Arthur H. Clark, 1965.

Wilson, Neill G. *Silver Stampede: The Career of Death Valley's Hell-Camp, Old Panamint.* New York: Macmillan, 1937.

Winther, Oscar Osburn. *Via Western Express & Stagecoach.* Palo Alto, Calif.: Stanford University Press, 1945.

Wixom, Hartt. *Hamblin: A Modern Look at the Frontier Life and Legend of Jacob Hamblin.* Springville, Utah: Cedar Fort Incorporated, 1996.

Zobel, Albert L., Jr. *Sentinel in the East: A Biography of Thomas L. Kane.* Salt Lake City: Nicholas G. Morgan, 1965.

Articles, Papers, and Maps

Alexander, Thomas G., and Leonard James Arrington. "Camp in the Sagebrush: Camp Floyd, Utah, 1858–1861." *Utah Historical Quarterly* 34 (winter 1966): 4–21.

Auerbach, Herbert S. "Map Showing the Several Mail Routes Through the Indian Country From 1858 to 1861 and Indian Depredations Committed Upon Mail Trains." *Utah Historical Quarterly* (1941), 13–63.

Bailey, Lynn R. "Lt. Sylvester Mowry's Report on His March in 1855 From Salt Lake City to Fort Tejon." *Arizona and the West* 7, no. 4 (winter 1965): 329–46.

Bennion, Israel. "Before the Arrowhead Trail." *Improvement Era* 29, no. 6 (April 1926): 542–44.

Brooks, Juanita. "Indian Relations on Mormon Frontier." *Utah Historical Quarterly* 12, nos. 1–2 (January–April 1944): 1–48.

Campbell, Eugene E. "Brigham Young's Outer Cordon—A Reappraisal." *Utah Historical Quarterly* 41, no. 3 (summer 1983): 220–53.

Caughey, John Walton. "Southwest From Salt Lake in 1849." *Pacific Historical Review* 6 (1937): 143–64.

Cheesman, David W. "By Ox Team From Salt Lake to Los Angeles, 1850: A Memoir by David W. Cheesman." Ed. Mary E. Foy. *Historical Society of Southern California* 14 (1930): 271–337.

Clark, William. "A Trip Across the Plains in 1857." *The Iowa Journal of History and Politics* 20, no. 22 (April 1922): 163–223.

Desmond, Lucille H. "Henry Clay Daulton, I." *Madera County Historian* 9, no. 3 (July 1969): 1–5.

Flint, Dr. Thomas. "Diary of Dr. Thomas Flint: California to Maine and Return, 1851–1855." Ed. Walter Westergaard. *Annual Publications Historical Society of Southern California* 12 (1923): 53–107.

Fufkin, Don. "The Lost County of Pah-Ute." *Arizoniana: The Journal of Arizona History* 5, no. 2 (1964): 1–11.

Gillette, J. W. "Some Indian Experiences." *History of Southern California Annual* (1904): 158–63.

Haenszel, Arda M. "History of Pioneer Days, by J. F. Pike, as told to A. B. Clyde." *Heritage Tales* 8 (City of San Bernardino Historical and Pioneer Society, 1985): 17–21.

Hafen, LeRoy R. "The Butterfield's Overland Mail." *California Historical Society Quarterly* 11, no. 3 (October 1923): 211–22.

Hensher, Alan. "Ivanpah—Pioneer Mojave Desert Town." *Heritage Tales* 7 (San Bernardino Society of California Pioneers, 1984): 37–58.

Holladay, Fred. "The Stoddard Boys." *Heritage Tales* 11 (San Bernardino: San Bernardino Society of California Pioneers, 1988): 44–47.

Hunter, Milton R. "The Mormon Corridor." *Pacific Historical Review* 8 (1939): 179–200.

Ivins, Anthony. "Traveling Over Forgotten Trails: Indian Revenge and a Brother's Devotion." *Improvement Era* 19, no. 7 (May 1916): 603–7.

———. "Traveling Over Forgotten Trails: The Old Spanish Trail." *Improvement Era* 26, no. 9 (July 1923): 771–84.

Jones, Sondra. "'Redeeming the Indian': The Enslavement of Indian Children in New Mexico and Utah." *Utah Historical Quarterly* 67 (summer 1999): 220–41.

Leavitt, Francis H. "Steam Navigation on the Colorado River."

California Historical Society Quarterly 22 (March 1943): 1–26.

Lyman, Edward Leo. "Larger Than Texas: Proposals to Combine California and Mormon Deseret as One State." *California History* 80 (spring 2001): 19–23.

———. "From the City of Angels to the City of the Saints: The Struggle to Build a Railroad From Los Angeles to Salt Lake City." *California History* 70, no. 1 (spring 1991): 76–93.

———. "Outmaneuvering the Octopus: Atchison, Topeka and Santa Fe." *California History* 67 (June 1988): 94–110.

———. "The Arrowhead Trails Highway: California's Predecessor to Interstate 15." *Southern California Quarterly* 81, no. 3 (fall 1999): 315–40.

———. "The Arrowhead Trails Highway: The Beginnings of Utah's Other Route to the Pacific Coast." *Utah Historical Quarterly* 67 (summer 1999): 242–64.

Lyman, [Edward] Leo, and Clifford Walker. "Water Holes to California: Emigrant Travel Over the Most Difficult Portion of the Southern Route from Utah to California." *San Bernardino County Museum Quarterly* 44, no. 2 (spring 1997): 64–65.

"Map of a Reconnaissance of the Snow Mountain (N.W. of Camp Cady, California) made by 1st Lt. B. F. Davis, 1st Dragoons U.S.A." In Dennis G. Casebier, *Carleton's Pah-Ute Campaign.* Norco, Calif.: Privately printed, 1972.

McKenney, J. Wilson. "Gold Builds a Road." *Desert Magazine* 1, no. 2 (December 1937): 8–9, 24.

Meacham, Frank G. "The Discovery and Location of the Silver King Mine in Calico Mountain." *Pioneer Cabin News.* Ed. Harold B. Meacham (San Bernardino: San Bernardino Society of California Pioneers), no date (probably 1969). Preliminary to a successor journal, *Heritage Tales.*

Morgan, Dale L[owell]. "The Significance and Value of the Overland Journal." Presented at the Western History Association conference at Santa Fe, New Mexico, in 1961. Copy in Dale Lowell Morgan Papers, microfilm reel 55, 257–67. The Bancroft Library, University of California, Berkeley.

Newaygo. "Saving a Wagon Train." *Juvenile Instructor* 21 (1886): 140–41.

Pleasants, J. E. "Ranging on the Mojave River in 1864." *Touring Topics* 22 (Automobile Club of Southern California) (March 1930): 42–43.

Rice, William B. "Early Freighting on the Salt Lake—San Bernardino Trail." *Pacific Historical Review* 9, no. 1 (March 1942): 73–80.

Schneider, Joan S., Elizabeth J. Lawlor, and Deborah L. Dozier. "Roasting Pits and Agave in the Mojave Desert: Archaeological, Ethnobotanical and Ethnographic Data." *San Bernardino County Museum Quarterly* 43, nos. 1–2 (winter and spring 1996): 29–33.

Smith, Gerald A., ed. "Rousseau Diary: Across the Desert to California From Salt Lake City to San Bernardino in 1864." *Quarterly of San Bernardino County Museum Association* 6, no. 2 (spring 1986): 1–17.

Smith, Melvin T. "Colorado River Exploration and the Mormon War." *Utah Historical Quarterly* 38 (summer 1970), 207–23.

———. "Mormon Exploration in the Lower Colorado River Area." In *The Mormon Role in the Settlement of the West.* Ed. Richard H. Jackson. Charles Redd Monograph no. 9. Provo, Utah: Brigham Young University Press, 41–49, 63.

Snow, Edwina Jo. "William Chandless: British Overlander, Mormon Observer and Amazon Explorer." *Utah Historical Quarterly* 54, no. 2 (spring 1986): 116–36.

Richard D. Thompson, ed., "Silas C. Cox: Daniel Boone of the West," *San Bernardino County Museum Association Quarterly* 22, no. 1 (fall 1974): 20–24.

Townley, John M. "Stalking Horse for the Pony Express: The Chorpenning Mail Contracts Between California and Utah, 1851–1860." *Arizona and the West* 24, no. 3 (autumn 1982): 229–44.

Waitman, Leonard B. "The Watch Dogs of San Bernardino Valley: Chief Juan Antonio and Lorenzo Trujillo." *San Bernardino Museum Quarterly* 30 (winter 1991): 1–30.

Walker, Henry P., ed. "Soldier in the California Column: The Diary of John W. Teal (1864)." *Arizona and the West* 13 (spring 1971): 69–79.

Waters, Louisa Brown. "Trail Blazers of Cajon Pass." *Westways* 1 (January 1939): 8–9.

West, Elliott. "A Longer, Grimmer, But More Interesting Story." In *Trails: Toward a New Western History.* Ed. Patricia Nelson Limerick, Clyde A. Milner II, and Charles E. Rankin. Lawrence: University of Kansas Press, 1991.

Theses

Christie, Blanche. "Phineas Banning: With Special Reference to the Development of Transportation in Southern California." Unpublished master's thesis, University of Southern California, 1932.

Hunter, Milton Reed. "Brigham Young the Colonizer." Unpublished doctoral dissertation, University of California, 1937.

Kowalewski, Jane Percy. "Strange Bedfellows: Mormon and Miners in Southern Nevada." Unpublished master's thesis, University of Nevada, Las Vegas, 1984.

Law, Wesley R. "Mormon Indian Missions—1855." Unpublished master's thesis, Brigham Young University, 1959.

McBride, Ralph L. "Utah Mail Service Before the Coming of the Railroad, 1869." Unpublished master's thesis, Brigham Young University, 1957.

Miller, David H. "The Impact of the Gunnison Massacre on

Mormon–Federal Relations: Colonel Edward Jenner Steptoe's Command in Utah Territory, 1854–1855." Unpublished master's thesis, University of Utah, 1968.

Peterson, Paul. "The Mormon Reformation." Unpublished doctoral dissertation, Brigham Young University, 1981.

Pugh, Byron Grant. "History of Utah–California Wagon Freighting." Unpublished master's thesis, University of California, Berkeley, 1949.

Reeder, Ray M. "The Mormon Trail: A History of the Salt Lake to Los Angeles Route to 1869." Unpublished doctoral dissertation, Brigham Young University, 1966.

Smith, Melvin T. "The Colorado River: Its History in the Lower Canyons Area." Unpublished doctoral dissertation, Brigham Young University, 1972.

Warren, Elizabeth von Till. "Armijo's Trace Revisited: A New Interpretation of the Impact of the Antonio Armijo Route of 1829–1830." Unpublished master's thesis, University of Nevada, Las Vegas, 1974.

Published Travel Accounts and Biographical Sketches

Babcock, Leonard. "Recollections." In Hafen and Hafen, *Supplement to Journals of Forty-niners*, 64–70.

Bigler, Henry W. "Journal." In Hafen and Hafen, *Journals of Forty-niners*, 142–80.

Brown, James S. "Account." In Hafen and Hafen, *Journals of Forty-niners*, 112–28.

Brown, Judge H. S. "Account." In Hafen and Hafen, *Supplement to Journals of Forty-niners*, 23–25.

Cannon, George Q. "Narrative." In Hafen and Hafen, *Journals of Forty-niners*, 218–72.

Carter, Harvey L. "Calvin Jones." In Hafen and Hafen, *Mountain Men*, vol. 6, 207–8.

Choteau, Ben. "Log." In Hafen and Hafen, *Old Spanish Trail*, 365–66.

Derr, Peter. "Experiences." In Hafen and Hafen, *Journals of Forty-niners*, 51–53.

Egan, Howard. "Diary." In Hafen and Hafen, *Journals of Forty-niners*, 307–19.

Erkson, Alexander C. "Account." In Hafen and Hafen, *Journals of Forty-niners*, 133–38.

Farrer, William. "Diary." In Hafen and Hafen, *Journals of Forty-niners*, 193–218.

Granger, Lewis. "Letter." In Hafen and Hafen, *Supplement to Journals of Forty-niners*, 59–63.

Gruwell, Jacob [D]. "Report to Hayes." In Hafen and Hafen, *Supplement to Journals of Forty-niners*, 29–30.

Gruwell, J[acob]. D. "Account." In Hafen and Hafen, *Journals of Forty-niners*, 53–55.

Hamelin, Joseph P., Jr. "Journal." In Hafen and Hafen, *Supplement to Journals of Forty-niners*, 79–101.

Hayes, Benjamin. "Notes." In Hafen and Hafen, *Journals of Forty-niners*, 55–57.

Humpherys, Alfred Glen. "Thomas L. (Peg-leg) Smith." In Hafen and Hafen, *Mountain Men*, vol. 4, 328–30.

Kealy, Thomas. "Letter." In Hafen and Hafen, *Supplement to Journals of Forty-niners*, 104–7.

Journal of Discourses, by Brigham Young, His Two Counselors and the Twelve Apostles, vol. 4. Liverpool: Latter-day Saint Booksellers Depot, 1857.

Larson, Gustive O. "Wakara, Ute Chief." In Hafen and Hafen, *Mountain Men*, vol. 2, 339–44.

Lorton, William Birdsall. "Letter." In Hafen and Hafen, *Supplement to Journals of Forty-niners*, 71–75.

Moody, Ransom G. "Reminiscent Account." In Hafen and Hafen, *Supplement to Journals of Forty-niners*, 108–16.

Parrish, Enoch. "Diary of Enoch Parrish." In *The Story of Oak Glen and the Yucaipa Valley*. Comp. O. W. Willits. Yucaipa, Calif.: Cobb's Printing Enterprise, 1971.

Pearson, G. C. "Recollections." In Hafen and Hafen, *Supplement to Journals of Forty-niners*, 42–52.

Pettit, Edwin. "[Auto]Biography." In Hafen and Hafen, *Journals of Forty-niners*, 293–96.

Pratt, Addison. "Diary." In Hafen and Hafen, *Journals of Forty-niners*, 66–113.

Pratt, Louisa Barnes. "Journal." In *Heart Throbs of the West*, vol. 8. Ed. Kate B. Carter. Salt Lake City: Daughters of Utah Pioneers, 1947, 189–256.

Pratt, Orville C. "Journal." In Hafen and Hafen, *Old Spanish Trail*, 341–59.

Pratt, Sarah. "Journal." In *Covered Wagon Women*, vol. 4. Ed. Kenneth L. Holmes. Glendale, Calif.: Arthur H. Clark, 1985.

Randolph, W. C. "Statement." In Hafen and Hafen, *Supplement to Journals of Forty-niners*, 20–22.

Rich, Charles C. "Diary." In Hafen and Hafen, *Journals of Forty-niners*, 181–92.

Seeley, David. "Sketch." In Hafen and Hafen, *Journals of Forty-niners*, 296–98.

Shackleford, Ruth. "To California by the Mormon Trail, 1865." In *Covered Wagon Women: Diaries & Letters from the Western Trails, 1840–1890*, vol. 9. Ed. and comp. Kenneth L. Holmes. Spokane, Wash.: Arthur H. Clark, 1990, 141–45.

Shearer, Arthur. "Journal." In Hafen and Hafen, *Supplement to Journals of Forty-niners*, 31–41.

Stoddard, Sheldon. "Sketch." In Hafen and Hafen, *Journals of Forty-niners*, 271–72.

Stover, Jacob Y. "Narrative." In Hafen and Hafen, *Journals of Forty-niners*, 274–91.

Stuart, Charles V. "Trip." In Hafen and Hafen, *Supplement to Journals of Forty-niners*, 17–19.

Thurber, Albert K. "Journal and Diary." In *Treasures of Pioneer History*, vol. 3. Ed. Kate B. Carter. Salt Lake City: Daughters of Utah Pioneers, 1954, 274–320.

———. "Journal." In Hafen and Hafen, *Supplement to Journals of Forty-niners*, 117–24.

Van Dyke, Walter. "Account." In Hafen and Hafen, *Journals of Forty-niners*, 300–305.

Voelker, Frederick E. "William Sherley (Old Bill) Williams." In Hafen and Hafen, *Mountain Men*, vol. 8, 381–82.

Waite, Sidney P. "Sketch." In Hafen and Hafen, *Journals of Forty-niners*, 128–30.

Young, Sheldon. "Log." In Hafen and Hafen, *Journals of Forty-niners*, 60–66.

Newspapers

Alta California (San Francisco), 1850–69.
Deseret News (Salt Lake City), 1849–70.
Las Vegas *Review-Journal*, 1976.
Las Vegas *Sun*, 1970.
Los Angeles *Southern California*, 1855.
Los Angeles *Southern News*, 1862.
Los Angeles *Southern Vineyard*, 1858.
Los Angeles *Star*, 1851–65.
Millennial Star (Liverpool, England), 1852–70.
New York *Sun*, 1850.
New York *Times*, 1857.
Sacramento *Union*, 1854.
Salt Lake *Daily Telegraph*, 1865.
San Bernardino *Guardian*, 1867–70.
San Bernardino *Sun*, 1938, 1966.
San Diego *Herald*, 1857–58.
San Francisco *Bulletin*, 1857–77.
Sentinel and Gazette (Milwaukee, Wisconsin), 1850.
Western Standard (San Francisco), 1856–57.
San Francisco *Western Standard*, 6 March 1857.

Public Documents

State of California. *California State Assembly Proceedings, 1855.*
———. *Journal of the Senate of the State of California, 1850.*
———. *Journal of the Senate of the State of California, 1942.*
United States Census, San Bernardino County, California, 1860, manuscript, family listings.
United States Government. S. G. Brock. "Utah Report." In *Report on the Internal Commerce of the United States for the Year 1890 of Commerce and Navigation*, vol. 2. Washington, D.C.: U.S. Government Printing Office, 1891.

———. George M. Wheeler, [Army] Corps of Engineers. *Preliminary Report Concerning Explorations and Survey Principally in Nevada and Arizona, 1871*. Washington, D.C.: U.S. Government Printing Office, 1872.
Utah Expedition Documents, 35th Cong. 1st Sess. House Ex. Docs. 10:71–88, no. 956.
Utah Territorial Manuscript Census, Utah County, 1850 [actually taken in March 1851].

Manuscripts

Beattie, George William, and Helen Pruitt Beattie. "Papers." The Huntington Libary, San Marino, California.

Beckwith, Frank. "Shameful Friday: A Critical Study at the Mountain Meadows Massacre." The Huntington Libary, San Marino, California.

Beebe, Nelson Paul. "Diary and Life." Historical Department and Archives, Church of Jesus Christ of Latter-day Saints, Salt Lake City, Utah (hereinafter HDA).

Bleak, James G. "Annals of the Southern Mission." Books A and B. Family History Center, Church of Jesus Christ of Latter-day Saints, St. George, Utah.

Boyle, Henry G. "Diary." Harold B. Lee Library, Brigham Young University, Provo, Utah.

Brigham Young Discourse, Tabernacle, 16 August 1857, reported by George D. Watt, HDA.

Brown, John Jr. "Diary." George William Beattie and Helen Pruitt Beattie Papers. The Huntington Libary, San Marino, California.

Brown, Lorenzo. "Journal." Harold B. Lee Library, Brigham Young University, Provo, Utah.

Carleton, James H. *"Special Report: The Mountain Meadows Massacre," to Maj. W. W. Mackall, Assistant Adjutant General, United States Army, San Francisco, California.* Spokane, Wash.: Arthur H. Clark, 1995.

Christian, J. Ward, to Hon. Benj. I. Hayes, 25 October 1857. Benjamin I. Hayes Scrapbooks 94. The Bancroft Library, University of California, Berkeley.

Cox, Silas C. "Autobiographical Sketch." Typescript. San Bernardino County Library, San Bernardino, California, 15–16.

Cox, William J., to Brigham Young, 7 September 1857, Brigham Young Papers. HDA.

Cox, William J., to A[masa] M. Lyman, 7 October 1857, both in Amasa M. Lyman Papers. HDA.

Cox, William J., and William Crosby, 1 October 1857. Brigham Young Papers. HDA.

Crosby, Caroline Barnes. "Diary." Utah State Historical Society, Salt Lake City, Utah.

Earle, David D. "Indians of the Upper Mojave River and Victor

Valley: The Historic Period." Paper and videotape commissioned by Victor Valley College lecture series, September 1991. Copies in Special Collections, Victor Valley College Library, Victorville, California.

Gillette, J. W., to Mrs. H. E. Parrish, 31 March 1866. In George William Beattie and Helen Pruitt Beattie Papers. The Huntington Libary, San Marino, California.

Ginn, John L. "Mormon and Indian Wars: The Mountain Meadows Massacre and Other Tragedies and Transactions Incident to the Mormon Rebellion of 1857, Together With the Personal Recollections of a Civilian Who Witnessed Many of the Thrilling Scenes Described." Copy in HDA. Also in Dale Lowell Morgan Papers, The Bancroft Library, University of California, Berkeley.

Hanks, Ebenezer, to Brigham Young, 6 February 1858. Thomas L. Kane Papers. HDA.

Hayes, Benjamin I. "Scrapbooks 5, 94." The Bancroft Library, University of California, Berkeley.

Hayes, W. R. "Diary." The Bancroft Library, University of California, Berkeley.

Heybourne, Melissa Keziah Rollins. "Autobiographical Sketch, John Henry Rollins." HDA.

"Historian's Office Journal." September 1857. HDA.

Hollister, William W. "Statement of a few facts on California in 1852 to 1860." Gathered by Hubert H. Bancroft, interviewer, 1878. The Bancroft Library, University of California, Berkeley.

Hoover, Vincent A. "Diary." The Huntington Libary, San Marino, California.

Hopkins, Richard R. "Journal of Expedition." 1852. HDA.

Hoth, Hans Peter Emanuel. "Journal." The Bancroft Library, University of California, Berkeley. Copy courtesy of Susan B. Doyle.

Huntington, Dimick Baker. "Journal," 18 August, 1 September 1857. HDA.

Hurt, Garland, to Superintendent Forney, Docs., 10:71:88, no. 956, Fiche 2 (microfiche).

Jensen, Andrew. "History of San Bernardino Branch (1851–1857)." HDA.

"Journal History of the Church of Jesus Christ of Latter-day Saints, 1849–1869." HDA.

Kenney, Scott G. "Early Trials of Joseph F. Smith." Unpublished chapter of Joseph F. Smith biography. Copy in possession of Edward Leo Lyman.

Kinney, Judge J. F., to Brigham Young, 23 February 1865. Brigham Young Papers. HDA.

Leithead, James, to Erastus Snow, 24 November 1870. In James G. Bleak, "Annals of the Southern Mission," Book A, 147. Copy in Family History Center, Church of Jesus Christ of Latter-day Saints, St. George, Utah.

Liston, Commodore Perry. "Sketch of Commodore Perry Liston Autobiography." Utah State Historical Society, Salt Lake City.

Lorton, William Birdsall. "Journal." The Bancroft Library, University of California, Berkeley.

Lyman, Amasa Mason. "Journal." HDA.

Lyman, Amasa Mason, to Brigham Young, 25 December 1857, 20 January 1858. Brigham Young Papers, HDA.

Lyman, Edward Leo. "History of Millard County: Unedited Edition (prior to ruthless cutting by Utah State Historical Society editors)." Copy in Great Basin Museum, Delta, Utah; also at Delta Public Library. Typescript.

———. "History of Victor Valley." Copy in Victor Valley College Library, Victorville, California. Incomplete manuscript.

Lyman, Francis Marion. "Journal." 1892–1895. HDA. (Use is now restricted by the LDS church; extensive notes in possession of Edward Leo Lyman).

Lyman, Francis Marion to A[masa] M[ason] Lyman, 4 October 1857. HDA.

Moorman, Donald. "Papers." Weber State University Library, Ogden, Utah.

Morgan, Dale Lowell. "Papers." The Bancroft Library, University of California, Berkeley.

Morris, Thomas. "Journal." Utah State Historical Society, Salt Lake City.

Mowry, Lt. Sylvester, to Col. S. Cooper, Adjt. Genl. U.S. Army United States. 23 July 1855. National Archives, Washington, D.C. Copy in Utah State Historical Society, Salt Lake City.

Osborne, Mary, and Melissa Lee Haybourne. "A Life Sketch of James Henry Rollins." Undated ms., HDA.

Parrish, Marionette. "Account." In Alexander Kier Jr. Folder, George William Beattie and Helen Pruitt Beattie Papers. The Huntington Libary, San Marino, California.

Peck, Washington. "Diary." Oregon California Trails Association Collection in Mattes Library. National Frontier Trails Center. Independence, Missouri.

Price, Lt. Col. William Redwood, to Maj. J. P. Sherburne, A.A.G. [Assistant Adjutant General], Dept. of California, 22 November 1867. National Archives, Records of the United States Army. Copy of letter in possession of Edward Leo Lyman, courtesy of Dennis G. Casebier.

Rich, Charles Colson. "Journal." HDA. Copy in George William Beattie and Helen Pruitt Beattie Papers. The Huntington Libary, San Marino, California.

Riser, John. "Mormon Battalion Memoir," no date. Riser Family Collection, Utah State Historical Society, Salt Lake City.

———. "Autobiography." The Bancroft Library, University of California, Berkeley, 1887.

Rogerson, Josiah. "Journal." HDA.

"Scrapbook Notes, Beaver Dam." Desert Valley Museum, Mesquite, Nevada.

Seeley, David Randolph, to George William Beattie, 7 April 1937. George William Beattie and Helen Pruitt Beattie Papers. The Huntington Libary, San Marino, California.

Severance, Mark Sibley. "Journal." Original in private possession. Copy in files of Edward Leo Lyman.

Shearer, Arthur. "Journal," 10 November 1849. The Bancroft Library, University of California, Berkeley.

Smith, George A., to Jacob Hamblin, 3 November 1863. Historian's Office Letterpress Copybooks, vol. 2, p. 9. HDA.

Smith, Jesse N. "Journal." HDA.

Steele, John. "Journal." Harold B. Lee Library, Brigham Young University, Provo, Utah.

Stickney. "Log." Dale Lowell Morgan Papers. The Bancroft Library, University of California, Berkeley.

Tanner, Nathan. "Diaries." HDA.

Thompson, Samuel, to Brigham Young, 20 March 1857. Brigham Young Papers, HDA.

Unsigned. From LDS First Presidency's office to Bishop Aaron Johnson, 3 February 1857. President's Office Journal. HDA.

———. From LDS First Presidency's office to Bishop Lewis Brunson and Presidents William H. Dame and Isaac C. Haight, 6 February 1857. President's Office Journal. HDA.

Welch, Adonijah S. "Diary Fragments." Copy in Dale Lowell Morgan Papers. The Bancroft Library, University of California, Berkeley.

Wilson, Bushrod W. "Journal." Daughters of Utah Pioneers Museum, Salt Lake City, Utah.

Wylly, Thomas S. "Westward Ho—in 1849: Memoirs of Captain Thomas S. Wylly." Typescript. The Bancroft Library, University of California, Berkeley.

Young, Brigham, Heber C. Kimball, and Willard Richards to Amasa M. Lyman and Charles C. Rich, 17 March 1851. First Presidency Papers. HDA.

Young, Brigham, to Amasa Lyman, 1 June 1855. Amasa Mason Lyman Papers. HDA.

Young, Brigham, to Amasa M. Lyman, 4 February 1858. Brigham Young Papers, HDA.

Young, Brigham, to Amasa M. Lyman and Charles C. Rich. 1 June 1855. Brigham Young Papers. HDA.

Young, Brigham, to Charles C. Rich, 28 September 1855, 28 May 1856. Charles Colson Rich Papers. HDA.

Young, Brigham, to George W. Manypenny, Commissioner, Washington, D.C., 31 March 1857. President's Office Journal. HDA.

Young, Brigham, to Isaac Haight and John D. Lee, 2 November 1857, Brigham Young Office Journal. HDA.

Young, Brigham, to Jacob Hamblin, 18 August 1857. HDA.

Young, Brigham, to James W. Denver, Commissioner of Indian Affairs, 12 September 1857, 6 January 1858. HDA. President's Office Journal. HDA.

Young, Brigham, to Judge J. F. Kinney, 23 December 1864. Brigham Young Papers. HDA.

Young, Brigham, to Maj. George W. Armstrong, 14 March 1857. President's Office Journal. HDA.

Young, Brigham, to Miles Anderson, 4 October 1856. Brigham Young Papers. HDA.

Young, Brigham, to Nathaniel V. Jones, 3 September 1856. Brigham Young Papers. HDA.

Young, Brigham, to Phillip K. Smith, 7 January 1857. Brigham Young Papers. HDA.

Young, Brigham, to Samuel Thompson, 7 January, 4 February, 20 March 1857. Brigham Young Papers. HDA.

Young, Brigham, to the bishops and others on the Muddy, 17 September 1870. In James G. Bleak, "Annals of the Southern Mission," Book A, 147. Copy in Family History Center, Church of Jesus Christ of Latter-day Saints, St. George, Utah.

Young, Brigham, to the Piedes at Las Vegas, 8 October 1856. Brigham Young Papers. HDA.

Index

Note: *Italic page numbers refer to illustrations.*

on Beaver Dam Wash, 6; and Colorado River freight promotion, 208; exploration from San Bernardino and San Diego, 88; first trip over Southern Route by, 38, 41; and freighting, 161, 174; and Gruwell family, 47; as guide on Southern Route, 46, 52–53, 54, 58–62, 76, 83, 84, 243n47; and mail service, 93; and Mormon Battalion, 38, 40–41, 93, 161; and Mormon colonization party, 82; on Mountain Meadows Massacre, 138–39; portrait of, *59;* and road improvements, 156; and search for water, 61–62, 243n57, 243n61; secession of travelers from Hunt-Baxter company, 62–65, 68; shortcut mistakes of, 61–62; sons of, 181, 184; threats against, 63, 243–44n65; travelers' return to main route with, 63–68, 69, 74
Hunt, John, 41, 93, 180, 181, 192–93
Hunt, Lois, 180
Hunt-Baxter company, 58–67, 243n47
Hunter, Milton R., 87
Huntfitter, 145
hunting, 13, 34–35, 36, 53, 65, 69, 72, 89, 92, 96, 109, 196, 233
Huntington, Caroline, 225
Huntington, Dimick Baker, 99, 119, 128–29, 144, 231, 251n21, 260n49
Huntington, Heber "Pete," 144, 225
Huntington (Henry E.) Library, 57
Huntington, Lot, 260n49
Huntington, William D., 144–45, 180, 225
Huntington–Horace Clark party, 144–45
Huntington way station, 225, 264n64
Huntsman's hill, 7
Hurt, Garland, 107, 126, 129, 136, 251n14
Hyde, John, 251n18
Hyde, William, 246n62

ice, 4, 55, 111, 181
Illinois, 123
illness: anthrax, 131; of children, 108, 194–95; cholera, 45, 88, 114, 231; diarrhea, 64; from eating mistletoe berries, 154; fever, 68; of Kane, 149; malaria, 212, 213; mountain fever, 194, 244n79; of Native Americans, 142, 186; and rest stops for ill travelers, 60, 61; of Rousseau, 193; scurvy, 216; smallpox, 186, 259n22; of women, 57, 180, 194. *See also* deaths; physicians
Impassable Pass, 12–13, 52, 55, 66, 68, 79, 237n28
Independence, Mo., 114
Independent Pioneer Company, 46–58, 60, 61, 67–68, 242n18

Indian Bureau, 191
Indian Springs, 115–16
Indian Territory (Oklahoma), 39, 223
Indians. *See* Native Americans; *and specific tribes*
insect infestation, 158–59
inspection of livestock, 27
Interstate 15, xiii, xiv, 1, 22, 69, 140, 235n6
Iowa City, Iowa, 121
Iron Battalion, 132
Iron County, Utah, 5, 33–34, 83–84, 87, 92, 95, 107, 124, 129, 132, 133
Iron Mission, 5, 95
Iron Springs, 5, 84, 95, 248n24
Isaac, Chief, 146, 183, 208. *See also* Tosho (or Touche), Chief
Isaac, John, 143, 255n74
Ivanpah, 218, 221, 224, 225
Ives, Joseph C., 107, 148, 149–50
Ives, William C., *148*
Ivins, Anthony W., xi, 102, 133, 203, 261n64

Jackman, Jehu (Parmeno), 189–90, 192
Jackson (African American), 57
Jackson, Alden A. M., 149, 195
Jackson, Caroline, 149, 195
Jackson, Chief, 136–37, 185, 208, 253n43
Jackson, David E., 22
Jackson, William H., 3, 168–69, *169*, 175–78, *177*
Jacobi, 194, 260n43
James, Jimmy, 196
Jarvis, George, 211–12
Jayhawk mine, 207
Jayhawkers, 59, 62, 63, 243n60
Jedediah Smith Butte, 20, 24
Jennings, W. W., 172
Johns, Neal, 235–36n8
Johnson, Aaron, 126, 251n16
Johnson, J. Neely, 82
Johnson, Nephi, 135, 136, 255n80
Johnston, Albert Sidney, 142, 148–49, 189–90, 208
Johnston, Joaquin, 188–89
Jones, Calvin, 28–29
Jones, M. G., 163
Jones, Marcus, 168
Jones, Nathaniel V., 118–19
Joshua trees, 14
journals. *See* overland journals and diaries
Juab Valley, 3
Juan Antonio, Chief, 30
Junction City, 210
juniper trees and berries, 4, 34, 35, 56

Kahseebats, Chief, 37
Kaibab Plateau, 33, 35
Kane, Thomas L., 149, 182, 232, 255n80
Kanosh, Chief: commitment of, to peace with whites, 144, 145–46, 255n79; confrontation between Parashot (Parashant) and, 145, 146; family of, 37,

145; and Flint party, 94; and Gunnison massacre, 255n79; mobility of, 37; and Mountain Meadows Massacre, 146, 253n52, 255n79; portrait of, 103, *145;* and safety for travelers against Indian attacks, 144, 145–46, 232; at Salt Lake City conference with Young, 128, 129, 251–52n22; village of, near Meadow Creek, 4
Kanosh, Utah, 4, 131, 217
Kanosh Indians. *See* Pahvant Indians
Kansas, 184
Katz, Marcus, 199
Kealy, Thomas, 74, 82
Kearny, Stephen W., 29–30, 190
Keil Ranch, 117
Kelly, Charles, 41
Kelsey, Eli, 130
Kenderdine, Thaddeus S., 161–62, 255n76, 263n47
Kern, Edward, *32*
killings. *See* deaths
Kimball, Heber C., 83, 152, 174, 249n48
Kimball, William, 249n48
Kingston, C. L., 11, 73
Kingston Springs, 11, 104, 105, 108, 110, 112, 150, 155, 172, 175–77, 199, 233
Kingston Springs cutoff, 11, 104, 108, 155
Kinney, John F., 209
Kinney (mountain man), 44
Kino, Eusebio, 19
Kirk (U.S. marshal), 188–89
Kirk, William, 218
Kirtland, Ohio, 250
Klingensmith, Phillip, 119, 124, 134, 135
Knapp, Albert, 214
Knapp, William, 207, 214
Knight, Samuel, 133, 140
Koosharem Indians, 33
Kwiengomit Indians, 33

La Puente ranch, 67
Lake City, Utah, 2–3
Lake Powell, 25
Lamphere, George, 102
Lane, Aaron G., 187, *187*, 188, 219, 220
Lane, Mr., 254n64
Lane's Crossing, 201
Larson, Andrew Karl, 213
Larson, Gustave O., 28
Las Flores Ranch, 29, 201
Las Flores Ranch killings, 196–98, 260n51, 261n53
Las Vegas: abandoned goods and dead livestock near, 104; abandoned goods near, 52; burial of dead near, 93; Carvalho on, 104; and Cheesman party, 78; and emigrations in 1852, 90; and establishment of Mormon corridor, 88; farming at, 207; Ginn party surrounded by Paiutes at, 146; and Independent Pioneer Company, 50–51, 52, 55;

Lyman on, 84; Mowry's detachment at, 106, 108; Native Americans in Vegas–Muddy River region, 149; Rich party at, 108; and Rynierson-Granger party, 64; and Sanford freighting expedition, 157; water puddles between Muddy River and, 55, 65
Las Vegas army outpost, 214–17
Las Vegas Indians, 73, 92, 113, 182, 215–16
Las Vegas mission, 41, 101, 110, 111, 115–21, *120*, 123, 182–83, 214, 230
Las Vegas Springs, 8–9, 25, 26, 33, 91, 147, 176, 238n22
Las Vegas *Sun*, 203
Las Vegas Wash, 26, 150
Lasenby, Robert, 250n4
Lathrop, Asahel A., 41
Latter-day Saints. *See* Mormons
Lawrence, Mr., 219
LDS. *See* Mormons
Leach, James B., 106, 112, 118, 156
Leach Canyon, 248n24
Leach Cutoff, 5, 108, 112, 113, 155–56, 248n24
Leach Springs, 133
lead mining, 118–20
Leany, William, 132
Leavitt, Dudley, 133, 140–41, 150, 185
Leavitt, LaVoid, xii, 235–36n8, 262n27
Lecouvreur, Frank, 110, 186
Lee, John D.: and Huntington–Horace Clark party, 144; and military presence in southwestern Utah, 208; and Mountain Meadows Massacre, 98, 132, 133–36, 142, 143, 231, 253n47; portrait of, *135;* public lodging houses owned by, 207; on rustlers, 260n49; and Southern Indian Mission, 98–101; territorial court proceedings against, 143
Leese, Jacob, 28
Lehi, Utah, 2, 111
Leithead, Bishop James, 212, 213
Leonard, Glen M., xii
Levan ridge, 3
Levick, William, 90
Lewis, Benjamin, 99
Lewis, David, 99
Lewis, Nat, 214
Lewis, Tarleton, 252n38
Lightfoot, Mr. and Mrs. Frank, 219–20
Limerick, Patricia Nelson, 36
limestone, 9
Lincoln, Abraham, 76
liquor. *See* alcoholic beverages
Liston, Perry, 142, 144, 254n70
Little, Feramorz, 92
Little, James A., 41, 76
Little Salt Lake, 22, 26, 39, 42, 61
livestock: abandonment of, 50, 51, 52, 55; and anthrax, 131; Caine's advice on, 69–70, 72; and Cajon Pass, 56, 89, 180; and California Wash, 8; death of, 1,